AIA

PAPER 9
MANAGEMENT INFORMATION

S T U D Y

T E X T

In this 2020 edition

- A **user-friendly format** for easy navigation
- **Exam-centred topic coverage**, directly linked to AIA's syllabus
- **Exam focus points** showing you what the examiner will want you to do
- Regular **fast forward** summaries emphasising the key points in each chapter
- **Questions** and **quick quizzes** to test your understanding
- **Exam question bank** containing exam standard questions with answers
- **2 mock exams** containing the November 2017 and May 2018 papers
- **A full index**

FOR EXAMS IN 2020

First edition 2007
Eleventh edition January 2020

ISBN 9781 5097 8724 1
(previous ISBN 9781 5097 2507 6)

eISBN 9781 5097 2896 1
(previous eISBN 9781 5097 2574 8)

British Library Cataloguing-in-Publication Data
A catalogue record for this book is available from the British Library

Published by

BPP Learning Media Ltd
BPP House, Aldine Place
142-144 Uxbridge Road
London W12 8AA

www.bpp.com/learningmedia

Printed in the United Kingdom

> Your learning materials, published by BPP Learning Media Ltd, are printed on paper obtained from traceable sustainable sources.

All rights reserved. No part of this publication may be reproduced, stored in a retrieval system or transmitted in any form or by any means, electronic, mechanical, photocopying, recording or otherwise, without the prior written permission of BPP Learning Media. Contains public sector information licensed under the Open Government Licence v3.0.

The contents of this book are intended as a guide and not professional advice. Although every effort has been made to ensure that the contents of this book are correct at the time of going to press, BPP Learning Media makes no warranty that the information in this book is accurate or complete and accept no liability for any loss or damage suffered by any person acting or refraining from acting as a result of the material in this book.

We are grateful to the Association of International Accountants for permission to reproduce past examination questions. The suggested solutions in the exam answer bank have been prepared by BPP Learning Media Ltd.

©
BPP Learning Media Ltd
2020

A note about copyright

Dear Customer

What does the little © mean and why does it matter?

Your market-leading BPP books, course materials and e-learning materials do not write and update themselves. People write them on their own behalf or as employees of an organisation that invests in this activity. Copyright law protects their livelihoods. It does so by creating rights over the use of the content.

Breach of copyright is a form of theft – as well as being a criminal offence in some jurisdictions, it is potentially a serious breach of professional ethics.

With current technology, things might seem a bit hazy but, basically, without the express permission of BPP Learning Media:

- Photocopying our materials is a breach of copyright
- Scanning, ripcasting or conversion of our digital materials into different file formats, uploading them to facebook or e-mailing them to your friends is a breach of copyright

You can, of course, sell your books, in the form in which you have bought them – once you have finished with them. (Is this fair to your fellow students? We update for a reason.) Please note the e-products are sold on a single user licence basis: we do not supply 'unlock' codes to people who have bought them secondhand.

And what about outside the UK? BPP Learning Media strives to make our materials available at prices students can afford by local printing arrangements, pricing policies and partnerships which are clearly listed on our website. A tiny minority ignore this and indulge in criminal activity by illegally photocopying our material or supporting organisations that do. If they act illegally and unethically in one area, can you really trust them?

Contents

Page

Introduction

The introduction pages contain lots of valuable advice and information. They include tips on studying for and passing the exam, also the content of the syllabus and what has been examined.

How the BPP Learning Media Study Text can help you pass – Help yourself study for your AIA exams – Syllabus – Command words and learning outcomes – The exam paper – Revision of IAS 1: New terminology

Part A: Techniques to support business decisions

1	Correlation and regression	3
2	Sampling theory and significance testing	33
3	Linear programming	59
4	Network analysis	91
5	Simulation	121
6	Decision theory	131

Part B: Information systems

7	Information systems – types and applications	149
8	Systems modelling	187
9	Systems development and organisation	211
10	Systems strategies and management issues	241
11	Control and security	259
12	Technology, selection and acquisition	281
13	The internet as a strategic business tool	307

Answers to end of chapter questions 331
Exam question bank 353
Exam answer bank 375
Mock exam 1 413
Mock exam 2 425
Mathematical tables 437
Index 445

How the BPP Learning Media Study Text can help you pass

> It provides you with the knowledge and understanding, skills and application techniques that you need to be successful in your exams

This Study Text has been targeted at the **Management Information** syllabus.

- It is **comprehensive**. It covers the syllabus content. No more, no less.
- It is written at the **right level**. Each chapter is written with AIA's syllabus in mind.
- It is aimed at the **exam**. We have taken account of recent exams, guidance the examiner has given and the assessment methodology.

> It allows you to study in the way that best suits your learning style and the time you have available, by following your personal Study Plan (see page vii)

You may be studying at home on your own or you may be attending a course. You may like to read every word, or you may prefer to do a fast read through and learn through doing practice questions the rest of the time. However you study, you will find the BPP Learning Media Study Text meets your needs in designing and following your personal Study Plan.

Help yourself study for your AIA exams

Exams for professional bodies such as AIA are very different from those you have taken at college or university. You will be under **greater time pressure before** the exam – as you may be combining your study with work. Here are some hints and tips.

The right approach

1 **Develop the right attitude**

Believe in yourself	Yes, there is a lot to learn. But thousands have succeeded before and you can too.
Remember why you're doing it	You are studying for a good reason: to advance your career.

2 **Focus on the exam**

Read through the Syllabus	This tells you what you are expected to know and is supplemented by **Exam focus points** in the text.
Study the Exam paper section	Past papers are likely to be good guides to what you should expect in the exam.

3 **The right method**

See the whole picture	Keeping in mind how all the detail you need to know fits into the whole picture will help you understand it better. • The **Introduction** of each chapter puts the material in context. • The **Syllabus content** and **Exam focus points** show you what you need to **grasp**.
Use your own words	To absorb the information (and to practise your written communication skills), you need to **put it into your own words**. • **Take notes**. • Answer the **questions** in each chapter. • Draw **mindmaps**. • Try **'teaching' a subject** to a colleague or friend.
Give yourself cues to jog your memory	The Study Text uses **bold** to **highlight key points**. • Try **colour coding** with a highlighter pen. • Write **key points** on cards.

4 **The right recap**

Review, review, review	Regularly reviewing a topic in summary form can **fix it in your memory**. The Study Text helps you review in many ways. • **Chapter roundups** summarise the 'Fast forward' key points in each chapter. Use them to recap each study session. • The **Quick quiz** actively tests your grasp of the essentials. • Go through the **Examples** in each chapter a second or third time.

Developing your personal Study Plan

BPP recommends that you follow a study plan. Planning and sticking to the plan are key elements of learning successfully.

There are five steps you should work through.

Step 1 **How do you learn?**

What types of intelligence do you display when learning? You might be advised to brush up on certain study skills before launching into this Study Text, but refer to the 'tackling your studies' section below which will help.

Step 2 **What do you prefer to do first?**

If you prefer to get to grips with a theory before seeing how it is applied, we suggest you concentrate first on the explanations we give in each chapter before looking at the examples and case studies. If you prefer to see first how things work in practice, read through the detail in each chapter, and concentrate on the examples and case studies, before supplementing your understanding by reading the detail.

Step 3 **How much time do you have?**

Work out the time you have available per week, given the following.

- The standard you have set yourself
- The other exam(s) you are sitting
- Practical matters such as work, travel, exercise, sleep and social life

	Hours
Note your time available in box A. A	

Step 4 **Allocate your time**

- Take the time you have available per week for this Study Text shown in box A, multiply it by the number of weeks available and insert the result in box B.   B

- Divide the figure in box B by the number of chapters in this text and insert the result in box C.   C

Remember that this is only a rough guide. Some of the chapters in this book are longer and more complicated than others, and you will find some subjects easier to understand than others.

Step 5 **Implement**

Set about studying each chapter in the time shown in box C, following the key study steps in the order suggested by your particular learning style.

This is your personal **Study Plan**. You should try to combine it with the study sequence outlined below. You may want to modify the sequence to adapt it to your **personal style**.

Tackling your studies

The best way to approach this Study Text is to tackle the chapters in order. Taking into account your individual learning style, you could follow this sequence for each chapter.

Key study steps	Activity
Step 1 **Topic list**	This topic list helps you navigate each chapter; each numbered topic is a numbered section in the chapter.
Step 2 **Introduction**	This sets your objectives for study by giving you the big picture in terms of the context of the chapter. The content is referenced to the syllabus, and Exam guidance shows how the topic is likely to be examined. The Introduction tells you **why** the topics covered in the chapter need to be studied.
Step 3 **Knowledge brought forward boxes**	These highlight information and techniques that it is assumed you have 'brought forward' with you from your earlier studies. Remember that you may be tested on these areas in the exam. If you are unsure of these areas, you should consider revising your more detailed study material from earlier papers.
Step 4 **Fast forward**	Fast forward boxes give you a quick summary of the content of each of the main chapter sections. They are listed together in the roundup at the end of each chapter to help you review each chapter quickly.
Step 5 **Explanations**	Proceed methodically through each chapter, particularly focusing on areas highlighted as significant in the chapter introduction, or areas that are frequently examined.
Step 6 **Key terms and Exam focus points**	• Key terms can often earn you **easy marks** if you state them clearly and correctly in an exam answer. They are highlighted in the index at the back of this text. • Exam focus points state how the topic has been or may be examined, difficulties that can occur in questions about the topic, and examiner feedback on common weaknesses in answers.
Step 7 **Note taking**	Take brief notes, if you wish. Don't copy out too much. Remember that being able to record something yourself is a sign of being able to understand it. Your notes can be in whatever format you find most helpful; lists, diagrams, mindmaps.
Step 8 **Examples**	Work through the examples very carefully as they illustrate key knowledge and techniques.
Step 9 **Case studies**	Study each one, and try to add flesh to them from your own experience. They are designed to show how the topics you are studying come alive in the real world.
Step 10 **Questions**	Attempt each one, as they will illustrate how well you have understood what you have read.
Step 11 **Answers**	Check yours against ours, and make sure you understand any discrepancies.
Step 12 **Chapter roundup**	Review it carefully, to make sure you have grasped the significance of all the important points in the chapter.
Step 13 **Quick quiz**	Use the Quick quiz to check how much you have remembered of the topics covered and to practise questions in a variety of formats.
Step 14 **Question practice**	Attempt the Question suggested at the very end of the chapter. These are all AIA past exam questions, so provide an excellent indication of the type and standard of question that you can expect in your real exam. Some of these questions cover more than one subject area, which is a common feature of exam questions.

INTRODUCTION

AIA Achieve

AIA provides an interactive course of study AIA Achieve, which offers students the tools, resources and learning environment to study for the exams. The study tools include a course of study e-book, marked practice questions, marked mock exam paper and feedback and technical advice via an e-Tutor. Contact the Study Support team at: Achieve@aiaworldwide.com.

Moving on…

When you are ready to start revising, you should still refer back to this Study Text.

- As a source of **reference** (you should find the index particularly helpful for this)
- As a way to **review** (the Fast forwards, Exam focus points, Chapter roundups and Quick quizzes help you here)

Syllabus

Aims

The objective of the paper is to ensure candidates have:

- A working knowledge of management science applications and management information systems development and implementation in business
- An understanding of mathematical, statistical and systems modelling techniques, their limitations and appropriateness in business and management contexts

The paper will examine candidates' understanding through the eyes of a user, a designer, a manager and an evaluator.

FIG. 9 INTER-RELATIONSHIP OF UNITS

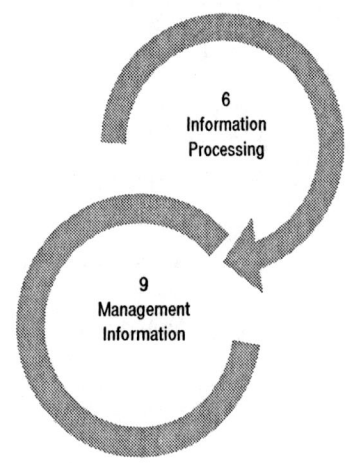

Candidates will be expected to explain, distinguish and interpret results of:

- Selected mathematical and statistical methods; candidates will not be expected to display in-depth mathematical ability nor derive or prove any mathematical formulae
- Selected methods in the strategic development and design of management information systems, including both hardware and software, and relevant methods of selection, acquisition, organisation, management and security of the processes and technology involved
- Candidates will be expected to demonstrate an appreciation and understanding of the implementation of management information systems in real cases and be aware of their pitfalls and limitations. Candidates however, will not be expected to display an in-depth knowledge of the science of computing

Descriptors

After successfully completing this paper candidates should be able to:

- Apply appropriate techniques and interpret the results to support a range of business decisions
- Discuss the features of information systems and technology to a given set of requirements
- Apply systems modeling, design, development and implementation tools and techniques to solve and evaluate organisational and informational problems

Structure of the paper

A three hour 15 minutes paper consisting of two sections. All questions must be attempted. Where appropriate the allocation of marks to individual parts of questions is stated on the paper. Relevant formulae, statistical and mathematical tables are printed on the question paper.

Section A

This section comprises a scenario based question worth 25 marks.

INTRODUCTION

This section relates to the management science part of the syllabus; the questions will generally be partly computational, partly explanation and partly interpretation.

Section B

This section comprises three main questions, each carrying 25 marks.

This section comprises questions from the management information systems part of the syllabus; the questions will be partly descriptive, partly evaluative, and are generally of the essay type, but candidates are expected to demonstrate techniques where appropriate.

Syllabus

Management Science

9.1 Correlation and Regression

Topic Weighting   5%

Candidates should demonstrate their understanding of calculations and interpretations of the techniques of simple and multiple correlation and linear regression when applied to business data. Candidates will also be expected to understand the significance of the coefficient of determination, and forecasting by regression.

9.2 Sampling Theory and Significance Testing

Topic Weighting   10%

Candidates must show an appreciation of the Central Limit theorem as the basis of classical sampling theory and significance testing. Point and interval estimation of the mean and proportion through sampling is a key element of this section of the syllabus, as are the hypothesis tests on a mean, a proportion, and the difference between two means or two proportions. The Chi-Squared significance test of association is also part of this section.

9.3 Linear Programming

Topic Weighting   10%

Candidates must be able to formulate simple linear programmes, involving two decision variables, solve them graphically, and interpret the results in the form of a report to management. The interpretation of the simplex solution is also a part of this section of the syllabus – note: candidates are not expected to derive simplex solutions.

Further, candidates should be able to apply the concept of sensitivity analysis to the graphical solution of a linear programme, and articulate their conclusions in a form of a report.

9.4 Network Analysis

Topic Weighting   5%

The drawing up of a network using either the activity-on-arrow or the activity-on-node notations is fundamental to this topic. Candidates should further be able to calculate the critical path and apply time, cost and resource-usage analyses to unique projects.

9.5 Simulation

Topic Weighting   5%

Candidates must be able to apply the sampling-based technique of Monte Carlo simulation to any of a selection of business problems. An understanding of the use of random numbers, and of tabulating the sampling from given distributions of factors subject to risk, as well as reporting conclusions from a small sample, are required in this topic section.

9.6 Decision Theory

Topic Weighting   5%

The concepts of expected value and risk through standard deviation are fundamental to the study of decisions under risk. Candidates should be able to apply these concepts as well as that of the coefficient of variation (relative risk) to business situations involving elements of risk. Further, the use of decision trees and payoff tables will be examined, as will techniques used in the analysis of problems involving uncertainty.

Management Information

9.7 Information Systems – Types and Applications

Topic Weighting   10%

Candidates are expected to demonstrate an understanding of the language and terminology, as well as the attributes of information systems and their general and specific applications. Systems such as MIS, DSS, SMIS, EIS, Expert and Accounting Information Systems are integral subjects in this part of the syllabus. Further, candidates will be expected to describe the organisation of files including those in database systems.

9.8 Systems Modelling

Topic Weighting   10%

Candidates should be able to present both manual and logic flowcharts of proposed systems, use dataflow diagrams to analyse new systems, and devise decision tables to analyse logic.

9.9 System and Development and Organisation

Topic Weighting   20%

Description of the stages of the systems life cycle, systems development methods SSM, SSADM, JSD, Object-oriented approaches must be known and compared, together with prototyping and the use of CASE tools. The location and distribution and general organisation of information systems is a major component of this section of the syllabus.

9.10 Systems Strategies and Management Issues

Topic Weighting   5%

Candidates must be able to explain and discuss the role of information systems (IS) in strategic planning as well as be aware of the issues involved in setting and managing IS tasks, operations, strategies; similarly, candidates must be able to discuss the features of ethics, law, audit and their implications for information systems.

9.11 Control and Security

Topic Weighting   10%

The control of an information system is an important dimension to its use, whether the system is to be controlled remotely or directly by the user.

Similarly, security of the investment in systems is well within this section of the syllabus in terms of access and risk analysis and handling.

9.12 Technology, Selection and Acquisition

Topic Weighting   5%

Knowledge of the components of hardware and software that may make up an information system are the essential elements of this section; candidates must be able to describe such components and be aware of their uses and limitations. Equally, candidates should be able to explain means of procuring hardware and software, and generally be able to justify alternative means of acquiring these elements, as well as information systems services. Knowledge of outsourcing and payment methods is also expected.

Relationship to Overall Syllabus

While accountants do not necessarily need to possess the level of knowledge and expertise equivalent to a qualified statistician, systems analyst or designer, they must be able to speak to such professionals and understand their language. The Management Information paper seeks to ensure that accountants can mix and liaise with such professionals by testing their understanding and knowledge of particular key elements within these realms. Accountants deal in financial data which is the basis of management information that can lead to particular future decisions and actions; they therefore must be familiar with a range of techniques and methodologies that may be employed to refine data into information that supports the taking of decisions. Indeed, accountants may well serve as a team member on projects also involving statisticians or systems specialists, or progress to becoming such specialists themselves after qualification.

Ethics

Candidates are advised that the standards outlined in The IFAC Code of Ethics for Professional Accountants issued by the International Ethics Standards Board for Accountants (IESBA Code) are implicit in, and examinable throughout, the AIA syllabus. The Code can be accessed via the AIA website at www.aiaworldwide.com

Recommended Reading

You can purchase any of the books listed quickly and easily on the AIA website through the AIA essential reading list webpage.

AIA Magazine – International Accountant

ISSN: 1465 - 5144

AIA Text Book

Paper 9 Management Information

Publisher: BPP Learning Media
ISBN: 9781 5097 8724 1

The e-Book is available at: exams@aiaworldwide.com

Contact our publisher BPP for information on purchasing a hard copy of the text book at: https://www.bpp.com/learning-media-listing/lmlist/6293

You can purchase any of the books listed below quickly and easily through the publisher's website or link stated below.

Business Information Systems: Analysis, Design and Practice (6th Edition)

Author: Curtis, G and Cobham, D
Publisher: Pearson Education Limited
ISBN: 9780273713821
Website: www.pearsoned.co.uk/bookshop/detail.asp?WT.oss=9780273713821&WT.oss_r=1&item=100000000248231

Quantitative Methods for Business (5th Edition)

Author: Waters, D
Publisher: Pearson Education Limited
ISBN: 9780273739470
Website: http://www.pearsoned.co.uk/bookshop/detail.asp?WT.oss=9780273739470&WT.oss_r=1&item=100000000370117

Essential Quantitative Methods for Business, Management and Finance

Author: Oakshott, Les
Publisher: Palgrave
6th edition, 2016
ISBN: 1137518553

Business Information: A Systems Approach (3rd Edition)

Author: Harry, M
Publisher: Pearson Education Limited
ISBN: 9780273646709
Website: http://www.pearsoned.co.uk/bookshop/detail.asp?WT.oss=Business%20Information%20A%20Systems%20Approach&WT.oss_r=1&item=100000000008600

INTRODUCTION

Command words and learning outcomes

The following list contains active command words and generic learning outcomes appropriate for use at each stage of the AIA qualification. Reference to the learning outcomes and use of the command words is essential to understanding how the assessment is applied in AIA exams.

Professional Level 1 Command Words

WORD	DEFINITION
ADVISE	To inform as necessary
ANALYSE	Examine in detail in order to interpret its meaning or essential features
APPLY	To use information or a technique
CALCULATE	Work out a value mathematically
CATEGORISE	To put into a group things or people with common qualities
COMPARE & CONTRAST	To explain the similarities and differences between things in order to interpret them
DEMONSTRATE	To show or prove by reasoning or evidence
DERIVE	To formulate or decide based on a particular source of information
DEVELOP	To bring to a more advanced stage
DIFFERENTIATE	To show the difference between
DISCUSS	To examine in detail by argument
IMPLEMENT	To carry out
INTERPRET	To explain the meaning of and to work out the significance of
ILLUSTRATE USING THE CASE	To clarify or explain by use of example or comparison
PRIORITISE	Place in order of importance
PRODUCE	To create or bring into existence
RELATE	To have reference or relation to
SOLVE	Find an answer to
VALUE	To assess the worth of something

Notes

1. The word 'Calculate' may be used at all levels of the syllabus

    CALCULATE   Select the appropriate method and techniques and apply your knowledge and understanding to work out and show how figures were arrived at.

2. The word 'Advise' may be used at all levels of the syllabus

    ADVISE   Notify or inform

3. For the Professional Level 1 exams, examiners may include a command word from the Foundation Level providing it is linked to another command word selected from the Professional 1 list. For example:

    '... prepare and discuss a set of accounts...'

4. For the Professional Level 2 exams, examiners may include a command word from the Foundation and Professional Level 1 providing it is linked to another command word from the Professional 2 list. For example:

    '...recommend the appropriate action and prepare a memo...'

The exam paper

Analysis of past papers

The analysis below shows the topics which were examined in all sittings of the current syllabus so far.

May 2018

Section A

1 Linear regression, hypothesis testing, critical path analysis

Section B

2 Anthony hierarchy, decision structure
3 Database management systems, entity relationship diagram
4 Expert systems

November 2017

Section A

1 Simulation, confidence intervals, decision theory

Section B

2 System development objectives and analysis, systems design process, user involvement
3 Cost effective hardware/software acquisition and installation process, security measures
4 DDP

May 2017

Section A

1 Linear regression, confidence intervals, linear programming

Section B

2 Decision making in Anthony hierarchy, DSS, ESS
3 Database management systems
4 Dataflow diagram

November 2016

Section A

1 Activity-on-the-node, critical path, simulation

Section B

2 Management information system development approaches, DSS
3 MIS technologies for virtual organisations, security of information
4 Dataflow diagram, entity models, prototyping

May 2016

Section A

1 Trend and seasonal variations, confidence interval, linear programming

Section B

2   SSADM, RAD, CASE
3   Customer relationship management, database management system
4   Data flow diagram, business activity modelling

November 2015

Section A

1   Coefficient of correlation and determination, linear programming, significance testing, pay-off tables, simulation

Section B

2   Operating systems, utility/systems, programming tools, off-the-shelf packages
3   Decision table, ERM, ERH, data flow diagram
4   Feasibility studies, MIS/ESS/ES, system integrity for LAN and WAN, audit trail system

May 2015

Section A

1   Linear programming, regression, sample size/confidence intervals, network analysis, chi-squared test

Section B

2   Data flow diagrams, ERM, decision table
3   Off-the-shelf package, systems development methodologies, JAD, structured walkthroughs and CASE tools
4   Security measures, information systems and strategic planning, expert systems, outsourcing and service provision

November 2014

Section A

1   Coefficient of correlation/determination, regression, confidence limits, network diagram, simulation

Section B

2   Systems development methodologies, SSADM, RAD
3   Data integrity, systems integrity, input controls, disaster recovery, back up controls and archiving
4   ESS/expert systems/DSS/MIS, off-the-shelf packages, decision table

May 2014

Section A

1   Correlation and regression, spreadsheets, linear regression, significance testing (central limit theorem) and sampling errors

Section B

2   Feasibility study, structured walkthroughs, tender evaluation using benchmark tests and weighted ranking scores
3   Decision table, manual flowchart
4   Levels of information, information systems and strategic planning, Earl's three leg analysis

November 2013

Section A

1. Linear programming, Simplex, coefficient of correlation, linear regression, significance testing (central limit theorem)

Section B

2. Information policy, security, disaster recovery plans, audit trail software
3. Data flow diagrams, logic flowchart, decision table
4. Software packages, bespoke software development methods, homeworking

May 2013

Section A

1. Linear programming, Simplex, linear regression, Chi-squared and significance, trend

Section B

2. Expert system, MIS, decision tables, flowchart
3. Security
4. Information strategy, bespoke vs off-the-shelf software

November 2012

Section A

1. Least squares regression, coefficient of correlation/ determination, linear programming

Section B

2. Computer system introduction
3. Information strategy in strategic planning, outsourcing
4. MIS, accounting software

May 2012

Section A

1. Linear regression
2. Chi-square and significance
3. Linear programming

Section B

4. Computer systems and management information
5. Decision tables
6. Data files and databases
7. Client-server architecture, websites and intranet

November 2011

Section A

1. Network diagrams, Gantt charts and histograms
2. Least squares regression, coefficient of correlation, coefficient of determination, forecasting
3. Simulation and expected values

INTRODUCTION

Section B

4 Changeover strategies, questionnaires, interviews, prototyping
5 Dataflow diagrams, ERM
6 Website benefits, extranet advantages and disadvantages, e-commerce strategy, computer hacking
7 Information systems, WAN, EDI

May 2011

Section A

1 Linear regression
2 Chi-square and significance
3 Linear programming

Section B

4 Computer systems and management information
5 Decision tables
6 Data files and databases
7 Client-server architecture, websites and intranet

November 2010

Section A

1 Linear regression
2 Network diagram
3 Sampling and standard deviation

Section B

4 Computer software
5 Earl's three-leg approach and CSFs
6 Computer system risks and controls
7 Computer system introduction

May 2008

Section A

1 Linear regression
2 Network diagram
3 Expected value

Section B

4 Management information and systems
5 Data entry and data capture
6 Computer system controls
7 Data files and databases

November 2007

Section A

1. Significance testing
2. Transportation problem
3. Network diagram

Section B

4. Data flow diagram
5. Computer system controls
6. E-commerce
7. Software languages

May 2007

Section A

1. Sampling and significance testing
2. Expected values and sensitivity analysis
3. Linear programming

Section B

4. Systems development
5. Computer controls
6. Information processing
7. Software packages

November 2006

Section A

1. Sampling and significance testing
2. Simulation, standard deviation and mean
3. Linear programming

Section B

4. Systems development
5. Decision tables
6. Systems analysis and feasibility reports
7. Information systems – types and applications

May 2006

Section A

1. Linear programming
2. Network analysis
3. Sampling and significance testing

Section B

4. Systems strategies
5. Technology, selection and acquisition
6. Security and controls
7. Data flow diagrams

INTRODUCTION

November 2005

Section A

1. Linear programming
2. Sampling and tests of significance
3. Management science techniques

Section B

4. Systems strategies
5. Decision support systems
6. Systems development and prototyping
7. Systems implementation

May 2005

Section A

1. Linear programming
2. Expected value and mean
3. Sampling and significance testing

Section B

4. Data flow diagrams
5. Systems analysis and design
6. Systems strategies
7. Technology, selection and design

November 2004

Section A

1. Linear programming
2. Sampling and significance testing
3. Network analysis

Section B

4. Computer systems audit
5. Data flow diagrams
6. Security and control
7. Project management

May 2004

Section A

1. Mean, standard deviation and probability
2. Linear programming
3. Network analysis

Section B

4. Systems analysis and design
5. Decision tables
6. End-user computing
7. Security and control

Revision of IAS 1: New terminology

Introduction

A revised IAS 1 *Presentation of Financial Statements* was issued in September 2007. The revised standard is covered in detail in the relevant financial accounting study texts.

The revised standard changes much of the terminology used in IASs and IFRSs. The new terminology has been used throughout this Study Text.

It is unlikely that you would lose marks in an exam if you accidentally said 'balance sheet', but it is better – and easier in the long run – to get into the habit of referring to the statements by their new names.

Most important terminology changes

Old standard	New standard
Balance sheet	Statement of financial position
Income statement	Statement of comprehensive income (one statement) *or*
	Income statement (separate) and statement of comprehensive income (two statements)
Statement of recognised income and expense	'Other comprehensive income' section of new comprehensive income statement. 'Other comprehensive income' for short
Cash flow statement	Statement of cash flows
Recognised in the income statement	Recognised in profit or loss (Note **or** not **and**)

Other terminology/wording changes

Old standard	New standard
'On the face of'	'in'
'Reporting date'	'end of the reporting period'
'Each balance sheet date'	'the end of each reporting period'
'Events after the balance sheet date'	'events after the reporting period'
'Equity holders'	'owners'
'Removed from equity and recognised in profit or loss' (recycling)	'reclassified from equity to profit or loss as a reclassification adjustment'
'Standard or interpretation'	'IFRS'

Changes to titles of IFRS

Old title	New title
IAS 7 *Cash flow statements*	IAS 7 *Statement of cash flows*
IAS 10 *Events after the balance sheet date*	IAS 10 *Events after the reporting period*

PART A

Techniques to support business decisions

Correlation and regression

Topic list	Syllabus reference
1 Forecasting using historical data	9.1
2 The high-low method	9.1
3 Linear regression analysis	9.1
4 Scatter diagrams and correlation	9.1
5 Sales forecasting	9.1
6 Regression and forecasting	9.1
7 The components of time series	9.1
8 Finding the trend	9.1
9 Finding the seasonal variations	9.1
10 Time series analysis and forecasting	9.1
11 Forecasting problems	9.1
12 Using spreadsheet packages to build business models	9.1

Introduction

In this chapter we will look at where the figures which go into business data such as budgets. To produce a budget calls for the **preparation of forecasts of costs and revenues**. Various quantitative techniques can assist with these **'number-crunching' aspects of budgeting.** This chapter aims to provide an understanding of those techniques within their budgetary context.

There is a certain amount of truth in the comment that **budgeting is more a test of forecasting skill than anything else**. Forecasts need to be made of sales volumes and prices, wage rates, material availability and prices, rates of inflation, the cost of bought-in services and overheads such as power. It is not sufficient to simply add a percentage to last year's budget in the hope of achieving a realistic forecast.

A **forecast** is a **best estimate** of what might happen in the future, based on certain assumptions about the conditions that are expected to apply. A **budget**, in contrast, is a **plan** of what the organisation is aiming to achieve and what it has set as a target. A budget should be **realistic** and so it will be based to some extent on forecasts prepared. In formulating a budget, management will try to establish some control over the conditions that will apply in the future.

PART A TECHNIQUES TO SUPPORT BUSINESS DECISIONS

1 Forecasting using historical data

FAST FORWARD

Two important quantitative methods the management accountant can use to obtain information for inclusion in budgets based on historical data, are the high-low method and linear regression analysis.

Numerous techniques have been developed for using past costs incurred as the basis for forecasting future values. These techniques range from simple arithmetic and visual methods to advanced computer-based statistical systems. With all techniques, however, there is the **presumption that the past will provide guidance to the future**. Before using any extrapolation techniques, the **past data** must therefore be critically examined to **assess their appropriateness for the intended purpose**. The following checks should be made.

(a) The **time period** should be long enough to include any periodically paid costs but short enough to ensure that averaging of variations in the level of activity has not occurred.

(b) The **data** should be examined to ensure that any non-activity level factors affecting costs were roughly the same in the past as those forecast for the future. Such factors might include changes in technology, changes in efficiency, changes in production methods, changes in resource costs, strikes, weather conditions and so on. Changes to the past data are frequently necessary.

(c) The **methods of data collection** and the accounting policies used should not introduce bias. Examples might include depreciation policies and the treatment of by-products.

(d) Appropriate choices of **dependent** and **independent variables** must be made.

The two forecasting methods which we are going to look at (the scatter diagram method and linear regression analysis) are based on the assumption that a **linear relationship** links levels of cost and levels of activity.

> **Knowledge brought forward from earlier studies**

Linear relationships

- A **linear relationship** can be expressed in the form of an equation which has the general form $y = a + bx$

    where   y   is the **dependent** variable, depending for its value on the value of x

    x   is the **independent** variable, whose value helps to determine the value of y

    a   is a **constant**, a fixed amount

    b   is a constant, being the **coefficient of x** (that is, the number by which the value of x should be multiplied to derive the value of y)

- If there is a linear relationship between total costs and level of activity, y = total costs, x = level of activity, a = fixed cost (the cost when there is no activity level) and b = variable cost per unit.

- The graph of a linear equation is a **straight line** and is determined by two things, the **gradient** (or slope) of the straight line and the point at which the straight line crosses the y axis (the **intercept**).

    – Gradient = b in the equation $y = a + bx = (y_2 - y_1)/(x_2 - x_1)$ where (x_1, y_1), (x_2, y_2) are two points on the straight line

    – Intercept = a in the equation $y = a + bx$

2 The high-low method

FAST FORWARD

The **high-low method** is a relatively simple way of determining the **fixed** and **variable** cost elements of **semi-variable** costs.

You may have encountered the high-low method in your earlier studies. It is used to identify the fixed and variable elements of costs that are **semi-variable**.

2.1 High-low method

Follow the steps below to estimate the fixed and variable elements of semi-variable costs.

Step 1 Review records of costs in previous periods:
- Select the period with the **highest** activity level.
- Select the period with the **lowest** activity level.

Step 2 If inflation makes it difficult to compare costs, adjust by indexing up or down.

Step 3 Determine the following:
- Total cost at high activity level
- Total costs at low activity level
- Total units at high activity level
- Total units at low activity level

Step 4 Calculate the following:

$$\frac{\text{Total cost at high activity level} - \text{Total cost at low activity level}}{\text{Total units at high activity level} - \text{Total units at low activity level}} = \text{variable cost per unit (v)}$$

Step 5 The fixed costs can be determined as follows. (Total cost at high activity level) − (total units at high activity level × variable cost per unit)

The following graph demonstrates the high-low method.

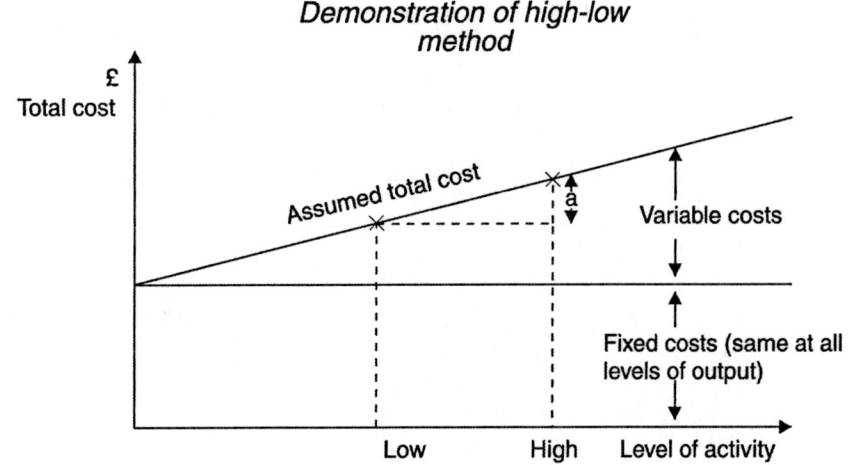

Demonstration of high-low method

2.2 Example: The high-low method with inflation

DG Co has recorded the following total costs during the last five years.

Year	Output volume Units	Total cost $	Average price level index
20X0	65,000	145,000	100
20X1	80,000	179,200	112
20X2	90,000	209,100	123
20X3	60,000	201,600	144
20X4	75,000	248,000	160

Required

Calculate the total cost that should be expected in 20X5 if output is 85,000 units and the average price level index is 180.

Solution

Step 1
- Period with highest activity = 20X2
- Period with lowest activity = 20X3

Step 2
- Adjust costs so that they can be compared.

- 20X2 indexed cost = $209,100 × $\frac{100}{123}$ = $170,000

- 20X0 indexed cost = $201,600 × $\frac{100}{144}$ = $140,000

Step 3
- Total cost at high activity level = 170,000
- Total cost at low activity level = 140,000
- Total units at high activity level = 90,000
- Total units at low activity level = − 60,000

Step 4 Variable cost per unit = $\frac{\text{Total cost at high activity level} - \text{Total cost at low activity level}}{\text{Total units at high activity level} - \text{Total units at low activity level}}$

= $\frac{170,000 - 140,000}{90,000 - 60,000}$ = $\frac{30,000}{30,000}$ = $1 per unit

Step 5 Fixed costs = (total cost at high activity level) − (total units at high activity level × variable cost per unit)

= 170,000 − (90,000 × 1) = 170,000 − 90,000 = $80,000

Therefore the costs in 20X5 for output of 85,000 units are as follows:

		$
Variable costs	85,000 × $1	85,000
Fixed costs		80,000
		165,000

However, we must now index up the 20X5 costs to reflect 20X5 price levels.

$165,000 × $\frac{180}{100}$ = $297,000

The step-by-step guide has been covered in order that you fully understand the process involved.

Question — High-low method

The Valuation Department of a large firm of surveyors wishes to develop a method of predicting its total costs in a period. The following past costs have been recorded at two activity levels.

	Number of valuations (V)	Total cost (TC)
Period 1	420	82,200
Period 2	515	90,275

The total cost model for a period could be represented by what equation?

Answer

Although we only have two activity levels in this question we can still apply the high-low method.

	Valuations V	Total cost $
Period 2	515	90,275
Period 1	420	82,200
Change due to variable cost	95	8,075

∴ Variable cost per valuation = $8,075/95 = $85.

Period 2: fixed cost = $90,275 − (515 × $85)
= $46,500

Therefore total costs = 46,500 + (85 × number of valuations)

3 Linear regression analysis

FAST FORWARD — Linear regression analysis (least squares technique) involves determining a **line of best fit**.

Linear regression analysis, also known as the **'least squares technique'**, is a **statistical method** of estimating costs using historical data from a number of previous accounting periods.

Linear regression analysis is used to derive a **line of best fit which has the general form y = a + bx**

where

y, the dependent variable = total cost

x, the independent variable = the level of activity

a, the intercept of the line on the y axis = the fixed cost

b, the gradient of the line = the variable cost per unit of activity

Historical data is collected from previous periods and adjusted to a common price level to remove inflationary differences. This provides a number of readings for activity levels (x) and their associated costs (y). Then, by substituting these readings into the formulae below for a and b, estimates of the fixed cost and variable cost per unit are provided.

PART A TECHNIQUES TO SUPPORT BUSINESS DECISIONS

Formula to learn

If $y = a + bx$, $b = \dfrac{n\Sigma xy - \Sigma x \Sigma y}{n\Sigma x^2 - (\Sigma x)^2}$ and $a = \dfrac{\Sigma y}{n} - \dfrac{b\Sigma x}{n}$

where n is the number of pair of data for x and y

Exam focus point

Note that you don't need to learn this formula, or the one in Section 4, as they are provided in the exam. But it would be very easy to make a mistake when copying them down so always double check back to the exam paper.

3.1 Example: Least squares method

The transport department of Norwest Council operates a large fleet of vehicles. These vehicles are used by the various departments of the Council. Each month a statement is prepared for the transport department comparing actual results with budget. One of the items in the transport department's monthly statement is the cost of vehicle maintenance. This maintenance is carried out by the employees of the department. To facilitate control, the transport manager has asked that future statements should show vehicle maintenance costs analysed into fixed and variable costs.

Data from the six months from January to June inclusive are given below.

	Vehicle maintenance cost $	Vehicle running hours
January	13,600	2,100
February	15,800	2,800
March	14,500	2,200
April	16,200	3,000
May	14,900	2,600
June	15,000	2,500

Required

Analyse the vehicle maintenance costs into fixed and variable costs, based on the data given, utilising the least squares method.

Solution

If $y = a + bx$, where y represent costs and x represents running hours (since costs depend on running hours) then $b = (n\Sigma xy - \Sigma x \Sigma y)/(n\Sigma x^2 - (\Sigma x)^2)$, when n is the number of pairs of data, which is 6 in this problem.

x '000 hrs	y $'000	xy	x²
2.1	13.6	28.56	4.41
2.8	15.8	44.24	7.84
2.2	14.5	31.90	4.84
3.0	16.2	48.60	9.00
2.6	14.9	38.74	6.76
2.5	15.0	37.50	6.25
15.2	90.0	229.54	39.10

Variable cost per hour, b = (6(229.54) − (15.2)(90.00))/(6(39.1) − (15.2)²)
= (1,377.24 − 1,368)/(234.6 − 231.04) = 9.24/3.56 = $2.60

Fixed costs (in $'000), a = (Σy/n) − (bΣx/n) = (90/6) − (2.6(15.2)/6) = 8.41 approx, say $8,400

 Cost levels

You are given the following data for output at a factory and costs of production over the past five months.

Month	Output '000 units x	Costs $'000 y
1	20	82
2	16	70
3	24	90
4	22	85
5	18	73

Required

(a) Calculate an equation to determine the expected cost level for any given output volume.
(b) Prepare a budget for total costs if output is 22,000 units.

Answer

(a) *Workings*

x	y	xy	x^2	y^2
20	82	1,640	400	6,724
16	70	1,120	256	4,900
24	90	2,160	576	8,100
22	85	1,870	484	7,225
18	73	1,314	324	5,329
Σx = 100	Σy = 400	Σxy = 8,104	Σx^2 = 2,040	Σy^2 = 32,278

n = 5 (There are five pairs of data for x and y values)

b = $(n\Sigma xy - \Sigma x \Sigma y)/(n\Sigma x^2 - (\Sigma x)^2)$ = $((5 \times 8,104) - (100 \times 400))/((5 \times 2,040) - 100^2)$
  = (40,520 − 40,000)/(10,200 − 10,000) = 520/200 = 2.6

a = $\bar{y} - b\bar{x}$ = (400/5) − (2.6 × (100/5)) = 28

y = 28 + 2.6x

where y = total cost, in thousands of pounds and x = output, in thousands of units.

(b) If the output is 22,000 units, we would expect costs to be 28 + 2.6 × 22 = 85.2 = $85,200.

3.2 The conditions suited to the use of linear regression analysis

The conditions which should apply if linear regression analysis is to be used to estimate costs are as follows.

(a) A **linear cost function should be assumed**. This assumption can be tested by measures of reliability, such as the correlation coefficient and the coefficient of determination (which ought to be reasonably close to 1). We will be looking at these concepts later in the chapter.

(b) When calculating a line of best fit, there will be a range of values for x. In the previous question, the line y = 28 + 2.6x was predicted from data with output values ranging from x = 16 to x = 24. Depending on the degree of correlation between x and y, we might safely use the estimated line of best fit to forecast values for y, provided that the value of x remains within the range 16 to 24. We would be on less safe ground if we used the equation to predict a value for y when x = 10, or 30, or any other value outside the range 16 to 24, because we would **have to assume that costs behave in the same way outside the range of x values used to establish the line in the first place.**

PART A   TECHNIQUES TO SUPPORT BUSINESS DECISIONS

Key terms

> **Interpolation** means using a line of best fit to predict a value within the two extreme points of the observed range.
>
> **Extrapolation** means using a line of best fit to predict a value outside the two extreme points.

(c) The **historical data** for cost and output should be **adjusted to a common price level** (to overcome cost differences caused by inflation) and the historical data should also be **representative of current technology, current efficiency levels and current operations** (products made).

(d) As far as possible, **historical data should be accurately recorded** so that variable costs are properly matched against the items produced or sold, and fixed costs are properly matched against the time period to which they relate. For example, if a factory rental is $120,000 per annum, and if data is gathered monthly, these costs should be charged $10,000 to each month instead of $120,000 in full to a single month.

(e) Management should either be **confident that conditions** which have existed in the past **will continue into the future or amend the estimates** of cost produced by the linear regression analysis to **allow for expected changes** in the future.

(f) As with any forecasting process, the **amount of data available is very important**. Even if correlation is high, if we have fewer than about ten pairs of data, we must regard any forecast as being somewhat unreliable.

(g) It must be assumed that the **value of one variable, y, can be predicted or estimated from the value of one other variable, x.**

Question   Linear regression model

The relationship between total operating cost and quantity produced (in a manufacturing company) is given by the linear regression model TC = 5,000 + 500Q, where TC = total operating cost (in $) per annum and Q = quantity produced per annum (kg).

What reservations might you have about relying on the above model for decision-making purposes?

Answer

(a) The reliability of the model is unknown if we do **not know the correlation coefficient**. A low correlation would suggest that the model may be unreliable.

(b) The model is probably **valid only over a certain range** of quantity produced. Outside this range, the relationship between the two variables may be very different.

(c) The model is **based on past data**, and assumes that what has happened in the past will happen in the future.

(d) The model **assumes that a linear relationship exists** between the quantity produced per annum and the total operating costs per annum. It is possible that a non-linear relationship may exist.

(e) The **fixed costs** of $5,000 per annum may be **misleading** if they include an element of allocated costs.

4 Scatter diagrams and correlation

4.1 The scatter diagram method of forecasting

FAST FORWARD

Scatter diagrams can be used to estimate the fixed and variable components of costs.

By this method of cost estimation, cost and activity data are plotted on a graph. A **'line of best fit'** is then drawn. This line should be drawn through the middle of the plotted points as closely as possible so that the distance of points above the line are equal to distances below the line. Where necessary costs should be adjusted to the same indexed price level to allow for inflation.

Scatter diagram method of estimating costs

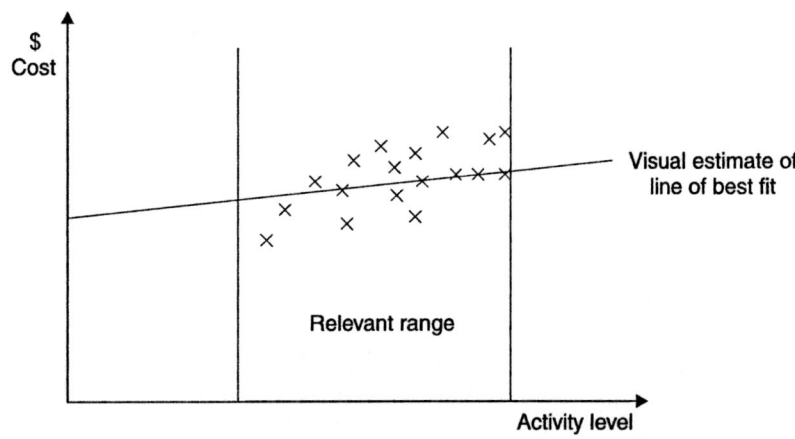

The fixed cost is the intercept of the line of best fit on the vertical axis. Suppose the fixed cost is $500 and that one of the plotted points (which is very close to the line or actually on it) represents output of 100 units and total cost of $550. The variable cost of 100 units is therefore calculated as $(550 − 500) = $50 and so the variable cost per unit is $0.50. The equation of the line of best fit is therefore **approximately** y = 500 + 0.5x.

If the company to which this data relate wanted to forecast total costs when output is 90 units, a forecast based on the equation would be 500 + (0.5 × 90) = $545. Alternatively the **forecast could be read directly from the graph using the line of best fit.**

The disadvantage of the scatter diagram method is that the cost line is drawn by visual judgement and so is a **subjective approximation**.

4.2 Correlation

FAST FORWARD

Correlation describes the extent to which the values of two variables are related. Two variables might be **perfectly** correlated, **partly** correlated or **uncorrelated**. The correlation may be **positive** or **negative**.

(a)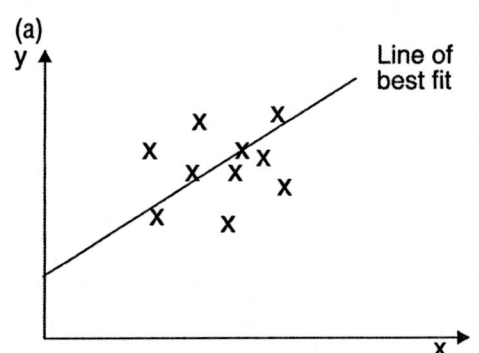

(b)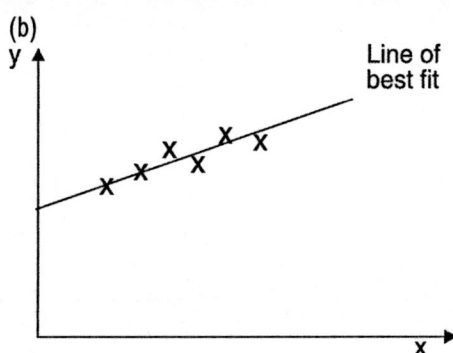

In the scatter diagrams above, you should agree that a line of best fit is more likely to reflect the 'real' relationship between x and y in (b) than in (a). In (b), the pairs of data are all close to the line of best fit, whereas in (a), there is much more scatter around the line.

In the situation represented in scatter diagram (b), forecasting the value of y from a given value for x would be more likely to be accurate than in the situation represented in (a). This is because there would be greater correlation between x and y in (b) than in (a).

> **Key term**
>
> **Correlation** is the degree to which change in one variable is related to change in another – in other words, the interdependence between variables.

4.3 Degrees of correlation

Two variables might be **perfectly correlated**, **partly correlated**, **uncorrelated** or subject to **non-linear correlation**.

(a) **Perfect correlation**

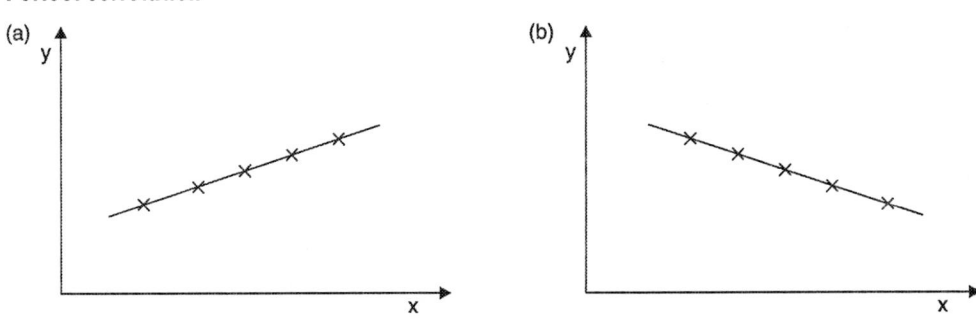

All the pairs of values lie on a straight line. An **exact linear relationship** exists between the two variables.

(b) **Partial correlation**

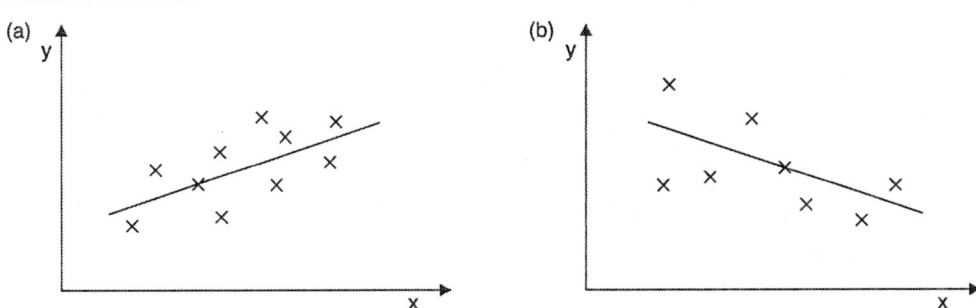

In the left hand diagram, although there is no exact relationship, **low values of x tend to be associated with low values of y, and high values of x with high values of y.**

In the right hand diagram, there is no exact relationship, but **low values of x tend to be associated with high values of y and vice versa.**

(c) **No correlation**

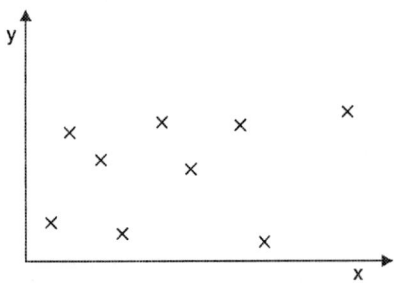

The values of these two variables are not correlated with each other.

(d) **Non-linear or curvilinear correlation**

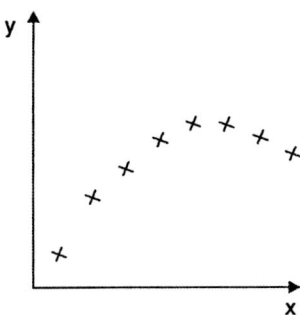

There is a relationship between x and y since the points are on an obvious curve but it is not a linear relationship.

4.3.1 Positive and negative correlation

Correlation, whether perfect or partial, can be **positive** or **negative**.

Key terms

Positive correlation is the type of correlation where low values of one variable are associated with low values of the other, and high values of one variable are associated with high values of the other.

Negative correlation is the type of correlation where low values of one variable are associated with high values of the other, and high values of one variable with low values of the other.

Question — Positive correlation

Which of the diagrams in Paragraph 4.3 demonstrate positive correlation?

Answer

The left hand diagrams for perfect and partial correlation.

4.4 Measures of correlation

FAST FORWARD

The degree of correlation between two variables can be measured using the **Pearsonian coefficient of correlation, r**. The **coefficient of determination** indicates the variations in the dependent variable that can be explained by variations in the independent variable.

4.4.1 The coefficient of correlation, r

The **degree of correlation between two variables** can be measured using the **Pearsonian coefficient of correlation** (also called the **product moment correlation coefficient**).

r has a value between –1 (perfect negative correlation) and +1 (perfect positive correlation). If r = 0 then the variables are uncorrelated.

Formula to learn

The **coefficient of correlation**, r, is calculated as follows.

$$r = \frac{n\Sigma xy - \Sigma x \Sigma y}{\sqrt{[n\Sigma x^2 - (\Sigma x)^2][n\Sigma y^2 - (\Sigma y)^2]}}$$

Look back at the example in Paragraph 3.1. Suppose that we wanted to know the correlation between vehicle maintenance costs and vehicle running hours. We can use a lot of the numbers that we calculated to find the variable and fixed costs in Paragraph 3.1, to determine r.

$$r = \frac{6(229.54) - (15.2)(90.0)}{\sqrt{[6(39.1) - (15.2)^2][6\Sigma y^2 - (90.0)^2]}} = \frac{1{,}377.24 - 1{,}368}{\sqrt{[(234.6 - 231.04)(6\Sigma y^2 - 8{,}100)]}}$$

All we need to calculate is Σy^2.

							Total
y ($'000)	13.60	15.80	14.50	16.20	14.90	15.00	90.00
y^2	184.96	249.64	210.25	262.44	222.01	225.00	1,354.30

$$r = \frac{9.24}{\sqrt{(3.56)(6 \times 1{,}354.30) - 8{,}100}} = 0.96$$

A **fairly high degree of positive correlation** between x (vehicle running hours) and y (vehicle maintenance cost) is indicated here **because r is quite close to +1**.

4.4.2 The coefficient of determination, r^2

Key term

> The **coefficient of determination** is a measure of the proportion of the change in the value of one variable that can be explained by variations in the value of the other variable.

In our example, $r^2 = (0.96)^2 = 0.9216$, and so 92% of variation in the value of y (cost) can be explained by a linear relationship with x (running hours). This leaves only 8% of variations in y to be predicted from other factors. It is therefore **likely that vehicle** running hours could be used with a high degree of confidence to predict costs during a period.

4.5 Correlation and causation

If two variables are well correlated this may be due to pure chance or there may be a reason for it. The **larger the number of pairs of data, the less likely it is that the correlation is due to chance**, though that possibility should never be ignored.

If there is a reason, it may not be causal. Monthly net income is well correlated with monthly credit to a person's bank account, for the logical (rather than causal) reason that for most people the one equals the other. **Even if there is a causal explanation** for a correlation, it **does not follow that variations in the value of one variable cause variations in the value of the other**. Sales of ice cream and of sunglasses are well correlated, not because of a direct causal link but because the weather influences both variables.

Having said this, it is of course possible that where two variables are correlated, there is a direct causal link to be found.

4.6 The interactions of r^2 and r with linear regression

The successful application of linear regression models depends on x and y being closely linearly related. r measures the strength of the linear relationship between two variables but **what numerical value of r is suggestive of sufficient linearity in data to allow one to proceed with linear regression?** The lower the value of r, the less chance of forecasts made using linear regression being adequate.

If there is a perfect linear relationship between the two variables ($r = \pm 1$), we can predict y from any given value of x with great confidence. If correlation is high (for example $r = 0.9$), the actual values will all be quite close to the regression line and so predictions should not be far out. If correlation is below about 0.7, predictions will only give a very rough guide to the likely value of y.

If $r = 0.75$, say, you may feel that the linear relationship between the two variables is fairly strong. But $r^2 = 56.25\%$ indicates that only just over half of the variations in the dependent variable can be explained by a linear relationship with the independent variable. The low figure could be because a non-linear relationship is a better model for the data or because extraneous factors need to be considered (and hence multiple regression analysis should be used). It is a common rule of thumb that $r^2 \geq 80\%$ indicates that linear regression may be applied for the purpose of forecasting.

4.7 Multiple regression and multiple correlation

Simple linear regression assumes that the value of one variable (the dependent variable) depends on the value of one other variable (the independent variable), so that it becomes possible to predict a value for the dependent variable given the value of the independent variable, and to measure a simple correlation coefficient r for the two variables.

Multiple linear regression analysis is based on the assumption that the value of the dependent variable depends on the values of two or more variables. For example:

$z = a + bx + cy$

In this formula, the value of a variable z depends on the values of both x and y.

Multiple regression analysis may be more appropriate than simple regression analysis in some situations, such as:

(a) Trying to relate the quantity of wheat production on a wheat farm to given amounts for both rainfall and the quantity of fertilisers used; or

(b) Estimating the costs of customer order handling from both the number of orders received and the number of customer complaints dealt with.

When multiple linear regression analysis is used, a multiple correlation coefficient R^2 can be calculated. This has a value between 0 and 1, with a value of 1 indicating perfect correlation.

5 Sales forecasting

> **FAST FORWARD**
>
> Sales are often the **principal budget factor**. Forecasting sales requires marketing information, and makes use of such techniques as **time series** and **'What if?'** analysis.

The sales budget is frequently the first budget prepared since **sales is usually the principal budget factor**, but before the sales budget can be prepared a sales forecast has to be made. Sales forecasting is difficult but management can use a number of forecasting methods, often combining them to reduce the level of uncertainty.

(a) **Sales personnel** can be asked to provide estimates.

(b) **Market research** can be used (especially for new products or services).

(c) **Mathematical** models can be set up so that repetitive computer simulations can be run which permit managers to review the results that would be obtained in various circumstances.

(d) Various **mathematical techniques** can be used to estimate sales levels. We will cover these in the remainder of the chapter.

6 Regression and forecasting

> **FAST FORWARD**
>
> Regression can be used to find a **trend line**, such as the trend in sales over a number of periods.

The same regression techniques as those considered earlier in the chapter can be used to **calculate a regression line (a trend line) for a time series**. A time series is simply a series of figures or values recorded over time (such as total annual costs for the last ten years). The determination of a trend line is particularly useful in forecasting. (We will be looking at time series and trend lines in more detail in the next section.)

The **years (or days or months) become the x variables in the regression formulae** by **numbering them from 0 upwards.**

6.1 Example: Regression and forecasting

Sales of product B over the seven year period from 20X1 to 20X7 were as follows.

Year	20X1	20X2	20X3	20X4	20X5	20X6	20X7
Sales of B ('000 units)	22	25	24	26	29	28	30

There is high correlation between time and the volume of sales.

Required

Calculate the trend line of sales, and forecast sales in 20X8 and 20X9.

Solution

Workings

Year	x	y	xy	x^2
20X1	0	22	0	0
20X2	1	25	25	1
20X3	2	24	48	4
20X4	3	26	78	9
20X5	4	29	116	16
20X6	5	28	140	25
20X7	6	30	180	36
	$\Sigma x = 21$	$\Sigma y = 184$	$\Sigma xy = 587$	$\Sigma x^2 = 91$

n = 7

Where y = a + bx
b = ((7 × 587) − (21 × 184))/((7 × 91) − (21 × 21)) = 245/196 = 1.25
a = (184/7) − ((1.25 × 21)/7) = 22.5357, say 22.5
y = 22.5 + 1.25x where x = 0 in 20X1, x = 1 in 20X2 and so on.

Using this trend line, predicted sales in 20X8 (year 7) would be 22.5 + 1.25 × 7 = 31.25 = 31,250 units.

Similarly, for 20X9 (year 8) predicted sales would be 22.5 + 1.25 × 8 = 32.50 = 32,500 units.

Exam focus point | Correlation and regression are examined regularly in the Paper 9 exam. Ensure you are comfortable with the techniques covered in this chapter.

7 The components of time series

A **time series** is a series of figures or values recorded over time. A time series has four components: a **trend**, **seasonal variations**, **cyclical variations** and **random variations**.

Key term | A **time series** is a series of figures or values recorded over time.

The following are examples of time series.

- Output at a factory each day for the last month
- Monthly sales over the last two years
- The Retail Prices Index each month for the last ten years

Key term

> A graph of a time series is called a **historigram**.

(Note the letters 'ri'; this is not the same as a histogram.) For example, consider the following time series.

Year	20X0	20X1	20X2	20X3	20X4	20X5	20X6
Sales ($'000)	20	21	24	23	27	30	28

The historigram is as follows.

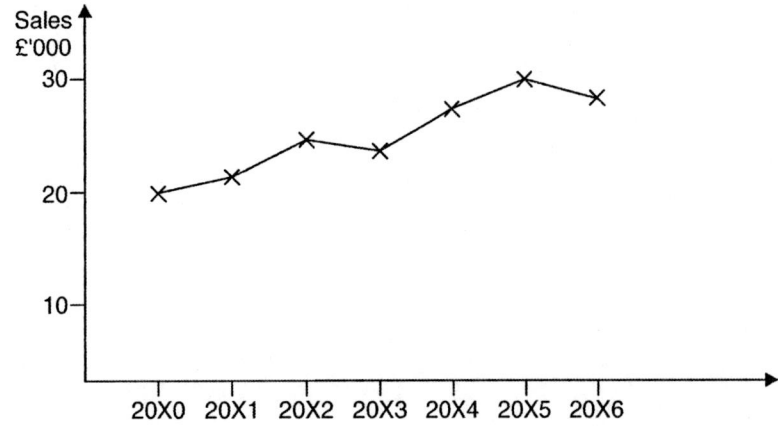

The horizontal axis is always chosen to represent time, and the vertical axis represents the values of the data recorded.

There are several **components of a time series** which it may be necessary to identify.

(a) A **trend**.

(b) **Seasonal variations** or fluctuations.

(c) Cycles, or **cyclical variations**.

(d) Non-recurring, **random variations**. These may be caused by unforeseen circumstances such as a change in government, a war, technological change or a fire.

7.1 The trend

Key term

> The **trend** is the underlying long-term movement over time in values of data recorded.

In the following examples of time series, there are three types of trend.

	Output per labour hour Units	Cost per unit $	Number of employees
20X4	30	1.00	100
20X5	24	1.08	103
20X6	26	1.20	96
20X7	22	1.15	102
20X8	21	1.18	103
20X9	17	1.25	98
	(A)	(B)	(C)

(a) In time series **(A)** there is a **downward trend** in the output per labour hour. Output per labour hour did not fall every year, because it went up between 20X5 and 20X6, but the long-term movement is clearly a downward one.

(b) In time series **(B)** there is an **upward trend** in the cost per unit. Although unit costs went down in 20X7 from a higher level in 20X6, the basic movement over time is one of rising costs.

(c) In time series **(C)** there is **no clear movement** up or down, and the number of employees remained fairly constant. The trend is therefore a static, or level one.

7.2 Seasonal variations

Key term

> **Seasonal variations** are short-term fluctuations in recorded values, due to different circumstances which affect results at different times of the year, on different days of the week, at different times of day, or whatever.

Here are two examples of seasonal variations.

(a) Sales of ice cream will be higher in summer than in winter.

(b) The telephone network may be heavily used at certain times of the day (such as mid-morning and mid-afternoon) and much less used at other times (such as in the middle of the night).

'Seasonal' is a term which may appear to refer to the seasons of the year, but its meaning in time series analysis is somewhat broader, as the examples given above show.

7.3 Example: A trend and seasonal variations

The number of customers served by a company of travel agents over the past four years is shown in the following historigram.

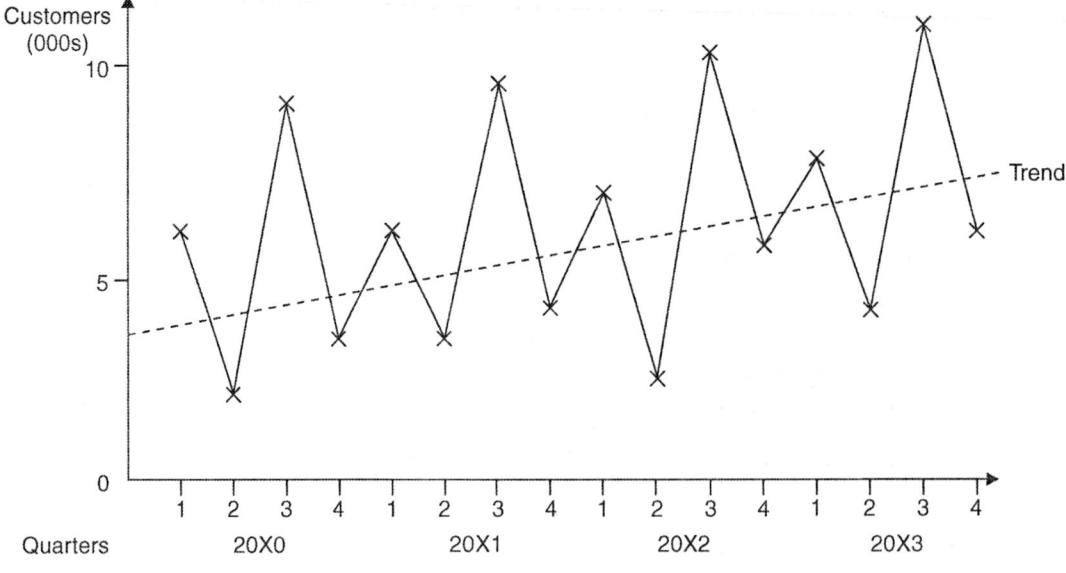

In this example, there would appear to be large seasonal fluctuations in demand, but there is also a basic upward trend.

7.4 Cyclical variations

Cyclical variations are **medium-term changes in results caused by circumstances which repeat in cycles**. In business, cyclical variations are commonly associated with economic cycles, successive booms and slumps in the economy. Economic cycles may last a few years. Cyclical variations are longer term than seasonal variations.

7.5 Summarising the components

In practice a time series could incorporate all of the four features we have been looking at and, to make reasonably accurate forecasts, the four features often have to be isolated. We can begin the process of isolating each feature by summarising the components of a time series as follows.

The **actual time series, Y = T + S + C + R**
where Y = the actual time series   C = the cyclical component
       T = the trend series   R = the random component
       S = the seasonal component

Though you should be aware of the cyclical component, it is unlikely that you will be expected to carry out any calculation connected with isolating it. The mathematical model which we will use, the **additive model**, therefore excludes any reference to C and is **Y = T + S + R**.

Key term

The **additive model** expresses a time series as Y = T + S + R.

We will begin by looking at how to find the trend in a time series.

8 Finding the trend

FAST FORWARD

Trend values can be determined by a process of **moving averages**.

Look at these monthly sales figures.

	August	September	October	November	December
Sales ($'000)	0.02	0.04	0.04	3.20	14.60

It looks as though the business is expanding rapidly – and so it is, in a way. But when you know that the business is a Christmas card manufacturer, then you see immediately that the January sales will no doubt slump right back down again.

It is obvious that the business will do better in the Christmas season than at any other time – that is the seasonal variation. Using the monthly figures, how can he tell whether or not the business is doing well overall – whether there is a rising sales trend over time other than the short-term rise over Christmas?

One possibility is to compare figures with the equivalent figures of a year ago. However, many things can happen over a year to make such a comparison misleading – new products might now be manufactured and prices will probably have changed.

In fact, there are a number of ways of overcoming this problem of distinguishing trend from seasonal variations. One such method is called **moving averages**. This method attempts to **remove seasonal (or cyclical) variations from a time series by a process of averaging so as to leave a set of figures representing the trend**.

A **moving average** is an average of the results of a fixed number of periods. Since it is an average of several time periods, it is **related to the mid-point of the overall period**.

8.1 Example: Moving averages

Year	Sales Units
20X0	390
20X1	380
20X2	460
20X3	450
20X4	470
20X5	440
20X6	500

Required

Take a moving average of the annual sales over a period of three years.

Solution

(a) Average sales in the three year period 20X0 – 20X2 were (390 + 380 + 460)/3 = 1,230/3 = 410. This average relates to the middle year of the period, 20X1.

(b) Similarly, average sales in the three year period 20X1 – 20X3 were (380 + 460 + 450)/3 = 1,290/3 = 430. This average relates to the middle year of the period, 20X2.

(c) The average sales can also be found for the periods 20X2 – 20X4, 20X3 – 20X5 and 20X4 – 20X6, to give the following.

Year	Sales	Moving total of 3 years sales	Moving average of 3 years sales (÷ 3)
20X0	390		
20X1	380	1,230	410
20X2	460	1,290	430
20X3	450	1,380	460
20X4	470	1,360	453
20X5	440	1,410	470
20X6	500		

Note the following points.

(i) The **moving average series has five figures** relating to the years 20X1 to 20X5. The **original series had seven figures** for the years from 20X0 to 20X6.

(ii) There is an upward trend in sales, which is more noticeable from the series of moving averages than from the original series of actual sales each year.

The above example averaged over a three-year period. Over what period should a moving average be taken? The answer to this question is that the **moving average which is most appropriate will depend on the circumstances and the nature of the time series**.

(a) A moving **average which takes an average of the results in many time periods will represent results over a longer term** than a moving average of two or three periods.

(b) On the other hand, with a moving average of results in many time periods, the **last figure in the series will be out of date by several periods**. In our example, the most recent average related to 20X5. With a moving average of five years' results, the final figure in the series would relate to 20X4.

(c) When there is a **known cycle** over which seasonal variations occur, such as all the days in the week or all the seasons in the year, the **most suitable moving average would be one which covers one full cycle**.

8.2 Moving averages of an even number of results

In the previous example, moving averages were taken of the results in an *odd* number of time periods, and the average then related to the mid-point of the overall period.

If a **moving average** of results was taken in an **even number of time periods**, the basic technique would be the same, but the mid-point of the overall period would not relate to a single period. For example, suppose an average were taken of the following four results.

Spring	120	
Summer	90	
Autumn	180	Average 115
Winter	70	

The average would relate to the mid-point of the period, between summer and autumn.

The trend line average figures need to relate to a particular time period; otherwise, seasonal variations cannot be calculated. To overcome this difficulty, we take a **moving average of the moving average**. An example will illustrate this technique.

8.3 Example: Moving averages over an even number of periods

Calculate a moving average trend line of the following results of Linden Co.

Year	Quarter	Volume of sales '000 units
20X5	1	600
	2	840
	3	420
	4	720
20X6	1	640
	2	860
	3	420
	4	740

Solution

A moving average of four will be used, since the volume of sales would appear to depend on the season of the year, and each year has four quarterly results. The moving average of four does not relate to any specific period of time; therefore a second moving average of two will be calculated on the first moving averages.

Year	Quarter	Actual volume of sales '000 units (A)	Moving total of 4 quarters' sales '000 units (B)	Moving average of 4 quarters' sales '000 units (B ÷ 4)	Mid-point of 2 moving averages Trend line '000 units (C)
20X5	1	600			
	2	840			
	3	420	2,580	645.0	650.00
	4	720	2,620	655.0	657.50
20X6	1	640	2,640	660.0	660.00
	2	860	2,640	660.0	662.50
	3	420	2,660	665.0	
	4	740			

By taking a mid point (a moving average of two) of the original moving averages, we can relate the results to specific quarters (from the third quarter of 20X5 to the second quarter of 20X6).

9 Finding the seasonal variations

FAST FORWARD

> **Seasonal variations** can be estimated using the **additive** model or the **proportional (multiplicative)** model.

Once a trend has been established we can find the seasonal variations. As we saw earlier, the additive model for time series analysis is $Y = T + S + R$. We can therefore write $Y - T = S + R$. In other words, if we deduct the trend series from the actual series, we will be left with the seasonal and residual components of the time series. If we assume that the random component is relatively small, and hence negligible, the **seasonal component can be found as $S = Y - T$**, the de-trended series.

The actual and trend sales for Linden Co (as calculated in Paragraph 8.3) are set out below. The **difference between the actual results for any one quarter (Y) and the trend figure for that quarter (T)** will be the seasonal variation for that quarter.

Year	Quarter	Actual	Trend	Seasonal variation
20X5	1	600		
	2	840		
	3	420	650.00	−230.00
	4	720	657.50	62.50
20X6	1	640	660.00	−20.00
	2	860	662.50	197.50
	3	420		
	4	740		

Suppose that seasonal variations for the third and fourth quarters of 20X6 and the first and second quarters of 20X7 are −248.75, 62.50, −13.75 and 212.50 respectively. The variation between the actual result for a particular quarter and the trend line average is not the same from year to year, but an **average of these variations can be taken**.

	Q1	Q2	Q3	Q4
20X5			−230.00	62.50
20X6	−20.00	197.50	−248.75	62.50
20X7	−13.75	212.50		
Total	−33.75	410.00	−478.75	125.00
Average (÷ 2)	−16.875	205.00	−239.375	62.50

Variations around the basic trend line should cancel each other out, and add up to zero. At the moment, they do not. We therefore **spread the total of the variations (11.25) across the four quarters (11.25 ÷ 4) so that the final total of the variations sum to zero.**

	Q1	Q2	Q3	Q4	Total
Estimated quarterly variations	−16.8750	205.0000	−239.3750	62.5000	11.250
Adjustment to reduce variations to 0	−2.8125	−2.8125	−2.8125	−2.8125	−11.250
Final estimates of quarterly variations	−19.6875	202.1875	−242.1875	59.6875	0
These might be rounded as follows	Q1: −20,	Q2: 202,	Q3: −242,	Q4: 60,	Total: 0

9.1 Seasonal variations using the proportional model

The method of estimating the seasonal variations in the above example was to use the differences between the trend and actual data. This model **assumes that the components of the series are independent** of each other, so that an increasing trend does not affect the seasonal variations and make them increase as well, for example.

The alternative is to use the **proportional model** whereby each actual figure is expressed as a proportion of the trend. Sometimes this method is called the **multiplicative model**.

Key term

The **proportional (multiplicative) model** summarises a time series as $Y = T \times S \times R$.

The **trend component** will be the **same whichever model is used** but the values of the **seasonal and random components** will **vary according to the model being applied**.

The example on Linden Co can be reworked on this alternative basis. The trend is calculated in exactly the same way as before but we need a different approach for the seasonal variations. The proportional model is $Y = T \times S \times R$ and, just as we calculated $S = Y − T$ for the additive model above we can calculate **$S = Y/T$** for the proportional model.

Year	Quarter	Actual (Y)	Trend (T)	Seasonal percentage (Y/T)
20X5	1	600		
	2	840		
	3	420	650.00	0.646
	4	720	657.50	1.095
20X6	1	640	660.00	0.970
	2	860	662.50	1.298
	3	420		
	4	740		

Suppose that seasonal variations for the next four quarters are 0.628, 1.092, 0.980 and 1.309 respectively. The summary of the seasonal variations expressed in proportional terms is therefore as follows.

	Q1 %	Q2 %	Q3 %	Q4 %
20X5			0.646	1.095
20X6	0.970	1.298	0.628	1.092
20X7	0.980	1.309		
Total	1.950	2.607	1.274	2.187
Average	0.975	1.3035	0.637	1.0935

Instead of summing to zero, as with the additive approach, the **averages should sum (in this case) to 4.0, 1.0 for each of the four quarters**. They actually sum to 4.009 so 0.00225 has to be deducted from each one.

	Q1	Q2	Q3	Q4
Average	0.97500	1.30350	0.63700	1.09350
Adjustment	–0.00225	–0.00225	–0.00225	–0.00225
Final estimate	0.97275	1.30125	0.63475	1.09125
Rounded	0.97	1.30	0.64	1.09

Note that the **proportional model is better than the additive model when the trend is increasing or decreasing over time**. In such circumstances, seasonal variations are likely to be increasing or decreasing too. The additive model simply adds absolute and unchanging seasonal variations to the trend figures whereas the proportional model, by multiplying increasing or decreasing trend values by a constant seasonal variation factor, takes account of changing seasonal variations.

10 Time series analysis and forecasting

FAST FORWARD

Forecasts can be made by calculating a **trend line** (using moving averages or linear regression), using the trend line to forecast future trend line values, and adjusting these values by the **average seasonal variation** applicable to the future period.

By extrapolating a trend and then adjusting for seasonal variations, forecasts of future values can be made.

Forecasts of future values should be made as follows.

(a) **Find a trend line using moving averages or using linear regression analysis.**

(b) **Use the trend line to forecast future trend line values.**

(c) **Adjust these values by the average seasonal variation applicable to the future period, to determine the forecast for that period.** With the additive model, add (or subtract for negative variations) the variation. With the multiplicative model, multiply the trend value by the variation proportion.

Extending a trend line outside the range of known data, in this case forecasting the future from a trend line based on historical data, is known as **extrapolation**.

10.1 Example: Forecasting

The sales (in $'000) of swimwear by a large department store for each period of three months and trend values found using moving averages are as follows.

Quarter	20X4 Actual $'000	20X4 Trend $'000	20X5 Actual $'000	20X5 Trend $'000	20X6 Actual $'000	20X6 Trend $'000	20X7 Actual $'000	20X7 Trend $'000
First			8		20	40	40	57
Second			30	30	50	45	62	
Third			60	31	80	50	92	
Fourth	24		20	35	40	54		

Using the additive model, seasonal variations have been determined as follows.

Quarter 1	Quarter 2	Quarter 3	Quarter 4
−$18,250	+$2,750	+$29,750	−$14,250

Required

Predict sales for the last quarter of 20X7 and the first quarter of 20X8, stating any assumptions.

Solution

We might guess that the trend line is rising steadily, by (57 − 40)/4 = 4.25 per quarter in the period 1st quarter 20X6 to 1st quarter 20X7 (57 being the prediction in 1st quarter 20X7 and 40 the prediction in 1st quarter 20X6). Since the trend may be levelling off a little, a quarterly increase of +4 in the trend will be assumed.

		Trend	Seasonal variation	Forecast
1st quarter	20X7	57		
4th quarter	20X7 (+ (3 × 4))	69	−14.25	54.75
1st quarter	20X8 (+ (4 × 4))	73	−18.25	54.75

Rounding to the nearest thousand, the forecast sales are $55,000 for each of the two quarters.

Note that you could actually plot the trend line figures on a graph, extrapolate the trend line into the future and read off forecasts from the graph using the extrapolated trend line.

If we had been using the proportional model, with an average variation for (for example) quarter 4 of 0.8, our prediction for the fourth quarter of 20X7 would have been 69 × 0.8 = 55.2, say $55,000.

Question — Sales forecast

The trend in a company's sales figures can be described by the linear regression equation y = 780 + 4x, where x is the month number (with January 20X3 as month 0) and y is sales in thousands. The average seasonal variation for March is 106%.

Required

Forecast the sales for March 20X5.

Answer

x = 26

Forecast = 1.06 × [780 + (4 × 26)] = 937.04 = $937,040 or about $937,000.

11 Forecasting problems

FAST FORWARD

Errors can be expected in forecasting due to unforeseen changes. This is more likely to happen the further into the future the forecast is for, and the smaller the quantity of data on which the forecast is based.

All forecasts are subject to error, but the likely errors vary from case to case.

- The **further into the future** the forecast is for, the **more unreliable** it is likely to be.
- The **less data** available on which to base the forecast, the **less reliable** the forecast.
- The historic **pattern** of trend and seasonal variations **may not continue** in the future.
- **Random variations** may upset the pattern of trend and seasonal variation.
- **Extrapolation** of the **trend line** is done by judgment and can introduce errors.

There are a number of changes that also may make it difficult to forecast future events.

Type of change	Examples
Political and economic changes	Changes in interest rates, exchange rates or inflation can mean that future sales and costs are difficult to forecast.
Environmental changes	The opening of high-speed rail links might have a considerable impact on some companies' markets.
Technological changes	These may mean that the past is not a reliable indication of likely future events. For example new faster machinery may make it difficult to use current output levels as the basis for forecasting future production output.
Technological advances	Advanced manufacturing technology is changing the cost structure of many firms. Direct labour costs are reducing in significance and fixed manufacturing costs are increasing. This causes forecasting difficulties because of the resulting changes in cost behaviour patterns, breakeven points and so on.
Social changes	Alterations in taste, fashion and the social acceptability of products can cause forecasting difficulties.

Management should have reasonable **confidence** in their estimates and forecasts. The assumptions on which the forecasts/estimates are based should be properly understood and the methods used to make a forecast or estimate should be in keeping with the nature, quantity and reliability of the data on which the forecast or estimate will be based. There is no point in using a 'sophisticated' technique with unreliable data; on the other hand, if there is a lot of accurate data about historical costs, it would be a waste of the data to use the scatter diagram method for cost estimating.

11.1 Illustration: domestic appliance

A domestic electrical appliance was introduced on the market in 20X2. At the point of sale customers are offered the chance to purchase an insurance policy to cover repairs and parts for the first five years of operation; these policies cannot be purchased later on, only when the appliance is bought. The table below shows the total industry sales of this appliance for the years 20X2 to 20X8 together with the number of insurance policies sold.

Year	Sales of appliance $m	Policy sales (number)
20X2	3	400
20X3	5	300
20X4	7	600
20X5	10	1,200
20X6	15	1,700
20X7	18	2,200
20X8	26	2,100

PART A   TECHNIQUES TO SUPPORT BUSINESS DECISIONS

Required

(a) Calculate the coefficient of determination between the appliance sales figures and the insurance policy sales, and interpret your value.

(b) Calculate the least squares regression equation to predict insurance policy sales from deflated appliance sales.

(c) The total sales of the electrical appliance in 20X9 are estimated at $51,000,000. Use the least squares regression equation to obtain a forecast of insurance policy sales for 20X9.

(d) Comment on why using this type of approach for predicting insurance policy sales in 20X9 may be problematic.

Solution

(a)

Appliance sales	Policy sales			
x	y	x^2	y^2	xy
$m	Hundreds			
3	4	9	16	12
5	3	25	9	15
7	6	49	36	42
10	12	100	144	120
15	17	225	289	255
18	22	324	484	396
26	21	676	441	546
84	85	1,408	1,419	1,386

The formula for r is provided in the exam.

$$r = \frac{n\Sigma xy - \Sigma x \Sigma y}{\sqrt{[n\Sigma x^2 - (\Sigma x)^2][n\Sigma y^2 - (\Sigma y)^2]}}$$

$$r^2 = \frac{(7 \times 1{,}386 - 84 \times 85)^2}{(7 \times 1{,}408 - 84^2)(7 \times 1{,}419 - 85^2)} = 0.87$$

This shows that **87% of the variation in policy sales is explained by variation in appliance sales.**

(b) For a regression line $y = a + bx$

$$b = \frac{n\Sigma xy - \Sigma x \Sigma y}{n\Sigma x^2 - (\Sigma x)^2} \text{ and } a = \frac{\Sigma y}{n} - \frac{b\Sigma x}{n}$$

$$\therefore b = \frac{7 \times 1{,}386 - 84 \times 85}{7 \times 1{,}408 - 84^2} = 0.915$$

$$\therefore a = \frac{85}{7} - 0.915 \times \frac{84}{7} = 1.163$$

y = 1.163 + 0.915x

Note. y is in hundreds of policies and x in millions of pounds.

(c) Predicted policy sales = 1.163 + 0.915 × 51 = 47.828 = 4,783 policies

(d) This prediction is based on the **assumption** that there is a **linear relationship** between appliance sales and policy sales. In fact, a non-linear relationship may exist, and there could well be other influences on policy sales.

12 Using spreadsheet packages to build business models

FAST FORWARD

> Spreadsheet packages can be used to build business models to assist the forecasting and planning process. They are particularly useful for 'what if?' analysis.

A spreadsheet is a type of general purpose software package that may be used in a wide range of business situations. It **can be used to build a model** in which data is presented in **rows and columns** and manipulated by the spreadsheet program. The most widely used spreadsheet package is Microsoft Excel.

A spreadsheet **model** is constructed as follows.

(a) Identify what data goes into each row and column and by **inserting text** (for example, row and column headings or labels).

(b) **Specify how the numerical data in the model should be derived.** Numerical data might be derived using one of the following methods.

   (i) **Insertion into the model via keyboard input.**

   (ii) **Calculation from other data in the model** by means of a formula specified within the model itself. The model builder must insert these formulae into the spreadsheet model when it is first constructed.

   (iii) **Retrieval from another file.**

12.1 The advantages of spreadsheets

Spreadsheets are a flexible tool, able to be applied to a wide range of tasks. Some of the more **common accounting applications** are listed below.

- Statements of financial position
- Cash flow analysis/forecasting
- General ledger
- Inventory records
- Job cost estimates
- Market share analysis and planning
- Profit projections
- Profit statements
- Project budgeting and control
- Sales projections and records
- Tax estimation

The great value of spreadsheets derives from their **simple format** of rows, columns and worksheets of data, and the ability to manipulate data using mathematical formulae. Spreadsheets bring powerful computer modelling within the everyday reach of data users.

12.2 The disadvantages of spreadsheets

Spreadsheets have disadvantages if they are not properly used.

(a) A **minor error in the design** of a model at any point can **affect the validity of data** throughout the spreadsheet. Such errors can be very difficult to trace.

(b) Even well-designed spreadsheets are **easy to corrupt** by accidentally changing a cell or inputting data in the wrong place.

(c) It is possible to **become over-dependent on them**, so that simple one-off tasks that can be done in seconds with a pen and paper are done on a spreadsheet instead.

(d) The possibility for experimentation with data is so great that it is possible to **lose sight of the original intention** of the spreadsheet.

(e) Spreadsheets **struggle to take account of qualitative factors** since they are invariably difficult to quantify. Decisions should not be made on the basis of quantitative information alone.

In summary, spreadsheets should be seen as a **tool in planning and decision making**. The user must make the decision.

12.3 'What if' analysis

Once a model has been constructed the consequences of changes in any of the variables may be tested by asking **'what if' questions, a form of sensitivity analysis**. For example, a spreadsheet may be used to develop a cash flow model, such as that shown below.

	A	B	C	D
1		Month 1	Month 2	Month 3
2	Sales	1,000	1,200	1,440
3	Cost of sales	(650)	(780)	(936)
4	Gross profit	350	420	504
5				
6	Receipts:			
7	Current month	600	720	864
8	Previous month		400	480
9		–	–	–
10		600	1,120	1,344
11	Payments	(650)	(780)	(936)
12		(50)	340	408
13	Balance b/f	–	(50)	290
14	Balance c/f	(50)	290	698

Typical 'what if' questions for sensitivity analysis

(a) What if the cost of sales is 68% of sales revenue, not 65%?

(b) What if payment from receivables is received 40% in the month of sale, 50% one month in arrears and 10% two months in arrears, instead of 60% in the month of sale and 40% one month in arrears?

(c) What if sales growth is only 15% per month, instead of 20% per month?

Using the spreadsheet model, the answers to such questions can be obtained simply and quickly, particularly if the variables such as gross profit percentage are held in a single cell, and referenced by other formulae. The information obtained should **provide management with a better understanding of what the cash flow position in the future might be**, and **what factors are critical to ensuring that the cash position remains reasonable**. For example, it might be found that the cost of sales must remain less than 67% of sales value to achieve a satisfactory cash position.

Chapter roundup

- Two important quantitative methods the management accountant can use to obtain information for inclusion in budgets based on historical data, are the high-low method and linear regression analysis.

- The **high-low method** is a relatively simple way of determining the **fixed** and **variable** cost elements of **semi-variable** costs.

- **Linear regression analysis** (least squares technique) involves determining a **line of best fit.**

- **Scatter diagrams** can be used to estimate the fixed and variable components of costs.

- **Correlation** describes the extent to which the values of two variables are related. Two variables might be **perfectly** correlated, **partly** correlated or **uncorrelated**. The correlation may be **positive** or **negative**.

- The degree of correlation between two variables can be measured using the **Pearsonian coefficient of correlation, r**. The **coefficient of determination** indicates the variations in the dependent variable that can be explained by variations in the independent variable.

- Sales are often the **principal budget factor**. Forecasting sales requires marketing information, and makes use of such techniques as **time series** and **'What if?'** analysis.

- Regression can be used to find a **trend line**, such as the trend in sales over a number of periods.

- A **time series** is a series of figures or values recorded over time. A time series has four components: a **trend**, **seasonal variations**, **cyclical variations** and **random variations**.

- **Trend** values can be determined by a process of **moving averages**.

- **Seasonal variations** can be estimated using the **additive** model or the **proportional (multiplicative)** model.

- **Forecasts** can be made by calculating a **trend line** (using moving averages or linear regression), using the trend line to forecast future trend line values, and adjusting these values by the **average seasonal variation** applicable to the future period.

- Errors can be expected in forecasting due to unforeseen changes. This is more likely to happen the further into the future the forecast is for, and the smaller the quantity of data on which the forecast is based.

- **Spreadsheet packages** can be used to build business **models** to assist the forecasting and planning process. They are particularly useful for 'what if?' analysis.

PART A   TECHNIQUES TO SUPPORT BUSINESS DECISIONS

Quick quiz

1   If the relationship between production costs and output is connected by the linear relationship y = 75x + 47,000, what is 47,000?

    A   The number of units produced
    B   Total production costs
    C   The production cost if 75 units are produced
    D   The fixed production costs

2   The costs of production runs consist of a mix of fixed and variable elements. The lowest number of production runs during the year was 120 during February, the highest number 150 during October. If the total costs of production runs in February were $80,000 and in October were $95,000, calculate the fixed and variable cost elements.

3   Fill in the missing words.

    Extrapolation involves using a .... of best .... to predict a value .... the two extreme points of the observed range.

4   Between sales of suntan cream and sales of cold drinks, one would expect (assuming spending money to be unlimited)

    A   Positive, but spurious, correlation
    B   Negative, but spurious, correlation
    C   Positive correlation indicating direct causation
    D   Negative correlation indicating direct causation

5   Which of the following statements is/are true of the coefficient of determination?

		True	False
(a)	It is the square of the Pearsonian coefficient of correlation.		
(b)	It can never quite equal 1.		
(c)	If it is high, this proves that variations in one variable cause variations in the other.		

6   What variable is used to signify 'time' in the regression equation y = a + bx when regression analysis is used for forecasting?

    A   x
    B   a
    C   b
    D   y

7   Which of the four components of a time series is missing from the list below?

    Trend
    Seasonal variations
    Random variations

8   Fill in the gaps with the appropriate mathematical symbols.

    Additive model of time series   Y = T .... S .... R
        Seasonal component, S   S = Y .... T
    Proportional model of time series   Y = T .... S .... R
        Seasonal component, S   S = Y .... T

Answers to quick quiz

1   D   The fixed production costs

2

	Number of runs	Total costs
		$
High	150	95,000
Low	120	80,000
	30	15,000

Variable costs per run = $\frac{15,000}{30}$ = $500

Fixed costs = 95,000 − (500 × 150) = $20,000

3   Line
    Fit
    Outside

4   A   When cold drinks sell well, so will suntan cream. Neither sales level causes the other; both are caused by the weather.

5   Statement (a) is true. The coefficient of determination is r^2.
    Statement (b) is false. r can reach 1 or −1, so r^2 can reach 1.
    Statement (c) is false. Correlation does not prove a causal link.

6   A   The correct answer is x.

7   Cyclical variations

8   Additive model of time series   =   T + S + R
        Seasonal component, S   =   Y − T
    Proportional model of time series   =   T × S × R
        Seasonal component, S   =   Y ÷ T

End of chapter questions

1   A plant nursery has estimated that when it grows 20,000 plants during a year its total costs will be $95,000 while if it grows 40,000 plants its costs are $170,000. Using the high-low method how much should it budget for costs if it expects to grow 35,000 plants next year?   **(5 marks)**

2   Identify and explain the components of a time series analysis.   **(5 marks)**

3   Using PEST analysis, give five examples of factors that might affect the level of sales of a national newspaper in the future. At least one example should be given for each PEST factor.   **(5 marks)**

PART A TECHNIQUES TO SUPPORT BUSINESS DECISIONS

Sampling theory and significance testing

Topic list	Syllabus reference
1 Population and samples	9.2
2 The theory of sampling (means)	9.2
3 The theory of sampling (proportions)	9.2
4 Significance testing	9.2

Introduction

It is often necessary to draw conclusions about a whole population by examining only a small sample taken from that population. In order to be able to do this successfully, it is very important that the sample is truly representative of the population.

PART A TECHNIQUES TO SUPPORT BUSINESS DECISIONS

1 Population and samples

FAST FORWARD

Population is the term used to mean all the items under consideration.

A sample is the group of items drawn from that population.

1.1 Definitions

Key terms

The term **population** is used to mean all the items under consideration.

A **sample** is a group of items drawn from a population.

The population may consist of items; it need not be people.

The purpose of sampling is to gain as much information as possible about the population by observing only a small proportion of that population, ie by observing the sample.

For example, in order to ascertain which television programmes are most popular, a sample of the total viewing public is monitored and, based on these results, the programmes can be listed in order of popularity with all viewers.

1.2 Why is sampling necessary?

Key term

A **sampling frame** is a list of all the members of the population. It can be used for selecting the sample. For example, if the population is electors, the sampling frame is the electoral register.

There are three main reasons why sampling is necessary:

(a) The whole population may not be known.

(b) Even if the population is known the process of testing every item can be extremely costly in time and money.

For example, checking the weight of every packet of tea coming off a production line would be a lengthy process.

(c) The items being tested may be completely destroyed in the process.

In order to check the lifetime of an electric light bulb it is necessary to leave the bulb burning until it breaks and is of no further use.

The characteristics of a population can be ascertained by investigating only a sample of that population provided that the following two rules are observed:

(a) The sample must be of a certain size. In general terms the larger the sample the more reliable will be the results.

(b) The sample must be chosen in such a way that each member of the population has an equal chance of being selected. This is known as random sampling and it avoids bias in the results.

There are several methods of obtaining a sample and these are considered in turn.

FAST FORWARD

There are various methods of sampling – random sampling, systematic sampling, stratified sampling, multi-stage sampling, quota sampling.

1.3 Random sampling

A simple random sample is defined as a sample taken in such a way that every member of the population has an equal chance of being selected. To achieve this, every item in the population must be numbered in

order. If a sample of, say, 20 items is required then 20 numbers from a table of random numbers are taken and the corresponding items are extracted from the population to form the sample, eg in selecting a sample of invoices for an audit. Since the invoices are already numbered this method can be applied with the minimum of difficulty.

This method has obvious limitations when either the population is extremely large or, in fact, not known. The following methods are more applicable in these cases.

1.4 Systematic sampling

If the population is known to contain 50,000 items and a sample of size 500 is required, then 1 in every 100 items is selected. The first item is determined by choosing randomly a number between 1 and 100, eg 67, then the second item will be the 167th, the third will be the 267th . . . up to the 49,967th item.

Strictly speaking, systematic sampling (also called quasi-random) is not truly random as only the first item is so selected. However, it gives a very close approximation to random sampling and it is very widely used, eg in selecting a sample of bags of sugar coming off a conveyor belt.

There is danger of bias if the population has a repetitive structure. For example, if a street has five types of house arranged in the order, A B C D E A B C D E . . . etc, an interviewer visiting every fifth home would only visit one type of house.

1.5 Stratified sampling

If the population under consideration contains several well defined groups (called strata), eg men and women, smokers and non-smokers, different sizes of metal bars, etc, then a random sample is taken from each group. This is done in such a way that the number in each sample is proportional to the size of that group in the population and is known as sampling with **probability proportional to size** (pps).

For example, in selecting a sample of people in order to ascertain their leisure habits, age could be an important factor. So if 20% of the population are over 60 years of age, 65% between 18 and 60 and 15% are under 18, then a sample of 200 people should contain 40 who are over 60 years old, 130 people between 18 and 60 and 30 under 18 years of age, ie the subsample should have sizes in the ratio 20 : 65 : 15.

This method ensures that a representative cross-section of the strata in the population is obtained, which may not be the case with a simple random sample of the whole population.

The method is often used by auditors to choose a sample to confirm receivable balances. In this case a greater proportion of larger balances will be selected.

1.6 Multi-stage sampling

If a nationwide survey is to be carried out, then this method is often applied.

Step 1   The country is divided into areas (counties) and a random sample of areas is taken.

Step 2   Each area chosen in Step 1 is then subdivided into towns and cities or boroughs and a random sample of these is taken.

Step 3   Each town or city chosen in Step 2 is further divided into roads and a random sample of roads is then taken.

Step 4   From each road chosen in Step 3 a random sample of houses is taken and the occupiers interviewed.

This method is used for example, in selecting a sample for a national opinion poll of the type carried out prior to a general election.

1.7 Cluster sampling

This method is similar to the previous one in that the country is split into areas and a random sample taken. Further sub-divisions can be made until the required number of small areas have been determined. Then every house in each area will be visited instead of just a random sample of houses. In many ways this is a simpler and less costly procedure as no time is wasted finding particular houses and the amount of travelling by interviewers is much reduced.

1.8 Quota sampling

With quota sampling the interviewer will be given a list comprising the different types of people to be questioned and the number or quota of each type, eg 20 males, aged 20 – 30 years, manual workers. 15 females, 25 – 35, housewives (not working). 10 males, 55 – 60, professional men . . . etc. The interviewer can use any method to obtain such people until the various quotas are filled. This is very similar to stratified sampling, but no attempt is made to select respondents by a proper random method, consequently the sample may be very biased.

1.9 Statistical enquiries

Many of the problems met in a business situation are capable of being treated statistically. The steps in a statistical enquiry are as follows:

Step 1   Define the problem. The population to be investigated must be clearly defined at this stage as well as the problem itself.

Step 2   Select the sample to be examined. The size of the sample and the method used to select the sample will have to be determined, and will depend on the degree of accuracy and budgeted cost of the enquiry.

Step 3   Draft the questionnaire. A pilot survey is conducted to test the questionnaire before it is finalised, as it cannot be amended once distributed.

Step 4   Collect the data. Data is collected in various ways where it has not already been collected for some other statistical purpose.

Step 5   Check the returned questionnaires. Responses to questionnaires are checked and sometimes coded before data tabulation can take place.

Step 6   Organise the data. Some data will need to be reorganised before it can be tabulated, ie items counted or values totalled.

Step 7   Analyse and interpret the data. Information collected has to be presented in a form that is easy to understand, ie tables, charts and graphs from which conclusions can be reached about the sample collected.

Step 8   Write the report. The conclusions arrived at in (7) above will form the basis of a report which will recommend a certain course of action.

1.10 Survey methods

Primary data can be collected in the following ways:

(a)   **Postal questionnaire**
This allows respondents to remain anonymous if desired. The main disadvantage is that many people will not bother to return the questionnaire, resulting in a low response rate. Those who do respond may do so because they have a special interest in the subject, resulting in bias.

(b) **Personal interview**
Questions are asked by a team of interviewers. A set questionnaire is still used to ensure that all interviewers ask the same questions in the same way, to minimise interviewer bias. The response rate is usually higher than (a), but employment of trained interviewers is costly.

(c) **Telephone interview**
Similar to personal interview, but only suitable where all members of the population have a telephone (eg business surveys). It is cheap and produces results quickly.

(d) **Observation**
Only suitable for obtaining data by counting (eg number of cars passing a traffic census point) or measuring (eg time taken to perform a task in work study).

1.11 Misleading statistics

Before leaving the topic of published statistics, it is necessary to mention a word of caution when dealing with statistical data.

All graphs, charts, tables, diagrams, etc must be carefully studied for units, scales, dates, etc.

All statements must be read and analysed for ambiguities and bias.

The following example may help to underline this last point.

1.12 Example

Badly worded statements can bring the subject of statistics into disrepute.

You are required to consider the following statements and:

(a) Explain briefly where they mislead or fail to make sense

(b) Re-word them in a more acceptable form

    (i) 'Nine out of ten people in this country would oppose a policy of state intervention in the Z industry'.

    (ii) 'Unemployment up 10% . . .' as stated in newspaper A;

        'Unemployment down 10% . . .' as stated in newspaper B, both on the same day.

    (iii) 'There are 2.41 children per family in the country of Y'.

    (iv) '80% of car accidents occurred within three miles of the driver's home, therefore, longer journeys must be safer'.

Solution

(i) (a) The statement presumably gives the opinion of a **sample** of people, and the proportion of 'nine out of ten' must be an **average** figure. With the present wording, the statement implies, however, that **exactly** nine out of ten people in the population **as a whole** would oppose state intervention in the Z industry.

    (b) A better wording would be:

'In a sample of 2,500 people interviewed recently, about 90% said that they were opposed to state intervention in the Z industry'.

(ii) (a) Although the statements seem at first sight to be incompatible, this is not necessarily the case since no base dates are given. Also, it may be that one newspaper was quoting actual unemployment and the other was quoting seasonally adjusted values.

PART A   TECHNIQUES TO SUPPORT BUSINESS DECISIONS

(b) The alternative wordings:

'Unemployment up 10% since July 1988'; 'Unemployment down 10% since March 1993' renders the statements compatible.

(iii) (a) The figure of 2.41 is clearly an average: no family can have exactly 2.41 children. Further, the precise figure is not particularly helpful.

(b) An adequate wording would be:

'On average, there are between two and three children per family in the country of Y'.

(iv) (a) Longer journeys might perhaps be safer, but such an inference cannot be drawn from the first part of the statement. If the majority of journeys are made within three miles of people's homes, then one would expect the majority of accidents to occur there.

(b) The false conclusion should be omitted so that the statement reads: 'The majority of car accidents occurred within three miles of the driver's home'.

2 The theory of sampling (means)

FAST FORWARD The most commonly used statistics are the mean and the standard deviation.

2.1 Using data from samples

A sample may be taken to obtain a quantitative measurement. For example we may take a sample measurement of the number of hours spent by teenage children on a mobile phone each day in a particular city. From the sample we could measure:

(a) The average time on a mobile for the children in the sample ($\bar{x}$).

(b) The spread of times: not all children spend the same length of time in the day on a mobile phone. A common statistical measurement for spread of values within a sample is the standard deviation of the sample (s).

If there is only one sample, we can use the sample to estimate values for the entire population from which the sample was drawn. In the example above, we could use the sample results for the average time on the mobile and assume that the same applies to for all children in the city.

(a) We could assume that the population mean (μ) equals the sample mean ($\bar{x}$).

(b) We can also estimate the standard deviation of values within the population (σ) from the standard deviation of the single sample (s).

2.2 Unbiased estimates

If just one sample is randomly selected from a given population, the mean ($\bar{x}$) of the sample will give the best (ie unbiased) estimate of the population mean (μ).

When the standard deviation of a population is estimated from a sample rather than from measuring every member of the population, this is denoted by placing the symbol ^ over the symbol for standard deviation. Thus:

σ = Exact population standard deviation, obtained by measuring every item in the population.
$\hat{\sigma}$ = Population standard deviation estimated from a sample (called 'sigma hat').
s = Sample standard deviation (ie the standard deviation of the items in the sample).

It is a proven fact that the sample standard deviation tends to underestimate the population standard deviation. It is said to be a biased estimator. A better, unbiased, estimate is obtained by multiplying the sample standard deviation by:

$$\sqrt{\frac{n}{n-1}}$$

This is known as Bessel's correction. However, when $n \geq 30$, this correction factor makes little difference and its use is then optional:

$\mu = \bar{x}$ for all values of n

$\hat{\sigma} = s \times \sqrt{\frac{n}{n-1}}$ for all values of n

$\simeq s$ for $n \geq 30$

Note on formulae for calculating standard deviations

By definition, $s = \sqrt{\frac{\Sigma(x-\bar{x})^2}{n}}$ or $\sqrt{\frac{\Sigma x^2}{n} - \left(\frac{\Sigma x}{n}\right)^2}$

Applying Bessel's correction:

$\hat{\sigma} = \sqrt{\frac{\Sigma(x-\bar{x})^2}{n}} \times \sqrt{\frac{n}{n-1}}$ or $\sqrt{\frac{\Sigma x^2 - \frac{(\Sigma x)^2}{n}}{n}} \times \sqrt{\frac{n}{n-1}}$

$= \sqrt{\frac{\Sigma(x-\bar{x})^2}{n-1}}$ or $\sqrt{\frac{\Sigma x^2 - \frac{(\Sigma x)^2}{n}}{n-1}}$

Thus, when $n-1$ is used as the divisor for calculating the standard deviation, it is $\hat{\sigma}$ that is being calculated, not s.

2.3 Example

A random sample of 15 metal bars is taken from a day's production. The weights of the bars in kg are:

1,205, 1,205, 1,208, 1,215, 1,260, 1,270, 1,271, 1,272, 1,283, 1,286, 1,289, 1,290, 1,291, 1,292, 1,293.

Using this data, the best possible point estimates of the mean and standard deviation of the weights of all such bars are calculated as follows:

(a) Estimate the mean of the population.

$\bar{x} = \frac{\Sigma x}{n}$

$= \frac{1{,}205 + 1{,}205 + 1{,}208 + \ldots + 1{,}293}{15}$ kg

$= \frac{18{,}930}{15}$ kg

$= 1{,}262$ kg

$\therefore \bar{x} = 1{,}262$ kg. This is the mean of the sample and can be used as an estimate of the population mean.

ie $\mu = 1{,}262$ kg. This is the estimate of the mean of the population based on the sample data

(b) Estimate the standard deviation of the population

Step 1 Calculate the standard deviation of the sample.

$$x^2 = 1{,}452{,}025,\ 1{,}452{,}025,\ 1{,}459{,}264,\ 1{,}476{,}225,\ 1{,}587{,}600,$$
$$1{,}612{,}900,\ 1{,}615{,}441,\ 1{,}617{,}984,\ 1{,}646{,}089,\ 1{,}653{,}796,$$
$$1{,}661{,}521,\ 1{,}664{,}100,\ 1{,}666{,}681,\ 1{,}669{,}264,\ 1{,}671{,}849$$

$$\Sigma x^2 = 23{,}906{,}764$$

$$s = \sqrt{\frac{\Sigma x^2 - \frac{(\Sigma x)^2}{n}}{n}} = \sqrt{\frac{\Sigma x^2}{n} - \left(\frac{\Sigma x}{n}\right)^2}$$

$$= \sqrt{\frac{23{,}906{,}764}{15} - \left(\frac{18{,}930}{15}\right)^2}$$

$$= 33.77 \text{ kg}$$

Step 2 Estimate the standard deviation of the population using $\hat{\sigma} = s \times \sqrt{\frac{n}{n-1}}$

$$\hat{\sigma} = 33.77 \times \sqrt{\frac{15}{14}}$$

$$= 34.96 \text{ kg}$$

or

$$\hat{\sigma} = \sqrt{\frac{\Sigma x^2 - \frac{(\Sigma x)^2}{n}}{n-1}}$$

$$= \sqrt{\frac{23{,}906{,}764 - \frac{(18{,}930)^2}{15}}{14}}$$

$$= 34.96 \text{ kg as before}$$

∴ the unbiased estimate of the population standard deviation = 35 kg (2 sf.).

2.4 Further example

A further example illustrating when to use n and when to use $n-1$ in the calculation of standard deviations:

A random sample of 5 wooden tables was selected from a large production run (the 'population').

The lengths of the 5 tables, in metres, were found to be:

1.25, 1.30, 1.32, 1.26, 1.21.

It is required to obtain:

(a) The mean length of the 5 tables selected (ie the sample mean).

(b) The standard deviation of length of the 5 tables selected (ie the standard deviation of the sample).

(c) The mean length of all tables in the production run (ie the population mean).

(d) The standard deviation of length of all tables in the production run (ie the population standard deviation).

Solution

Note. As every table made in the large production run was not measured, it is not possible to calculate the exact mean and standard deviation of the population; they must be estimated from the sample of 5 selected, which is why the sample was taken.

Initial calculations:

$\Sigma x = 1.25 + 1.30 + 1.32 + 1.26 + 1.21 = 6.34$ metres

$\Sigma x^2 = (1.25)^2 + (1.30)^2 + (1.32)^2 + (1.26)^2 + (1.21)^2 = 8.0466$ square metres

(a) The mean length of the five tables is $\bar{x}$, where

$$\bar{x} = \frac{\Sigma x}{n} = \frac{6.34}{5} = 1.27 \text{ metres (to 3 sig figs)}$$

This is the sample mean.

(b) The standard deviation of length of the five tables is s. This is where n is used as the divisor, hence

$$s = \sqrt{\frac{\Sigma x^2}{n} - \left(\frac{\Sigma x}{n}\right)^2}$$

$$= \sqrt{\frac{8.0466}{5} - \left(\frac{6.34}{5}\right)^2}$$

$$= 0.0387 \text{ metres (3 sf)}$$

This is the sample standard deviation.

(c) The estimated mean length of the whole production run is the same as the mean of the sample, hence

Estimated population mean = 1.27 metres.

(d) The estimated standard deviation of length of table for the whole production run is $\hat{\sigma}$. This is where $n - 1$ is used as the divisor, hence

$$\hat{\sigma} = s\sqrt{\frac{n}{n-1}} = 0.0387 \times \sqrt{\frac{5}{4}}$$

$$= 0.0433 \text{ metres (3 sf)}$$

This is the estimated population standard deviation.

In sampling theory, it is usually the estimated population standard deviation rather than the sample standard deviation that is required so if you are still in doubt as to which formula to use, use the one with $n - 1$ as the divisor, as this will more likely be the correct one.

2.5 The Central Limit Theorem

Estimates of a population mean from a single sample may be unreliable, and the sample mean is likely to be different from the mean of the population as a whole. The purpose of taking samples in statistics is to learn about the population as a whole.

Instead of using just one sample to estimate a population mean, we could take a number of different samples, and compare the sample results. If the population has a normal distribution of values, the Central Limit Theorem will then apply.

The Central Limit Theorem states that, if a sufficient number of samples of a given size n are taken from a population with normally-distributed values, the sample means will have:

(a) A mean value equal to the population mean μ.

(b) Values that are normally distributed around this population mean.

(c) A standard deviation of their mean values equal to a value called the standard error (explained later).

In other words, if we have a large number of samples from the same population:

(a) The mean of the sample means will equal the population mean; and

(b) These sample means will be normally distributed around the population mean with a standard deviation of mean values equal to the standard error.

The Central Limit Theorem applies not only to populations whose values are normally distributed, but also to populations whose values are not normally distributed, **provided that the sample sizes are sufficiently large.**

2.6 Distribution of sample means

FAST FORWARD

If a large number of samples of the same size are drawn from a given population and the mean of each calculated, the mean of all the samples means will be the population mean.

The standard deviation of the sampling distribution is known as the standard error.

If two samples of the same size are drawn from a given population they will not be identical, even though each has been randomly selected. So if the mean of each sample is calculated, two different values will result, each of which could be used to estimate the population mean.

If a large number of samples of the same size (n) are drawn from a given population and the mean of each calculated, a distribution of values will be obtained. This is known as the **sampling distribution of the mean** or the **distribution of sample means.**

When large samples are taken (ie n ≥ 30) this distribution is found to be normally distributed irrespective of the form of the distribution of the parent population.

Furthermore, the mean of all the sample means is the population mean. So the distribution of sample means will be of the type:

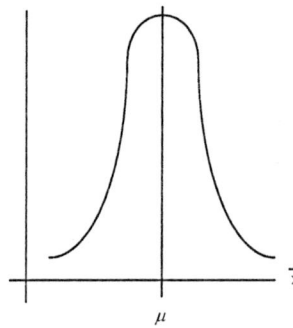

Any normal distribution is completely defined by its mean and standard deviation. To avoid confusion, the standard deviation of **this** sampling distribution is called the **standard error** and its value is $\dfrac{\sigma}{\sqrt{n}}$ (ie the population standard deviation divided by the square root of the sample size).

The larger the sample size (n) the smaller will be the value of the standard error $\dfrac{\sigma}{\sqrt{n}}$ and the less dispersed will be the sample means about the population mean. **This means that we can expect larger samples to provide more reliable estimates of the population mean.**

2: SAMPLING THEORY AND SIGNIFICANCE TESTING

A sample mean will not equal the population mean, but we can use the standard error, as a standard deviation of sample means, to estimate a range of values or confidence interval within which the population mean probably lies.

Since the distribution of sample means is normal with mean μ and the standard deviation of sample means (or standard error) related to the population standard deviation as shown above, the following 'z score' can be used with normal distribution tables to make probability estimates about the population mean:

$$z = \frac{\bar{x} - \mu}{\frac{\sigma}{\sqrt{n}}}$$

where the z score is the difference between the population mean and the sample mean, divided by the standard error of the sample means. This is the number of standard deviations between the population mean and the sample mean, and this can be used in statistical analysis of the population mean.

The following points should be noted:

(a) The population from which the samples are drawn need not itself be normally distributed, provided that the sample sizes are sufficiently large. It is the sample means that are normally distributed about the population mean.

(b) The standard error, $\frac{\sigma}{\sqrt{n}}$ of the means is **not** the sample standard deviation **nor** the population standard deviation; it is an entirely separate value that measures the spread (or dispersion) of the sample means. It happens to depend on σ and n which is not surprising, though this need not be proved at this level.

(c) n is the size of each sample and **not** the number of samples that are taken. In general, only one sample is available and all conclusions are based on the one set of data as will be seen shortly.

(d) The main reason for taking samples is so that inferences can be made about the population under consideration. It is, therefore, very likely that σ will not be known and therefore *s*, the sample standard deviation, must be used to estimate σ.

(e) It is assumed that the population is very large, so that any sample forms only a very small proportion of that population (less than 5%).

(f) A further necessary assumption is that the sample size is ≥ 30.

2.7 Example

The mean length of a component is specified as 20cm with a standard deviation of 0.51cm. The probability that a sample of 100 rods will have a mean less than 19.85cm is calculated as follows:

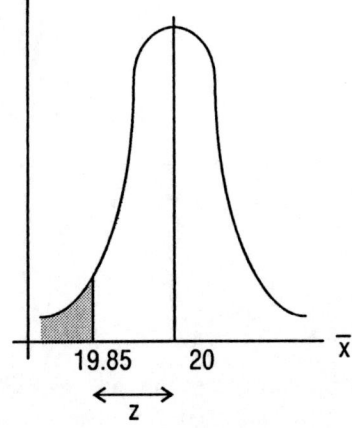

μ = 20,   σ = 0.51,   n = 100, $\bar{x}$ = 19.85

$$\text{standard error} = \frac{\sigma}{\sqrt{n}}$$

$$= \frac{0.51}{\sqrt{100}}$$

$$= 0.051 \text{ cm}$$

Standardising: $z = \dfrac{19.85 - 20}{0.051}$

$$= \frac{-0.15}{0.051}$$

$= -2.94$ Area $= 0.5 - 0.4984$

$$= 0.0016$$

(ie 19.85 is 2.94 standard errors below the population mean of 20.)

∴ $P(\bar{x} < 19.85)$ = $P(z < -2.94)$
= 0.0016
= 0.16%

2.8 Confidence intervals

FAST FORWARD

Instead of giving just a point estimate of the population mean, it is possible to give a probable range of values in which the population mean lies together with the probability that it lies in this range – known as a confidence interval.

Instead of giving just a point estimate of the population mean, it is possible to give a probable range of values in which the population mean lies and the probability that it does in fact lie within this range. This range of values is known as a **confidence interval**. The lower and upper limits of this interval are called **confidence limits, or precision limits**. The probability that the population value lies within this range is known as the **confidence level**.

In order to calculate the limits of a confidence interval, the following critical values must first be understood.

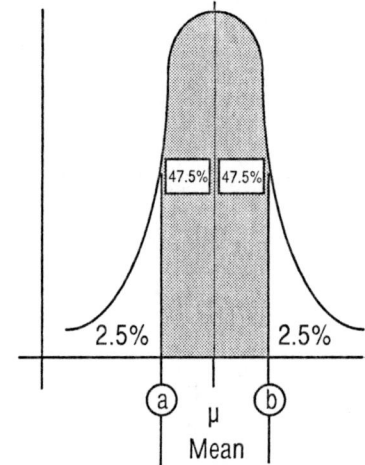

$-1.96 \dfrac{\sigma}{\sqrt{n}}$ $+1.96 \dfrac{\sigma}{\sqrt{n}}$

95% of the area under any normal curve is contained within ± 1.96 standard deviations of the mean. This can be checked from normal curve tables. 1.96 standard deviations corresponds to 0.475 or 47.5 % of the area; twice this (remembering that the tables are one-sided) gives 95%.

So, for a sampling distribution, the range from $\mu - 1.96\dfrac{\sigma}{\sqrt{n}}$ to $\mu + 1.96\dfrac{\sigma}{\sqrt{n}}$

((a) to (b) above) contains 95% of all the sample means. Therefore, the probability that a sample mean lies within this range is 0.95 and the probability that a sample mean lies outside this range is 0.05. So ninety-five samples out of every 100 would yield a mean value in this range and only five samples in every 100 would yield a value outside this range.

Also:

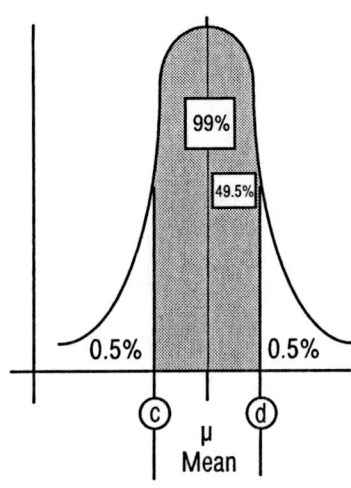

$-2.58\dfrac{\sigma}{\sqrt{n}}$ $+2.58\dfrac{\sigma}{\sqrt{n}}$

99% of the area under any normal curve is contained within ± 2.58 standard deviations of the mean. So for a sampling distribution the range from

$\mu - 2.58\dfrac{\sigma}{\sqrt{n}}$ to $\mu + 2.58\dfrac{\sigma}{\sqrt{n}}$ ((c) to (d) above)

contains 99% of all sample means. Therefore, the probability that a sample mean lies within this range is 0.99 and the probability that it falls outside the range is 0.01. So out of every 100 samples ninety-nine would yield a value within the range and only one would give a value outside it.

It therefore follows that there is a 95% probability that the population mean lies within ± 1.96 standard errors of a sample mean, ie in the range:

$\bar{x} - 1.96\dfrac{\sigma}{\sqrt{n}}$ to $\bar{x} + 1.96\dfrac{\sigma}{\sqrt{n}}$

There is a 99% probability that the population mean lies within ± 2.58 standard errors of a sample mean, ie in the range

$\bar{x} - 2.58\dfrac{\sigma}{\sqrt{n}}$ to $\bar{x} + 2.58\dfrac{\sigma}{\sqrt{n}}$

These ranges of values are known as the 95% and 99% confidence intervals for the population mean. Any size of confidence interval can be set up, by using the appropriate number of standard errors, but these are two very commonly used values.

2.9 Summary

95% confidence limits = $\bar{x}$ ± 1.96 standard errors

99% confidence limits = $\bar{x}$ ± 2.58 standard errors

where the standard error $= \dfrac{\sigma}{\sqrt{n}}$

If σ is not known, use $\hat{\sigma} = s\sqrt{\dfrac{n}{n-1}} \cong s$ if n is large, say ≥ 30.

2.10 Example

The mean and standard deviation of the height of a random sample of 100 students are 168.75 cm and 7.5 cm, respectively. The 95% and 99% confidence intervals for the mean height of all students are calculated as follows.

Solution

As the standard deviation of the population is not known, and $n > 30$, the standard deviation of the sample can be used to calculate the standard error. Hence:

Standard error $= \dfrac{7.5}{\sqrt{100}}$ cm

$= 0.75$ cm

The 95% confidence limits are 168.75 ± 1.96 Standard errors = 168.75 ± 1.96 × 0.75
= 168.75cm ± 1.47 cm

This means that there is a 95% probability that the mean height of all students is between 167.28 and 170.22 cm.

The 99% confidence limits are 168.75 ± 2.58 Standard errors = 168.75 ± 2.58 × 0.75
= 168.75cm ± 1.94 cm

This means that there is a 99% probability that the mean height of all students is between 166.81 and 170.69 cm.

It is important to note that it is impossible to infer an exact value of the population mean from a sample. We can only state that there is a specified probability that the population mean is within specified limits. This uncertainty is known as sampling error. The only way to eliminate sampling error and obtain an exact value for the population mean is to measure every item in the population.

The result of **increasing** the degree of confidence (from 95% to 99%) is that the precision of the estimate is reduced, ie a wider interval is calculated for μ.

2.11 Sample size for a given error

$1.96 \dfrac{\sigma}{\sqrt{n}}$ and $2.58 \dfrac{\sigma}{\sqrt{n}}$ are known as **errors** in the estimates of μ. It is possible to reduce the size of this error by increasing the value of *n*, the sample size.

2.12 Example

In measuring the reaction time of individuals, a psychologist estimates that the standard deviation of all such times is 0.05 seconds.

Calculate the smallest sample size necessary in order to be (a) 95% and (b) 99% confident that the error in the estimate will not exceed 0.01 seconds.

(a) 95% confidence limits are $\bar{x} \pm 1.96 \dfrac{\sigma}{\sqrt{n}}$

∴ error in estimate $= 1.96 \dfrac{\sigma}{\sqrt{n}} = 1.96 \times \dfrac{0.05}{\sqrt{n}}$

and this must be less than or equal to 0.01 seconds.

∴ $1.96 \times \dfrac{0.05}{\sqrt{n}} \leq 0.01$

∴ $\dfrac{1.96 \times 0.05}{0.01} \leq \sqrt{n}$

$9.80 \leq \sqrt{n}$

$96.04 \leq n$ (squaring both sides to remove square root)

The sample size should be 97 since n must be greater than or equal to 96.04.

(b) 99% confidence limits are $\bar{x} \pm 2.58 \dfrac{\sigma}{\sqrt{n}}$

∴ error in estimate $= 2.58 \dfrac{\sigma}{\sqrt{n}} = 2.58 \times \dfrac{0.05}{\sqrt{n}}$

and this must be at most 0.01 seconds.

∴ $\dfrac{2.58 \times 0.05}{\sqrt{n}} \leq 0.01$

$\dfrac{2.58 \times 0.05}{0.01} \leq \sqrt{n}$

$12.90 \leq \sqrt{n}$

$166.41 \leq n$ (squaring both sides)

The sample size should be 167.

By increasing the sample size from 97 to 167, we can be more confident that the mean reaction time is within the required limits.

Question — Confidence interval

A sample of 100 items from a production line has a mean length of 8.4 cm with standard deviation 0.5 cm. What is the 95% confidence interval for the mean length of all items from that production line?

Answer

95% confidence interval $= \bar{x} \pm 1.96 \dfrac{\sigma}{\sqrt{n}}$

Using s to estimate σ,

95% confidence interval $= 8.4 \pm 1.96 \times \dfrac{0.5}{\sqrt{100}}$ cm $= 8.4 \pm 1.96 \times 0.05$ cm

∴ $8.302 < \mu < 8.498$ cm

PART A　TECHNIQUES TO SUPPORT BUSINESS DECISIONS

3 The theory of sampling (proportions)

FAST FORWARD

In some cases rather than trying to estimate a mean it is necessary to estimate the proportion of the population which possesses a particular attribute.

3.1 Introduction

It is often necessary to estimate a population proportion from a sample, rather than estimating a mean. For example, in public polls, sample enquiries are made to estimate the proportion of people in favour of government policies. In consumer research, it may be required to estimate the proportion of consumers who would use a new product in order to estimate the demand. This type of enquiry is known as **sampling for attributes**, as the object is to estimate the proportion of the population who possess the attribute under investigation.

If $n \geq 30$, the normal distribution can be used as an approximation to this distribution, hence, provided the sample size is not less than 30, the theory is the same as that for means, except that a different formula is used for the standard error.

Standard error of a proportion = $\sqrt{\dfrac{pq}{n}}$

where p = proportion of the population possessing the attribute
q = $1 - p$ = proportion not possessing the attribute
n = size of sample

If the proportion of the population is not known, the proportion of the sample can be used as an estimate.

Note. To be consistent with the convention of using Greek letters for population parameters, π (pi) should be used rather than p. However, it is more common to see p used, and we have therefore done so here.

3.2 Example

Past experience with an examination in Law has shown that only 50% of the students pass. The probability that 55% or more of a group of 200 students will pass is calculated as follows:

The population proportion is 50%, ie $\dfrac{50}{100}$ = 0.5. Hence:

$p = 0.5$, ∴ $q = 1 - 0.5 = 0.5$ and $n = 200$

$$
\begin{aligned}
\text{Standard error} &= \sqrt{\dfrac{pq}{n}} \\
&= \sqrt{\dfrac{0.5 \times 0.5}{200}} \\
&= \sqrt{0.00125} \\
&= 0.03536
\end{aligned}
$$

Given sample proportion = 0.55

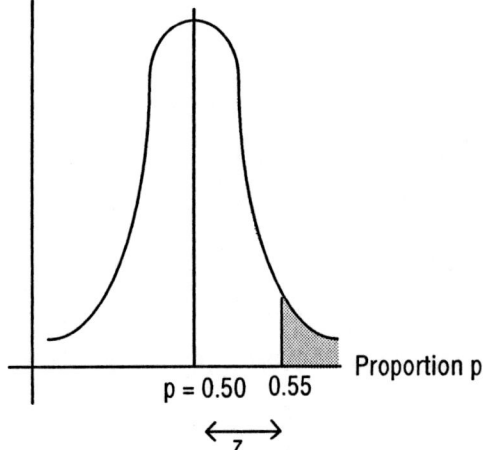

Standardising the value 0.55:

$$z = \frac{0.55 - 0.5}{0.03536}$$

$$= 1.41$$

Area = 0.4207 (from table at front of text)

∴ the required probability = 0.5 − 0.4207
= 0.0793

The chances of 55% (or more) passing are 0.0793 or approximately 8 in 100.

3.3 Confidence intervals

The 95% and 99% confidence limits for the population proportion are obtained in the same way as those for the sample mean, using the formula for the standard error of a proportion, ie:

95% confidence limits = sample proportion ± 1.96 SE
99% confidence limits = sample proportion ± 2.58 SE

where $SE = \sqrt{\dfrac{pq}{n}}$

If the population proportion is not known, use the sample proportion to calculate the standard error.

3.4 Example

Calculate the 95% and 99% confidence limits for the proportion of all voters in favour of candidate A if a random sample of 100 voters had 55% in favour of A.

Solution

As the population proportion is not known the sample proportion must be used to calculate the standard error. Hence:

$p = 0.55$, $q = 1 - 0.55 = 0.45$ and $n = 100$

$$\text{Standard error} = \sqrt{\frac{pq}{n}}$$

$$= \sqrt{\frac{0.55 \times 0.45}{100}}$$

$$= 0.04975$$

95% confidence limits = 0.55 ± 1.96 × 0.04975
= 0.55 ± 0.0975

The 95% confidence interval is therefore (0.55 − 0.0975) to (0.55 + 0.0975) = 0.45 to 0.65 (2 d.p.)

This means that there is a 95% probability that the proportion of all voters in favour of candidate A is between 45% and 65%.

The 99% confidence limits = 0.55 ± 2.58 × 0.04975
= 0.55 ± 0.128

The 99% confidence interval is therefore (0.55 − 0.128) to (0.55 + 0.128) = 0.42 to 0.68 (2 d.p.)

This means that there is a 99% probability that the proportion of all voters in favour of candidate A is between 42% and 68%.

There is obviously a very large sampling error, indicating that a larger sample should have been used.

Note. The nature of the inference that can be drawn from the sample. It does not follow that because 55% of the sample were in favour, 55% of the population will be in favour. We can only infer that there is a specified probability that the proportion will be within specified limits. If the candidate assumed from the sample result that he would win the election, he might well be disappointed.

3.5 Problems of sample size for a given error

The standard error and hence the error in the estimate can be reduced by increasing the sample size n.

At the 95% level, the error in the estimate is 1.96 standard errors and at the 99% level 2.58 standard errors.

3.6 Example

An advertising firm claims that its recent promotion reached 30% of the families living in the city. The company who hired the firm doubts this assertion and wishes to take a sample survey of its own. Calculate the sample size necessary to be at least 95% confident that the estimate will be within 3% of the true value.

Here, the only estimate available of the population proportion is 30% or 0.3. This value must therefore be used to calculate the standard error.

Hence: $p = 0.3$
$q = 1 - 0.3 = 0.7$

Standard error $= \sqrt{\dfrac{pq}{n}}$

$= \sqrt{\dfrac{0.3 \times 0.7}{n}}$

but we require the value of n to be such that 1.96 standard errors = 0.03 (ie 3%)

$\therefore \quad 0.03 = 1.96 \times \sqrt{\dfrac{0.3 \times 0.7}{n}}$

$\therefore \quad \sqrt{n} = \dfrac{1.96 \times \sqrt{0.3 \times 0.7}}{0.03}$

$\therefore \quad n = \dfrac{1.96^2 \times 0.3 \times 0.7}{0.03^2}$ (squaring both sides)

$= 896.4$

A sample size of 897 should be taken.

Note. In order to calculate the standard error, it is necessary to have an assumed value of the population proportion p. If the survey is completely new, there will be no means of knowing what value of p would be reasonable to assume. In this case, the method used is to take the worst possible case giving the highest standard error. This is when $p = q = 0.5$.

Thus in the previous example, if it was not valid to assume $p = 30\%$, the calculation would be as follows:

Take $p = q = 0.5$

Standard error $= \sqrt{\dfrac{0.5 \times 0.5}{n}}$

$= \sqrt{\dfrac{0.25}{n}}$

We require $0.03 = 1.96 \sqrt{\dfrac{0.25}{n}}$

$n = \left(\dfrac{1.96}{0.03}\right)^2 \times 0.25$

$= 1{,}067.1$

A sample of size 1,068 would be required.

Question — 99% confidence

In a random sample of 144 people, 63% preferred the flavour of a new brand of instant coffee to that of the other brands tested.

What are the 99% confidence limits for the proportion of the total population preferring the new brand?

Answer

Estimated $p = 0.63$, $q = 1 - 0.63 = 0.37$, $n = 144$

99% confidence limits = sample proportion ± 2.58 standard errors

$= 0.63 \pm 2.58 \sqrt{\dfrac{0.63 \times 0.37}{144}}$

$= 0.63 \pm 0.10$

∴ $0.53 < p < 0.73$

or $53\% < p < 73\%$

Exam focus point

Sampling theory has been examined regularly.

3.7 Illustration

A manufacturer of electric light bulbs needs to estimate the average 'burning life' of the bulbs he makes. A random sample of 100 bulbs was found to have a mean life of 340 hours with a standard deviation of 30 hours.

Calculate

(a) The standard error of the mean
(b) The 95% and 99% confidence intervals for the population mean
(c) The sample size necessary to provide a degree of accuracy within 3 hours at the 95% level

Solution

$\bar{x} = 340$ hours, $s = 30$ hours $= \hat{\sigma}$ $(n > 30)$ $n = 100$

(a) Standard error $= \dfrac{\hat{\sigma}}{\sqrt{n}}$

$= \dfrac{30}{\sqrt{100}}$

$= 3$ hours

(b) 95% confidence interval for μ:

$\bar{x} \pm 1.96 \times \dfrac{\hat{\sigma}}{\sqrt{n}} = 340 \pm 1.96 \times 3$

$= 340 \pm 5.88$
$= 334.12$ to 345.88 hours
$= 334$ hours to 346 hours

99% confidence interval for μ:

$\bar{x} \pm 2.58 \times \dfrac{\hat{\sigma}}{\sqrt{n}} = 340 \pm 2.58 \times 3$

$= 340 \pm 7.74$
$= 332.26$ to 347.74 hours
$= 332$ hours to 348 hours

(c) The error in the estimate $= 3$ hours

$\therefore 1.96 \times \dfrac{\hat{\sigma}}{\sqrt{n}} = 3$

$\therefore 1.96 \times \dfrac{30}{\sqrt{n}} = 3$

$\therefore \dfrac{1.96 \times 30}{3} = \sqrt{n}$

$19.6 = \sqrt{n}$

$384.16 = n$

$\therefore$ it is necessary to use a sample of at least 385.

4 Significance testing

FAST FORWARD

Significance tests such as the Chi-squared test measure the likelihood that the association between variables is caused by chance.

A result or relationship is considered statistically significant if it is unlikely to have occurred by chance. A 'statistically significant' difference or relationship simply means there is statistical evidence of a difference or relationship. A difference does not need to be large to be considered statistically significant.

Significance tests measure the likelihood that the association between variables is caused by chance.

4.1 The Chi-squared test

A widely used significance test is the Chi-squared test.

A chi-square of .05 is a conventionally accepted threshold of statistical significance (what this means will be demonstrated later). Chi-square values less than .05 are considered 'statistically significant'. When the chi-square is less than .05, we reject the possibility that no association exists between the independent and dependent variables.

Let's consider a simple example.

4.2 Example

We want to determine if a coin is fair – that the odds of flipping a head are the same as those for flipping a tail.

We toss the coin 200 times, resulting in 108 'heads' and 92 'tails'. Does this indicate the coin is biased towards heads? To establish this, we will analyse the data using a chi-squared test.

To perform a chi-square test we first establish our null hypothesis. In this example, our null hypothesis is that the coin is equally likely to land head-up or tails-up. Therefore, our null hypothesis stated in expected frequencies is that for 200 tosses we would expect 100 heads and 100 tails.

We can now prepare a table showing observed values and the expected values (based on the null hypothesis), with totals.

	Heads	Tails	Total
Observed	108	92	200
Expected	100	100	200
Total	208	192	400

Next, we calculate Chi-squared.

Chi-squared = (observed−expected)^2/(expected)

We have two classes to consider in this example, heads and tails.

$$\text{Chi-squared} = (108 - 100)^2/100 + (92 - 100)^2/100$$
$$= (8)^2/100 + (-8)^2/100$$
$$= 0.64 + 0.64$$
$$= 1.28$$

We now consult Chi-squared distribution tables (tables are provided for you in the exam, and at the back of this book). For this example, use the table extract provided below.

The left-most column lists the degrees of freedom (df). The relevant degree of freedom is calculated by subtracting one from the number of classes. In this example, we have two classes (heads and tails), so our relevant degree of freedom is one (2−1).

					Probability					
df	0.99	0.95	0.90	0.80	0.70	0.50	0.30	0.20	0.10	0.05
1	0.00013	0.0039	0.016	0.64	0.15	0.46	1.07	1.64	2.71	3.84

From our earlier calculation, our Chi-squared value is 1.28. We now look across the one degree of freedom row in our table until we find the values that bound (sit either side of) our Chi-squared value of 1.28. In the table above, the values are 1.07 (corresponding to a probability of 0.30) and 1.64 (corresponding to a probability of 0.20).

We now know the probability of getting 108 heads out of 200 coin tosses with a fair coin lies between 0.2 (20%) and 0.3 (30%). Our Chi-squared will therefore be greater than 0.05, so we can accept the null hypothesis as true, and conclude that the coin is fair.

If required, we could use interpolation to establish a more accurate probability for our Chi-squared value of 1.28.

PART A   TECHNIQUES TO SUPPORT BUSINESS DECISIONS

The illustration that follows, taken from the May 2007 exam, further illustrates the use of the Chi-squared test.

4.3 Illustration

Power4U provides domestic electricity supplies. Analysis of a random sample of 4,300 of its customers in 2005 gave the following results:

		Type of customer		
		Owns home	Rents home	
	Direct	1,071	1,273	
Payment	Quarterly	519	907	
method	Defaulted	210	320	
	Total	1,800	2,500	4,300

Direct payments are made automatically monthly to Power4U through the customers' bank accounts; quarterly payments are made by customers on receiving 3-monthly bills from Power4U. Customers who do not pay, or initially pay then stop, are termed 'defaulted'. The sample excludes customers who have pre-payment meters.

Required

(a) Power4U's director of finance feels that there are differences in the proportions of customers paying by different methods, between those who own their homes and those who rent their homes. You are required to investigate this assertion by conducting a Chi-squared contingency table test at the 5% level of significance.

Note. The expected frequencies calculated in this test should be rounded to the nearest whole number prior to calculating the value of Chi-squared. **(11 marks)**

(b) Report your conclusions on the test fully to the finance director and justify the test result by reference to any observed differences in proportions in the sample data. **(4 marks)**

(c) Throughout the year 2005 Power4U invested in advertising the benefits to customers of paying for their electricity consumption by the direct method. A sample of 1100 homeowner customers in 2006 shows that 753 are paying by the direct method.

Taking the corresponding proportion of 2005 customers to be 60%, conduct a single sample proportion test designed to show whether there has been a significant increase in the proportion of 2006 customers paying by the direct method over the proportion in 2005; use a 5% level of significance. Report your conclusion clearly. **(10 marks)**

(Total = 25 marks)

Solution

(a) A Chi-squared contingency table test is a multiple test between proportions, such as those between customers who own their home and those who rent, those who pay by the direct method and those who pay after being billed quarterly, or those who default. The following test will comprehensively test all comparison proportions in both dimensions of the sample table. But it will look for one overall significant result, and as such it will mask significant and insignificant differences between the several proportions in the two-way table of sample results. However, if there is a significant result to the test, it is possible to investigate the raw figures in the sample to see where the main differences lie.

Test H_0: There is no association between customer home-owning status and the payment method used, against.

H_1: There is some significant association between these attributes.

2: SAMPLING THEORY AND SIGNIFICANCE TESTING

Test statistic: Chi-squared = $\dfrac{S(O-E)^2}{E}$

Where 'O' represents the observed frequencies in the sample table, and 'E' represents the expected frequencies in the table if H_0 is true.

Level of significance: $a = 0.05$ (5%).

Critical region: Reject H_0 if Chi-squared > 5.991 with 2 degrees of freedom (df are calculated by number of rows less one times by number of columns less one = $(3-1) \times (2-1)$). Assuming H_0 is true then we calculate the E-values by the formula:

$$E = \dfrac{\text{Row total} \times \text{Column total}}{\text{Overall total}}$$

where these totals relate to the table of sample observed frequencies. The following table presents the necessary calculations under H_0 for the expected frequencies (rounded to whole numbers) and the value of Chi-squared:

O	E			$\dfrac{(O-E)^2}{E}$
1071	$2,344 \times 1,800/4,300$	=	981	8.26
519	$1,426 \times 1,800/4,300$	=	597	10.19
210	$530 \times 1,800/4,300$	=	222	0.65
1273	$2,344 \times 2,500/4,300$	=	1363	5.94
907	$1,426 \times 2,500/4,300$	=	829	7.34
320	$530 \times 2,500/4,300$	=	308	0.47
				32.85

Conclusion: since chi-squared = 32.85 is greater than the theoretical value of 5.991, we must reject H_0 at the 5% significance level. It would appear that there is some association between the two attributes of home-ownership status and payment method.

(b) The test of association between attributes gave a significant result. This means that at least some of the proportions of customers paying by a particular method are significantly different between those customers owning their own home and those renting their home. Looking into the detail of the sample, and looking at the differences in the 'O' and corresponding 'E' values, we see that the larger Chi-squared values derive from the two payment methods of direct and quarterly billing, rather than from the defaulting payment customers. For example, in the sample data, 1,071/1,800 = 59.5% of home-owning customers paid direct while 1,273/2,500 = 50.9% of renting customers paid direct. And, 519/1,800 = 28.8% of homeowning customers paid quarterly while 36.3% paid quarterly. The proportion of customers defaulting on their payment in 2005 was 11.7% of home-owners and 12.8% of renters.

Thus the sample suggests (strongly) that a higher proportion of home-owning customers pay by the direct method, but a higher proportion of renting customers pay by the quarterly method. This is where the significances lie.

(c) The required test in this case is a test on a proportion ie that the proportion of homeowning customers in 2006 who pay by the direct method is not significantly higher than the corresponding proportion in 2005. Note that the null hypothesis is always that there has not been a change.

Test H_0: $p = 0.6$, against
H_1: $p > 0.6$

Test statistic: $\dfrac{(x/n) - p}{\sqrt{p(1-p)/n}}$

where x is the sample number of customers paying direct in 2006, and n is the sample size in 2006.

Level of significance: a = 0.05

Critical region: reject H_0 if $z > 1.645$, otherwise accept H_0.

Assuming that H_0 is true, $z = \dfrac{(753/1{,}100) - 0.60}{\sqrt{0.6 \times 0.4 / 1{,}100}} = 5.72$

Conclusion: the calculated value of z is very much greater than 1.645 and thus H_0 must be firmly rejected at the 5% significance level.

There is therefore very strong evidence in the 2006 sample that the proportion of customers electing to pay for their electricity consumption by the direct method is significantly greater than the 60% in 2005. It would appear from the 2006 sample that Power4U's advertising campaign has been successful.

Chapter roundup

- Population is the term used to mean all the items under consideration.
- A sample is the group of items drawn from that population.
- There are various methods of sampling – random sampling, systematic sampling, stratified sampling, multi-stage sampling, quota sampling.
- The most commonly used statistics are the mean and the standard deviation.
- If a large number of samples of the same size are drawn from a given population and the mean of each calculated, the mean of all the sample means will be the population mean
- The standard deviation of the sampling distribution is known as the standard error.
- Instead of giving just a point estimate of the population mean, it is possible to give a probable range of values in which the population mean lies together with the probability that it lies in this range – known as a confidence interval.
- In some cases rather than trying to estimate a mean it is necessary to estimate the proportion of the population which possesses a particular attribute.
- Significance tests such as the Chi-squared test measure the likelihood that the association between variables is caused by chance.

Quick quiz

1. What is Bessel's correction?
2. What is a distribution of sample means?
3. What are confidence intervals?
4. What confidence level is given by the interval $\bar{x} \pm 1.96$ standard errors?
5. What is the formula for the standard error of a proportion?

Answers to quick quiz

1. To obtain an unbiased estimate of a population standard deviation multiply the sample standard deviation by $\sqrt{\dfrac{n}{n-1}}$

2. The mean of each sample drawn from the same population.

3. The range in which a population statistic will lie and the probability that it will lie in this range.

4. 95%

5. $\sqrt{\dfrac{pq}{n}}$

End of chapter question

Printex (AIA November 2007)

Printex is a company offering a litho-printing service mainly to business customers. Printex is keen to hold on to its existing customers and to attract new ones; it wrote to all existing customers six months ago informing them that it will be freezing all its prices for the coming year at last year's levels. On delivery of a print job to a customer Printex requires payment within one month.

A census of last year's print jobs showed that the average value of a job was $378 with a standard deviation of $83; further, the proportion of customers paying their bills within one month of receiving their printed work was 72%.

A random sample of the print jobs completed by Printex in the first six months of this year has the following characteristics:

- Sample size, n = 66
- Sample mean print job value = $359
- Sample proportion of customers paying within one month = 65% (43 customers)

Required

(a) Use a statistical test of significance on the mean value of a print job to determine whether the average value of a print job this year has decreased. Test at the 5% level of significance. **(9 marks)**

(b) Use a statistical test of significance on the proportion of customers paying their bills within one month of receiving their printed work to determine whether the proportion this year has decreased compared to last year. Test at the 5% level of significance. **(9 marks)**

(c) For each test in (a) and (b) calculate the minimum level of significance at which the test would conclude in a significant result, and outline a report explaining the tests and their results to the managing director of Printex. **(7 marks)**

(Total = 25 marks)

Linear programming

Topic list	Syllabus reference
1 The problem	9.3
2 Formulating the problem	9.3
3 Graphing the model	9.3
4 Finding the best solution	9.3
5 Interpretation of a graphical solution: sensitivity analysis	9.3
6 Two-plus variable models	9.3
7 Interpretation of a simplex solution: sensitivity analysis	9.3

Introduction

We are now going to look at a decision-making technique which involves **allocating resources in order to achieve the best results**. The name **'linear programming'** sounds rather formidable and the technique **can** get very complicated. Don't worry though: you are only expected to be able to analyse the simplest examples, using a graphical technique (ie draw lines!) and using equations. Get a ruler and sharpen your pencil!

PART A   TECHNIQUES TO SUPPORT BUSINESS DECISIONS

1 The problem

FAST FORWARD

Linear programming is a technique for solving problems of profit maximisation or cost minimisation and resource allocation. 'Programming' has nothing to do with computers: the word is simply used to denote a series of events.

A typical business problem is to decide how a company should **divide up its production among the various types of product** it manufactures in order to obtain the **maximum possible profit**. A business cannot simply aim to produce as much as possible because there will be **limitations** or **constraints** within which the production must operate. Such constraints could be one or more of the following.

- Limited quantities of raw materials available
- A fixed number of man-hours per week for each type of worker
- Limited machine hours

Moreover, since the profits generated by different products vary, it may be better not to produce any of a less profitable line, but to concentrate all resources on producing the more profitable ones. On the other hand limitations in market demand could mean that some of the products produced may not be sold.

2 Formulating the problem

FAST FORWARD

Linear programming, at least at this fairly simple level, is a technique that can be carried out in a fairly 'handle turning' manner once you have got the basic ideas sorted out. The steps involved are as follows.

1   Define variables
2   Establish constraints
3   Construct objective function
4   Graph constraints
5   Establish feasible region
6   Add iso-profit/contribution line
7   Determine optimal solution

Let us imagine that B Co makes just two models, the Super and the Deluxe, and that the **only constraint** faced by the company is that **monthly machine capacity is restricted to 400 hours**. The Super requires 5 hours of machine time per unit and the Deluxe 1.5 hours. Government restrictions mean that the maximum number of units that can be sold each month is 150, that number being made up of any combination of the Super and the Deluxe.

Let us now work through the steps involved in setting up a linear programming model.

Step 1   **Define variables**

What are the quantities that the company can vary? Obviously not the number of machine hours or the maximum sales, which are fixed by external circumstances beyond the company's control. The only things which it can determine are the number of each type of unit to manufacture. It is these numbers which have to be determined in such a way as to get the maximum possible profit. Our variables will therefore be as follows.

Let x = the number of units of the Super manufactured.
Let y = the number of units of the Deluxe manufactured.

Step 2   **Establish constraints**

Having defined these two variables we can now translate the two constraints into inequalities involving the variables.

Let us first consider the machine hours constraint. Each Super requires 5 hours of machine time. Producing five Supers therefore requires $5 \times 5 = 25$ hours of machine time and, more generally, producing x Supers will require 5x hours. Likewise producing y Deluxes will

require 1.5y hours. The total machine hours needed to make x Supers and y Deluxes is 5x + 1.5y. We know that this cannot be greater than 400 hours so we arrive at the following inequality.

5x + 1.5y ≤ 400

We can obtain the other inequality more easily. The total number of Supers and Deluxes made each month is x + y but this has to be less than 150 due to government restrictions. The sales order constraint is therefore as follows.

x + y ≤ 150

Non-negativity

The variables in linear programming models should usually be non-negative in value. In this example, for instance, you cannot make a negative number of units and so we need the following constraints.

x ≥ 0; y ≥ 0

Do not forget these non-negativity constraints when formulating a linear programming model.

Step 3 **Construct objective function**

We have yet to introduce the question of profits. Let us assume that the profit on each model is as follows.

	$
Super	100
Deluxe	200

The **objective** of B Co is to **maximise profit** and so the **function** to be maximised is as follows.

Profit (P) = 100x + 200y

The problem has now been reduced to the following four inequalities and one equation.

5x + 1.5y ≤ 400
x + y ≤ 150
x ≥ 0
y ≥ 0
P = 100x + 200y

Have you noticed that **the inequalities are all linear expressions**? If plotted on a graph, they would all give **straight lines**. This explains why the technique is called **linear programming** and also gives a hint as to how we should proceed with trying to find the solution to the problem.

Question — Constraints

Patel plc manufactures two products, X and Y, in quantities x and y units per week respectively. The contribution is $60 per X and $70 per Y. For practical reasons, no more than 100 Xs can be produced per week. If Patel plc uses linear programming to determine a profit-maximising production policy and on the basis of this information, which one of the following constraints is correct?

A   x ≤ 60   C   x ≤ 100
B   y ≤ 100   D   60x + 70y ≤ 100

Answer

The correct answer is C because the question states that the number of Xs produced cannot exceed 100 and so $x \leq 100$.

Option A has no immediate bearing on the number of units of X produced which must be ≤ 100. ($60 represents the contribution per unit of X).

We have no information on the production volume of Product Y and option B is therefore incorrect.

The contribution earned per week is given by $60x + 70y$ but we have no reason to suppose that this must be less than or equal to 100. Option D is therefore incorrect.

Exam focus point

Students often have problems with constraints of the style 'the quantity of one type must not exceed twice that of the other'. This can be interpreted as follows: the quantity of one type (say X) must not exceed (must be less than or equal to) twice that of the other (2Y) (ie $X \leq 2Y$).

We have looked at how to **formulate a problem** and in the next section we will look at solving a problem using graphs.

3 Graphing the model

FAST FORWARD

A graphical solution is only possible when there are two variables in the problem. One variable is represented by the x axis and one by the y axis of the graph. Since non-negative values are not usually allowed, the graph shows only zero and positive values of x and y.

A linear equation with one or two variables is shown as a straight line on a graph. Thus $y = 6$ would be shown as follows.

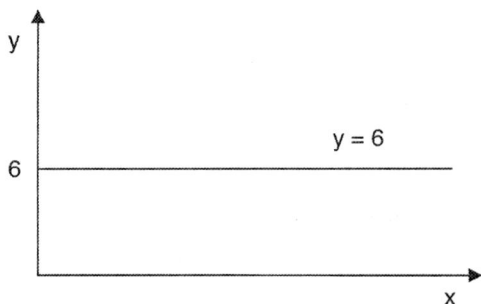

If the problem included a constraint that y could not exceed 6, the **inequality** $y \leq 6$ would be represented by the shaded area of the graph below.

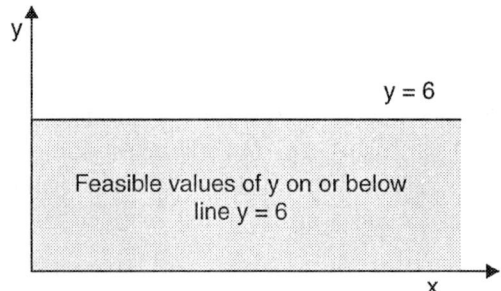

The equation 4x + 3y = 24 is also a straight line on a graph. To draw any straight line, we need only to plot two points and join them up. The easiest points to plot are the following.

(a) x = 0 (in this example, if x = 0, 3y = 24, y = 8)
(b) y = 0 (in this example, if y = 0, 4x = 24, x = 6)

By plotting the points, (0, 8) and (6, 0) on a graph, and joining them up, we have the line for 4x + 3y = 24.

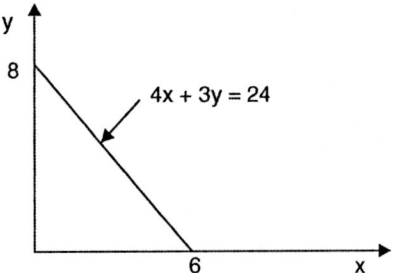

If we had a constraint 4x + 3y ≤ 24, any combined value of x and y within the shaded area below (on or below the line) would satisfy the constraint.

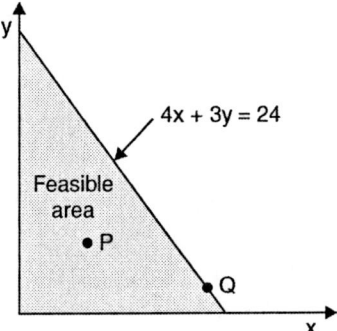

For example, at point P where (x = 2, y = 2) 4x + 3y = 14 which is less than 24; and at point Q where x = 5.5, y = 2/3, 4x + 3y = 24. Both P and Q lie within the **feasible area** (the area where the inequality is satisfied, also called the feasible region). A **feasible area** enclosed on all sides may also be called a **feasible polygon**.

The inequalities y ≥ 6, x ≥ 6 and 4x + 3y ≥ 24, would be shown graphically as follows.

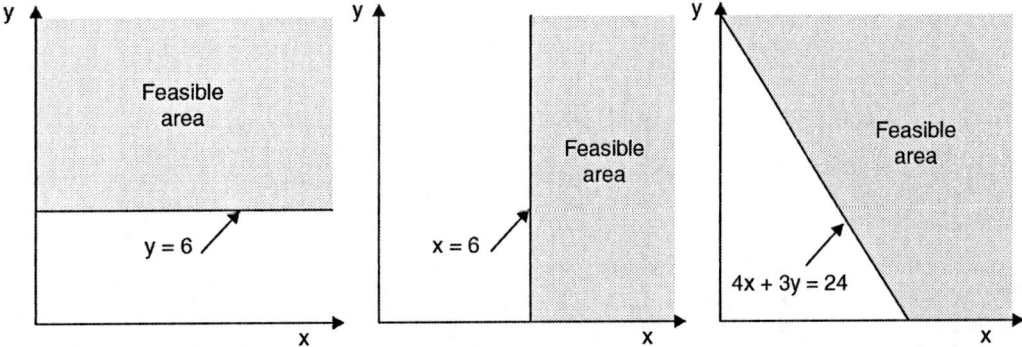

When there are several constraints, the feasible area of combinations of values of x and y must be an area where all the inequalities are satisfied.

Thus, if y ≤ 6 **and** 4x + 3y ≤ 24 the feasible area would be the shaded area in the graph following

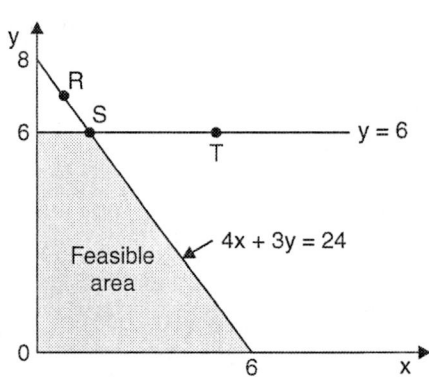

(a) Point R (x = 0.75, y = 7) is not in the feasible area because although it satisfies the inequality 4x + 3y ≤ 24, it does not satisfy y ≤ 6.

(b) Point T (x = 5, y = 6) is not in the feasible area, because although it satisfies the inequality y ≤ 6, it does not satisfy 4x + 3y ≤ 24.

(c) Point S (x = 1.5, y = 6) satisfies both inequalities and lies just on the boundary of the feasible area since y = 6 exactly, and 4x + 3y = 24. Point S is thus at the intersection of the two equation lines.

Similarly, if y ≥ 6 and 4x + 3y ≥ 24 but x ≤ 6, the feasible area would be the shaded area in the graph below.

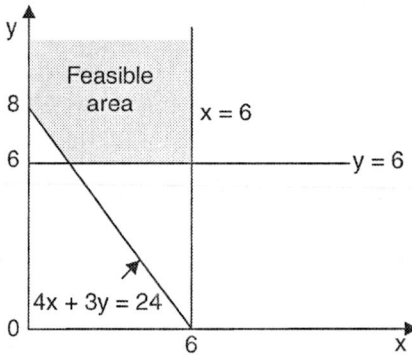

 Question — Feasible region

Draw the feasible region which arises from the constraints facing B Co (see Section 2).

Answer

If 5x + 1.5y = 400, then if x = 0, y = 267 and if y = 0, x = 80.
If x + y = 150, then if x = 0, y = 150 and if y = 0, x = 150.

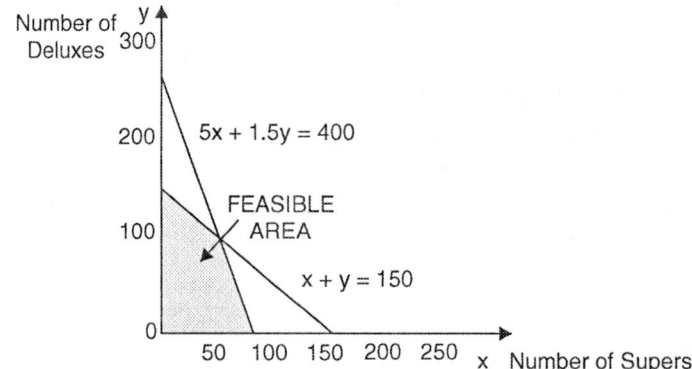

Linear programming problem

In a linear programming problem, one of the constraints is given by $2x \leq 3y$. Which of the following statements about the graphical presentation of this constraint is correct?

I   The constraint line passes through the point $x = 2$, $y = 3$.
II   The constraint line passes through the origin.
III   The constraint line passes through the point $x = 3$, $y = 2$.
IV   The region below the constraint line is part of the feasible area.

A   I and II only
B   I and III only
C   II and III only
D   II, III and IV only

Answer

When $x = 0$ then y must also equal 0, therefore statement II is correct.

When $x = 3$, $6 = 3y$ and hence $y = 2$, therefore statement III is correct.

Statements II and III are correct and therefore option C is the right answer.

Statement I is incorrect since when $x = 2$, $4 = 3y$ and $y = 1.33$ and y does not equal 3 when $x = 2$.

Statement IV is incorrect since $3y$ is greater than $2x$ above the line, not below it.

4 Finding the best solution

4.1 Introduction

Having found the **feasible region** (which includes all the possible solutions to the problem) we need to find which of these possible solutions is **'best'** in the sense that it yields the **maximum possible profit**. We could do this by finding out what profit each of the possible solutions would give, and then choosing as our 'best' combination the one for which the profit is greatest.

Consider, however, the feasible region of the problem faced by B Co (see the solution to the question entitled Feasible region). Even in such a simple problem as this, there are a great many possible solution points within the feasible area. Even to write them all down would be a time consuming process and also an unnecessary one, as we shall see.

4.2 Example: Finding the best solution

Let us look again at the graph of B Co's problem.

Consider, for example, the point A at which 40 Supers and 80 Deluxes are being manufactured. This will yield a profit of $((40 \times 100) + (80 \times 200)) = \$20,000$. We would clearly get more profit at point B, where the same number of Deluxes are being manufactured but where the number of Supers being manufactured has increased by five, or from point C where the same number of Supers but 10 more Deluxes are manufactured. This argument suggests that **the 'best' solution is going to be a point on the edge of the feasible area rather than in the middle of it.**

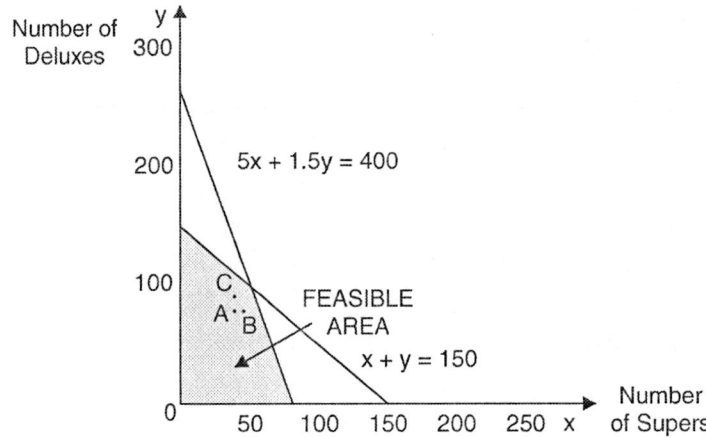

This still leaves us with quite a few points to look at but there is a way we can narrow down the candidates for the best solution still further. Suppose that B Co wish to make a profit of $10,000. The company could sell the following combinations of Supers and Deluxes.

(a) 100 Super, no Deluxe

(b) No Super, 50 Deluxe

(c) A proportionate mix of Super and Deluxe, such as 80 Super and 10 Deluxe or 50 Super and 25 Deluxe

The possible combinations of Supers and Deluxes required to earn a profit of $10,000 could be shown by the straight line $100x + 200y = 10,000$.

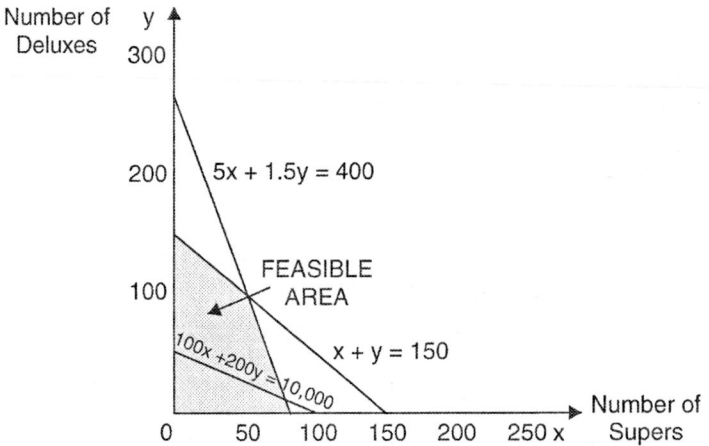

For a total profit of $15,000, a similar line $100x + 200y = 15,000$ could be drawn to show the various combinations of Supers and Deluxes which would achieve the total of $15,000.

Similarly a line $100x + 200y = 8,000$ would show the various combinations of Supers and Deluxes which would earn a total profit of $8,000.

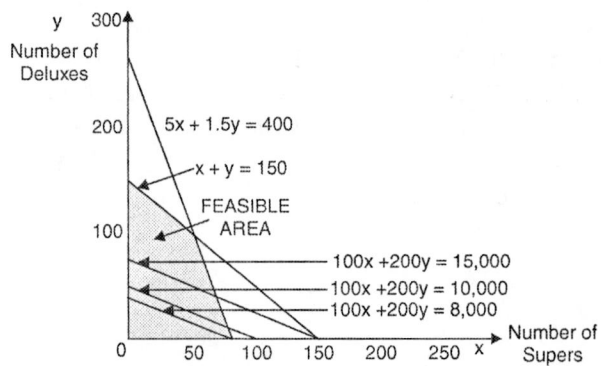

These profit lines are all parallel. (They are called **iso-profit lines**, 'iso' meaning equal.) A similar line drawn for any other total profit would also be parallel to the three lines shown here. This means that if we wish to know the slope or gradient of the profit line, for any value of total profit, we can simply draw one line for any convenient value of profit, and we will know that all the other lines will be parallel to the one drawn: they will have the same slope.

Bigger profits are shown by lines further from the origin (100x + 200y = 15,000), **smaller profits by lines closer to the origin** (100x + 200y = 8,000). As B Co try to **increase possible profit** we need to **slide the profit line outwards from the origin**, while always keeping it **parallel** to the other profit lines.

As we do this there will come a point at which, if we were to move the profit line out any further, it would cease to lie in the feasible region and therefore larger profits could not be achieved in practice because of the constraints. In our example concerning B Co this will happen, as you should test for yourself, where the profit line is just passing through the intersection of x + y = 150 with the y axis (at (0, 150)). The point (0, 150) will therefore give us the best production combination of the Super and the Deluxe, that is, to produce 150 Deluxe models and no Super models.

4.3 Example: A maximisation problem

Brunel Co manufactures plastic-covered steel fencing in two qualities, standard and heavy gauge. Both products pass through the same processes, involving steel-forming and plastic bonding.

Standard gauge fencing sells at $18 a roll and heavy gauge fencing at $24 a roll. Variable costs per roll are $16 and $21 respectively. There is an unlimited market for the standard gauge, but demand for the heavy gauge is limited to 1,300 rolls a year. Factory operations are limited to 2,400 hours a year in each of the two production processes.

Gauge	Processing hours per roll	
	Steel-forming	Plastic-bonding
Standard	0.6	0.4
Heavy	0.8	1.2

What is the production mix which will maximise total contribution and what would be the total contribution?

Solution

(a) Let S be the number of standard gauge rolls per year.

Let H be the number of heavy gauge rolls per year.

The objective is to maximise 2S + 3H (contribution) subject to the following constraints.

$$0.6S + 0.8H \leq 2,400 \text{ (steel-forming hours)}$$
$$0.4S + 1.2H \leq 2,400 \text{ (plastic-bonding hours)}$$
$$H \leq 1,300 \text{ (sales demand)}$$
$$S, H \geq 0$$

Note that **the constraints are inequalities**, and are not equations. There is no requirement to use up the total hours available in each process, nor to satisfy all the demand for heavy gauge rolls.

(b) If we take the production constraint of 2,400 hours in the steel-forming process

$$0.6S + 0.8H \leq 2,400$$

it means that since there are only 2,400 hours available in the process, output must be limited to a maximum of either:

(i) $\dfrac{2,400}{0.6}$ = 4,000 rolls of standard gauge

(ii) $\dfrac{2,400}{0.8}$ = 3,000 rolls of heavy gauge

(iii) A proportionate combination of each

This maximum output represents the boundary line of the constraint, where the inequality becomes the equation:

0.6S + 0.8H = 2,400.

(c) The line for this equation may be drawn on a graph by joining up two points on the line (such as S = 0, H = 3,000; H = 0, S = 4,000).

(d) The other constraints may be drawn in a similar way with lines for the following equations.

0.4S + 1.2H = 2,400 (plastic-bonding)
H = 1,300 (sales demand)

(e)

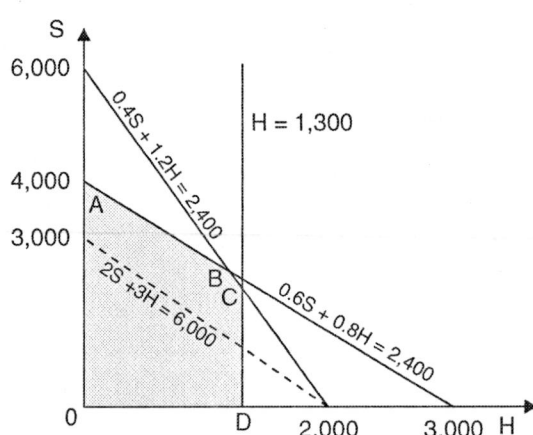

To satisfy all the constraints simultaneously, the values of S and H must lie on or below each constraint line. The outer limits of the **feasible polygon** are the lines, but all combined values of S and H within the shaded area are **feasible solutions**.

(f) The next step is to find the **optimal solution**, which **maximises the objective function**. Since the objective is to **maximise contribution**, the solution to the problem must involve relatively high values (within the feasible polygon) for S, or H or a combination of both.

If, as is likely, there is only one combination of S and H which provides the optimal solution, this combination will be one of the **outer corners of the feasible polygon**. There are four such corners, A, B, C and D. However, it is possible that any combination of values for S and H on the boundary line between two of these corners might provide solutions with the same total contribution.

(g) To solve the problem we establish **the slope of the iso-contribution lines**, by drawing a line for any one level of contribution. In our solution, a line 2S + 3H = 6,000 has been drawn. (6,000 was chosen as a convenient multiple of 2 and 3). **This line has no significance except to indicate the slope, or gradient, of every iso-contribution line for 2S + 3H.**

Using a ruler to judge at which corner of the feasible polygon we can draw an **iso-contribution line** which is as far to the right as possible, (away from the origin) but which still touches the **feasible polygon**.

(h) This occurs at corner B where the constraint line 0.4S + 1.2H = 2,400 crosses with the constraint line 0.6S + 0.8H = 2,400. At this point, there are simultaneous equations, from which the exact values of S and H may be calculated.

0.4S +	1.2H	=	2,400	(1)
0.6S +	0.8H	=	2,400	(2)
1.2S +	3.6H	=	7,200	(3) ((1) × 3)
1.2S +	1.6H	=	4,800	(4) ((2) × 2)
	2H	=	2,400	(5) ((3) – (4))
	H	=	1,200	(6)

Substituting 1,200 for H in either equation, we can calculate that S = 2,400.

The contribution is maximised where H = 1,200, and S = 2,400.

	Units	Contribution per unit $	Total contribution $
Standard gauge	2,400	2	4,800
Heavy gauge	1,200	3	3,600
			8,400

Question
Linear programming model

The Dervish Chemical Company operates a small plant. Operating the plant requires two raw materials, A and B, which cost $5 and $8 per litre respectively. The maximum available supply per week is 2,700 litres of A and 2,000 litres of B.

The plant can operate using either of two processes, which have differing contributions and raw materials requirements, as follows.

Process	Raw materials consumed (litres per processing hour)		Contribution per hour
	A	B	$
1	20	10	70
2	30	20	60

The plant can run for 120 hours a week in total, but for safety reasons, process 2 cannot be operated for more than 80 hours a week.

Formulate a linear programming model, and then solve it, to determine how many hours process 1 should be operated each week and how many hours process 2 should be operated each week.

Answer

The decision variables are processing hours in each process. If we let the processing hours per week for process 1 be P_1 and the processing hours per week for process 2 be P_2 we can formulate an objective and constraints as follows.

The objective is to maximise $70P_1 + 60P_2$, subject to the following constraints.

$20P_1 + 30P_2 \leq 2,700$	(material A supply)
$10P_1 + 20P_2 \leq 2,000$	(material B supply)
$P_2 \leq 80$	(maximum time for P_2)
$P_1 + P_2 \leq 120$	(total maximum time)
$P_1, P_2 \geq 0$	(non-negativity)

PART A TECHNIQUES TO SUPPORT BUSINESS DECISIONS

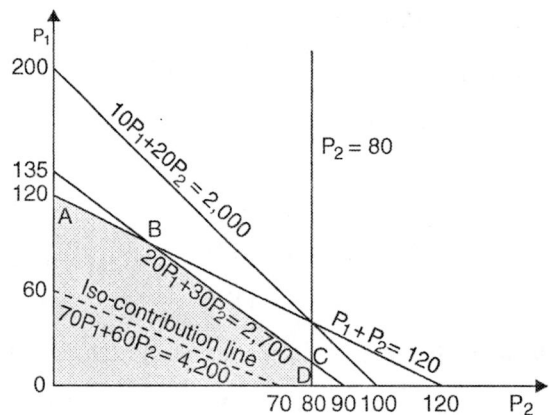

The feasible area is ABCDO. The optimal solution, found by moving the iso-contribution line outwards, is at point A, where $P_1 = 120$ and $P_2 = 0$. Total contribution would be $120 \times 70 = \$8,400$ a week.

Question — Constraints

WX Co manufactures two products, A and B. Both products pass through two production departments, mixing and shaping. The organisation's objective is to maximise contribution to fixed costs.

Product A is sold for $1.50 whereas product B is priced at $2.00. There is unlimited demand for product A but demand for B is limited to 13,000 units per annum. The machine hours available in each department are restricted to 2,400 per annum. Other relevant data are as follows.

Machine hours required	Mixing hrs	Shaping hrs
Product A	0.06	0.04
Product B	0.08	0.12

Variable cost per unit	$
Product A	1.30
Product B	1.70

In a report to management, use graphical linear programming to calculate the optimum number of each product which WX Co should make assuming it wishes to maximise contribution.

Answer

To: Management
From: Assistant accountant
Date: xx/xx/xx
Subject: Optimum numbers of product

There are constraints that will prevent WX from producing and selling as much of each product as it chooses.

The constraints are machine hours in each department and sales demand for product B. There is no restriction on the availability of labour hours. Selling price cannot be a constraint. We can use the linear programming steps to calculate the optimum numbers of each product to produce.

Step 1 Define the variables

The variables are the items whose value we are trying to decide. In this problem, the variables are the two products that WX can make and sell; we want to decide the quantities of product A and product B that should be made in order to maximise contribution (and profit).

For the graphical method of linear programming to be possible, there can be only two variables. The variables in this problem will therefore be stated as follows.

Let x = number of units of product A produced and sold.

Let y = number of units of product B produced and sold.

Step 2 Establish the constraints

Constraints are anything that sets a maximum or a minimum limit on the solution. Typically, there may be a maximum limit to the sales demand for each product, or a maximum limit to the amount of a production resource available, such as the quantity of a material, labour time or machine time.

In this problem there are constraints for the maximum sales demand for product B, the maximum machine hours in the Mixing Department and the maximum machine hours in the Shaping Department.

In a linear programming problem there may also be a minimum constraint, such as a minimum quantity of a product that must be made and sold to meet a confirmed customer order.

There are also non-negativity constraints. In this example, the values of x and y cannot be negative. (You cannot produce a negative quantity of a product.)

Each constraint must now be stated as a formula or 'inequality'. An inequality is similar to an equation except that the symbol 'less than or equal to' ($\leq$) or 'greater than or equal to' ($\geq$) is used instead of the equation sign (=).

(a) Consider the Mixing Department machine hours constraint.

  (i) **Each unit of product A** requires 0.06 hours of machine time. Producing five units therefore requires 5×0.06 hours of machine time and, more generally, **producing x units will require 0.06x hours**.

  (ii) Likewise, producing **y units of product B will require 0.08y hours**.

  (iii) The total machine hours needed in the mixing department to make x units of product A and y units of product B is $0.06x + 0.08y$.

  (iv) We know that this **cannot be greater in total than 2,400 hours** and so we arrive at the following inequality.

$0.06x + 0.08y \leq 2,400$

The constraint facing the Shaping Department can be written as follows.

$0.04x + 0.12y \leq 2,400$

The constraint has to be a 'less than or equal to' inequality, because the amount of resource used ($0.04x + 0.12y$) has to be 'less than or equal to' the amount available of 2,400 hours.

(b) The final inequality is easier to obtain. The **number of units of product B produced and sold is y** but this has to be **less than or equal to 13,000**. Our inequality is therefore as follows.

$y \leq 13,000$

(c) We also need to add **non-negativity constraints** ($x \geq 0, y \geq 0$) since negative numbers of products cannot be produced. (Linear programming is simply a mathematical tool and so there is nothing in this method which guarantees that the answer will 'make sense'. An unprofitable product may produce an answer which is negative. This is mathematically correct but nonsense in operational terms. Always remember to include the non-negativity constraints. The examiner will not appreciate 'impossible' solutions.)

Step 3 Construct the objective function

The objective function is a formula that states what we are trying to achieve as a solution to the problem. The objective function is always an objective of wanting to maximise something or minimise something. Typically, the objective function will be to maximise total contribution or to minimise total cost.

In the problem we are looking at here, the objective function is to maximise total contribution. We must put this into a formula.

We know that the **contribution on each type of product** is as follows.

			$ per unit
Product A	$(1.50 – 1.30)	=	0.20
Product B	$(2.00 – 1.70)	=	0.30

The **objective of the company is to maximise contribution** and so the **objective function to be maximised** is as follows.

Maximise contribution (C): $0.2x + 0.3y$

The problem has now been reduced to the following four inequalities and one equation.

Maximise contribution (C) = $0.2x + 0.3y$, subject to the following constraints:

$$0.06x + 0.08y \leq 2{,}400$$
$$0.04x + 0.12y \leq 2{,}400$$
$$y \leq 13{,}000$$
$$x, y \geq 0$$

Steps 4 and 5 Graph constraints and establish feasible region

Drawing the constraints

In addition to the non-negativity constraints for x and y, there are three constraints in the problem.

(a) Mixing Department hours: $0.06x + 0.08y \leq 2{,}400$

Draw a line for the equation $0.06x + 0.08y = 2{,}400$

If $x = 0$, $y = 30{,}000$

If $y = 0$, $x = 40{,}000$

Plot these two points on the graph and join them up to shown the boundary line of the constraint.

(b) Shaping Department hours: $0.04x + 0.12y \leq 2{,}400$

Draw a line for the equation $0.04x + 0.12y = 2{,}400$

If $x = 0$, $y = 20{,}000$

If $y = 0$, $x = 60{,}000$

Plot these two points on the graph and join them up to shown the boundary line of the constraint.

(c) **Maximum sales demand for Product B: y ≤ 13,000**

Draw the line y = 13,000.

This is a horizontal line on the graph at the point where y = 13,000, and for all value of x.

The graph should look like this.

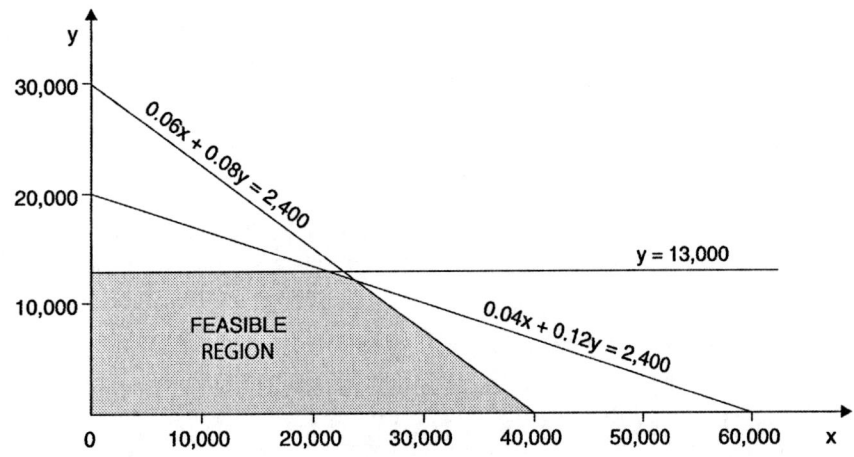

Step 6 Add iso-contribution line

Suppose that WX wishes to earn contribution of $3,000. Given that the contribution per unit of Product A is $0.2 and the contribution per unit of Product B is $0.3, the company could sell the following combinations of the two products.

(a) 15,000 units of A, no B (x = 15,000, y = 0)

(b) No A, 10,000 units of B (x = 0, y = 10,000).

(c) A suitable mix of the two, such as 7,500 A and 5,000 B.

The possible combinations required to earn contribution of $3,000 could be shown by the straight line 0.2x + 0.3y = 3,000

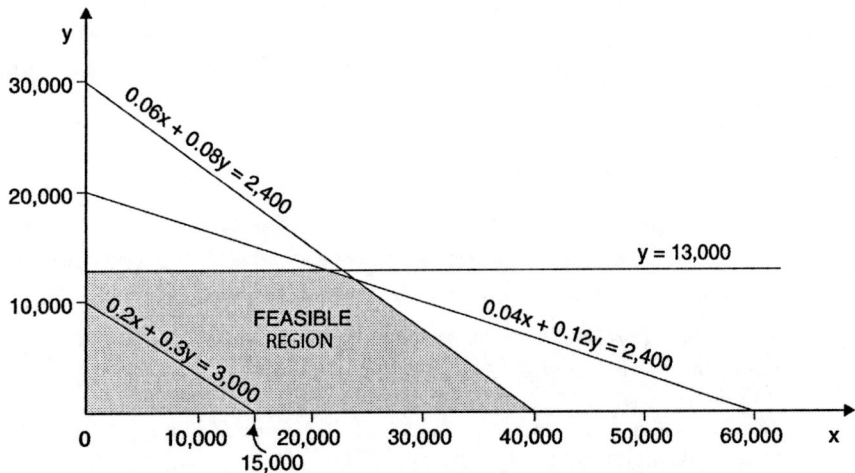

Step 7 Determine optimal solution

As WX tries to increase possible contribution, we need to 'slide' any contribution line outwards from the origin.

As we do this there will come a point at which, if we were to move the contribution line out any further, it would cease to lie in the feasible region. Greater contribution could not be achieved, because of the constraints. This will happen where the contribution line just passes through the intersection of $0.06x + 0.08y = 2,400$ and $0.04x + 0.12y = 2,400$ (at co-ordinates (24,000, 12,000)).

The point (24,000, 12,000) will therefore give us the optimal allocation of resources (**to produce 24,000 units of A and 12,000 units of B**).

4.4 Multiple solutions

It is possible that the optimum position might lie, not at a particular corner, but all along the length of one of the sides of the feasibility polygon. This will occur if the iso-contribution line is exactly parallel to one of the constraint lines.

If this happens then there is no one optimum solution but a **range of optimum solutions**. All of these will maximise the objective function at the same level. However, **any** value of the decision variables that happens to satisfy the constraint between the points where the constraint line forms part of the feasibility region would produce this optimum level of contribution.

4.5 Minimisation problems in linear programming

Although decision problems with limiting factors usually involve the maximisation of contribution, there may be a requirement to **minimise costs**. A graphical solution, involving two variables, is very similar to that for a maximisation problem, with the exception that instead of finding a contribution line touching the feasible area as far away from the origin as possible, we look for a **total cost line touching the feasible area as close to the origin as possible.**

4.5.1 Example: A minimisation problem

Claire Speke Co has undertaken a contract to supply a customer with at least 260 units in total of two products, X and Y, during the next month. At least 50% of the total output must be units of X. The products are each made by two grades of labour, as follows.

	X Hours	Y Hours
Grade A labour	4	6
Grade B labour	4	2
Total	8	8

Although additional labour can be made available at short notice, the company wishes to make use of 1,200 hours of Grade A labour and 800 hours of Grade B labour which has already been assigned to working on the contract next month. The total variable cost per unit is $120 for X and $100 for Y.

Claire Speke Co wishes to minimise expenditure on the contract next month. How much of X and Y should be supplied in order to meet the terms of the contract?

Solution

(a) Let the number of units of X supplied be x, and the number of units of Y supplied be y.

The objective is to minimise 120x + 100y (costs), subject to the following constraints.

x + y	≥	260	(supply total)
x	≥	0.5 (x + y)	(proportion of x in total)
4x + 6y	≥	1,200	(Grade A labour)
4x + 2y	≥	800	(Grade B labour)
x, y	≥	0	

The constraint x ≥ 0.5 (x + y) needs simplifying further.

x	≥	0.5 (x + y)
2x	≥	x + y
x	≥	y

In a graphical solution, the line will be x = y. Check this carefully in the following diagram.

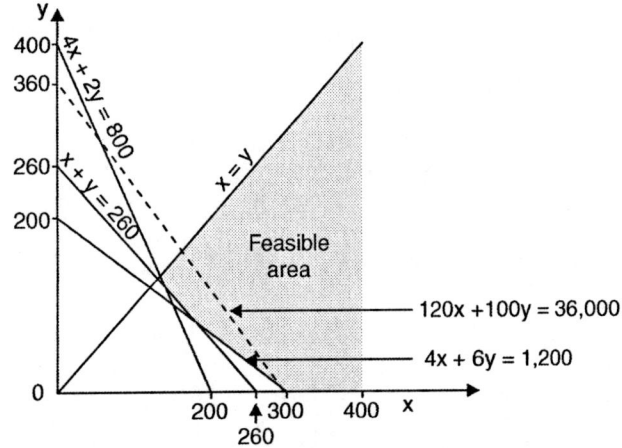

(b) The cost line 120x + 100y = 36,000 has been drawn to show the slope of every cost line 120x + 100 y. **Costs are minimised where a cost line touches the feasible area as close as possible to the origin of the graph.** This occurs where the constraint line 4x + 2y = 800 crosses the constraint line x + y = 260. This point is found as follows.

x + y	=	260	(1)
4x + 2y	=	800	(2)
2x + y	=	400	(3) ((2) ÷ 2)
x	=	140	(4) ((3) – (1))
y	=	120	(5)

(c) Costs will be minimised by supplying the following.

	Unit cost	Total cost
	$	$
140 units of X	120	16,800
120 units of Y	100	12,000
		28,800

The proportion of units of X in the total would exceed 50%, and demand for Grade A labour would exceed the 1,200 hours minimum.

4.6 The use of simultaneous equations

You might think that a lot of time could be saved if we started by solving the simultaneous equations in a linear programming problem and did not bother to draw the graph.

Certainly, this procedure may give the right answer, but in general, it is **not** recommended until you have shown graphically which constraints are effective in determining the optimal solution. (In particular, if a question requires 'the graphical method', you **must** draw a graph). To illustrate this point, consider the following graph.

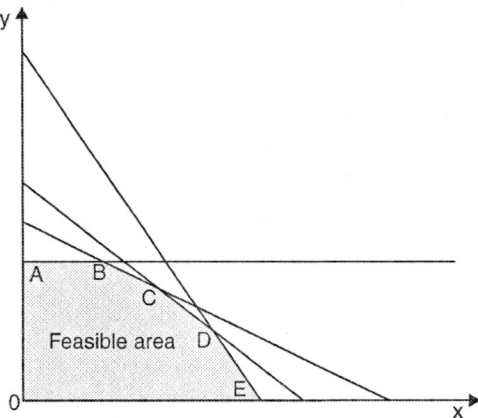

No figures have been given on the graph but the feasible area is OABCDE. When solving this problem, we would know that the optimum solution would be at one of the corners of the feasible area. We need to work out the profit at each of the corners of the feasible area and pick the one where the profit is greatest.

Once the optimum point has been determined graphically, simultaneous equations can be applied to find the exact values of x and y at this point.

5 Interpretation of a graphical solution: sensitivity analysis

A graphical solution to a linear programming problem can be interpreted and more useful analytical information can be obtained using sensitivity analysis. The solution in Paragraph 4.3 will be used here to illustrate an approach to interpretation.

In the optimal solution to this problem, H = 1,200 and S = 2,400, and we can calculate from this that the total contribution is $8,400. We can also see from the graph that at this level of output the total quantities of steel-forming hours and plastic-forming hours are utilised.

We can now ask the question:

What would be the optimal solution if one additional steel-forming hour could be made available? In other words, what is the **shadow price or dual price** of steel-forming hours?

By looking at the graph, it may be apparent that a new constraint for steel-forming hours (0.6S + 0.8H = 2,401) will be very similar to the original constraint line (0.6S + 0.8H = 2,400), and the optimal solution will still be at the point where the constraint lines for steel-forming hours and plastic-forming hours intersect.

At this point:

0.4S + 1.2H = 2,400; and

0.6S + 0.8H = 2,401.

We can solve these simultaneous equations to get H = 1,199 and S = 2,403. At this level of output and sales, total contribution = (1,199 × $3) + (2,403 × $2) = $8,403.

This is $3 more than the original optimal solution, which means that contribution can be increased by $3 if just one extra steel-forming hour can be made available. The shadow price or dual price of steel-forming hours is $3 per hour.

We can ask another question:

By how much would the contribution per unit of standard gauge rolls need to increase before the optimal solution moves from the current level of output (H = 1,200, S = 2,400) to one where we produce only standard-gauge rolls and no heavy gauge rolls. From the graph, we can see that this is where S = 4,000 and H = 0.

The optimal solution would switch from H = 1,200, S = 2,400 to H = 0, S = 4,000 when the slope of the iso-contribution line is exactly the same as the slope of the constraint line 0.6S + 0.8H = 2,400.

This is a line where the ratio of the value of S to H = 0.6: 0.8.

If we assume that the contribution be unit of S increases, but the contribution per unit of H remains at 3, the contribution per unit of S on the iso-contribution line would need to be $3 \times 0.6/0.8 = \$2.25$.

This means that if the contribution per unit of S increases from $2 to $2.25, we would be indifferent between producing H = 1,200, S = 2,400 or H = 0, S = 4,000. If the contribution per unit of S increases above $2.25, with no change in the contribution per unit of H, we would want to make 4,000 units of S and 0 units of H in order to maximise contribution.

This can be shown mathematically. If the contribution per unit of S = 2.25 and the contribution per unit of H = 3:

- Total contribution when H = 1,200, S = 2,400: $(1,200 \times \$3) + (2,400 \times \$2.25) = \$9,000$
- Total contribution when H = 0, S = 4,000: $(0 \times \$3) + (4,000 \times \$2.25) = \$9,000$.

6 Two-plus variable models

FAST FORWARD

> The graphical method cannot be used when there are more than two decision variables. A method called the **simplex method** is available in these circumstances, but in practice it is much easier to use a computer.

You need to have a **basic understanding** of how to formulate the equations for two-plus variable problems. You will not, however, be required to interpret computer output.

The formulation of the problem using the **simplex method** is similar to that required when the graphical method is used but **slack variables** must be incorporated into the constraints and the objective function.

6.1 General points about the simplex method

Exam focus point

> A **slack variable** represents the amount of a constraint that is unused.
>
> In any feasible solution, if a problem involves n constraints and m variables (decision plus slack), n variables will have a positive value and (m–n) variables will have a value of zero.
>
> Feasible solutions to a problem are shown in a **tableau**.

Before introducing an example to explain the technique, we will make a few introductory points. Don't worry if you get confused, working through the example will make things clearer.

(a) The simplex method involves **testing one feasible solution after another**, in a **succession of tables or tableaux, until the optimal solution is found**. It can be used for problems with **any number of decision variables, from two upwards**.

(b) In addition to the decision variables, the method introduces additional variables, known as **slack variables** or **surplus variables**. There will be **one slack (or surplus) variable for each constraint in the problem (excluding non-negativity constraints)**.

For example, if a linear programming problem has three decision variables and four constraints, there will be four slack variables. With the three decision variables, there will therefore be a total of seven variables and four constraints in the problem.

(c) The technique is a **repetitive, step-by-step process**, with each step having the following **purposes**.

   (i) To **establish a feasible solution** (in other words, a feasible combination of decision variable values and slack variable values) and the **value of the objective function** for that solution.

   (ii) To **establish** whether that particular **solution** is one that **optimises** the value of the objective function.

(d) Each feasible solution is tested by drawing up a **matrix** or **tableau** with the following rows and columns.

   (i) **One row per constraint, plus a solution row**

   (ii) **One column per decision variable and per slack variable, plus a solution column**

(e) **Every variable**, whether a decision variable, slack variable or surplus variable, **must be ≥ 0 in any feasible solution**.

(f) A feature of the simplex method is that if there are **n constraints**, there will be **n variables with a value greater than 0 in any feasible solution**. Thus, if there are seven variables in a problem, and four constraints, there will be four variables with a positive value in the solution, and three variables with a value equal to 0.

Keep these points in mind as we work through an example.

Example: The simplex method

An organisation produces and sells two products, X and Y. Relevant information is as follows.

	Materials Kg	Labour Hours	Machine time Hours	Contribution per unit $
X, per unit	5	1	3	20
Y, per unit	2	3	2	16
Total available, each week	3,000	1,750	2,100	

Required

Use the simplex method to determine the profit-maximising product mix.

6.2 Formulating the problem

We have just two decision variables in this problem, but we can still use the simplex method to solve it.

Step 1 **Define variables**

Let x be the number of units of X that should be produced and sold.

Let y be the number of units of Y that should be produced and sold.

Step 2 **Establish objective function**

Maximum contribution (C) = 20x + 16y subject to the constraints below.

Step 3 Establish constraints

The constraints are as follows.

Materials	$5x + 2y \leq 3{,}000$	Machine time	$3x + 2y \leq 2{,}100$
Labour	$x + 3y \leq 1{,}750$	Non-negativity	$x \geq 0, y \geq 0$

Step 4 Introduce slack variables

Begin by turning each constraint (ignoring the non-negativity constraints now) into an equation. This is done by introducing slack variables.

Let S_1 be the quantity of unused materials, S_2 be the number of unused labour hours and S_3 be the number of unused machine hours.

Step 5 Values of variables – non-negative or zero?

In this example, there are **five variables** (x, y, S_1, S_2 and S_3) and **three equations**, and so in any **feasible solution** that is tested, **three variables** will have a **non-negative value** (since there are three equations) which means that **two variables** will have a value of **zero**.

Step 6 Express objective function as an equation

It is usual to express the objective function as an equation with the right-hand side equal to zero. In order to keep the problem consistent, the slack (or surplus) variables are inserted into the objective function equation, but as the quantities they represent should have no affect on the objective function they are given zero coefficients. In our example, the objective function will be expressed as follows.

Maximise contribution (C) given by $C - 20x - 16y + 0S_1 + 0S_2 + 0S_3 = 0$.

Key term

Slack variable. 'Amount of each resource which will be unused if a specific linear programming solution is implemented.'
(CIMA Official Terminology)

6.3 Drawing up the initial tableau and testing the initial feasible solution

---

Exam focus point

You will not be required to do this in the assessment, but seeing how the initial tableau is drawn up will give you additional insight into the technique.

We begin by testing a solution that **all the decision variables have a zero value**, and **all the slack variables have a non-negative value**.

Obviously, this is **not going to be the optimal solution**, but it gives us a starting point from which we can develop other feasible solutions.

Simplex tableaux can be **drawn in several different ways**, and if you are asked to interpret a given tableau in an examination question, you may need to adapt your understanding of the tableau format in this Study Text to the format in the question. The following points apply to all tableaux, however.

(a) There should be a **column for each variable** and also a **solution column**.

(b) It helps to add a **further column on the left**, to **indicate the variable which is in the solution to which the corresponding value in the solution column relates**.

(c) There is a **row for each equation** in the problem, and a **solution row**.

PART A TECHNIQUES TO SUPPORT BUSINESS DECISIONS

Here is the initial matrix for our problem. Information on how it has been derived is given below.

Variables in solution	x	y	S_1	S_2	S_3	Solution
A (materials)	5	2	1	0	0	3,000
B (labour)	1	3	0	1	0	1,750
C (machine time)	3	2	0	0	1	2,100
Solution	−20	−16	0	0	0	0

(a) The **figures in each** row correspond with the **coefficients of the variables in each of the initial constraints**. The bottom row or **solution row** holds the **coefficients of the objective function**. For example the materials constraint $5x + 2y + S_1 = 3{,}000$ gives us the first row, 5 (number of x), 2 (number of y), 1 (number of S), then zeros in the S_2 and S_3 columns (since these do not feature in the constraint equation) and finally 3,000 in the solution column.

(b) The **variables in the solution are S_1, S_2 and S_3** (the unused resources).

 (i) The **value of each variable is shown in the solution column**. We are testing a solution that all decision variables have a zero value, so there is no production and hence no resources are used. The total resource available is therefore unused.

 (ii) The **column values** for each variable in the solution are as follows.
  – 1 in the variable's own solution row
  – 0 in every other row, including the solution row

(c) The **contribution per unit obtainable from x and y** is given in the **solution row**. These are the **dual prices** or **shadow prices** of the products X and Y. The minus signs are of no particular significance, except that in the solution given here they have the following meanings.

 (i) A **minus shadow price** indicates that the **value of the objective function can be increased by the amount of the shadow price per unit** of the variable that is introduced into the solution, given no change in the current objective function or existing constraints.

 (ii) A **positive shadow price** indicates the amount by which the **value of the objective function would be decreased** per unit of the variable introduced into the solution, given no change in the current objective function or the existing constraints.

6.4 Interpreting the tableau and testing for improvement

We can see that the **solution is testing $S_1 = 3{,}000$, $S_2 = 1{,}750$ and $S_3 = 2{,}100$, contribution = 0. The coefficients for the variables not in this solution, x and y, are the dual prices or shadow prices** of these variables, given the solution being tested. A **negative value** to a dual price means that the **objective function can be increased**; therefore the **solution in the tableau is not the optimal solution**.

The **shadow prices** in the initial solution (tableau) indicate the following.

(a) The profit would be increased by $20 for every extra unit of x produced (because the shadow price of x is $20 per unit).

(b) Similarly, the profit would be increased by $16 for every extra unit of y produced (because its shadow price is $16 per unit).

Since the **solution is not optimal**, the **contribution may be improved by introducing either x or y into the solution**.

6.5 The next step

The next step is to **test another feasible solution**. We do this by **introducing one variable into the solution, in the place of one variable that is now removed**. In our example, we **introduce x or y in place of S_1, S_2 and S_3**.

3: LINEAR PROGRAMMING

The simplex technique continues in this way, producing a feasible solution in each successive tableau, until the optimal solution is reached.

6.6 Interpreting the final tableau

If the shadow prices on the bottom (solution) row of a tableau are all positive, the tableau shows the optimal solution.

- The solution column shows the optimal production levels and the units of unused resource.
- The figure at the bottom of the solution column/right-hand side of the solution row shows the value of the objective function.
- The figures in the solution row indicate the shadow prices of resources.

After a number of iterations, the following tableau is produced.

Variables in solution	x	y	S_1	S_2	S_3	Solution column
X	1	0	0	−0.2857	0.4286	400
S_1	0	0	1	0.5714	−1.8571	100
Y	0	1	0	0.4286	−0.1429	450
Solution row	0	0	0	1.1428	6.2858	15,200

This can be interpreted as follows.

(a) The solution in this tableau is the **optimal** one, because the **shadow prices on the bottom row are all positive**.

(b) The optimal solution is to **make and sell 400 units of X and 450 units of Y, to earn a contribution of $15,200**.

(c) The solution will leave **100 units of material unused**, but will use up all available labour and machine time.

(d) The **shadow price of labour time (S_2) is $1.1428 per hour**, which **indicates the amount by which contribution could be increased if more labour time could be made available at its normal variable cost**.

(e) The **shadow price of machine time (S_3) is $6.2858 per hour**, which **indicates the amount by which contribution could be increased if more machine time could be made available, at its normal variable cost**.

(f) The **shadow price of materials is nil**, because there are 100 units of **unused** materials in the solution.

Question
TDS

TDS manufactures two products, X and Y, which earn a contribution of $8 and $14 per unit respectively. At current selling prices, there is no limit to sales demand for Y, but maximum demand for X would be 1,200 units. The company aims to maximise its annual profits, and fixed costs are $15,000 per annum.

In the year to 30 June 20X2, the company expects to have a limited availability of resources, and estimates of availability are as follows.

Skilled labour maximum 9,000 hours

Machine time maximum 4,000 hours

Material M maximum 1,000 tonnes

PART A TECHNIQUES TO SUPPORT BUSINESS DECISIONS

The usage of these resources per unit of product are as follows.

	X	Y
Skilled labour time	3 hours	4 hours
Machine time	1 hour	2 hours
Material M	½ tonne	¼ tonne

Required

(a) Formulate the problem using the simplex method of linear programming.

(b) Determine how many variables will have a positive value and how many a value of zero in any feasible solution.

Answer

(a) The linear programming problem would be formulated as follows.

Define variables

Let x and y be the number of units made and sold of product X and product Y respectively.

Establish objective function

Maximise contribution (C) = 8x + 14y subject to the constraints below.

Establish constraints

$3x + 4y \leq 9{,}000$ (skilled labour)*

$x + 2y \leq 4{,}000$ (machine time)

$0.5x + 0.25y \leq 1{,}000$ (material M)

$x \leq 1{,}200$ (demand for X)

$x, y \geq 0$

*This constraint is that skilled labour hours cannot exceed 9,000 hours, and since a unit of X needs 3 hours and a unit of Y needs 4 hours, 3x + 4y cannot exceed 9,000. The other constraints are formulated in a similar way.

Introduce slack variables

Introduce a slack variable into each constraint, to turn the inequality into an equation.

Let S_1 = the number of unused skilled labour hours

S_2 = the number of unused machine hours

S_3 = the number of unused tonnes of material M

S_4 = the amount by which demand for X falls short of 1,200 units

Then

$3x + 4y + S_1 = 9{,}000$ (labour hours)

$x + 2y + S_2 = 4{,}000$ (machine hours)

$0.5x + 0.25y + S_3 = 1{,}000$ (tonnes of M)

$x + S_4 = 1{,}200$ (demand for X)

And maximise contribution (C) given by $C - 8x - 14y + 0S_1 + 0S_2 + 0S_3 + 0S_4 = 0$

(b) There are six variables (x, y, S_1, S_2, S_3, S_4) and four equations. In any feasible solution, four variables will have a non-negative value (as there are four equations), while two variables will have a value of zero.

7 Interpretation of a simplex solution: sensitivity analysis

7.1 Shadow prices

FAST FORWARD

The **shadow price** (or **dual price**) of a resource is the amount by which the value of the objective function (contribution) will go up (or down) if one unit more (or less) of the resource were made available.

Here is the final tableau to the question above called TDS, which shows the **contribution-maximising** solution.

Variables in the solution	x	y	a	b	c	d	Solution column
x	1	0	1	−2	0	0	1,000
y	0	1	−0.5	1.5	0	0	1,500
c	0	0	−0.375	0.625	1	0	125
d	0	0	−1	2	0	1	200
Solution row	0	0	1	5	0	0	29,000

The value of the **objective function** – here, the **total contribution** – is in both the solution row and the solution column. Here it is $29,000.

The shadow prices are as follows.

(a) $1 per labour hour
(b) $5 per machine hour

The **solution row** gives the shadow prices of each variable.

This means that if more labour hours could be made available **at their normal variable cost per hour** total contribution could be increased by $1 per extra labour hour. Similarly, if more machine time could be made available, **at its normal variable cost**, total contribution could be increased by $5 per extra machine hour.

The shadow or dual price is the opportunity cost of the scarce resources, which is the amount of benefit forgone by not having the availability of the extra resources.

You need to understand the interpretation of a solution to a linear programming problem using the simplex method. Study the following example carefully.

7.2 Interpretation of a solution: example

A business makes two products, X and Y, using the same direct materials, labour and machines. The following information is available.

Product	Material quantity per unit	Labour hours per unit	Machine hours per unit	Contribution per unit
X	40	4	2	$40
Y	20	10	3	$32
Maximum available per day	600	100	38	

PART A   TECHNIQUES TO SUPPORT BUSINESS DECISIONS

Materials must be consumed on the day they are purchased.

A linear program can be formulated to solve this problem with the simplex method.

Let:

x = number of units of X produced each day and y = number of units of Y produced each day

a, b and c = the number of unused units of materials, unused labour hours and unused machine hours per day respectively.

The problem is formulated as follows:

Maximise 40x + 32y   (Daily contribution)

Subject to the following constraints:

Materials: $40x + 20y \leq 600$

Labour: $4x + 10y \leq 100$

Machine hours: $2x + 3y \leq 38$

x, y, a, b, c $\geq$ 0

The optimal solution is shown in the following table.

Variables in solution	x	y	a	b	c	Solution
x	1	0	0.0375	0	(0.25)	13
b	0	0	0.1	1	(4.0)	8
y	0	1	(0.025)	0	0.5	4
Solution	0	0	0.7	0	6	648

Interpreting the optimal solution

This table gives us the following information:

(a) The solution being tested is that the variables in the solution are x, y and b (= number of units of X and Y and unused labour hours).

(b) From the Solution column, we can see that the values are x = 13, y = 4 and s2 = 8. This means that we should produce 13 units of X, 4 units of Y and this will leave 8 unused labour hours.

(c) Variables a and c are not in this solution, so their values are 0. There will be no unused materials or machine hours.

(d) The total daily contribution from this solution (= the value of the objective function) is shown in the bottom right-hand corner of the table, and in the optimal table it is = $648.

(e) The bottom row gives us the **dual prices or shadow prices** for each variable. This is the amount by which the value of the objective function would change if a unit of that variable were to be introduced into the solution.

(f) When a variable has a positive shadow price or dual price, this shows the amount by which:

  (i) The value of the objective function would be reduced if this variable were to be introduced into the solution, for each unit of the variable that is introduced.

  (ii) The value of the objective function could be improved if one extra unit of the variable were made available.

  (iii) The value of the objective function would be reduced if one less unit of the variable were available.

Interpreting shadow prices (dual prices)

The table shows that if it were possible to increase the availability of materials from 600 to 601, the value of the objective function would increase by $0.7, and if it were possible to increase the availability of materials from 600 to 602, the value of the objective function would increase by (2 × 0.7) = $1.4.

It is also showing that if one unit less of materials were available, so that only 599 units were available, the value of the objective function would be reduced by $0.7.

The same analysis can be applied to slack variable c (machine hours), whose dual price is $6. If the available machine hours could be increased, the total contribution could be increased by $6 for each extra machine hour that is available.

The table tells us even more. Look at the figures in the c column for machine hours, whose shadow price is 6. If one extra machine hour were made available, so that 39 hours were available instead of 38 (= the original constraint):

(a) The value of x would fall by 0.25 units, from 13 to 12.75
(b) The value of b would fall by 4 units, from 8 to 4
(c) The value of y would increase by 0.5, from 4 to 4.5

Contribution would be (12.75 × $40) + (4.5 × $32) = $654. This is 6 higher than the optimal solution, showing that the shadow price or dual price of machine hours is $6.

Chapter roundup

- **Linear programming** is a technique for solving problems of profit maximisation or cost minimisation and resource allocation. 'Programming' has nothing to do with computers: the word is simply used to denote a series of events.

- **Linear programming**, at least at this fairly simple level, is a technique that can be carried out in a fairly 'handle-turning' manner once you have got the basic ideas sorted out. The steps involved are as follows.

    1. Define variables
    2. Establish constraints
    3. Construct objective function
    4. Graph constraints
    5. Establish feasible region
    6. Add iso-profit/contribution line
    7. Determine optimal solution

- A graphical solution is only possible when there are two variables in the problem. One variable is represented by the x axis and one by the y axis of the graph. Since non-negative values are not usually allowed, the graph only shows zero and positive values of x and y.

- The graphical method cannot be used when there are more than two decision variables. A method called the **simplex method** is available in these circumstances, but in practice it is much easier to use a computer.

- The **shadow price** (or **dual price**) of a resource is the amount by which the value of the objective function (contribution) will go up (or down) if one unit more (or less) of the resource were made available.

Quick quiz

1. What are the three main steps involved in setting up a linear programming model?

   Step 1 ....
   Step 2 ....
   Step 3 ....

2. Draw the inequality $4x + 3y \leq 24$ on the graph below.

   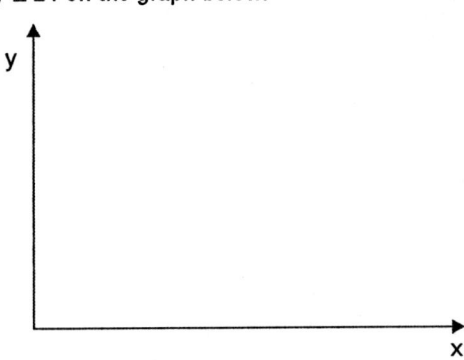

3. A feasible area enclosed on all sides may also be called a ....

4. How does the graphical solution of minimisation problems differ from that of maximisation problems?

5. The graphical method cannot be used when there are more than two decision variables.

   True ☐   False ☐

6. When there are more than two decision variables a method called the .... method is available in these circumstances.

7. What is a shadow price?

Answers to quick quiz

1. **Step 1** Define variables
   Step 2 Establish constraints
   Step 3 Establish objective function

2.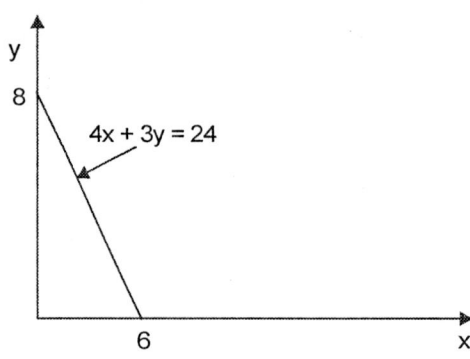

3. Feasible polygon.

4. Instead of finding a contribution line touching the feasible area as far away from the origin as possible, we look for a total cost line touching the feasible area **as close to the origin as possible**.

5. True

6. Simplex

7. The **shadow price** of a resource is the amount by which the value of the objective function (contribution) will go up (or down) if one unit more (or less) of the resource were made available. The shadow price is also known as the **dual price.**

End of chapter questions

1 **Bang Demolition Ltd (AIA May 2005)**

Bang Demolition Ltd has been awarded the contract to demolish and clear the site of an old power station. In addition to a range of demolition workers and machinery Bang owns a number of tipper trucks which will be used to remove rubble to a waste site. Bang needs to decide upon the mix of 10 and 15 cubic metre (m^3) capacity trucks to apply to the contract; any such trucks used on the contract will incur an opportunity cost of not being available for other work. These opportunity costs are estimated as $750 per day for a 10$m^3$ capacity truck and $900 per day for a 15$m^3$ capacity truck. Each 10m^3 truck could make six round trips a day and each 15m^3 truck could make four round trips a day, between the contract site and the waste site. These data include allowance for travel, loading and unloading times.

Bang wishes to minimise the total opportunity cost per day of using the trucks on the contract but has decided that no more than twenty trucks in total can be applied to the contract; at least five of these should be the 10m^3 capacity trucks and at least five should be the 15m^3 capacity trucks. Further, Bang has agreed with the contract site owner to remove not less than 900m^3 of rubble from the site each day.

Required

(a) Formulate this situation as a linear programme and present a diagram on graph paper of the region of feasible mixes of 10m^3 and 15m^3 trucks to be applied each day. **(10 marks)**

(b) Present a solution method to the problem and state:

  (i) The optimal mix of trucks

  (ii) The minimum total daily opportunity cost

  (iii) The amount of rubble in m^3 of waste to be removed each day

  (iv) The number of days the contract will last if there are 15000m^3 of waste to be removed in total **(6 marks)**

(c) If Bang decided after 10 working days on the contract that, because it has just agreed another special contract to start immediately, the minimum number of 15m^3 trucks to be applied to the power station contract must be raised from five to ten trucks henceforth, what effect would this have on your answers in (b)? **(9 marks)**

(Total = 25 marks)

2 **KG Co**

KG Co makes two products, the Purse and the Handbag. Each purse earns $5 contribution and each handbag earns $6. Inputs are as follows:

	Purse	*Handbag*
Leather	1½ m^2	2m^2
Skilled labour	45 min	30 min

There are six skilled labourers each working a 35 hour week and delivery contracts limit the amount of leather available to 600m^2 each week.

KG Co has an EU quota ruling whereby it has to produce at least as many handbags as it does purses. Leather costs $8 per m^2, wages are paid at $4.20 per hour.

Required

Formulate the linear programming model. **(5 marks)**

PART A TECHNIQUES TO SUPPORT BUSINESS DECISIONS

Network analysis

Topic list	Syllabus reference
1 Projects and project management	9.4
2 Management tools and techniques	9.4
3 Network analysis	9.4
4 Project management software	9.4
5 Planning the tasks: Work Breakdown Schedule (WBS)	9.4
6 Gantt charts	9.5
7 Critical path analysis (CPA)	9.5
8 Other project planning techniques	9.5

Introduction

In this chapter we study the stages a project moves through from initiation to completion. Be aware that other books may refer to **project stages** with different names or may include more or fewer stages. This does not mean one description is incorrect. The principles behind the process and techniques are more important than the labels used.

Later in the chapter we study the various **management tools and techniques** used in project management – covering areas such as project documentation and risk management.

We conclude by looking at the use of computers in this area.

1 Projects and project management

A project is a major task, with a clearly defined start and a clearly defined objective and end. In business, a project can be distinguished from regular or routine business operations, which are continuous and ongoing. An example of a project is the development and implementation of a new computer system.

Successful projects call for effective planning, effective use of resources and control over costs. Management also need to ensure that work on the project progresses, so that it is completed within the target length of time.

This chapter looks at several techniques that are used to help with the management of projects.

2 Management tools and techniques

> Various **tools and techniques** are available to plan and control projects including the project plan, project budget, Work Breakdown Structure, Gantt charts, network analysis, resource histogram and specialist software.

2.1 The project budget

Key term

> A **project budget** is the amount and distribution of resources allocated to a project.

Building a project budget should be an orderly process that attempts to establish a realistic estimate of the cost of the project.

2.2 Work breakdown structure (WBS)

Key term

> **Work breakdown structure** is the analysis of the work of a project into different units or tasks. WBS:
>
> (a) Identifies the work that must be done in the project
> (b) Determines the resources required
> (c) Sequences the work done, to allocate resources in the optimum way

Work breakdown structure is used as a starting point for many project management functions including budgeting and **scheduling**. As a simple example of WBS, **wiring** a house can be **sub-divided** into connecting the mains, fitting light sockets and power points etc. Dealing with the foundations involves digging, filling, area marking, damp proofing and disposal of soil.

The process of work breakdown continues until the smallest sub-units are reached. Digging the foundations for example would be analysed so that the number of labour hours needed, and hence the cost, could be determined.

2.2.1 WBS and estimates of expenditure

WBS can be used in devising estimates. From the WBS it is possible to compile a complete list of **every task** that is going to attract expenditure.

Estimating the costs identified with each task has several benefits:

(a) It provides a basis for budgeting the project costs.
(b) It assists with project **cost control**.
(c) It provides evidence, in any dispute with the project client, that the costs are reasonable.

The overall level of cost estimates will be influenced by:

(a) **Project goals**. If a high level of quality is expected, costs will be higher.

(b) **Staff availability**. If internal staff are unavailable, potentially expensive contractors may be required.

(c) **Time schedules**. The quicker a task is required to be done the higher the cost is likely to be – particularly with external suppliers.

In project management, a balance must always be found between project objectives, available resources, time and cost.

2.3 Gantt charts

A Gantt chart, named after the engineer Henry Gantt who pioneered the procedure in the early 1900s, is a horizontal bar chart used to plan the **time scale** for a project and to estimate the amount of **resources** required.

The Gantt chart displays the **time relationships** between tasks in a project. Two lines are usually used to show the time allocated for each task, and the actual time taken.

A simple Gantt chart, illustrating some of the activities involved in a network server installation project, follows.

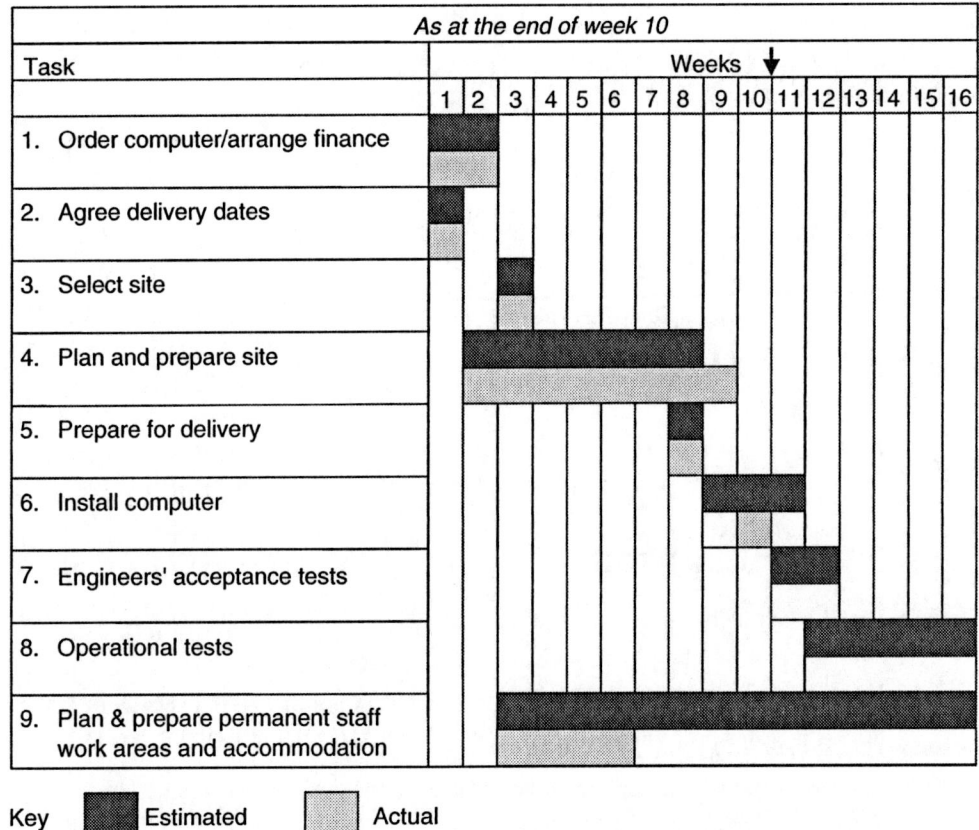

The chart shows that at the end of the tenth week Activity 9 is running behind schedule. More resources may have to be allocated to this activity if the staff accommodation is to be ready in time for the changeover to the new system.

Activity 4 was not completed on time, and this has resulted in some disruption to the computer installation (Activity 6), which may mean further delays in the commencement of Activities 7 and 8.

A Gantt chart does not show the interrelationship between activities as clearly as a **network diagram** (covered next in this chapter). A combination of Gantt charts and network analysis will often be used for project planning and resource allocation.

3 Network analysis

FAST FORWARD

> **Network analysis**, also known as **Critical path analysis** (CPA), is a useful technique to help with planning and controlling large projects, such as construction projects, research and development projects and the computerisation of systems.

The purpose of network analysis is to help management with control over the duration of the project and trying to ensure that it is completed on time and that the work does not overrun.

Key term

> **Network analysis** requires breaking down the project into tasks with estimated durations and establishing a logical sequence of tasks that identifies which tasks must be completed before others can begin, and the expected time for completing each task. This enables the minimum possible duration of the project to be found.

CPA aims to ensure the progress of a project, so the project is completed in the **minimum amount of time**.

It pinpoints the tasks which are on the **critical path**. The critical path activities are those tasks which, if their starting time is delayed beyond earliest possible time for starting them, would **delay the completion** of the project as a whole.

Critical path analysis is quite a simple technique. The events and activities making up the whole project are represented in the form of a **diagram**. Drawing the diagram or chart involves the following steps.

Step 1   Estimating the time needed to complete each individual activity or task that makes up a part of the project.

Step 2   Sorting out what activities must be done one after another, and which can be done at the same time, if required.

Step 3   Representing these in a network diagram.

Step 4   Identifying the critical path, and its duration. This is the shortest possible time for completing the project, given the estimated completion times for each project activity.

3.1 The critical path

The duration of the whole project will be fixed by the time taken to complete the largest path through the network. This path is called the **critical path** and activities on it are known as **critical activities**.

Activities on the critical path **must be started and completed by the scheduled time**, otherwise the total project time will be extended.

Network analysis shows the **sequence** of tasks and how long they are going to take. The diagrams are drawn from left to right. To construct a network diagram you need to know the activities involved in a project, the expected duration of each activity, and the sequence or 'precedences' of the activities (which preceding activities must be completed before the next activity can begin).

3.1.1 Example

The table below shows the activities, activity durations and precedences of a simple project.

Activity	Expected duration	Preceding activity
A	3	–
B	5	–
C	2	B
D	1	A
E	6	A
F	3	D
G	3	C, E

This information can be used to construct a network diagram. There are two mehods of drawing a network diagram:

- As **an activity-on-arrow diagram**, where each activity in the project is represented by an arrowed line. Activities are linked by starting and completion 'events'.

- As **an activity-on-node diagram**, where activities are represented by boxes or 'nodes' linked sequentially.

3.2 Activity-on-arrow presentation

An activity-on-arrow network diagram for this simple project is shown below.

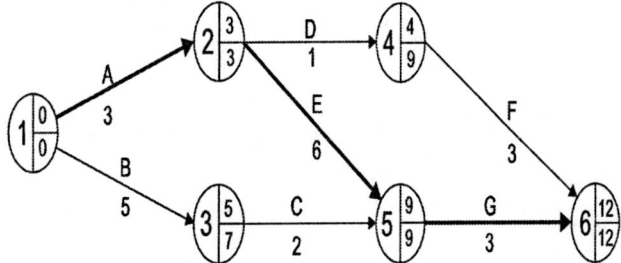

Points to note from the diagram:

(a) Tasks are represented by arrowed lines, each with an estimated duration. The logical sequence of activities is shown by linking the activities through 'events'. An event represents the start and/or the completion of one or more activities.

(b) When two or more activities can begin at the same time after a preceding activity has ended, these activities can all begin from the same event where the previous activity end. In this example, both activities D and E can begin when activity A has ended, so both activities can start at the same event.

(c) When one activity cannot begin until two or more previous activities have ended, the previous activities may all end at the same event where the subsequent activity begins. In this example activity G cannot start until both C and E have finished. Activities C and E can therefore end at the same event 5, and the subsequent activity G can start from this event.

(d) The times are entered in the diagram by showing an earliest starting time and a latest finishing time for each event. These are the times in the top and bottom right hand sections of each event circle.

(e) The earliest starting times are entered first, starting with the first event (starting time 0) and working from left to right through the diagram. The earliest starting time for each subsequent event is calculated by adding the duration for the preceding activity to the earliest start time of the preceding event. When two activities end at the same event, the earliest starting time should be the higher of the two figures. For example, at event 5 the earliest starting time for the next activity G is the higher of (3 + 6) = 9 and (5 + 2) = 7.

(f) The latest finishing times are entered next. Start at the right hand side of the diagram and work back towards the left. The latest finishing time at the final event is the same as the earliest finishing time. The latest finishing time at each event is the latest finishing time at the subsequent event minus the duration of the subsequent activity. For example the latest finishing time at event 4 is (12 – 3) = 9. When two subsequent activities start from the same event, take the lower of the two figures. In this example, the latest finishing time at event 2 is the lower of (9 – 1) = 8 and (9 – 6) = 3.

(g) The **critical path** is the sequence of activities joined by events where the earliest starting time and latest finishing time are the same. In this example is it the path AEG. It is the longest path (in terms of time) through the network – which is the **minimum amount of time** that the project will take. The critical path may be distinguished by making the arrows on the critical path thicker.

3.2.1 Float and activity-on-arrow diagrams

When activities are not on the critical path, they have some float. Float is the amount of time by which the activity (or a small chain of activities) can be delayed without affecting the completion time for the project as a whole. Delay would mean starting the activity later than the earliest possible starting time, or taking longer than the estimated time to complete.

(a) **Total float** on a job is the time available (earliest start date to latest finish date) **less** time needed for the job. If, for example, job A's earliest start time was day 7 and its latest end time was day 17, and the job needed four days, total float would be:

(17 – 7) – 4 = 6 days

(b) **Free float** is the delay possible in an activity on the assumption that all preceding jobs start as early as possible and all subsequent jobs also start at the earliest time.

(c) **Independent float for an individual activity** is the delay possible if all preceding jobs have finished as late as possible, and all succeeding jobs have started as early as possible.

In this example, there is a float of 5 days on the **non-critical chain of activities** DF. This is because the latest finishing time at event 2 is day 3 and the latest finishing time at event 6 is day 12. This gives 9 days to complete D and F, but only 4 days (1 + 3) should be needed.

The **free float** for activity D is 9 – 3 – 1 = 5 days.

Similarly the free float for activity F is 12 – 4 – 3 = 5 days.

Activity D can begin any time between days 3 and 8, and activity F can begin at any time between days 4 and 9, thus giving the project manager a degree of flexibility.

However, this is a combined float for activities D and F together. The **independent float** for each activity is 0.

There is also float on chain of activities BC. A total time of 9 days is available to complete these activities, without affecting the project completion time, but only 7 days is needed for the two activities. This gives a combined float of 2 days on B and C.

3.3 Activity-on-node presentation

Network diagrams may also be drawn using activity-on-node presentation which is similar in style to that used by the **Microsoft Project** software package. With an activity-on-node network diagram, activities are shown by boxes or 'nodes', joined by arrows. The arrows indicate the sequence of events, but have no other significance.

3.3.1 Example: Activity on Node

Suppose that a project includes three activities, C, D and E. Neither activity D nor E can start until activity C is completed, but D and E could be done simultaneously if required.

This would be represented as follows.

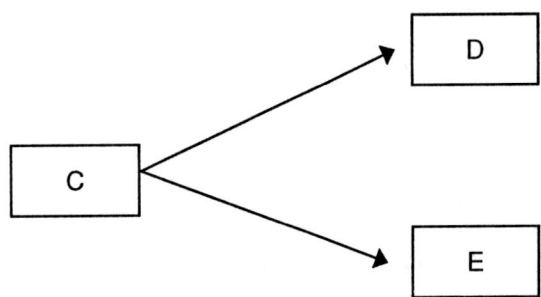

Notes

1. An **activity** within a network is represented by a rectangular box. (Each box is a **node**.)
2. The **'flow'** of activities in the diagram should be from **left to right**.
3. The diagram clearly shows that **D and E must follow C**.

A second possibility is that an activity cannot start until two or more activities have been completed. If activity H cannot start until activities G and F are both complete, then we would represent the situation like this.

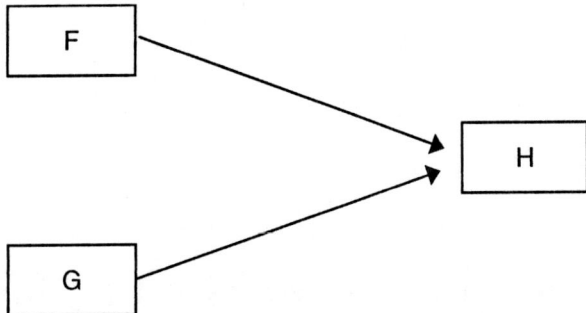

In some conventions an extra node is introduced at the start and end of a network. This serves no purpose (other than to ensure that all the nodes are joined up), so we recommend that you do not do it.

Just in case you ever see a network presented in this way, both styles are shown in the next example.

3.4 Example showing start and end nodes

Draw a diagram for the following project. The project is finished when both D and E are complete.

Activity	Preceding activity
A	–
B	–
C	A
D	B and C
E	B

The first solution that follows excludes start and end nodes – the second solution includes them.

Solution

3.4.1 Microsoft Project style

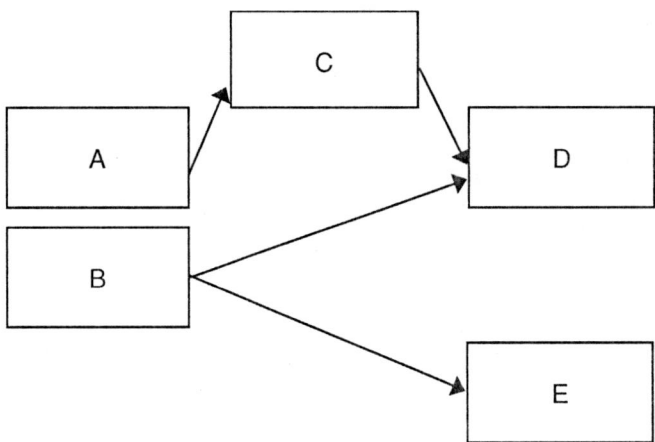

3.4.2 With start and end nodes

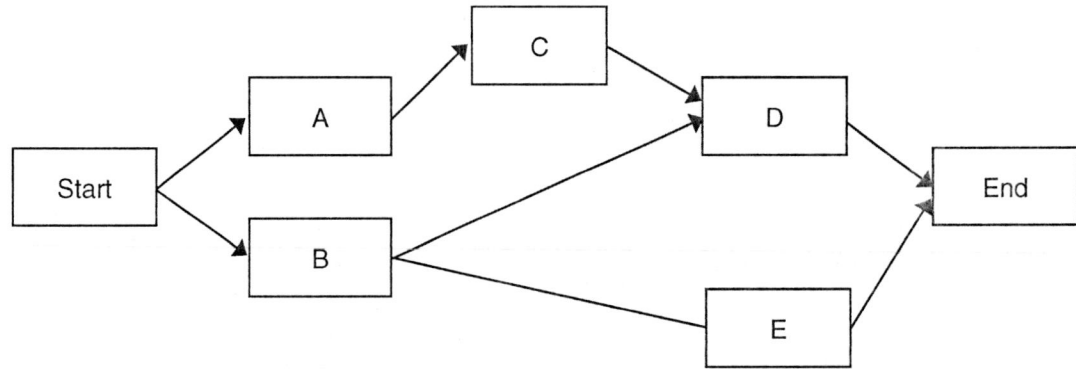

Any network can be analysed into a number of different paths or routes. A path is simply a sequence of activities which can take you from the start to the end of the network.

In the example above, there are just three possible routes or paths (based on the precedences given earlier).

(a) A C D
(b) B D
(c) B E

3.5 Showing the duration of activities

The time needed to complete each individual activity in a project must be estimated. This **duration** may be shown within the node as follows. The meaning of the other boxes is explained later.

Task A	
ID	6 days

Note. There are a range of acceptable notation styles for network diagrams. You should learn the principles of the technique so you are able to interpret diagrams presented in a variety of formats (with an explanatory key).

3.6 Example: The critical path

Activity	Immediately preceding activity	Duration Weeks
A	–	5
B	–	4
C	A	2
D	B	1
E	B	5
F	B	5
G	C, D	4
H	F	3
I	F	2

(a) What are the paths through the network?
(b) What is the critical path and its duration?

Solution

The first step in the solution is to draw the network diagram, with the time for each activity shown.

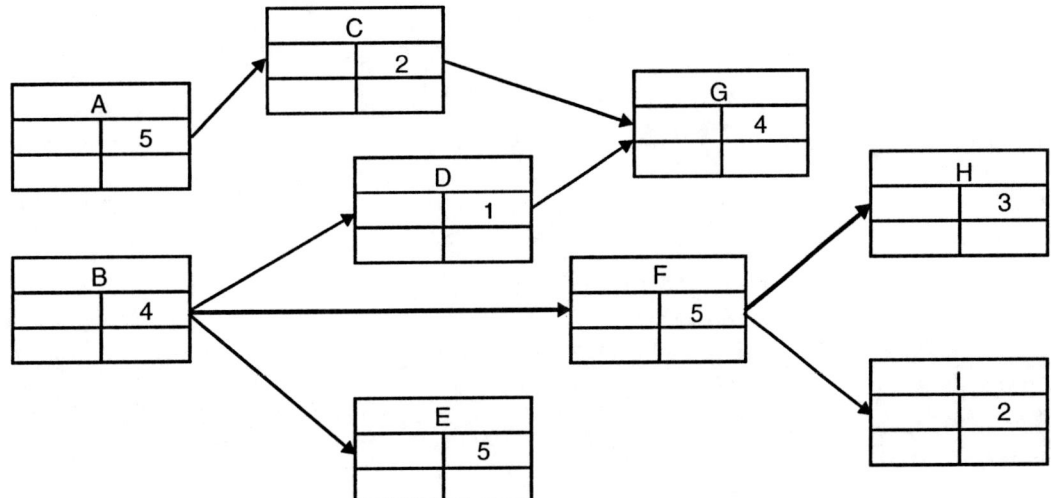

We could list the paths through the network and their overall completion times as follows.

Path	Duration	Weeks
A C G	(5 + 2 + 4)	11
B D G	(4 + 1 + 4)	9
B E	(4 + 5)	9
B F H	(4 + 5 + 3)	12
B F I	(4 + 5 + 2 + 0)	11

The critical path is the longest, **BFH**, with a duration of 12 weeks. This is the **minimum time needed** to complete the project.

The **critical path** may be indicated on the diagram by drawing **thick** arrows. In Microsoft Project the arrows and the nodes are highlighted in red.

Listing paths through the network in this way should be easy enough for small networks, but it becomes a **long and tedious task** for bigger and more complex networks. This is why **software packages** are used in real life.

Conventionally it has been recognised as useful to calculate the **earliest and latest times for activities to start or finish**, and show them on the network diagram. This can be done for networks of any size and complexity.

3.7 Example: Earliest and latest start times

One way of showing earliest and latest start times for activities is to divide each node into sections. These sections record the following data.

(a) The **name** of the activity, for example activity A.

(b) An **ID number** which is unique to that activity. This helps computer packages to understand the diagram, because it is possible that two or more activities could have the same name.

(c) The **duration** of the activity.

(d) The **earliest start time**. Conventionally for the first node in the network, this is time 0.

(e) The **latest start time**.

(**Note**. Don't confuse start times with the 'event' times that are calculated when using the **activity-on-arrow** method, even though the approach is the same.)

Activity D	
ID number: 4	Duration: 6 days
Earliest start: Day 4	Latest start: Day 11

3.7.1 Earliest start times

To find the earliest start times, always start with activities that have no predecessors and give them an earliest starting time of 0. In the example we have been looking at, this is week 0.

Then work along each path from **left to right** through the diagram calculating the earliest time that the next activity can start. For example, the earliest time for activity C is week 0 + 5 = 5. The earliest time activities D, E and F can start is week 0 + 4 = 4.

To calculate an activity's earliest time, simply look at the box for the **preceding** activity and add the bottom left figure to the top right figure. If **two or more** activities precede an activity take the **highest** figure as the later activity's earliest start time: it cannot start before all the others are finished!

3.7.2 Latest start times

The latest start times are the latest times at which each activity can start **if the project as a whole is to be completed in the earliest possible time**, in other words in 12 weeks in our example.

Work backwards from **right to left** through the diagram calculating the latest time at which the activity can start, if it is to be completed at the latest finishing time. For example the latest start time for activity H is 12 − 3 = week 9 and for activity E is 12 − 5 = week 7.

Activity F might cause difficulties as two activities, H and I, lead back to it.

(a) Activity H must be completed by week 12, and so must start by week 9.

(b) Activity I must also be completed by week 12, and so must start by week 10.

(c) Activity F takes 5 weeks so its latest start time F is either 9 − 5 = week 4 or 10 − 5 = week 5. However, if it starts in week 5 it will not be possible to start activity H on time and the whole project will be delayed. We therefore take the **lower** figure.

The final diagram is now as follows.

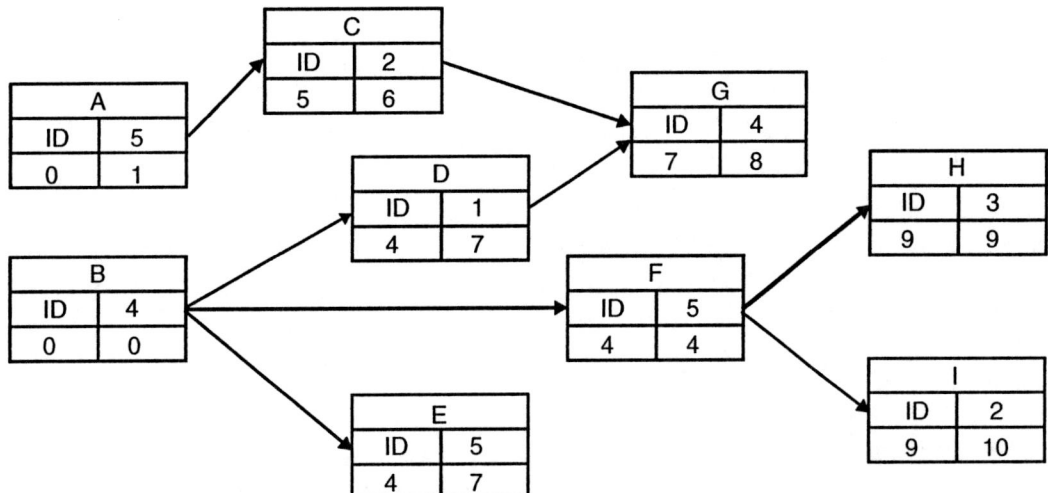

Critical activities are those activities which must be started on time, otherwise the total project time will be increased. It follows that each event on the critical path must have the same earliest and latest start times. The critical path for the above network is therefore **B F H**.

3.7.3 Float and activity-on-node diagrams

For each activity, float is the difference between the earliest and latest starting times, but float is sometimes shared between a chain of non-critical activities. In this example, there is a **free float** of 1 week on activities A, C and G. however this is a shared float time because these activities are a non-critical chain. A delayed start of 1 week on activity A for example would mean that activities C and G become critical.

Activity D, on the other hand, has **independent float** of 2 weeks. If all preceding activities finish as late as possible, B must finish by the end of week 4. If all succeeding activities start as early as possible, G will begin after the end of week 7. This gives three weeks to complete activity D, but only one week is needed for the work.

3.8 Criticisms of critical path/network analysis

The following criticisms are often made in relation to network analysis.

(a)　It is not always possible to devise an effective WBS for a project.

(b)　**It assumes a sequential relationship** between activities. For example, in the diagram above it assumes that activity C starts after activity A has finished. In reality, a part of a subsequent activity may be started before a preceding activity has ended.

(c)　There are **problems in estimation of duration times** for activities. Estimates may be inexact – and incorrect or unrealistic.

3.9 Example: Network analysis and Gantt charts

This example is provided as an illustration of how Gantt charts may be used to manage resources efficiently. A company is about to undertake a project about which the following data is available.

Activity	Preceded by activity	Duration Days	Workers required
A	–	3	6
B	–	5	3
C	B	2	4
D	A	1	4
E	A	6	5
F	D	3	6
G	C, E	3	3

There is a multi-skilled workforce of nine workers available, each capable of working on any of the activities. Draw the network to establish the duration of the project and the critical path. Then draw a Gantt chart, using the critical path as a basis, assuming that jobs start at the earliest possible time.

Solution

Here are the diagrams.

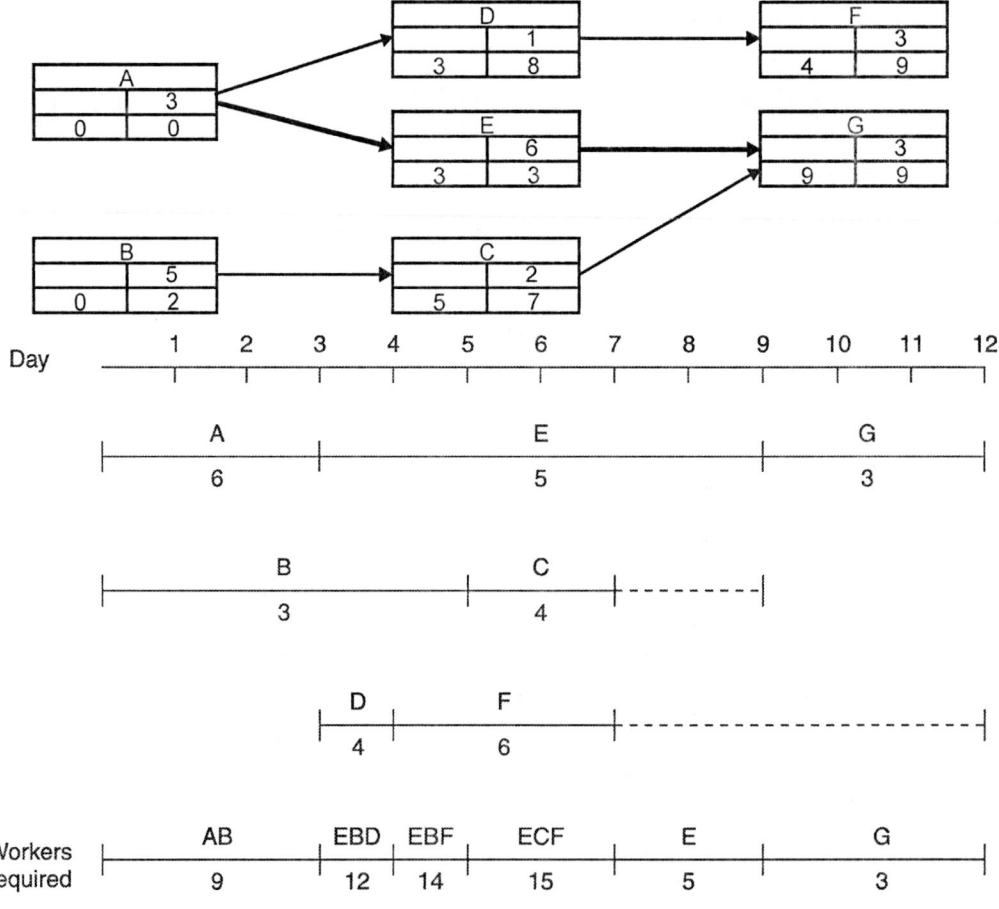

It can be seen that if all activities start at their earliest times, as many as 15 workers will be required on days 6–7 whereas on other days there would be idle capacity (days 8–12).

The problem can be reduced, or removed, by using up spare time on non-critical activities. Suppose we **deferred the start** of activities D and F until the latest possible days. These would be days 8 and 9, leaving four days to complete the activities by the end of day 12.

The Gantt chart would be redrawn as follows.

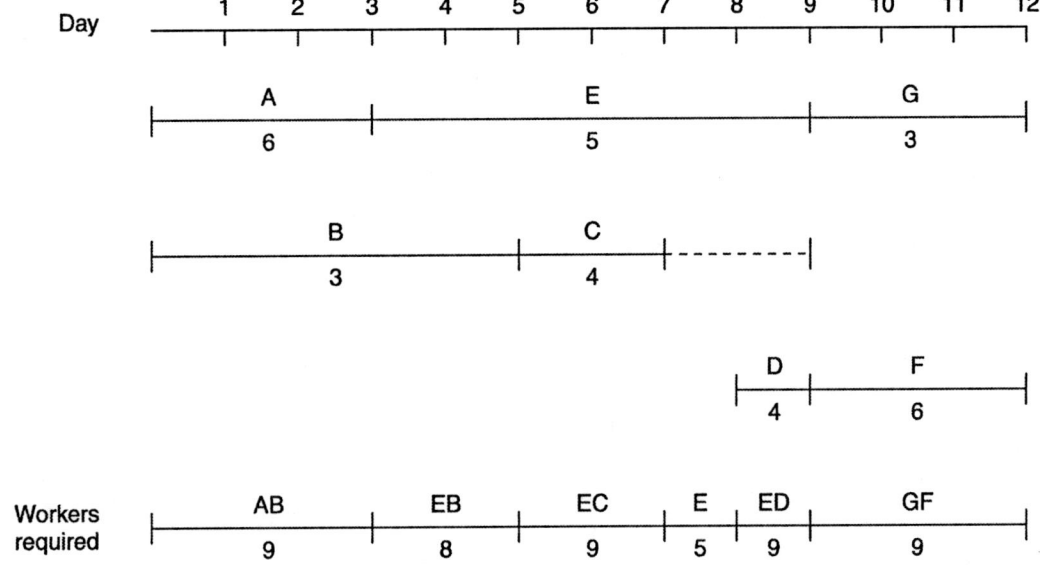

3.9.1 Resource histogram

A useful planning tool that shows the amount and timing of the requirement for a resource (or a range of resources) is the resource histogram.

Key term

A **resource histogram** shows a view of project data in which resource requirements, usage, and availability are shown against a time scale.

A simple resource histogram showing programmer time required on a software development program is shown below.

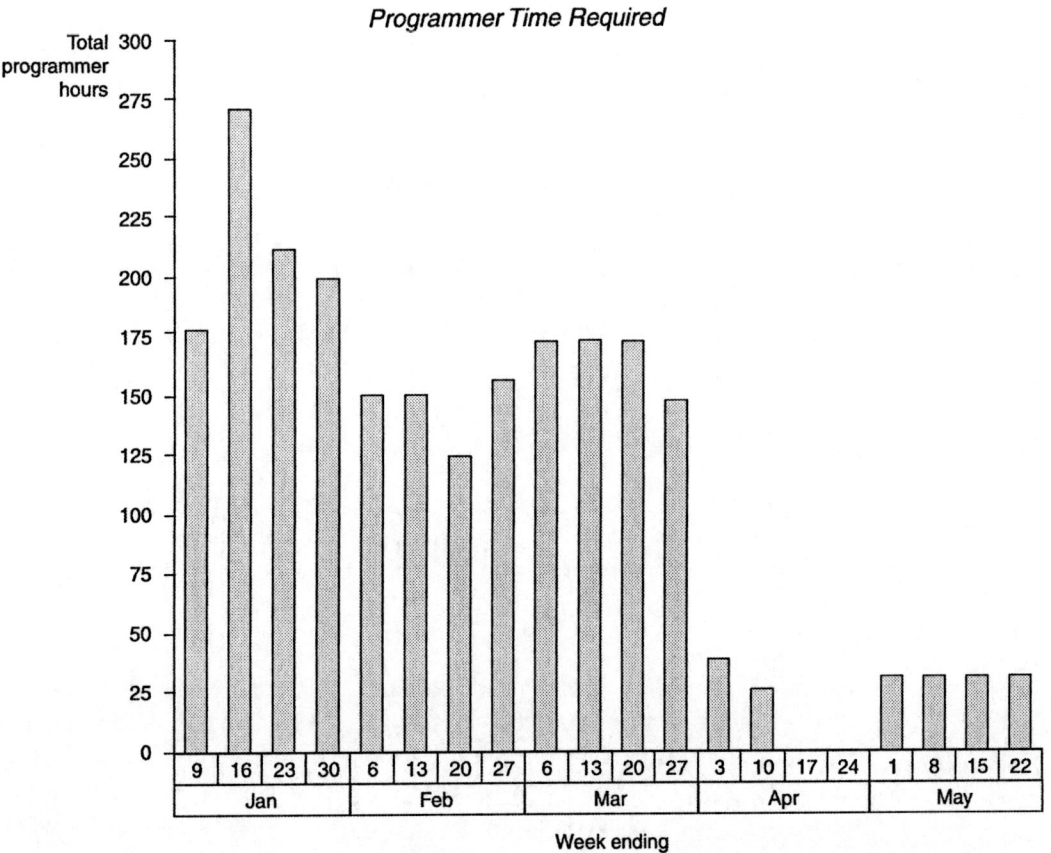

Some organisations add another bar (or a separate line) to the chart showing resource availability. The chart then shows any instances when the required resource hours exceed the available hours. Plans should then be made to either obtain further resource for these peak times, or to re-schedule the work plan. Alternatively the chart may show times when the available resource is excessive, and should be re-deployed elsewhere. An example follows.

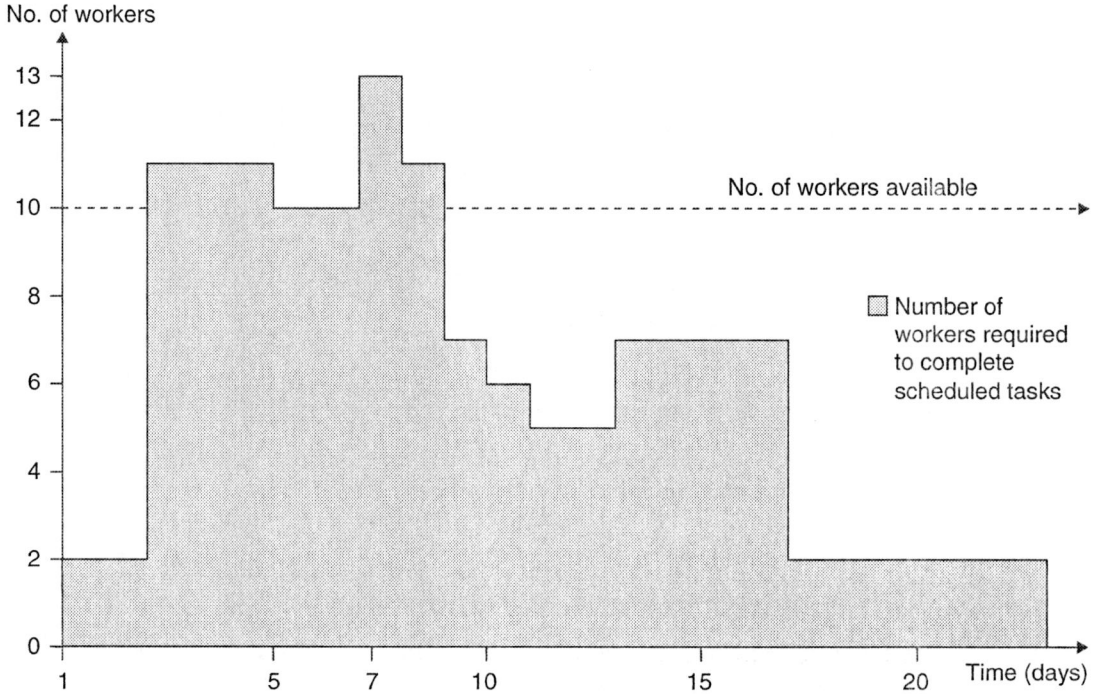

The number of workers required on the seventh day is 13. Can we re-schedule the non-critical activities to reduce the requirement to the available level of 10? We might be able to re-arrange activities so that we can make use of the workers available from day 9 onwards.

Exam focus point

Network analysis is examined regularly. Ensure you are comfortable drawing, and interpreting, network diagrams.

4 Project management software

FAST FORWARD

Project management software may be used to help produce project documentation, diagrams and reports.

Project management software packages have been available for a number of years. Microsoft Project and Micro Planner X-Pert are two such packages.

Software might be used for a number of purposes.

(a) **Planning**
Network diagrams (showing the critical path) and Gantt charts (showing resource use) can be produced automatically once the relevant data is entered. Packages also allow a sort of 'what if?' analysis for initial planning, trying out different levels of resources, changing deadlines and so on to find the best combination.

(b) **Estimating**
As a project progresses, actual data will become known and can be entered into the package and collected for future reference. Since many projects involve basically similar tasks (interviewing users and so on), actual data from one project can be used to provide more accurate estimates for the next project. The software also facilitates and encourages the use of more sophisticated estimation techniques than managers might be prepared to use if working manually.

(c) **Monitoring**
Actual data can also be entered and used to facilitate monitoring of progress and automatically updating the plan for the critical path and the use of resources as circumstances dictate.

(d) **Reporting**
Software packages allow standard and tailored progress reports to be produced, printed out and circulated to participants and senior managers at any time, usually at the touch of a button. This helps with co-ordination of activities and project review.

4.1 Time, cost and quality

A project is affected by a number of factors, often in **conflict** with each other.

(a) **Quality** of the system required, in terms of basic system requirements.

(b) **Time**, both to complete the project, and in terms of the opportunity cost of time spent on this project which could be spent on others.

(c) **Costs** and resources allocated to the project.

The balance between the constraints of time, cost and quality will be different for each project.

(a) If a system aims to provide competitive advantage then time will tend to be the dominant factor.

(b) If safety is paramount, then quality will be most important.

(c) If the sole aim of a project is to meet administrative needs that are not time dependent, then cost may be the dominant factor.

The relationship can be shown as a triangle.

The Time/Cost/Quality Triangle

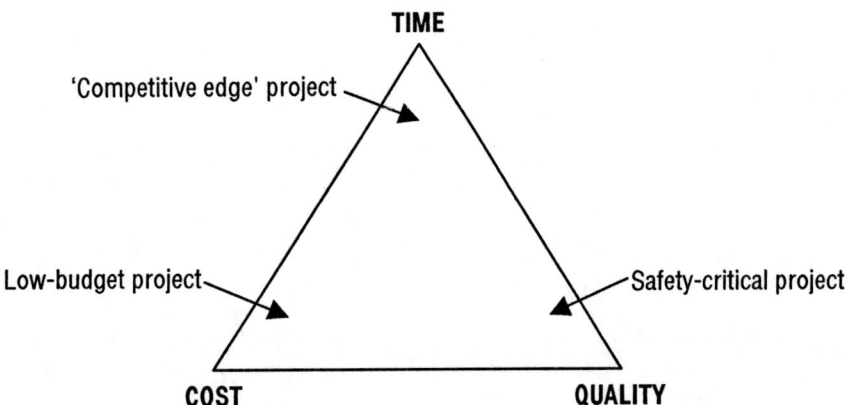

The balance of time, cost and quality will influence decision making throughout the project – for example whether to spend an extra $5,000 to fix a problem completely or only spend $1,000 on a quick fix and implement a user work-around?

4.2 Dealing with slippage

'Slippage' or slipping behind schedule is a common problem.

When a project has slipped behind schedule there is a range of options open to the project manager. Some of these options are summarised in the following table.

Action	Comment
Do nothing	After considering all options it may be decided that things should be allowed to continue as they are.
Add resources	If capable staff are available and it is practicable to add more people to certain tasks it may be possible to recover some lost ground. Could some work be subcontracted?
Work smarter	Consider whether the methods currently being used are the most suitable – for example could prototyping be used?
Re-plan	If the assumptions the original plan was based on have been proved invalid a more realistic plan should be devised.
Reschedule	A complete re-plan may not be necessary – it may be possible to recover some time by changing the phasing of certain deliverables.
Introduce incentives	If the main problem is team performance, incentives such as bonus payments could be linked to work deadlines and quality.
Change the specification	If the original objectives of the project are unrealistic, given the time and money available, it may be necessary to negotiate a change in the specification.

5 Planning the tasks: Work Breakdown Structure (WBS)

The project manager must identify all the work that needs to be done in order to complete the project, and the order in which the work has to be done. Some tasks cannot be started until other tasks have been finished. For example, a new system cannot be tested until it has been designed and developed.

To help them with identifying and planning the work, project managers may use a technique called Work Breakdown Structure (WBS). A WBS is a technique for defining and organising the tasks that must be done in order to complete a project tree structure. A well-designed WBS describes planned outcomes instead of planned actions. Outcomes are the desired ends of project activity, and can be predicted accurately.

A **work breakdown structure** is an analysis of the work involved in a project into smaller and smaller tasks, until the project consists of a large number of 'work packages'. These can then be included in the project plan as project activities.

Since WBS breaks down the work into smaller and smaller activities, it provides a hierarchical view of the project tasks. The activities that are identified by WBS can then be included in plans for resource allocation to the project and for scheduling the work, using techniques such as Gantt charts and critical path analysis (CPA).

6 Gantt charts

A Gantt chart may be used to plan a project schedule and monitor progress towards completion.

A Gantt chart is a chart that shows all the activities in a project. Each activity is shown in the chart as a bar. The chart also shows the time frame for the project: the earliest activities are shown on the left of the chart and the sequence of activities is shown from left to right.

Gantt charts can be used both for planning the work and also for recording completion (or part-completion) of tasks as the project work progresses.

7 Critical path analysis (CPA)

FAST FORWARD

Critical path analysis (CPA) is a technique for planning and controlling large projects. It aims to get the project done in the minimum time and with the most effective use of resources.

Critical path analysis (CPA) is a technique for planning and controlling large projects. It aims to get the project done in the minimum time and with the most effective use of resources.

When a project involves carrying out a large number of different tasks, the project planner and controller has to decide three things.

(i)   What tasks must be done first before others can be started.

(ii) What tasks can be done at the same time.

(iii) What tasks must be done 'now' and completed on schedule in order to complete the whole project in the shortest possible time.

7.1 Drawing a CPA diagram

The more usual type of CPA diagram is an **'activity-on-arrow' diagram**, which means that each individual activity within a project is represented on the diagram by an arrowed line.

- A project is analysed into its separate tasks or activities and the sequence of activities is presented in a network diagram. The 'flow' of activities in the diagram is from left to right.

- An activity within a network is represented by an arrowed line, running between one 'event' and another 'event'.

- An event is simply the start and/or completion of an activity, which is represented on the network diagram by a circle.

7.2 Example: Critical path analysis

(a) Let us suppose that in a certain project there are two activities A and B, and activity B cannot be started until activity A is completed. This will be represented as follows.

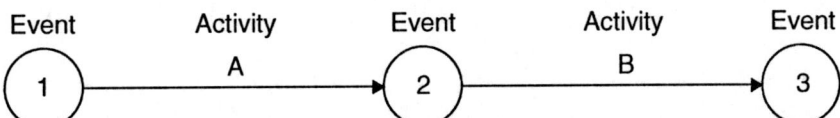

Events are usually numbered, just to identify them. In this example, event 1 is the start of activity A, event 3 is the completion of activity B, and event 2 is both the completion of A and the start of B.

(b) Let us now suppose that another project includes three activities, C, D and E. Neither activity D nor E can start until activity C is completed, but D and E could be done simultaneously if required. This would be represented as follows.

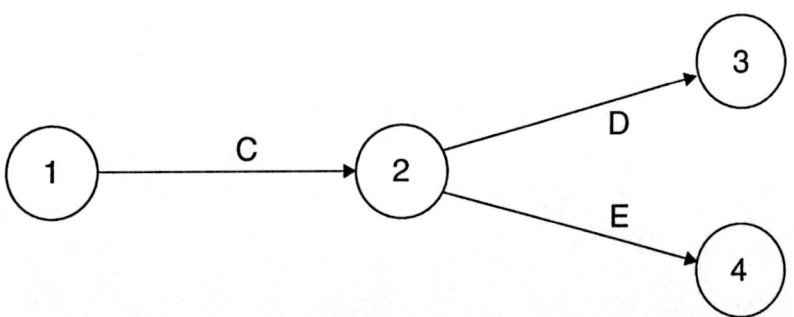

In this diagram, event 2 represents the point when activity C is completed and also the point when activities D and E can start, so the diagram clearly shows that D and E must follow C.

(c) A third possibility is that an activity cannot start until two or more activities have been completed. If activity H cannot start until activities G and F are both complete, then we would represent the situation like this.

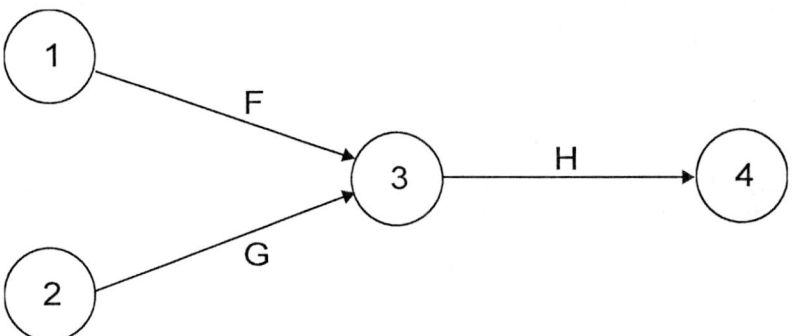

 Question — Network diagram

Draw a network diagram for the activities listed below.

Activity	Preceding activity
A	–
B, C & D	A
E & F	B
G	E
H	F
I	G & H
J	C
K	D
L	I, J & K

Answer

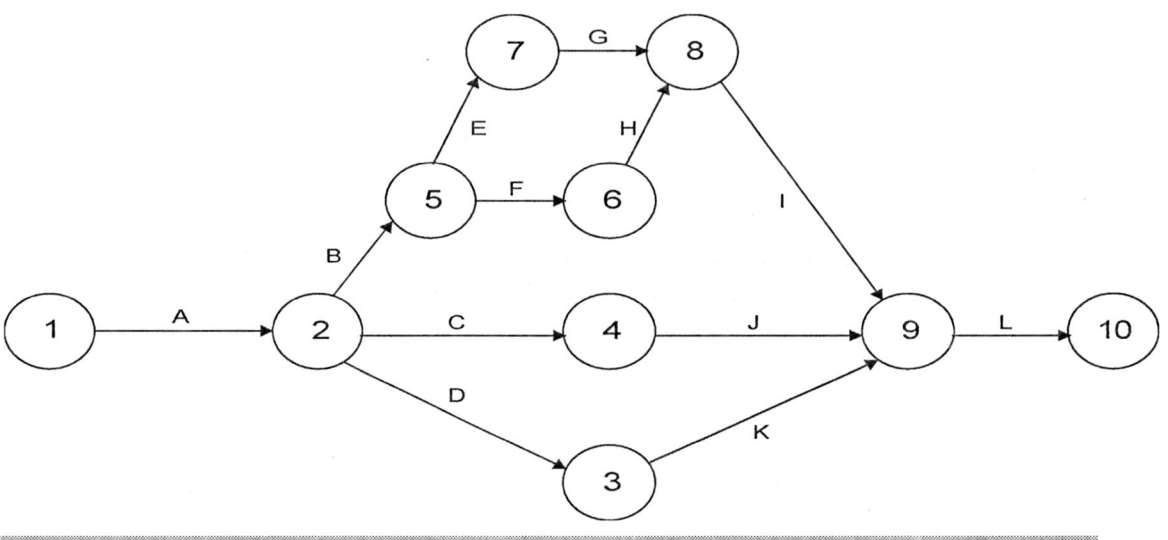

7.3 Dummy activities

It is a convention in network analysis that two separate activities do not have the same starting and finishing event numbers; in other words, two activities should not be drawn between the same events. This problem is overcome by introducing a dummy activity, which is represented by a broken arrowed line.

7.4 Example: Dummy activities

(a) Suppose that the sequence of activities in a project is as follows.

Activity	Preceding activity
A	–
B & C	A
D	B & C

In theory, we could draw the network as follows.

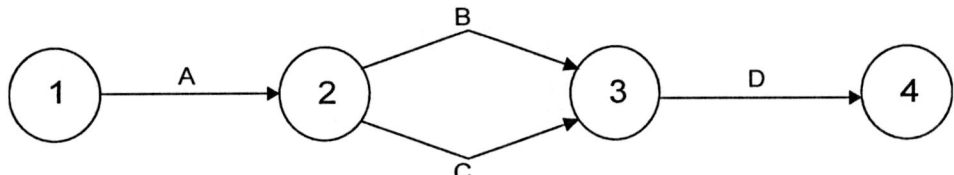

By convention, this would be incorrect. **Two separate activities must not start and end with the same events**. The correct representation is shown below.

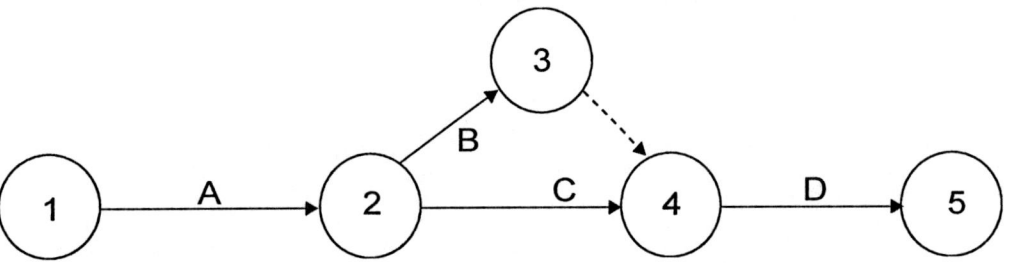

The dummy activity is introduced. It preserves the logic of the sequence of events, and at the same time avoids the need for two activities to share the same starting and completion nodes.

(b) Sometimes it is necessary to use a dummy activity not just to comply with the convention, but to **preserve the basic logic of the network**.

Activity	Preceding activity
A	–
B	–
C	A
D	B & C
E	B

The project is finished when both D and E are complete.

The problem arises because D can only start when both B and C have been finished, whereas E is only required to follow B. The problem is solved by using a **dummy activity**.

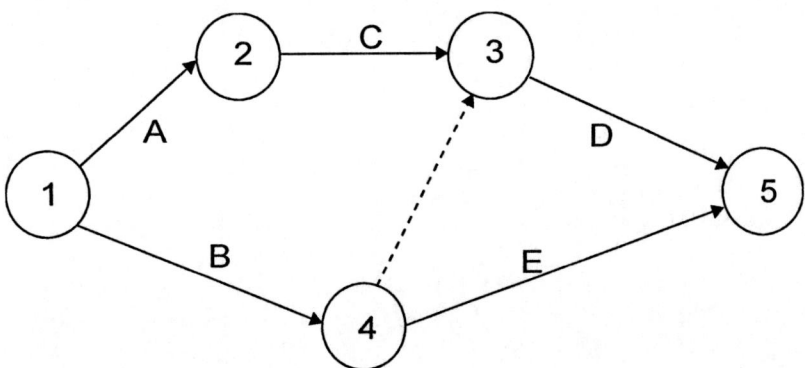

7.5 The critical path

Any network can be analysed into a number of different **paths** or **routes**.

A **path** is simply a sequence of activities which can take you from the start to the end of the network.

In the example above there are three routes or paths.

- A C D
- B Dummy D
- B E

The time needed to complete each individual activity in a project must be estimated. This time is shown on the network above or below the line representing the activity. The duration of the whole project will be fixed by the time taken to complete the largest path through the network. This path is called the critical path and activities on it are known as critical activities. Activities on the critical path must be started and completed on time; otherwise the total project time will be extended.

7.6 Example: Dummy activities

Activity	Immediately preceding activity	Duration (weeks)
A	–	5
B	–	4
C	A	2
D	B	1
E	B	5
F	B	5
G	C, D	4
H	F	3
I	F	2

(a) What are the paths through the network?
(b) What is the critical path and its duration?

Solution

(a) The first step in the solution is to draw the network diagram, with the time for each activity shown. A network should have just **one start node** and **one completion node**, and in the diagram below, this is achieved by introducing a **dummy activity** after activity 1.

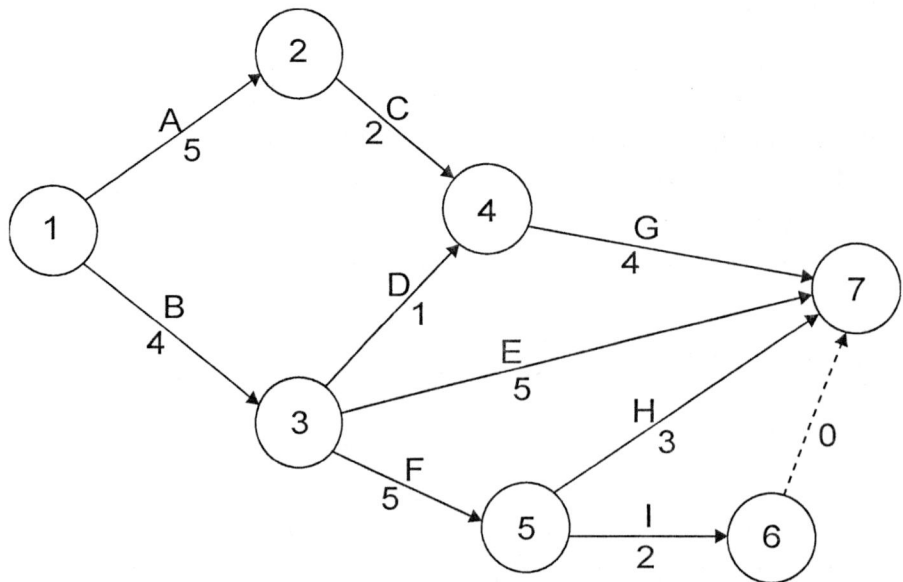

(b) The paths through the network and their overall completion times are as follows.

Path	Duration (weeks)	
A C G	(5 + 2 + 4)	11
B D G	(4 + 1 + 4)	9
B E	(4 + 5)	9
B F H	(4 + 5+ 3)	12
B F I Dummy	(4 + 5 + 2 + 0)	11

The critical path is the longest, BFH, with a duration of 12 weeks. This is the **minimum time** needed to **complete the project**. Listing paths through the network in this way should be easy enough for small networks, but it becomes a long and tedious task for bigger and more complex networks.

7.7 Earliest event times and latest event times

Another way of calculating the critical path is to include **earliest times** and **latest times** for each event, and show them on the network diagram.

- The **earliest event time** is the earliest time that any subsequent activities can start.

- The **latest event time** is the latest time that any preceding activity must be completed if the project as a whole is to be completed in the minimum time.

One way of showing earliest and latest event times is to divide each event node into three sections. These will record the following three things.

- The event number.
- The earliest event time. For the starting node in the network, this is time 0.
- The latest event time.

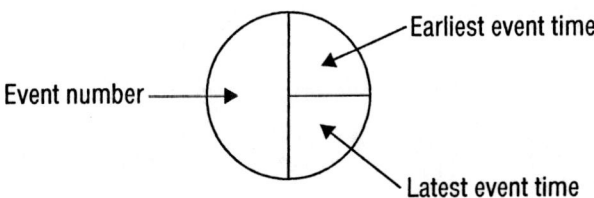

The next step is to calculate the **earliest event times**. Always start at event 1 with its earliest starting time of 0. In the example we have been looking at, this is week 0. **Work from left to right through the diagram** calculating the earliest time that the next activity following the event can start. For example, the earliest event time at event 2 is the earliest time activity C can start. This is week 0 + 5 = 5. Similarly, the earliest event time at event 3 is the earliest time D, E and F can start, which is week 0 + 4 = 4, and the earliest time at event 5 is the earliest time activity H and I can start, which is 4 + 5 = week 9.

A slight problem occurs where more than one activity ends in the same node. For example, event 4 is the completion node for activities C and D. Activity G cannot start until both C and D are complete, therefore the earliest event time at event 4 is the longer duration of A + C or B + D, ie the **higher value** of the following.

- Earliest event time, event 2 + duration of C = 5 + 2 = 7 weeks
- Earliest event time, event 3 + duration of D = 4 + 1 = 5 weeks

The earliest event time at event 4 is seven weeks.

Similarly, the earliest event time at event 7 is the highest value of the following.

- Earliest event time, event 3 + duration of E = 4 + 5 = 9
- Earliest event time, event 4 + duration of G = 7 + 4 = 11
- Earliest event time, event 5 + duration of H = 9 + 3 = 12
- Earliest event time, event 6 + duration of dummy activity = 11 + 0 = 11

The highest value is 12 weeks. This also means that the minimum completion time for the entire project is 12 weeks.

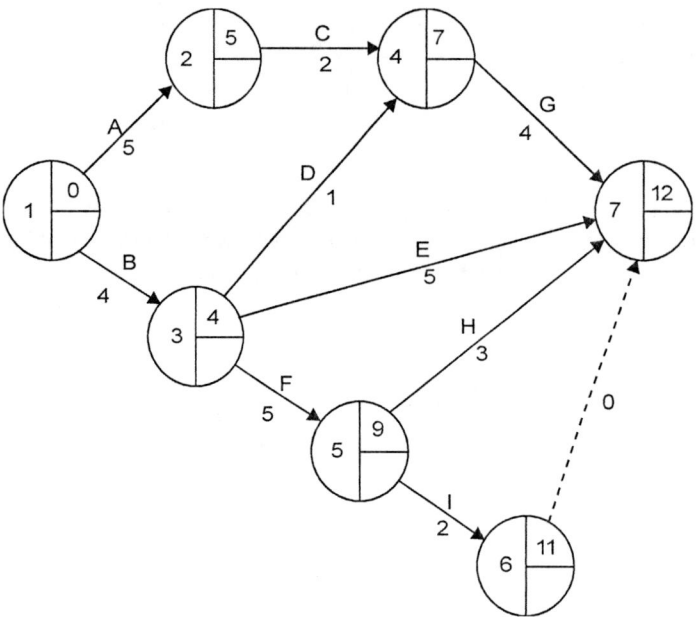

7.8 Latest event times

The next step is to calculate the **latest event times**.

Latest event times are the latest times at which each event can occur if the project as a whole is to be completed in the earliest possible time.

The latest event time at the final event must be the same as the earliest event time, which in this example is 12 weeks.

Work from right to left through the diagram calculating the latest time at which the activity can start, if it is to be completed at the latest finishing time. The latest finishing time for events 4, 6 and 2 is as follows.

- Event 4 is 12 – 4 = week 8
- Event 6 is 12 – 0 = week 12
- Event 2 is 8 – 2 = week 6

Event 5 might cause difficulties as two activities, H and I lead back to it.

(a) Activity H must be completed by week 12, and so must start at week 9.
(b) Activity I must also be completed by week 12, and so must start at week 10.

The latest event time at node 5 is the **lower** of week 9 or week 10, ie week 9. This is simply saying that all activities leading up to node 5, which in this case is just F, must be completed by week 9 so that both H and I can be completed by or before week 12.

The latest event time at event 3 is calculated in the same way. It must be the earliest time which enables all subsequent activities to be completed within the required time. Thus, at event 3, we have the following:

Subsequent event	Latest time of that event (a)	Intermediate activity	Duration of the activity (b)	Required event time at event 3 (a) – (b)
(4)	8	D	1	7
(5)	9	F	5	4*
(7)	12	E	5	7

*All activities before event 3 must be completed by week 4, to enable all subsequent activities to be completed within the required time. Similarly, the latest event time at event 1 is the lowest value of the following:

Latest event time, event 2 minus duration of A = 6 – 5 = 1
Latest event time, event 3 minus duration of B = 4 – 4 = 0

The latest event time at event 1 is therefore 0. **It must always be 0**. If your calculations find it to be any other value, you will have made an error.

The final network diagram is now as follows.

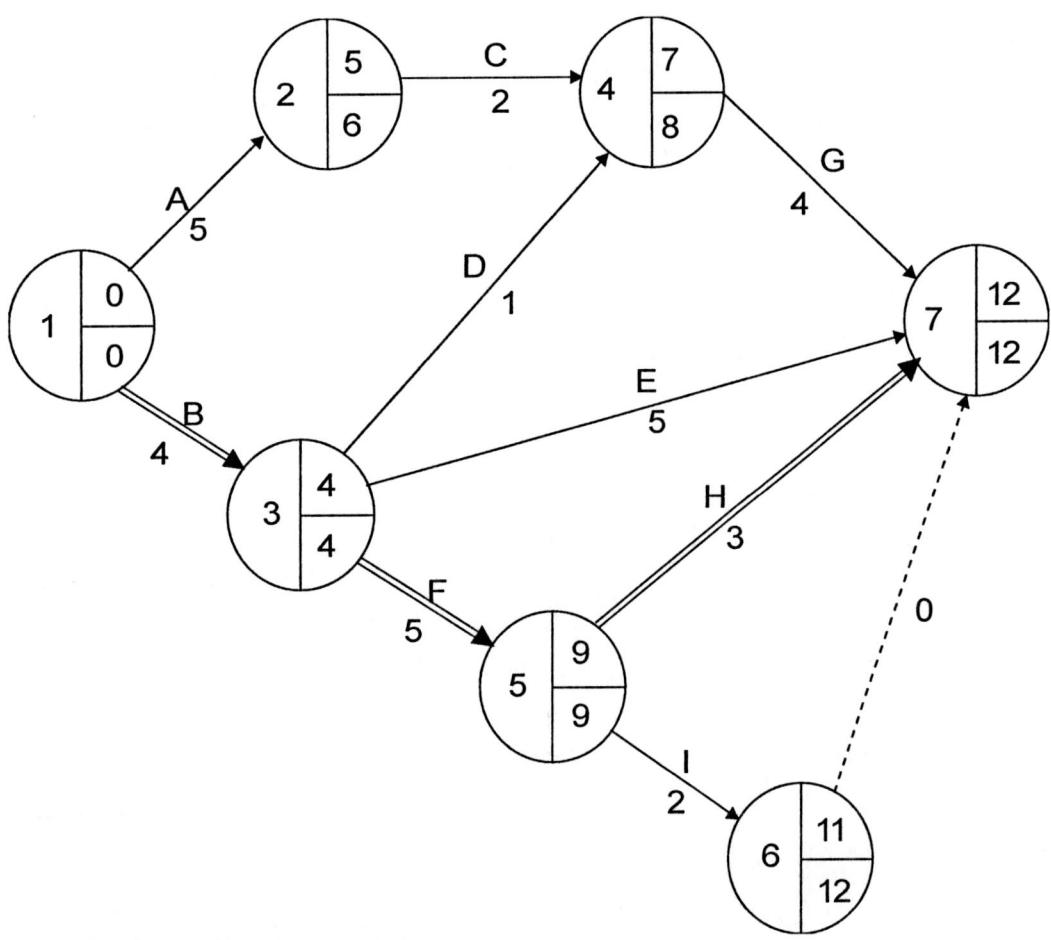

7.9 Finding the critical path

Key term

> **Critical activities** are those activities which must be started on time, otherwise the total project time will be increased. It follows that each event on the critical path must have the same earliest and latest times.

The critical path for the above network is therefore B F H (ie events 1, 3, 5, 7).

When finding the critical path, you should select that path which goes through all of the events which have the same earliest and latest times. You may well find that an activity connects two critical events but is not itself critical. For example, in the following extract from the network events 3 and 7 are on the critical path.

PART A TECHNIQUES TO SUPPORT BUSINESS DECISIONS

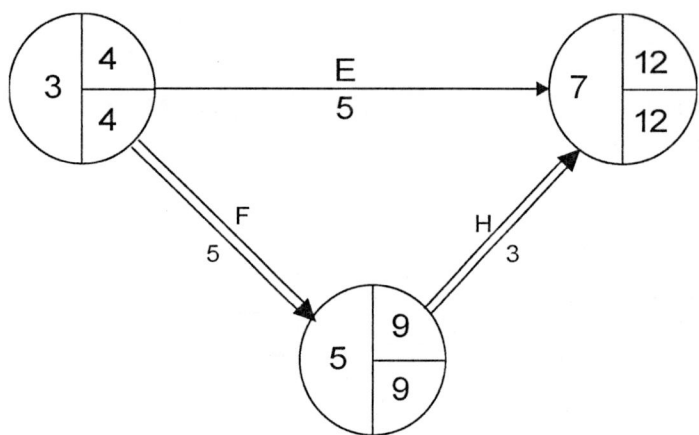

Activity E, however, is not critical as the critical path goes through event 5. If you are in doubt as to whether an activity is on the critical path you should check to see whether it has a float (see below).

All critical activities have zero total float.

7.10 Float

FAST FORWARD Float is the amount of slack time associated with a non-critical activity.

Activities which are not on the critical path are non-critical and they can, within limits, either start late, and/or take longer than the time specified without holding up the completion time of the project as a whole.

Key term

Float is the name given to amount of slack time associated with a non-critical activity. Floats can be categorised into different types.

- Total float
- Free float

7.11 Total float

Key term

The **total float** for any activity is the amount of time by which the duration of an activity can be delayed without delaying the whole project.

The **total float** for any activity is the amount of time by which the duration of an activity can be delayed without delaying the whole project.

When calculating the total float for an activity, the effect on the time available for subsequent activities is ignored. The total float is the **maximum permissible delay** and so is calculated as follows.

(a) **Total float** = Latest finish time – Earliest finish time; or alternatively, as
(b) **Total float** = Latest start time – Earliest start time

The total float for activity C in the previous example is one week, and it is calculated as follows.

	Week
Latest finish time	8
Earliest finish time	(7)
	1

The total float for activity D is three weeks, and is calculated as follows.

	Week
Latest finish time	8
Earliest finish time	(5)
	3

7.12 Free float

Key term

The **free float** for any activity is the amount of time an activity can be delayed without delaying the whole project or subsequent activities.

To calculate the free float of an activity, its earliest finish time must be compared to the earliest start times of all immediate successors.

(a) Let us consider activity C. The earliest finish time of C is seven weeks. The earliest start time of its immediate successor G is seven weeks. Hence free float on C is zero.

(b) Consider activity D. The earliest finish time of D is five weeks. The earliest start time of its immediate successor G is seven weeks. Hence free float on D is two weeks.

It is important to appreciate that the immediate successor refers to the next real activity. Dummy activities should be treated as an extension of the main activity. The next real successor to I would have earliest start time of twelve weeks. Hence the free float on activity I is the difference between the earliest finish time of eleven weeks and twelve weeks. This is one week.

Question — Critical path

A project will consist of six phases, A to F, as follows.

Phase	Must be preceded by	'Normal' days taken
A	–	8
B	–	4
C	Phase B	2
D	–	4
E	Phases A, C, D	3
F	Phase E	3

Required

Calculate the minimum time required for the project, and state the critical path. Draw up a network diagram showing the earliest start and finish times and the latest start and finish times for each activity.

Answer

The network might look like this (some variations in the layout are possible).

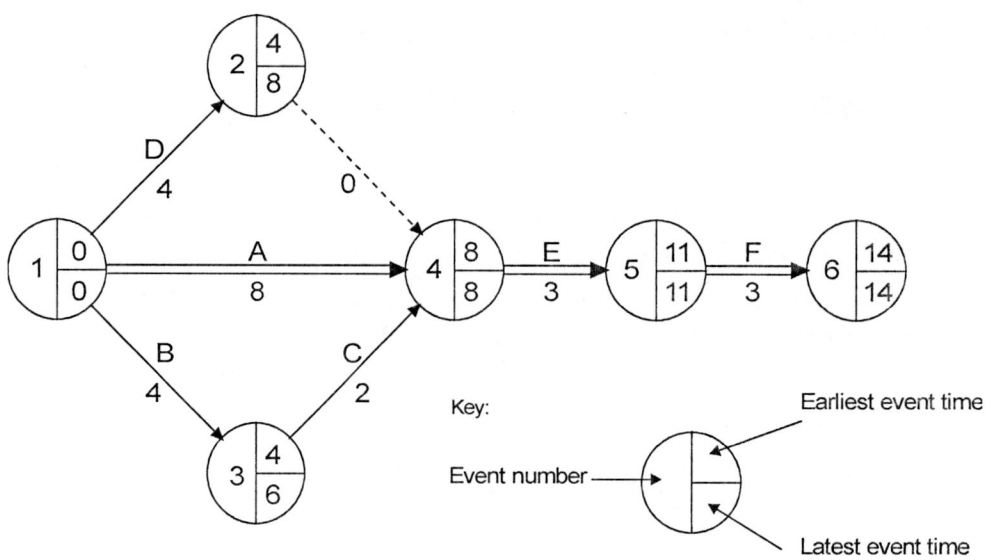

A dummy activity has been introduced since A and D can both start at time 0, and E cannot start until both A and D are completed.

There are three routes, or chains of activity, through the network.

(a) D Dummy E F: Time in days 4 + 0 + 3 + 3 = 10
(b) A E F: Time in days 8 + 3 + 3 = 14
(c) B C E F: Time in days 4 + 2 + 3 + 3 = 12

The critical path is AEF, which will require 14 days to complete.

8 Other project planning techniques

FAST FORWARD

Other project planning techniques include using gates and milestones and resource histograms.

In this section we briefly consider some other project planning techniques. Other project planning techniques include:

(a) **Gates and milestones**. A large project can be divided into several phases. The progress towards completion of the project involves reaching 'milestones' along the way. Each milestone is a completion of one of the phases of the project. Gates and milestones, by breaking up the project into parts, may help management to plan and control the project more easily.

(b) **Resource histograms**. Resource histograms are bar charts showing the amount of resources required for the project in each day, week or month. There is a bar chart for each time period, and the bar may be analysed into the different resources required in that time period – such as the number of different types of worker or the amount of equipment.

4: NETWORK ANALYSIS

Chapter roundup

- Various **tools and techniques** are available to plan and control projects including the project plan, project budget, Work Breakdown Structure, Gantt charts, network analysis, resource histogram and specialist software.

- **Network analysis,** also known as **Critical path analysis** (CPA), is a useful technique to help with planning and controlling large projects, such as construction projects, research and development projects and the computerisation of systems.

- Project management software may be used to help produce project documentation, diagrams and reports.

- A Gantt chart may be used to plan a project schedule and monitor progress towards completion.

- Critical path analysis (CPA) is a technique for planning and controlling large projects. It aims to get the project done in the minimum time and with the most effective use of resources.

- **Float** is the amount of slack time associated with a non-critical activity.

- Other project planning techniques include using gates and milestones and resource histograms.

Quick quiz

1   What is Work Breakdown Structure?

2   What is the purpose of a Gantt chart?

3   Briefly outline the relationship between quality, cost and time in the context of an information systems project.

4   Fill in the blanks.

    In an activity on arrow diagram for a CPA chart, an activity is represented by …………… and an event is represented by …………………… .

5   It is usual to enter earliest finishing times and latest starting times in a CPA chart. True or false?

6   Float is the maximum amount of time that the completion of an activity may be delayed before it affects the completion date for a project. True or false?

7   Fill in the blank.

    In CPA analysis, float can be analysed into total float and …………………… .

PART A   TECHNIQUES TO SUPPORT BUSINESS DECISIONS

Answers to quick quiz

1   Work Breakdown Structure (WBS) is the process of breaking down the project into manageable tasks.

2   A Gantt chart displays the time relationships between tasks in a project. It is a horizontal bar chart used to estimate the amount and timing of resources required.

3   The quality of information system produced is dependent upon (among other things) the time available to develop the system and the resources (ie cost) available to the project. Insufficient time and / or resources will have an adverse effect on the quality of system produced.

4   Arrowed line. Circle.

5   False. CPA charts show earliest starting times and latest finishing times. The **earliest event time** is the earliest time that any subsequent activities can start. The **latest event time** is the latest time that any preceding activity must be completed if the project as a whole is to be completed in the minimum time.

6   True. This is a definition of float in CPA analysis.

7   Free float.

End of chapter questions

1 Landscapro Ltd (AIA November 2007)

Landscapro Ltd is a business with the purpose of undertaking large garden re-design projects. Generally Landscapro uses manual labour but can also utilise special machines such as mechanical diggers, tillers and a turf-laying machine, to speed up a project's completion time.

Landscapro has been invited to tender for a project with the following characteristics:

Activity	A	B	C	D	E	F	G	H	I	J	K	L
Duration	2	1	3	4	1	2	2	3	3	4	2	3
Precedence	–	–	–	A	B, D	B, D	B, D	C	E	G, H	I	F, J

The activity durations have been estimated in days.

Required

(a)   Draw a network diagram for this project and determine the estimated number of days of completion time. **(9 marks)**

(b)   The project has been costed using only manual labour at $400 per day of its length. However, If Landscapro uses its special machines the following lists those activities for which the estimated duration can be shortened:

Activity	C	D	G	H	I	J
Minimum duration	2	2	1	1	2	2
Extra cost $	200	300	200	600	200	500

The extra costs are linear with shortened duration. Thus, if activity C is executed in 2 rather than 3 days there will be an increase in Landscapro's project costs of $200; if activity D is executed in 2 rather than 4 days, Landscapro's project costs increase by $300. But activity D could be executed in 3 days in which case the extra costs are only $150. Shortening the project's completion time saves the manual labour cost per day. Calculate the optimal project completion time for Landscapro. **(10 marks)**

(c) For the optimal project schedule determined in (b):
   (i) What is the total project cost
   (ii) Which activities are critical
   (iii) What are the floats of each non-critical activity **(6 marks)**

(Total = 25 marks)

2 In the context of project management, explain the difference between top-down budgeting and bottom-up budgeting. **(5 marks)**

PART A TECHNIQUES TO SUPPORT BUSINESS DECISIONS

Simulation

Topic list	Syllabus reference
1 Introduction to simulation	9.5
2 Continuous and discrete simulation models	9.5
3 Designing a simulation model	9.5

Introduction

In this chapter we will look at the steps involved in setting up a simulation and analysis of a complex situation.

1 Introduction to simulation

FAST FORWARD — Simulation models provide managers with a way to imitate real-world conditions and relationships, to test the impact of different events, decisions or changes.

1.1 Analogue and mathematical models

Simulation means 'imitation' and simulation models are built which imitate real-world conditions. One form of simulation model is an **analogue model**, where a model is constructed that imitates the **physical characteristics of a practical situation**. An example is the use of an analogue model to represent the flight deck of an aeroplane, to help with the training of airline pilots. It would obviously be impractical to teach the trainees how to deal with engine failures and crash landings in a real aeroplane, and so an analogue is used to simulate conditions for a pilot on a flight deck.

More usually in business, simulation involves **mathematical simulation models**, rather than analogue models. A simulation model is a mathematical model which reflects the relationships between certain variables in real-world conditions.

1.2 Monte Carlo simulation

The term 'simulation' model is often used more specifically to refer to modelling which makes use of **random numbers**. This is the **'Monte Carlo' method of simulation**. The method is used for the study of a dynamic system over time, where the relationships between variables, or the values of variables are changeable, and are not constant. In the business environment for example, simulation models can be used to examine inventory, queuing, production scheduling and forecasting problems.

Monte Carlo simulation models imitate real world conditions using random numbers and probabilities in place of what is called 'chance' in the real world. **Simulation models** imitate real world conditions using random numbers and probabilities in place of what is called 'chance' in the real world.

1.3 Advantages of simulation

The **advantages of simulation** are as follows.

(a) It provides a means of **solving problems** or **providing information** in situations where the **use of other quantitative analytical methods would be unsuitable**.

(b) Fewer simplifying assumptions are used in simulation models compared with other quantitative methods and models. In other words, **more variables can be introduced**, and **fewer simplifications are necessary**.

(c) Carrying out a properly-designed simulation is, in essence, much the same as observing the real system. In simulation, however, **the researcher is able to control the system** rather than being controlled by it. This means that he can experiment with the system by altering its parameters and decision rules at will.

(d) A computer simulation model can assess the performance of the real-world system over a lengthy time span.

1.4 Disadvantages of simulation

There are two **disadvantages with simulation models**.

(a) To obtain representative information, **the amount of calculations required** in all but the simplest **will be substantial** (hence the need for computers).

(b) Unlike some other mathematical models, **simulation is non-optimising** and does not indicate the optimal solution for management of the situation that is modelled. If a simulation model is intended to help with decision making, the user selects a preferred solution after testing several alternative options. There is the possibility that the best option will not be tested or selected.

1.5 Planning a simulation

Step 1 Analyse the problem, determining what decisions are involved and by what criteria the results are to be measured.

Step 2 Data about the problem must be collected to assist in formulating and testing the model.

Step 3 The model must be formulated and exhaustively tested with the collected data to ensure that it is valid. Testing may indicate areas in which the model has been over-simplified, or conversely where simplifications can be made.

Step 4 The parameters of the variables must be estimated from collected data and assessed for interdependence of variables.

Step 5 The hypotheses to be tested are determined.

Step 6 The simulation run is now carried out, using random data determined by the parameters of the variables. The simulation can be undertaken manually or by computer: in the latter case there is the additional step of writing and testing the computer program.

2 Continuous and discrete simulation models

In this section we look at the difference between continuous and discrete simulation models, then use discrete simulation to simulate the behaviour of a queue and the demand for inventory.

Simulation models may be either continuous or discrete models.

(a) **Continuous models** can be used to represent a system continuously over the simulated time span. They are used when it is desirable to record how the system might **develop over time**.

(b) In **discrete models**, the system is simulated by observing it only at selected moments in time.

These points in time are chosen so that they coincide with the occurrence of certain events which are crucial to the system's performance. This is the most commonly-used type of simulation model.

2.1 Discrete simulation

To build a discrete simulation model we have to identify the events that describe the behaviour of the system. Each event is the start or end of one or more activities.

Example: Monte Carlo simulation for a simple queuing system

A discrete simulation model could be constructed for a queuing system with a single queue.

The simulation model may assume that a customer who arrives in the queue will patiently wait until he is served and that he will not leave the queue if he has to wait too long. The two key events in this queuing model will then be:

- The arrival of customers (and how frequently these occur)
- The departure of customers on completion of service (and so how long it takes to serve the customer)

When an **arrival** occurs, the **queue will grow in size** unless there happens to be nobody being served, so that the customer can be served straightaway. When a **departure** occurs the next customer can be served, if there is someone waiting in the queue.

It is only necessary to observe the system at the **discrete points** in time when an **arrival** or **departure** occurs. These points in time will be decided in the simulation model in accordance with defined **probability distributions** and **the generation of random numbers**.

The table below illustrates what the output from the simulation model may be, although many more arrivals and departures from the queue will be simulated.

Time (minutes)	Inter-arrival time (based on probability distributions and generation of random numbers)	Service time (based on probability distributions and generation of random numbers)	Length of queue	Time in queue (including service time)
0				
2	2		0	
		6		
5	3		1	
6	1		2	
8		4	1	6
9	3		2	
12			1	7
13	4		2	
14	1		3	

This model would help management to assess what the average length of the queue might be. By experimenting with a different service procedure, such as employing more people to serve customers in the queue or introducing measures to speed up service times, management can also make a decision about how the queue should be operated to optimise the queue length and waiting times.

3 Designing a simulation model

In a simulation model, there are some variables whose value is uncertain. In the example of the simple queue, the uncertain variables were inter-arrival times and service times.

Exam focus point

> To construct a Monte Carlo simulation model, probability distributions must be established for each uncertain variable that reflects the real system most accurately.

For example, suppose that we are constructing a simulation model where one of the uncertain variables is the volume of sales demand per day. The estimated probability distribution may be as follows:

Demand per day	Probability
Units	
100	0.10
125	0.20
150	0.25
175	0.30
200	0.08
225	0.07

When probabilities are assessed to two decimal places, random numbers 00 – 99 are assigned so that each possible quantity for sales demand each day is given a random number allocation that reflects the probability that this value will occur.

In this example, the allocation of random numbers would be as follows.

Demand per day Units	Probability	Random number allocation
100	0.10	00 – 09
125	0.20	10 – 29
150	0.25	30 – 54
175	0.30	55 – 84
200	0.08	85 – 92
225	0.07	93 – 99

The Monte Carlo simulation model will generate random numbers for daily sales demand. The actual sales demand each day will be an output value from the model. The volume of demand each day will depend on the random number that is generated and its corresponding value for sales demand.

For example if the model is used to simulate demand over a ten day period, the random numbers generated might be as follows: 19007174604721296802. (**Note.** Random numbers can be generated by a computer program, or by using random number tables.)

The model would then assign values to the demand per day.

Day	Random number	Sales demand Units
1	19	125
2	00	100
3	71	175
4	74	175
5	60	175
6	47	150
7	21	125
8	29	125
9	68	175
10	02	100

You might notice that demand is neither 200 nor 225 on any of these 10 days, because the random numbers generated did not include any value in the range 85 – 99. As you might therefore appreciate, when a simulation model is used, there must be a large enough 'sample' to present a **true representation** of the system and its **potential variations**.

3.1 Designing a simulation model: identifying the variables

The first step in designing a simulation model is to **identify the reason for constructing a model**. What is the problem? What are we trying to establish or decide? There must be a reason for constructing a model; otherwise it would be a waste of time and effort.

Variables

The next step is to identify the key variables in the situation, which will be included in the model.

- What are the **key variables**?
- How are these variables **inter-related**?
- Which variables have a known, **certain value** and which have a **changeable value**? What is the **probability distribution** of values for these changeable variables?

Variables can be analysed into three broad categories.

- **Input variables** (or 'exogenous' variables): these are the variables that create the situation in the model.
- **Status variables**: these variables describe the state of the system under study at any point in time. For example if the demand for an item of inventory varies according to the season of the year, a status variable will be required to specify the season that applies.
- **Output variables** (or 'endogenous' variables). These are the measured 'results' from the model. They are the outcome from the interaction of the input variables, given the status variables that apply. These outputs are the data that management will use to assess the situation that is modelled.

For example in an inventory system, output variables may be the balance of units of an inventory item, the number of stock-outs, and the total costs of holding inventory, re-ordering and stock-outs.

3.2 Developing, testing and implementing a simulation model

A simulation model should be designed and developed so as to **incorporate all the significant variables in the situation**, and the **key relationships between them**. A simulation model is normally a computer model, and the program instructions will specify the logical sequence of events that must be carried out to run the model.

3.2.1 Example

A small farm produces blocks of cheese and sells them to local retailers. The farm is capable of producing between 8 and 14 blocks of cheese each day, depending on working conditions, and the owner of the farm is wondering whether to increase output capacity in order to meet sales demand more successfully. The daily demand for blocks of cheese and the current output capacity of the farm have been analysed as follows.

Daily demand (blocks)	Probability	Output capacity (blocks)	Probability
9	0.06	8	0.07
10	0.08	9	0.10
11	0.10	10	0.12
12	0.40	11	0.23
13	0.19	12	0.32
14	0.17	13	0.13
		14	0.03

When output capacity on any day exceeds the sales demand, the surplus can be stored and sold the next day. When demand exceeds the ability of the farm to supply on any day, the unsatisfied excess demand is lost.

Required

Simulate the business over a period of two weeks (14 days) using the following random numbers for supply and demand respectively.

- For supply 95011268379935267076511059200
- For demand 15664104932049238301911322199

Suggest whether you think that the farm should take measures to increase its output capacity.

3.2.2 Solution

Daily demand (blocks)	Probability	Random number allocation	Output capacity (blocks)	Probability	Random number allocation
9	0.06	00 – 05	8	0.07	00 – 06
10	0.08	06 – 13	9	0.10	07 – 16
11	0.10	14 – 23	10	0.12	17 – 28
12	0.40	24 – 63	11	0.23	29 – 51
13	0.19	64 – 82	12	0.32	52 – 83
14	0.17	83 – 99	13	0.13	84 – 96
			14	0.03	97 – 99

Using the random numbers given, the 14-day simulation can be presented as follows:

Day	Demand Random number	Units	Supply Random number	Units	Opening stock Units	Sales Units	Closing stock Units	Unsatisfied demand Units
1	95	14	15	10	0	10	0	4
2	01	9	66	12	0	9	3	0
3	12	10	41	11	3	10	4	0
4	68	13	04	8	4	12	0	1
5	37	12	93	13	0	12	1	0
6	99	14	20	10	1	12	0	3
7	35	12	49	11	0	11	0	1
8	26	12	23	10	0	10	0	2
9	70	13	83	12	0	12	0	1
10	76	13	01	8	0	8	0	5
11	51	12	91	13	0	12	1	0
12	10	10	13	9	1	10	0	0
13	59	12	22	10	0	10	0	2
14	20	11	19	10	0	10	0	1
		167		147		147		20

The simulation model can be run for many more days, to build up a more representative picture of probable outcomes. From this 14-day analysis, it would appear that a substantial amount of potential sales demand is lost (20 units in 14 days). A decision can be made about whether it would be profitable to increase production capacity slightly in order to reduce unsatisfied demand.

PART A   TECHNIQUES TO SUPPORT BUSINESS DECISIONS

Chapter roundup

- Simulation models provide managers with a way to imitate real-world conditions and relationships, to test the impact of different events, decisions or changes.

Quick quiz

1   What is the 'Monte Carlo' method of simulation?

2 | Demand | 0-2 | 3-5 | 6-8 |
    |-------------|-----|-----|-----|
    | Probability | 0.2 | 0.5 | 0.3 |

   What range of random numbers would you allocate to the 3-5 range, assume you start allocating from random digit 0?

3   What is the problem with allocating random numbers in the previous question?

Answers to quick quiz

1. The 'Monte Carlo' method is a method of simulation which uses probabilities and random numbers to generate a series of possible outcomes, which can then be analysed.

2. Range 3–5 is 50% of the total range. Allocate random numbers 20–69 to these values, since random numbers 00–19 will be allocated to the values 0–2 (20% of the total).

3. The problem is that the random numbers are allocated to a range of values. In designing the simulation model, a decision has to be made about what a value in the range 3–5 represents. For example, would the mid-point value 4 be used to represent an item in the range 3–5?

End of chapter question

AB Travel Agency

The AB Travel Agency deals with numerous personal callers each day and prides itself on its level of service. The time to deal with each caller depends on the client's requirements which range from, say, a request for a brochure to booking a round-the-world cruise. If clients have to wait more than 10 minutes for attention it is AB's policy for the manager to see them personally and to give them a $5 holiday voucher.

Observations have shown that the time taken to deal with clients and their arrival patterns follow the distributions below:

Time to deal with clients		Time between arrivals	
Minutes	Probability	Minutes	Probability
2	0.05	1	0.2
4	0.10	8	0.4
6	0.15	15	0.3
10	0.30	25	0.1
14	0.25		1.00
20	0.10		
30	0.05		
	1.00		

Required

(a) Describe how you would simulate the operation of the Travel Agency based on the use of Random Number Tables. **(5 marks)**

(b) Simulate the arrival and serving of 12 clients and show the number of customers who receive a voucher (use line 1 of the Random Numbers below to derive the arrival pattern and Line 2 for the serving times).

Random Numbers

| Line 1 | 03 | 47 | 43 | 73 | 86 | 36 | 96 | 47 | 36 | 61 | 46 | 98 |
| Line 2 | 63 | 71 | 62 | 33 | 26 | 16 | 80 | 45 | 60 | 11 | 14 | 10 |

(9 marks)

(c) Calculate the weekly cost of vouchers, assuming the proportion receiving vouchers derived from (b) applies throughout a week of 50 opening hours. **(3 marks)**

(d) Describe the advantages and disadvantages of simulation. **(8 marks)**

(Total = 25 marks)

PART A TECHNIQUES TO SUPPORT BUSINESS DECISIONS

Decision theory

Topic list	Syllabus reference
1 Decision analysis – single decisions	9.6
2 Decision analysis – multiple decisions	9.6
3 Using standard deviation to measure risk	9.6

Introduction

In this chapter we will consider what a decision is and look at decisions made under conditions of certainty and uncertainty. We will also look at the techniques of expected values and decision trees in decision making.

PART A TECHNIQUES TO SUPPORT BUSINESS DECISIONS

1 Decision analysis – single decisions

> Some decisions are taken under conditions of certainty, as all possible outcomes are known and can be considered. More complex decisions involve uncertainty.

1.1 What is a decision?

A decision is a choice between two or more alternatives.

1.2 Decisions made under certainty?

Decisions may be taken under conditions of certainty, for example,

I have received an offer to sell my car for $5,000. Should I accept the offer?

The decision has a simple yes/no choice which can be evaluated:

Accept – receive $5,000 and lose the car
Reject – keep the car but do not receive $5,000

1.3 Decisions made under uncertainty

> The techniques of expected value pay-off tables and decision trees may be used to evaluate decisions made under conditions of uncertainty.

Most decisions which a company's management has to make can be described as **decisions made under uncertainty**. The essential features of making a decision under uncertain conditions are:

(a) The decision-maker is faced with a choice between several alternative courses of action.

(b) Each course of action may have several possible outcomes, dependent on a number of uncertain factors, ie even when a decision has been made the outcome is by no means certain.

(c) Which choice is made will depend upon the criteria used by the decision-maker in judging between the outcomes of the possible courses of action.

1.4 Expected values

> The expected value is the weighted average of the possible outcomes.

Key term

> **Expected value** is the value obtained by multiplying the financial forecast of an outcome by the probability of achieving that outcome.

In order to have a **rational** basis for decision-making it is necessary to have some estimate of the probabilities of the various outcomes and then to use them in a decision criterion. One such criterion is the **maximisation of expected value**.

The expected value $\bar{x}$ of a particular action is defined as the **sum of the values of the possible outcomes, each multiplied by their respective probabilities** (it is analogous to the arithmetic mean): $\bar{x} = \sum px$

1.5 Example

Using the following data, apply the criteria of **maximisation of expected value** to decide the best course of action for the company, assuming the following probabilities:

P (low demand)	0.1
P (medium demand)	0.6
P (high demand)	0.3
	1.0

A company has three new products A, B and C, of which it can introduce only one. The level of demand for **each** course of action might be low, medium or high. If the company decides to introduce product A, the net income that would result from the levels of demand possible are estimated at $20, $40 and $50 respectively. Similarly, if product B is chosen, net income is estimated at $80, $70 and – $10, and for product C, $10, $100 and $40, respectively.

The expected value of the decision to introduce product A is given by the following summation:

$0.1 \times \$20 + 0.6 \times \$40 + 0.3 \times \$50 = \$41$

(ie on 10% of all occasions demand will be low and net income $20, on 60% of all occasions demand will be medium and net income $40 and on 30% of all occasions demand will be high and net income $50. Thus, on average, net income will be the weighted average of all three net incomes, weighted by their respective probabilities.)

The expected value of all the products may be calculated by a table:

Table of expected values

State of the world (demand)	Prob of state of the world	Product					
		A		B		C	
		Income $	Income × Prob $	Income $	Income × Prob $	Income $	Income × Prob $
Low	0.1	20	2	80	8	10	1
Medium	0.6	40	24	70	42	100	60
High	0.3	50	15	(10)	(3)	40	12
Total	1.0		$41		$47		$73

Thus, if the criterion is to maximise the expected value, it means that the product with the highest expected value will be chosen, in this case product C.

1.5.1 Example: Expected values and pay-off tables

IB Newsagents stocks a weekly lifestyle magazine. The owner buys the magazines for $0.30 each and sells them at the retail price of $0.50 each.

At the end of the week unsold magazines are obsolete and have no value. The estimated probability distribution for weekly demand is shown below.

Weekly demand in units	Probability
20	0.20
30	0.55
40	0.25
	1.00

PART A TECHNIQUES TO SUPPORT BUSINESS DECISIONS

Required

What is the expected value of demand?

If the owner is to order a fixed quantity of magazines per week how many should that be?

Assume no seasonal variations in demand.

Solution

EV of demand (units per week) = $(20 \times 0.20) + (30 \times 0.55) + (40 \times 0.25)$ = 30.5 units per week

The next step is to set up a decision matrix of possible strategies (numbers bought) and possible demand.

The 'pay-off' from each combination of action and outcome is then computed.

No sale = cost of $0.30 per magazine

Sale = profit of $0.20 per magazine ($0.50 – $0.30)

		Decision (number bought)		
Probability	Outcome (number demanded)	20 $	30 $	40 $
0.20	20	4.00	1.00*	(2.00)
0.55	30	4.00	6.00	3.00
0.25	40	4.00	6.00	8.00
1	EV	4.00	5.00**	3.25

* Buy 30 and sell only 20 gives a profit of $(20 \times \$0.5) - (30 \times \$0.3) = \$1$

** $(0.2 \times 1) + (0.55 \times 6) + (0.25 \times 6) = 5$

The strategy which gives the highest expected pay-off is to stock 30 magazines each week.

1.6 Applicability of expected values

The criterion of expected value is only valid where the decision being made is either:

(a) One that is **repeated regularly** over a period of time; or

(b) A **one-off** decision, but where its size is fairly small in relation to the total assets of the firm, and many similar decisions are faced regularly.

The **law of averages** will apply in the long run, but the result of any single action must, by definition, be one of the specified outcomes. Thus, while the expected value of introducing product C is $73, each actual outcome will result in either $10, $100 or $40 net income, and it is only if a whole series of product introductions were involved that the **average** over a period of time would approach $73.

Therefore, it is quite acceptable to adopt the expected value as the decision-making criterion for the company in the example, so long as it has several other products and the same sort of marketing decision arises fairly regularly.

To illustrate the distinction being made, consider a man insuring his house against fire damage for a year. Suppose the house is worth $50,000 and the probability of the house being burnt down is 0.0001 (the only other outcome being that the house is not burnt down with a probability of 0.9999). The man would be quite prepared to pay, say, $15 pa to insure his house even though the expected value if he did not (or expected cost in this case) is only $0.0001 \times \$50,000 + 0.9999 \times 0 = \$5$. The man cannot afford to pay $50,000 out more than once in his lifetime and therefore cannot afford to **play the averages** by using expected value as his decision criterion (if so he would refuse to pay a premium greater than $5). However, to the insurance company, $50,000 is not a large sum, most of their transactions being for similar or greater amounts and therefore expected value would be appropriate as a decision criterion for them.

In fact, the expected value of the insurance company's decision to insure the house at $15 pa is:

0.0001 × (−$49,985) + 0.9999 × $15

or −$4.9985 + $14.9985 = $10

and any positive expected value would, in theory, have made it worth their while to insure.

Question
Possible outcomes

If the three possible outcomes of a decision are profits of $10, $50 and $80 with probabilities of 0.3, 0.3 and 0.4 respectively, what is the expected profit?

Answer

Expected profit = 0.3 × $10 + 0.3 × $50 + 0.4 × $80 = $50

1.7 Payoff tables

FAST FORWARD — Pay-off tables show the best, worst and most likely outcomes from a decision.

A pay-off table will show the **full range of possible outcomes** from a decision. This helps decision making, for example a course of action may be rejected because the worst possible outcome would result in insolvency.

1.7.1 Preparing pay-off tables

Pay-off tables identify and record the **range of possible outcomes (or pay-offs)** in situations where the action taken affects the outcomes.

1.7.2 Example: worst/best possible outcomes

Omelette Co is trying to set the sales price for one of its products. Three prices are under consideration, and expected sales volumes and costs are as follows.

Price per unit	$4	$4.30	$4.40
Expected sales volume (units)			
Best possible	16,000	14,000	12,500
Most likely	14,000	12,500	12,000
Worst possible	10,000	8,000	6,000

Fixed costs are $20,000 and variable costs of sales are $2 per unit.

Which price should be chosen?

Solution

We prepare a pay-off table showing pay-offs (contribution) at different levels of demand and different selling prices.

Price per unit	$4	$4.30	$4.40
Contribution per unit	$2	$2.30	$2.40
Total contribution towards fixed costs	$	$	$
Best possible	32,000	32,200	30,000
Most likely	28,000	28,750	28,800
Worst possible	20,000	18,400	14,400

(a) The highest contribution based on **most likely** sales volume would be at a price of $4.40. Arguably a price of $4.30 would be better than $4.40, since the most likely profit is almost as good, the worst possible profit is not as bad, and the best possible profit is better.

(b) However, only a price of $4 guarantees that the company would **not make a loss**, even if the worst possible outcome occurs. (Fixed costs of $20,000 would just be covered.) A risk averse management team might therefore prefer a price of $4.

2 Decision analysis – multiple decisions

FAST FORWARD

A **decision tree** is a way of applying the expected value criterion to situations where a number of decisions are made sequentially. It is so called because the decision alternatives are represented as **branches** in a **tree** diagram.

2.1 Decision trees

So far only a single decision has had to be made. However, many managerial problems consist of a rather long, drawn-out structure involving a whole sequence of actions and outcomes. Where a number of decisions have to be made sequentially the complexity of the decision-making process increases considerably. By using **decision trees**, however, highly complex problems can be broken down into a series of simpler ones while providing, at the same time, opportunity for the decision-maker to obtain specialist advice in relation to each stage of his problem.

2.2 Decision points and random outcome points

2.2.1 Example

A retailer must decide whether to sell a product loose or packaged. In either case, the product may sell, or not sell.

The decision facing the retailer can be represented by a tree diagram:

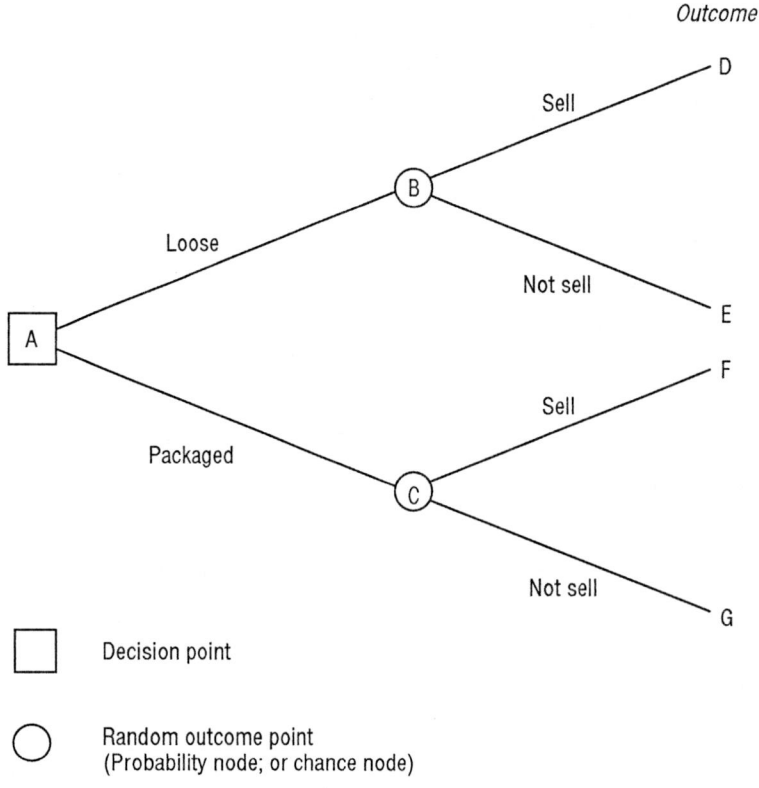

As you can see, in a decision tree there are two types of events (points where a branch occurs).

- **Decision points**, signified by a ☐ in the tree. At this point the decision or branch taken can be chosen by the decision-maker. In this example the decision point is [A] where the decision-maker can choose whether to sell the product loose or packaged.

- **Random outcome points**, signified by a ◯. At this point the branch taken is completely outside the control of the decision-maker. In the example above, the random outcome points are at and (C); the retailer has no control over which branch is followed from this point, the product will either sell or it won't.

Question
Decision tree

Using the data given below, draw a decision tree and mark clearly on the tree the decision points and the random outcome points.

Mr A is a microcomputer retailer who has recently bought a large consignment of popular micros, of which he knows some will be faulty. He has to decide whether or not to inspect every micro of this type prior to sale. If he does do the inspection, there is still a chance that he will not pick up the fault in the faulty micros. However, if Mr A sells a faulty micro it is equally likely that either the customer will return it for repair or will have it repaired elsewhere and discontinue trading with him.

Answer

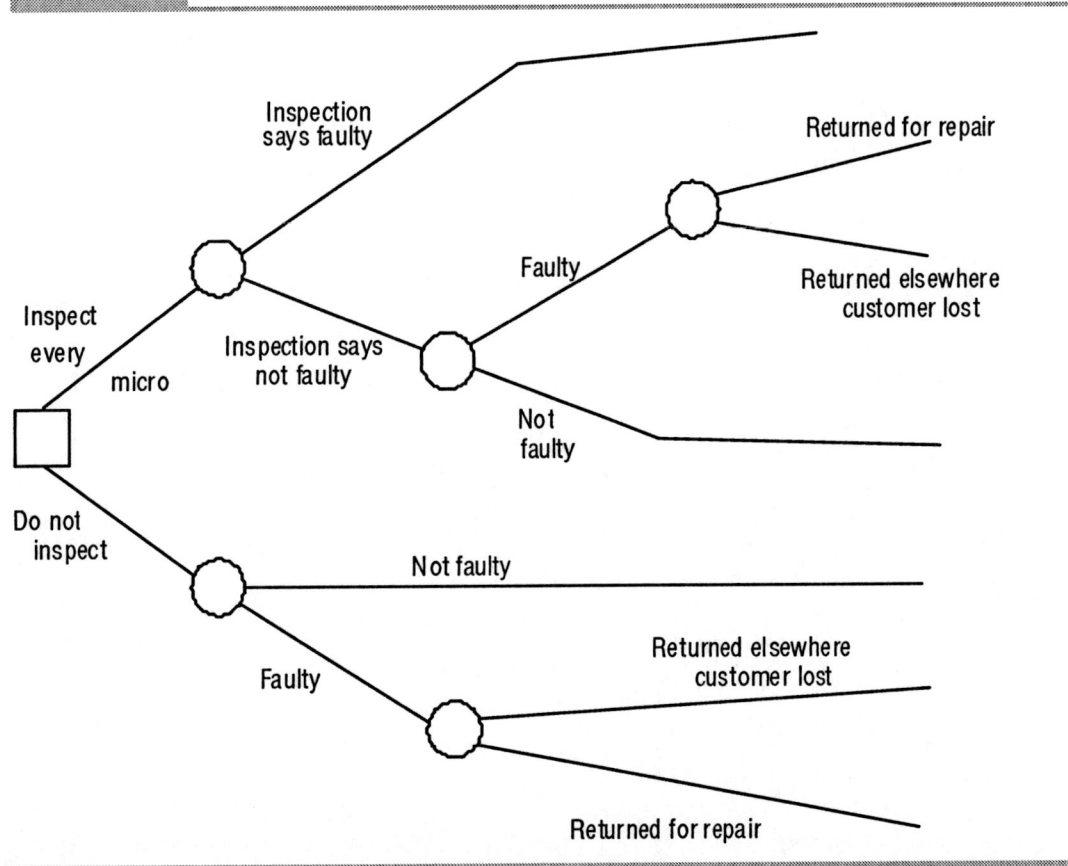

2.3 Expected values and the roll back method

Now return to the previous example about packaging or selling a product loose. The profitability of selling packaged products is $10, loose products $15. The loss through not selling is $5 in either case. The probability of the product being sold is 0.7 for packaged products, 0.5 for loose products.

You are required to evaluate the expected values of each decision alternative.

Step 1 Add all the relevant information ie, probabilities and profits and losses, to the decision tree ending at the right hand side of the tree with a column for outcomes.

Step 2 Evaluate the decision tree by working back from right to left towards the first decision under consideration. In this example it is decision point (A). At each random outcome point calculate the EV of revenue, cost, profit or whatever type of pay off the question gives.

Step 3 Block off all other routes from the decision point (sometimes called a decision **fork**) with a double parallel line '//'. (This is important when trees have several decision forks.)

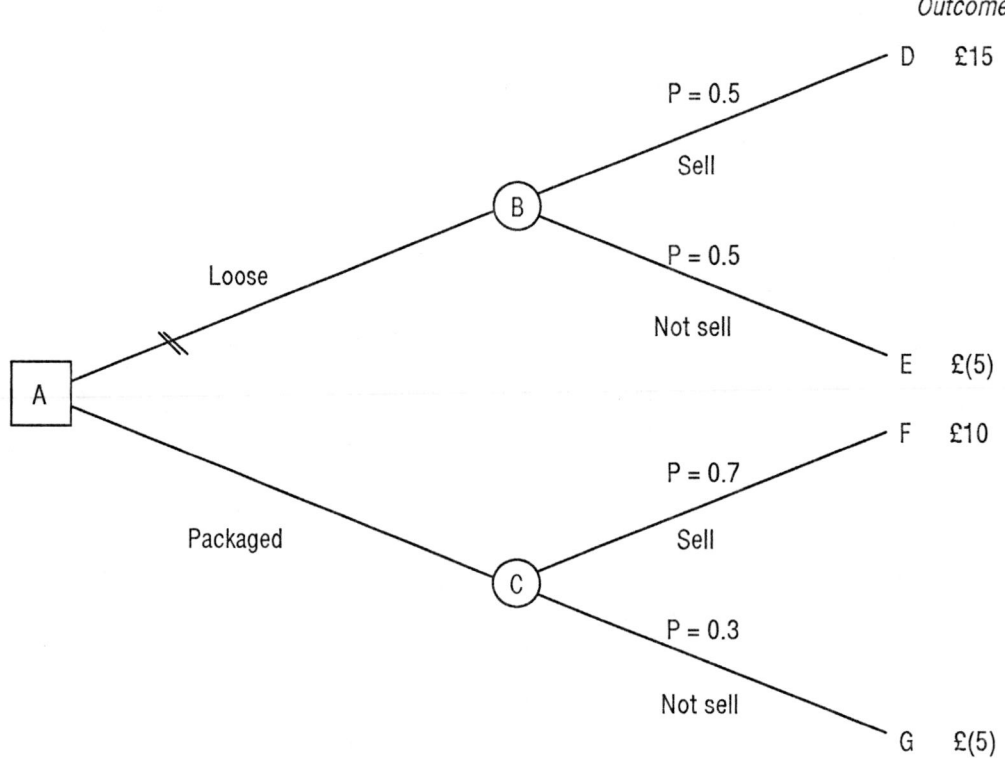

The diagram is evaluated as follows (using obvious notation):

EV_B = $(0.5 \times EV_D) + (0.5 \times EV_E)$
     = $(0.5 \times \$15) + (0.5 \times (-\$5))$
     = $5

EV_C = $(0.7 \times EV_F) + (0.3 \times EV_G)$
     = $(0.7 \times \$10) + (0.3 \times (-\$5))$
     = $5.5

∴ At decision point A the retailer will choose to go towards node C as this has the higher EV. The discarded routes are indicated by drawing two short parallel lines across that particular path.

Therefore, the decision to sell a packaged product has the higher expected value.

The method just described is known as the **rollback technique**.

Note. The expected values here (EV) are sometimes called expected monetary values (EMV). At point C the probability that the product will sell is 0.7, therefore the probability that it will not is 1 – 0.7 = 0.3. The total probability at any chance fork must be 1.00.

Question — Tree diagram

A company manufactures a single product which it may sell directly to the public or via a retailer. If it sells directly to the public the profit is $100; whereas via the retailer the profit is only $70.

The probability of the product being sold if the retailer is used is 0.8 whereas the use of direct selling techniques have a sale probability of 0.6. If a sale is not made the resulting losses are:

Direct selling method $30
Retail method $50

Advise the company which technique to use, illustrating your solution using a tree diagram.

Answer

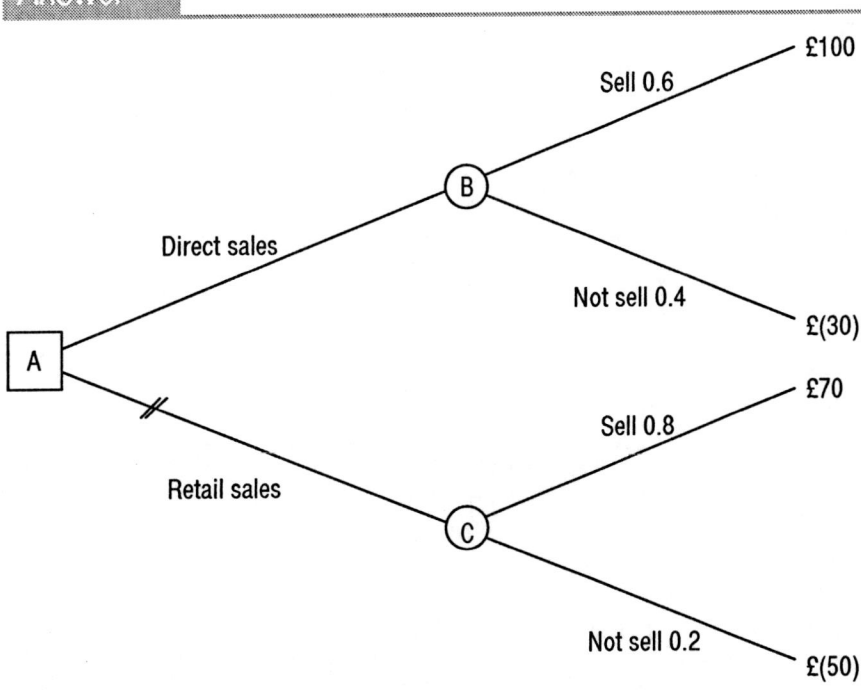

$EV_B = (0.6 \times \$100) + (0.4 \times \$(30)) = \$48$

$EV_C = (0.8 \times \$70) + (0.2 \times \$(50)) = \$46$

The direct sales route is recommended because it has the higher expected value.

2.4 Decision trees – a comprehensive example

The last problem could have been solved without a tree diagram, but the technique comes into its own in a more complex situation, as illustrated by the next example. If in doubt it is always safer to draw a tree.

2.4.1 Example

The manager of a newly formed specialist machinery manufacturing subsidiary has to decide whether to build a small plant or a large plant for manufacturing a new piece of machinery with an expected market life of ten years.

PART A   TECHNIQUES TO SUPPORT BUSINESS DECISIONS

One of the major factors influencing his decision is the size of the market that the company can obtain for its product. He estimates that there is a 70% chance of a high level of demand and a 30% chance of a low level of demand if a large plant is built. However, if a small plant is originally constructed there is only a 50% chance of there being a high demand.

The level of demand will not change throughout the project's life.

If the company initially builds a large plant, it must live with it for the whole ten years, regardless of the market demand. If it builds a small plant, it also has the option, after two years, of expanding the plant but this expansion would cost more overall, when taken with the initial cost of building small, than starting by building a large plant.

Various pieces of information have been collected, or estimated by the management.

(a) **Annual income estimates**

   (i) For a large plant with high demand annual earnings will be $1m. This applies whether the plant was originally constructed as 'large' or had to be extended.

   (ii) For a large plant with low market demand annual earnings will be $0.1m.

   (iii) For a small plant with low demand annual earnings will be $0.4m.

   (iv) For a small plant with high demand annual earnings will be $0.6m.

(b) **Capital costs**

   (i) Initial cost of building a large plant $3m
   (ii) Initial cost of building a small plant $1.3m
   (iii) Additional cost of expanding a small plant $2.6m

Using expected value as the decision criterion, advise the manager on what choice of plant to make.

Ignore the time value of money and taxation.

Solution

Step 1   The first stage in solving a problem of this nature, which involves more than one decision being made over a period of time, is to construct a decision tree to demonstrate the structure of the decisions which have to be made.

6: DECISION THEORY

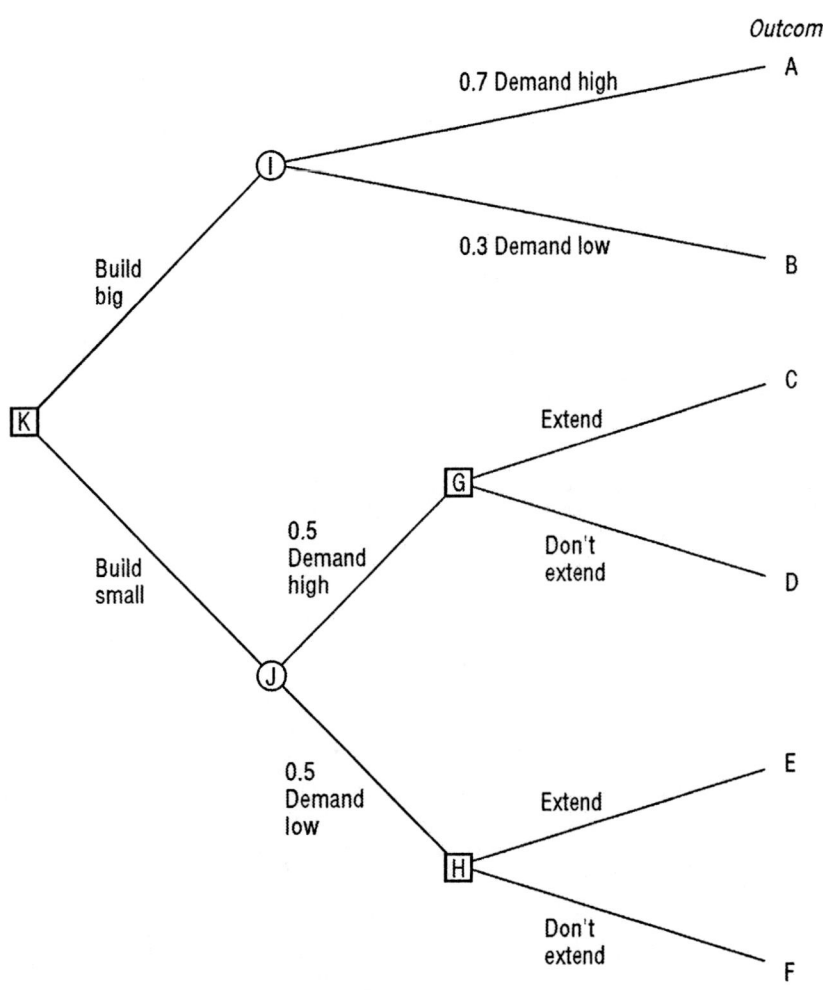

Notes

1. ☐ Decision point.
   ○ Random outcome point, probabilities given.

2. Each path represents a different series of events and eventual outcome. For example, outcome C is reached by originally building a small plant, finding that demand is high and subsequently extending the plant.

Step 2 It is now necessary to evaluate the monetary value of the outcomes. This is best achieved by tabulation, in order to avoid needless repetition.

			$m			
Outcome	A	B	C	D	E	F
Total revenue in years 1–2	2	0.2	1.2	1.2	0.8	0.8
Total revenue in years 3–10	8	0.8	8.0	4.8	0.8	3.2
Original cost	(3)	(3)	(1.3)	(1.3)	(1.3)	(1.3)
Cost of extension	–	–	(2.6)	–	(2.6)	–
Net income/(cost)	7	(2)	5.3	4.7	(2.3)	2.7

Step 3 Having found the outcomes the tree is worked through right to left,

- At random outcome points taking a weighted average of the possible outcomes, and
- At decision points taking the route with the higher expected value ('EV').

Thus:

EV_I = $0.7 \times EV_A + 0.3 \times EV_B$
= $0.7 \times 7 + 0.3 \times (-2)$
= 4.3

EV_G = greater of EV_C and EV_D
= greater of 5.3 and 4.7
= 5.3

∴ At that point the decision would be to extend the plant.

EV_H = greater of EV_E and EV_F
= greater of –2.3 and 2.7
= 2.7

∴ At that point the decision would be not to extend the plant (in accordance with common sense).

A double line would now be placed along lines GD and HE.

EV_J = $0.5 \times EV_G + 0.5 \times EV_H$
= $0.5 \times 5.3 + 0.5 \times 2.7$
= 4

EV_K = greater of EV_I and EV_J
= greater of 4.3 and 4
= 4.3

∴ The decision should be to build a large plant immediately, since the expected value of doing so, $4.3m, is greater than that of building a small plant.

However, it should be noted that if this decision were to be taken there is a possibility of incurring losses of $2m. If the decision were taken instead to build the small plant, and extend it only if demand is high, the worst that can happen is that the firm makes net revenues of only $2.7m. It may well be, therefore, that this less risky option is preferred, notwithstanding the higher EV available through the other route. This shows that maximising EV is not necessarily the best strategy in all situations, but that the amount of risk is also a factor that must be taken into account.

2.5 Other decision criteria

Whilst expected value is the most commonly used measure of outcomes used to evaluate decisions made under conditions of uncertainty it is not the only technique.

Expected value takes an average position; other factors which influence the decisions are the risk attitudes of the decision maker – the pessimist would look to maximise the benefit from the worst possible outcome whereas the optimist would seek to maximise the benefit from the best possible outcome. This is outside the syllabus.

3 Using the standard deviation to measure risk

FAST FORWARD

Risk can be measured by the possible variations of outcomes around the expected value. One useful measure of such variations is the standard deviation of the expected value.
The coefficient of variation is a measure of relative risk. It is computed by dividing the standard deviation by the expected value.

> The standard deviation is $s = \sqrt{\Sigma p(x - \bar{x})^2} = \sqrt{\text{variance}}$
>
> where $\bar{x}$ is the EV of profit
> x represents each possible profit
> p represents the probability of each possible profit

The decision maker can then **weigh up the EV of each option against the risk** (the standard deviation) that is **associated with it**.

Example: measuring risk

The management of RC is considering which of two mutually exclusive projects to select. Details of each project are as follows.

	Project S		Project T
Probability	Profit $'000	Probability	Profit $'000
0.3	150	0.2	(400)
0.3	200	0.6	300
0.4	250	0.1	400
		0.1	800

Required

Determine which project seems preferable, S or T.

Solution

On the basis of EVs alone, T is marginally preferable to S, by $15,000.

	Project S			Project T	
Probability	Profit $'000	EV $'000	Probability	Profit $'000	EV $'000
0.3	150	45	0.2	(400)	(80)
0.3	200	60	0.6	300	180
0.4	250	100	0.1	400	40
			0.1	800	80
	EV of profit	205		EV of profit	220

Project T is more risky, however, offering the prospect of a profit as high as $800,000 but also the possibility of a loss of $400,000.

One measure of this risk is the **standard deviation of the EV of profit**.

(a) **Project S**

Probability p	Profit x $'000	$x - \bar{x}$	$p(x - \bar{x})^2$
0.3	150	−55	907.5*
0.3	200	−5	7.5
0.4	250	45	810.0
		Variance	1,725.0

* $0.3 \times (-55)^2$

Standard deviation = $\sqrt{1,725}$ = 41.533 = $41,533

PART A   TECHNIQUES TO SUPPORT BUSINESS DECISIONS

(b) **Project T**

Probability p	Profit x $'000	$x - \bar{x}$	$p(x - \bar{x})^2$
0.2	(400)	−620	76,880
0.6	300	80	3,840
0.1	400	180	3,240
0.1	800	580	33,640
		Variance	117,600

Standard deviation = $\sqrt{117,600}$ = 342.929 = $342,929

If the management are **risk averse**, they might therefore **prefer project S** because, although it has a smaller EV of profit, the possible profits are subject to less variation.

The **risk associated with project T can be compared with the risk associated with project S** if we calculate the **coefficient of variation** for each project: the **ratio of the standard deviation of each project to its EV**.

	Project S	Project T
Standard deviation	$41,533	$342,929
EV of profit	$205,000	$220,000
Coefficient of variation (standard deviation/EV of profit)	0.20	1.56

Project T has a higher coefficient of variation and is therefore considered to be more risky.

Chapter roundup

- Some decisions are taken under conditions of certainty, as all possible outcomes are known and can be considered. More complex decisions involve uncertainty.
- The techniques of expected value pay-off tables and decision trees may be used to evaluate decisions made under conditions of uncertainty.
- The expected value is the weighted average of the possible outcomes.
- Pay-off tables show the best, worst and most likely outcomes from a decision.
- A **decision tree** is a way of applying the expected value criterion to situations where a number of decisions are made sequentially. It is so called because the decision alternatives are represented as **branches** in a **tree** diagram.
- Risk can be measured by the possible variations of outcomes around the expected value. One useful measure of such variations is the standard deviation of the expected value. The coefficient of variation is a measure of relative risk. It is computed by dividing the standard deviation by the expected value.

Quick quiz

1. What is a decision?
2. What is an expected value?
3. The criterion of expected value is only valid under certain conditions. What are they?
4. A pay-off table shows only the best and worst possible outcomes. **True** or **false**?
5. What is a decision tree?
6. Describe the rollback technique.
7. What is the decision criterion for following one route compared to another?

PART A TECHNIQUES TO SUPPORT BUSINESS DECISIONS

Answers to quick quiz

1. A choice between two or more alternatives.
2. The sum of the values of the possible outcomes each multiplied by their respective probabilities.
3.
   - Where the decision is one which is repeated regularly over time.
   - Where the decision is a one-off decision but where is it is fairly small in terms of value and one which the firm will face many times over a period of time.
4. False. Pay-off tables show the best, worst and most likely outcomes.
5. A method of applying the expected value criterion to situations where a number of decisions are made sequentially.
6. The rollback method is where you start considering expected values and therefore decisions from the furthest right hand element of the decision tree and then work backwards to the initial decision.
7. Go down the route with the highest expected value.

End of chapter question

Country house (AIA May 2008)

A country house and its landscaped gardens are to be renovated for future commercial use. The owner is considering turning the premises into one of the following investments: A – a small conference centre, B – a quality restaurant, or C – a museum. Each of these alternatives has been researched in terms of conversion costs, and much information on potential markets has been obtained. The total costs of renovation and the costs of starting up each venture over the first two years have been assessed as

A: $0.8 million   B: $0.7 million   C: $ 0.5 million

Similarly, operating profits over each of the years 3 to 7 have been estimated on a yearly basis as follows:

A		B		C	
Annual profit $m	Prob.	Annual profit $m	Prob.	Annual profit $m	Prob.
0.2 – < 0.3	0.2	0.3 – < 0.4	0.5	0.1 – < 0.3	0.4
0.3 – < 0.4	0.4	0.4 – < 0.5	0.3	0.3 – < 0.5	0.5
0.4 – < 0.5	0.3	>= 0.5	0.2	0.5 – < 0.7	0.1
>=0.5	0.1				

After year 7 the owner intends selling the property whichever use has been applied, but he needs to make a decision between the three alternatives to begin the appropriate renovation and to begin operating the new business venture.

Required

(a) Use the technique of expected value to calculate the net operating profit over the years 1 to 7 for each of the alternatives A, B and C. **(12 marks)**

(b) (i) Report your conclusions to the owner and provide notes on the limitations of using expected value in situations subject to variation in potential financial rewards.

   (ii) Suggest and explain a measure of risk that could be applied to provide an additional means of assessment of the worth of each alternative. **(6 marks)**

(c) Provide calculations of the additional measure suggested in (b)(ii) for each alternative, and advise the owner which use you would recommend him to elect. **(7 marks)**

(Total = 25 marks)

Information systems

Information systems – types and applications

Topic list	Syllabus reference
1 Information systems in a computerised environment	9.7
2 The computer	9.7
3 Software	9.7
4 Types of information system	9.7
5 Types of transaction processing system	9.7
6 System architecture	9.7
7 Local Area Networks (LANs) and Wide Area Networks (WANs)	9.7
8 The internet	9.7
9 Organisation of files: file-based systems	9.7
10 Databases	9.7
11 Developments in technology and systems	9.7

Introduction

We will now look at some of the ways that organisations use information technology to construct information systems for different applications and uses. We shall consider some aspects of IT technology including the organisation of files, and also the various types of information system.

While working through this chapter remember that the examiner does **not** expect you to be an expert on the technical aspects of information technology (IT), but you are expected to understand the language and terminology of IT systems.

What is required in Paper 9 is an awareness of how **IT** may be used in the development of information systems that **help an organisation achieve its goals.**

1 Information systems in a computerised environment

An information system is, quite simply, a system that provides information to information users. In business, information is needed to perform day-to-day operations as well as to assist management with decision-making.

Systems used for routine day-to-day operational processing purposes are sometimes called data processing systems. 'Information' is sometimes defined as 'processed data'.

In principle, computerised information and data processing systems are similar to manual systems, but computerised systems have the distinct advantages of:

- Ability to process much greater volumes of data and to store, analyse and use greater quantities of information
- Much greater speed of processing
- Ability to perform complex processing and analysis
- Greater flexibility and scope of usage
- Greater accuracy in processing and reliability/completeness of information
- Access to many more sources of information

2 The computer

You are possibly very familiar with computers and computer systems. If so, this section contains information that you should already know. It provides fundamental knowledge that you need for Section B of the syllabus.

A computer is a device which accepts input data, processes it according to programmed rules, calculates results and then stores and/or outputs these results. A computer system contains:

- One or more computers
- Input devices for input of data into the system
- Output devices for output of results from the system
- Input/output devices that are used for both input and output
- Storage devices for holding data and information: storage devices hold files that provide input for processing and receive output from processing (for filing)
- Communication (telecommunication or data communication) networks or systems
- Software

2.1 Types of computer

FAST FORWARD

> Computers can be classified as supercomputers, mainframes, minicomputers and microcomputers or PCs.

Computers can be classified as follows:

- Supercomputers
- Mainframe computers
- Minicomputers
- Microcomputers, now commonly called PCs

A **supercomputer** is used to process **very large amounts of data very quickly**. They are particularly useful for occasions where high volumes of calculations need to be performed, for example in meteorological or astronomical applications.

A **mainframe** computer system uses a powerful central computer, linked by cable or telecommunications to terminals. A mainframe has many times more **processing power** than a PC and offers **extensive data storage** facilities.

Mainframes are used by organisations such as banks that have very large volumes of processing to perform and have special security needs. Many organisations have now replaced their old mainframes with networked 'client-server' systems of mid-range computers and PCs because this approach is thought to be cheaper and offer more flexibility.

A **minicomputer** is a computer whose size, speed and capabilities lie somewhere between those of a mainframe and a PC. The term was originally used before PCs were developed, to describe computers which were cheaper but less well-equipped than mainframe computers.

With the advent of PCs and of mainframes that are much smaller than in the past, the definition of a minicomputer has become rather vague. There is really no definition which distinguishes adequately between a PC and a minicomputer.

Microcomputers (or PCs) are now the norm for small to medium-sized business computing and for home computing, and most larger businesses now use them for day-to-day needs such as word-processing. Often they are linked together in a **network** to enable sharing of information between users.

2.2 Portables

The original portable computers were heavy, weighing around five kilograms, and could only be run from the mains electricity supply. Subsequent developments allow true portability.

> **FAST FORWARD**
>
> The amount of **RAM** and the **processor speed** are key determinants of computer performance. Hard drive size is another important factor.

2.3 The processor or Central Processing Unit (CPU)

The processor is the **'brain'** of the computer. The processor may be defined as follows. The processor (sometimes referred to as the central processing unit or CPU) is divided into three areas:

- Arithmetic and logic unit (ALU)
- Control unit
- Main store or memory

The processing unit may have all its elements – arithmetic and logic unit, control unit, and the input/output interface on a single **'chip'**. A chip is a small piece of silicon upon which is etched an integrated circuit, on an extremely small scale.

The most common chips are those made by the Intel Company. Each generation of Intel CPU chip has had its performance improved over previous versions. This is achieved by increasing the number of operations per cycle, and the number of cycles per second. This has the effect of increasing the amount of work it can get through per second and therefore its speed.

2.3.1 MHz and clock speed

The processor receives program instructions and sends signals to peripheral devices. The signals are co-ordinated by a **clock** which sends out a 'pulse' – a sort of tick-tock sequence called a **cycle** – at regular intervals.

The **number of cycles** produced per second is usually measured in **MegaHertz** (MHz) or **GigaHertz** (GHz).

- 1 MHz = one **million** cycles per **second**
- 1 GHz = one **billion** (a thousand million or 10^9) cycles per **second**

2.4 Memory

The computer's memory is also known as main store or internal store. The memory will hold the following.

- Program instructions
- The input data that will be processed next
- The data that is ready for output to an output device

The processing capacity of a computer is in part dictated by the capacity of its memory. Capacity is calculated in kilobytes (1 kilobyte = 2^{10} (1,024) bytes) and megabytes (1 megabyte = 2^{20} bytes) and gigabytes (2^{30}). These are abbreviated to Kb, Mb and Gb.

2.4.1 Bits and bytes

Each individual storage element in the computer's memory consists of a simple circuit which can be switched **on** or **off**. These two states can be conveniently expressed by the numbers 1 and 0 respectively.

Each 1 or 0 is a **bit**. Bits are grouped together in groups of eight to form **bytes**. A byte may be used to represent a **character**, for example a letter, a number or another symbol.

2.4.2 RAM

RAM (Random Access Memory) is memory that is directly available to the processing unit. It holds the data and programs in current use. RAM in microcomputers is 'volatile' which means that the contents of the memory are erased when the computer's power is switched off.

2.4.3 Cache

The **cache** is a small capacity but **extremely fast** part of the memory which saves a second copy of the pieces of data most recently read from or written to main memory. When the cache is full, older entries are 'flushed out' to make room for new ones.

2.4.4 ROM

ROM (**read-only memory**) is **a memory chip into which fixed data is written permanently** at the time of its manufacture. When you turn on a PC you may see a reference to **BIOS** (basic input/output system). This is part of the ROM chip containing all the programs needed to control the keyboard, screen, disk drives and so on.

2.5 Hard disks

Disks offer **direct access** to data. Almost all PCs have an **internal hard disk** to store software and data. The size of the hard disk installed will be determined by what the user intends to use the PC for.

2.6 Tape storage

Magnetic tape cartridges are still used as a **backing storage** medium. Fast tapes which can be used to create a back-up file very quickly are known as **tape streamers**.

Like an audio or video cassette, data has to be recorded **along the length** of a computer tape and so it is **more difficult to access** than data on other storage devices (ie direct access is not possible with tape). Reading and writing are separate operations.

2.7 CD-ROM (Compact Disc – Read Only Memory)

CD recorders are available for general business use with blank CDs (CD-R) and **rewritable disks** (CD-RW).

2.8 DVD (Digital Versatile Disc)

DVD development was encouraged by the advent of multimedia files with video graphics and sound – requiring greater disk capacity.

CD-ROMs and DVDs are examples of optical, rather than magnetic, storage media.

2.9 Memory stick or 'Pen drive'

A pen drive or memory stick is a physically small external storage device usually connected via a USB (universal serial bus) port. Capacity has increased significantly over recent years.

Question — Storage devices

Briefly outline two features and one common use of hard disks, magnetic tapes and optical disks.

Answer

(a) **Hard disks** offer fast access times, direct access to data and offer suitability for multi-user environments. Hard disk storage is therefore the predominant storage medium in most commercial applications currently. Direct access is essential for many commercial applications (eg databases) particularly where speed is important.

(b) **Magnetic tapes** offer cheap data storage, portability and serial or sequential access only. Magnetic tape is most valuable as a back-up medium.

(c) **Optical disks** (eg CD and DVDs) have the capacity to store vast amounts of data but offer slower access speeds than magnetic disks. They are most suitable for archiving.

3 Software

> **FAST FORWARD**
>
> Five types of software are:
> - Operating systems
> - Utilities
> - Programming tools
> - Off-the-shelf applications
> - Bespoke application software

Computer software can be classified into five types, as shown in the following table.

Type	Comment
Operating systems	Operating systems software keeps the computer itself operating smoothly and efficiently. This software is loaded into main memory and it is always resident in the main memory when the computer is operating. The operating system provides the interface between the computer hardware and both the user and the other software. An operating system will typically perform the following tasks. • Initial set-up of the computer, when it is switched on • Managing storage devices and the transfer of data between the main memory and storage devices • Management of data in main memory, allocating storage space in main memory to the different elements of software in operation at the time • Managing job scheduling and multiprogramming: large computers can execute more than one application simultaneously. The most widely-used operating system is Microsoft Windows. Other operating systems include UNIX, the Apple Macintosh O/S system and Linux.
Utilities/systems software	Software utilities are relatively small software packages, usually designed to perform a task related to the general operation of a computer system. For example, computers include standard software which enables the computer to send output from the system to a printer. Systems software performs functions associated with the needs of the computer – they control the operation of the computer to ensure efficient and uninterrupted action. Examples include copying the contents of one disk to another disk or reorganising the contents of a file (stored data).
Programming tools	Some software is designed specifically to help programmers produce computer programs. Examples include program compilers and assemblers, and Computer Assisted Software Engineering (CASE) tools.
Off-the-shelf applications	This term is used to describe software produced by a software manufacturer and released in a form that is ready to use. 'Office' type software (spreadsheet, word processing, database software) and integrated accounting systems such as Sage are examples.
Bespoke applications	Bespoke software is tailor-made to meet the needs of an organisation. Bespoke software is relatively expensive, but may be the only feasible solution in unusual situations.

3.1 Applications software and packages

Applications software is software for computer users to perform data processing (for example, processing accounting transactions) and other standard tasks such as word processing.

Applications software may be developed especially for one user, but purpose-made computer systems are expensive to develop and are only justifiable for very large systems. More commonly, applications software is purchased as a 'package' from a computer manufacturer or a software house, which sells the same package to different customers/ user organisations. Applications packages are sometimes called 'off-the-shelf' software.

Small computer applications may be written by individuals for their own use, or for the use of a work team. Small computer applications may be developed in-house with standard spreadsheet or database software packages, for example to develop forecasting models (with spreadsheets).

3.1.1 Advantages and limitations of packages

Standard applications packages are widely used in preference to purpose-written systems for several important reasons.

(a) Cost: Off-the-shelf application packages are much cheaper to acquire than developing in-house systems.

(b) Speed of implementation: An off-the-shelf package is ready to use as soon as it has been purchased and well-established packages should be error-free. An in-house system can take a long time to develop and may initially contain errors so that the system must be 'de-bugged' after it has been implemented.

(c) Portability: Applications software may be used on the computers of different manufacturers, provided that the operating system is compatible.

There are some **possible problems** with using standard application packages.

(a) An applications package is written for many different computer users, and it provides standard methods of processing for standard types of application.

(b) A user of the package may need to adapt its operational procedures to suit the demands of the package.

(c) A package may not contain some processing features that the computer user would like to have.

(d) Application packages are not available for large or complex systems. These systems should be developed as a bespoke system.

4 Types of information system

FAST FORWARD

> There are different **types of information system**. Each has different characteristics and service a different purpose.

Although opinions differ and not all categories are agreed, we can identify seven **types of information system**.

- Office Automation Systems (OAS)
- Transaction Processing Systems (TPS)
- Management Information Systems (MIS)
- Decision Support Systems (DSS)
- Knowledge Work Systems (KWS)
- Executive Support Systems (ESS)
- Expert systems

4.1 Office Automation Systems (OAS)

Key term

> **Office Automation Systems (OAS)** are computer systems designed to increase the productivity of data and information workers.

Office automation systems, as their name suggests, are used to automate routine office functions such as document management, communication and managing data. Examples of OAS include:

- Word processing and desktop publishing
- Digital filing systems and desktop databases
- Email, voicemail, videoconferencing, groupware, schedulers
- Intranets
- Spreadsheets

4.2 Transaction Processing Systems (TPS)

Key term

A **Transaction Processing System (TPS)** performs and records routine transactions.

TPS are used for **routine tasks** in which data items or transactions must be processed so that operations can continue. A feature of TPS is that there are:

- 'Master files' of records for items, containing standing data and cumulative transaction data for each record
- 'Transaction files' or 'transaction entries' which are input to the system to update the master file records and produce processed output from the system

TPS support most business functions in most types of organisation. In a manufacturing company, for example, there may be separate transaction processing systems for sales, inventory and purchasing, production planning, accounting and human resources. The following table shows a number of TPS applications and indicates the nature of master files, transactions and outputs from the system.

Sales system	
Master files	Customer file, products/prices file
Transactions	Sales order details, updated sales prices
Output	Sales orders

Purchasing system	
Master files	Inventory file, suppliers file
Transactions	Materials used, purchased materials received
Output	Purchase orders

Accounting system	
Master files	General ledger, receivables ledger, payables ledger
Transactions	Credit sales, invoices received, cash receipts, cash payments
Output	Sales invoices, credit notes, accounting statements

Within any TPS it should be possible to identify master files, transactions (inputs to the system) and outputs from the system.

4.3 Management Information Systems (MIS)

Key term

Management Information Systems (MIS) convert data from **mainly internal sources** into information (eg summary reports, exception reports). This information enables managers to make timely and effective decisions for planning, directing and controlling the activities for which they are responsible.

An MIS provides regular reports and (usually) online access to the organisation's current and historical performance.

MIS usually transform data from underlying transaction processing systems into summarised files that are used as the basis for management reports. For example, a sales processing system is a transaction processing system, but it is also used to produce sales reports and other management information that may be of use and value to management.

Management accounting systems may be examples of MIS. A cost and management accounting system may include a budget file or standard cost data. Transaction processing data into the system should include data about actual costs, and the MIS will compare actual costs with budgeted or standard costs and produce variance reports for management control purposes.

MIS have the following characteristics:

- Support **structured** decisions at operational and management control levels
- Designed to report on **existing** operations
- Relatively **inflexible**
- Have an **internal** focus, because the sources of the information produced by the system are primarily internal records

4.4 Decision Support Systems (DSS)

Key term

> **Decision Support Systems (DSS)** combine data and analytical models or data analysis tools to support semi-structured and unstructured decision making.

A Decision Support System (DSS) is a computerised system for providing information and 'tools' to help with decision making by management. A DSS does not provide the decision for management. It simply provides information that should be of assistance to a manager in reaching a decision or judgement. DSS analyse and condense large volumes of data into a form that aids managers make decisions. The objective is to allow the manager to consider a number of **alternatives** and evaluate them under a variety of potential conditions.

DSS are used by management to assist in making decisions on issues which are subject to high levels of uncertainty about the problem, the various **responses** which management could undertake or the likely **impact** of those actions.

However, many decisions by management are '**semi-structured**'. This means that the decision situation has some structured element that can be quantified and analysed. A DSS is also able to take data and transform this into information that can assist management in reaching their decisions. For example, a DSS in a bank can help a credit manager to assess the creditworthiness of an applicant for a loan, to assist the credit manager in deciding whether the bank should agree to provide the loan.

Managers should also be able to **ask questions and obtain answers** from a DSS, and the system should therefore provide a facility that enables the system user to enter questions in the system.

A user may be connected to a DSS through a desk-top computer or laptop/portable computer. For example, desktop computers may be linked through a local area network (LAN) to a central computer.

DSSs can be grouped into three types or categories:

(a) Data retrieval and analysis DSS
(b) DSS providing computational support for structured decisions
(c) Decision support involving modelling

Data retrieval and analysis. This type of DSS interacts with an existing database to retrieve and analyse data, for the purpose of producing information to assist with decision-making. With this type of DSS, managers are able to interrogate the files to obtain immediate answers to a question or to produce instant reports. Examples are:

- The ability to interrogate an inventory file to establish the current stock of an inventory item, for the purpose of making an operational decision.
- The ability to interrogate a receivables file to produce an aged receivables report, for the purpose of making decisions relating to chasing customers for late payments.

DSSs providing computational support for structured decisions. An example of a structured decision is a decision by a banker about whether or not to agree to a loan application, and if so on what terms (for example, what interest rate). With this type of DSS, information is extracted from a central database and the DSS user makes some additional calculations on the data and then reaches a decision.

Decision support involving modelling. Some DSS are constructed as decision-making models. The model user can input data to the model to obtain information that can help with decision-making. Spreadsheet models for forecasting and planning are an example of this type of DSS. Linear programming models, to make decisions when there are known constraints or limitations on resources, is another.

4.5 Knowledge Work Systems (KWS)

Key terms

> **Knowledge Work Systems (KWS)** are information systems that facilitate the creation and integration of new knowledge into an organisation.
>
> **Knowledge Workers** are people whose jobs consist of primarily creating new information and knowledge. They are often members of a profession such as doctors, engineers, lawyers and scientists.

KWS help knowledge workers create new knowledge and expertise. Examples include:

- Computer Aided Design (CAD)
- Computer Aided Manufacturing (CAM)
- Specialised financial software that analyses trading situations

4.6 Executive Support Systems (ESS)

Key term

> An **Executive Support System (ESS)** pools data from internal and external sources and makes information available to senior managers in an easy to use form. ESS help senior managers make strategic, unstructured decisions.

An ESS combines data from both internal and external sources, and makes information available to senior managers in a form that is easy to use. Whereas a DSS may assist management with semi-structured decisions, ESS helps senior managers make strategic **unstructured decisions**. ESS systems are useful for senior management in large organisations who need to process large amounts of varied data in order to reach decisions about business strategy. (However, an ESS has also been described as a specialised form of DSS, providing enterprise-wide decision support for senior executives.)

An ESS summarises and tracks strategically critical information, possibly drawn from internal MIS and DSS, but also including data from external sources, eg competitors, government departments (legislation), and external databases such as Reuters and Bloomberg.

An ESS usually includes flexible but sophisticated data analysis and modelling tools. A model of a typical ESS follows.

An Executive Support System (ESS)

```
                    ESS workstation
                         |
                    • Menus
                    • Graphics
                    • Communications
                    • Local processing

ESS workstation ──[ Internal data          External data       ]── ESS workstation
                   TPS/MIS data            Share prices
• Menus            Financial data          Market research       • Menus
• Graphics         Office systems          Legislation           • Graphics
• Communications   Modelling/analysis      Competitors           • Communications
• Local processing                                               • Local processing
```

4.6.1 Advantages and disadvantages of ESS

Although ESS have lost some popularity in recent years, they offer some benefits for senior managers.

- They are easy to use and extensive familiarity with computers is not required.
- They can provide prompt summaries of company-wide information.
- Senior executives are able to reach decisions more quickly by having access to information.
- They can improve the understanding of senior executives.

ESS also have some disadvantages.

- They have limited functionality. Functionality is limited by the design of the system.
- They may provide senior executives with too much information to absorb and understand.
- The benefits of having an ESS are difficult to measure.
- They can be expensive.

4.7 Expert systems

Key term

> An **expert system** is a computer program that captures human expertise in a limited domain of knowledge.

Expert system software uses a **knowledge base** that consists of **facts**, **concepts** and the **relationships** between them on a particular domain of knowledge and uses pattern-matching techniques to 'solve' problems.

For example, many financial institutions now use expert systems to process straightforward **loan applications**. The user enters certain key facts into the system such as the loan applicant's name and most recent addresses, their income and monthly outgoings, and details of other loans. The system will then:

(a) **Check the facts** given against its database to see whether the applicant has a good previous credit record.

(b) **Perform calculations** to see whether the applicant can afford to repay the loan.

(c) **Make a judgement** as to what extent the loan applicant fits the lender's profile of a good risk (based on the lender's previous experience).

(d) Suggest a decision.

An organisation can **use an expert system** when a number of **conditions** are met.

(a) The problem is **well defined**.
(b) The expert can define **rules** by which the problem can be solved.
(c) The **investment** in an expert system is cost-justified.

Other examples of an expert system might be:

(a) A medical diagnosis system that provides a diagnosis of a medical condition in response to input of symptoms of a medical disorder.
(b) A legal system that indicates the law in a particular situation, in response to input of facts about the case.

The key feature of an expert system is that its files contain data about an areas of expertise, and the user of the system is able to input data and ask questions in order to obtain expert information from the system. Expert systems are an example of the use of Artificial Intelligence or AI.

4.7.1 Advantages and disadvantages of expert systems

Advantages of expert systems are as follows.

(a) They provide consistent answers for repetitive decisions.
(b) They hold a very large quantity of information about a particular area of expertise.
(c) When reaching a decision, an expert system never forgets to ask a question in the decision-making process – unlike humans, who may forget to ask an important question.

Expert systems also have **disadvantages**.

(a) The logic used by the system may be imperfect. Occasionally an expert system may reach a decision that lacks common sense.
(b) The knowledge in the knowledge base of an expert system may contain errors, leading at times to imperfect decisions.
(c) An expert system cannot make a creative decision by 'looking outside the box' – unlike humans.
(d) The logic used within an expert system may not be apparent to the user.
(e) The knowledge base in an expert system must be continually updated; otherwise it cannot adapt to changes and developments in the area of expertise.

4.8 Accounting information systems

In many organisations, the main purpose of an accounting system is to process accounting transactions.

Many accounting systems are available in modular form, and users can purchase and use whichever modules they want. Output from one module can be used as input to another module.

The most common modules are a general ledger module, a receivables ledger module and a payables ledger module. Organisations may also have a payroll module and other modules such as a cost accounting module.

Major advantages of accounting systems for transaction processing, compared with manual accounting systems, are greater speed and efficiency of processing, the ability to handle larger volumes of transactions, fewer errors in processing and automated production of documents such as invoices statements and payslips.

In a fully-integrated modular system, a 'day book' transaction is entered into the system once, and it is subsequently posted to the relevant accounts in the relevant ledgers automatically.

4.8.1 Accounting information

Accounting systems are not simply used for transaction processing. Computer systems also provide accountants with:

- A greater amount of information for analysis
- Various techniques and models for analysing data, and consequently
- Better-quality information

Managers in many organisations are provided with personal computing facilities, in the form of a desk-top PC or a portable or laptop computer that can link into the company's network and central data files. This enables them, to some extent, to retrieve data from the central files and prepare their own models for personal use or for the use of their work team. The use of spreadsheet models by managers is an example of decision support systems. PC for spreadsheet modelling.

4.8.2 Spreadsheets and accounting information

Accountants make extensive use of spreadsheets, in particular for planning and forecasting. **Spreadsheet models** are used extensively for accounting activities such as:

- Budgeting and risk analysis in budgets
- Financial forecasting
- Investment appraisal
- Budgetary control reporting
- Cost and profitability analysis

Spreadsheets are particularly suitable for tasks requiring the production of reports, such as income statements and statements of financial position, and reports on quantitative data which include the presentation of the information in graphs or other visual form (such as pie charts).

With spreadsheets, it is a simple task to ask 'what if' questions by changing the values of parameters within the spreadsheet model. This easy facility to carry out sensitivity analysis on the assumptions in a model has greatly improved the quality of risk analysis in forecasting and planning.

There are several limitations to the use of spreadsheets, however.

- Spreadsheet models are based on a matrix format of rows and columns, and are suited only to applications involving large amounts of calculations.

- The design of personal spreadsheet models can take up a lot of management time and the benefits may not justify the effort.

- Spreadsheet models written by one manager may be useful for the individual, but others may not want to use it because they do not understand the assumptions that have been made in constructing the model.

- Spreadsheets can be very large – too large to display in full on a computer screen or include in a single sheet of printout.

5 Types of transaction processing system

Transaction processing can be divided into two broad types: **batch processing** and **real-time processing**. Batch processing systems are becoming less common, particularly if the process concerned impacts on customer service.

5.1 Batch processing

In a **batch processing system,** transactions are put into batches for input to the system. Transactions are then input in one or more batches at a time.

(a) Batch processing may be appropriate when there is a very large number of input transactions for processing. Grouping them into batches provides a simple system of control. Each batch is identified by a code number, and for each batch the total number of records is included in a batch entry record. Batch identification and batch totals provide a form of check to make sure that all transactions have been input and processed. Grouping transactions into batches may also help with finding individual transactions in the event that they need to be re-input due to an input error.

(b) Batch processing may also be appropriate when transactions are processed at regular intervals, such as once every week. Transactions are accumulated over a period of time and then are input at the same time in a batch run. Some **delay** in processing the transactions must therefore be acceptable. Because data is not input as soon as it is received the system will not always be up-to-date.

The lack of up-to-date information means batch processing is usually not suitable for systems involving customer contact. Batch processing is suitable for internal, regular periodic tasks such as payroll.

5.2 Online processing

Online processing involves transactions being input for processing individually, as soon as they are received, without grouping them into batches.

The term 'online' refers to the fact that the individual who inputs the transactions has continual access to the processing system and its files, and so is to input new transactions at any time, and receive immediate notification from the system either that the transaction has been processed successfully, or that it has been rejected because of an error.

Another feature of an online system is that the user can often interact with the computer program, responding to prompts that appear on the computer screen.

An online transaction processing system may also be a **real-time system**. This means that the master file is updated by the transaction immediately, and subsequent transactions will use the updated master file.

An example of a real-time system is an online booking system, such as a system for reserving seats on an airline flight, or seats for the theatre. Each transaction that makes a booking selects and reserves seats. Any subsequent transaction to reserve seats will find all seats taken that have been reserved by previous transactions. Unless the seating plan can be updated in real time, there is an obvious risk that the same seats will be double-booked.

Online real-time processing is appropriate when immediate processing is required, and the delay implicit in batch processing would not be acceptable.

Online real-time systems are practically the **norm** in modern business. **Other examples** include the following.

(a) As a sale is made in a department store or a supermarket, the item barcode is scanned on the **point of sale terminal** and the inventory records are updated immediately.

(b) In **banking and credit card** systems whereby customer details are often maintained in a real-time environment. There can be immediate access to customer balances, credit position etc and authorisation for withdrawals (or use of a credit card).

The features of both batch and online processing methods are shown in the following diagram.

Batch processing and online processing

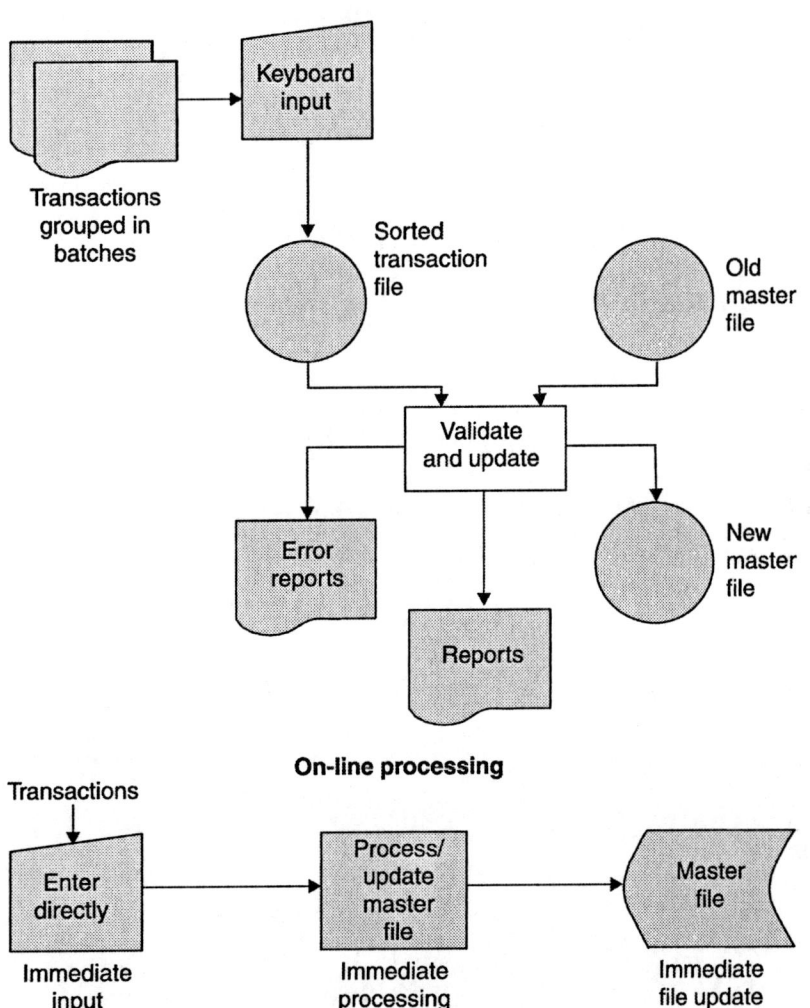

6 System architecture

The term **system architecture** refers to the way in which the various components of an information system are linked together, and the way they relate to each other.

(a) At one extreme an organisation may have just a **single** 'stand-alone' computer.

(b) At the other extreme, an organisation may have **hundreds** of computers, all in use simultaneously and able to communicate with each other.

6.1 Networks

Key term

The term **network** is a general term used to describe any computing architecture that includes connected autonomous processors. A network is therefore a system of linked computers and other devices, with some common files.

There are two main network architectures – client-server and peer-to-peer.

> **FAST FORWARD**
> The main network architectures are **client-server** and **peer-to-peer**. Client-server systems aim to ensure best utilisation of computing resources.

6.2 Client-server architecture

The term 'client-server' is a way of describing the relationship between the devices in a network. 'Client-server' describes a network architecture in which each computer or process on the network is either a client or a server.

Servers are powerful computers or processors within a network. Servers may have a specific function, and may be dedicated to managing disk drives (file servers), managing shared printers (print servers), or managing network traffic (network servers).

Clients are PCs or workstations on which the users of the network run their computer applications. Clients rely on servers for resources such as files (and storage), other devices such as printers, and sometimes processing power.

Key terms

> A **client** is a machine which requests a service, for example a PC running a spreadsheet application which the user wishes to print out.
>
> A **server** is a machine which is dedicated to providing a particular function or service requested by a client. Servers include file servers (see below), print servers, email servers and fax servers.

6.2.1 Client-server hardware

A typical client-server system includes three **hardware** elements.

- A central server (sometimes called the corporate server)
- Local servers (sometimes called departmental servers)
- Client workstations

A server computer (such as a file server) may be a powerful PC or a minicomputer. As its name implies, it **serves** the rest of the network offering a generally-accessible hard disk and sometimes offering other resources, such as a **shared printer**.

A client-server architecture is shown below. (**Note.** A local area network is explained later.)

Client-server architecture

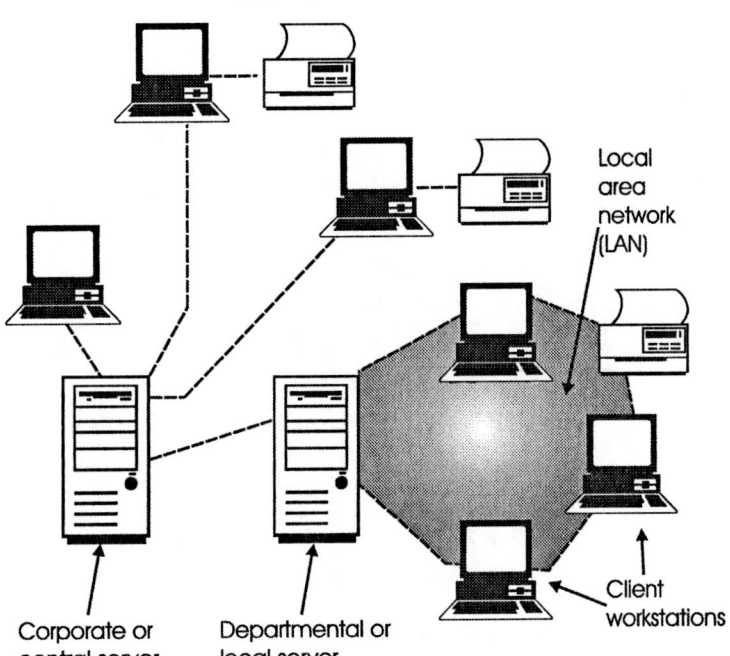

6.2.2 Client-server software

Client-server systems aim to locate software where it is most efficient – based on the number and location of users requiring access and the processing power required. There are three main types of software applications.

(a) **Corporate applications** are run on the central (or corporate) server. These applications are accessed by people spread throughout the organisation, and often require significant processor power (eg a centralised Management Information System).

(b) **Local applications** are used by users within a particular section or department, and therefore are run on the relevant local or departmental server (eg a credit-scoring expert system may be held on the server servicing the loans department of a bank).

(c) **Client applications** may be unique to an individual user, eg a specialised ESS. Other software that may be run on client hardware could include 'office' type software, such as spreadsheet and word processing programs. Even though many people may use these applications, individual copies of programs are often held on client hardware – to utilise the processor power held on client machines.

6.3 The advantages of a client-server architecture

Advantage	Comment
Greater resilience	Processing is spread over several computers. If one server breaks down, other locations can carry on processing.
Scalability	They are highly scalable. Instead of having to buy computing power in large quantities you can buy just the amount of power you need to do the job.
Shared programs and data	Program and data files held on a file server can be shared by all the PCs in the network. With stand-alone PCs, each computer would have its own data files, and there might be unnecessary duplication of data. A system where everyone uses the same data will help to improve data processing and decision making.
Shared work-loads	The processing capability of each computer in a network can be utilised. For example, if there were separate stand-alone PCs, A might do job 1, B might do job 2 and C might do job 3. In a network, any PC, (A, B or C) could do any job (1, 2 or 3). This is more efficient.
Shared peripherals	Peripheral equipment can be shared. For example, five PCs might share a single printer.
Communication	Local area networks (LANs) can be linked up to the office communications network, thus adding to the processing capabilities in an office. Electronic mail, calendar and diary facilities can also be used.
Compatibility	Client/server systems are likely to include interfaces between different types of software used on the system, making it easier to move information between applications.
Flexibility	For example, if a detailed analysis of existing data is required, a copy of this data could be placed on a separate server, allowing data to be manipulated without disrupting the main system.

6.4 The disadvantages of a client/server architecture

The client/server approach has some drawbacks.

(a) A single **mainframe computer** may be more efficient performing some tasks, in certain circumstances, than a network of servers and clients. For example, where there is routine processing of a very large number (eg millions) of transactions.

(b) It is easier to **control** and **maintain** a centralised system. In particular it is easier to keep data **secure**.

(c) It may be **cheaper** to 'tweak' an existing mainframe system rather than throwing it away and starting from scratch.

(d) Each location may need its own **network administrator** to keep things running smoothly – there may be unnecessary duplication of **skills** and staff.

(e) Duplication of information may be a problem if individual users do not follow a disciplined approach.

6.5 Peer-to-peer architecture

'Peer-to-peer' refers to a type of network in which each workstation has equivalent capabilities and responsibilities. This differs from client/server architectures, in which some computers are dedicated to serving the others. Peer-to-peer networks are generally simpler, but they usually do not offer the same performance under heavy workloads.

7 Local Area Networks (LANs) and Wide Area Networks (WANs)

Client-server and peer-to-peer describe the relationship between devices within a network. Another way of classifying networks is the geographical area that they cover.

A local area network (LAN) is a computer network that spans a relatively small area. Most LANs are confined to a single building or group of buildings. However, one LAN can be connected to other LANs over any distance via telephone lines and radio waves. A system of LANs connected in this way is called a wide-area network (WAN).

A WAN is a computer network that spans a relatively large geographical area. Typically, a WAN consists of two or more LANs. Computers connected to a WAN are often connected through public networks, such as the telephone system. They can also be connected through leased lines or satellites. The largest WAN in existence is the internet.

The **main differences** between a LAN and a WAN are as follows.

(a) The **geographical area** covered by a WAN is greater, not being limited to a single building or site.

(b) WANs will send data over **telecommunications links.** The computer equipment in a LAN are commonly linked by cable.

(c) WANs will often use a **larger computer** as a file server.

(d) WANs will often be larger than LANs, with **more terminals or computers** linked to the network.

(e) A WAN can link two or more LANs, using **gateways**.

7.1 Centralised processing

Data processing may be either centralised or decentralised.

To gain economies of scale the original trend in IT systems was to centralise them into one geographical location. This was the era of specialised computer centres with large rooms housing mainframe computer systems and specialist IT operating staff on site to manage all the IT operations.

With the development of networks and online processing, it is still possible to centralise data processing within the organisation. A central mainframe computer may perform all the processing centrally, for transactions that are input for processing from remote **'dumb' terminals** in different parts of the organisation.

A dumb terminal is capable of communicating with a central computer, for the input data and receipt of on-screen output, but it has no data processing capability of its own. All the processing is performed by the central computer.

A centralised processing approach has a number of disadvantages:

(a) The system is vulnerable to a problem at the central location, such as flood, fire, industrial action or bad weather, or of a breakdown in communications between the remote terminals and the central processing unit.

(b) It supports centralisation of management within the organisation, because the processing is performed centrally, and the various departments and divisions within the organisation depend on centralised operations for their information. When the organisation has a culture of centralised management, centralised processing may be the most appropriate arrangement. However, centralised management can be demoralising for 'local' managers because:

- Decision-making may be slowed down if information is held centrally at head office
- 'Local' managers are not given much opportunity to perform when they are continually instructed what to do by head office.

7.2 Decentralised processing

Decentralised processing is the opposite of centralised processing. In a distributed system, computer hardware is located at different geographical sites. Instead of processing transactions and other data in a centralised location, processing takes place at different locations, usually under the control of different departmental or regional management.

With a decentralised processing system, data processing capability must be distributed through the network.

(a) As a minimum requirement, remote terminals linked to a central mainframe computer should be 'intelligent terminals, such as desk-top computers, with their own processing capability.

(b) When data processing is decentralised and distributed to a greater extent, servers may be located at different places around the network, so that local processing makes use of more powerful computers than intelligent desk-top computers.

Decentralised processing may involve stand-alone file systems, which are discussed later. Alternatively, decentralised processing may involve some processing at different locations within the organisation, but if these locations are linked together in a network, the data and files in one location can be shared by all other users in the network.

Decentralised processing does not have to be 100% decentralised. Processing may be partially decentralised and partially centralised.

(a) Data processed locally (decentralised processing) may be transferred through the network to head office, for further centralised processing.

(b) Some processing may be carried out locally, and some may be performed centrally.

There are some possible problems with decentralised processing:

(i) With decentralised processing, there may be a risk of loss of standardisation of data within the network, because local managers may introduce their own adjustments to processing features or data storage. If local processing ceases to conform to standard, there may be problems with data communication and data sharing through the network.

(ii) The same data may be held in files at different sites. This creates duplication of input and may lead to inconsistencies and discrepancies if the 'duplicated' data is updated locally.

7.3 Distributed processing

Distributed processing describes an arrangement where the organisation has significant processing power situated in a number of different geographical locations. It originated in the armed forces where there was an awareness of the potential for disruption if the enemy destroyed the centralised facility, or knocked out decentralised ones.

Unlike decentralised processing, which leave the processing under the management of the local division, distributed processing is still managed centrally, and the sites are linked together by high bandwidth connections so that large scale work, such as running month end reports, can be shared across the sites.

The benefits of distributed processing include the following.

(a) Reduction in vulnerability: if a computer in one location suffers an operational breakdown and suspension of service, processing in the rest of the network will be unaffected.

(b) It should be cheaper than fully decentralised processing: this would require that each division owns sufficient capacity to run its most intensive applications. This might be needed only a few days a year. It can now 'borrow' capacity on slack systems in other divisions.

7.4 Networks: centralised and distributed processing

Network systems provide great flexibility in choice of processing arrangements.

(a) Networks allow users to have distributed processing as an alternative to centralised computers.

(b) Networks can be used for centralised processing, with input to the central system from remote online terminals. Users at remote terminals can also access centralised files to obtain information.

(c) Networks can also be used for decentralised processing, where there is local data processing, perhaps with LANs.

(d) LANs can be linked in WANs, so that any data can be transferred anywhere through the network.

Networks may also provide their users with access to the internet.

7.5 Intranets and extranets

Organisations are increasingly using **intranets** and **extranets** to **disseminate information**.

(a) An **intranet** is like a mini version of the internet (see the next section). Organisation members use networked computers to access information held on a server. The user interface is a browser – similar to those used on the internet. The intranet offers access to information on a wide variety of topics, and often includes access to the internet.

(b) An **extranet** is an intranet that is also accessible to **authorised outsiders**, who must use a valid username and password to gain access to the system. The username will have access rights attached – determining which parts of the extranet can be viewed. Extranets are becoming a very popular means for business partners to exchange information.

8 The internet

FAST FORWARD

Many organisations are now utilising **the internet** as a means of gathering and disseminating information, and conducting transactions.

Key term

The **internet** is a global network connecting millions of computers.

The internet is the name given to the technology that allows any computer with a telecommunications link to **send and receive information** from any other suitably equipped computer.

The **World Wide Web** is the multimedia element which provides facilities such as full-colour, graphics, sound and video. Websites are points within the network created by members who wish to provide an information point for searchers to visit and benefit by the provision of information and/or by entering into a transaction.

Almost all companies have a **website** on the internet. A site is a collection of screens providing **information in text and graphic form**, any of which can be viewed simply by clicking the appropriate button, word or image on the screen.

8.1 Current uses of the internet

The scope and potential of the internet are still developing. Its uses already embrace the following:

(a) **Dissemination** of information.

(b) **Product/service development** – through almost instantaneous test marketing.

(c) **Transaction processing** (electronic commerce or e-commerce) – both business-to-business and business-to-consumer.

(d) **Relationship enhancement** – between various groups of stakeholders.

(e) **Recruitment** and job search – involving organisations worldwide.

(f) **Entertainment** – including music, humour, art, games and some less wholesome pursuits!

It is estimated that approximately 60% of the adult population of the UK use the internet on a regular basis.

The internet provides opportunities to organise for and to automate tasks which would previously have required more costly interaction with the organisation. These have often been called low-touch or zero-touch approaches.

8.1.1 Websites

Tasks which a **website may automate** include:

(a) **Frequently Asked Questions (FAQs)**: carefully-structured sets of answers can deal with many customer interactions.

(b) **Status checking**: major service enquiries (Where is my order? When will the engineer arrive? What is my bank balance?) can also be automated, replacing high-cost human service processes, and also providing the opportunity to proactively offer better service and new services.

(c) **Keyword search**: the ability to search provides web users with opportunities to find information in large and complex websites.

(d) **Wizards** (interview style interface) and **intelligent algorithms**: these can help diagnosis, which is one of the major elements of service support.

(e) **Email and systems to route and track inbound email**: the ability to route and/or to provide automatic responses will enable organisations to deal with high volumes of email from actual and potential customers.

(f) **Bulletin boards**: these enable customers to interact with each other, thus facilitating self-activated customer service and also the opportunity for product/service referral. Cisco in particular has created communities of Cisco users who help each other – thus reducing the service costs for Cisco itself.

(g) **Call-back buttons**: these enable customers to speak to someone in order to deal with and resolve a problem; the more sophisticated systems allow the call-centre operator to know which web pages the users were consulting at the time.

8.2 Problems with the internet

To a large extent the internet has grown organically **without any formal organisation**. There are specific communication rules, but it is not **owned** by any one body and there are no clear guidelines on how it should develop.

The **quality** of much of the information on the internet leaves much to be desired.

Speed is a major issue. Data only downloads onto the user's PC at the speed of the slowest telecommunications link – downloading data can be a painfully **slow** procedure.

So much information and entertainment is available that employers worry that their **staff will spend too much time** browsing through non-work-related sites.

Connecting an information system to the internet exposes the system to numerous **security issues**. We will explore these issues in Chapter 13.

Case Study

Internet service providers such as Virgin and Sky have upgraded their broadband speeds in response to customer demand for services such as video and music.

9 Organisation of files: file-based systems

In principle there are several ways of considering the organisation of files.

(a) One approach is to consider the location of files within a network. In a centralised processing system, all the main files are held in a central location. With networks and decentralised processing, data files may be located in different places around the network.

(b) Another approach is to consider whether files should be maintained for a specific application or use, or whether there should be a shared database available for different users and different uses.

A **file-based system** is a system that has its own separate files. The system has a specific purpose and the files are unique to the system. They are not accessible to other users and other systems.

For example, a human resources department may have its own separate employee files which are used for purposes specific to the HR department. The employee records would be updated by HR staff and used exclusively for HR purposes, such as identifying individuals who may require training, calculating annual inflation-linked pay rises and estimating future recruitment requirements.

When an organisation has file-based computer systems, it may have a large number of separate systems, each with its own files, input transactions and uses.

Data files are associated with specific transaction applications and different departments and departmental managements.

Different systems may all hold similar information, but in different (and incompatible) formats. For example, a sales system and an accounting system may both hold records about sales. The sales records in the separate file systems may hold some data about the same items, and so to some extent may duplicate each other. However the data on file in the two systems may be held in incompatible formats.

When two or more file-based application systems hold the same data, this data has to be input into each system separately. This creates unnecessary work, (time, resources and cost) compared with a database system, where all data is held in common files accessible to all users.

Each separate file-based system has its own management. No one has responsibility management information on an organisation-wide basis.

9.1 Possible advantages of file-based systems

File-based systems often create unnecessary duplication of data in the various different systems, and shared databases are used extensively as a means of avoiding the wasted effort and cost of duplication.

However, there are some situations where the use of file-based systems may be preferable to database systems.

(a) A system may use data that no other system in the organisation requires.

(b) The users of a system may have a fixed set of processing requirements that are not expected to change in the future. If so, there is no value in the ability to use a database for developing new uses and applications for data.

(c) When there is a large amount of time-critical transaction data, a file-based system gives management closer control over data input operations and procedures.

A commonly-used alternative to file-based systems is a database.

10 Databases

FAST FORWARD

> A **database** is a collection of data organised to service many applications. The database provides convenient access to data for a wide variety of users and user needs. A Database Management System (**DBMS**) is the software that centralises data and manages access to the database. It is a system which allows numerous applications to extract the data they need without the need for separate files.

The way in which data is held on a system affects the ease with which the data is able to be accessed and manipulated.

Key terms

> A **database** is a collection of data organised to service many applications. The database provides convenient access to data for a wide variety of users and user needs.
>
> A **Database Management System** (**DBMS**) is the software that centralises data and manages access to the database. It is a system which allows numerous applications to extract the data they need without the need for separate files.
>
> The **logical structure** of a database refers to how various application programs access the data. The **physical structure** relates to how data is organised within the database.
>
> The independence of data items from the programs which access them is referred to as **data independence**.
>
> Duplication of data items is referred to as **data redundancy**.
>
> In a database environment, the ease with which applications access the central pool of data is referred to as **integration**.
>
> **Integrity** relates to data accuracy and consistency. Data independence and integration should reduce data redundancy resulting in improved data integrity.

10.1 The characteristics of a database system

A database system has the following characteristics.

(a) **Shared**. Different users are able to access the same data for their own processing applications. This removes the need for duplicating data on different files.

(b) **Controls** to preserve the **integrity** of the database. Users should not be able to alter the data on file so as to **spoil** the database records for other users. However, users must be able to make **valid** alterations to the data.

(c) **Flexibility.** The database system should provide for the **needs of different users**, who each have their own processing requirements and data access methods. The database should be capable of **evolving** to meet **future** needs.

10.2 Database structures

There are three logical database models.

- The **hierarchical** model
- The **network** model
- The **relational** model

10.3 The hierarchical model

The hierarchical model is an example of **a logical database model**. It shows data in a tree-like format. Upper segments of the model are connected to lower segments in a parent-child relationship. A parent can have more than one child, but a child can have only one parent. Such relationships can be expressed conveniently in a **hierarchy**. Each data item is related to only one item above it in the hierarchy, but to any number of data items below it.

In a customer database, for example, the hierarchical model might be used to show customers and customer orders. An extract from a **parts department database** might be structured as follows.

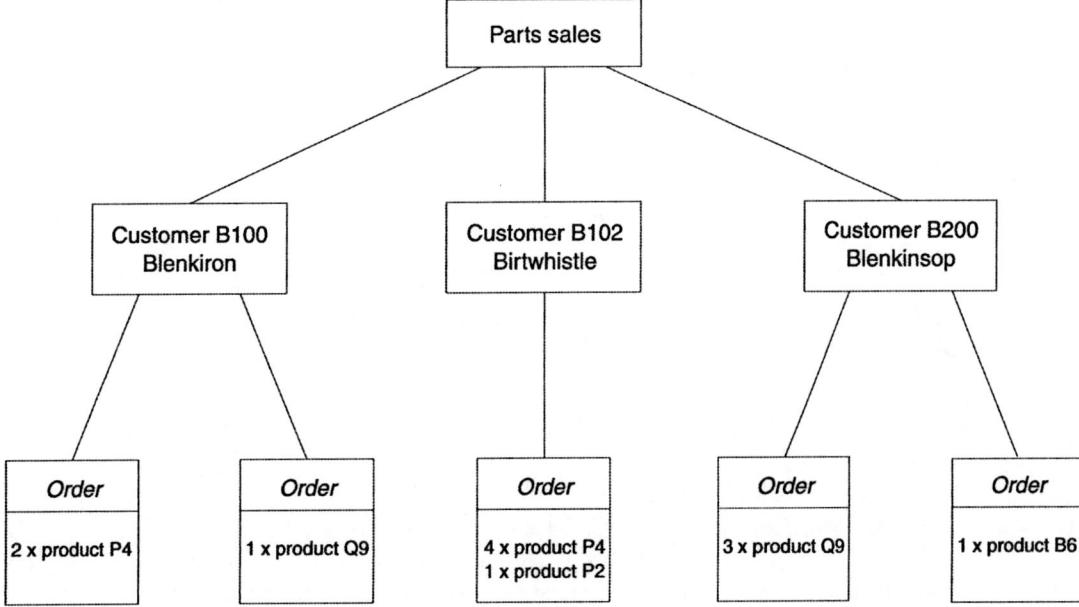

In the diagram above, the starting point (Part sales) is known as the **root segment**. Three child segments are shown below the root and further child segments below these.

The hierarchical nature of the model makes it **unsuitable for situations involving many-to-many relationships**.

For example, say we wish to model a purchases system using a Part code number as the root segment. If we buy Part X from three suppliers (A, B and C) the root segment (X) will have three children (A, B and C). The hierarchical model can show this relationship effectively. However, if we also buy another part (Y) from supplier A, a separate model would be needed to show this relationship – as a child (A) can have only one parent (X). If a hierarchical model was used in this situation, supplier A data would have to be held in more than one location (data redundancy).

Hierarchical structures are appropriate when systems must handle large numbers of routine requests for information eg an airline reservation system.

10.4 The network model

The network model is **another logical database model**. Whereas a hierarchical data structure only allows a **one-to-many** relationship between data items, a **network** database allows **many-to-many** relationships. In other words, parents can have many children and children can have many parents.

The relationship between courses run by an educational institution (such as BPP) and students (such as you) can be shown in a network data model. A student could take many courses and a course will (hopefully) have many students.

Network Data Model

```
        Paper 3.4       Paper 3.5       Paper 3.6
         Course          Course          Course


 Student 1   Student 2   Student 3   Student 4   Student 5
```

The data in the diagram above could be structured hierarchically but this would require data redundancy as student details would have to be stored separately for each course enrolled in.

Returning to our Part sales example, a network model is shown below.

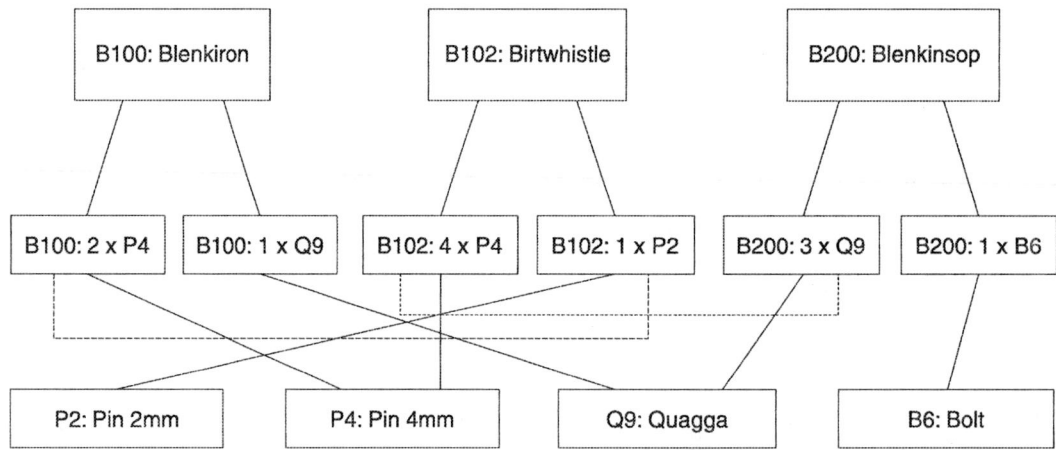

Using the network structure allows student details to be stored just once and should provide quicker response time to queries. To facilitate this, network databases require widespread use of **pointers**. Pointers are data elements attached to record segments on disk giving the location of related records. Hierarchical databases also use pointers but not to the extent they are required in network databases.

10.5 The relational model

The relational model is the third type of logical database model, designed to overcome some of the limitations of the other two models. A relational model organises data elements in a series of **two-dimensional tables** consisting of rows and columns. A row represents a record (or entity). Each column is a field or attribute eg address, telephone number, part number.

In a **relational data structure** the relationships between different entity types have been determined at the outset, and are not embodied in the records themselves. A relational database thus does not have to navigate through other data before reading the required record.

Any data element can be recognised by its record number or field name. The **primary key** is used to identify a record. Data redundancy is eliminated. Data in one table can point to data in another table, as long as there is one data attribute that exists in both tables.

Customer table			Product table			Order table		
B100	Blenkiron		B6	Bolt		B100	P4	2
B102	Birtwhistle		P2	Pin 2mm		B100	Q9	1
B200	Blenkinsop		P4	Pin 4mm		B102	P4	4
			Q9	Quagga		B102	P2	1
						B200	Q9	3
						B200	B6	1

Using the DBMS, data from these tables can be extracted and combined to produce reports, provided that any two share a common data element. For example, the customer code could be used to link the *Customer table* with the *Order table*. Once the link has been established between two or more tables a query can permit any combination of the data from the tables to be viewed.

These views are obtained by using enquiry tools such as **Structured Query Language** (SQL). This permits an application to create a unique data set (record) from a common set of data (database) in a fashion that meets the application requirements.

Basic SQL operations include:

- Select – creates a subset of rows (records) based on stated criteria
- Join – combines tables to provide more information
- Project – creates new tables containing only the columns required

10.6 The advantages and disadvantages of database systems

FAST FORWARD

> **Advantages of a database system** include the avoidance of data duplication, management is encouraged to manage data as a valuable resource, data consistency across the organisation, and the flexibility for answering ad-hoc queries.

The **advantages** of a database system are as follows.

(a) **Avoidance of unnecessary duplication of data**. It recognises that data can be used for many purposes but only needs to be input and stored once.

(b) **Multi-purpose data**. From (a), it follows that although data is input once, it can be used for several purposes.

(c) **Data for the organisation as a whole, not just for individual departments**. The database concept encourages management to regard data as a resource that must be **properly managed** just as any other resource. Database systems encourage management to analyse data, relationships between data items, and how data is used in different applications.

(d) **Consistency**. Because data is only held once, it is easier to ensure that it is up-to-date and consistent across departments.

(e) **New uses for data**. Data is held independently of the programs that access the data. This allows greater flexibility in the ways that data can be used. New programs can be easily introduced to make use of existing data in a different way.

(f) **New applications**. Developing new application programs with a database system is easier as a central pool of data is already available to be drawn upon.

(g) **Flexibility**. Relational systems are extremely flexible, allowing information from several different sources to be combined and providing answers to ad hoc queries.

> **Disadvantages of a database system** include initial development costs and the potential problems of data security.

The **disadvantages** of a database systems relate mainly to security and control.

(a) There are potential problems of **data security** and **data privacy**. Administrative procedures for data security should supplement software controls.

(b) Since there is only one set of data, it is essential that the data should be **accurate** and free from corruption. A back-up routine is essential.

(c) Initial **development costs** may be high.

(d) For hierarchical and network structures, the access paths through the data must be **specified in advance**.

(e) Both hierarchical and network systems require intensive **programming** and are **inflexible**.

10.6.1 Database alternatives

The following table compares the three database alternatives we have looked at.

Type	Hierarchical	Network	Relational
Programming effort required	High	High	Low
User-friendliness	Low	Low to medium	High
Processing efficiency	High	Medium to high	Low (improving)
Flexibility	Low	Low to medium	High

10.7 Knowledge Management Systems

> **Knowledge Management Systems (KMS)** record and store the knowledge held within an organisation. KMS are an example of how a database may be used.

Information held on a KMS is easily accessed and shared by employees. Examples of information held in a KMS include facts, solutions to problems, relevant legislation and intellectual property.

A KMS is primarily of benefit to **knowledge based organisations**, such as those involved in research and development or providing services such as legal advice. This is because their information is best suited to storing and sharing by a database.

Benefits of a KMS include:

(a) **Valuable data is preserved** for the future and not lost, for example, where an employee leaves.

(b) The data is **easily shared**.

(c) **Data duplication** (or data redundancy) is **avoided**.

(d) It allows employees to 'get up to speed' on knowledge quickly and easily and this may **reduce the time they need to spend training**.

10.8 Customer relationship management systems

FAST FORWARD

Customer relationship management (CRM) systems are software applications which specialise in providing information concerning an organisation's products, services and customers. They are another example of the use of a database.

Most CRM systems are based on a **database** which stores data about customers such as their **order history** and **personal information** such as address, age and any marketing feedback they have provided. These systems allow a personalised service to be provided to the customer as well as a swift reply to their queries.

CRM systems are often used by customer facing staff who handle **customer enquiries**, **orders** or **complaints** and who need to understand the customer's immediate needs and provide an appropriate response.

10.9 Enterprise-wide systems

FAST FORWARD

Enterprise-wide systems are designed to co-ordinate all business functions, resources and information.

Under an enterprise-wide system, each business area (such as accounts, HR, production and sales) is provided with a system that fulfils its needs, however each module shares a **common database** that is the basis of all the information within the organisation.

The central database allows each business area to **access** and **update information** in **real-time** and this means that information is **easy to share**, **available** to all business areas, and above all, **reliable**.

In some enterprises, even though the system spans the whole organisation individual locations have their own specific data processing capability, via a direct link to the central database. This is an example of **Distributed Data Processing (DDP)**. The link is provided by either a **Local Area Network** (LAN) or a **Wide Area Network** (WAN), depending upon how far apart the different locations are.

10.10 Database management system

A database management system is software that controls all access to the database and provides an interface between the database and users and user applications. There is (usually) one person, the database administrator, responsible for all the data and the database structure.

The major features of a database management system are as follows:

(a) It handles all access by users and application programmes.

(b) It provides the user with a logical view of data within the database that is relevant to the user's requirements.

(c) It ensures data consistency for all users of the database.

(d) It can allow access to some restricted parts of the database only to authorised users.

A database management system also includes various utility programs, such as:

(a) Report generators. These are pieces of software to assist users with the production of reports from the database.

(b) Automatic back-up of data and recovery in case of loss of data. The DBMS occasionally copies the database content on to a secure storage medium. Between making back-up copies, the DBMS automatically records every database transaction that occurs, so that if a serious failure occurs in the database, the DBMS can reconstruct it from the most recent back-up copy and the subsequent transactions.

(c) Control over concurrent usage. Concurrent usage happens when two database users are trying to access and amend the same data on the database at the same time. This DBMS utility software prevents more than one modification to a data item at the same time.

(d) Data dictionaries. A database dictionary is utility software that defines the types of data held on the database (for example by means of characteristics such as record type, and field type). It is a 'centralized repository of information about data such as meaning, relationships to other data, origin, usage, and format' (*IBM Dictionary of Computing*). This helps to define the database structure and can assist programmers who are writing new or amended software applications.

11 Developments in technology and systems

In this section we discuss some of the most significant developments in technology and how these developments are changing the characteristics of information systems and the way that organisations operate.

11.1 Digital transmission

New technologies require **transmission systems** capable of delivering substantial quantities of data at great speed across a wide network.

For data transmission through the existing 'analogue' telephone network to be possible, there has to be a device at each end of the telephone line that can:

- Convert (MOdulate) the data from digital form to analogue form for transmission over the analogue network; and
- (DEModulate) the data at the other end, from analogue form back into digital form.

This conversion of data is done by devices called **modems**.

More recent communication technologies such as ISDN and ADSL provide data transmission speeds far superior than possible using standard modems and telephone lines. These faster communication technologies are collectively referred to as **broadband**.

(a) An **ISDN line** enables the sending of voice, data, video and fax communications from a single desktop computer system over the telecommunication link, without using a modem.

(b) ADSL offers data transfer rates faster than ISDN over ordinary copper wires, and simultaneously with the normal telephone service. A special ADSL modem is required.

The effect of these developments has been to make possible even faster transmission of even greater quantities of data.

11.2 Mobile communications

Networks for mobile or cellular phones have been developed extensively in recent years. Mobile services available are developing all the time. Here are some examples.

(a) **Messaging services** such as: voice mail; short message service (SMS) or 'text messaging'.

(b) **Call handling services** such as: call barring, conference calls and call divert.

(c) **Corporate services** such as: integrated numbering, so that people have a single contact number for both the phone on their desk and for their mobile.

(d) **Dual mode handsets** which allow users to use both cheap cordless technology when in the office and cellular technology when outside.

(e) **Internet access** using laptops or hand-held devices (eg an iPhone and other smartphone devices for wireless email).

11.3 E-commerce

No doubt you are familiar with online commerce or e-commerce. This involves purchasing goods or services by visiting the website of a supplier and placing an order.

(a) The purchased item may be delivered electronically, if this is possible. Alternatively it may be delivered physically.

(b) E-commerce systems allow customers to pay by debit or credit card, or electronically (for example through PayPal).

E-commerce has several significant commercial features.

(a) It can bring suppliers into direct contact with potential customers, through their website. This cuts out the 'middle man' such as a retailer.

(b) It can bring suppliers into contact with potential new markets and customers who could not have been reached in the days before e-commerce.

(c) It provides customers with more information. Customers know immediately whether the goods they want to buy are available. They may also be able to follow the progress of their order through an electronic tracking system.

Berens (2006) identified the following points to consider when building a website with e-commerce capability.

(a) Ensure transactions are **secure**, and tell customers they are. Customer trust is essential.
(b) Comply with all applicable consumer, privacy and data protection legislation.
(c) Have clear **terms of use** for the site.
(d) Don't require customers to provide excessive amounts of information as this may deter them.
(e) Maintain **on-going communication** with willing customers, for example by email.

11.4 Electronic Funds Transfer (EFT)

EFT describes a system whereby organisations are able to use their computer system to **transfer funds** – for example make payments to a **supplier**, or pay salaries into **employees'** bank accounts.

Electronic transfers of funds has also helped to improve international trade. Most international trade is now conducted in a similar way to domestic trade, with payment by customers effected by bank transfer at the end of an agreed period of credit.

11.5 Electronic Data Interchange (EDI)

EDI is a form of computer-to-computer **data** interchange. Instead of sending each other reams of paper in the form of invoices, statements and so on, details of inter-company transactions are sent via telecoms links, **avoiding the need for output** and paper at the sending end, and **for re-keying of data** at the receiving end.

A feature of EDI is that it enables two different organisations to exchange documents from their computer systems. Documents produced by one computer system can be read successfully by the other system.

Two companies, one a regular supplier of goods to the others, may use EDI to send and acknowledge receipt of computer-produced purchase orders, delivery notes and invoices.

11.6 Social networking websites

Websites such as Facebook and Twitter have recently attempted to expand into business communication. Other sites, such as LinkedIn, encourage collaboration and communication between business people.

11.7 Videoconferencing

Videoconferencing is the use of computer and communications technology to **conduct meetings**.

Videoconferencing has become increasingly common as the internet and webcams have brought the service to desktop PCs at reasonable cost. More expensive systems feature a **separate room with several video screens**, which show the images of those participating in a meeting.

11.8 Cloud computing

Cloud computing is the provision of computer resources (hardware and software) from 'cloud providers' to other users, as a service over the internet.

(a) Users of cloud computing make use of the cloud provider's services to store and process data over the internet.

(b) The cloud provider makes available an infrastructure and platform for users to run their computer applications.

Organisations may benefit from cloud computing by:

(a) Improving the quantity and quality of computing resources that they use

(b) Sharing large data files between distant users (possibly worldwide) where the files are too large to send as email attachments

11.9 SMI-S

SMI-S is the Storage Management Initiative – Specification. This is a standard for storage of electronic data, developed by the Storage Networking Industry Association.

This standard was developed in response to the problem that storage devices from different manufacturers required data to be held in different formats. Data formatted for one manufacturer's storage devices could not be held on the devices of other manufacturers.

As a result, manufacturers of software (for example, operating systems) and manufacturers of hardware 'teamed up' together in bilateral agreements to create storage systems for software that were tied in to the hardware of a specific manufacturer. It was therefore impossible for software to be replaced without also replacing the storage hardware.

The purpose of SMI-S has been to overcome this problem by creating an industry standard for the interface between software and hardware storage devices, so that a computer user can buy the hardware of supplier X and use the software of supplier Y on the hardware. Most manufacturers have adopted SMI-S for the hardware storage devices they now produce. They no longer need to make different storage devices for different operating systems.

An important incentive for the creation of an industry standard has been the growth in demand for **storage area networking**. A storage area network or SAN is 'a network of storage devices that can be accessed by multiple computers. Each computer on the network can access hard drives in the SAN as if they were local disks connected directly to the computer. This allows individual hard drives to be used by multiple computers, making it easy to share information between different machines.

While a single server can provide a shared hard drive to multiple machines, large networks may require more storage than a single server can offer. For example, a large business may have several terabytes of data that needs to be accessible by multiple machines on a local area network (LAN). In this situation, a SAN could be set up instead of adding additional servers. Since only hard drives need to be added instead of complete computer systems, SANs are an efficient way to increase network storage' (www.techterms.com).

Cloud computing therefore is an example of a development that has benefited from SMI-S.

11.10 Homeworking or remote working

Advances in communications technology have, for some tasks, **reduced the need for the actual presence of an individual in the office.**

11.10.1 Advantages for the organisation

The **advantages to the organisation** of homeworking are as follows.

(a) **Cost savings on space.** Office rental costs and other charges can be very expensive. If firms can move some of their employees on to a homeworking basis, money can be saved.

(b) A **larger pool of labour.** The possibility of working at home might attract more applicants for clerical positions, especially from people who have other demands on their time (eg going to and from school) which cannot be fitted round standard office hours.

(c) If the homeworkers are **freelance**, then the organisation **avoids the need to pay them** when there is insufficient work, when they are sick, on holiday etc.

11.10.2 Advantages for the individual

The **advantages to the individual** of homeworking are as follows.

(a) No time and money is wasted commuting.
(b) Work can be organised around domestic commitments.

11.10.3 Possible disadvantages for the organisation

Problems for the organisation might be as follows.

(a) **Co-ordination** of the work of different homeworkers. The job design should ensure that homeworkers perform to the required standard.

(b) **Training.** If a homeworker needs a lot of help on a task, this implies that the task has not been properly explained.

(c) **Culture.** A homeworker is relatively isolated from the office and therefore, it might be assumed, from the firm. However, questions of loyalty and commitment do not apply for an organisation's sales force, whose members are rarely in the office.

(d) A loss of direct **control.**

11.10.4 Possible disadvantages for the individual

Problems for homeworkers may include:

- Isolation
- Interruptions
- Adequate space
- Possibly fewer employment rights (if employed on a 'casual' basis)

> **Exam focus point**
>
> The internet and websites may be examined in the context of e-commerce, which we cover in more detail in Chapter 13.

Chapter roundup

- **Computers** can be classified as supercomputers, mainframes, minicomputers and microcomputers or PCs.
- The amount of **RAM** and the **processor speed** are key determinants of computer performance. Hard drive size is another important factor.
- Five types of software are:
  - **Operating systems**
  - **Utilities**
  - **Programming tools**
  - **Off-the-shelf applications**
  - **Bespoke application software**
- There are different **types of information system**. Each has different characteristics and service a different purpose.
- Transaction processing can be divided into two broad types: **batch processing** and **real-time processing**. Batch processing systems are becoming less common, particularly if the process concerned impacts on customer service.
- The main network architectures are **client-server** and **peer-to-peer**. Client-server systems aim to ensure best utilisation of computing resources.
- Many organisations are now utilising **the internet** as a means of gathering and disseminating information, and conducting transactions.
- A **database** is a collection of data organised to service many applications. The database provides convenient access to data for a wide variety of users and user needs. A database management system (**DBMS**) is the software that centralises data and manages access to the database. It is a system which allows numerous applications to extract the data they need without the need for separate files.
- **Advantages of a database system** include the avoidance of data duplication, management is encouraged to manage data as a valuable resource, data consistency across the organisation, and the flexibility for answering ad-hoc queries.
- **Disadvantages of a database system** include initial development costs and the potential problems of data security.
- **Knowledge Management Systems (KMS)** record and store the knowledge held within an organisation. KMS are an example of how a database may be used.
- **Customer relationship management (CRM)** systems are software applications which specialise in providing information concerning an organisation's products, services and customers. They are another example of the use of a database.
- **Enterprise-wide systems** are designed to co-ordinate all business functions, resources and information.

Quick quiz

1. List four reasons why manual office systems may be less beneficial than computerised systems.
2. What is RAM?
3. List four types of software.
4. What is a database management system (DBMS)?
5. Distinguish between batch and real-time processing.
6. What is EDI and how could it encourage a closer relationship between organisations?
7. Distinguish between an intranet and an extranet.
8. List four general business uses of the internet.
9. List five tasks a website may automate.
10. Do you agree with the statement 'information derived from the internet is unreliable'? Justify your answer.

PART B INFORMATION SYSTEMS

Answers to quick quiz

1. Manual systems may be slower, more prone to error, require more labour and may be unable to handle large volumes of data. (This assumes the computerised system is operating correctly, is reliable and that staff know how to utilise it fully.)

2. RAM stands for Random Access Memory. It holds the data and programs in current use. RAM and processor speed are important indicators of processing power.

3. Operating systems, utilities, off-the-shelf packages, bespoke packages.

4. A database management system (DBMS) is the software that manages access to a database. This allows multiple users and applications to access the same files.

5. Batch processing is the processing as a group of a number of transactions of a similar kind in a batch. Real-time processing is the continual receiving and processing of data. Real-time processing uses an 'online' computer system to interrogate or update files as requested, rather than batching for subsequent processing.

6. Electronic Data Interchange (EDI) is a form of computer-to-computer data interchange. Instead of sending reams of paper in the form of invoices, statements and so on, details of transactions are sent via telecoms links. An efficient EDI link encourages a closer relationship between organisations as it encourages organisations to do business with those organisations it has EDI links with. Faster document transmission should reduce order lead times.

7. An intranet is available to those inside an organisation – members use networked computers to access information held on a server. The user interface is a browser – similar to those used on the internet. An extranet is an intranet that is accessible to authorised outsiders. Extranets are becoming a very popular means for business partners to exchange information.

8. Four of the following:
    - External email
    - Dissemination of information
    - Product/service development – through almost instantaneous test marketing
    - Transaction processing (electronic commerce or e-commerce)
    - Relationship enhancement – between various groups of stakeholders
    - Recruitment and job search – involving organisations worldwide

9. Five of the following:
    - Frequently Asked Questions (FAQs)
    - Status checking service enquiries
    - Keyword search
    - Recruitment and job search – involving organisations worldwide
    - Bulletin boards that enable customers to interact with each other
    - Call-back buttons that enable customers to request a customer services representative contacts them

10. The internet provides a means of accessing information from a wide range of organisations. Some of these organisations will provide good quality information (eg AIA, BBC etc), others may provide information that proves to be unreliable. Who is behind the information is a more significant indicator of reliability than the fact that the information was transmitted over the internet.

End of chapter question

Jean-Genie Stores (AIA May 2005)

Jean-Genie Stores has recently expanded from one to three outlets by opening two more shops selling casual clothing in a large shopping mall. Prior to this with only one shop the proprietor operated an entirely manual business administration system on cash and cheque sales. Given that the expanded business is more complex with three outlets, more business and more staff, the proprietor is considering automating some of the major aspects of the business. In particular, she wishes to consolidate the operations of all three shops to centralise administration and to move to computer processing of payroll, purchasing and credit card transactions. It has been proposed that the proprietor purchase and install a local area network (LAN) computer system to provide the automation.

Required

(a) (i) Describe the hardware appropriate to this situation that could be utilised.
    (ii) Describe the facilities a LAN would offer the proprietor of Jean-Genie. **(9 marks)**

(b) What advantages would there be to the proprietor of Jean-Genie from installing a local area network to provide the desired automation? **(7 marks)**

(c) Detail the types of application software that Jean-Genie could run on its network if it implemented the proposal, and what support the proprietor would require from the start. **(9 marks)**

(Total = 25 marks)

PART B INFORMATION SYSTEMS

Systems modelling

Topic list	Syllabus reference
1 Investigating user requirements	9.8
2 Modelling the system	9.8
3 Process modelling: data flow diagrams	9.8
4 Process modelling: flowcharts	9.8
5 Decision tables	9.8
6 Logical data modelling: Entity Relationship Model	9.8
7 An event model: Entity Life History	9.8
8 Object-oriented approach to modelling	9.8

Introduction

We start this chapter with a look at some **common techniques of systems investigation**, including the use of **interviews** and **questionnaires**.

In the second half of the chapter we demonstrate the recording and **documenting tools** used during the analysis and design of information systems.

1 Investigating user requirements

> **FAST FORWARD**
>
> During the **systems investigation** the project team examines the inputs, outputs, processing methods and volumes, controls, staffing and costs of the current system. This may involve fact finding by means of questionnaires, interviews, observation and reviewing documents.

When a decision is taken to introduce a new or amended processing or information system, the development project begins with an investigation of the current system, to establish what it does and what is does not do. An analysis of the current system provides a starting platform for developing a new and improved system.

A systems investigation is a detailed fact-finding exercise about the information system under consideration.

The project team has to determine the inputs, outputs, processing methods and volumes of the current system. It also examines controls, staffing and costs and reviews the organisational structure. It should also consider the expected growth of the organisation and its future requirements.

The stages involved in this phase of the study are as follows.

(a) **Fact finding** by means of questionnaires, interviews, observation, reading handbooks, manuals, organisation charts, or from the knowledge and experience of members of the study team.

(b) **Fact recording** using flowcharts, decision tables, narrative descriptions, organisation and responsibility charts.

(c) **Evaluation**, assessing the strengths and weaknesses of the existing system.

At this phase, when the team is trying to discover the details of a system with which they may be unfamiliar, they will be interested in the organisational context of the system, as it is important to have an overall view of what the system does. Consequently, fact finding in a user department can cover a broad area, as demonstrated by a few examples, below. The emphasis will be on the potential for **improvement**.

(a) **Plans and objectives.** Does the department have clear plans and objectives and are these consistent with the objectives of the organisation as a whole?

(b) **Organisation structure.** Is the structure geared towards achieving the department's objectives? Are responsibilities clearly delegated and defined?

(c) **Policies, systems and procedures**. How has the department established its current policies? Are they written down and formally reviewed? How does management ensure that policies are adhered to?

(d) **Personnel**. Are there adequate systems/procedures for job specifications and appraisals? Are there adequate systems for staff development and training?

(e) **Equipment and the office.** What is the general condition of office equipment? Is it used to full advantage?

(f) **Operations and control.** What exceptional cases are dealt with, and how are they dealt with? Are there bottlenecks in operations; if so, what can be done to ease them?

There are many items about which facts ought to be obtained, and so the systems investigators should begin by drafting a **checklist of points** before they start asking questions.

This 'top-down' approach **focuses first on management needs** and ignores operational needs until later on. Top management's needs in controlling the organisation are of great importance in systems design.

1.1 Interviews

FAST FORWARD

Interviews can be an effective method of fact finding, although they can be time consuming and therefore expensive.

Interviews with members of staff can be an effective method of fact finding, although they can be **time consuming** for the analyst, who may have several to conduct, and therefore expensive.

(a) In an interview, **attitudes** not apparent from other sources may be obtained.

(b) **Immediate clarification** can be sought to unsatisfactory/ambiguous responses.

(c) Interviews **require a response** – some staff may ignore a questionnaire.

(d) A well-conducted interview should provide staff with some reassurance regarding the upcoming change.

Some **guidelines** to consider when conducting fact-finding interviews are explained below.

(a) The interviewer may be dealing with many individuals each with different attitudes and personalities. The approach to each interview should be adapted to suit the individual interviewee.

(b) The interviewer should be **fully prepared**, having details of the interviewee's name and job position, and a plan of questions to ask.

(c) **Employees ought to be informed** before the interview that a systems investigation is taking place, and its **purpose explained**.

(d) The interviewer must ask questions at the **level appropriate** to the employee's position within the organisation.

(e) The interview should be allowed to develop into a **conversation** whereby the interviewee offers his opinions and suggestions, but the focus must remain on what the interview hopes to achieve.

(f) The interviewer must not **jump to conclusions** or confuse opinions with facts, accepting what the interviewee has to say (for the moment) and refraining from interrupting.

(g) The interviewer should gain the **interviewee's confidence** by explaining what is going on. This confidence may be more easily obtained by allowing the interview to take place on the interviewee's 'home ground' (desk or office). The purpose of note taking should also be explained.

(h) If possible, the interviewer may find it helps understanding to move **progressively** through the system, for example interviewing operational staff first, then supervisors, then managers.

(i) The interview should be **long** enough for the interviewer to obtain the information required and to ensure an understanding of the system, but **short** enough to ensure that concentration does not wander.

(j) The interview should be **concluded** by a résumé of its main points and the interviewer should **thank** the interviewee for their time.

Question — Fact finding interviews

Draw up a checklist of dos and don'ts for conducting fact-finding interviews.

Answer

A useful checklist for **guidance in conducting interviews** is suggested by Daniels and Yeates in *Basic Training in Systems Analysis* as follows:

Do	Don't
Plan	Be late
Make appointments	Be too formal or too casual
Ask questions at the right level	Interrupt
Listen	Use technical jargon
Use the local terminology	Confuse opinion with fact
Accept ideas and hints	Jump to conclusions
Hear both sides	Argue
Collect documents and forms	Criticise
Check the facts back	Suggest
Part pleasantly	

1.2 Questionnaires

The use of **questionnaires** may be useful whenever a **limited** amount of **information** is required from a **large number of individuals** or where the individuals or **geographically dispersed**.

1.2.1 Designing a questionnaire

When designing a questionnaire, the following guidelines should be considered.

(a) Questionnaires should **not contain too many questions** (people tend to lose interest quickly and become less accurate in their answers).

(b) They should be **organised in a logical sequence**.

(c) Ideally, they should be designed so that each question can be answered with a limited range of answers, such as **'yes' or 'no'** or a 'tick' in a numbered box eg 1 = Strongly agree, 4 = Strongly disagree.

(d) They should be **tested independently** before being issued. This should enable the systems analyst to establish the effectiveness of the questions.

(e) Questionnaires should take into account the **sensitivity** of individuals in respect of any threat to their job security, change of job definition etc.

(f) Employees ought to be informed of the questionnaire's **purpose**. This should remove any staff suspicion and hopefully ensure a good proportion of sensible responses.

(g) Question design is a very important issue. Questions should obtain the specific information necessary for the study, but should not be worded in such a way as to influence the response given.

(h) Questionnaires must not be too long – a questionnaire of many pages is likely to end up in a 'pending' tray indefinitely, or worse, the bin.

1.2.2 Advantages of questionnaires

(a) Questionnaires may be used as the **groundwork for interviews** with some respondents being interviewed subsequently.

(b) Many respondents find questionnaires **less imposing than interviews** and may therefore be more prepared to express their opinion.

(c) Staff may prefer **anonymity**. This should result in greater honesty, but has the disadvantage of preventing follow-up of uncompleted questionnaires, and of 'interesting' responses.

(d) There is **less chance** of the interviewer attempting to **'put words into the mouth'** of the interviewees rather than let the interviewee think for themselves.

(e) Questionnaires enable users dispersed over a **wide geographical area** to be questioned by the use of email or website.

Questionnaires, by themselves, are useful for gathering specific information. In a systems development context, it is likely that further methods of gathering information, such as interview or observation, would also be required.

1.3 Observation

> **FAST FORWARD** **Observation** may be used to check facts obtained by interview or questionnaire. Staff may work differently to the answers provided in interviews and specified in written policies and procedures.

An analyst, after establishing the methods and procedures used in the organisation, may wish to undertake further investigation through **observing operations**.

The observer must remember that staff may act differently simply because they know they are being observed – this is a difficult problem to overcome as observing staff without their knowledge may not be **ethical**.

1.4 Facilitated user workshops

> **FAST FORWARD** **Facilitated user workshops** are often used in systems analysis to help establish and record user requirements.

A workshop is a meeting with the emphasis on **practical exercises.** User workshops are often used in systems analysis to help establish and record user requirements.

At a user workshop, user input is obtained by the analyst to analyse business functions and define the data associated with the current and future systems. An outline of the proposed new system is produced, which is used to design more detailed system procedures.

Depending on the complexity of the system, the workshop may devise a **plan for implementation**. More complex systems may conduct a workshop early in the design stage and hold a later workshop with the aim of producing a **detailed system model. Prototyping** may be used at such a workshop to prepare preliminary screen layouts.

User workshops should be facilitated by a **facilitator.** The facilitator co-ordinates the workshop activities with the aim of ensuring the objectives of the session are achieved.

The facilitator would most likely be a systems analyst with excellent **communication** and leadership skills. The skills of the person in this role are critical to the success of the workshop.

Many user workshops also utilise a **scribe**. The scribe is an active participant who is responsible for producing the outputs of the workshop. The scribe may use a **CASE tool**.

1.5 Document review

An analysis of existing **system documentation** should help the analyst estimate future processing requirements and volumes.

The systems analyst must investigate the **documents** that are used in the system for input and output. One way of recording facts about document usage is the **document description form**, which is simply a standard form which the analyst can use to describe a document.

This may be a wide ranging investigation, using for example organisation charts, procedures manuals and standard operational forms.

One risk, however, is that **staff do not follow** documented policies and procedures or that these documents have **not been properly updated**. Document review should therefore be used in tandem with one or more other investigative techniques.

An analysis of documents, together with historical operational data, should help the analyst estimate future processing requirements and volumes.

1.6 Existing computerised systems

Existing computer systems can provide much information relevant to the requirements for a new computerised system. Areas where an existing system could provide useful information include:

- File structures
- Transaction volumes and processor speed
- Screen design
- User satisfaction and user complaints
- Help-desk/Information centre records
- Causes of system crashes

It is important to remember however that a duplicate of the existing system is not required. The aim is to produce a better system – which is likely to involve changes to existing working methods.

1.7 Requirements creep

If user requirements are investigated and established effectively, an accurate picture should be established of what the new system should achieve. This should prevent a common problem occurring later in the project, the problem of 'requirements creep'.

Requirements creep refers to the situation where users appear to change their requirements throughout the development process. Requirements creep may be due to actual changes in user requirements, but it is often caused by an inaccurate original system specification.

2 Modelling the system

When information has been obtained about the current system, the systems analyst has to make sense of it. To make sense of an information system, the systems analyst will create one or more models.

The same approaches to modelling are used for defining the current system and also for developing a new or improved system. The approaches to systems modelling described in this chapter are therefore also relevant to systems development, which is described in the next chapter.

There are three broad approaches to systems modelling:

(a) A **process-oriented approach**, which focuses on the processes that occur in the system.

(b) A **data-oriented approach**, which focuses on the data that is used in the system and how data is inter-related.

(c) An **object-oriented approach**, which defines a system in terms of classes (groups of similar objects) and objects. An object combined both data and processing.

Each of these approaches to modelling is described briefly in this chapter. You need to understand the techniques and approach to modelling for each method, because you may be required to construct your own simple model in the examination.

3 Process modelling: data flow diagrams

> **FAST FORWARD**
>
> **Process models** may be used to model business systems. Two examples of process models are **data flow diagrams** and **flowcharts**.

Business systems (which may include manual and computerised components) involve the input, processing and output of data. Process models may be used to model business systems and to show the movement and processing actions data is subjected to.

The syllabus refers to two process models, Data flow diagrams (DFDs) and flowcharts. We will look at both.

3.1 Data flow diagrams (DFD)

As its name suggests, a data flow diagram is used to model the flow of data within a system and how the data is processed. Four symbols are used in data flow diagrams as shown below.

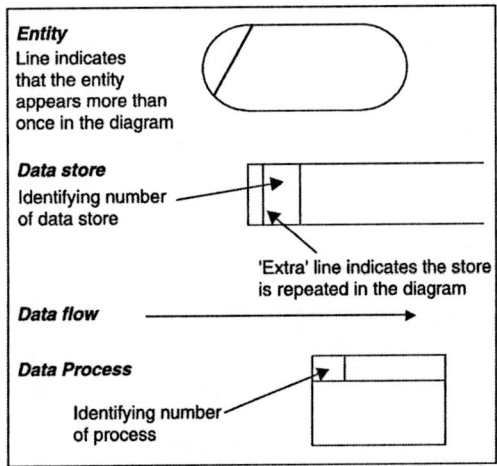

Key terms

An **external entity** is a **source** or **destination** of data which is considered **external to the system** (not necessarily external to the organisation). It may be people or groups who provide data or input information or who receive data or output information.

A **data store** is a point which receives a data flow and holds data. Most data stores would be either digital (ie computer files) or paper.

A **data flow** represents the movement or transfer of data from one point in the system to another.

Data processes involve data being used or altered. The processes could be manual, mechanised or computerised.

A data flow is any **movement of data or information**. This could include a product code, employee name or salary. When a data flow occurs, a copy of the data transferred may also be retained at the transmitting point.

A process could involve **changing the data** in some way, or simply using the data. For example, a mathematical computation or a process such as sorting would alter data, whereas printing data out does not change data – the process makes the same data available in a different form.

DFDs may be drawn to represent different levels of detail. The top level (least detailed) diagram would show one process only. The source of the data for this process, and its destination(s) are also shown. This type of diagram is known as a **Level-0 DFD**, or a Context diagram.

The Level-0 DFD may be 'exploded' into a more detailed data flow diagram, known as a **Level-1 DFD**. Further detail can be represented on a **Level-2 DFD**, and so on until all individual entities, stores, flows and processes are shown.

The diagram below illustrates how **levels of DFDs** are built up.

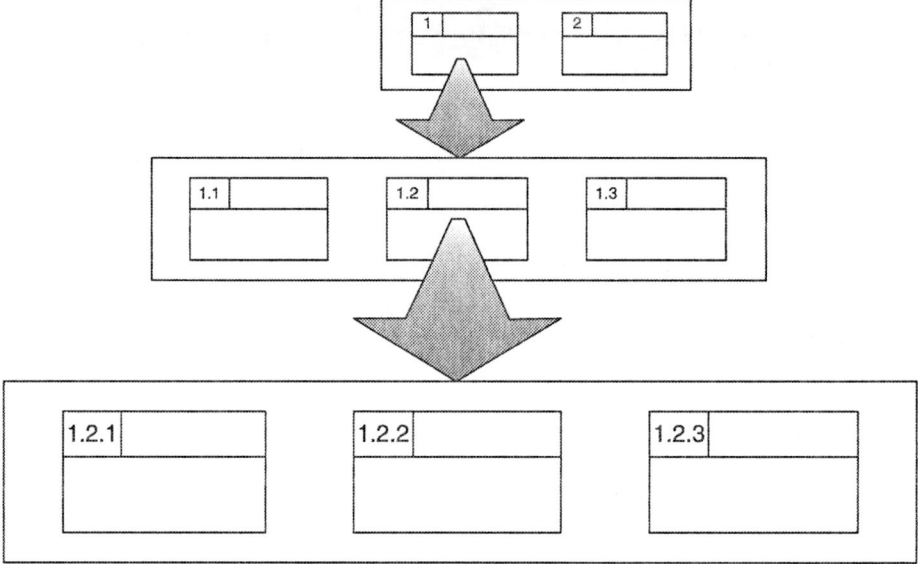

3.2 Example: Data flow diagram

The example used here is a system used for purchasing in a manufacturing company. Three data flow diagrams are shown; each is prepared to record a certain level of detail.

3.2.1 Level-0 DFD (context diagram)

The Level-0 DFD or context diagram would show the source of the purchasing process, its destination and the inputs and outputs. (Data stores are not shown on Context diagrams).

The central box represents the purchasing system as a whole. In this case only one external entity is shown. In some cases more than one entity will be required, but a context diagram will only ever show one process.

Note that we are only showing flows of data. The physical resources (the goods supplied) can be shown (by means of broad arrows ⇨), but this tends to overcomplicate the diagram.

8: SYSTEMS MODELLING

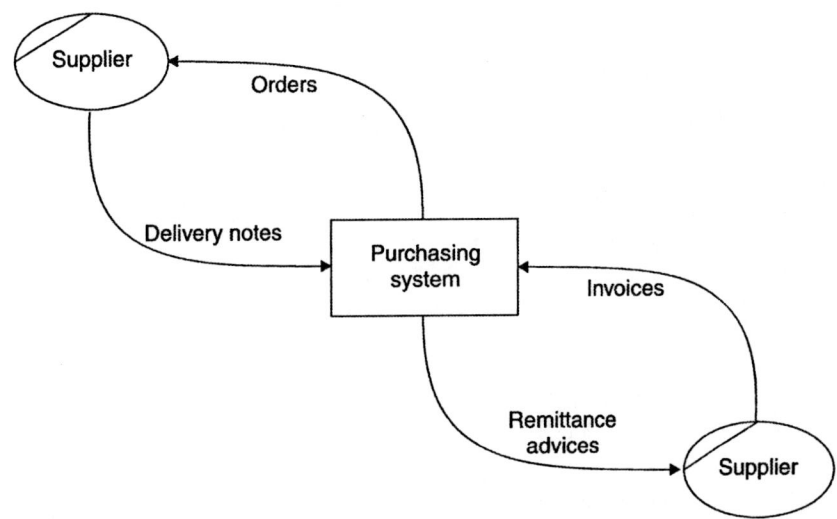

Exam focus point

If you are required to draw a Data Flow Diagram in the exam the level of detail required may be established by the information you are asked to model. For example, you might be required to first produce a Level-0 DFD, and then to provide underlying detail in a Level-1 DFD.

3.2.2 Level 1 DFDs

Within the purchasing system as a whole in this organisation there are two **subsystems**: the **Stores department** places requests for purchases and accepts delivery of the goods themselves; the **Purchasing department** places orders, and receives and pays invoices.

A **Level-1 DFD** for the **purchasing department** is shown below. GRN means goods received note.

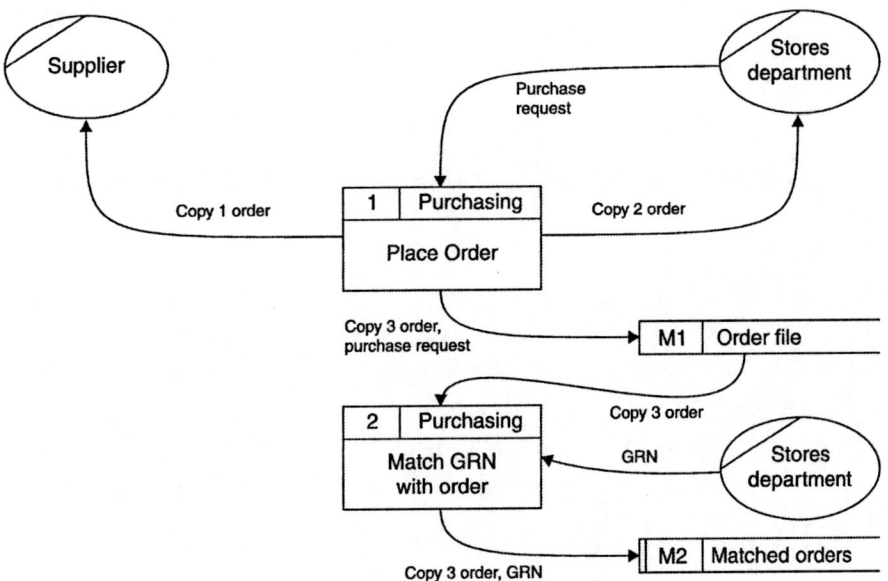

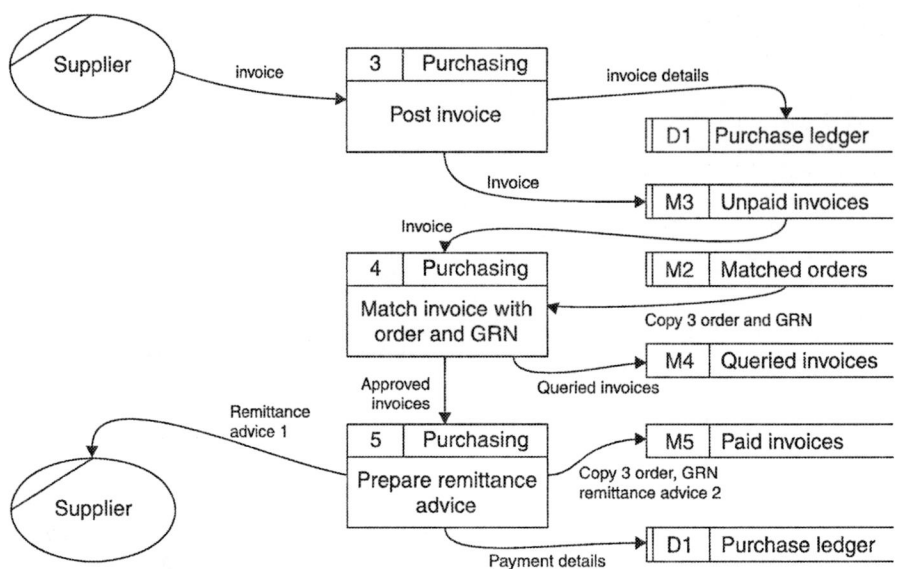

Notes

1. Some analysts prefer to also show a **system boundary**. This usually involves drawing a single line around the diagram enclosing everything except the Entities (ie all Entities would be shown outside the system boundary). This reflects the point-of-view that although Entities interact with the system, the focus of the model is the process that occurs inside the system boundary.

2. If a boundary was added to the diagram above, the two Stores department entity symbols and the three Supplier entity symbols would be shown outside the system boundary. They may also be referred to as 'External entities' – this refers to being external to the process being focussed on rather than necessarily being external to the organisation. Other analysts prefer not to show a boundary – you should be aware of what the boundary is in case you are presented with a diagram that includes a boundary.

3. Each process is numbered, but this is only for ease of identification: the numbers are not meant to show the strict sequence of events.

4. Each process box has a heading, showing where the process is carried out or who does it. The description of the process should be a clear verb like 'prepare', 'calculate', 'check' (not 'process', which is too vague).

5. The same entity or store may appear more than once on the same diagram (to prevent diagrams becoming overly complicated with arrows crossing each other). When this is done an additional line is put within the symbol. The supplier entity and several of the data stores have extra lines for this reason.

6. Data stores are given a reference number (again sequence is not important). Some analysts like to use 'M' with this number if it is a **manual** store, and a 'D' if it is a digital or **computerised** store.

3.2.3 Level-2 DFDs

A **separate** DFD (Level-2) could be prepared for **each of the numbered processes** shown in the Level 1 DFD. This is known as decomposing a process.

For example, the diagram below shows the data flows for process 1, Place Order.

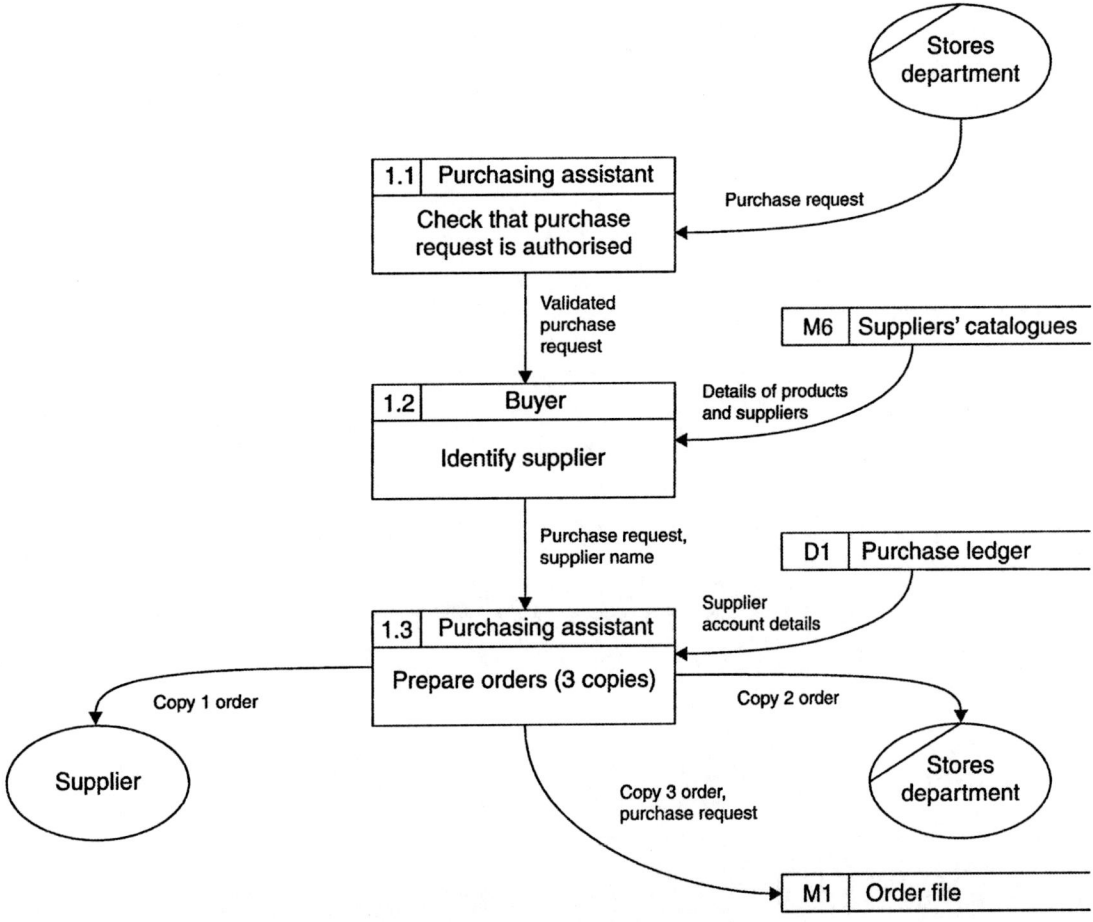

In turn, box 1.1 could be **further decomposed** in a Level-3 DFD, with processes 1.1.1, 1.1.2 and so on, and box 1.2 could be decomposed into processes 1.2.1, 1.2.2 etc.

4 Process modelling: flowcharts

Flowcharts are another type of a process model. Flowcharts use special shapes to represent different types of actions or steps in a process. Lines and arrows show the sequence of the steps, and the relationships among them.

Below are examples of commonly used flowcharting symbols. You should remember though that different people and organisations may use different symbols, or may use only some of the symbols below. Factors such as the complexity of the process being modelled and simple personal preference play a part.

Exam focus point

In an examination, if you draw a flowchart you should provide a Key that explains the symbols you use. You should ensure your diagram is clear, logical – and able to be understood by the marker. Before the exam, ensure you are proficient in at least one of either DFDs or Flowcharts.

Flowcharting symbols

Start/End

This symbol marks the starting or ending point of the system.

Action or process

A box can represent a single step ('add two cups of flour'), or an entire sub-process ('make bread') within a larger process.

Document

A printed document or report. This symbol is not always used – it depends upon the level of detail required in the model.

Decision

A decision or branching point. Lines representing different decisions emerge from different points of the diamond.

Input/ Output

Represents material or information entering or leaving the system, such as customer order (input) or a product (output). Again, the use of this symbol is not consistent – some people may identify a customer placing an order at a retail counter as an action – others may identify it as Input.

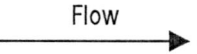
Flow

This arrow indicate the sequence of steps and the direction of flow.

4.1 Example: Flowchart

The following example shows how flowcharts may be used to model and re-design a process. Analysts studying the process of ordering at a fast-food chain noticed that many customers ordered a burger, fries and a drink. They decided they could streamline this process.

The 'before' and 'after' flowcharts follow. The flowcharts shown below include very little detail. More detailed models could be drawn if required – for example showing any receipt given to the customer and the customer leaving the counter. (In an examination the level of detail required would be able to be established from the information supplied.)

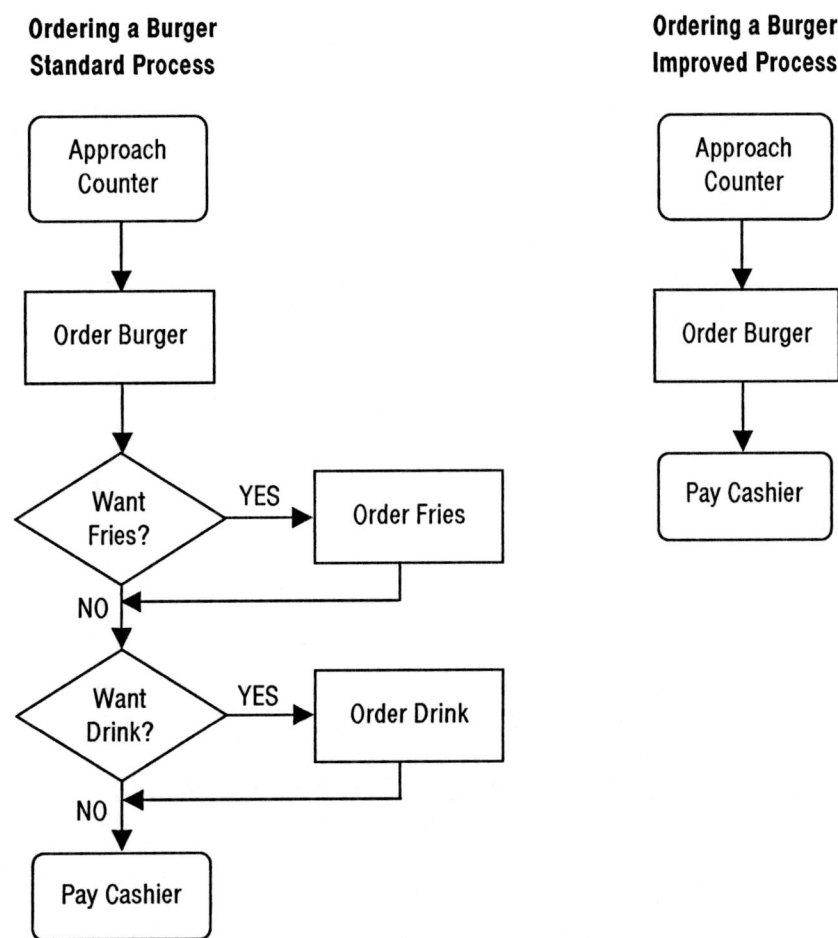

Exam focus point

There are some **variations in the use of flowcharting symbols**. For example, the chart above classifies 'Order Burger' as an Action. It could also justifiably be classified as an Input and a different symbol used.

In the examination always provide an explanatory **'key' explaining the notation used in your model**.

5 Decision tables

Decision tables (also known as cause-effect charts) are used as a method of demonstrating the effect of a process or action in a concise manner. Decision tables are useful in deciding what action to take if an error is identified when following a test script.

FAST FORWARD

Decision tables show the effect of a process, decision or action. They are often used in the context of system testing, but they can also be used to model individual decision processes within a system.

Before we look at an example in the context of system testing, we will work through a simple example to demonstrate the workings of a decision table. The purpose of a decision table is to set out the logic of how a decision is reached within a process.

(a) The table sets out the various conditions or situations that may exist.

(b) For each condition or situation that may exist, the table sets out what the decision or action (or actions) should be.

A decision table consists of four quadrants, as shown below.

Condition stub	Condition entry
Action stub	Action entry

(c) Condition stub: The condition stub contains a list of all the conditions that need to be tested in order to reach the decision Before we look at an example in the context of system testing, we will work through a simple example to demonstrate the workings of a decision table. A decision table consists of four quadrants, as shown below.

5.1 Example : A simple decision table

Suppose the decision is whether to wear a coat and take an umbrella when going outside. The decision may depend on two conditions, whether it is raining and whether the outside air temperature is cold.

(a) The conditions are a combination of rain and air temperature, and for each condition the only conditions are either Yes' or 'No'. Because a condition can only apply or not apply (Yes or No), the number of combinations (or 'rules') is 2^n, where n is the number of conditions.

In our example there are 2 conditions: the weather and the temperature, so n = 2 and the number of combinations is $2^2 = 4$. There are four columns for condition entries.

(b) The conditions can either have a Yes or No answer (Y or N). The four columns should be used to enter the four possible combinations of conditions that may apply. A letter Y can represent Yes, and the letter N can represent No.

(c) Now **consider what action** you would take if the condition(s) specified in each column applied. In this example, there are three possible actions – wear a coat, take an umbrella or do nothing. These are shown in the action stub of the table.

(d) For each combination of possible conditions, we indicate the decision or action in the action entry part of the decision table. In a simple decision table, the action can be indicated with a cross X.

The decision table can be constructed as follows.

Conditions				
Raining?	Y	Y	N	N
Cold?	N	Y	N	Y
Actions				
Wear coat		X		X
Take umbrella	X	X		
Take nothing			X	

In more complicated problems you may find that there are some combinations of conditions that are not possible. When this happens, the impossible combination of conditions can be omitted from the table, and the number of columns in the entry side of the table is reduced accordingly.

8: SYSTEMS MODELLING

Simple decision table

Jed decided to draw up a decision table demonstrating the decision-making process he executed when he woke up each day.

He identified three conditions, mirroring his early-morning thought processes, and two possible actions.

Conditions   *Is it 8 o' clock yet? Is it a weekday? Is it the weekend?*

Actions   *Get up. Stay in bed.*

If it is a weekday and if it is 8 o'clock, he will get up. Otherwise he will stay in bed.

Draw the decision table.

Answer

Jed identified three conditions, so we should expect to have a decision table with 8 (= 2^3) condition entries and so 8 columns.

	1	2	3	4	5	6	7	8
Is it 8 o' clock yet?	Y	Y	Y	Y	N	N	N	N
Is it a weekday?	Y	Y	N	N	Y	Y	N	N
Is it the weekend?	Y	N	Y	N	Y	N	Y	N
Get up		X						
Stay in bed			X			X	X	

Columns 1, 4, 5 and 8 do not have any Xs because it cannot be both a weekday **and** a weekend. These are impossible conditions. (In more complex decision situations it may only become clear that certain combinations are impossible once the table has been drawn up.)

In this example we can simplify the table by deleting columns 1, 4, 5 and 8.

5.2 Example: Decision table and system testing

Decision tables can be used to test the logic of a system as well as to describe a decision-making process.

- The **condition stub** specifies what is being tested.
- The **condition entry** shows the outcome for the condition stub, in the form of Ys and Ns.
- The **action stub** shows the range of possible actions.
- The **action entry** shows the action or actions that will be performed, in the form of Xs.

An accounts payable module includes a facility for entering invoices.

A test script has been devised to ensure the checks built-in to the 'Value' field within the Invoice entry field are operating as intended.

Possible actions to be taken depending on the results of testing have been laid out in a decision table, as shown below.

Invoice entry screen: value field testing	Rules															
	1	2	3	4	5	6	7	8	9	10	11	12	13	14	15	16
Field not empty	Y	N	Y	N	Y	N	Y	N	Y	N	Y	N	Y	N	Y	N
Numeric values only	Y	Y	Y	Y	Y	Y	Y	Y	N	N	N	N	N	N	N	N
Positive values only	Y	Y	Y	Y	N	N	N	N	Y	Y	Y	Y	N	N	N	N
Maximum value 999,999.99	Y	Y	N	N	Y	Y	N	N	Y	Y	N	N	Y	Y	N	N
Test passed	X															
Amend exit condition for Invoice entry screen		X		X		X		X		X		X		X		X
Amend field properties - maximum value			X	X			X	X			X	X			X	X
Amend field properties - minimum value					X	X	X	X					X	X	X	X
Amend field properties - numeric only									X	X	X	X	X	X	X	X

6 Logical data modelling: Entity Relationship Model

An **Entity Relationship Model (ERM)** (also known as an entity model or a logical data structure) provides an understanding of the logical data requirements of a system independently of the system's organisation and processes. An ERM is an example of a **static structure model**.

Instead of, or in addition to, a process-oriented approach to system modelling, a systems analyst may construct a model for the data within the system.

An **entity**, as we have seen, is an item (a person, a job, a business, an activity, a product or stores item etc) about which information is stored.

Key term

> An **entity** is any item, role, object, organisation, activity or person that is relevant to the data held in a system.

An **attribute** is a characteristic or property of an entity. It may also be called a data **item** or **field**. For a customer, attributes include customer name and address, amounts owing, date of invoices sent and payments received, credit limit etc.

The following table shows examples of common entities and their attributes.

Entities	Attributes
PRODUCT TYPE	**Product-type-code**, product-type-description
PRODUCT	**Product-code**, price, product-description
ORDER LINE (= individual line in an order)	**Product-code, order-no**, order-quantity, *customer-no
ORDER	**Order-no**, order-date, *customer-no
CUSTOMER	**Customer-no**, name, address, *region-code, *customer-category-code
SALES REGION	**Region-code**, region-description
CUSTOMER CATEGORY	**Customer-category-code**, customer-category-description

Key:	
ENTITY TYPE NAME:	**Keyfield**, *foreign-key-field, other-fields

8: SYSTEMS MODELLING

Key term

> An **Entity Relationship Model (ERM)** (also known as an **entity model** or a **logical data structure**) provides an understanding of the logical data requirements of a system independently of the system's organisation and processes.

FAST FORWARD

> An **ERM** may show **three** main **types of relationship**:
> - One-to-one relationship **(1:1)**
> - One-to-many relationship **(1:M)**, could be expressed as a Many-to-one relationship **(M:1)**
> - Many-to-many relationship **(M:M)**

The following relationships may be identified between attributes and entities.

6.1 One-to-one relationship (1:1)

With a one-to-one relationship, an entity is related to only one of the other entity shown. For example, a one-to-one relationship exists between **company** and **finance director**. The model below represents the situation were one specific company employs one specific finance director. (These diagrams are sometimes called Bachmann diagrams.)

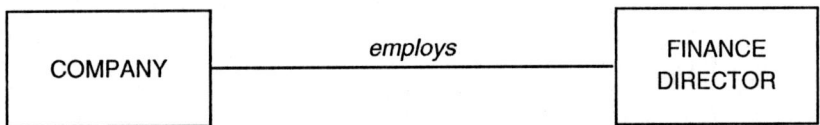

6.2 One-to-many relationship (1:M)

For example, the relationship **employs** also exists between the **company** and all their **directors**. This **company** employs many **directors**, a **director** is employed by, at most, one **company**.

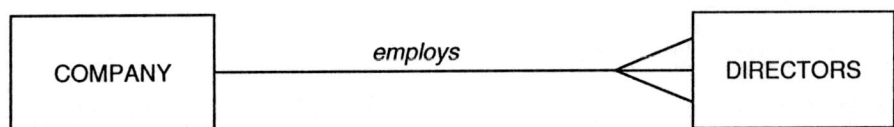

6.3 Many-to-one relationship (M:1)

This is really the same as the previous example, but **viewed from the opposite direction**. For example, a **sales manager** reports to at most one **sales director**. A **sales director** is reported to by many **sales managers**.

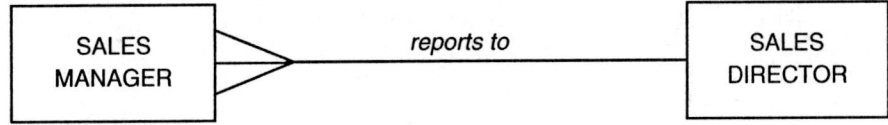

6.4 Many-to-many relationship (M:M)

The relationship between **product** and **part** is **many-to-many**. A product is composed of many parts, and a part might be used in many products.

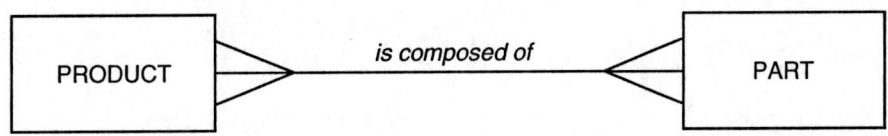

When analysing relationships the correct classification is important. If the one-to-many relationship customer order lists products is incorrectly described as one-to-one, a system designed on the basis of this ERM might allow an order to be entered for one product and one product only. Also, a product could only appear on one order.

6.5 Example: Building an ERM

The following diagram models part of a warehousing and despatch system. It indicates that:

(a) A customer may make many orders, and an order is for only one customer.

(b) That an order form can contain several order lines, and an order line appears on only one order.

(c) That each line on the order form can only detail one product, but that one product can appear on many order lines.

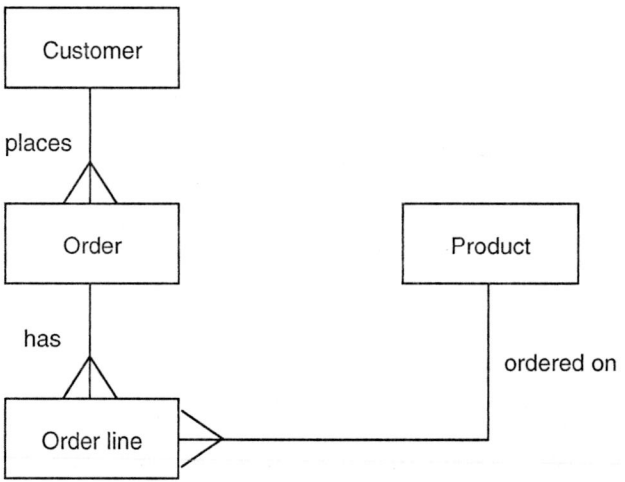

Question   ERM

Convert the text shown in the following table into an ERM.

Entity	Relationship	Entity
Customer	Places many	Orders
Order	Has many	Deliveries
Product	Is ordered on many	Orders
Product	Is ordered on many	Purchase orders
Supplier	Receives many	Purchase orders
Invoice	Is for one	Delivery
Customer	Receives many	Invoices

Answer

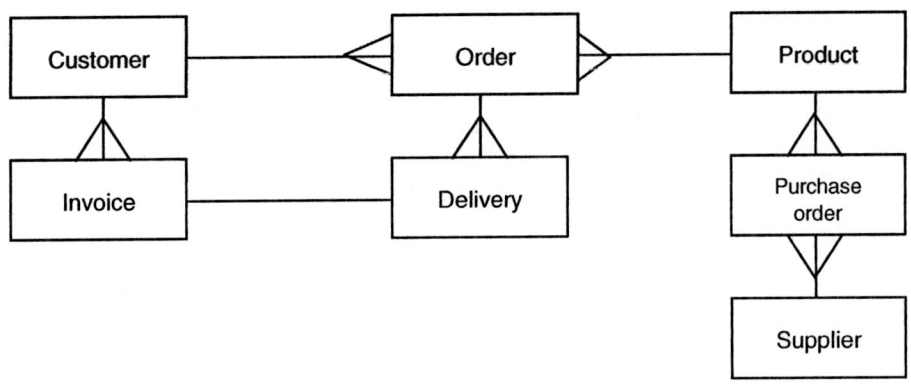

7 An event model: Entity Life History

As we have seen, **Entity Relationship Models** take a **static** view of data. We will now look at a modelling tool that focuses on events that happen to an entity.

FAST FORWARD

> An **Entity Life History (ELH)** documents the events that happen to an entity. An ELH is a type of **Event model**.

Key term

> An **Entity Life History (ELH)** is a diagram of the **events** that happen to an **entity**. An entity life history gives a **dynamic** view of the data.

Data items do not always remain unchanged – they may come into existence by a specific operation and be destroyed by another. For example, a customer order forms part of a number of processes, and is affected by a number of different events. At its simplest, an entity life history displays the following structure.

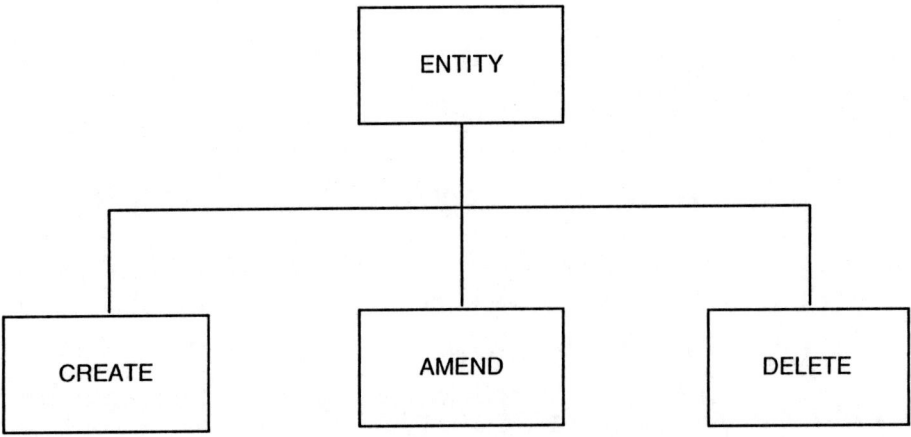

Entity life histories identify the various states that an entity can legitimately be in. It is really the functions and events which cause the state of the entity to change that are being analysed, rather than the entity itself.

The following notation rules are used for entity life histories.

(a) Three symbols are used. The main one is a rectangular box. Within this may be placed an asterisk or a small circle, as explained below.

(b) At the top level the first box (the 'root node') shows the entity itself.

(c) At lower levels the boxes represent events that affect the life of the entity.

(d) The second level is most commonly some form of 'create, amend, delete', as explained earlier (or birth, life, death if you prefer). The boxes are read in **sequence** from top to bottom and left to right.

(e) If an event may affect an entity many times (**iteration**) this is shown by an **asterisk** in the top right hand corner of the box. A customer account, for example, will be updated many times.

(f) If events are alternatives (**selection**) – for example accept large order or reject large order – a **small circle** is placed in the top right hand corner.

Note. Three types of process logic referred to above:

- Sequence
- Iteration (or repetition)
- Selection

Here is a very simple example.

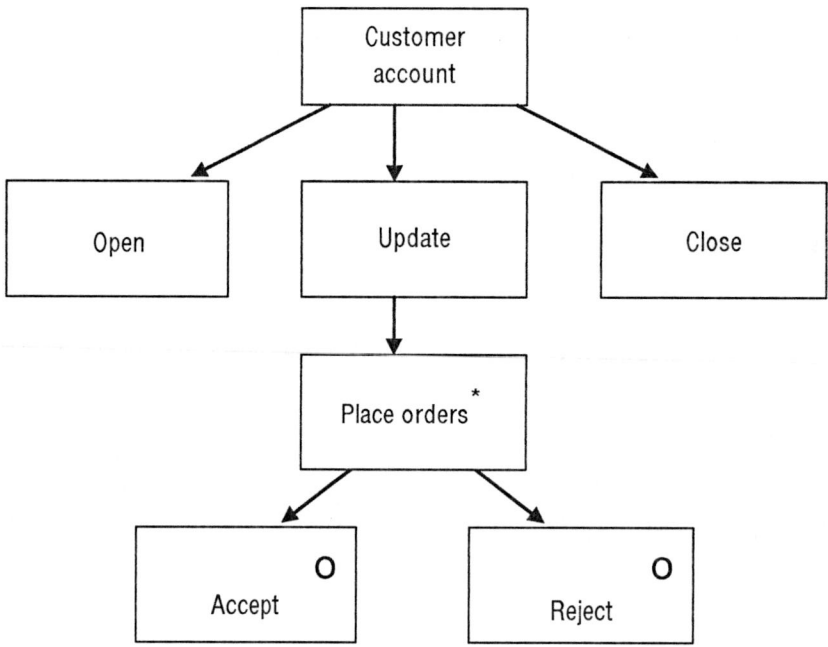

8 Object-oriented approach to modelling

An object-oriented (OO) approach to system modelling is based on classes of objects, and individual objects within each class.

A system is defined as a set of different objects that combine to accomplish various tasks

(a) Each object carries out actions when asked to do so (when prompted by a message).
(b) Each object maintains its own data.

In process-oriented modelling, a system is defined in terms of a set or series of procedures that will combine with data, and the procedures are modelled separately from the data. In OO modelling, each object has data that 'belongs' to it and also contains 'methods' or procedures that process this data.

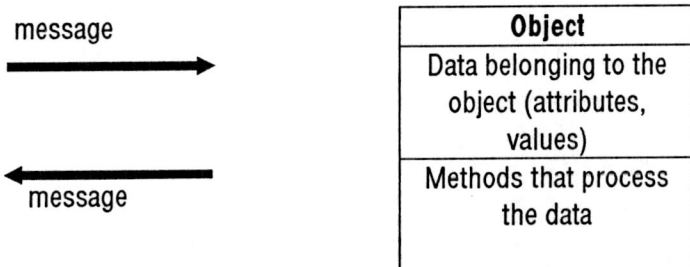

Messages are the means by which objects interact with each other.

Objects are problem-domain objects, GUI (graphical user interface) objects or data access objects (relating to interaction with a database)

(a) Problem-domain objects are specific to the particular system application. For example, classes of objects may be customers, sales orders and products. Within each class of objects there are individual objects – for example, individual customers, sales orders and products.

(b) GUI objects are objects that provide an interface between the user of the system and the system itself. They are items on a computer screen for entering instructions to the system.

In an OO approach to system modelling, the model identifies:

- The attributes for each object
- The 'methods' for each object

The example below illustrates this process.

Problem domain objects	Attributes	Methods
Customer	Name, address, telephone number	Set name; Set address; Add new order for customer
Order	Order number, date, amount	Set date, calculate order amount, add product to order, schedule delivery
Product	Product number, description, price	Set description, add to order, get price
GUI objects		
Button	Size, shape, colour, location on screen	Click, enable, disable, hide, show
Label	Size, shape, colour, location on screen, text	Set text, get text, hide, show

OO modelling goes on to define how objects respond to messages, and how they interact with each other.

This chapter has now provided a description of the various system modelling methods that may be used. The next chapter will describe different approaches to system development and how the methods of modelling are used within these approaches.

Chapter roundup

- During the **systems investigation** the project team examines the inputs, outputs, processing methods and volumes, controls, staffing and costs of the current system. This may involve fact finding by means of questionnaires, interviews, observation and reviewing documents.
- **Interviews** can be an effective method of fact finding, although they can be time consuming and therefore expensive.
- The use of **questionnaires** may be useful whenever a **limited** amount of **information** is required from a **large number of individuals**, or where the individuals are **geographically dispersed**.
- **Observation** may be used to check facts obtained by interview or questionnaire. Staff may work differently to the answers provided in interviews and specified in written policies and procedures.
- **Facilitated user workshops** are often used in systems analysis to help establish and record user requirements.
- An analysis of existing **system documentation** should help the analyst estimate future processing requirements and volumes.
- **Process models** may be used to model business systems. Two examples of process models are **dataflow diagrams** and **flowcharts**.
- **Decision tables** show the effect of a process, decision or action. They are often used in the context of system testing, but they can also be used to model individual decision processes within a system.
- An **Entity Relationship Model (ERM)** (also known as an entity model or a logical data structure) provides an understanding of the logical data requirements of a system independently of the system's organisation and processes. An ERM is an example of a **static structure model**.
- An **ERM** may show **three** main **types of relationship**:
    - One-to-one relationship **(1:1)**
    - One-to-many relationship **(1:M)**, could be expressed as a Many-to-one relationship **(M:1)**
    - Many-to-many relationship **(M:M)**
- An **Entity Life History (ELH)** documents the events that happen to an entity. An ELH is a type of **Event model**.

Quick quiz

1. List three advantages of conducting user interviews to establish user requirements, rather than sending users a written questionnaire.
2. List three advantages of using a written questionnaire to establish user requirements, rather than conducting user interviews.
3. Give two examples of a process-oriented model.
4. What four symbols are used in data flow diagrams?
5. List the three types of relationship an Entity Relationship Model (ERM) may portray.
6. What three types of process logic may an Entity Life History (ELH) show?
7. Distinguish between logical design and physical design of a system.

Answers to quick quiz

1. Any three of the following (you may have thought of other valid points). In an interview, attitudes not apparent from other sources may be obtained. Interviews allow immediate clarification to be sought to unsatisfactory/ambiguous responses. Interviews require a response – some staff may ignore a questionnaire. A well-conducted interview should provide staff with some reassurance regarding the upcoming change.

2. Any three of the following (you may have thought of other valid points). Using questionnaires allows focus to be maintained – interview discussions may lose focus. Questionnaires can be 100% anonymous. Questionnaires can be sent to widespread locations very cheaply. People may find questionnaires less imposing than interviews and may therefore be more prepared to express their opinion.

3. Data flow diagrams and flowcharts.

4. The four symbols used in Data Flow Diagrams are:

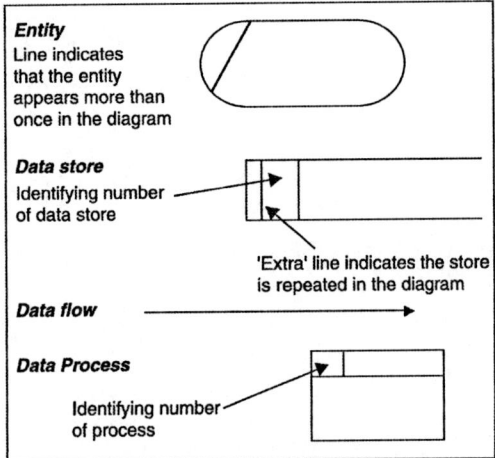

5. One-to-one (1:1), one-to-many (1:M) (or many-to-one M:1), and many-to-many (M:M).

6. Sequence, iteration, selection.

7. Logical design is concerned with the purpose and processes of the system. Physical design involves the physical aspects including hardware, software, data storage and presentation.

   In general, the logical design is more relevant to the systems analyst while programmers will require details of physical design.

PART B INFORMATION SYSTEMS

End of chapter question

Showex (AIA November 2007)

Showex is a growing company that organises and manages medium and large-scale exhibitions and country shows. Showex has recently gained the contract to organise a 3-day Country and Leisure Show in the southern area. The Show is expected to enjoy an average visitor number of 25,000 per day and it will have numbers of event participants and have a large number of exhibitors; exhibitors will demonstrate their services and sell their wares to Show visitors who also watch Show events.

The tasks of accepting applications for exhibition stands and booking participants for a wide range of demonstrations and events has recently begun. The exhibitors and participants apply to attend for 1, 2 or all 3 days of the show and pay a fee to Showex which varies with the number of days, type of activity, size, format and location of the stand and space required at the Show site.

As an IT employee of Showex, you have been asked to monitor and study Showex's current manual approach to booking exhibitors and participants with a view to helping with the computerisation of the company's pre-exhibition administration in the near future. Your observations to date include:

- A participant/exhibitor applies to Showex with full details of their requirements
- Showex staff process this order (some applications require amendment due to timing and space limitations)
- Reference is made to Showex's price list and previous customers records file in processing each order
- Ultimately the participant/exhibitor is sent an acceptance and an invoice – a copy of the latter is also sent to Showex's accounting department
- Then two months prior to the actual Show taking place, participants/exhibitors are sent a package of information indicating the space reserved, for which day(s), a brochure and exhibition plan; this issue is referred to as the joining instructions

Required

(a) Prepare and present a Level 0 data flow diagram to indicate the overall data processing structure of the pre-show administration that Showex applies. Your Level 0 diagram should include one process, one data source, two data sinks and two data stores. **(8 marks)**

(b) Showex intends to use the following when it computerises this administration:

    Data sources/sinks   – Participants/exhibitors (customers)
                                  – Accounting department
                                    – Joining instructions

    Data processes   – Generation of orders
                                    – Generation of invoices
                                    – Generation of joining instructions

    Data stores   – Existing customers
                                    – Price list
                                    – Company order store
                                    – Joining instructions

Present a Level 1 data flow diagram to show the processing structure with this detail. **(11 marks)**

(c) Briefly explain the role of a data dictionary in supporting the work of a systems analyst, and provide as an example the typical contents for the data item 'invoice' in the above Showex example.

(6 marks)

(Total = 25 marks)

Systems development and organisation

Topic list	Syllabus reference
1 Systems development lifecycles	9.9
2 The waterfall model	9.9
3 The spiral model	9.9
4 Systems development methodologies	9.9
5 SSADM	9.9
6 Soft Systems Methodology (SSM)	9.9
7 Jackson System Development (JSD)	9.9
8 Object-Oriented (OO) approach to system design	9.9
9 Software support for the systems development process	9.9
10 User involvement	9.9
11 The feasibility study	9.9

Introduction

In this chapter we consider the **approaches to systems development** which may be used on Information Systems projects. These approaches are often referred to as **lifecycle models**.

Later we look at how **methodologies** can assist the development process. The chapter concludes by exploring the impact of **software development tools**.

PART B INFORMATION SYSTEMS

1 Systems development lifecycles

Key term

> The term **systems development lifecycle** describes the stages a system moves through from inception until it is discarded or replaced.

In the context of information systems projects a **distinction** can be made between the **project lifecycle** and the **systems development lifecycle**. As a project has a definite end it is unlikely that **ongoing maintenance** would be included in the scope of a project, but it does fall within our definition of the system development lifecycle.

In the early days of computing, systems development was **piecemeal**, involving automation of existing procedures rather than forming part of a planned strategy. The development of systems was **not properly planned**. The consequences were often poorly designed systems, which cost too much to make and which were not suited to users' needs.

This led to the development of systems development lifecycle models. Among the first models was one developed by the National Computing Centre in the 1960s. This **disciplined approach** to systems development identified several stages of development.

Stage	Comment
Identification of a problem or opportunity	This involves an analysis of the organisation's information requirements.
Feasibility study	This involves a review of the existing system and the identification of a range of possible alternative solutions. A feasible (technical, operational, economic, social) solution will be selected – or a decision not to proceed made. We cover feasibility studies, in detail, later in this chapter.
Systems investigation	A fact finding exercise which investigates the existing system to assess its problems and requirements and to obtain details of data volumes, response times and other key indicators.
Systems analysis	Once the workings of the existing system have been documented, they can be analysed. This process examines why current methods are used, what alternatives might achieve the same, or better, results, and what performance criteria are required from a system.
Systems design	This is a technical phase which considers both computerised and manual procedures, addressing, in particular, inputs, outputs, program design, file design and security. A detailed specification of the new system is produced.
Systems implementation	This stage carries development through from design to operations. It involves acquisition (or writing) of software, program testing, file conversion or set-up, acquisition and installation of hardware and 'going live'.
Review and maintenance	This is an ongoing process which ensures that the system meets the objectives set during the feasibility study, that it is accepted by users and that its performance is satisfactory.

In the early 1970s a similar systems development lifecycle model was published by Royce – the waterfall model. The sequential approach described by the National Computing Centre and the waterfall model is sometimes referred to as the **'traditional approach'**.

FAST FORWARD

> The term **systems development lifecycle** describes the stages a system moves through from inception until it is discarded or replaced. Traditional lifecycle models such as **Royce's waterfall model** break the systems development process into **sequential stages** – with the output from a stage forming the input to the following stage.

9: SYSTEMS DEVELOPMENT AND ORGANISATION

Exam focus point

You may be asked to discuss one or more of the stages in the systems development lifecycle in an exam.

2 The waterfall model

Royce's waterfall model (like the National Computing Centre model) breaks the systems development process into sequential stages – with the output from a stage forming the input to the following stage. The model is shown in the following diagram.

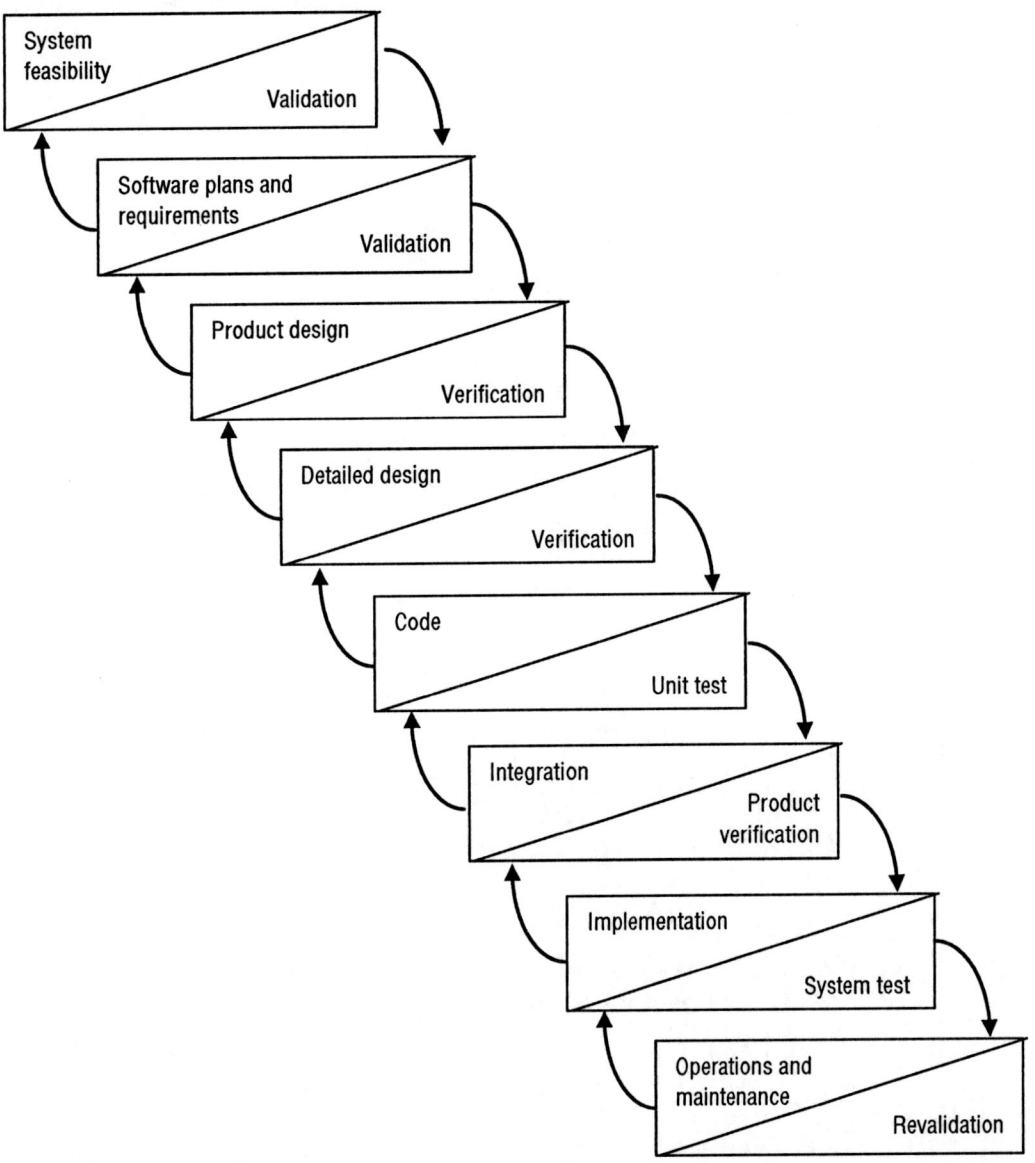

As shown on the diagram, each stage is divided into two parts – the actual work associated with the stage followed by a procedure to check what has been done. **Verification** in this context is concerned with ensuring required specifications have been met ('Have we built the system in the correct way?'). **Validation** is concerned with ensuring the system is fit for its operational role ('Have we built the correct product?').

The term 'waterfall model' is now used to describe any system development model that is made up of a number of sequential stages – regardless of the name given to the stages. It works reasonably well where the system requirements are well understood by users and developers.

2.1 Drawbacks of the waterfall approach

The waterfall approach is an efficient means of computerising existing procedures within easily defined processing requirements. It produces systems modelled on the manual systems they are replacing.

Sequential models restricted user input throughout much of the process. This often resulted in substantial and costly modifications late in the development process. It becomes increasingly difficult and expensive to change system requirements the further a system is developed.

Time overruns were the norm. The sequential nature of the process meant a hold-up on one stage would stop development completely – contributing to time overruns. Time pressures and lack of user involvement often resulted in a poor quality system and blame for the developers.

Operations and maintenance are treated as if the activity had a distinct start and end. Maintenance is in fact on-going and open-ended. **Birrel** and **Ould** devised **the 'b' model** to address this issue.

The 'b' model

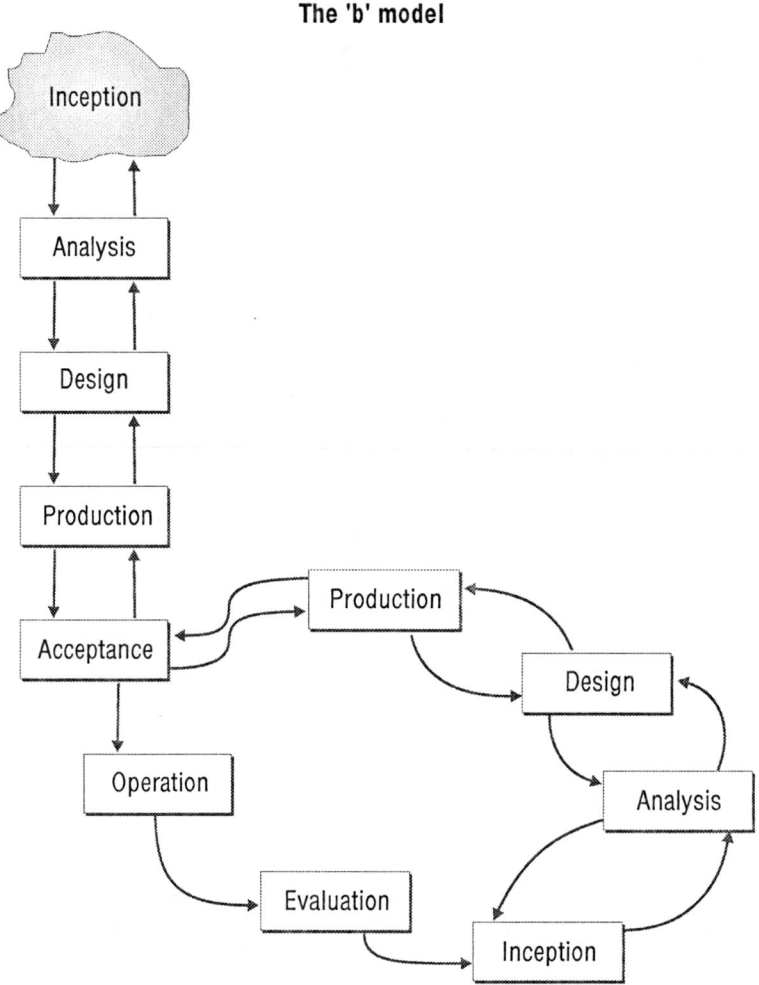

The 'b' model shows that enhancements or changes to the system (ie system maintenance) are made through a series of cycles that follow the same sequence as the original system development. Each change will go through the stages of feasibility, analysis, design production and operation.

3 The spiral model

FAST FORWARD

The **spiral approach** involves carrying out the same activities over a number of cycles in order to clarify requirements and solutions.

When developing systems where requirements are difficult to specify it is unrealistic to follow a sequential process which relies on getting things correct at each stage of development before starting subsequent activities. In these more complex situations the spiral approach is appropriate.

The spiral model represents an evolutionary approach to systems development. It involves carrying out the same activities over a number of cycles in order to clarify requirements and solutions.

The first spiral model was developed by **Boehm**. The model is shown below.

Boehm's spiral model

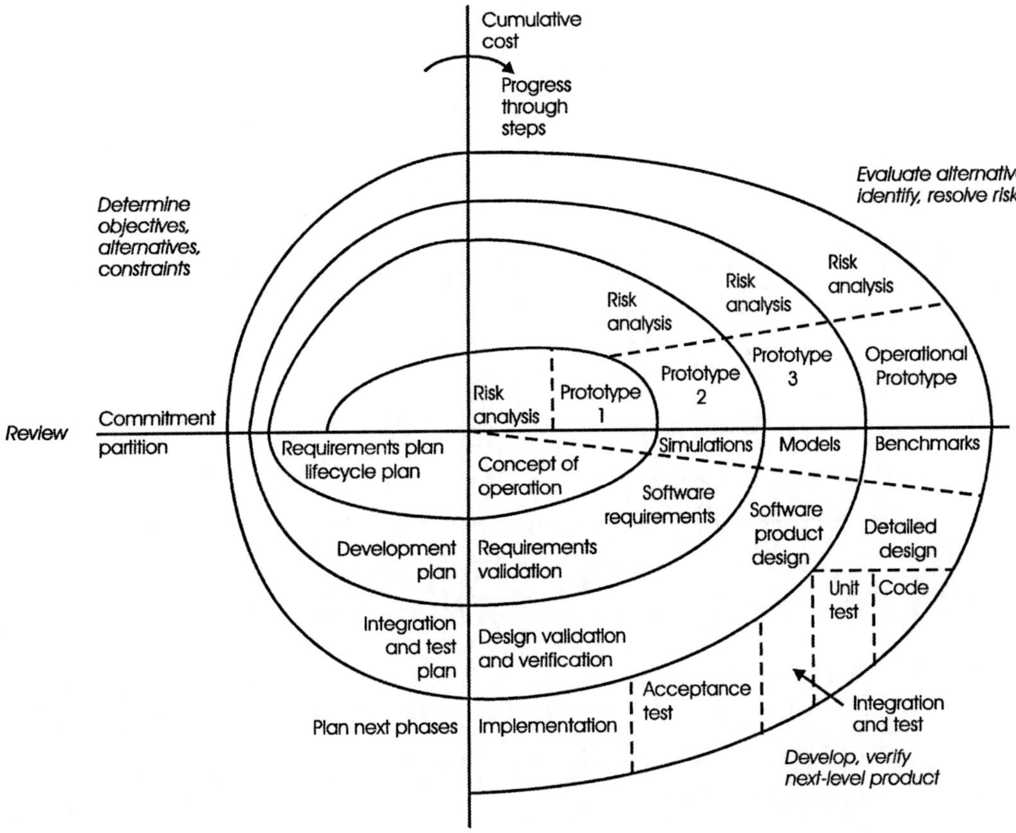

The development process starts at the centre of the spiral. At the centre requirements are not well defined. System requirements are refined with each rotation around the spiral. The longer the spiral, the more complex the system and the greater the cost.

The model is divided into **four quadrants**.

(a) **Top left**

   (i) Objectives determined
   (ii) Alternatives and constraints identified

(b) **Top right**

   (i) Alternatives evaluated
   (ii) Risks identified and resolved

(c) **Bottom right**

  (i) System development
  (ii) Covers the activities described in the waterfall model (including implementation)

(d) **Bottom left**

  The next phase in the development process is planned

Boehm's spiral model of system development includes the processes of objective setting and risk management that we have previously identified as key elements of project management.

The spiral approach aims to avoid the problems of the waterfall model (lack of user involvement, long delays). It is usually used in conjunction with prototyping which we look at later in this chapter.

Before looking at different methods for system development, it will be useful to recognise that when a new system is developed, it is now usual to consider the **logical design** of the system before its **physical design**.

3.1 Logical design

Logical design involves describing the purpose of a system – **what the system will do**. Logical design does not include any specific hardware or software requirements – it is more concerned with the **processes** to be performed.

Models such as Data Flow Diagrams (for example) or written descriptions may be used to show and explain what a system will do. In some cases logical design may also include the identification of the main data files that will be required by the system (eg these may be established from a DFD).

3.2 Physical design

Physical design refers to the actual 'nuts and bolts' of the system – it includes technical specifications for the hardware and software required. Physical design involves the following tasks.

(a) **Initial physical design** – obtaining the design rules from the chosen system and applying them to the logical data design drawn up in the previous stages.

(b) Further define the **processing** required. For instance requirements for **audit, security and control** are considered, such as **controls over access** to the system; controls **incorporated within programs** (eg data validation, error handling); and **recovery procedures**, in case processing is interrupted.

(c) **Program specifications** are created. These provide in detail exactly what a particular program is supposed to achieve.

(d) Program specifications are assessed for their **performance** when implemented. It should be possible to estimate the times that programs will take to run.

(e) File and data specifications are **finalised**.

(f) **Operating instructions** are drawn up (user documentation). These will include such items as error correction and detailed instructions for operators and users (eg the sort of screen format that will appear).

4 Systems development methodologies

The waterfall and spiral models of IT system development are general forms of development method. In practice there are many different methods, some more well-known than others.

Key term

> A systems development **methodology** is a collection of procedures, techniques, tools and documentation aids which will help systems developers in their efforts to implement a new information system.

The various systems development methods share several characteristics.

Characteristic	Comment
Separation of logical from physical design	The initial focus is on business benefits – on what the system will achieve (the logical design). Physical design and implementation issues are looked at later.
User involvement	Users' information requirements determine the type of data collected or captured by the system. Users are involved throughout the development process.
Diagrams as documentation	Diagrams rather than text-based documentation are used as much as possible to ensure the focus is on what the system is trying to achieve – and to aid user understanding of the process.
Data-driven	Some structured methods focus on data items regardless of the processes they are related to. The type of data within an organisation is less likely to change than either the processes which operate on it or the output information required of it.
Defined structure	Most methodologies prescribe a consistent structure to ensure a consistent and complete approach to the work. For example, the Structured Systems Analysis and Design Method (**SSADM**) suggests five modules: Feasibility, Requirements Analysis, Requirements Specification, Logical Systems Specification and Physical Design.

FAST FORWARD

A **methodology** is a collection of procedures, techniques, tools and documentation aids which are designed to help systems developers in their efforts to implement a new system. Methodologies are usually broken down into phases.

4.1 Advantages and disadvantages of methodologies

The **advantages** of using a methodology are as follows.

(a) Detailed **documentation** is produced.

(b) **Standard methods** allow less qualified staff to carry out some of the analysis work, thus **cutting the cost** of the exercise.

(c) Using a standard development process leads to **improved system specifications**.

(d) Systems developed in this way are **easier to maintain and improve**.

(e) **Users are involved** with development work from an early stage and are required to sign off each stage.

(f) The emphasis on **diagramming** makes it easier for relevant parties, including users, to **understand** the system than if purely narrative descriptions were used.

(g) The structured framework of a methodology **helps with planning**. It defines the tasks to be performed, sets out when they should be done and identifies an end product. This allows control by reference to actual achievements rather than to estimates of progress.

(h) A logical design is produced that is **independent of hardware and software**.

(i) Techniques such as data flow diagrams, logical data structures and entity life histories **allow information to be cross-checked** between diagrams and ensure that the system delivered does what is required.

The use of a methodology in systems development also has **disadvantages**.

(a) It has been argued that methodologies are ideal for analysing and documenting processes and data items at an operational level, but are perhaps **inappropriate for information of a strategic nature** that is collected on an ad hoc basis.

(b) Some are a little **too limited in scope**, being too concerned with systems design, and not with their impact on actual work processes or social context of the system.

In this chapter, **four approaches or methodologies will be described**:

(a) Structured Systems Analysis and Design Method (SSADM)
(b) Soft systems methodology
(c) Jackson System Development (JSD) method
(d) Object-oriented systems analysis (OOA) and design (OOD)

5 Structured Systems Analysis and Design Method (SSADM)

The SSADM is a waterfall method of systems development. SSADM was developed for the UK government Treasury Department.

SSADM makes use of three methods of system modelling:

(a) **Logical data modelling**: modelling the data requirements of the system. Data is separated into entities (things that the system needs to record data or information about) and relationships (associations between the entities). Entity Relationship models can be used for this purpose.

(b) **Data flow modelling**: identifying and modelling how data moves around the information system. Data Flow Diagrams are used for this purpose.

(c) **Entity behaviour modelling**: modelling the events that affect each entity during its life, and the sequence in which these events occur. Entity Life History modelling can be used for this purpose.

5.1 The stages of SSADM

SSADM has seven stages.

Stage	Module	Comment
0	Feasibility study	A feasibility study is described later. The main objectives of a feasibility study are to consider: • Technical feasibility: whether the project is technically feasible • Financial feasibility: whether the organisation can afford to develop and implement the system • Organisational feasibility: whether the new system will be compatible with current practices • Ethical feasibility: whether the impact of the new system will be ethically and socially acceptable
1	Investigation of current system	This is an important stage in SSADM. This involves the use of interviews, questionnaires, observation and examination of existing documentation for the system.

Stage	Module	Comment
2	Business system options	Having investigated the current system, the systems analyst must devise a general or broad design for the new system. Initially several different options are considered. The different options may vary in terms of the degree of automation, the degree of centralisation or decentralisation in processing, impact and cost-benefit. Each option may be documented with a Level 1 DFD and a logical data structure model. The system user selects one of the options suggested.
3	Requirements specification	This stage involves defining the data and processes that will be used in the new system. A detailed logical specification for the system is designed and documented. This documentation includes data flow diagrams, entity-relationship models and entity life histories for the new system.
4	Technical system options	This stage considers different options for the technology for the new system, such as the hardware architecture, any networks that will be required, software to use in the system, staffing required and the form of the human-computer interface. At the end of this stage, the technology for the new system is selected.
5	Logical system design	The logical system design specifies the main methods of interaction between humans (the users) and the computer, in terms of items such as menu structures and command structures.
6	Physical design	The logical data structure is converted to actual physical data specifications, for example the 'real' hardware and software. The logical data structure is converted into a 'physical' database structure. The end result is a system specification that programmers can use to write the software for the new system.

6 Soft systems methodology (SSM)

The term 'soft' systems methodology (SSM) is used to distinguish this approach to systems development with a 'hard' systems approach. A soft systems approach considers the system conceptually, whereas a hard approach considers the system in terms of a computer system and/or a communications system or another type of physical system.

SSM is consistent with approaches to systems development such as SSADM, which look at the logical aspects of a system, and SSM may be used at the early stage of systems development.

In particular SSM is useful for defining a complex system in which there is a problem, but there is no agreement about what the exact nature of the problem is. SSM is also used as an early 'front end' stage in computer systems design and is consistent with approaches to systems development such as SSADM, which look at the logical aspects of a system.

Originally, SSM was defined as a seven-stage method by Peter Checkland. This methodology can be applied to any soft system, and is not unique to information systems. The seven stages in SSM were:

1. Enter the problem situation
2. Express the problem situation
3. Formulate **root definitions** for relevant systems
4. Build Conceptual Models of Human Activity systems. In this stage of SSM, a simple conceptual model is produced for each 'stakeholder' in the system, which represents the stakeholder's view of what the system does and the activities that happen within it.
5. Compare these models with the 'real world'
6. Define changes to the system that are both desirable and feasible
7. Take action to improve the 'real world'

Stages 2, 3 and 4 are iterative processes that are repeated until an acceptable broad conceptual design for the system is reached.

6.1 Root definitions: CATWOE

The root definition of a relevant system should include specification of several features or criteria, which have been given the mnemonic CATWOE. The letters CATWOE stand for:

C	Clients	Who are the beneficiaries or 'victims' of this system? Who would benefit or suffer from its operations?
A	Actors	Who are responsible for implementing the system and making the system function?
T	Transformation	What transformation does this system produce? What are the inputs to the system and what transformation do they go through to become outputs?
W	Weltanschaung or 'World view'	What point of view (view of the world) justifies the existence of this system?
O	Owner	Who has the authority to abolish this system or change its measures of performance?
E	Environmental constraints	What are the environmental constraints on this system?

7 Jackson System Development (JSD)

Jackson System Development (JSD) is another approach to system development, where the sequence of events within the system is an important aspect of the system. SSADM was developed out of JSD in the 1970s.

JSD is based on the view that the 'real world' system contains objects and entities that engage in activities that occur sequentially in time (either once only, or repetitively).

Systems development using JSD goes through several stages.

(a) **Modelling stage**. The modelling phase identifies the sequential events affecting each entity in the system, and the attributes of each event. It also involves the construction of an Entity Life History for each entity in the system.

Michael Jackson, writing in the Wiley Encyclopaedia of Software Engineering (1992) used a library system to illustrate the JSD approach. Within a library system the following sequential events occur:

Event		Attribute
ACQUIRE	Library acquires a book	Book ID, date, ISBN
CLASSIFY	A book is classified	Book ID, class
JOIN	A new member joins the library	Member ID, name, address, date
LEAVE	A new member leaves the library	Member ID, name, date
BORROW	A member borrows a book from the library	Book ID, member ID, date
RETURN	A member returns a book to the library	Book ID, member ID, date
SELL	The library sells one of its books	Book ID, Date, price

In this example, there are two entities in the system, Members, and Books. For each of these entities, an Entity Life History model is constructed. Conceptually, JSD has identified the actions in a system, which entities are affected by each action, and the sequence in which they occur.

(b) **Network phase**. In the network phase of JSD, a set of sequential processes is defined that models the 'real world', and the connections between these processes within the system are shown in a System Specification Diagram (SSD). This stage of the system development also specifies the inputs and outputs for each process.

(c) **Implementation phase**. In this stage of JSD, there are two main issues: how the processes in the system specification are to be scheduled and how the data (typically in a database) is to be organised and managed.

8 Object-Oriented (OO) approach to system design

It was explained in the previous chapter that in object-oriented systems design (OOD), the system is modelled in terms of objects and the system model provides the basis for programming the system and the construction of an object-oriented database design (a relational database structure).

The development of a system involves:

(a) Identifying classes, objects, attributes and methods.

(b) Developing 'use cases'. A use case is a description of a sequence of events that result in the system doing something 'useful'. Each use case describes one or more scenarios', and each scenario explains how the system should interact with its users ('actors'). Users may be end users of the system or another system.

(c) Producing system sequence diagrams (SSDs) for each scenario in a use case, showing the events that external actors generate and the sequence in which they occur.

9 Software support for the systems development process

There are a number of software tools that can be used to facilitate the systems development process. We will examine three of the most widely used software tools – CASE tools, fourth generation languages and prototypes.

9.1 Computer Aided Software Engineering (CASE) tools

Computer Aided Software Engineering tools are used in systems development to automate some development tasks, such as the production of documentation, and to provide an efficient tool to control developmental activities.

PART B INFORMATION SYSTEMS

Key term

> **CASE tools** are software tools used to automate some tasks in the development of information systems eg generating documentation and diagrams. The more sophisticated tools facilitate software prototyping and code generation.

FAST FORWARD

> A CASE tool may be used to support the construction and maintenance of a system model – often allowing the construction of a prototype.

There is a range of CASE tools available. Some focus on certain phases of development such as analysis and design, others may be used throughout the complete development lifecycle.

The range of facilities offered by CASE tools is shown in the following table.

Stage of system development project	Possible use of CASE tools
Project initiation	Generate project schedules in various formats
Analysis and design	• Produce diagrams eg flowcharts, DFDs, ERMs, ELHs • Generate data dictionary
Design (logical and physical)	• Produce system model diagrams • Data structures • Automate screen and report design
Implementation	• Installation schedule • Program code generator
Maintenance	• Version control • Change specification and tracking

CASE tools can be grouped into Upper CASE tools (sometimes referred to as analysts' workbenches) and Lower CASE tools (sometimes referred to as programmers' workbenches).

9.1.1 Upper CASE tools (analysts' workbenches)

Upper CASE tools are geared towards automating tasks associated with systems analysis. They include:

(a) **Diagramming tools** that automate the production of diagrams using a range of modelling techniques.

(b) **Analysis tools** that check the logic, consistency and completeness of system diagrams, forms and reports.

(c) A **CASE repository** that holds all data and information relating to the system. The **Data dictionary** records all data items held in the system and controls access to the repository. The dictionary will list all data entities, data flows, data stores, processes, external entities and individual data items.

9.1.2 Lower CASE tools (programmers' workbenches)

Lower CASE tools are geared towards automating tasks later in the development process (after analysis and design). They include:

(a) **Document generators** that automate the production of diagrams using a range of modelling techniques.

(b) **Screen and report layout generators** that allow prototyping of the user-interface to be produced and amended quickly.

(c) **Code generators** that automate the production of code based on the processing logic input to the generator.

9.1.3 Advantages of using CASE tools

Advantages of CASE include the following.

(a) **Document/diagram preparation** and amendment is quicker and more efficient.

(b) **Accuracy of diagrams** is improved. Diagram drawers can ensure consistency of terminology and maintain certain standards of documentation.

(c) **Prototyping** (see later in this section) is made easier, as re-design can be effected very quickly.

(d) **Blocks of code can be re-used.** Many applications incorporate similar functions and processes; blocks of software can be retained in a library and used (or modified) as appropriate.

9.1.4 Examples of CASE tools

Examples of CASE tools include Select's SSADM Professional, Rational's ClearCase and AxiomSys from STG.

Example 1: Automated diagram production

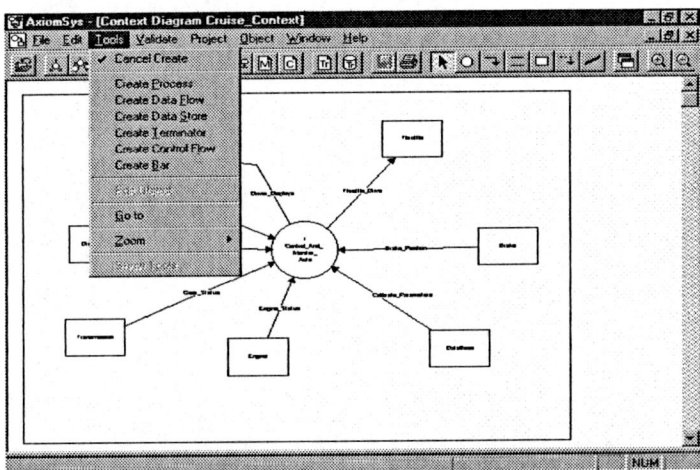

Example 2: Code generating and checking

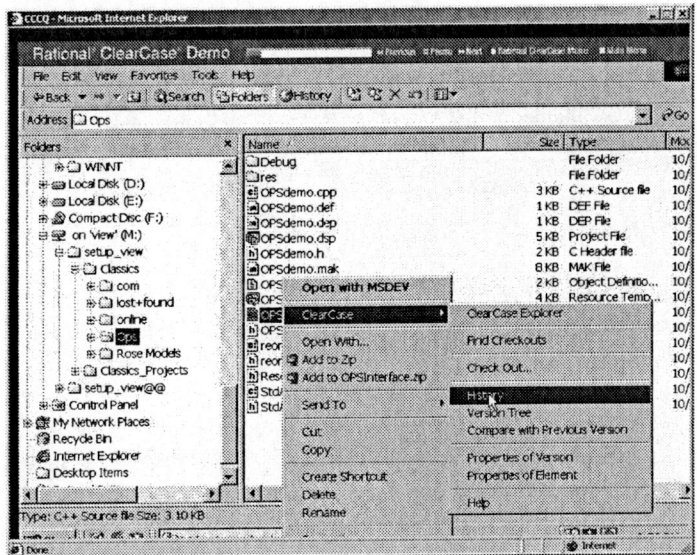

Example 3: Version/change control

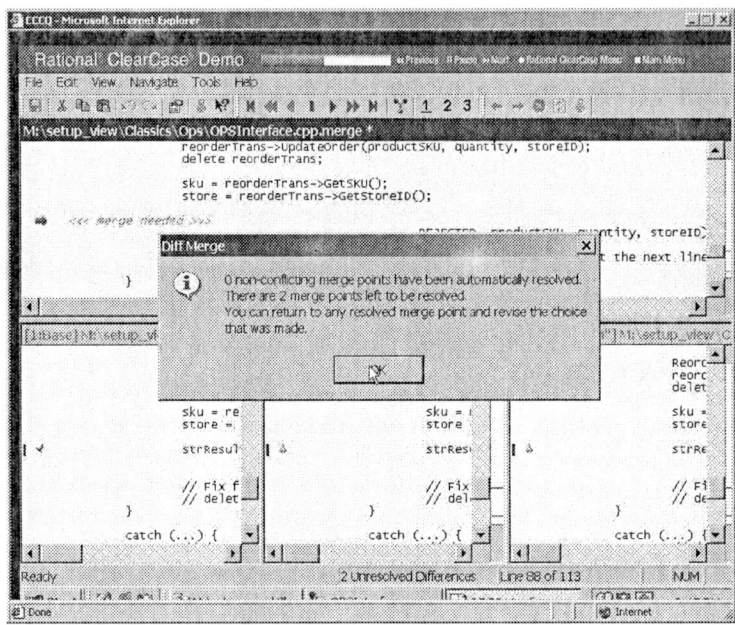

9.2 Fourth generation languages (4GLs)

As computer languages have developed over time, certain types of computer languages have become identified with a generation of languages. The four generations are explained in the following table.

Generation	Comment
First	Machine code. Program instructions were written for individual machines in binary form (a series of 1s and 0s).
Second	Assembly languages. Still machine specific, programs were written using symbolic code which made them easier to understand and maintain.
Third	High-level languages such as COBOL, BASIC and FORTRAN. These languages have a wider vocabulary of words, enabling commands to be closer to everyday language. Programs produced are able to be moved between similar computers.
Fourth	There is no formal definition of a Fourth Generation Language (4GL). Fourth-generation languages are programming languages closer to human languages than typical high-level or third generation languages. Most 4GLs use simple query language such as 'FIND ALL RECORDS WHERE NAME IS 'JONES''

A fourth generation language is a programming language that is easier to use than languages like COBOL, PASCAL and C++. Well known examples include **Informix** and **Powerhouse**.

Key term

A **Fourth Generation Language (4GL)** is a high-level computer language that uses commands that are closer to everyday speech than previous languages. 4GLs usually also include a range of features intended to automate software production.

A **4GL** enables programs to be constructed more quickly and allows greater flexibility in the development process.

Most fourth generation languages use a graphical user interface. Icons, objects, help facilities, pull down menus and templates present programmers with the options for building the software. Sections of code are often treated as components, which may be used (maybe with slight modifications) in a variety of applications.

A 4GL will often include the following features (many of these features could also be provided by a CASE tool):

- Relatively easy to learn and use
- Often centred around a database
- Includes a data dictionary
- Uses a relatively simple query language
- Includes facilities for screen design and dialogue box design
- Includes a report generator
- Code generation is often automated
- Documenting and diagramming tools

4GLs are often used to facilitate **object-oriented programming**. With object-oriented programming, programmers define the types of operations (functions) that can be applied to data structures (in programming, a data structure refers to a scheme for organising related pieces of information). In this way, the data structure becomes an object that includes both data and functions. In addition, programmers can create relationships between one object and another. For example, objects can inherit characteristics from other objects.

One of the principal advantages of object-oriented programming techniques over procedural programming techniques is that they enable programmers to create modules that do not need to be changed when a new type of object is added. A programmer can simply create a new object that inherits many of its features from existing objects. This makes object-oriented programs easier to modify (a group of objects with some common properties may be referred to as a **class**).

4GLs enable a more flexible approach to be taken to software production than under the traditional Systems Development Lifecycle. Using a 4GL, changes to the program design and to the code itself can be made relatively easily and quickly. This allows development to follow a pattern like the Spiral model, with users able to make amendments based on prototypes.

9.2.1 Examples taken from 4GLs

The following screenshots are taken from the Metamill 4GL.

Example 1: Automated diagram production

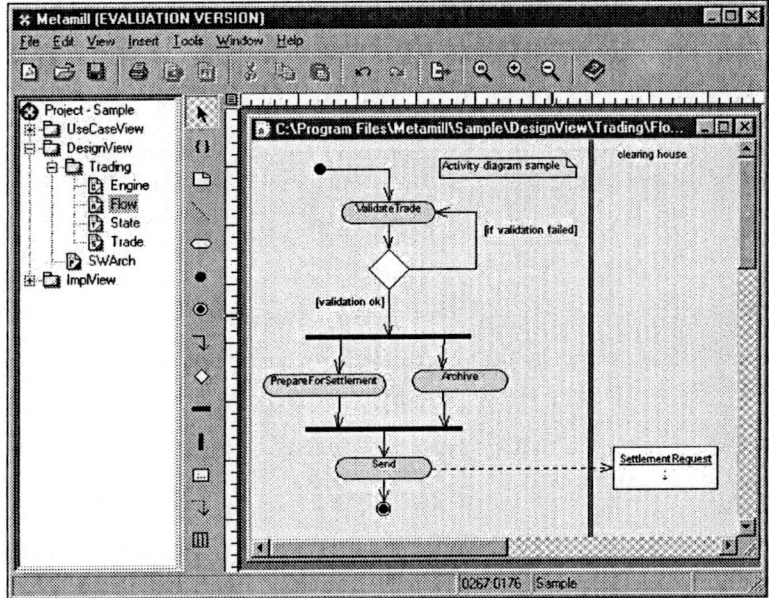

Example 2: Class properties window

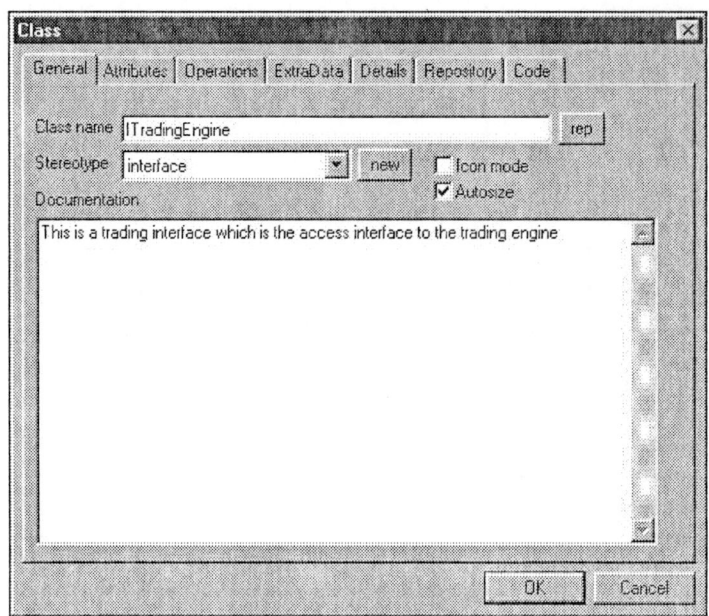

Exam focus point

An exam question could require you to distinguish between machine code, assembly language and high level languages.

9.3 Prototyping

The use of 4GLs, together with the realisation that users need to see how a system will look and feel to assess its suitability, have contributed to the increased use of **prototyping**.

Key term

A **prototype** is a model of all or part of a system, built to show users early in the design process how it is envisaged the completed system will appear.

As a simple example, a prototype of a formatted screen output from a system could be prepared using a graphics package, or even a spreadsheet model. This would describe how the screen output would appear to the user. The user could make suggested amendments, which would be incorporated into the next model.

FAST FORWARD

Prototyping enables programmers to write programs more quickly and allows the user to see a 'preview' of the system that is envisaged.

Using prototyping software, the programmer can develop **a working model of an application program quickly**. The model can then be checked against user needs and amended appropriately.

The prototyping process

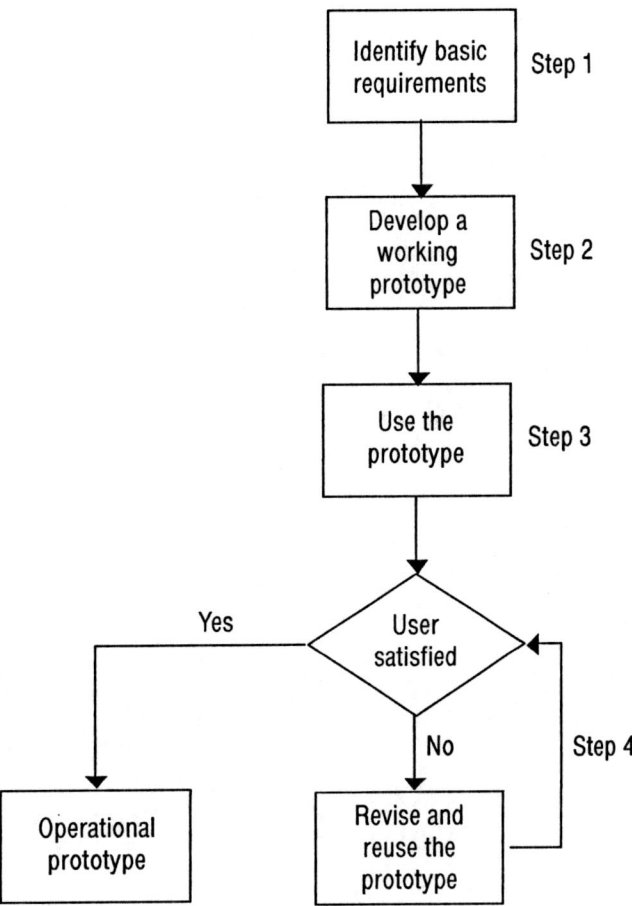

9.3.1 Advantages and disadvantages of prototyping

The **advantages** of prototyping.

(a) It makes it possible to present a 'mock-up' version of an envisaged system to users **before a substantial amount of time and money** have been committed. The user can judge the prototype before things have gone too far to be changed.

(b) The process facilitates the production of **'custom built' application software** rather than off-the-shelf packages which may or may not suit user needs.

(c) It makes **efficient use of programmer time** by helping programmers to develop programs more quickly. Prototyping may speed up the 'design' stage of the systems development lifecycle.

(d) A prototype does not necessarily have to be written in the language of the final system, so prototyping is not only a tool, but a **design technique**.

(e) A prototype may be a 'throwaway' design tool, but could also evolve into the final system.

Disadvantages of prototyping.

(a) Some prototyping tools are **tied** to a particular make of **hardware**, or a particular **database system**.

(b) It is sometimes argued that prototyping tools are **inefficient** in the program codes they produce, so that programs are bigger and require more memory than a more efficiently coded program.

(c) Prototyping may help users to steer the development of a new system towards an **existing system**.

(d) As prototyping encourages the attitude that changes and amendments are likely, some believe prototyping tools encourage programmers to produce programs quickly, but to neglect program quality.

10 User involvement

The importance of user involvement in the development process cannot be over-estimated. This section looks at a number of approaches intended to ensure that the required level of involvement is achieved.

10.1 Structured walkthroughs

FAST FORWARD

A **structured walkthrough** usually takes the form of a meeting in which the output from a phase or stage of development is presented to users for discussion and for formal approval.

Structured walkthroughs are a technique used (often in conjunction with SSADM) by those responsible for the design of some aspect of a system (particularly analysts and programmers) to present their design to interested **user groups** – in other words to 'walk' them through the design. Structured walkthroughs are **formal meetings**, in which the **documentation produced during development is reviewed and checked** for errors or omissions.

These presentations are used both to **introduce and explain** the new systems to users and also to offer the users the opportunity of **making constructive criticism** of the proposed systems, and suggestions for further amendments/improvements, before the final systems specification is agreed.

Users are involved in structured walkthroughs because their knowledge of the desired system is more extensive than that of the systems development personnel. Walkthroughs are sometimes referred to as **user validation**. A structured walkthrough has similarities with facilitated user workshops covered in Chapter 8.

10.1.1 The importance of signing off work

At the end of each stage of development, the resulting output is presented to users for their approval. There must be a **formal sign-off** of each completed stage before work on the next stage begins.

This **minimises reworking**, as if work does not meet user requirements, only the immediately preceding stage must be revisited. More importantly, it clarifies responsibilities and leaves little room for later disputes.

(a) If the systems developers fail to deliver something that both parties formally agreed to, it is the **developers' responsibility** to put it right, at their own expense, and compensate the user for the delay.

(b) If users ask for something extra or different, that was not formally agreed to, the developers cannot be blamed and **the user must pay** for further amendments and be prepared to accept some delay.

Question — Benefits of a structured walkthrough

What, besides identification of mistakes (errors, omission, inconsistencies etc), would you expect the benefits of a walkthrough to be?

Answer

(a) Users become involved in the systems analysis process. Since this process is a critical appraisal of their input, they should have the opportunity to provide feedback on the appraisal itself.

(b) The output from the development is shown to people who are not systems development personnel. This encourages its originators to prepare it to a higher quality and in user-friendly form.

(c) Because the onus is on users to approve the design, they are more likely to become committed to the new system and less likely to 'rubbish' it.

(d) The process focuses on quality of and good practice in operations generally.

(e) It avoids disputes about who is responsible for what.

10.2 Joint applications development (JAD)

FAST FORWARD

Joint Applications Development (JAD) describes a close partnership between users and developers.

Joint Applications Development (JAD) describes the partnership between users and system developers. JAD was originally developed by IBM to promote a more participative approach to systems development. The potential value to an organisation may be as follows.

(a) It creates a **pool of expertise** comprised of interested parties from all relevant functions.

(b) Reduced risk of systems being **imposed** by systems personnel.

(c) This **increases user ownership** and responsibility for systems solutions.

(d) Emphasises the **information needs of users** and their relationship to business needs and decision making.

There are a number of possible **risks** affecting the potential value of JAD.

(a) The relative **inexperience of many users** may lead to misunderstandings and possibly unreasonable expectations/demands on the system performance.

(b) The danger of **lack of co-ordination** leading to fragmented, individual, possibly esoteric information systems.

The shift of emphasis to applications development by end-users must be well managed and controlled. An organisation may wish to set up an **information centre** to provide the necessary support and co-ordination.

10.3 Rapid applications development (RAD)

FAST FORWARD

Rapid Applications Development (RAD) combines a less structured approach to systems development with the use of other tools such as prototyping.

Rapid Applications Development (RAD) can be described as a quick way of building software. It combines a managed approach to systems development with the use of other tools such as **prototyping**. RAD also involves the **end-user** heavily in the development process.

RAD has become increasingly popular as the pace of change in business has increased. To develop systems that provide **competitive advantage** it is often necessary to build and implement the system quickly.

RAD can create **difficulties for the project manager** as RAD relies to a certain extent on a **lack of structure** and control.

10.4 User groups

User groups enable users to **share ideas and experience** relating to a particular product; usually a software package.

User groups can provide valuable insights and suggestions when system upgrades are being considered.

PART B INFORMATION SYSTEMS

11 The feasibility study

FAST FORWARD

A **feasibility study** is a formal study to decide whether a project is viable. When considering an information systems project the study would investigate the type of system that could be developed to meet the needs of the organisation, and if it is possible to produce such a system within the relevant constraints.

Key term

A **feasibility study** is a formal study to decide what type of system can be developed which best meets the needs of the organisation. A study may be undertaken before a decision is taken to go ahead with a new system development, especially when the system is large and/or the new development will be expensive.

A feasibility study was mentioned earlier in this chapter as the first stage in the SSADM approach to system development. This chapter ends with a discussion of a feasibility study. This may help to provide a useful summary of the issues involved in systems development more generally.

11.1 The feasibility study team

A feasibility study team should be appointed to carry out the study (although individuals might be given the task in the case of smaller projects). It may be worthwhile employing a professional systems analyst to work with the team on larger projects.

(a) Members of the team should be drawn from the **departments affected by the project**.

(b) At least one person must have a **detailed knowledge of computers and systems design** (in a small concern it may be necessary to bring in a systems analyst from outside).

(c) At least one person should have a **detailed knowledge of the organisation** and in particular of the workings and staff of the departments affected. Managers with direct knowledge of how the current system operates will know what the **information needs** of the system are, and whether any proposed new system (for example an off-the-shelf software package) will do everything that is wanted. They are also most likely to be in a position to recognise **improvements that can be made in the current system**.

(d) It is possible to hire **consultants** to carry out the feasibility study, but their **lack of knowledge about the organisation** may adversely affect the usefulness of their proposals.

(e) Before selecting the members of the study group, the steering committee must ensure that they possess **suitable personal qualities**, eg the ability to be **objectively critical**.

(f) All members of the study group should ideally have some knowledge of information technology and systems design. They should also be encouraged to read as widely as possible and take an **active interest in current innovations**.

11.2 Identifying and selecting IS projects

A planned approach is needed when identifying and selecting new information systems projects. The following actions should be considered.

(a) IS projects almost always utilise IT. IT is critical to the success of many organisations. This means that an **IT strategy** should form a **core part of the overall corporate strategy** and should be developed/updated whenever the organisation's strategy is reviewed or as otherwise necessary. IT needs can then be identified in the context of **overall business needs**.

(b) Because IT is critical, it requires adequate **representation at senior management level**. It is no longer suitable for IT to be under the control of the managing director, finance director or computer centre manager. It really needs a separate Board level person responsible, such as an **Information**

Director or an **IS director**. This will help to ensure that IT is given adequate consideration at strategic level.

(c) The IT development can no longer function as a subsystem of accounting, administration or finance. It should be given **separate departmental or functional status** in the organisation with its own reporting lines and responsibilities.

(d) Once the IT department has been set up, its **funding** must be considered. A simplistic approach would be to treat it as an overhead; this is simple but inefficient. There are various approaches possible to the recovery of IT costs from user departments, and the IT department may even operate as a commercial concern providing services to third parties at a profit.

(e) A **strategic plan for the use of IT** should be developed. This should take in separate elements such as information technology and information systems. It should also acknowledge the importance of the organisation's information resource.

(f) If new computer systems are to be introduced regularly, the organisation may set up a **steering committee** to oversee **systems development**. A steering committee can also be set up for a one-off project. The role of the steering committee includes approving or rejecting individual projects and where appropriate submitting projects to the Board for approval. The composition and determination of terms of reference for the steering committee must be agreed.

(g) The **approach** of the organisation to individual projects must be decided. Will it follow the traditional **life cycle** or will it use a **methodology**? Commercial methodologies impose discipline on the development process.

(h) Procedures for **evaluating and monitoring performance** both during and after a project need to be put in place. Many methodologies require formal sign-off of each stage, but this does not obviate the need for good project management or for post-implementation evaluation.

(i) Details of the **systems development procedures** must be agreed. If a commercial methodology is used, many of these procedures will be pre-determined. Areas to be considered include the approach to **feasibility studies**, methods of **cost-benefit analysis**, **design specifications** and conventions, development **tools** and **techniques**, **reporting** lines, contents of standard **invitations to tender**, drawing up of **supplier conditions** and procedures for **testing** and **implementation**.

11.3 Conducting the feasibility study

Some of the work performed at the feasibility study stage may be similar to work performed later on in the development of the project. This is because both processes include the need to define the current situation or problem.

A **feasibility study** should be carried out before undertaking an information systems project because a new or amended system may:

(a) Be complicated and costly
(b) Disrupt operations during development and implementation (eg staff and management time)
(c) Have far reaching consequences in the way an organisation conducts future business
(d) Impact on organisation strategy and structure

11.3.1 Terms of reference

The **terms of reference for a feasibility study** group may be set out by a steering committee, the information director or the board of directors, and might consist of:

(a) To investigate and report on an existing system, its procedures and costs
(b) To define the systems requirements
(c) To establish whether these requirements are being met by the existing system
(d) To establish whether they could be met by an alternative system
(e) To specify performance criteria for the system

(f) To recommend the most suitable system to meet the system's objectives
(g) To prepare a detailed cost budget, within a specified budget limit
(h) To prepare a draft plan for implementation within a specified timescale
(i) To establish whether the hoped-for benefits could be realised
(j) To establish a detailed design, implementation and operating budget
(k) To compare the detailed budget with the costs of the current system
(l) To set the date by which the study group must report back
(m) To decide which operational managers should be approached by the study group

The remit of a feasibility study may be narrow or wide. The feasibility study team must engage in a substantial effort of **fact finding**.

11.3.2 Problem definition

In some circumstances the **'problem'** (for example the necessity for a real-time as opposed to a batch processed application) may be quite **exact**, in others it may be characterised as **'soft'** (related to people and the way they behave).

The problem definition stage should result in the production of a set of documents which define the problem.

(a) A set of **diagrams** representing, in overview:

   (i) The current physical flows of data in the organisation (**documents**).
   (ii) The activities underlying them (**data flows**).

(b) A description of all the people, jobs, activities and so on (**entities**) that make up the system, and their relationship to one another.

(c) The **problems/requirements** list established from the terms of reference and after consultation with users.

11.3.3 The problems/requirements list

The problems/requirements list or catalogue can cover, amongst other things, the following areas.

(a) The data **input** to the current system
(b) The nature of the **output** information (contents, timing etc)
(c) Methods of **processing**
(d) The expected **growth** of the organisation and so **future volumes** of processing
(e) The systems **control** in operation
(f) **Staffing** arrangements and organisational **structure**
(g) The **operational costs** of the system
(h) **Type of system** (batch, online)
(i) **Response times**
(j) Current organisational **problems**

11.3.4 Option evaluation

This stage involves suggesting a number of **options** for a new system, evaluating them and recommending one for adoption. It concludes with a final **feasibility study report**.

Step 1   Create the **base constraints** in terms of expenditure, implementation and design time, and system requirements, which any system should satisfy.

(a) **Operations** (for example faster processing, larger volumes, greater security, greater accuracy, better quality, real-time as opposed to other forms of processing).

(b) Information **output** (quality, frequency, presentation, eg GUIs, database for managers, EIS facilities).

9: SYSTEMS DEVELOPMENT AND ORGANISATION

(c) **Volume of processing**.

(d) **General system requirements** (eg accuracy, security and controls, audit trail, flexibility, adaptability).

(e) **Compatibility/integration** with existing systems.

Step 2 Create outlines of **project options**, describing, in brief, each option. The number will vary depending on the complexity of the problem, or the size of the application, but is typically between three and six.

Step 3 Assess the **impact** each proposal has on the work of the relevant user department and/or the organisation as a whole.

Step 4 **Review** these proposals with users, who should indicate those options they favour for further analysis.

11.3.5 System justification

A new system should not be recommended unless it can be justified. The justification for a new system would have to come from:

(a) An evaluation of the **costs and benefits** of the proposed system; and/or
(b) Other **performance criteria**.

11.4 Key areas of feasibility

FAST FORWARD

> There are four key areas in which a project must be feasible if it is to be selected. It must be justifiable on **technical, operational, social and economic** grounds.

There are four key areas of feasibility:

- Technical feasibility
- Operational feasibility
- Social feasibility
- Economic feasibility

11.4.1 Technical feasibility

The requirements, as defined in the feasibility study, must be technically achievable. This means that any proposed solution must be capable of being implemented using available hardware, software and other technology. Technical feasibility considerations could include the following.

- **Volume** of transactions which can be processed within a given time
- **Capacity** to hold files or records of a certain size
- **Response times** (how quickly the computer does what you ask it to)
- **Number of users** which can be supported without deterioration in the other criteria

11.4.2 Operational feasibility

Operational feasibility is a key concern. If a solution makes technical sense but **conflicts with the way the organisation does business**, the solution is not feasible. Thus an organisation might reject a solution because it forces a change in management responsibilities, status and chains of command, or does not suit regional reporting structures, or because the costs of redundancies, retraining and reorganisation are considered too high.

11.4.3 Social feasibility

An assessment of social feasibility will address a number of areas, including the following.

- **Personnel** policies
- Redrawing of **job specifications**
- Threats to **industrial relations**
- Expected **skills requirements**
- **Motivation**

11.4.4 Economic feasibility

Any project will have economic costs and economic benefits. Economic feasibility has three strands.

(a) The benefits must justify the costs.

(b) The project must be the 'best' option from those under consideration for its particular purpose.

(c) The project must compete with projects in other areas of the business for funds. Even if it is projected to produce a positive return and satisfies all relevant criteria, it may not be chosen because other business needs are perceived as more important.

11.4.5 The costs of a proposed system

In general the best cost estimates will be obtained for systems bought from an **outside vendor** who provides a cost quotation against a specification. Less concrete cost estimates are generally found with development projects where the work is performed by the organisation's own employees.

The costs of a new system will include costs in a number of different categories.

Cost	Example
Equipment costs	<ul><li>Computer and peripherals</li><li>Ancillary equipment</li><li>The initial system supplies (disks, tapes, paper etc)</li></ul>
Installation costs	<ul><li>New buildings (if necessary)</li><li>The computer room (wiring, air conditioning if necessary)</li></ul>
Development costs	These include costs of measuring and analysing the existing system and costs of looking at the new system. They include software/consultancy work and systems analysis and programming. Changeover costs, particularly file conversion, may be very considerable.
Personnel costs	<ul><li>Staff training</li><li>Staff recruitment/relocation</li><li>Staff salaries and pensions</li><li>Redundancy payments</li><li>Overheads</li></ul>
Operating costs	<ul><li>Consumable materials (tapes, disks, stationery etc)</li><li>Maintenance</li><li>Accommodation costs</li><li>Heating/power/insurance/telephone</li><li>Standby arrangements, in case the system breaks down</li></ul>

11.4.6 Capital and revenue costs

The distinction between capital costs and revenue costs is important.

(a) The costs-benefit analysis of a system ought to include **cash flows and DCF**.

(b) The annual charge against profits shown in the financial accounts is of interest to **stakeholders.**

Capital items will be capitalised and then depreciated, and revenue items will be expensed as incurred as a regular annual cost.

In practice, **accounting treatment** of such development costs may **vary widely** between organisations depending on their accounting policies and on agreement with their auditors.

Question
System costs

Draw up a table with three headings: capital cost items, one-off revenue cost items and regular annual costs. Identify at least three items to be included under each heading. You may wish to refer back to the preceding paragraphs for examples of costs.

Answer

Capital cost items	'One-off' revenue cost items	Regular annual costs
Hardware purchase costs	Consultancy fees	Operating staff salaries/wages
Software purchase costs	Systems analysts' and programmers' salaries	Data transmission costs
Purchase of accommodation (if needed)	Costs of testing the system (staff costs, consumables)	Consumable materials
Installation costs (new desks, cables, physical storage etc)	Costs of converting the files for the new system	Power
	Staff recruitment fees	Maintenance costs
		Cost of standby arrangements
		Ongoing staff training

11.4.7 The benefits of a proposed system

The benefits from a proposed new system must also be evaluated. Possible examples are outlined below

(a) **Savings** because the **old system** will no longer be operated. Savings may include:

    (i) Savings in **staff costs**.
    (ii) Savings in **other operating costs**, such as consumable materials.

(b) Extra **savings** or revenue benefits because of the improvements or enhancements that the **new system** should bring:

    (i) Possibly **more sales revenue** and so additional contribution.

    (ii) **Better inventory control** (with a new inventory control system) and so fewer inventory losses from obsolescence and deterioration.

    (iii) Further savings in **staff time**, resulting perhaps in reduced future staff growth.

(c) Possibly, some one-off revenue benefits from the **sale of equipment** which the existing system uses, but which will no longer be required. Second-hand computer equipment does not have a high value, however! It is also possible that the new system will use **less office space**, and so there will be benefits from selling or renting the spare accommodation.

Some benefits might be **intangible**, or impossible to give a money value to.

(a) Greater **customer satisfaction**, arising from a more prompt service (eg because of a computerised sales and delivery service).

(b) Improved **staff morale** from working with a 'better' system.

(c) **Better decision making** is hard to quantify, but may result from better MIS, DSS or EIS.

11.4.8 The feasibility study report

FAST FORWARD

Once each area of feasibility has been investigated a number of possible projects may be put forward. The results are included in a **feasibility report**.

Once each area of feasibility has been investigated a number of possible projects may be put forward. The results of the study should be compiled into a report that makes a recommendation regarding future action (eg a new system, modify the existing system, or to remain with the status quo).

The feasibility study report may be submitted to the organisation's steering committee for consideration – or perhaps to the likely project manager (this will depend upon the size and nature of the project and the preferences of the organisation).

A typical feasibility study report may include the following sections.

- Terms of reference
- Description of existing system
- System requirements
- Details of the proposed system(s)
- Cost/benefit analysis
- Development and implementation plans
- Recommendations as to the preferred option

Chapter roundup

- The term **systems development lifecycle** describes the stages a system moves through from inception until it is discarded or replaced. Traditional lifecycle models such as **Royce's waterfall model** break the systems development process into **sequential stages** – with the output from a stage forming the input to the following stage.
- The **spiral approach** involves carrying out the same activities over a number of cycles in order to clarify requirements and solutions.
- A **methodology** is a collection of procedures, techniques, tools and documentation aids which are designed to help systems developers in their efforts to implement a new system. Methodologies are usually broken down into phases.
- A **CASE tool** may be used to support the construction and maintenance of a system model – often allowing the construction of a prototype.
- A **4GL** enables programs to be constructed more quickly and allows greater flexibility in the development process.
- **Prototyping** enables programmers to write programs more quickly and allows the user to see a 'preview' of the system that is envisaged.
- A **structured walkthrough** usually takes the form of a meeting in which the output from a phase or stage of development is presented to users for discussion and for formal approval.
- **Joint Applications Development (JAD)** describes a close partnership between users and developers.
- **Rapid Applications Development (RAD)** combines a less structured approach to systems development with the use of other tools such as prototyping.
- A **feasibility study** is a formal study to decide whether a project is viable. When considering an information systems project the study would investigate the type of system that could be developed to meet the needs of the organisation, and if it is possible to produce such a system within the relevant constraints.
- There are four key areas in which a project must be feasible if it is to be selected. It must be justifiable on **technical, operational, social and economic** grounds.
- Once each area of feasibility has been investigated a number of possible projects may be put forward. The results are included in a **feasibility report**.

PART B INFORMATION SYSTEMS

Quick quiz

1. List the seven stages identified in the National Computing Centre systems development lifecycle model.
2. What is the key feature of the waterfall model?
3. What shortcoming of the waterfall model did the 'b' model address?
4. What is the key feature of the spiral model?
5. Define 'systems development methodology'.
6. What would a CASE tool be used for?
7. Explain one advantage of prototyping.
8. Distinguish between JAD and RAD.
9. List three reasons why an organisation considering the implementation of a new information system should undertake a feasibility study.
10. What four areas of feasibility should be evaluated by a feasibility study?
11. Give three reasons why it is difficult to place a monetary value on the benefits of an information system.
12. List the contents of a typical feasibility study report.

Answers to quick quiz

1. Identification of a problem or opportunity, Feasibility study, Systems investigation, Systems analysis, Systems design, Systems implementation, Review and maintenance.

2. The waterfall model, like the National Computing Centre model, breaks the systems development process into sequential stages, with the output from a stage forming the input to the following stage.

3. The 'b' model recognised that operations and maintenance are on-going.

4. The spiral approach involves carrying out the same activities over a number of cycles in order to clarify requirements and solutions.

5. A systems development methodology is a collection of procedures, techniques, tools and documentation aids which will help systems developers in their efforts to implement a new information system.

6. A CASE tool is used to aid system design and program coding.

7. Prototyping makes it possible for developers to present a 'mock-up' version of the envisaged system without committing too much time and effort. Users can then suggest improvements which can be incorporated in the actual system.

8. Joint Applications Development (JAD) describes the partnership between users and system developers. Rapid Applications Development (RAD) is a quick way of building software. It combines a managed approach to systems development with the use of modern software tools such as prototyping and object-oriented design methods. As RAD involves the end-user heavily in the development process it is one example of JAD.

9. A feasibility study should be undertaken when considering a new information system because new systems can:

    - Be complicated and cost a great deal to develop.
    - Be disruptive during development and implementation.
    - Have far-reaching consequences in the way an organisation conducts its business or is structured.

10. Technical, Operational, Social and Economic.

11. Many benefits are intangible and hard to measure eg better quality decision-making. Many benefits will accrue in the future – it is difficult to accurately account for the time value of money. Many benefits are uncertain, for example a system may provide competitive advantage depending on what systems competitors introduce.

12. A typical report might include:

    (a) Terms of reference
    (b) Description of existing system
    (c) System requirements
    (d) Details of the proposed system
    (e) Cost/benefit analysis
    (f) Development and implementation plans
    (g) Recommendations as to the preferred option

PART B INFORMATION SYSTEMS

End of chapter question

Fourth-generation languages (AIA November 2007)

(a) Explain and distinguish between the computer software types: machine code, Assembly Language (AL), and High Level Languages (HLL). **(10 marks)**

(b) (i) What are the disadvantages of these pre-fourth generation languages that together identified the need for a different approach to software development that concentrates upon the needs of end-users of computing? **(6 marks)**

(ii) Describe the particular features of Fourth Generation Languages (4GL) that have made them so useful in modern computing. **(5 marks)**

(iii) Briefly explain **two** disadvantages to the use of 4GLs. **(4 marks)**

(Total = 25 marks)

Systems strategies and management issues

Topic list	Syllabus reference
1 Organisational information requirements	9.10
2 Business strategy and information systems strategy	9.10
3 Developing a strategy for Information Systems and Information Technology	9.10
4 Critical success factors	9.10

Introduction

In this chapter we examine the relationships between **business strategy**, **information systems** (IS) and **information technology** (IT).

1 Organisational information requirements

> **FAST FORWARD**
>
> All organisations require information for a range of **purposes** including:
> - Planning
> - Controlling
> - Recording transactions
> - Performance measurement
> - Decision making

1.1 Planning

Planning requires a knowledge of the available resources, possible time-scales and the likely outcome under alternative scenarios. Information is required that helps **decision making**, and how to implement decisions taken.

1.2 Controlling

Once a plan is implemented, its actual performance must be controlled. Information is required to assess **whether it is proceeding as planned** or whether there is some unexpected deviation from plan. It may consequently be necessary to take some form of corrective action.

1.3 Recording transactions

Information about **each transaction or event** is required. Reasons include:

(a) Documentation of transactions can be used as **evidence** in a case of dispute.

(b) There may be a **legal requirement** to record transactions, for example for accounting and audit purposes.

(c) **Operational information** can be built up, allowing control action to be taken.

1.4 Performance measurement

Just as individual operations need to be controlled, so overall performance must be measured. **Comparisons against budget or plan** are able to be made. This may involve the collection of information on, for example, costs, revenues, volumes, time-scale and profitability.

1.5 Decision making

Strategic planning, management control and operational control may be seen as a hierarchy of planning and control decisions. (This is sometimes called the Anthony hierarchy, after the writer **Robert Anthony**.)

> **FAST FORWARD**
>
> A **strategy** is a general statement of long-term objectives and goals and the ways by which these will be achieved. **Strategic planning** is the formulation, evaluation and selection of strategies for the purpose of preparing a long-term plan of action to attain objectives.

Strategic planning is a complex process which involves taking a view of the **organisation** and the **future** that it is likely to encounter, and then attempting to organise the structure and resources of the organisation accordingly.

10: SYSTEMS STRATEGIES AND MANAGEMENT ISSUES

Key terms

> **Strategy** can be defined as 'a course of action, including the specification of resources required, to achieve a specific outcome'.
> *(CIMA Official Terminology)*
>
> **Strategic planning** is the formulation, evaluation and selection of strategies for the purpose of preparing a long-term plan of action to attain objectives.

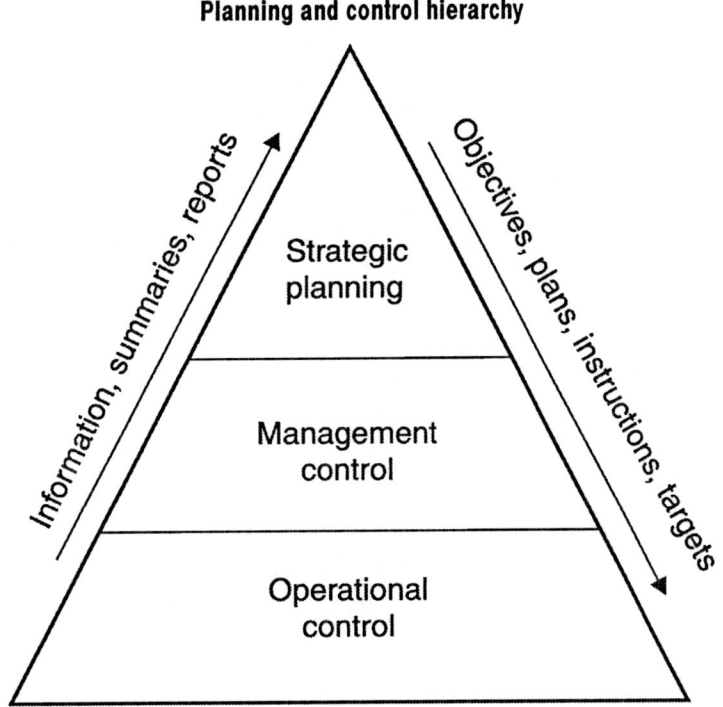

Planning and control hierarchy

1.5.1 Strategic information

Strategic information is used to **plan** the **objectives** of the organisation, and to **assess** whether the objectives are being met in practice. Such information includes overall profitability, the profitability of different segments of the business, future market prospects, the availability and cost of raising new funds, total cash needs, total manning levels and capital equipment needs.

Strategic information is:

- Derived from both **internal and external** sources
- **Summarised** at a high level
- Relevant to the **long term**
- Concerned with the **whole organisation**
- Often prepared on an **'ad hoc'** basis
- Both **quantitative** and **qualitative**
- **Uncertain**, requiring assumptions to be made regarding the future

1.5.2 Tactical information

Tactical information is used to decide **how the resources of the business should be employed**, and to **monitor** how they are being and have been employed. Such information includes productivity measurements (output per hour) budgetary control or variance analysis reports, and cash flow forecasts, staffing levels and profit results within a particular department of the organisation, labour turnover statistics within a department and short-term purchasing requirements.

Tactical information is:

- Primarily generated internally (but may have a limited external component)
- **Summarised** at a relatively low level
- Relevant to the **short-** and **medium**-terms
- Concerned with **activities** or **departments**
- Prepared **routinely** and regularly
- Based on **quantitative** measures

1.5.3 Operational information

Operational information is used to ensure that **specific operational tasks** are planned and carried out as intended.

In a payroll office, for example, operational information would include the hours worked by each employee and the rate of pay per hour.

Operational information is:

- Derived from **internal** sources
- **Detailed**, being the processing of raw data
- Relevant to the **immediate term**
- **Task-specific**
- Prepared very **frequently**
- Largely **quantitative**

1.6 The qualities of good information

'Good' information is information that adds to the understanding of a situation. The qualities of good information are outlined in the following table.

Quality	Example
Accurate	Figures should add up, the degree of rounding should be appropriate, there should be no typos, items should be allocated to the correct category, assumptions should be stated for uncertain information.
Complete	Information should include everything that it needs to include, for example external data if relevant, or comparative information.
Cost-beneficial	It should not cost more to obtain the information than the benefit derived from having it. Providers of information should be given efficient means of collecting and analysing it. Presentation should be such that users do not waste time working out what it means.
User-targeted	The needs of the user should be borne in mind, for instance senior managers need summaries, junior ones need detail.
Relevant	Information that is not needed for a decision should be omitted, no matter how 'interesting' it may be.
Authoritative	The source of the information should be a reliable one (**not**, for instance, 'Joe Bloggs Predictions Page' on the internet unless Joe Bloggs is known to be a reliable source for that type of information).
Timely	The information should be available when it is needed.
Easy to use	Information should be clearly presented, not excessively long, and sent using the right medium and communication channel (email, telephone, hard-copy report etc).

Exam focus point

> You will **not be asked simply to produce a list** of the qualities of good information in the exam. Exam questions will expect you to be able to **recognise information deficiencies** and **suggest improvements**.

1.7 Improvements to information

The table below contains suggestions as to how poor information can be **improved**.

Feature	Example of possible improvements
Accurate	Use computerised systems with automatic input checks rather than manual systems.
	Allow sufficient time for collation and analysis of data if pinpoint accuracy is crucial.
	Incorporate elements of probability within projections so that the required response to different future scenarios can be assessed.
Complete	Include past data as a reference point for future projections.
	Include any planned developments, such as new products.
	Information about future demand would be more useful than information about past demand.
	Include external data.
Cost-beneficial	Always bear in mind whether the benefit of having the information is greater than the cost of obtaining it.
User-targeted	Information should be summarised and presented together with relevant ratios or percentages.
Relevant	The purpose of the report should be defined. It may be trying to fulfil too many purposes at once. Perhaps several shorter reports would be more effective.
	Information should include exception reporting, where only those items that are worthy of note – and the control actions taken by more junior managers to deal with them – are reported.
Authoritative	Use reliable sources and experienced personnel.
	If some figures are derived from other figures the method of derivation should be explained.
Timely	Information collection and analysis by production managers needs to be speeded up considerably, probably by the introduction of better information systems.
Easy-to-use	Graphical presentation, allowing trends to be quickly assimilated and relevant action decided upon.
	Alternative methods of presentation should be considered, such as graphs or charts, to make it easier to review the information at a glance. Numerical information is sometimes best summarised in narrative form or vice versa.
	A 'house style' for reports should be devised and adhered to by all. This would cover such matters as number of decimal places to use, table headings and labels, paragraph numbering and so on.

PART B   INFORMATION SYSTEMS

Exam focus point

> In the exam, you may need to adapt or apply your knowledge to answer the specific question asked. For example, you could be required to discuss the information characteristics of time horizon, level of detail, source, degree of certainty and frequency.

2 Business strategy and information systems strategy

The relationship between corporate, business and operational strategies is shown in the following diagram.

Levels of strategy

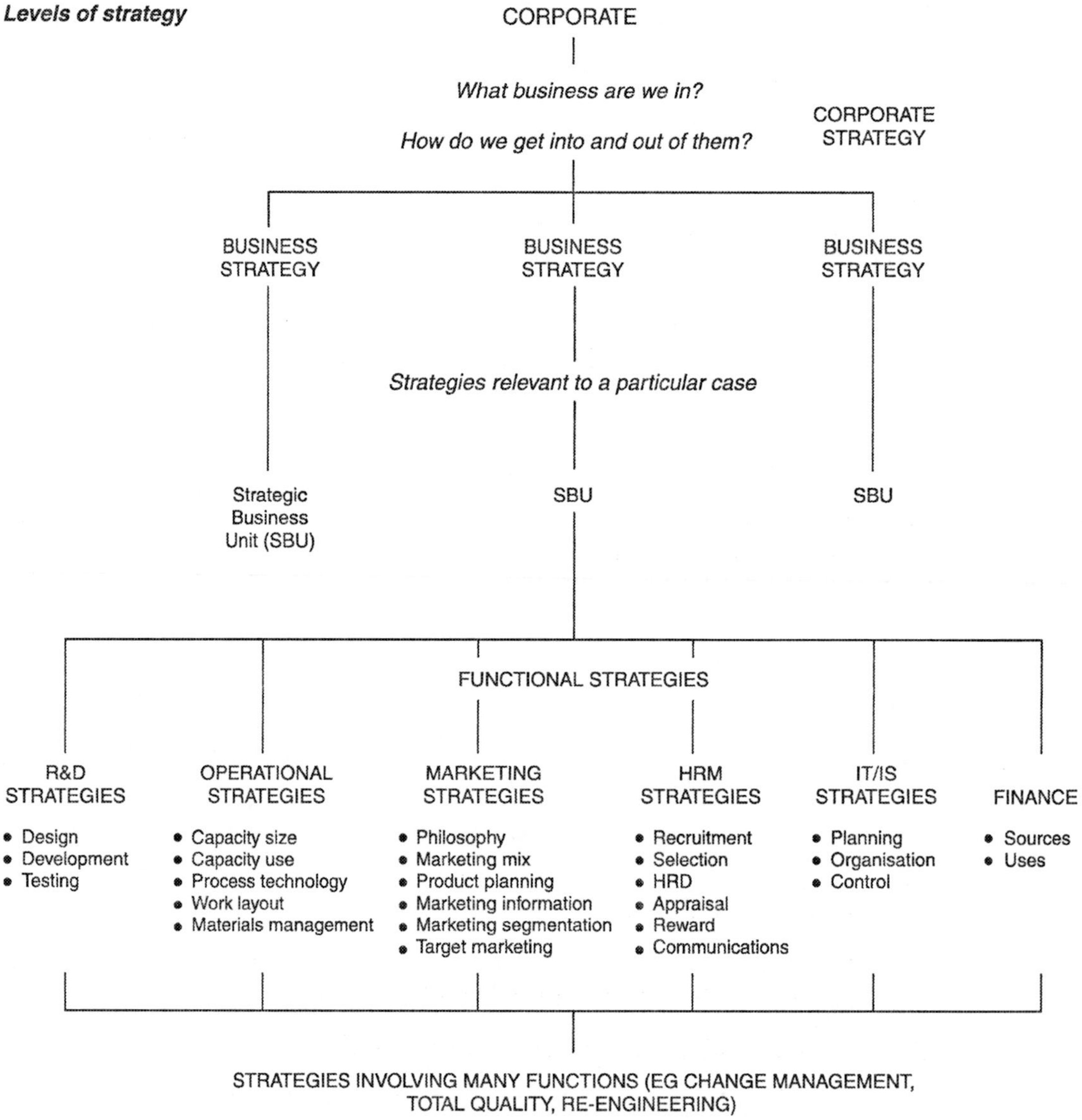

```
                              CORPORATE
                                  |
                     What business are we in?
                                                      CORPORATE
                 How do we get into and out of them?   STRATEGY
        ┌─────────────────────┼─────────────────────┐
   BUSINESS              BUSINESS              BUSINESS
   STRATEGY              STRATEGY              STRATEGY
                            |
              Strategies relevant to a particular case

   Strategic               SBU                    SBU
   Business
   Unit (SBU)
```

```
                        FUNCTIONAL STRATEGIES
   ┌──────────┬──────────────┬──────────┬──────────┬──────────┬──────────┐
   R&D        OPERATIONAL    MARKETING   HRM        IT/IS      FINANCE
   STRATEGIES STRATEGIES     STRATEGIES  STRATEGIES STRATEGIES

   • Design   • Capacity size • Philosophy • Recruitment • Planning     • Sources
   • Development • Capacity use • Marketing mix • Selection • Organisation • Uses
   • Testing  • Process technology • Product planning • HRD • Control
              • Work layout  • Marketing information • Appraisal
              • Materials management • Marketing segmentation • Reward
                             • Target marketing • Communications
```

STRATEGIES INVOLVING MANY FUNCTIONS (EG CHANGE MANAGEMENT, TOTAL QUALITY, RE-ENGINEERING)

2.1 Functional/operational strategies; information systems strategy

FAST FORWARD

> IS/IT strategy is an example of a functional/operational strategy, but may have **strategic implications**.

Information systems strategy is an example of a **functional/operational strategy** (although in some cases it may have strategic implications). Functional/operational strategies deal with specialised areas of activity.

Functional area	Comment
Information systems	A firm's information systems are becoming increasingly important, as an item of expenditure, as administrative support and as a tool for competitive strength.
Marketing	Devising products and services, pricing, promoting and distributing them, in order to satisfy customer needs at a profit.
Production	Factory location, manufacturing techniques, outsourcing etc.
Finance	Ensuring that the firm has enough financial resources to fund its other strategies.
Human resources	Secure personnel of the right skills in the right quantity at the right time.
R&D	New products and techniques.

Question — Strategy and information systems

List five ways in which corporate and business strategy are relevant to the types of information system required in an organisation.

Answer

Five ways are shown below. You may have come up with others.

(a) Information is needed to shape corporate and business strategy.

(b) Information systems provide information that monitors progress towards strategic objectives.

(c) Business objectives are becoming increasingly customer focused. Good customer service requires good quality information available on demand.

(d) A strategy of growth will require a corresponding increase in the information system.

(e) A change of strategy may mean a new information system is required.

2.2 Information systems and business strategy

It is widely accepted that an organisation's information system should **support** corporate and business strategy. In some circumstances an information system may have a greater influence and actually help **determine** strategy. For example:

(a) IS/IT may provide a possible source of competitive advantage. This could involve new technology not yet available to others or simply using existing technology in a different way.

(b) The information system may help in formulating business strategy by **providing information** from internal and external sources.

(c) Developments in IT may provide **new channels** for distributing and collecting information, and /or for conducting transactions eg the internet.

An important role of both the finance and information technology functions is to help ensure the agreed business strategy is proceeding according to plan. The table that follows (devised by the US Institute of Management Accountants) outlines the rationale behind this view.

PART B INFORMATION SYSTEMS

	Traditional view	Strategic implications
Cost	The finance and information technology functions can be relatively expensive.	Shared services and outsourcing could be used to capture cost savings.
IT	IT has traditionally been transaction based.	IT/IS should be integrated with business strategy.
Value	The finance and IT functions do not add value.	Redesign the functions.
Strategy	Accountants and IT managers are seen as scorekeepers and administrators rather than as a business partner during the strategic planning process.	Change from cost-orientated to market-orientated, ie development of more effective strategic planning systems.

3 Developing a strategy for Information Systems and Information Technology

Key terms

Information Systems (IS) include all systems and procedures involved in the collection, storage, production and distribution of information.

Information Technology (IT) describes the equipment used to capture, store, transmit or present information. IT provides a large part of the information systems infrastructure.

Information management refers to the approach an organisation takes towards the management of its information systems, including:

- Planning IS/IT developments
- Organisational environment of IS
- Control
- Technology

FAST FORWARD

The term **Information Systems (IS) strategy** refers to the long-term plan concerned with exploiting IS and IT either to support business strategies or create new strategic options.

3.1 Vision and reality

A company that has a **vision** of its own future, and some idea of how information technology can be used to turn that vision into **reality**, may be able to use new technologies for strategic advantage.

One approach to creating a vision is to adopt a familiar three step approach, involving answering three questions about the organisation.

- Where are we now?
- Where do we want to be?
- How will we get there?

The first question can be answered using standard techniques such as a strengths, weaknesses, opportunities, threats **(SWOT) analysis**. This approach ensures that both internal and external factors are considered. We cover SWOT analysis in the context of information systems development in Chapter 4.

Answering the second question requires vision. This does not have to be a continuation in the organisation's current direction. It must be challenging, attainable and communicated to those who will implement it.

Once this has been done, the strategy (in answer to the third question) can be defined.

A second approach takes the view that insiders are too tied to 'the way we do things now', and recommends the involvement of **outsiders**. An outsider may be able to more readily anticipate dramatic shifts which might occur in the future. Additionally, an outsider does not have the insider's investment in **maintaining the status quo**.

3.2 Information systems, strategy and competitive advantage

It is now recognised that information can be used as a source of competitive advantage. The realisation that information (and therefore information systems and information technology) may be a source of competitive advantage and be key to achieving organisational goals, has led to increased emphasis on the importance of formal management strategies and plans for information and information systems.

A strategy is needed for areas in which decisions have the potential to have a major impact on an organisation. Many organisations have recognised the importance of information and developed an **information strategy**, covering both IS and IT.

In commercial organisations it could be argued that one of the main aims of any strategy is competitive advantage – as success ultimately depends upon doing something better than competitors do. Business objectives, if achieved, should result in competitive advantage in one or more areas. This process is contributed to by ensuring the organisation's strategy for information and information systems is **tied to business objectives**.

(a) The **corporate strategy** is used to plan functional **business plans** which provide guidelines for information-based activities.

(b) On a year by year basis, the **annual plan** would try to tie in business plans with **information systems projects**, perhaps through a **steering committee**.

3.3 Information systems strategy

An IS strategy therefore deals with the integration of an organisation's information requirements and information systems planning with its **long-term overall goals** (customer service etc). IS strategy is formulated at the level of business where specific customer needs etc can be delineated. It deals with what applications should be developed, and where resources should be deployed.

The **information technology (IT) strategy** leads on from the IS strategy above. It deals with the **technologies** of:

- Computing
- Communications
- Data
- Application systems

This provides a framework for the analysis and design of the **technological infrastructure** of an organisation. This strategy indicates how the information systems strategies that rely on technology will be **implemented**.

3.4 Why have an IS/IT strategy?

FAST FORWARD

A strategy is needed for IS/IT because these areas involve **high costs**, are **critical to the success** of many organisations, can be used as a **strategic weapon** and affect internal and external **stakeholders**. IS/IT are sufficiently important and widespread to require proper **planning** and management attention.

A strategy for information systems and information technology is **justified** on the grounds that IS/IT:

- Involves **high costs**
- Is **critical to the success** of many organisations
- May be utilised as part of the commercial strategy in the battle for **competitive advantage**

- Can significantly change the business environment
- Affects **all levels of management**
- Affects the way **management information** is created and presented
- **Requires effective management** to obtain the maximum benefit
- Involves many **stakeholders** inside and outside the organisation

3.4.1 IS/IT is a high cost activity

Many organisations invest large amounts of money in IS, but not always wisely.

The unmanaged proliferation of IT is likely to lead to expensive mistakes. Two key benefits of IT – the ability to **share** information and the avoidance of duplication – are likely to be lost.

All IT expenditure should therefore require approval to ensure that it enhances rather than detracts from the overall information management strategy.

3.4.2 IS/IT is critical to the success of many organisations

When developing an IS/IT strategy a firm should assess **how important IT is** in the provision of products and services. The role that IT fills in an organisation will vary depending on the type of organisation. IS/IT could be:

- A **support** activity
- A **key** operational activity
- **Potentially** very important
- A **strategic** activity (without IT the firm could not function at all)
- A source of **competitive advantage**

3.4.3 IT can significantly change the business environment

IT is an **enabling** technology, and can produce dramatic changes in individual businesses and whole industries. For example, the deregulation of US airline system encouraged the growth of computerised seat-reservation systems (eg SABRE, as used by American Airlines which always displayed American Airlines flights preferentially). IT can be both a **cause** of major changes in doing business and a **response** to them.

3.4.4 IT affects all levels of management

IT has become a routine feature of office life, **a facility for everyone to use**. IT is no longer used solely by specialist staff.

3.4.5 IT and its effect on management information

> **FAST FORWARD**
>
> IT developments have increased the **amount of information available** to organisations. It is important to ensure information is useful – that it is of **good quality**.

The use of IT has permitted the design of a range of **Management Information Systems (MIS)**. Executive Information Systems (EIS), Decision Support Systems (DSS), and expert systems can be used to enhance the flexibility and depth of MIS.

IT has also had an effect on **production processes**. For example, Computer Integrated Manufacturing (CIM) changed the methods and cost profiles of many manufacturing processes. The techniques used to **measure and record costs** have also adapted to the use of IT.

3.4.6 IT and stakeholders

Parties interested in an organisation's use of IT are as follows.

(a) **Other business users** – for example to facilitate Electronic Data Interchange (EDI).

(b) **Governments** – eg telecommunications regulation, regulation of electronic commerce.

(c) **IT manufacturers** looking for new markets and product development. User-groups may be able to influence software producers.

(d) **Consumers** – for example as reassurance that product quality is high, consumers may also be interested if information is provided via the internet.

(e) **Employees** – as IT affects work practices.

3.5 Developing an IS/IT strategy

FAST FORWARD

Developing strategy involves taking a number of steps, from setting strategic objectives right through to evaluating actual performance. Three basic issues are the organisation's **overall business objectives** and in consequence its **IS/IT needs**, the organisation's **current IT usage** and the potential **opportunities** that IT can bring.

An IS/IT strategy should be developed with the aim of ensuring IS/IT is utilised as efficiently and effectively as possible in the pursuit of organisational goals and objectives.

The inputs and outputs of the IS/IT strategic planning process are summarised on the following diagram.

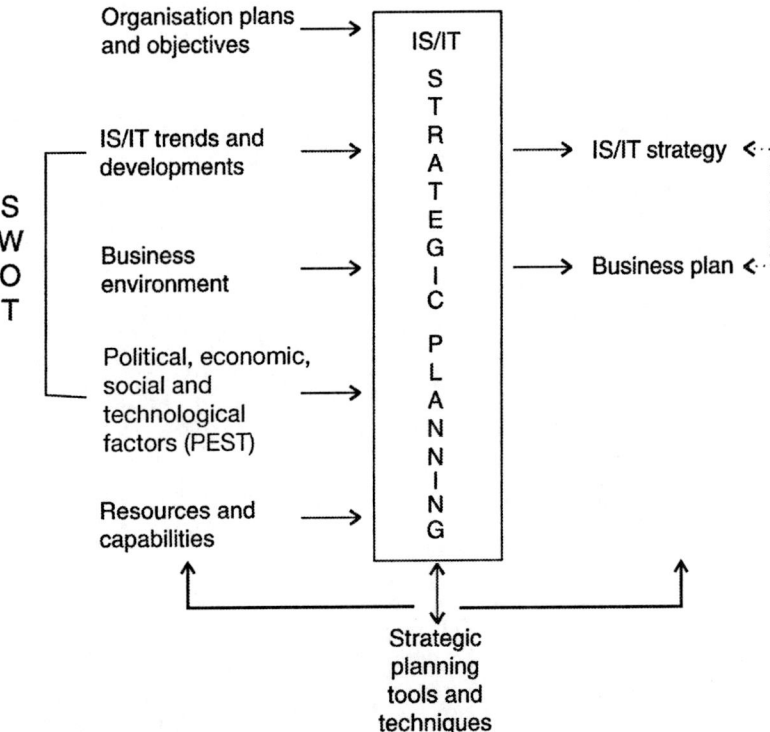

An IS strategy therefore deals with the integration of an organisation's information requirements and information systems planning with its **long-term overall goals** (customer service etc). IS strategy deals with what applications should be developed and where resources should be deployed.

3.6 Establishing organisational information requirements

The identification of organisational information needs and the information systems framework to satisfy them is at the heart of a strategy for information systems and information technology.

The IS and IT strategies should complement the overall strategy for the organisation. It follows therefore that the IS/IT strategy should be considered whenever the organisation prepares other long-term strategies such as marketing or production.

3.7 Earl's three leg analysis

The writer Earl identified **three legs of IS strategy development**:

- Business-led (top-down emphasis, focuses on **business plans and goals**)
- Infrastructure-led (bottom-up emphasis, focuses on **current systems**)
- Mixed (inside-out emphasis, focuses on **IT/IS opportunities**)

A diagrammatic representation of the three legs follows:

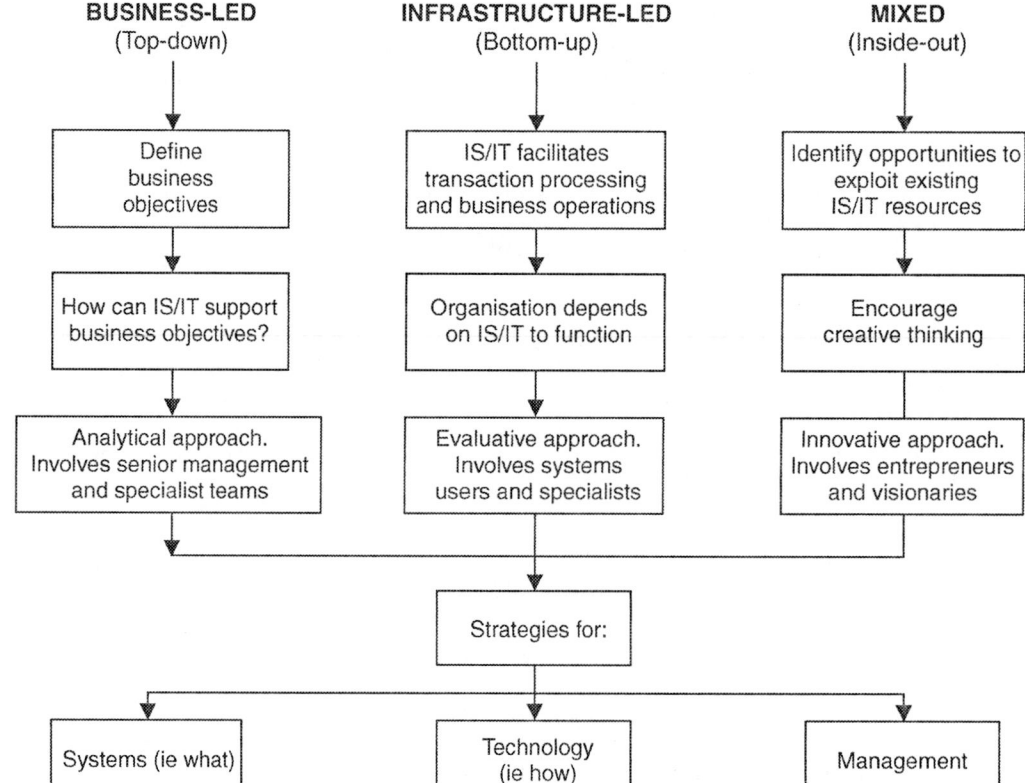

Earl's three leg analysis is explained in the following table.

Leg or approach	Comment
Business-led (top-down)	The overall objectives of an organisation are identified and then IS/IT systems are implemented to enable these objectives to be met. This approach relies on the ability to break down the organisation and its objectives to a series of business objectives and processes and to be able to identify the information needs of these. This is an analytical approach. The people usually involved are senior management and specialist teams.
Infrastructure-led (bottom-up)	Computer based transaction systems are critical to business operations. The organisation focuses on systems that facilitate transactions and other basic operations. This is an evaluative approach. The people usually involved are system users and specialists.
Mixed (inside-out)	The organisation encourages ideas that will exploit existing IT and IS resources. Innovations may come from entrepreneurial managers or individuals outside the formal planning process. This is an innovative/creative approach. The people involved are entrepreneurs and/or visionaries.

Question — IS/IT and competitive advantage

Think about the role of Information Systems (IS) and Information Technology (IT) in achieving business objectives and securing an advantage over competitors. Try to think of an example of each of the following.

(a) The use of IT to 'lock out' competitors.
(b) The use of IS/IT to reduce the likelihood of customers changing suppliers.
(c) The use of IS/IT to secure a performance advantage.
(d) How IT may generate a new product or service.

Answer

(a) An example is an organisation that invests so heavily in technology that potential competitors lack both the expertise and the funds to compete successfully. Microsoft has not completely locked competitors out of the office software market but its domination is increasing.

(b) Once a bank customer has gone to the effort of installing a home banking system, he or she is unlikely to make a decision to change banks.

(c) Accurate stock systems that facilitate Just-In-Time stock management, and organisations participating in Electronic Data Interchange (EDI) are two examples of how IT can increase efficiency and facilitate better service – providing an advantage over competitors. (They may also make an organisation more dependent on existing suppliers therefore discouraging the changing of suppliers.)

(d) Internet Service Providers (ISPs) did not exist before the advent of the internet.

PART B INFORMATION SYSTEMS

4 Critical success factors

Critical success factors are a small number of key operational goals vital to the success of an organisation. CSFs may be used to establish organisational information requirements.

The use of **critical success factors (CSFs)** can help to determine the information requirements of an organisation. CSFs are operational goals. If operational goals are achieved the organisation should be successful.

Key term

> **Critical success factors** are a small number of key operational goals vital to the success of an organisation. CSFs may be used to establish organisational information requirements.

The CSF approach is sometimes referred to as the **strategic analysis** approach. The philosophy behind this approach is that managers should focus on a small number of objectives, and information systems should be focussed on providing information to enable managers to monitor these objectives.

4.1 Types of CSF

Two separate types of critical success factor can be identified. A **monitoring** CSF is used to keep abreast of existing activities and operations. A **building** CSF helps to measure the progress of new initiatives and is more likely to be relevant at senior executive level.

- **Monitoring** CSFs are important for **maintaining** business
- **Building** CSFs are important for **expanding** business

4.2 Revising CSFs

One approach to **determining the factors** which are critical to success in performing a function or making a decision is as follows.

- List the organisation's **objectives** and **goals**
- Determine which factors are **critical** for accomplishing the objectives
- Determine a small number of **key performance indicators** for each factor

4.3 Key Performance Indicators (KPIs)

The determination of measures or **key performance indicators** to monitor CSFs is not necessarily straightforward. Some measures might use **factual**, verifiable data, while others might make use of 'softer' concepts, such as opinions, perceptions and hunches.

For example, the reliability of stock records can be measured by means of physical stock counts, either at discrete intervals or on a rolling basis. Forecasting of demand variations will be much harder to measure.

Where measures use quantitative data, performance can be measured in a number of ways.

- In **physical quantities**, for example units produced or units sold
- In **money terms**, for example profit, revenues, costs or variances
- In **ratios** and **percentages**

4.4 Sources of CSFs

In general terms Rockart identifies four **sources** of CSFs.

(a) The **industry** that the business is in.
(b) The **company** itself and its situation within the industry.

(c) The **environment**, for example consumer trends, the economy, and political factors of the country in which the company operates.

(d) Temporal organisational factors, which are areas of corporate activity that may cause **concern** from time to time, for example, high stock levels.

4.5 Possible specific sources of CSFs and KPIs

More specifically, possible internal and external data sources for CSFs include the following.

(a) The **existing system**. The existing system can be used to generate reports showing failures to meet CSFs.

(b) **Customer service department**. This department will maintain details of **complaints, refunds** and **queries**.

(c) **Customers**. A survey of customers, provided that it is properly designed and introduced, would reveal (or confirm) those areas where **satisfaction** is high or low.

(d) **Competitors**. Competitors' operations, pricing structures and publicity should be closely monitored.

(e) **Accounting system**. The **profitability** of various aspects of the operation would be a key factor in any review of CSFs.

(f) **Consultants**. A specialist consultancy might be able to perform a detailed review of the organisation to identify CSFs.

4.6 The CSF approach

The CSF approach to IS/IT planning is illustrated in the following diagram. MIS, DSS, KWS and ESS are different types of information system which are explained in Chapter 7, Section 9.9.

The critical success factor approach to IS/IT planning

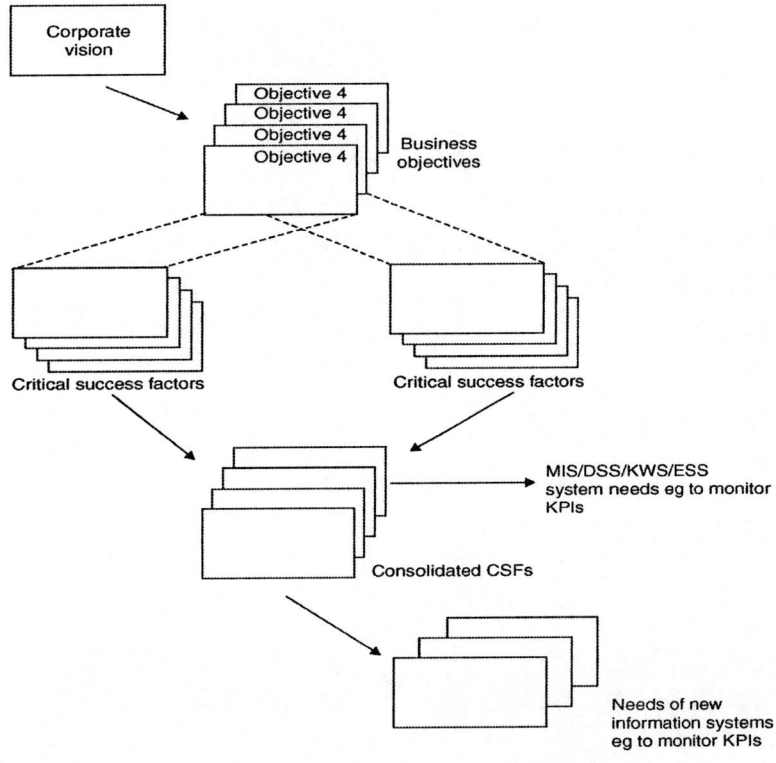

Source: *IT Strategy for Business*, Joe Peppard
Chapter 4, Garret Hickey

4.7 Example

An organisation has an objective to maintain a high level of service direct from stock without holding uneconomic stock levels. This is quantified in the form of a **goal**, which might be to ensure that 95% of orders for goods can be satisfied directly from stock, while minimising total stockholding costs and stock levels. **CSFs** and **KPIs** might then be identified as the following.

CSF	KPI
Supplier performance	Average order lead time
Stock records reliability	Number of discrepancies found
Accurate demand forecasting	Difference between forecast and actual demand

4.8 CSF approach: strengths and weaknesses

CSF approach – strengths	Comment
Takes into account environmental changes	The CSF approach requires managers to examine the environment and consider how it influences their information requirements.
Focuses on information	The approach doesn't just aim to establish organisational objectives. It also looks at the information and information systems required to establish and monitor progress towards these objectives.
Facilitates top management participation in system development	The clear link between information requirements and individual and organisational objectives encourages top management involvement in system (DSS, EIS) design.

CSF approach – weaknesses	Comment
Aggregation of individual CSFs	Wide-ranging individual CSFs need to be aggregated into a clear organisational plan. This process relies heavily on judgement. Managers who feel their input has been neglected may be alienated.
Bias towards top management	When gathering information to establish CSFs it is usually top management who are interviewed. These managers may lack knowledge of operational activities.
CSFs change often	The business environment, managers and information systems technology are subject to constant change. CSFs and systems must be updated to account for change.

Chapter roundup

- Organisations **require information for a variety of purposes** including:
    - **Planning**
    - **Controlling**
    - **Recording transactions**
    - **Measuring performance**
    - **Decision making**

- A **strategy** is a general statement of long-term objectives and goals and the ways by which these will be achieved. **Strategic planning** is the formulation, evaluation and selection of strategies for the purpose of preparing a long-term plan of action to attain objectives.

- IS/IT strategy is an example of a functional/operational strategy, but may have **strategic implications**.

- The term **Information Systems (IS) strategy** refers to the long-term plan concerned with exploiting IS and IT either to support business strategies or create new strategic options.

- A strategy is needed for IS/IT because these areas involve **high costs**, are **critical to the success** of many organisations, can be used as a **strategic weapon** and affect internal and external **stakeholders**. IS/IT are sufficiently important and widespread to require proper **planning** and management attention.

- IT developments have increased the **amount of information available** to organisations. It is important to ensure information is useful – that it is of **good quality**.

- Developing strategy involves taking a number of steps, from setting strategic objectives right through to evaluating actual performance. Three basic issues are the organisation's **overall business objectives** and in consequence its **IS/IT needs**, the organisation's **current IT usage** and the potential **opportunities** that IT can bring.

- **Critical success factors** are a small number of key operational goals vital to the success of an organisation. CSFs may be used to establish organisational information requirements.

Quick quiz

1. List five general purposes an organisation may use information for.
2. 'Operational information is derived mainly from external sources.' **True** or **false**?
3. List four features of strategic information.
4. List five reasons why an organisation should have a strategy for IS/IT.
5. What three issues must an IS/IT strategy deal with?
6. Identify three general sources of CSFs.
7. 'A well thought out CSF will always be valid for at least two years'. **True** or **false**?

PART B INFORMATION SYSTEMS

Answers to quick quiz

1. Planning, controlling, recording transactions, measuring performance, making decisions.
2. False.
3. Four of the following:
   - Derived from both internal and external sources
   - Summarised at a high level
   - Relevant to the long term
   - Concerned with the whole organisation
   - Often prepared on an 'ad hoc' basis
   - Both quantitative and qualitative
   - Uncertain, as the future cannot be accurately predicted
4. Five of the following:
   - IT involves high costs.
   - IT is critical to the success of many organisations.
   - IT is now used as part of the commercial strategy in the battle for competitive advantage.
   - IT is required by customers.
   - IT affects all levels of management.
   - IT affects the way management information is created and presented.
   - IT requires effective management to obtain the maximum benefit.
   - IT involves many stakeholders inside and outside the organisation.
5.
   - The organisation's overall business needs
   - The organisation's current use of IT
   - The potential opportunities and threats that IT can bring
6.
   - The industry that the organisation is in
   - The environment that the organisation operates in
   - Factors within the organisation itself
7. False. There is no guarantee that any CSF will be valid for a particular period of time. Changes in the environment that invalidate the CSF may occur at any time.

End of chapter questions

Management information system (AIA May 2008)

1. A management information system should provide information about and for a wide range of management activities that are carried out within an organisation.

   (a) Distinguish clearly between strategic, tactical and operational management activities and decisions. **(9 marks)**

   (b) Management information has characteristics, the levels of which vary with the levels of management activity. Detail this variation in relation to the following five information characteristics: time horizon, level of detail, source, degree of certainty, and frequency. **(10 marks)**

   (c) (i) What are the factors that have contributed in the past 20 years to the growth in use of management information systems in both public and private organisations?

   (ii) What roles do an executive information system, a decision support system and a transaction processing system play in the wider context of management information systems? **(6 marks)**

   (Total = 25 marks)

2. What are critical success factors? List the four sources of critical success factors according to Rockhart. **(5 marks)**

Control and security

Topic list	Syllabus reference
1 Security	9.11
2 Physical threats	9.11
3 Physical access control	9.11
4 Building controls into an information system	9.11
5 Privacy and data protection	9.11
6 Internet security issues	9.11
7 Information systems and the accountant	9.11

Introduction

Organisations are becoming increasingly **reliant on computerised information systems**.

It is vital therefore to ensure these systems are secure – to protect the information held on them, to ensure operations run smoothly, to prevent theft and to ensure compliance with legislation.

Security and legal issues crop up regularly in the examination.

PART B   INFORMATION SYSTEMS

1 Security

FAST FORWARD

Security is the protection of data from accidental or deliberate threats and the protection of an information system from such threats.

1.1 The responsibilities of ownership

If you own **something that you value** – you **look after it**. **Information** is valuable and it deserves similar care.

Key term

Security, in information management terms, means the **protection of data** from accidental or deliberate threats which might cause unauthorised modification, disclosure or destruction of data, and the **protection of the information system** from the degradation or non-availability of services.

Security refers to **technical** issues related to the computer system, psychological and **behavioural** factors in the organisation and its employees, and protection against the unpredictable occurrences of the **natural world**.

Security can be subdivided into a number of aspects.

(a) **Prevention.** It is in practice impossible to prevent all threats cost-effectively.

(b) **Detection.** Detection techniques are often combined with prevention techniques: a log can be maintained of unauthorised attempts to gain access to a computer system.

(c) **Deterrence.** As an example, computer misuse by personnel can be made grounds for disciplinary action.

(d) **Recovery procedures.** If the threat occurs, its consequences can be contained (for example checkpoint programs).

(e) **Correction procedures.** These ensure the vulnerability is dealt with (for example, by instituting stricter controls).

(f) **Threat avoidance.** This might mean changing the design of the system.

2 Physical threats

FAST FORWARD

Physical threats to security may be natural or man made. They include fire, flooding, weather, lightning, terrorist activity and accidental damage.

The **physical environment** quite obviously has a major effect on information system security, and so planning it properly is an important precondition of an adequate security plan.

2.1 Fire

Fire is the **most serious hazard** to computer systems. Destruction of data can be even more costly than the destruction of hardware.

A fire safety plan is an essential feature of security procedures, in order to prevent fire, detect fire and put out the fire. Fire safety includes:

- **Site preparation** eg fireproof materials, fire doors
- **Detection equipment** eg smoke detector alarms
- **Extinguishing equipment** eg sprinklers and extinguishers
- **Staff awareness** of fire safety procedures

2.2 Water

Water is a serious hazard. Flooding and water damage are often encountered following firefighting activities elsewhere in a building.

This problem can be countered by the use of waterproof ceilings and floors together with the provision of adequate drainage.

In some areas flooding is a natural risk, for example in parts of central London and many other towns and cities near rivers or coasts. Basements are therefore generally not regarded as appropriate sites for large computer installations.

2.3 Weather

Wind, rain and storms can all cause substantial **damage to buildings**. In certain areas the risks are greater, for example the risk of typhoons in parts of Asia. Many organisations make heavy use of prefabricated and portable offices, which are particularly vulnerable.

Cutbacks in maintenance expenditure may lead to leaking roofs or dripping pipes, which can invite problems of this type, and maintenance should be kept up if at all possible.

2.4 Lightning

Lightning and electrical storms can play havoc with power supplies, causing power failures coupled with power surges as services are restored. Adjustments in power supplies may be enough to affect computer processing operations (characterised by lights which dim as the country's population turns on electric kettles following a popular television program).

One way of combating this is by the use of **uninterruptible (protected) power supplies**. This will protect equipment from fluctuations in the supply. Power failure can be protected against by the use of a **separate generator** or rechargeable battery. It may be sufficient to maintain power only long enough to close down the computer system in an orderly manner.

2.5 Terrorist activity

Political terrorism is the main risk, but there are also threats from individuals with **grudges.**

In some cases there is very little that an organisation can do: its buildings may just happen to be in the wrong place and bear the brunt of an attack aimed at another organisation or intended to cause general disruption.

There are some avoidance measures that should be taken, however.

(a) **Physical access** to buildings should be controlled (see the next section).

(b) Organisations involved in controversial activities may consider moving into other lines of business.

(c) The organisation should consult with police and fire authorities about potential risks, and co-operate with their efforts to avoid them.

(d) The organisation should not advertise its presence by displaying its name and logo on the building.

2.6 Accidental damage

People are a physical threat to computer installations: there can be few of us who have not at some time spilt a cup of coffee over a desk covered with papers, or tripped and fallen doing some damage to ourselves or to an item of office equipment.

Combating accidental damage is a matter of:

(a) Sensible **attitudes** to office behaviour
(b) Good office **layout**
(c) Eliminating hazards such as trailing cables

Question — Fire and flooding

You are the financial controller of your organisation. The company is in the process of installing a mainframe computer, and because your department will be the primary user, you have been co-opted onto the project team with responsibility for systems installation. You have a meeting at which the office services manager will be present, and you realise that no one has yet mentioned the risks of fire or flooding in the discussions about site selection. Make a note of the issues which you would like to raise under these headings.

Answer

(a) **Fire**. Fire security measures can usefully be categorised as preventative, detective and corrective. Preventative measures include siting of the computer in a building constructed of suitable materials and the use of a site which is not affected by the storage of inflammable materials (eg stationery, chemicals). Detective measures involve the use of smoke detectors. Corrective measures may include installation of a sprinkler system (water-based or possibly gas-based to avoid electrical problems), training of fire officers and good siting of exit signs and fire extinguishers.

(b) **Flooding**. Water damage may result from flooding or from fire recovery procedures. If possible, large installations should not be situated in basements.

3 Physical access control

FAST FORWARD

Physical access controls are designed to prevent **intruders** getting near to computer equipment and/or storage media.

Physical access controls including the following.

(a) **Personnel**, including receptionists and, outside working hours, security guards, can help control human access.

(b) **Door locks** can be used where frequency of use is low. (This is not practicable if the door is in frequent use.)

(c) Locks can be combined with:

  (i) A **keypad system**, requiring a code to be entered.
  (ii) A **card entry system**, requiring a card to be 'swiped'.

(d) Intruder **alarms**.

The best form of access control would be one which **recognised** individuals immediately, without the need for personnel or cards. However, machines that can identify a person's fingerprints or scan the pattern of a retina are relatively more **expensive**, so their use is less widespread.

It may not be cost effective or practical to use the same access controls in all areas. The **security requirements of different departments** should be estimated, and appropriate measures taken. Some areas will be very restricted, whereas others will be relatively open.

Important aspects of physical access of control are **door locks** and **card entry systems**. Computer theft is becoming more prevalent as equipment becomes smaller and more portable.

3.1 Personal identification numbers (PINs)

In some organisations staff are allocated an individual **personal identification number**, or PIN, which identifies him or her to the system. Based on the security privileges allocated, the person will be **allowed** access to certain parts of a building, but prevented from accessing other areas.

3.2 Door locks

Conventional door locks are of value in certain circumstances, particularly where users are only required to pass through the door a **couple of times a day**. If the number of people using the door increases and the frequency of use is high, it will be difficult to persuade staff to lock a door every time they pass through it.

A 'good' lock must be accompanied by a **strong door**. Similarly, other points of entry into the room/complex must be as well protected, otherwise the intruder will simply use a **window** to gain access.

One difficulty with conventional locks is the matter of **key control**. Each person authorised to use the door will need a key. Cleaners and other contractors might also be issued with keys. Practices such as lending out keys or taking duplicate keys may be difficult to prevent.

One approach to this is the installation of **combination locks**, where a numbered keypad is located outside the door and access allowed only after the correct 'code', or sequence of digits has been entered. This will only be fully effective if users ensure the combination is kept confidential, and the combination is **changed** frequently.

3.3 Card entry systems

Card entry systems are a more sophisticated means of control than the use of locks, as **cards can be programmed** to allow access to certain parts of a building only, between certain times.

Cards allow a high degree of monitoring of staff movements; they can for example be used instead of clock cards to record details of time spent on site. Such cards can be incorporated into **identity cards**, which also carry the photograph and signature of the user and which must be 'displayed' at all times.

3.4 Computer theft

As computer equipment becomes **smaller** and **more portable**, it can be 'smuggled' out of buildings with greater ease. Indeed much equipment is specifically **designed for use off-site**.

A **log of all equipment** should be maintained. This may already exist in basic form as a part of the non-current asset register. The log should include the **make, model** and **serial number** of each item, together with some other organisation-generated code which identifies the **department** which owns the item, the **individual** responsible for the item and its **location**. Anyone taking any equipment off-site should book it out and book it back in.

Smaller items of equipment, such as laptop computers and floppy disks, should always be **locked securely away**. Larger items cannot be moved with ease and one approach adopted is the use of **bolts** to secure them to desks. This discourages 'opportunity' thieves. Larger organisations may also employ site security guards and install closed circuit camera systems.

Other possible precautions include secured containers in cars for laptops, and the locking away of CDs and other storage media.

Question

Security measures

You are the chief accountant at your company. Your department, located in an open-plan office, has five networked desktop PCs, two laser printers and a dot matrix printer.

You have just read an article suggesting that the best form of security is to lock hardware away in fireproof cabinets, but you feel that this is impracticable. Make a note of any alternative security measures which you could adopt to protect the hardware.

Answer

(a) 'Postcode' all pieces of hardware. Invisible ink postcoding is popular, but visible marking is a better deterrent. Heated soldering irons are ideal for imprinting postcodes onto objects with a plastic casing.

(b) Mark the equipment in other ways. Some organisations spray their hardware with permanent paint, perhaps in a particular colour (bright red is popular) or using stencilled shapes.

(c) Hardware can be bolted to desks. If bolts are passed through the desk and through the bottom of the hardware casing, the equipment can be rendered immobile.

(d) Ensure that the organisation's standard security procedures (magnetic passes, keypad access to offices, signing in of visitors etc) are followed.

4 Building controls into an information system

FAST FORWARD

It is possible to **build controls into a computerised** information system. A **balance** must be struck between the degree of control and the requirement for a user friendly system.

Controls can be classified as:

- Security controls
- Integrity controls
- Contingency controls

4.1 Security controls

Key term

Security can be defined as 'The protection of data from accidental or deliberate threats which might cause unauthorised modification, disclosure or destruction of data, and the protection of the information system from the degradation or non-availability of services'.

(Lane, *Security of Computer Based Information Systems*, 1985)

Risks to data

- Human error
  - Entering incorrect transactions
  - Failing to correct errors
  - Processing the wrong files
- Technical error such as malfunctioning hardware or software
- Natural disasters such as fire, flooding, explosion, impact, lightning
- Deliberate actions such as fraud
- Commercial espionage
- Malicious damage
- Industrial action

4.2 Integrity controls

Key terms

> **Data integrity** in the context of security is preserved when data is the same as in source documents and has not been accidentally or intentionally altered, destroyed or disclosed.
>
> **Systems integrity** refers to system operation conforming to the design specification despite attempts (deliberate or accidental) to make it behave incorrectly.

Data will maintain its **integrity** if it is **complete** and **not corrupted**. This means that:

(a) The original **input** of the data must be controlled in such a way as to ensure that the results are complete and correct.

(b) Any **processing and storage** of data must maintain the completeness and correctness of the data captured.

(c) That reports or other **output** should be set up so that they, too, are complete and correct.

4.2.1 Input controls

Input controls should ensure the **accuracy, completeness and validity** of input.

(a) **Data verification** involves ensuring data entered matches source documents.

(b) **Data validation** involves ensuring that data entered is not incomplete or unreasonable. Various checks can be used, depending on the data type.

   (i) **Check digits**. A digit calculated by the program and added to the code being checked to validate it eg modulus 11 method.

   (ii) **Control totals**. For example, a batch total totalling the entries in the batch.

   (iii) **Hash totals**. A system generated total used to check processing has been performed as intended.

   (iv) **Range checks**. Used to check the value entered against a sensible range, eg statement of financial position account number must be between 5,000 and 9,999.

   (v) **Limit checks**. Similar to a range check, but usually based on a upper limit eg must be less than 999,999.99.

Data may be **valid** (for example in the **correct format**) but still **not match source documents**.

4.2.2 Processing controls

Processing controls should ensure the **accuracy and completeness of processing**. Programs should be subject to development controls and to rigorous testing. Periodic running of test data is also recommended.

4.2.3 Output controls

Output controls should ensure the accuracy, completeness and security of output. The following measures are possible.

- Investigation and follow-up of error reports and exception reports
- Batch controls to ensure all items processed and returned
- Controls over distribution/copying of output
- Labelling of disks/tapes

4.2.4 Back-up controls

> **FAST FORWARD**
>
> A **back-up** and **archive** strategy should include:
> - Regular back-up of data (at least daily)
> - Archive plans
> - A **disaster recovery** plan including off-site storage

Back-up controls aim to maintain system and data integrity. We have classified back-up controls as an integrity control rather than a contingency control (see later this section) because back-ups should be part of the day-to-day procedures of all computerised systems.

Key term

> **Back-up** means to make a copy in anticipation of future failure or corruption. A back-up copy of a file is a duplicate copy kept separately from the main system and only used if the original fails.

The **purpose of backing-up data** is to ensure that the most recent usable copy of the data can be recovered and restored in the event of loss or corruption on the primary storage media.

In a well-planned data back-up scheme, a copy of backed-up data is delivered (preferably daily) to a secure **off-site** storage facility.

A tape **rotation scheme** can provide a restorable history from one day to several years, depending on the needs of the business.

A well-planned **back-up and archive strategy** should include:

(a) A plan and schedule for the **regular back-up of critical data**.
(b) **Archive plans**.
(c) A **disaster recovery plan** that includes off-site storage.

Regular tests should be undertaken to **verify that data backed-up can be successfully restored**.

The **intervals** at which back-ups are performed must be decided. Most organisations back up their data daily, but back-ups may need to be performed more frequently, depending on the nature of the data and of the organisation.

Even with a well planned back-up strategy some re-inputting may be required. For example, if after three hours work on a Wednesday a file becomes corrupt, the Tuesday version can be restored – but Wednesday's work will need to be re-input.

4.2.5 Archiving

A related concept is that of **archiving.** Archiving data is the process of moving data from primary storage, such as a hard disk, to tape or other portable media for long-term storage.

Archiving provides a legally acceptable **business history**, while freeing up **hard disk space**. If archived data is needed, it can be restored from the archived tape to a hard disk. Archived data can be used to recover from site-wide disasters, such as fires or floods, where data on primary storage devices is destroyed. Archiving also helps avoid the slowdown in processing which may occur if large volumes of data build up on the main operational storage.

How long data should be retained will be influenced by:

- Legal obligations
- Other business needs

Data stored for a long time should be tested periodically to ensure it is **still restorable** – it may be subject to **damage** from environmental conditions or mishandling.

4.2.6 Passwords and logical access systems

Key term

A **password** is a set of characters which may be allocated to a person, a terminal or a facility which is required to be keyed into the system before further access is permitted.

Unauthorised persons may circumvent physical access controls. A **logical access system** can prevent access to data and program files, by measures such as the following.

- Identification of the user
- Authentication of user identity
- Checks on user authority

Virtually all computer installations use passwords. Failed access attempts may be logged. Passwords are not foolproof.

- Standard system passwords (such as 1234) given when old passwords are reset or provided to new employees, must be changed
- Passwords must never be divulged to others and must never be written down
- Passwords must be changed regularly – and changed immediately if it is suspected that the password is known by others
- Obvious passwords must not be used

Passwords are also used by administrators to control access rights for the reading, modifying and deleting functions.

Some laptop computers now include **fingerprint readers** able to recognise users with a simple swipe of a finger.

4.2.7 Administrative controls

Personnel selection is important. Some employees are always in a position of trust.

- Computer security officer
- Senior systems analyst
- Database administrator

Measures to control personnel include the following.

- Careful recruitment
- Job rotation and enforced vacations
- Systems logs
- Review and supervision

For other staff, **segregation of duties** remains a core security requirement. This involves division of responsibilities into separate roles.

- Data capture and data entry
- Computer operations
- Systems analysis and programming

4.2.8 Audit trail

FAST FORWARD

An **audit trail** shows who has accessed a system and the operations performed.

The original concept of an audit trail is to enable a manager or auditor to follow transactions stage-by-stage through a system to ensure that they have been processed correctly. The intention is to:

- **Identify errors**
- **Detect fraud**

Modern integrated computer systems have cut out much of the time-consuming stage-by-stage working of older systems, but there should still be some **means of identifying individual records** and the **input and output documents** associated with the processing of any individual transaction.

> **Key term**
>
> An **audit trail** is a record showing who has accessed a computer system and what operations he or she has performed. Audit trails are useful both for maintaining security and for recovering lost transactions. Accounting systems include an audit trail component that is able to be output as a report.
>
> In addition, there are separate audit trail software products that enable network administrators to monitor use of network resources.

An audit trail should be provided so that every transaction on a file contains a **unique reference** (eg a sales system transaction record should hold a reference to the customer order, delivery note and invoice).

Typical contents of an accounting software package audit trail include the following items:

(a) A system generated **transaction number**
(b) A meaningful reference number eg invoice number
(c) Transaction type eg reversing journal, credit note, cashbook entry etc
(d) Who input the transaction (user ID)
(e) Full **transaction details** eg net and gross amount, customer ID and so on
(f) The **PC or terminal** used to enter the transaction
(g) The **date** and **time** of the entry
(h) Any additional reference or **narration** entered by the user

4.2.9 Systems integrity with a PC

Possible **controls relevant to a stand-alone PC** are as follows:

(a) Installation of a **password** routine which is activated whenever the computer is booted up, and activated after periods of inactivity
(b) The use of additional passwords on 'sensitive' files eg employee salaries spreadsheet
(c) Any data stored on floppy disk, DVD or CD should be locked away
(d) **Physical access controls**, for example door locks activated by swipe cards or PIN numbers, to prevent access into the room(s) where the computers are kept

4.2.10 Systems integrity with a LAN

The main additional risk (when compared to a stand-alone PC) is the risk of a fault **spreading across the system**. This is particularly true of **viruses**. A virus introduced onto one machine could replicate itself throughout the network. All files coming in to the organisation should be scanned using **anti-virus software** and all machines should have anti-virus software running constantly.

A further risk, depending on the type of network configuration, is that an extra PC could be 'plugged in' to the network to gain access to it. The **network management software** should detect and prevent breaches of this type.

4.2.11 Systems integrity with a WAN

Additional issues, over and above those already described are related to the extensive communications links utilised by Wide Area Networks. Dedicated land lines for data transfer and encryption software may be required.

If **commercially sensitive data** is being transferred it would be necessary to specify high quality communications equipment and to use sophisticated network software to prevent and detect any security breaches.

11: CONTROL AND SECURITY

4.3 Contingency controls

Key term

A **contingency** is an unscheduled interruption of computing services that requires measures outside the day-to-day routine operating procedures.

The preparation of a contingency plan (also known as a disaster recovery plan) is one of the stages in the development of an organisation-wide security policy. A contingency plan is necessary in case of a major **disaster**, or if some of the **security measures** discussed elsewhere **fail**.

A **disaster** occurs where the system for some reason breaks down, leading to potential **losses** of equipment, data or funds. The system **must recover as soon as possible** so that further losses are not incurred, and current losses can be rectified.

Question — Cause of system breakdown

What actions or events might lead to a system breakdown?

Answer

System breakdowns can occur in a variety of circumstances, for example:

(a) Fire destroying data files and equipment
(b) Flooding
(c) A computer virus completely destroying a data or program file
(d) A technical fault in the equipment
(e) Accidental destruction of telecommunications links (eg builders severing a cable)
(f) Terrorist attack
(g) System failure caused by software bugs which were not discovered at the design stage
(h) Internal sabotage (eg logic bombs built into the software)

4.3.1 Disaster recovery plan

Any disaster recovery plan must provide for:

(a) **Standby procedures** so that some operations can be performed while normal services are disrupted.
(b) **Recovery procedures** once the cause of the breakdown has been discovered or corrected.
(c) **Personnel management** policies to ensure that (a) and (b) above are implemented properly.

4.3.2 Contents of a disaster recovery plan

FAST FORWARD

A **disaster recovery plan** must cover all activities from the initial response to a 'disaster', through to damage limitation and full recovery. Responsibilities must be clearly spelt out for all tasks.

The **contents of a disaster recovery** (or contingency) **plan** will include the following.

Section	Comment
Definition of responsibilities	It is important that somebody (a manager or co-ordinator) is designated to take control in a crisis. This individual can then delegate specific tasks or responsibilities to other designated personnel.
Priorities	Limited resources may be available for processing. Some tasks are more important than others. These must be established in advance. Similarly, the recovery program may indicate that certain areas must be tackled first.
Back-up and standby arrangements	These may be with other installations, with a company that provides such services (eg maybe the hardware vendor); or reverting to manual procedures.
Communication with staff	The problems of a disaster can be compounded by poor communication between members of staff.
Public relations	If the disaster has a public impact, the recovery team may come under pressure from the public or from the media.
Risk assessment	Some way must be found of assessing how big an impact on the organisation a 'contained' disaster would have. For example, would all systems be fully operational if running on temporary replacement hardware.

The contingency plan is dependent on effective **back-up procedures** for data and software, and arrangements for replacement – and even alternative premises.

5 Privacy and data protection

FAST FORWARD

Privacy is the right of the individual not to suffer unauthorised disclosure of information.

Key term

Privacy is the right of the individual to control the use of information about him or her, including information on financial status, health and lifestyle (ie prevent unauthorised disclosure).

5.1 Why is privacy an important issue?

In recent years, there has been a growing fear that the ever-increasing amount of **information** about individuals held by organisations could be misused.

In particular, it was felt that an individual could easily be harmed by the existence of computerised data about him or her which was inaccurate or misleading and which could be **transferred to unauthorised third parties** at high speed and little cost.

In the UK the current legislation covering this area is the **Data Protection Act 2018**.

5.2 The Data Protection Act 2018

FAST FORWARD

The (UK) **Data Protection Act 2018** protects individuals about whom data is held. Both manual and computerised information must comply with the Act.

The Data Protection Act 2018 is an attempt to protect the **individual**. The terms of the Act cover data about individuals – **not data about corporate bodies**.

5.3 Definitions of terms used in the Act

In order to understand the Act it is necessary to know some of the technical terms used in it.

Key terms

> **Personal data** is information about a living individual, including expressions of opinion about him or her. Data about organisations is not personal data.
>
> **Data users** are organisations or individuals who control personal data and the use of personal data.
>
> A **data subject** is an individual who is the subject of personal data.

5.3.1 The data protection principles

The UK Data Protection Act includes eight Data Protection Principles with which data users must comply.

DATA PROTECTION PRINCIPLES

Schedule 1 of the Act contains the data protection principles.

1. Personal data shall be processed fairly and lawfully and, in particular, shall not be processed unless:
   (a) At least one of the conditions in Schedule 2 is met (see paragraph 5.5.3 (c) later in this chapter).
   (b) In the case of sensitive personal data, at least one of the conditions in Schedule 3 is also met (see 5.5.3 (d)).
2. Personal data shall be obtained only for one or more specified and lawful purposes, and shall not be further processed in any manner incompatible with that purpose or those purposes.
3. Personal data shall be adequate, relevant and not excessive in relation to the purpose or purposes for which they are processed.
4. Personal data shall be accurate and, where necessary, kept up to date.
5. Personal data processed for any purpose or purposes shall not be kept for longer than is necessary for that purpose or those purposes.
6. Personal data shall be processed in accordance with the rights of data subjects under this Act.
7. Appropriate technical and organisational measures shall be taken against unauthorised or unlawful processing of personal data and against accidental loss or destruction of, or damage to, personal data.
8. Personal data shall not be transferred to a country or territory outside the European Economic Area unless that country or territory ensures an adequate level of protection for the rights and freedoms of data subjects in relation to the processing of personal data.

The Act has two main aims:

(a) To protect **individual privacy**. Previous UK law only applied to **computer-based** information. The 2018 Act applies to **all personal data, in any form.**

(b) To **harmonise data protection legislation** so that, in the interests of improving the operation of the single European market, there can be a **free flow of personal data** between the member states of the EU.

5.4 The coverage of the Act

Key points of the Act can be summarised as follows.

(a) **Data users** have to **register** under the Act with the **Data Protection Registrar**.
(b) **Individuals** (data subjects) are awarded certain **legal rights**.
(c) **Data holders** must adhere to the **data protection principles**.

5.4.1 Registration under the Act

The Data Protection Registrar keeps a Register of all data users. Only registered data users are permitted to hold personal data. The data user must only hold data and use data for the registered **purposes**.

5.4.2 The rights of data subjects

The Act establishes the following rights for data subjects.

(a) A data subject may seek **compensation** through the courts for damage and any associated distress caused by the **loss, destruction** or **unauthorised disclosure** of data about himself or herself or by **inaccurate data** about himself or herself.

(b) A data subject may apply to the courts for **inaccurate data** to be **put right** or even **wiped off** the data user's files altogether. Such applications may also be made to the Registrar.

(c) A data subject may obtain **access** to personal data of which he or she is the subject. (This is known as the 'subject access' provision.) In other words, a data subject can ask to see his or her personal data that the data user is holding.

(d) A data subject can **sue** a data user for any **damage or distress** caused to him by personal data about him which is **incorrect** or **misleading** as to matter of **fact** (rather than opinion).

5.4.3 Other features of the legislation

(a) Everyone has the right to go to court to seek redress for **any breach** of data protection law.

(b) Filing systems that are structured so as to facilitate access to information about a particular person now fall within the legislation. This includes systems that are **paper-based** or on **microfilm** or **microfiche**. Personnel records meet this classification.

(c) Processing of personal data is **forbidden** except in the following circumstances.
   (i) With the **consent** of the subject. Consent cannot be implied: it must be freely given, specific and informed agreement
   (ii) As a result of a **contractual arrangement**
   (iii) Because of a **legal obligation**
   (iv) To **protect the vital interests** of the subject
   (v) Where processing is in the **public interest**
   (vi) Where processing is required to exercise **official authority**

(d) The processing of **'sensitive data'** is forbidden, unless express consent has been obtained. Sensitive data includes data relating to **racial origin, political opinions, religious beliefs,** physical or mental **health, sexual orientation** and **trade union** membership.

(e) If data about a data subject is **obtained from a third party** the data subject must be given.
   (i) The identity of the **controller** of the data
   (ii) The **purposes** for which the data are being processed
   (iii) **What data** will be disclosed and **to whom**
   (iv) The existence of a right of subject **access** to the data

(f) Data subjects have a right not only to have a **copy of data** held about them but also the right to know **why** the data is required.

Question — Data protection

Your Managing Director has asked you to recommend measures that your company, which is based in the UK, could take to ensure compliance with data protection legislation. Suggest what measures should be taken.

11: CONTROL AND SECURITY

Answer

Measures could include the following.

- Obtain consent from individuals to hold any sensitive personal data you need.
- Supply individuals with a copy of any personal data you hold about them if so requested.
- Consider if you may need to obtain consent to process personal data.
- Ensure you do not pass on personal data to unauthorised parties.

6 Internet security issues

FAST FORWARD — Establishing organisational **links to the internet** brings numerous **security dangers**.

There are a numbers of security issues associated with the internet.

(a) Corruptions such as **viruses** on a single computer can spread through the network to all of the organisation's computers. (Viruses are described at greater length later in this section.)

(b) Disaffected employees have much greater potential to do **deliberate damage** to valuable corporate data or systems because the network could give them access to parts of the system that they are not really authorised to use.

(c) If the organisation is linked to an external network, persons outside the company (**hackers**) may be able to get into the company's internal network, either to steal data or to damage the system.

(d) Employees may **download inaccurate information** or imperfect or **virus-ridden software** from an external network. For example 'beta' (free trial) versions of forthcoming new editions of many major packages are often available on the internet, but the whole point about a beta version is that it is not fully tested and may contain bugs that could disrupt an entire system.

(e) Information transmitted from one part of an organisation to another may be **intercepted**. Data can be 'encrypted' (scrambled) in an attempt to make it unintelligible to eavesdroppers, this is covered later in this section.

(f) The **communications link itself may break down or distort data**. The worldwide telecommunications infrastructure is improving thanks to the use of new technologies, and there are communications 'protocols' governing the format of data and signals transferred.

6.1 Hacking

Hacking involves attempting to gain unauthorised access to a computer system, usually through telecommunications links.

Hackers require only limited programming knowledge to cause large amounts of damage. The fact that billions of bits of information can be transmitted in bulk over the public telephone network has made it **hard to trace** individual hackers, who can therefore make repeated attempts to invade systems. Hackers, in the past, have mainly been concerned to **copy** information, but a recent trend has been their desire to **corrupt it**.

Phone numbers and passwords can be guessed by hackers using **electronic phone directories** or number generators and by software which enables **rapid guessing** using hundreds of permutations per minute.

Default passwords are also available on some electronic bulletin boards and sophisticated hackers could even try to 'tap' messages being transmitted along phone wires (the number actually dialled will not be scrambled).

One of the most recent and very serious hacking incidents affected Sony Pictures Entertainment in November 2014. A vast number of internal emails were released to the public (in which some film stars were disparagingly referred to by Sony management), In addition, some scripts for future films and some unreleased films were also leaked. The hackers called themselves the 'Guardians of Peace'. At the time of writing, it has not been definitively established who the hackers are, though the FBI in the USA points its finger at North Korea as that country was incensed by a film (The Interview) that was about to be released and which poked fun at Kim Jong-un, the president of North Korea.

PART B INFORMATION SYSTEMS

6.2 Viruses

Key term

> A **virus** is a piece of software which infects programs and data and possibly damages them, and which replicates itself.

Viruses need an **opportunity to spread**. The programmers of viruses therefore place viruses in the kind of software which is most likely to be copied. This includes:

(a) Free software (for example from the internet)

(b) Pirated software (cheaper than original versions)

(c) Games software (wide appeal)

(d) **Email attachments**. Email has become the most common means of spreading the most destructive viruses. The virus is often held in an attachment to the email message. Recent viruses have been programmed to send themselves to all addresses in the user's electronic address book

The main types of viruses (and related programs) are explained in the following table.

Type of virus/program	Explanation/Example
File viruses	File viruses infect program files. When you run an infected program the virus runs first, performs an unauthorised act and copies itself to another file or to another location (replicating itself).
Boot sector or 'stealth' viruses	The boot sector is the part of every hard disk and diskette which is read by the computer when it starts up. These 'stealth' viruses hide from virus detection programs by hiding themselves in boot records or files. If the boot sector is infected, the virus runs when the machine starts.
Trojan	A Trojan (or Trojan Horse) is a small program that performs an unexpected function. The trojan is hidden inside a 'valid' program. Trojans therefore act like a virus, but they aren't classified as a virus as they don't replicate themselves.
Logic bomb	A logic bomb is a program that is executed when a specific act is performed. The logic bomb then performs an unexpected function, often designed to cause damage.
Time bomb	A time bomb is a logic bomb activated at a certain time or date, such as Friday the 13th or April 1st.
Worm	A worm is a type of virus that can replicate (copy) itself and use memory, but cannot attach itself to other programs.
Dropper	A dropper is a program that installs a virus while performing another function.
Macro viruses	A macro virus is a piece of self-replicating code written in an application's 'macro' language. Many applications have macro capabilities including all the programs in Microsoft Office. The distinguishing factor which makes it possible to create a virus with a macro is the existence of auto-execute events. Auto-execute events are opening a file, closing a file, and starting an application. Once a macro is running, it can copy itself to other documents, delete files, and create general havoc. Melissa was a well publicised macro virus.

6.3 Protecting against viruses

The main protection against viruses is **anti-virus software**. Anti-virus software, such as McAfee or Norton's searches systems for viruses and removes any that are found. Anti-virus programs include an auto-update feature that enables the program to download profiles of new viruses, enabling the software to check for all **known** or existing viruses. Very new viruses may go undetected by anti-virus software (until the anti-virus software vendor updates their package – and the organisation installs the update).

Additional precautions include disabling floppy disk drives to prevent viruses entering an organisation via floppy disk. However, this can disrupt work processes. At the very least, organisations should ensure all files received via floppy disk and email are virus checked.

External email links can be protected by way of a **firewall** that may be configured to virus check all messages, and may also prevent files of a certain type being sent via email (eg .exe files, as these are the most common means of transporting a virus).

6.4 Encryption and other safety measures

6.4.1 Encryption

Encryption aims to ensure the security of data during transmission. It involves the translation of data into secret code. To read an encrypted file, you must have access to a secret key or password that enables you to decrypt it. Unencrypted data is called plain text; encrypted data is referred to as cipher text.

Key term

> **Encryption** involves scrambling the data at one end of the line, transmitting the scrambled data, and unscrambling it at the receiver's end of the line.

6.4.2 Authentication

Authentication is a technique of making sure that a message has come from an authorised sender. Authentication involves adding an extra field to a record, with the contents of this field derived from the remainder of the record by applying an algorithm that has previously been agreed between the senders and recipients of data.

6.4.3 Firewalls and dial-back security

Systems can have **firewalls** (which disable part of the telecoms technology) to prevent unwelcome intrusions into company systems, but a determined hacker may well be able to bypass even these.

Dial-back security operates by requiring the person wanting access to the network to dial into it to identify themselves first. The system then dials the person back on their authorised number before allowing them access.

All attempted **violations of security** should be automatically **logged** and the log checked frequently. In a multi-user system, the terminal attempting the violation may be automatically disconnected.

6.5 Jokes and hoaxes

Some programs claim to be doing something destructive to your computer, but are actually 'harmless' jokes. For example, a message may appear suggesting that your hard disk is about to be reformatted. Unfortunately, it is **easy to over-react** to the joke and cause more damage by trying to eradicate something that is not a virus.

There are a number of common hoaxes, which are widely believed. The most common of these is **Good Times**. This hoax has been around for several years, and usually takes the form of a virus warning about viruses contained in email. People pass along the warning because they are trying to be helpful, but they are wasting the time of all concerned.

PART B INFORMATION SYSTEMS

6.6 The Computer Misuse Act

FAST FORWARD

The (UK) **Computer Misuse Act 1990** was enacted to respond to the growing threat of **hacking** to computer systems and data.

The (UK) Computer Misuse Act 1990 made hacking and the deliberate infection of computer systems with viruses criminal offences. The Act defines three levels of hacking, as shown in the following table.

Crime	Explanation
Unauthorised access	This means that a hacker, who, knowing he or she is unauthorised, tries to gain access to a computer system. It is the **attempt** which is the crime: the hacker's success or failure is irrelevant.
Unauthorised access with the **intention** of committing another offence	This results in **stricter penalties** than unauthorised access alone.
Unauthorised **modification** of data or programs	In effect this makes the deliberate introduction of computer **viruses** into a system a **criminal offence**. Guilt is based on the **intention to impair** the operation of a computer or program, or prevent or **hinder access** to data.

Although the legislation was originally aimed at external unauthorised users of the system, it can also be applied to internal users.

Possible sources of evidence that could be used in a case brought under The Computer Misuse Act include software audit trails, communications link records, internet Service Provider records and logs such as the operating system transaction log.

6.7 Denial of service attack

Another threat to internet websites and related systems is the 'Denial of Service (DoS)' attack. A denial of service attack is characterised by an attempt by attackers to prevent legitimate users of a service from using that service. Examples include attempts to:

- 'Flood' or bombard a site or network, thereby preventing legitimate network traffic (major sites such as Amazon.com have been targeted in this way)
- Disrupt connections and communications, thereby preventing access to a service
- Prevent a particular individual from accessing a service

Exam focus point

Exams often include questions based on topical issues. Keep up to date with IT developments and news. Aspects of control and security are examined regularly.

7 Information systems and the accountant

FAST FORWARD

In many organisations the **accountant** plays an **important role** in the **IS/IT** function.

Depending on the size and structure of the organisation, the responsibility for ensuring an organisation's information systems operate efficiently and comply with relevant legislation may fall to the accountant. In other organisations these responsibilities may rest with the Company Secretary or the Information Systems Manager.

Historically, accountants have played an important role in information systems installations. The accounting function was often the first area of an organisation to be computerised and many organisations lacked specialist IS/IT staff.

As the importance of IS/IT has increased large and medium sized organisations have created specialist IS/IT departments. In many smaller organisations the accountant still has responsibility for information systems.

Even in larger organisations, the accountant still has an important role to play in the information systems function. Key areas include:

- Investment appraisal
- Cost-benefit analysis
- Internal audit requirements
- Performance measurement eg metrics
- Presenting user concerns (eg accounts department staff)
- Assessing usability

PART B INFORMATION SYSTEMS

Chapter roundup

- **Security** is the protection of data from accidental or deliberate threats and the protection of an information system from such threats.
- **Physical threats** to security may be natural or man made. They include fire, flooding, weather, lightning, terrorist activity and accidental damage.
- **Physical access controls** are designed to prevent **intruders** getting near to computer equipment and/or storage media.
- Important aspects of physical access control are **door locks** and **card entry systems**. Computer theft is becoming more prevalent as equipment becomes smaller and more portable.
- It is possible to **build controls into** a **computerised** information system. A **balance** must be struck between the degree of control and the requirement for a user friendly system.
- A **back-up** and **archive** strategy should include:
    - Regular back-up of data (at least daily)
    - Archive plans
    - A **disaster recovery** plan including off-site storage
- An **audit trail** shows who has accessed a system and the operations performed.
- A **disaster recovery plan** must cover all activities from the initial response to a 'disaster', through to damage limitation and full recovery. Responsibilities must be clearly spelt out for all tasks.
- **Privacy** is the right of the individual not to suffer unauthorised disclosure of information.
- The (UK) **Data Protection Act 2018** protects individuals about whom data is held. Both manual and computerised information must comply with the Act.
- Establishing organisational **links to the internet** brings numerous **security dangers**.
- The (UK) **Computer Misuse Act 1990** was enacted to respond to the growing threat of **hacking** to computer systems and data.
- In many organisations the **accountant** plays an **important role** in the IS/IT function.

Quick quiz

1. List three physical access control methods.
2. List four risks to data.
3. What is the purpose of taking a back-up?
4. Why should certain duties be segregated between staff members?
5. List six possible items shown on an accounting package audit trail report.
6. What is 'personal data' under the (UK) Data Protection Act (1998)?
7. Does the (UK) Data Protection Act 2018 cover data held on manual system, on computerised systems or on both manual and computerised systems?
8. Briefly describe the process of encryption.
9. List the three levels of hacking referred to in the (UK) Computer Misuse Act 1990.
10. What is the most common method of spreading a virus?

Answers to quick quiz

1. Personnel (security guards), mechanical devices (eg keys), electronic devices (eg card-swipe systems, PIN keypads).

2.
   - Human error
   - Hardware error
   - Software error
   - Deliberate actions

   You may have come up with others.

3. To enable valid files to be restored in case of a future corruption or failure.

4. To reduce the opportunity for fraud and/or malicious damage.

5. Six of the following:
   - Transaction number
   - Transaction date and time
   - User ID
   - Transaction type
   - Amount
   - Terminal/PC used to input
   - User entered description or narration

6. Information about a living individual.

7. Both.

8. Encryption involves scrambling data at one end of the communications link, transmitting the scrambled data, then receiving and unscrambling the data at the other end of the link.

9. Unauthorised access, unauthorised access with the intention of modification and finally unauthorised modification.

10. Email.

End of chapter question

Controls (AIA November 2007)

Control and security of computerised information systems should be of prime importance to organisations and be a constant theme applied by new systems designers.

Required

(a) List and briefly explain the purposes of controls applied in designing computerised information systems. **(6 marks)**

(b) Controls exist over data movement into, through and out from computerised systems.

   (i) Describe **two** accuracy controls and **two** completeness controls often applied to data input to a system. **(8 marks)**

   (ii) Describe **three** controls that may be applied to ensure accuracy and continuing reliability of the data held in storage in a system. **(6 marks)**

(c) Briefly explain the concepts of parity bit control and echo check applied as data transmission controls within computer systems. **(5 marks)**

(Total = 25 marks)

PART B INFORMATION SYSTEMS

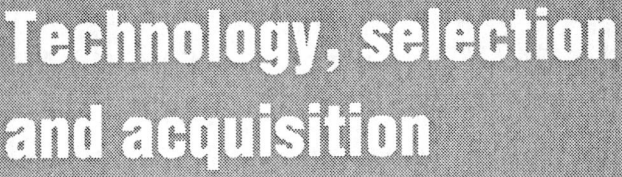

Technology, selection and acquisition

Topic list	Syllabus reference
1 Input devices	9.12
2 Data capture: choosing input devices for a computer system	9.12
3 Output devices	9.12
4 Storage devices	9.12
5 Software sources	9.12
6 Invitations To Tender (ITT)	9.12
7 Evaluating supplier proposals	9.12
8 The advantages and disadvantages of bespoke and off-the-shelf software	9.12
9 Software contracts and licences	9.12
10 Outsourcing	9.12

Introduction

In this chapter we look briefly at issues to consider when deciding upon **input**, **output** and **storage devices**, before turning our attention to the issues to consider when **acquiring software** for information systems.

We consider the options available when **sourcing software**, before examining the issues when obtaining and evaluating **supplier proposals**.

The relative advantages and disadvantages of **bespoke** and **off-the-shelf** software are covered next – and the chapter concludes with an outline of **software licensing** and **outsourcing** issues.

1 Input devices

> **FAST FORWARD**
>
> There are a range of **input** devices available. The most efficient method will depend on the circumstances of each situation.

1.1 The keyboard

The keyboard is the most often used tool for computer input.

Keying data into a computer using a keyboard can be a **labour-intensive** process. In many cases the process of inputting data is speeded up through some form of automated **data capture**. We will look at automatic input devices later in this section.

1.2 The VDU or monitor

A VDU (visual display unit) or 'monitor' displays text and graphics. The screen's **resolution** is the number of pixels that are lit up. A **pixel** is a picture element – a 'dot' on the screen, as it were. The fewer the pixels on screen, the larger each individual pixel will be, so fewer pixels mean lower resolution or image quality. A larger number of smaller pixels will provide a higher resolution display.

Touch-sensitive screens have been developed which allow the monitor to be used as an input device. Selections are made by users touching areas of the screen. Sensors, built into the screen surround, detect which area has been touched. These devices are widely used in vending situations, such as the selling of train tickets.

1.3 Mice and trackball devices

A **wheeled mouse** is a handheld device with a rubber ball protruding from a small hole in its base. The mouse is moved over a flat surface, and as it moves, internal sensors pick up the motion and convert it into electronic signals which **instruct the cursor on screen to move**.

The wheeled mouse is slowly being replaced by the **optical mouse**. The optical mouse has a small light-emitting diode (LED) that bounces light off the surface the mouse is moved across. The mouse contains sensors that convert this movement into co-ordinates the computer can understand.

A typical mouse has two or three **buttons** which can be pressed (**clicked**) to send specific signals. Newer mice also have a **wheel** used to scroll within pages or documents that can't all be displayed on a single screen.

Similar to the mouse is the **trackball**, which is often found on laptop computers. Trackballs comprise a casing fixed to the computer, and a ball which protrudes upwards. The user moves the ball by hand. Other mobile computers use a **touch-sensitive pad** for mouse functions; others have a tiny **joystick** in the centre of the keyboard.

1.4 Voice data entry (VDE)

Voice recognition software is now sufficiently developed to allow computers to accept **voice input** via a **microphone**. A particularly useful application is the use of VDE software and **translation programs** that allow users from different countries to communicate.

1.5 Automatic input devices

In the following paragraphs we explain some of the most common document reading methods. Document reading methods reduce the manual work involved in data input. This **saves time and money** and also **reduces errors**.

1.5.1 Magnetic ink character recognition (MICR)

Magnetic ink character recognition (**MICR**) involves the recognition by a machine of special formatted characters printed in magnetic ink. The characters are read using a specialised reading device. The main advantage of MICR is its speed and accuracy, but MICR documents are expensive to produce. The main commercial application of MICR is in the banking industry – on cheques and deposit slips.

1.5.2 Optical mark reading (OMR)

Optical mark reading involves the marking of a pre-printed form with a ballpoint pen or typed line or cross in an appropriate box. The card is then read by an OMR device which senses the mark in each box using an electric current and translates it into machine code. Applications in which OMR is used include **National Lottery** entry forms and answer sheets for multiple-choice questions.

1.5.3 Scanners and Optical Character Recognition (OCR)

A scanner is device that can **read text or illustrations printed on paper** and translate the information into a **form the computer can use**. To edit text read by an optical scanner, you need **optical character recognition (OCR)** software to translate the image into text. You may use a scanner and OCR to obtain 'digital' versions of paper documents. To enable the OCR software to recognise the characters correctly, the copy must be of good quality.

1.5.4 Barcodes and EPOS

Barcodes are groups of marks which, by their spacing and thickness, indicate specific codes or values. Electronic Point of Sale (**EPOS**) devices, which include barcode readers, enable supermarkets and other retailers to record and manage inventory movements – and provide detailed sales information.

1.5.5 Digital cameras

These capture images in digital form and allow easy transfer to a computer. Images may then be manipulated by image-processing software.

2 Data capture: choosing input devices for a computer system

When a computer user is planning a new computer system, one aspect of the system design is the choice of methods of data capture. Data capture is a term for getting data into the computer for processing.

The ideal method of data capture should be one that:

- Maximises convenience; and
- Minimises both cost and the risk of input errors.

At one time, large transaction processing systems captured data on to specially-designed forms, then converted this data into machine-readable form such as punched cards. The data was then input to the computer system through a card reader. This process, involving manual preparation of forms and conversion into a computer input medium was both time-consuming and error-prone.

With network systems, it is now common for computer users to input data by means of a keyboard and visual display screen. The use of on-screen prompts and a user-friendly interface can speed up the input process and limit the risk of input errors, but input from keyboard and screen terminals is still slow and error-prone.

For large transaction processing systems, it is therefore common for data capture to involve the use of input devices that can read pre-prepared information, such as bar codes on products in a store, which can be read at check-out desks and used by the computer system to calculate what the customer has to pay, produce a receipt and update the store's inventory. Similarly magnetic ink characters on bank cheques enable details of cheque payments to be read directly into the bank's computer system and also used for automated cheque clearing. simple printed characters on some standardised forms and documents (such a payment slips for utility bills and credit card payments) can be used by Optical Character Reader (OCR) devices.

The methods of data capture for use in a computer application will depend on several factors.

(a) **The type of application**. For some applications, the choice of data capture method is limited. For example, when a system requires interactive dialogue between the computer system and the computer user, input with a keyboard and mouse (or similar device) is probably necessary. For example, most word processing systems use keyboard input, although voice entry technology is improving.

(b) **Speed and volume of input**. Some systems involve only limited amounts of data entry, which is not time-critical. For these systems, input by keyboard and mouse may be sufficient. Some systems involve large volumes of input, where a more efficient and error-free data capture method is required.

(c) **Error tolerance**. When a system relies on a small level of errors – such as checkout systems in supermarkets and the processing of bank payments – the data capture method should be one that helps to minimise the risk of errors.

(d) **Cost**. The choice of data capture method should also have regard to cost. The cost of the data capture method should be appropriate for the system and its uses.

3 Output devices

> **FAST FORWARD**
>
> The most often used methods of computer **output** are **printers** and **screen display**.

3.1 Printers

Laser printers print a whole page at a time, rather than line by line. The **quality** of output is very **high**. Laser printers are relatively expensive to purchase, but compared with inkjet printers, running costs are relatively low.

Inkjet printers are small and reasonably cheap. They work by sending a jet of ink on to the paper to produce the required characters.

Older style printers, that use tractor-fed rolls of paper, are still used in some organisations for printing high volumes. An example is a **dot matrix** printer, which is a character printer which prints a single character at a time. Their main drawback is their **low-resolution**. They are also relatively **slow** and **noisy**.

3.2 The VDU or monitor

Screens were described earlier in this chapter, as they are used together with computer keyboards for **input**. It should also be clear that they can be used as an **output** medium, primarily where the output **volume is low** (for example, a single enquiry) and **no permanent output** is required (for example, the current balance on an account).

3.3 The choice of output medium

Choosing a suitable output medium depends on a number of factors.

Factor	Comment
Hard copy	Is a printed version of the output needed?
Quantity	For example, a VDU screen can hold a certain amount of data, but it becomes more difficult to read when information goes 'off-screen' and can only be read a 'page' at a time.
Speed	For example, if a single enquiry is required it may be quicker to make notes from a VDU display.
Suitability for further use	Output to a file would be appropriate if the data will be processed further, maybe in a different system.
Cost	The 'best' output device may not be justifiable on the grounds of cost – another output medium should be chosen.

Output devices for a computer system accept data or information or data from the computer and convert it into a suitable output form. The form of output may be:

- 'Hard copy' – in printed form
- 'Soft copy' – in the form of electronic data or information displayed on a screen.

With hard copy, the choice of printer depends on the volume and speed of output processing requirements. Laser printers are fast (printing pages at a time) but more expensive than line printers (which print one line at a time) and character printers that, although quite fast, print characters at a time (such as ink-jet printers).

Output on to a display screen is suitable when the user does not necessarily want a permanent hard copy. The user also has an option to print out screen displays, email messages and file attachments to emails.

The user may be satisfied with output on to an electronic medium, perhaps the internal memory of the user's personal computer. Information stored digitally can be retrieved at any time and, if required, printed out.

3.4 Audio output

Speakers provide output for audio files, such as MP3 files.

4 Storage devices

> **FAST FORWARD**
>
> Hard disks, flash drives and DVDs are common forms of storage.

We covered some storage devices in Chapter 7 section 2. **Memory** is a **computer's primary storage**, however the information stored will be lost when the machine is turned off. Therefore **backing** (or **secondary**) **storage** is required to save the information for future use.

Hard disks are the most common storage medium but in recent years, **flash drives** and **DVDs** (digital video/versatile disks) have become more popular due to **high speed access** and **storage capacity**.

5 Software sources

> **FAST FORWARD**
>
> An organisation has a range of options when sourcing software. The four main options are:
>
> - A standard **off-the-shelf** package
> - Amended standard package
> - Standard package plus additions
> - Have **bespoke** software written

An organisation has a range of options when sourcing software for information systems. The four main options are described in the following table.

Source	Comment
Standard off-the-shelf package	This is the simplest option. The organisation purchases and installs a ready-made solution.
Amended standard package	A standard package is purchased, but some customisation is undertaken so that the software meets the organisation's requirements. This may require access to the source code.
Standard package plus additions	The purchased standard package is not amended itself, but additional software that integrates with the standard package is developed. This also may require access to the source code.
Bespoke package	Programmers write an application to meet the specific needs of the organisation. This can be a time-consuming and expensive process.

In this chapter we discuss the process and relative advantages of the two main options – purchasing an application off-the-shelf and developing a bespoke solution. The other two options include elements of both of these two main options.

Key terms

Bespoke software is designed for a specific user or situation. It may be written either 'in-house' by the IS department or externally by a software house.

An **off-the-shelf package** is one that is sold to a wide range of users. The package is written to handle requirements that are common to a wide range of organisations.

5.1 Choosing an application package off-the shelf

FAST FORWARD

Off-the-shelf software is produced to meet requirements that are common to many organisations. The software is likely to be available **immediately** and **cost significantly less** than bespoke solutions. However, as it has not been written specifically for the organisation, it may not meet all their requirements.

Off-the-shelf packages are generally available for functions that are likely to be performed similarly across a range of organisations eg accounting. The following table describes some of the factors to consider when choosing an off-the-shelf application package.

Factor	Comment
User requirements	Does the package fit the user's particular requirements? Matters to consider include data volumes, data validation routines, number of users and the reports available.
Processing times	Are the processing times fast enough? If response times to enquiries are slow, the user might consider the package unacceptable.
Documentation	Is there full and clear documentation for the user? A comprehensive user manual, a quick reference guide and online help should be considered.
Compatibility	Is the package compatible with existing hardware and software? Can data be exchanged with other related systems?
Controls	Access and security controls (eg passwords) should be included, as should processing controls that enable the accuracy of processing operations to be confirmed.

Factor	Comment
User-interface	Users are most affected by the user-interface design. The interface should be clear, logical, and consistent, and should follow standard interface conventions such as those used on most packages produced for use with the Microsoft Windows operating system.
Modification	Can the package be modified by the user – allowing the user to tailor it to meet their needs?
Support, maintenance and updates	The availability and cost of support, such as a telephone help-line, should be considered, as should the arrangements for updates and upgrades. This is particularly important if software is likely to be affected by changes in legislation eg a payroll package.
Cost	An organisation should aim to purchase a package that will meet their requirements. However, a package should not be purchased if the cost outweighs the value of the benefits it should bring.

5.2 Developing a bespoke application

FAST FORWARD

Bespoke software should be written so as to **match** the organisation's requirements exactly. However, the software is likely to be considerably **more expensive** than an off-the-shelf package. Bespoke software may be designed and written 'in-house' by the IS department, or externally by a software house.

Producing a bespoke software system involves all the tasks included in the software development and testing cycle.

The process is summarised in the diagram below, and explained in the table that follows.

The software development cycle

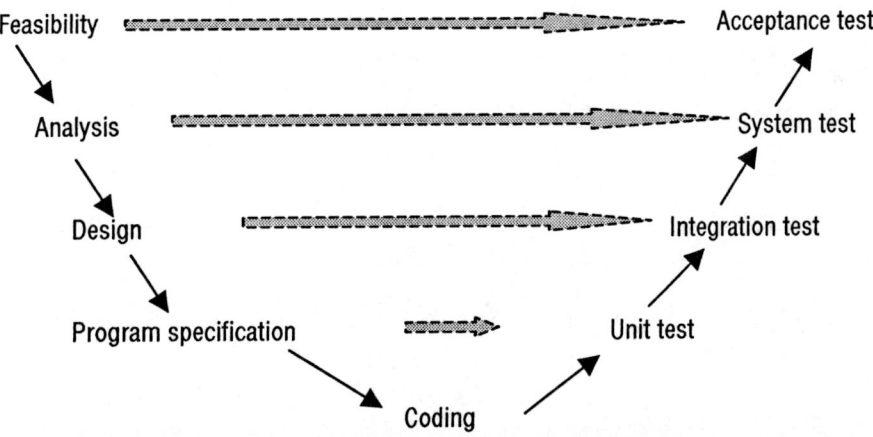

Stages of software development	Comment
Feasibility and analysis	The feasibility of software solutions would have usually been covered during the overall system feasibility study. An analysis of the software requirements should therefore be available.
Design and program specification	The software requirements are used to develop a systems design specification, which in turn is used to produce a detailed program specification. The specification would be used by in-house software developers, or would be distributed to software producers (as part of the invitation to tender – covered below).

Stages of software development	Comment
Coding	Software producers will decide how to build the package, for example identifying parts of existing programs that may be used, and establishing what will need to be coded (ie written) from scratch. Prototyping may be used to help ensure user requirements are met.
Testing Unit; Integration; System; Acceptance	Unit testing tests individual programs (or units) operating alone. Integration testing tests how two or more units of the software interact with each other. System testing tests the complete package and how it interacts with other software programs. User acceptance testing aims to ensure all user requirements included in the software specification have been met.

6 Invitations To Tender (ITT)

A number of suppliers may be invited to tender (bid) to supply specific software (the tendering procedure could also be used for hardware, or for a complete system).

Key term

> An **Invitation To Tender** is a document that invites suppliers to bid for the supply of specified software, or hardware, or both.

There are a number of possible options available to identify possible suppliers who may be in a position to submit a realistic tender:

- **Trade magazines and websites** may include software advertisements and reviews
- **Computer consultants** may have experience and/or knowledge of suitable suppliers
- **Establish who supplies other similar organisations** – it is likely these suppliers could also meet the requirements of a similar organisation

FAST FORWARD

> An organisation that requires bespoke software to be written may issue an **Invitation to Tender (ITT)** to a range of potential suppliers. The **contents of a typical ITT** could include:
>
> - Covering letter
> - Instructions
> - Detailed software requirements
> - Details of development model/methodology
> - Request for further details of the proposed software contract

The contents of a typical invitation to tender (ITT) are outlined in the following table. This format could be used when inviting tenders for bespoke or off-the-shelf software – although sections such as the development methodology would be shorter for off-the-shelf tenders, as this would refer only to any proposed amendments to the package.

ITT section	Comment
Covering letter	An ITT will include a letter inviting the supplier to tender. The letter should specify: • Contact names for queries relating to the tendering process and for technical queries • The closing date for submitting tenders
Instructions	Instructions to tenderers should specify the information required in a tender. Instructions are likely to require tenderers to specify: • Areas of their tender that do not comply with the software • Specification provided, and the reasons why • The period of validity for the tender • The basis for calculating prices, whether prices are estimates or a quote • An indication of timescale – when work could start and an approximate completion date • Alternative ways of approaching parts of the software design than indicated in the requirements specification
Detailed software requirements	The ITT must include a detailed requirements specification so tenderers know exactly what they are tendering for. This should include: • The purpose of the system • The volume of data to be processed • Processing requirements (including details of inputs and outputs, and interfaces with other systems) • The number of locations and users requiring access • The speed of processing required, eg response times • Expected life of the system • Possible upgrades or expansion anticipated When submitting their bids, some potential suppliers may come up with alternative specifications – these must be fully explained.
Details of development model/ methodology	This section of the ITT requires tenderers to provide a description of the methodology or systems development model used to develop their software. The aim is to ensure that the supplier produces software using accepted development techniques – reducing the possibility of poor quality software.
Request for details of the proposed software contract	The ITT document should request information from potential suppliers relating to the key terms of any future software contract. We cover software contracts later in this chapter.

7 Evaluating supplier proposals

Once vendor proposals have been obtained, they should be evaluated against what was requested within the ITT. There are many factors that should be considered when evaluating proposals. The factors to consider fit into three general categories:

- **Technical**, how well does the proposal meet the specified technical requirements?
- **Support**, what after-sales support is included?
- **Cost**, what do we get for our money?

Some of the main factors to consider when evaluating supplier proposals are described in the following table. Some of the relevant points are the same as those considered when choosing off-the-shelf software.

Factor	Comment
Organisation needs	How well does the software meet the requirements of the organisation? If some requirements aren't met, how important are they – can they be satisfied through other means?
Speed	Can the system cope with data volumes; is response time affected by high data volumes?
Documentation	Is there full and clear documentation for the user, and a technical manual that would allow further development?
Compatibility	Is the package compatible with existing hardware and software? Can data be exchanged with other related systems?
Controls	Access and security controls (eg passwords) should be included, as should processing controls that enable the accuracy of processing operations to be confirmed.
User-friendly	Software should be relatively easy to use and tolerant to user errors. Menu structures should be logical, the software should follow standard user-interface conventions.
Modification	Can the package be modified by the user – allowing the organisation to tailor it to meet their specific needs?
Demonstration	A demonstration version of the software may be available – this should provide a good idea of how the finished product would look, feel and operate.
Training provided	Training is essential for the organisation to utilise the software effectively.
Support, maintenance and updates	The availability and cost of support, such as a telephone help-line, should be considered, as should the arrangements for updates and upgrades. This is particularly important if software is likely to be affected by changes in legislation eg a payroll package.
Conditions included in the software contract	The software contract includes terms relating to the actual supply and use of the software.
Supplier size, reputation and customer base	Software suppliers that have been in business for a reasonable amount of time, and who have an established client base, are more likely to remain in business – and therefore be in a position to provide support. References may be available from existing customers, attesting to the quality of software and support.
Cost	An organisation should aim to purchase a package that will meet their requirements. However, a package should not be purchased if the cost outweighs the value of the benefits it should bring.

7.1 Comparing supplier proposals

An organisation may receive a number of apparently viable tenders. Tenders are likely to have different strengths and weaknesses – a process to establish the 'best' tender needs to be established. Two common ways of comparing software or systems are benchmark tests and weighted ranking scores.

Suppliers' proposals need to be evaluated, perhaps using **benchmark tests**. Other relevant factors include how well the software would meet **user requirements**, user-friendliness, **controls**, **compatibility** and **cost**. Supplier **reputation** and **reliability** should also be considered.

7.1.1 Benchmark tests

There are several factors involved in measuring the capability of a system. Benchmark tests are particularly useful to compare system speed and capacity.

Key term

> **Benchmark tests** test how long it takes a machine and program to run through a particular routine or set of routines.

Benchmark tests are carried out to compare the performance of a piece of hardware or software against pre-set criteria. Typical criteria which may be used as benchmarks include speed of performance of a particular operation, acceptable volumes before a degradation in response times is apparent and the general user-friendliness of equipment. Benchmarks can cover subjective tests such as user-friendliness, although it may be harder to reach definitive conclusions.

For example, an organisation comparing accounting software packages may test a number of different packages on its own existing hardware to see which performed the best according to various predefined criteria (eg speed of response, ability to process different volumes of transactions, reporting capabilities and so on).

Once the performance of the software package under consideration has been evaluated, the acquiring organisation should consider other features of the proposal, possibly using a weighted ranking system.

7.1.2 Weighted ranking

Key term

> A **weighted ranking** system involves establishing a number of factors important to a system, giving each factor a numerical weighting to reflect its importance, and using these weightings to calculate a score for each supplier (or software, or system).

FAST FORWARD

> A **weighted ranking** scoring system may be used to evaluate software proposals from a number of different vendors.

The factors chosen to be used in the weighted ranking, and the relative importance of each factor will vary according to the purpose of the software/system under consideration. Judgements need to be made in the selection of criteria, the weightings applied to the criteria and the scores allocated. These judgements must be made by people who have a good understanding of the software/system requirements.

The following example shows how weighted ranking scores could be calculated.

Case Study

An organisation must chose between three software suppliers.

The decision-makers within the organisation have decided on the relevant criteria and weightings that will be used to judge the suppliers. This information is shown in the following model, together with the scores that have been allocated to each supplier.

Weighted ranking							
Ranking scale: 3 = best supplier, 1 = worst		Supplier A software		Supplier B software		Supplier C software	
Criteria	Weight	Rank	Weighted rank score	Rank	Weighted rank score	Rank	Weighted rank score
User friendliness	9	2	18	3	27	1	9
Cost	4	1	4	2	8	3	12
Controls/Security	8	1	8	3	24	2	16
Processing speed	7	3	21	2	14	1	7
Support	10	2	20	1	10	3	30
		Total score	71	Total score	83	Total score	74

The weighted ranking calculation shows that the software supplied by Supplier B appears to best meet the organisation's needs.

8 The advantages and disadvantages of bespoke and off-the-shelf software

8.1 Bespoke software

Bespoke software is written to meet the specific needs of an organisation.

8.1.1 Advantages of bespoke software

Advantages of having software specially written include the following.

(a) If it is well-written, the software should meet the organisation's specific needs.

(b) Data and file structures may be chosen by the organisation rather than having to meet the structures required by standard software packages.

(c) The company may be able to do things with its software that competitors cannot do with theirs. In other words it is a source of competitive advantage.

(d) Similar organisations may wish to purchase the software.

(e) The software should be able to be modified to meet future needs.

8.1.2 Disadvantages of bespoke software

Key **disadvantages** are:

(a) As the software is being developed from scratch, there is a risk that the package may not perform as intended.

(b) There is a greater chance of 'bugs'. Widely used off-the-shelf software is more likely to have had bugs identified and removed.

(c) Development will take longer than purchasing ready-made software.

(d) The cost is considerable when compared with a ready-made package.

(e) Support costs are also likely to be higher than with off-the-shelf software.

8.1.3 Overcoming the risks of bespoke development

Building a bespoke software application involves much time, effort and money. The risks associated with such an undertaking are that the resulting software:

- Does not meet user needs
- Does not interact as intended with other systems
- Is produced late
- Is produced over-budget

These risks can be minimised or overcome by:

(a) Good project management.

(b) Involving users at all stages of development.

(c) Ensuring in-house IT staff are able to maintain and support bespoke systems supplied from outside parties.

(d) Ensuring the ITT document includes details of all file structures required, and details of interfaces with other systems.

8.2 Off-the-shelf packages

Advantages of an off-the-shelf package are:

(a) The software is likely to be available immediately.

(b) A ready-made package will almost certainly be cheaper because it is 'mass-produced''.

(c) The software is likely to have been written by software specialists and so should be of a high quality.

(d) A successful package will be continually updated by the software manufacturer.

(e) Other users will have used the package already, and a well-established package should be relatively free of bugs.

(f) Good packages are well-documented, with easy-to-follow user manuals or online help.

(g) Some standard packages can be customised to the user's specific needs (see below).

The **disadvantages** of ready-made packages are as follows.

(a) The organisation is purchasing a standard solution. A standard solution may not be well suited to the organisation's particular needs.

(b) The organisation is dependent on the supplier for maintenance of the package – ie updating the package or providing assistance in the event of problems. It is unlikely that the supplier would give access to the code that would allow organisations with the relevant expertise to amend the software themselves.

(c) Competitors may well use the same package, removing any chance of using IS/IT for competitive advantage.

(d) The package supplier may go out of business or be taken over which could affect the support the organisation receives.

8.3 Customised versions of standard packages

Standard packages can be customised so that they fit an organisation's specific requirements. This can be done by purchasing the source code of the package and making modifications in-house, or by paying the producer of the package to customise it.

Advantages of customisation are similar to those of producing a bespoke system, with the additional advantages that:

(a) Development time should be much quicker, given that most of the system will be written already.

(b) If the work is done in-house the organisation gains considerable knowledge of how the software works and may be able to 'tune' it so that it works more efficiently with the company's hardware.

Disadvantages of customising a standard package include the following.

(a) It may prove more costly than expected, because new versions of the standard package will also have to be customised.

(b) Customisation may delay delivery of the software.

(c) Customisation may introduce bugs that do not exist in the standard version.

(d) If done in-house, the in-house team may have to learn new skills.

(e) If done by the original manufacturer, the disadvantages of being dependent on the supplier for maintenance applies (as with off-the-shelf packages).

8.4 Add-ons and programming tools

Two other ways of trying to give a computer user more flexibility with packages are:

(a) The sale of 'add-ons' to a basic package, which an organisation may purchase if the add-ons suit their particular needs.

(b) The provision of programming tools (such as fourth generation languages) with a package, which allows users to write amendments to the software (without having to be a programming expert).

> **Exam focus point**
>
> An exam question could easily be set requiring you to discuss whether or not a company should opt for bespoke, off-the-shelf or customised software.

9 Software contracts and licences

9.1 Software contracts

> **FAST FORWARD**
>
> The agreement to supply bespoke software should be formally laid out in a contract. **Software contracts** include provisions relating to matters such as warranty, ownership and liability.

The agreement to supply bespoke software should be formally laid out in a contract. The contract to supply the software is likely to include terms relating to:

(a) The cost, and what this figure does and does not include.
(b) Delivery date.
(c) Ownership of the source code, sometimes referred to as ownership rights.
(d) Right to make copies.
(e) Number of licensed users.
(f) Performance criteria, such as what the software will and will not do, processing speed.
(g) Warranty period.
(h) Support available.
(i) Arrangements for upgrades.
(j) Maintenance arrangements.

9.2 Software licences

FAST FORWARD

A **software licence** typically covers issues such as the number of users, right to copy and a limitation of liability.

Packaged software generally has a licence, the **terms** of which users are deemed to have agreed to the moment the package is unwrapped or a seal is broken.

A licence typically covers the following areas:

(a) **How many users** can use the software.

(b) Whether the software may be **modified**.

(c) In what circumstances the licence is **terminated**.

(d) A **limitation of liability** should the software contain bugs or be misused (in an 'exclusion clause'). This is a complex area that is still developing. The representations that the software supplier makes regarding the package's capabilities would also be taken into account in any legal dispute.

When a user purchases software they are merely buying the **right to use** the software in line with the terms and conditions within the licence agreement. The licence will be issued with the software, on paper or in electronic form. It contains the terms and conditions of use, as set out by the software publisher or owner of the copyright. A breach of the licence conditions usually means the owner's copyright has been infringed. In the UK, computer software is defined as a 'Literary Work' in the Copyright, Designs and Patents Act (1988).

9.2.1 Software piracy

The **unauthorised copying** of software is referred to as software **piracy**. If an organisation is using illegal copies of software, the organisation may face a civil suit, and corporate officers and individual employees may have criminal liability.

In the UK, remedies for civil copyright infringement may include damages to compensate the copyright owners for damage caused to their business, including reputation, and for loss of sales. Criminal penalties can include unlimited fines and two years' imprisonment or both.

The most common type of software misuse in a business setting is referred to as **Corporate Over-Use**. This is the installation of software packages on more machines than there are licences for. For example if a company purchases five single-user licences of a software program but installs the software on ten machines, then they will be using five infringing copies. If a company is running a large network and more users have access to a software program than the company has licences for, this too is Corporate Over-Use.

A grey area is the additional installation of programs on portable or laptop computers for use off-site. Generally speaking, if a person has a program installed on their desktop in the office and the **same person** has the same program on their laptop for off-site use, then this usually counts as one user under the licence rather than two. However, the terms in different licences may differ.

To ensure they **do not infringe copyright** organisations should:

- Make sure they receive and keep licences – these are valuable documents
- Track the number of users with access to licensed programs
- Periodically check all computers for unlicensed software
- Buy from reputable dealers
- Get a written quote listing hardware/software specification and version
- Require an itemised invoice giving details of all hardware and software supplied

In the UK, the Copyright, Designs and Patents Act 1998 specifically allows the making of back-up copies of software, but only providing it is for lawful use.

Extracts from a typical licence for an off-the-shelf package follow.

Case Study

Program & licence

(a) The 'Program' means the licensed software programs as stored on the computer disks or compact disks included in this box.

(b) This Licence permits you to **install the Program on a single personal computer (or single network, where you have purchased this version**) and install data onto the Program for a single set of data at any one time (unless, and to the extent that, you have purchased the relevant licence for multiple users and/or multiple sets of data from X Co Ltd), whether for a company, partnership, group, person or otherwise, in the course of which you may make one copy of the Program in any computer readable format for back-up purposes. The copyright design right and any other intellectual property rights in the source and object codes of this Program vest exclusively in X Co Ltd ('X Co Ltd').

(c) The **Program may not be copied** without the express consent in writing of X Co Ltd under such terms as it shall determine. In particular, **the Program shall not be installed onto any additional network** (where you have purchased such version) **or onto any additional personal computer** including any lap-top or portable computer **without an additional user licence**, available at separate cost from X Co Ltd.

(d) This licence is personal to you. **you may not transfer** or part with possession of the programs or seek to sub-license or assign this licence or your rights under it.

You must not modify or merge (except by a X Co Ltd approved dealer, or otherwise with the written consent of X Co Ltd), reverse engineer or decompile the program. you must not copy the program except as expressly provided in (ii) above. any breach of this sub-clause (iv) will automatically terminate your licence.

(e) X Co Ltd does not warrant or guarantee that the program performs any particular function or operation which may be suitable for your requirements other than may be disclosed in relevant documentation published by X Co Ltd.

Case Study

Federation against Software Theft (FAST)

The Federation Against Software Theft (FAST), based in the UK, promotes the legal use of software and defends the intellectual property of software publishers.

www.fast.org

9.3 Escrow agreements

Escrow is a legal term which means 'money, goods or a written document, held by a trusted third party, pending the fulfilment of some condition'.

In a typical Software Escrow Agreement (SEA) the owner (the licensor) of the software provides a copy of the intellectual property (IP) including source code to an escrow agent (a trusted third party). The source code is the formula of any software program.

The agreement sets out certain events under which the above can be released to a licensed user of the software (the licensee). For example, if the licensor goes into bankruptcy or liquidation, a merger or acquisition takes place, or fails to properly maintain the software or perform under the licence agreement.

Today, many businesses are reliant upon third parties to supply bespoke software for their needs and to provide a maintenance service for this. Such an agreement is therefore essential in order to protect the licensee.

10 Outsourcing

FAST FORWARD

> **Outsourcing** is the contracting out of specified operations or services to an external vendor. There are various outsourcing options available, with different levels of control maintained 'in-house'. Outsourcing has **advantages** (eg use of highly skilled people) and **disadvantages** (eg lack of control).

Key term

> **Outsourcing** is the contracting out of specified operations or services to an external vendor.

10.1 Types of outsourcing

There are four **broad classifications** of outsourcing, as described in the following table.

Classification	Comment
Ad-hoc	The organisation has a short-term requirement for increased IS/IT skills. An example would be employing programmers on a short-term contract to help with the programming of bespoke software.
Project management	The development and installation of a particular IS/IT project is outsourced. For example, a new accounting system.
Partial	Some IT/IS services are outsourced. Examples include hardware maintenance, network management or ongoing website management.
Total	An external supplier provides the vast majority of an organisation's IS/IT services; eg third party owns or is responsible for IT equipment, software and staff.

10.2 Levels of service provision

The degree to which the provision and management of IS/IT services are transferred to the third party varies according to the situation and the skills of both organisations.

(a) **Time-share**. The vendor charges for access to an external processing system on a time-used basis. Software ownership may be with either the vendor or the client organisation.

(b) **Service bureaux** usually focus on a specific function. Traditionally bureaux would provide the same type of service to many organisations eg payroll processing. As organisations have developed their own IT infrastructure, the use of bureaux has decreased.

(c) **Facilities management (FM)**. The terms 'outsourcing' and 'facilities management' are sometimes confused. Facilities management traditionally involved contracts for premises-related services such as cleaning or site security.

In the context of IS/IT, facilities management involves an outside agency managing the organisation's IS/IT facilities. All equipment usually remains with the client, but the responsibility for providing and managing the specified services rests with the FM company. FM companies operating in the UK include Accenture and Cap Gemini.

The following table shows the main features of each of the outsourcing arrangements described earlier.

Feature	Outsourcing arrangement		
	Timeshare	Service bureaux	Facilities Management (FM)
Management responsibility	Mostly retained	Some retained	Very little retained
Focus	Operational	A function	Strategic
Timescale	Short-term	Medium-term	Long-term
Justification	Cost savings	More efficient	Access to expertise; higher quality service provision. Enables management to concentrate on the areas where they do possess expertise.

10.3 Organisations involved in outsourcing

10.3.1 Software houses

Software houses concentrate on the provision of **'software services'**. These services include feasibility studies, systems analysis and design, development of operating systems software, provision of application program packages, 'tailor-made' application programming, specialist systems advice, and so on. For example, a software house might be employed to write a computerised system for the London Stock Exchange.

10.3.2 Consultancy firms

Some consultancy firms work at a fairly **high level**, giving advice to management on the **general approach** to solving problems and on the types of system to use. Others specialise in giving more particular systems advice, carrying out feasibility studies and recommending computer manufacturers/software houses that will supply the right system. When a consultancy firm is used, the terms of the contract should be agreed at the outset.

The use of consultancy services enables management to learn directly or indirectly from the experience of others. Many larger consultancies are owned by big international accountancy firms; smaller consultancies may consist of one or two-person outfits with a high level of specialist experience in one area.

The following categories of **consulting activity** have been identified by **Beaumont** and **Sutherland**.

(a) **Strategic studies**, involving the development of a business strategy or an IS strategy for an organisation.

(b) **Specialist studies**, where the consultant provides a high level of expertise in one area, for example Enterprise Resource Management software.

(c) **Project management**, involving supervision of internal and external parties in the completion of a particular project.

(d) **Body-shopping**, where the necessary staff, including consultants, project managers, systems analysts and programmers, for a project are identified.

(e) **Recruitment**, involving the supply of permanent or temporary staff.

10.3.3 Hardware manufacturers and suppliers

Computer manufacturers or their designated suppliers will provide the **equipment** necessary for a system. They will also provide, under a **maintenance contract**, engineers who will deal with any routine servicing and with any breakdown of the equipment.

 **Case Study**

The retailer Sears outsourced the management of its vast information technology and accounting functions to Accenture. First year **savings** were estimated to be £5 million per annum, growing to £14 million in the following year, and thereafter. This is clearly considerable, although re-organisation costs relating to redundancies, relocation and asset write-offs are thought to be in the region of £35 million. About 900 staff were involved: under the transfer of undertakings regulations (which protect employees when part or all of a company changes hands), Accenture was obliged to take on the existing Sears staff. This provided new opportunities for the staff who moved, while those who remained at Sears are free to concentrate on strategy development and management direction.

10.4 Developments in outsourcing

Outsourcing arrangements are becoming increasingly flexible to cope with the ever-changing nature of the modern business environment. Three trends are:

(a) **Multiple sourcing**. This involves outsourcing different functions or areas of the IS/IT function to a range of suppliers. Some suppliers may form alliances to present a stronger case for selection.

(b) **Incremental approach**. Organisations progressively outsource selected areas of their IT/IS function. Possible problems with outsourced services are solved before progressing to the next stage.

(c) **Joint venture sourcing**. This term is used to describe an organisation entering into a joint venture with a supplier. The costs (risks) and possible rewards are split on an agreed basis. Such an arrangement may be suitable when developing software that could be sold to other organisations.

(d) **Application Service Providers (ASP)**. ASPs are third parties that manage and distribute software services and solutions to customers across a Wide Area Network. ASPs could be considered the modern equivalent of the traditional computer bureaux.

10.5 Managing outsourcing arrangements

Managing outsourcing arrangements involves deciding what will be outsourced, choosing and negotiating with suppliers and managing the supplier relationship.

When considering whether to outsource a particular service the following questions are relevant.

(a) Is the system of strategic importance? Strategic IS are generally not suited to outsourcing as they require a high degree of specific business knowledge that a third party IT specialist cannot be expected to possess.

(b) Can the system be relatively isolated? Functions that have only limited interfaces are most easily outsourced eg payroll.

(c) Do we know enough about the system to manage the outsourced service agreement? If an organisation knows very little about a technology it may be difficult to know what constitutes good service and value for money. It may be necessary to recruit additional expertise to manage the relationship with the other party.

(d) Are our requirements likely to change? Organisations should avoid tying themselves into a long-term outsourcing agreement if requirements are likely to change.

10.5.1 Service level agreement

A key factor when choosing and negotiating with external vendors is the contract offered and subsequently negotiated with the supplier. The contract is sometimes referred to as the **Service Level Contract** (SLC) or **Service Level Agreement** (SLA).

The key elements of the contract are described in the following table.

Contract element	Comment
Timescale	When does the contract expire? Is the timescale suitable for the organisation's needs or should it be renegotiated?
Service level	The contract should clearly specify minimum levels of service to be provided. Penalties should be specified for failure to meet these standards. Relevant factors will vary depending on the nature of the services outsourced but could include: • Response time to requests for assistance/information • System 'uptime' percentage • Deadlines for performing relevant tasks
Exit route	Arrangements for an exit route, addressing how transfer to another supplier, or the move back in-house, would be conducted.
Software ownership	Relevant factors include: • Software licensing and security • If the arrangement includes the development of new software who owns the copyright?
Dependencies	If related services are outsourced the level of service quality agreed should group these services together.
Employment issues	If the arrangement includes provision for the organisation's IT staff to move to the third party, employer responsibilities must be specified clearly.

The contract provides the framework for the **relationship** between the organisation and the service provider.

Question — Outsourcing

Do any organisations with which you are familiar use outsourcing? What is the view of outsourcing in the organisation?

Answer

One view is given below.

The PA Consulting Group's annual survey of outsourcing found that 'on average the top five strategic outsourcers out-performed the FTSE by more than 100 per cent over three years; the bottom five under-performed by more than 66%'.

However the survey revealed that of those organisations who have opted to outsource IT functions, only five per cent are truly happy with the results. A spokesman for the consultants said that this is because most people fail to adopt a proper strategic approach, taking a view that is neither long-term nor broad enough, and taking outsourcing decisions that are piecemeal and unsatisfactory.

This lack of prescience is compounded by a failure to take a sufficiently rigorous approach to selection, specification, contract drafting and contract management.

The survey found that a constant complaint among many of those interviewed is the lack of ability of outsourcing organisations to work together.

Twenty-five per cent of those asked would bring the functions they had outsourced back in-house if it were possible.

10.6 The advantages and disadvantages of outsourcing

10.6.1 Advantages of outsourcing

The **advantages** of outsourcing are as follows.

(a) Outsourcing can remove uncertainty about **cost**, as there is often a long-term contract where services are specified in advance for a **fixed price**. If computing services are inefficient, the costs will be borne by the FM company. This is also an incentive to the third party to provide a high quality service.

(b) Long-term contracts (maybe up to ten years) encourage **planning** for the future.

(c) Outsourcing can bring the benefits of **economies of scale**. For example, a FM company may conduct research into new technologies that benefits a number of their clients.

(d) A specialist organisation is able to retain **skills and knowledge**. Many organisations would not have a sufficiently well-developed IT department to offer IT staff opportunities for career development. Talented staff would leave to pursue their careers elsewhere.

(e) New skills and knowledge become available. A specialist company can **share** staff with **specific expertise** between several clients. This allows the outsourcing company to take advantage of new developments without the need to recruit new people or re-train existing staff, and without the cost.

(f) **Flexibility** (contract permitting). Resources may be able to be scaled up or down depending upon demand. For instance, during a major changeover from one system to another the number of IT staff needed may be twice as large as it will be once the new system is working satisfactorily.

An outsourcing organisation is more able to arrange its work on a **project** basis, whereby some staff will expect to be moved periodically from one project to the next.

10.6.2 Disadvantages of outsourcing

Some possible **disadvantages** are outlined below.

(a) It is arguable that information and its provision is an **inherent part of the business** and of management. Unlike office cleaning, or catering, an organisation's IT services may be too important to be contracted out. Information is at the heart of management.

(b) A company may have highly **confidential information** and to let outsiders handle it could be seen as **risky** in commercial and/or legal terms.

(c) If a third party is handling IS/IT services there is no onus upon internal management to keep up with new developments or to suggest new ideas. Consequently, opportunities to gain **competitive advantage** may be missed. Any new technology or application devised by the third party is likely to be available to competitors.

(d) An organisation may find itself **locked in** to an unsatisfactory contract. The decision may be very difficult to reverse. If the service provider supplies unsatisfactory levels of service, the effort and expense the organisation would incur to rebuild its own computing function or to move to another provider could be substantial.

(e) The use of an outside organisation does not encourage awareness of the potential **costs** and benefits of IS/IT within the organisation. If managers cannot manage in-house IS/IT resources effectively, then it could be argued that they will not be able to manage an arrangement to outsource effectively either.

PART B INFORMATION SYSTEMS

> **Exam focus point**
> Watch out for exam questions that ask for a discussion of whether or not a company should outsource its IT department.

Chapter roundup

- There are a range of **input** devices available. The most efficient method will depend on the circumstances of each situation.
- The most often used methods of computer **output** are **printers** and **screen display**.
- **Hard disks, flash drives** and **DVDs** are common forms of **storage**.
- An organisation has a range of options when sourcing software. The four main options are:
    - A standard **off-the-shelf** package
    - Amended standard package
    - Standard package plus additions
    - Have **bespoke** software written
- **Off-the-shelf software** is produced to meet requirements that are common to many organisations. The software is likely to be available **immediately** and **cost significantly less** than bespoke solutions. However, as it has not been written specifically for the organisation, it may not meet all their requirements.
- **Bespoke software** should be written so as to **match** the organisation's requirements exactly. However, the software is likely to be considerably **more expensive** than an off-the-shelf package. Bespoke software may be designed and written 'in-house' by the IS department, or externally by a software house.
- An organisation that requires bespoke software to be written may issue an **Invitation to Tender (ITT)** to a range of potential suppliers. The **contents of a typical ITT** could include:
    - Covering letter
    - Instructions
    - Detailed software requirements
    - Details of development model/methodology
    - Request for further details of the proposed software contract
- Suppliers' proposals need to be evaluated, perhaps using **benchmark tests**. Other relevant factors include how well the software would meet **user requirements**, **user-friendliness**, **controls**, **compatibility** and **cost**. Supplier **reputation** and **reliability** should also be considered.
- A **weighted ranking** scoring system may be used to evaluate software proposals from a number of different vendors.
- The agreement to supply bespoke software should be formally laid out in a contract. **Software contracts** include provisions relating to matters such as warranty, ownership and liability.
- A **software licence** typically covers issues such as the number of users, right to copy and a limitation of liability.
- **Escrow** is a legal term which means 'money, goods or a written document, held by a trusted third party, pending the fulfilment of some condition'.
- **Outsourcing** is the contracting out of specified operations or services to an external vendor. There are various outsourcing options available, with different levels of control maintained 'in-house'. Outsourcing has **advantages** (eg use of highly skilled people) and **disadvantages** (eg lack of control).

Quick quiz

1. List five ways an organisation could input or capture data.
2. List five factors to consider when choosing an off-the-shelf application package.
3. List eight stages of a typical software development project.
4. Why would an organisation issue an Invitation To Tender (ITT)?
5. What would you say is the main advantage of bespoke software?
6. What is the main disadvantage of bespoke software?
7. Briefly explain how a weighted ranking system works.
8. Define 'Corporate Over-Use'.
9. 'Information systems that are strategically important should be outsourced to ensure those working with these systems have excellent technical knowledge'. **True** or **false**?
10. List four advantages of outsourcing the IS/IT function.
11. List four disadvantages of outsourcing the IS/IT function.
12. What would a service level agreement (SLA) contain?

12: TECHNOLOGY, SELECTION AND ACQUISITION

Answers to quick quiz

1. Five of the following:
   - Touch sensitive screen
   - Voice recognition
   - Digital camera
   - Keyboard
   - Scanner and OCR
   - Tablet and pen
   - Mouse
   - MICR
   - OMR
   - EPOS

2. Any five of the following (you may have thought of other valid considerations). User requirements; Processing times; Documentation; Compatibility; Controls/security; User-interface; Modification; Support; Maintenance; Updates/upgrades; Cost.

3. Feasibility, Analysis, Design, Program specification, Coding, Unit test, Integration test, System test, Acceptance test.

4. To invite tenders (offers to supply) for the system specified in the ITT.

5. As it is written for a specific purpose, it should match user requirements very closely.

6. It's expensive when compared to off-the-shelf software.

7. A weighted ranking system involves establishing a number of factors important to a system, giving each factor a numerical weighting to reflect its importance, and using these weightings to calculate a score for each supplier (or software, or system).

8. The installation of software by more users than the organisation is licensed for.

9. False. Strategic IS are generally not suited to outsourcing as they require a high degree of specific business knowledge that a third party IS/IT specialist can not be expected to possess.

10. Four of the following:
    - Cost control – services are specified in advance for a fixed price.
    - Certainty – long-term contracts allow greater certainty in planning for the future.
    - Economies of scale. Several organisations will employ the same company.
    - Skills and knowledge are retained within the specialist company who can offer staff career development.
    - New skills and knowledge become available. A specialist company can share staff with specific expertise between several clients.
    - Flexibility – resources employed can be scaled up or down depending upon demand.

11. Four of the following:
    - An organisation's IS services may be too important to be contracted out. Information is at the heart of management.
    - Risky – confidential or commercially sensitive information could be leaked.
    - Opportunities may be missed to use IS/IT for competitive advantage – there is no onus upon internal management to keep up with new developments and have new ideas.
    - Locked in – an organisation may be locked into a contract with a poor service provider.

PART B INFORMATION SYSTEMS

- Hard to reverse – the effort and expense an organisation would have to incur to rebuild its own computing function and expertise would be enormous.
- Outsourcing does not encourage an awareness of the potential costs and benefits of IT amongst managers.

12 The Service Level Agreement (SLA) or Service Level Contract (SLC) is a vital aspect of any outsourcing arrangement. It should specify minimum levels of service, arrangements for an exit route, transfer arrangements and dispute procedures.

End of chapter questions

The senior administrator in a small charitable organisation is considering the introduction of some IT systems to assist with the clerical procedures. She has asked you as an IT adviser to provide her with the following information:

1 Describe some of the data entry devices which are commonly used as an alternative to the standard keyboard entry devices. **(5 marks)**

Some of the staff at the charity complain that they have never learnt to type on a keyboard. The senior administrator is considering alternatives to the keyboard for data input.

2 What are the advantages of keyboard input? **(5 marks)**

3 What are the disadvantages of keyboard input? **(5 marks)**

(Total = 15 marks)

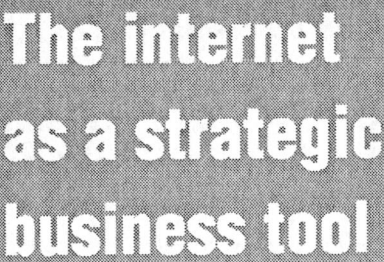

The internet as a strategic business tool

Topic list	Syllabus reference
1 The internet – an overview	9.7
2 Internet security issues	9.7
3 Electronic commerce	9.7
4 Developing a strategy for the internet and e-commerce	9.7

Introduction

The internet is potentially the most **significant communication development** since the advent of the telephone.

As with any technology the internet provides both opportunities and risks. In this chapter we look at how the **internet can be exploited** to provide enhanced value to businesses and their customers. We also cover the **security issues** associated with the internet and e-commerce.

We end this chapter with a discussion of **globalisation**, and how information systems can support an organisation's global business strategy.

1 The internet – an overview

> **FAST FORWARD**
>
> The **internet** is a global network linking millions of computers. The World Wide Web (**WWW**) is a system of internet servers that support specially formatted documents. A group of documents accessed from the same base web address is known as a **website**.

Key terms

> The **internet** is a global network connecting millions of computers (and other compatible devices).
>
> The **World Wide Web** (WWW) is a system of internet servers that support specially formatted documents. Most documents on the web are formatted in HTML (HyperText Markup Language) that supports links to other documents, as well as graphics, audio, and video files.
>
> A group of documents accessed from the same base web address is known as a **website**.

The internet is the name given to the technology that allows any computer (or other device) with a telecommunications link to **send and receive information** from any other suitably equipped device.

Connection to the internet is made via an internet Service Provider (ISP). ISPs, such as Virgin, provide their own information services in addition to internet access and email capability.

The internet is viewed through interface programs called **browsers**. The most widely used are Microsoft internet Explorer and Netscape Navigator. Searching the web is done using a **search engine** such as Google.

> **FAST FORWARD**
>
> Most organisations now have a **website** and some conduct **transactions** over the internet.

Most organisations now have a **website** on the internet. A website address will typically be given in the format of a **U**niversal **R**esource **L**ocator (**URL**) eg http://www.bbc.co.uk

1.1 Current uses of the internet

The scope and potential of the internet are still developing. Its uses already include the following:

(a) Dissemination of information.

(b) Product/service development – through almost instantaneous test marketing.

(c) Transaction processing – both business-to-business (B2B) and business-to-consumer (B2C).

(d) Relationship enhancement – between various groups of stakeholders, but principally (for our purposes) between consumers and product/service suppliers.

(e) Recruitment and job search – involving organisations worldwide.

(f) Entertainment – including music, humour, games and some less wholesome pursuits!

1.2 Growth of the internet

Being able to access the internet from home is now the norm in most UK households.

(a) Many households are now establishing **multiple internet access points** eg Digital TV set, PCs, hand-held devices including mobile phones.

(b) **Changes in the telecoms market** are likely to mean that internet connection is likely to become cheaper and connection speeds quicker.

(c) Digital television and internet enabled mobile phones provide further points of access.

(d) Many now access the internet using a hand-held **PDA (Personal Digital Assistant)**.

(e) Internet **kiosks** are becoming increasingly common in shopping centres, cafes etc.

1.3 Factors influencing internet use in business

The internet is not expanding at the same rate in every sphere of business. The rate of growth is influenced by:

(a) The degree to which the customer can be persuaded to believe that using the internet will **deliver some added-value** – in terms of quickness, simplicity and price.

(b) Whether there are 'costs' which the **customer** has to bear – not exclusively 'costs' in the financial sense, but also such psychological 'costs' as the isolated online shopping experience.

(c) The **market segment** to which the individual belongs. The internet is largely the preserve of younger, more affluent, more technologically competent individuals with above-average amounts of disposable income.

(d) The **frequency** of supplier/customer **contact** required.

(e) The availability of **incentives** which might stimulate internet acceptance. For example, interest rates on bank accounts which are higher than those available through conventional banks (Egg), the creation of penalties for over-the-counter transactions, and the expectations of important customers (IBM's relationships with its suppliers).

1.3.1 'Infomediaries'

Arguably, the most profitable pure internet companies, as well as the most influential, will be **business-to-business 'infomediaries'** (the term coined by John Hagel of McKinsey), because they can exploit the internet's most salient characteristics.

(a) **The internet shifts power from sellers to buyers by reducing switching costs.** Buyers may feel overwhelmed by this power, but they typically want one-stop shopping, with information they believe and advice they can trust. Sellers cannot be believed or trusted – but infomediaries may.

(b) **The internet reduces transaction costs and thus stimulates economic activity.** According to one US calculation, a banking transaction via the internet costs 1 cent, 27 cents at an ATM (automated teller machine) and 52 cents over the telephone. Infomediaries can enable significant savings to be enjoyed by small-scale or even single customers.

(c) **The speed, range and accessibility of information on the internet, and the low cost of capturing and distributing it, create new commercial possibilities.** Infomediaries can focus on particular product/service supply issues; by doing so, they attract specialised buyers and sellers; in turn they acquire more expertise which generates continued customer loyalty and participation.

> **Exam focus point**
>
> Material such as that provided above relating to 'infomediaries' is unlikely to be examined directly. However, this type of information helps broaden your overall understanding of how the internet may be utilised in a business context – which could be relevant to a number of examination questions.

1.3.2 B2B e-commerce

> **FAST FORWARD**
>
> The major growth of **e-commerce** so far has been in the Business to Business (B2B) sector.

Business to Business (B2B) e-commerce has grown rapidly over the past decade.

(a) **Major companies** have adopted e-business, for example, both Ford and General Motors have switched a major portion of their procurement and supply chain management to the web.

(b) IBM require major **suppliers to quote and invoice electronically**.

(c) Many firms are using the internet to exploit the **transparency of supplier prices** and to maximise their purchasing benefits from the availability of world-wide sourcing. Robert Bosch, the German kitchen appliance manufacturer, **requires all its suppliers to have web-based catalogues** and prices.

(d) Companies are also delivering customer service through the web. Dell, the computer company, has created **extranets for its major business customers**, enabling them to receive personalised customer support, their own price lists, and some free value-added services.

Case Study

Business and the internet

The internet has the potential to turn business upside down and inside out, to fundamentally change the way companies operate, whether in high-tech or metal-bashing. This goes far beyond buying and selling over the internet, or e-commerce, and deep into the processes and culture of an enterprise.

Some companies are using the internet to make direct connections with their customers for the first time. Others are using secure internet connections to intensify relations with some of their trading partners, and using the internet's reach and ubiquity to request quotes or sell off perishable inventories of goods or services by auction.

The internet is helping companies to lower costs dramatically across their supply and demand chains, take their customer service into a different league, enter new markets, create additional revenue streams and redefine their business relationships.

Some writers argue that companies can be either **'brick' or 'click'** businesses, but they can't be both: if they are a 'brick' operation – ie they have real premises, real shops, real factories and warehouses – then their culture will make it impossible for them fully to assimilate the drastic changes required in order to operate successfully in a 'click' environment. It is no accident, therefore, that companies like Prudential Assurance have initiated their internet activities through stand-alone enterprises, using newly-recruited people situated in geographically-distinctive locations.

1.3.3 Tasks suited to website automation

The internet provides opportunities to automate tasks which would previously have required more costly interaction with the organisation. These have often been called low-touch or zero-touch approaches.

> **FAST FORWARD**
>
> The internet provides opportunities to **automate tasks** which would previously have required human intervention.

Tasks which a website may automate include:

(a) **Frequently Asked Questions (FAQs)**: carefully-structured sets of answers can deal with many customer interactions.

(b) **Status checking**: major service enquiries (Where is my order? When will the engineer arrive? What is my bank balance?) can also be automated, replacing high-cost human service processes, and also providing the opportunity to proactively offer better service and new services.

(c) **Keyword search**: the ability to search provides web users with opportunities to find information in large and complex websites.

(d) **Wizards (interview style interface) and intelligent algorithms**: these can help diagnosis, which is one of the major elements of service support.

(e) **Email and systems to route and track inbound email**: the ability to route and/or to provide automatic responses will enable organisations to deal with high volumes of email from actual and potential customers.

(f) **Bulletin boards**: these enable customers to interact with each other, thus facilitating self-activated customer service and also the opportunity for product/service referral. Cisco in particular has created communities of Cisco users who help each other – thus reducing the service costs for Cisco itself.

(g) **Call-back buttons**: these enable customers to speak to someone in order to deal with and resolve a problem; the more sophisticated systems allow the call-centre operator to know which web pages the users were consulting at the time.

(h) **Transaction processing**: the taking of orders and payment online.

1.4 Problems with the internet

1.4.1 Lack of organisation

To a large extent the internet has grown **without any formal organisation**. There are specific communication rules, but it is not **owned** by any one body and there are no clear guidelines on how it should develop.

Inevitably, the **quality** of much of the information on the internet leaves much to be desired.

1.4.2 Connection speed

Speed is a major issue. Data only downloads onto the user's PC at the speed of the slowest telecommunications link – downloading data can be a time-consuming procedure. However, future developments will mean that speeds will improve.

A number of **faster services** collectively referred to as '**Broadband**' are available but are often perceived by consumers as being expensive.

(a) **Integrated Services Digital Network (ISDN)** is an international communications standard for sending voice, video, and data over digital telephone lines or normal telephone wires. ISDN supports data transfer rates three times faster than modems.

(b) **ADSL** (Asymmetric Digital Subscriber Line) is offers data transfer rates of up to **8 Mbps**, considerably faster than ISDN. ADSL allows information to be sent out over ordinary copper wires and simultaneous use of the normal telephone service.

1.4.3 Staff wasting time

So much information and entertainment is available that employers worry that their **staff will spend too much time** browsing through non-work-related sites.

1.4.4 Security

Security is perhaps the biggest worry of all; this is covered in the next section.

2 Internet security issues

> **FAST FORWARD**
>
> Establishing links to the internet brings **security risks**. Suitable systems, policies and procedures should be implemented to minimise these risks.

Establishing organisational links to the internet brings numerous security dangers.

PART B   INFORMATION SYSTEMS

(a) Corruptions such as **viruses** on a single computer can spread through the network to all of the organisation's computers. (Viruses are described at greater length later in this section.)

(b) Disaffected employees have much greater potential to do **deliberate damage** to valuable corporate data or systems because the network could give them access to parts of the system that they are not really authorised to use.

(c) If the organisation is linked to an external network, persons outside the company (**hackers**) may be able to get into the company's internal network, either to steal data or to damage the system.

(d) Employees may **download inaccurate information** or imperfect or **virus-ridden software** from an external network. For example 'beta' (free trial) versions of forthcoming new editions of many major packages are often available on the internet, but these are not fully tested and may contain bugs that could disrupt an entire system.

(e) Information transmitted from one part of an organisation to another may be **intercepted**. Data can be 'encrypted' (scrambled) in an attempt to make it unintelligible to eavesdroppers, this is covered later in this section.

(f) The **communications link itself may break down or distort data**. The worldwide telecommunications infrastructure is improving thanks to the use of new technologies, and there are communications 'protocols' governing the format of data and signals transferred.

2.1 Hacking

> **FAST FORWARD**
>
> **Hacking** involves attempting to gain unauthorised access to a computer system, usually through telecommunications links. A **virus** is a piece of software which infects programs and data and possibly damages them, and which replicates itself. Viruses often use email links to spread.

Hacking involves attempting to gain unauthorised access to a computer system, usually through telecommunications links. Hackers require only limited programming knowledge to cause large amounts of damage.

Phone numbers, network addresses and passwords can be guessed by hackers using software which enables **rapid guessing** using hundreds of permutations per minute.

Default passwords are also available on some internet websites and electronic bulletin boards.

2.2 Encryption and other safety measures

Encryption aims to ensure the security of data during transmission. It involves the translation of data into secret code. To read an encrypted file, you must have access to a secret key or password that enables you to decrypt it. Unencrypted data is called plain text; encrypted data is referred to as cipher text.

> **FAST FORWARD**
>
> **Encryption** aims to ensure the security of data during transaction. Encryption involves scrambling the data at one end of the line, transmitting the scrambled data, and unscrambling it at the receiver's end of the line.

Authentication is a technique of making sure that a message has come from an authorised sender. Authentication involves adding an extra field to a record, with the contents of this field derived from the remainder of the record by applying an algorithm that has previously been agreed between the senders and recipients of data.

Systems can have **firewalls** (which disable part of the telecoms technology) to prevent unwelcome intrusions into company systems, but a determined hacker may well be able to bypass even these.

Dial-back security operates by requiring the person wanting access to the network to dial into it and identify themselves first. The system then dials the person back on their authorised number before allowing them access.

All attempted **violations of security** should be automatically **logged** and the log checked regularly. In a multi-user system, the terminal attempting the violation may be automatically disconnected.

2.3 Viruses

Key term

> A **virus** is a piece of software which infects programs and data and possibly damages them, and which replicates itself.

Viruses need an **opportunity to spread**. The programmers of viruses therefore place viruses in the kind of software which is most likely to be copied. This includes:

(a) Free software (for example from the internet).

(b) Pirated software (cheaper than original versions).

(c) **Email attachments**. Email has become the most common means of spreading the most destructive viruses. The virus is often held in an attachment to the email message. Recent viruses have been programmed to send themselves to all addresses in the user's electronic address book.

2.4 Protecting against viruses

FAST FORWARD

> **Anti-virus software** and a **firewall** are essential security tools for any network (or PC) with access to the internet.

The main protection against viruses is **anti-virus software** such as McAfee or Nortons. This software searches systems for viruses and removes any that are found. The programs are periodically updated by downloading upgrades that include profiles of new known viruses. Very new viruses won't be detected by anti-virus software until the anti-virus software vendor updates their package – and the organisation installs the update.

Additional precautions include ensuring all files received via storage media and email are virus checked.

External email links can be protected by way of a **firewall** that may be configured to virus check all messages, and may also prevent files of a certain type being sent via email (eg .exe files, as these are the most common means of transporting a virus).

2.5 Hoaxes

There are a number of common hoaxes, the most common of these are based on the **Good Times** hoax. This hoax has been around for a few years, and usually takes the form of a virus warning about viruses contained in email.

People send these 'warning' emails to others in an attempt to be helpful, but this actually wastes the time of all concerned.

The security issues surrounding e-commerce, particularly regarding making payment over the internet are covered later in this chapter.

3 Electronic commerce

> **FAST FORWARD**
>
> **Electronic commerce** means conducting business electronically. An older technology that is covered under the electronic commerce umbrella is **Electronic Data Interchange** (EDI).

Key term

> **Electronic commerce** means conducting business electronically via a communications link.

3.1 Electronic Data Interchange (EDI)

EDI is a form of computer-to-computer data transfer. For instance instead of sending a customer a paper invoice through the post the data is sent over telecommunications links. This offers savings and **benefits** to organisations that use it.

3.1.1 Benefits of EDI

(a) It reduces the **delays** caused by postal paper chains.

(b) It avoids the need to **re-key** data and therefore saves time and reduces errors.

(c) It provides the opportunity to reduce administrative **costs** eg the costs associated with the creation, recording and storage of paper documents.

(d) It facilitates shorter **lead times** and reduced inventory holdings which allow reductions in working capital requirements (eg Just-In-Time policies).

(e) It provides the opportunity to improve **customer service**.

3.1.2 Possible problems setting up EDI

The general concept of having one computer talk directly to another might seem straightforward enough in principle, but **difficulties** may arise.

(a) Businesses hold records in computer files to their own **file structure** specifications. A translation mechanism may be required to allow transfer between the systems.

(b) The problem of **compatibility** between different makes or types of computer was a serious one in the past, and some form of interface between the computers had to be devised to enable data interchange to take place. Newer systems tend to include facilities for linking to other systems.

(c) Businesses often work to differing **time** schedules and time-zones. Organisations may conduct system maintenance late at night thinking this will not affect business. However, an overseas company in a different time zone, may need to access the system.

(d) As the number of trading partners grows the number of one-to-one links eventually becomes **unmanageable**.

3.2 E-commerce and the web

> **FAST FORWARD**
>
> Ensuring **'back-office' operations complement web-based operations** is vital.

Over the last few years, electronic commerce or **e-commerce** has increasingly been used to describe the use of the internet and websites in the sale of products or services. A simple definition is that 'e-commerce is the process of trading on the internet'.

3.2.1 Distribution

The internet can be used to get certain products **directly into people's homes**. Anything that can be converted into **digital form** can simply be uploaded onto the seller's site and then **downloaded** onto the customer's PC at home. The internet thus offers huge opportunities to producers of text, graphics/video, and sound-based products. Much computer software is now distributed in this way.

3.2.2 Electronic marketing

Besides its usefulness for tapping into worldwide information resources businesses are also using it to **provide information** about their own products and services.

For **customers** the internet offers a **speedy and impersonal** way of getting to know about the services that a company provides. For **businesses** the advantage is that it is much cheaper to provide the information in electronic form than it would be to employ staff to man the phones on an enquiry desk, and much more effective than sending out mailshots that people would either throw away or forget about when they needed the information.

Companies will need to develop new means of promoting their wares through the medium of the internet, as opposed to shop displays or motionless graphics. Websites can provide **sound and movement** and allow **interactivity**, so that the user can, say, drill down to obtain further information or watch a video of the product in use, or get a virtual reality experience of the product or service.

For many companies this will involve a rethink of current promotional activity.

Case Study

Peapod.com is an online supermarket and one of the more sophisticated recorders and users of customers' personal data and shopping behaviour. With over 200,000 customers in various US cities, Peapod's website sells groceries that are then delivered to customer's homes.

Peapod creates a database on each shopper that includes their purchase history (what they bought), their online shopping patterns (how they bought it), questionnaires about their attitudes and opinions, and demographic data (which Peapod buys from third parties). A shopper's profile is used to determine which advertisements to show and which promotions/electronic coupons to offer. Demographically identical neighbours are thus treated differently based on what Peapod has learned about their preferences and behaviours over time.

Shoppers seem to like this high-tech relationship marketing, with 94% of all sales coming from repeat customers. Manufacturers like it too. the more detailed customer information enables them to target promotions at customers who have repeatedly bought another brand, thereby not giving away promotion dollars to loyal customers.

3.2.3 Collecting information about customers

People who visit a site for the first time may be asked to **register**, which typically involves giving a name, physical address and post code, email address and possibly other demographic data such as age, job title and income bracket.

When customers come to the site on subsequent occasions (from the same computer) the website recognises them using a **cookie**, which is a small and **harmless** file containing a string of characters that uniquely identify the computer.

From the initial registration details the user record may show, say, that the user is male, aged 20 to 30, based in London. The **website can respond** to this by displaying products or services likely to appeal to this type of person.

3.2.4 Clickstreams

As users visit the site more often, more is learned about them by **recording what they click on**, since this shows what they are really interested in. On a news site for instance, one user may always go to the sports pages first, while another looks at the TV listings. In a retail sense this is akin to physically following somebody about the store recording everything they do (including products they pick up and put back) and everything they look at, whether or not they buy it.

3.3 Virtual companies and virtual supply chains (VSC)

Key terms

> A **virtual company** is a collection of separate companies, each with a specific expertise, who work together, sharing their expertise to compete for bigger contracts/projects than would be possible if they worked alone.
>
> A traditional **supply chain** is made up of the physical entities linked together to facilitate the supply of goods and services to the final consumer.
>
> A **Virtual Supply Chain (VSC)** is a supply chain that is enabled through e-business links (eg the web, extranets or EDI).

3.3.1 Virtual companies

The **virtual company** concept has been around since the mid-1990s. Initially, companies attempted to work together using fax and phone links. The concept only really became a reality when technology such as extranets came into common usage. Companies are now able to work together and exchange information online. For example, engineers from five companies could design a product together on the internet.

3.3.2 Virtual supply chains

Virtual Supply Chain networks have two types of organisation: producers and integrators.

(a) **Producers** produce goods and services. They have core competencies in production schedule execution. Producers must focus on delivery to schedule and within cost. The sales driver within these companies is on ensuring that their capacity is fully sold through their networking with co-ordinators. Producer are often servicing multiple chains, so managing and avoiding capacity and commercial conflicts becomes key.

(b) **Integrators** manage the supply network and effectively 'own' the end customer contact. The focus of the integrating firms is on managing the end customer relationship. Their core competence is in integrating and controlling the response of the company to customer requirements. This includes the difficult task of synchronising the responses and performance of multi-tiered networks, where the leverage of direct ownership is no longer available, and of often outsourced services such as warehousing and delivery.

Many of the most popular internet companies are integrators in virtual company's eg Amazon.com and Lastminute.com. These organisations 'own' customer contact and manage customer relationships for a range of producers.

3.4 How does the internet and e-commerce challenge traditional business thinking?

There are several features of the internet which make it **radically different** from what has gone before.

(a) It **challenges traditional business models** – because, for example, it enables product/service suppliers to interact directly with their customers, instead of using intermediaries (like retail shops, travel agents, insurance brokers, and conventional banks).

(b) Although the internet is global in its operation, its benefits are not confined to large (or global) organisations. **Small companies** can move instantly into a global market place, either on their own initiative or as part of what is known as a 'consumer portal'. For example, Ede and Ravenscroft is a small outfitting and tailoring business in Oxford: it could easily promote itself within a much larger 'portal' called OxfordHighStreet.com, embracing a comprehensive mixture of other Oxford retailers.

(c) It offers a **new economics of information** – because, with the internet, much information is free. Those with internet access can view all the world's major newspapers and periodicals without charge.

(d) It supplies an almost incredible **level of speed** – virtually instant access to organisations, plus the capacity to complete purchasing transactions within seconds. This velocity, of course, is only truly impressive if it is accompanied by equal speed so far as the delivery of tangible goods is concerned.

(e) It has created **new networks of communication** – between organisations and their customers (either individually or collectively), between customers themselves (through mutual support groups), and between organisations and their suppliers.

(f) It stimulates the appearance of **new intermediaries** and the disappearance of some existing ones. Businesses are finding that they can cut out the middle man, with electronic banking, insurance, publishing and printing as primary examples.

(g) It has led to **new business partnerships** through which small enterprises can gain access to customers on a scale which would have been viewed as impossible a few years ago. For example, a university can put its reading list on a website and students wishing to purchase any given book can click directly through to an online bookseller such as Amazon.com. The university gets a commission; the online bookseller gets increased business; the student gets a discount. Everyone benefits except the traditional bookshop.

(h) It promotes **transparent pricing** – because potential customers can readily compare prices not only from suppliers within any given country, but also from suppliers across the world.

(i) It facilitates **personalised attention** – even if such attention is actually administered through impersonal, yet highly sophisticated IT systems and customer database manipulation.

(j) It provides sophisticated **market segmentation** opportunities. Approaching such segments may be one of the few ways in which e-commerce entrepreneurs can create **competitive advantage**. As **Management Today** (March 2000) puts it:

'The starting point must be a neat niche, a funky few, a global tribe. You need to understand your particular tribe better than anyone else. The tribe is the basic unit of business... The good news is that there are lots of tribes out there – and some are enormous. It's just a question of identifying them, understanding them and meeting their needs better than anyone else.'

(k) The web can either be a **separate** or a **complementary** channel.

(l) A new phenomenon is emerging called **dynamic pricing**. Companies can rapidly change their prices to reflect the current state of demand and supply.

These new trends are creating **pressure** for companies. The main threat facing companies is that **prices will be driven down by consumers' ability to shop around.**

Case Study

(1) **Airlines**

The impact of the web is seen clearly in the transportation industry. Airlines now have a more effective way of bypassing intermediaries (ie travel agents) because they can give their customers immediate access to flight reservation systems.

(2) **Travel agents**

The web has also produced a new set of online travel agents who have lower costs because of their ability to operate without a High Street branch network. Their low-cost structure makes them a particularly good choice for selling low margin, cheap tickets for flights, package holidays, cruises and so forth.

(3) **Tesco**

Tesco is the UK's largest internet grocery business, but other companies are rapidly developing new initiatives. Some supermarkets now offer same day deliveries.

(4) **Financial services**

The impact of the internet is especially profound in the field of financial services. New intermediaries enable prospective customers to compare the interest rates and prices charged by different organisations for pensions, mortgages and other financial services. This means that the delivering companies are losing control of the marketing of their services, and there is a downward pressure on prices, especially for services which can legitimately be seen as mere commodities (eg house and contents insurance).

3.5 Disadvantages of e-commerce

E-commerce involves an unusual mix of people – security people, web technology people, designers, marketing people – and this can be very **difficult to manage**. The e-business needs supervision by expensive specialists.

Many e-businesses have only recently reported making any **profit**, the best-known example being **Amazon.com**.

A new technology installed will **need to link up with existing business systems** and procedures put in place that enables orders to be fulfilled.

The international availability of a website means that the **laws** of all countries that transactions may be conducted from have to be considered. The legal issues surrounding e-commerce are complex and still developing.

3.5.1 Lack of trust

In most cultures, consumers grant their trust to business parties that have a close **physical presence**: buildings, facilities and people to talk to. On the internet these familiar elements are simply not there.

Internet merchants need to elicit consumer trust when the level of **perceived risk** in a transaction is high. However, research has found that once consumers have built up trust in an internet merchant such concerns are reduced.

3.6 Cryptography, keys and signatures

The parties involved in e-commerce need to have confidence that any communication sent gets to its target destination **unchanged**, and **without being read by anyone else**.

One way of providing electronic signatures is to make use of what is known as **public key** (or asymmetric) **cryptography.** Public key cryptography uses **two keys – public and private**. The **private key** is only known to its owner, and is used to scramble the data contained in a file.

The 'scrambled' data is the electronic signature, and can be checked against the original file using the **public key** of the person who signed it. This confirms that it could only have been signed by someone with access to the private key. If a third party altered the message, the fact that they had done so would be easily detectable.

An alternative is the use of encryption products which support **key recovery,** also known as **key encapsulation.** Such commercial encryption products can incorporate the public key of an agent known as a **Key Recovery Agent (KRA).** This allows the user to recover their (stored or communicated) data by approaching the KRA with an encrypted portion of the message. In both cases the KRA neither holds the user's private keys, nor has access to the plain text of their data.

3.7 Customer service on the web

Effective, competent and acceptable customer service through the web is a combination of the following factors:

(a) **Rapid response time**. If the website is not fast, the transient potential shopper will simply click on to another. These 'fickle' visitors to a website will only allow around five to eight seconds: if the site has not captured their attention in that time-frame, they will move elsewhere.

(b) **Response quality**. The website must be legible, with appropriate graphics and meaningful, relevant information supplied. Generally speaking, website visitors are not interested in the company's history and size: they are much more concerned about what the company can offer them.

(c) **Navigability**. It is important to create a website which caters for every conceivable customer interest and question. Headings and category-titles should be straightforward and meaningful, not obscure and ambiguous.

(d) **Download times**. Again, these need to be rapid, given that many internet shoppers regard themselves (rightly or otherwise) as cash-rich and time-poor.

(e) **Security/Trust**. One of the biggest barriers to the willingness of potential internet customers actually to finalise a transaction is their fear that information they provide about themselves (such as credit card details) can be 'stolen' or used as the basis for fraud.

(f) **Fulfilment**. Customers must believe that if they order goods and services, the items in question will arrive, and will do so within acceptable time limits (which will generally be much faster than the time limits normally associated with conventional mail order). Equally, customers need to be convinced that if there is a subsequent need for service recovery, then speedy and efficient responses can be secured either to rectify the matter or to enable unsatisfactory goods to be returned without penalty.

(g) **Up-to-date**. Just as window displays need to be constantly refreshed, so do websites require frequent repackaging and redesign.

(h) **Availability**. Can the user reach the site 24 hours a day, seven days a week? Is the down-time minimal? Can the site always be accessed?

(i) **Site effectiveness and functionality**. Is the website intuitive and easy to use? Is the content written in a language which will be meaningful even to the first-time browser (ie the potential customer)?

Question   E-commerce

Initially, many companies ignored e-commerce. This approach appeared to be justified as a succession of much-publicised ventures struggled to translate success into profits.

Why, do you think, is this view increasingly untenable?

Answer

Relevant points include:

(a) The growth in e-commerce over the past few years has been immense.

(b) Every part of the value chain is up for grabs. Any participant in the value chain who lacks a web presence could find 'their' role taken by another organisation.

  (i) The free flow of information about buyers and sellers undermines the role of intermediaries.

  (ii) A book publisher could bypass retailers or distributors and sell directly.

  (iii) A book seller could decide to publish books, based on the information it has obtained about readers' interests.

(c) Established operators can secure important advantages over latecomers. They can use information about their customers to tailor their offerings and they may even be able to foster a sense of community among users.

4 Developing a strategy for the internet and e-commerce

FAST FORWARD

When developing a **strategy for e-commerce** consider:

- Organisation and culture
- Systems and infrastructure
- Training
- Customers

4.1 Broad approaches

Four broad approaches a company may adopt towards the internet and e-commerce are:

(a) Do not sell products through the internet at all, and if distribution is conducted through resellers, prevent them from doing so. Provide only product **information** on the internet. This may be an appropriate strategy where products are **large, complex and highly customised**, such as aircraft manufacturing.

(b) **Leave the internet business to resellers** and do not sell directly through the internet (ie do not compete with resellers). This can be appropriate, for instance, where manufacturers have already assigned exclusive territories to resellers.

(c) The manufacturer can **restrict internet sales exclusively to itself**. The problem with this is that most large manufacturers do not have systems that are geared to dealing with sales to end users who place numerous, irregular small orders.

(d) Open up internet sales to everybody and **let the market decide** who it prefers to buy from.

4.2 Example of potential strategies

On a more detailed level, in an article for *IT Consultancy* magazine, Laurence Holt offered 18 potential strategies for e-commerce.

Strategy	Comment
Outsource to your customers	What do we do for our customers that they would rather do for themselves and could probably do better? Examples: www.cisco.com, www.dell.com.
Cannibalise your own business	If there were an Amazon.com in our market, what would it be doing? Examples: www.barnesandnoble.com, www.egghead.com.
Host your competitors	How can we create a marketplace that includes our competitors, but that we own? Examples: www.sabre.com, www.jewellery.com.
Build one-to-one customer relationships	How can we make each customer feel that we built our organisation just for them? Examples: www.my.yahoo.com, www.netgrocer.com.
Make first contact	What is the first step our customers take in the chain of events that leads them to buy from us? How can we make contact with them? Examples: www.autobytel.com.
Be a process integrator	What other things do customers need or do when they buy from us? Examples: www.autobytel.com.
Catch rites of passage	What major life changes are customers going through when they come into contact with us? How can we help? Examples: www.usnews.com, www.citibank.com.
Create a community	What interests do our customers share? How can we create a place that people with those interests will keep coming back to? Examples: www.yahoo.com.
Create a niche portal	How can we make our site the portal our customers go to first? Examples: www.ft.com.
Pirate your value chain	How can we take over the roles of others in our value chain? Examples: www.dell.com.
Re-intermediate on information value	How can we boost the value we add through information? Examples: www.britannica.com.
Go pure cyberspace	What if we made the digital world our first priority and the physical world second? Examples: www.tiscali.com.
Be a fast follower	What are our competitors doing that looks likely to be successful? How can we do the same thing faster? Examples: www.barnesandnoble.com.
Think dream not transaction	What dream do our customers start with that leads them to buy from us? How can we realise that dream? Examples: www.expedia.com.
Beat the physical world	What can we do in the digital world that would be impossible or not feasible in the physical world? Examples: www.benjerry.com.
Leverage the froth	What simple ideas would capture most media and public attention, even if short-lived? Examples: www.travelocity.com, www.lastminute.com.
Change the pricing model	Would our customers benefit from a different way of pricing, perhaps micro-payments or auctions? Examples: www.priceline.com.
Convert atoms to bits	What physical world core competencies do we have that could be applied to the digital world? Examples: www.ups.com.

If the decision is made to enter into e-commerce, an e-business venture needs **support and long-term commitment from high-level management** such as a the chief executive or a board-level director.

4.3 Ten key steps to constructing an effective strategy for e-commerce

Step 1 **Upgrade customer interaction**

The first thing for the organisation to do is to **upgrade interaction with existing customers**.

(a) Create automated responses for FAQs (Frequently Asked Questions) so that customers become conditioned to electronic communication. Automated responses, perhaps surprisingly in view of their impersonal nature, can help to improve customer confidence and trust.

(b) Set fast response standards, at least to match anything offered by the competition.

(c) Use email in order to confirm actions, check understanding, and reassure the customer that their business is being taken forward.

(d) Establish ease of navigation around your website and enhance the site's 'stickiness' so that there is a measurably reduced likelihood that actual or potential customers will migrate elsewhere.

A study conducted by Rubic Inc in the USA ('Evaluating the 'Sticky' Factor of E-Commerce Sites') found that the majority of websites fail to communicate effectively with customers. Only 40 per cent had a strategy of personalisation for their email messages to customers; when customers responded to follow-up offers, only one quarter of websites recognised the fact that they were dealing with a repeat customer; 40 per cent of email enquiries went unanswered despite promises of replies within two days.

Step 2 **Understand customer segments**

The organisation preparing its e-commerce strategy should **understand its customer segments** and classify each segment against the likelihood that it will be receptive to an internet business route.

(a) Some will be eager to transfer to the new technology, others will do so if persuaded (or incentivised), and residual groups will prefer to remain as they are.

(b) Once the degree of profitability-per-customer has been established, efforts should be made to automate the provision of customer service and transaction capability so far as low-value customers are concerned.

(c) The organisation may establish personalised service relationships with key customers.

Step 3 **Understand service processes**

The organisation must **understand its customer service processes** in order to disentangle those processes which can safely be put on to the web and those which have to be delivered in other ways.

(a) Typically, organisations serving customers may find that there are between five and ten generic transaction types which describe their relationships with these customers (eg information query, complaint, and so forth).

(b) This analysis is essential for addressing such questions as: Which of these processes is appropriate for low-touch automation? Which of these processes will work better, from the customer's standpoint, if put on the web?

(c) Transaction costs also need to be investigated, again from the perspective of the organisation and its overheads, and also taking into account the transaction costs incurred by the customer. These may involve money, but customers are often more conscious about time and timeliness.

PART B INFORMATION SYSTEMS

Step 4   Define the role

The organisation needs to **define the role for live interaction with its customers**.

(a) Live interaction may be very useful if there is scope for cross-selling and the conversion of enquiries into sales.

(b) The availability of service supplied by human intervention can also be appropriate if the organisation needs to build trust (eg it is a new brand which must work hard to establish confidence) and secure diagnostic information from the customer before any product or service can be delivered.

(c) Email may not be sufficient as a communications route, especially if it involves a delay before replies or acknowledgements are forthcoming.

(d) Live interaction can be essential for customers who have a strong preference for human contact.

Step 5   Decide technology

Making the key technology decisions involves some tough choices. Given the pace of change and innovation in this arena, it is difficult to know whether to initiate a pilot programme immediately, with the full IT and people investment scheduled for later, or whether to go for full integration at once. The risk with a pilot programme is that the organisation can be overtaken by pioneering competitors; the risk with full integration is that new systems can be inadequate or may even collapse completely.

Step 6   Deal with the tidal wave

There is much evidence that offering an internet-based service can lead to a major increase in customer interaction, and so organisations need to develop strategies for **dealing with the tidal wave**. This might involve:

(a) Ensuring sufficient capacity is available for worst-case scenarios
(b) Using low-touch technologies and system design
(c) Setting targets for low-touch interaction
(d) Ensuring facilities are scaleable if demand rapidly outstrips supply

Step 7   Create incentives

The organisation may have to **create incentives for use of the lowest-cost channels**, with savings passed on the customer through discounts. The alternatives are:

(a) To create **incentives** to switch to the lowest-cost channels, through financial inducements, training and additional benefits.

(b) To introduce **disincentives** for continuing to use existing channels. Thus Abbey National has implemented a £5 charge for customers who pursue over-the-counter cash transactions in their branches. Such tactics almost invariably generate very hostile reactions from customers themselves and from consumer groups.

Step 8   Decide on channel choices

The eighth consideration involves the decision about **which channel choices to offer**, and whether, for instance, to confine operations to the 'click' route or whether to simultaneously maintain the 'brick' presence through a branch network. There are two crucial questions:

(a) **Whether to offer the customer a choice of channels**, eg face-to-face, post, phone and internet. Many banks offer all four; some have single-channel accounts (phone or internet only), whilst others (like **egg**) allow constrained choice.

(b) **How to balance the costs of different channels whilst managing the Customer Relationship Management (CRM) database.** In most customer service environments, the quality and scope of the CRM database is central to the successful delivery of service, so it becomes desirable not to operate each customer-communication channel separately, but to integrate existing channels around a single CRM database.

Step 9 Exploit the internet

The organisation should **exploit the internet in order to create new relationships and an experience**.

(a) It is desirable to create **tailor-made service** sites for significant customers.

(b) Proactive **product/service offerings** should be regularly incorporated into the website architecture.

(c) **Communities of users** and/or customers (depending on whichever is appropriate) should be facilitated, since these generate additional business through referral and may well undertake a large proportion of the customer-service activity among themselves. Such communities may also stimulate product/service innovation, new uses for existing products and services, and product/service extensions.

(d) Deliberate mechanisms need to be developed in order to **turn browsers into buyers**, and transform one-off customers into repeat purchasers.

(e) Any successful e-commerce strategy presupposes the likelihood that the product/service supplier can engage the potential customer **emotionally** despite the technology which surrounds internet availability.

It is vital for organisations to place themselves in the shoes of customers and ask the question: what are our customers really buying? The answer, 99 times out of 100, is that customers are buying benefits whilst companies are selling features. Further, if the transaction lacks any emotional commitment, then it also lacks any real likelihood of voluntary customer retention.

Step 10 Implement

No strategy is worth the paper is written on if it simply remains a document, gathering dust: as Peter Drucker once pointed out, 'Strategy is nothing until it degenerates into work'.

4.4 Important aspects of strategy implementation for e-commerce

4.4.1 Organisation and culture

When organisations move into an electronic age, some people (and functions) increase their corporate influence, whilst others move into the shadows. The increasing use of technology is unsettling, especially for senior people (ironically, employees lower down the hierarchy are likely to be much more comfortable about technological innovation). The internet promotes freedom of information, both upwards and downwards; this, for some managers, is equated with a loss of authority.

4.4.2 Systems and infrastructure

Implementation of e-commerce often requires integration of service systems, particularly call centres, the web, and CRM processes. This in turn may require a company to review its whole decision-making patterns and make some difficult choices about existing 'legacy' procedures.

4.4.3 Training

Effective e-commerce implementation requires both staff and customers to be trained. Dealing with electronic interaction demands different skills from those which are appropriate to staff who focus on voice communications. Dealing simultaneously with written and verbal interaction is likely to call for a new skill set.

Chapter roundup

- The **internet** is a global network linking millions of computers. The World Wide Web **(WWW)** is a system of internet servers that support specially formatted documents. A group of documents accessed from the same base web address is known as a **website**.

- Most organisations now have a **website** and some conduct **transactions** over the internet.

- The major growth of **e-commerce** so far has been in the Business to Business (B2B) sector.

- The internet provides opportunities to **automate tasks** which would previously have required human intervention.

- Establishing links to the internet brings **security risks**. Suitable systems, policies and procedures should be implemented to minimise these risks.

- **Hacking** involves attempting to gain unauthorised access to a computer system, usually through telecommunications links. A **virus** is a piece of software which infects programs and data and possibly damages them, and which replicates itself. Viruses often use email links to spread.

- **Encryption** aims to ensure the security of data during transmission. Encryption involves scrambling the data at one end of the line, transmitting the scrambled data, and unscrambling it at the receiver's end of the line.

- **Anti-virus software** and a **firewall** are essential security tools for any network (or PC) with access to the internet.

- **Electronic commerce** means conducting business electronically via a communications link. An older technology that is covered under the electronic commerce umbrella is **Electronic Data Interchange** (EDI).

- Ensuring **'back-office' operations complement web-based operations** is vital.

- When developing a **strategy for e-commerce** consider:
    - Organisation and culture
    - Systems and infrastructure
    - Training
    - Customers

Quick quiz

1. List five current uses of the internet.
2. What tasks are typically automated by a website?
3. How do ISDN and ADSL technologies improve internet efficiency?
4. Distinguish between encryption and authentication.
5. What is a virus?
6. List five ways in which the internet and e-commerce differ from normal business practices.

PART B INFORMATION SYSTEMS

Answers to quick quiz

1. Five of the following:
   - Dissemination of information
   - Product/service development (test marketing)
   - Transaction processing (B2B and B2C)
   - Relationship enhancement
   - Recruitment and job search
   - Entertainment

2. Frequently-Asked-Questions, order status checking, keyword search, interview style information gathering, email, bulletin boards and requests for personal contact.

3. Through allowing faster transfer of data.

4. Encryption involves scrambling and unscrambling data to prevent unauthorised 'eavesdroppers' obtaining useful data. Authentication ensures a message has come from an authorised sender.

5. A small program that infects systems and possibly damages them.

6.
   - It challenges traditional business models.
   - Benefits are available to organisations of all sizes.
   - It challenges the need to pay for some information.
   - It encourages speed of product/service delivery.
   - It creates new communication networks and business alliances.

End of chapter question

Insurance brokerage (AIA November 2007)

You work for a medium-size insurance brokerage company offering policies to the public and to companies for vehicle and buildings insurance. You have been asked to prepare an introductory seminar to the brokerage's directors on e-commerce and business via the internet. The directors wish to know more about this possibility before considering moving into internet based brokerage in the future.

Required

(a) (i) What are the key features of electronic commerce? **(6 marks)**

(ii) Explain **four** advantages to your company in developing and using an internet website.

(8 marks)

(b) Present your seminar notes under the following headings:

(i) Barriers to conducting business over the internet; and

(ii) Factors that encourage the business to adopt an internet-based dimension. **(11 marks)**

(Total = 25 marks)

Answers to end of chapter questions

Chapter 1

1

	Plants	Total cost
	P	$
Period – High production	40,000	170,000
Period – Low production	20,000	95,000
Change due to variable cost	20,000	75,000

∴ Variable cost per plant = $75,000/20,000 = $3.75

Period – High production: fixed cost = $170,000 – (40,000 × $3.75)

= $20,000

Therefore total costs = 20,000 + ($3.75 × number of plants)

When output = 35,000 plants,

Expected costs = 20,000 + ($3.75 × 35,000)

Expected costs = $151,250

2   A time series is a series of figures or values recorded over time. A time series has four components: a trend, seasonal variations, cyclical variations and random variations.

The trend is the underlying long-term movement over time in values of data recorded.

Seasonal variations are short-term fluctuations in recorded values, due to different circumstances which affect results at different times of the year, on different days of the week, at different times of day, or whatever.

Cyclical variations are medium-term changes in results caused by circumstances which repeat in cycles.

Random variations are non-recurring and unpredictable caused by unforeseen circumstances such as a change in government, a war, technological change or a fire.

3   Marks would be awarded for **any** valid examples such as:

Political	Government imposing maximum prices for newspapers
Economic	Change in income levels
	Change in unemployment
	Change in sales tax
Social	Attitudes towards newspaper companies (scandals and so on)
Technical	Development of tablet editions of major newspapers

ANSWERS TO END OF CHAPTER QUESTIONS

Chapter 2

(a) Test $H_0: \mu = 378$ against
$H_1: \mu < 378$

Test statistic: $z = \dfrac{\bar{x} - \mu}{x / \sqrt{n}}$

Level of significance: $a = 0.05$

Critical Region: Reject H_0 if $z < -1.645$, otherwise Accept H_0

Assuming that H_0 ($\mu = 378$) is true,

$z = \dfrac{359 - 378}{83 / \sqrt{66}} = -1.86$

Conclusion: since $z = -1.86 < -1.645$ we should reject H_0 in favour of H_1. There is therefore evidence in the sample that the mean value of print job values in the first six months of this year is less than last year's mean value.

(b) Test $H_0: p = 0.72$ against
$H_1: p < 0.72$

Test statistic: $z = \dfrac{x/n - p}{\sqrt{[p(1-p)/n]}}$

Level of significance: $a = 0.05$

Critical Region: Reject H_0 if $z < -1.645$, otherwise Accept H_0

Assuming that H_0 ($p = 0.72$) is true,

$z = \dfrac{0.65 - 0.72}{\sqrt{[(0.72 \times (1 - 0.72)/66]}}$

Conclusion: since $z = -1.27 > -1.645$ we should Accept H_0. There is thus evidence in the sample that the proportion of this year's customers paying within the allowed one month is not less than last year's proportion of 72%.

(c) For a test to end in a significant result H_0 must be rejected. In (i), H_0 is rejected at the 5% level of significance, while in (ii) this is not the case. In (i) the minimum level of significance to conclude that H_0 is rejected corresponds to a z-value of –1.86. Referring to the table of the standard Normal distribution, this corresponds to a significance level of 0.03144 or 3.1%. In (ii) the minimum level of significance to conclude that H_0 should be rejected corresponds to a z-value of –1.27. The standard Normal table gives this probability as 0.10204 or 10.2%.

To the Managing Director of Printex:

We have analysed a sample of customer accounts so far this year with a view to discovering whether, compared to last year, the average value of print jobs completed and the proportion of customers paying for their work within one month of completion have both decreased significantly. We have found that this is likely to be the case in the former, but unlikely to be the case in the latter, although both conclusions are based only on a sample of this year's customer accounts. We actually found that there is only a chance of 3.2% that the average value per customer print job is not less than that last year, but there is a chance of 10.2% that the proportion of this year's customers paying us within one month is not less than last year's proportion. Generally it is reckoned that a result with greater than a 5% chance of not being true should not be relied upon. It does appear that there has been a change this year, but only to the value of print jobs.

Chapter 3

1. (a) The minimisation linear programme of the mix of 10m³ and 15m³ capacity tipper trucks to apply to the contract to demolish the power station is as follows:

    Objective: to minimise the total daily opportunity cost of using the trucks

    Unknowns: the numbers of 10m³ and 15m³ trucks to use on the contract

    Constraints: limited – total numbers of trucks allocated: no more than 20

    - Number of 10m³ trucks allocated: at least 5
    - Number of 15m³ trucks allocated: at least 5
    - Total amount of rubble removed per day: at least 900m³

    Let the numbers of the two types of trucks be x and y, respectively. Then the LP is:

    Minimise 750 x + 900 y

    subject to
    - (1) x + y <= 20
    - (2) x >= 5
    - (3) y >= 5
    - (4) 60 x + 60 y >= 900

    Note. Since a 10m³ truck can make six round trips per day the amount of rubble it can dispose of is 60m³; similarly, the figure for a 15m³ truck is also 60m³. The graph of the feasible combinations of values of x and of y is presented below. The region has vertices A, B, C and D.

    (b) To minimise the total daily opportunity cost, evaluate the objective function at each corner of the feasible region:

Corner point	(x, y)	Value of 750 x + 900 y
A	(5,10)	12,750
B	(5,15)	17,250
C	(15,5)	15,750
D	(10,5)	12,000

    The optimal solution point is point D.

    (i) The optimal mix of trucks is therefore: ten 10m³ and five 15m³ trucks.

    (ii) The minimum total daily opportunity cost is £12,000.

    (iii) The total m³ of rubble waste that would be possible to remove each day is:

    $(60 \times 10) + (60 \times 5) = 900$ m³

    (iv) The number of days that the contract will last given that there are a total of 15000m³ of rubble to remove to the waste site is:

    15,000/ 900 = 16 ⅔ days

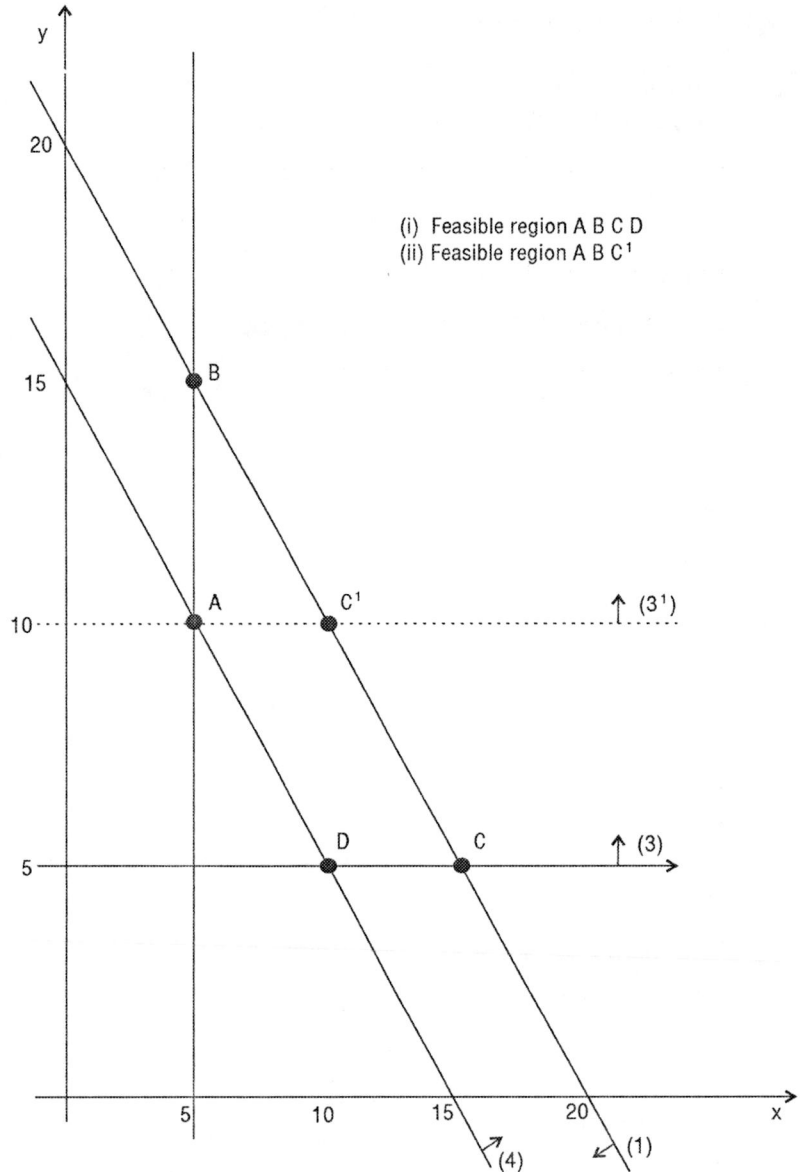

(c) After 10 working days on the contract, the amount of rubble so far removed would be 9,000m³, leaving another 6,000m³ to be removed. But now there will be at least 10 15m³ trucks assigned to the remainder of the contract. This alters the LP to:

Minimise 750 x + 900 y

Subject to (1) x + y <= 20
            (2) x >= 5
            (3) y >= 10
            (4) 60 x + 60y >= 900

The region of feasible solutions changes to A, B, C – refer to the diagram of feasible solutions.

Applying the solution method to this feasible region:

Corner point	(x, y)	750 x + 900 y
A	(5,10)	12,750
B	(5,15)	17,250
C¹	(10,10)	16,500

Thus, the optimal point is now A (5,10).

(i) The optimal mix of trucks is five $10m^3$ and ten $15m^3$ capacity trucks.

(ii) The remaining minimum total daily opportunity cost is £12,750.

(iii) The amount of rubble to be removed each day is:

$(5 \times 60) + (10 \times 60) = 900m^3$ still

(iv) The remaining number of days that the contract will last is:

6000/900 = 6⅔ days

Thus, the effect of the change to the minimum number of $15m^3$ capacity trucks is to alter the mix of trucks and to raise the daily minimum total opportunity cost by £750.

2 **Step 1**

Let p = weekly number of purses

h = weekly number of handbags

Step 2

Leather $1.5p + 2h \leq 600$

Skilled labour $0.75p + 0.5h \leq 210$

Quota $p - h \leq 0$

Non-negativity $p, h \geq 0$

Step 3

Objective:

Maximise $5p + 6h$

Chapter 4

1 (a) The activity-on-arrow network for this project is:

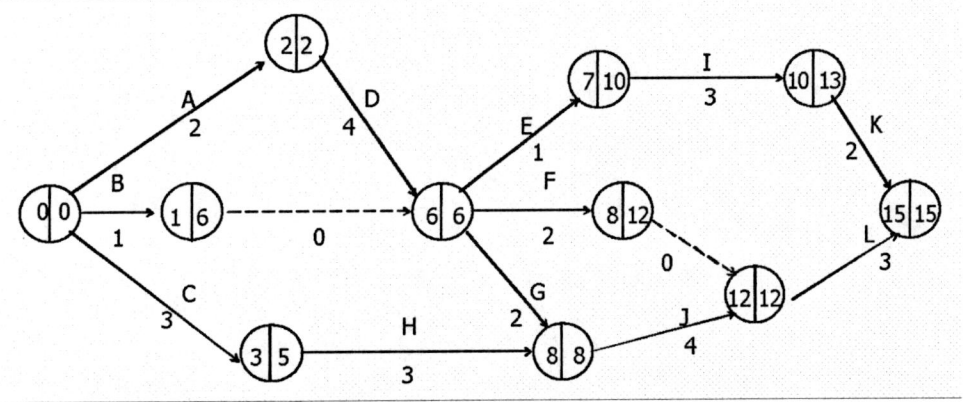

The critical path of activities is ADGJL; the estimated number of days of completion is 15.

(b) To determine the optimal cost project completion time we need to balance the extra costs of using the special machines on the indicated activities with savings in manual labour costs if days of normal completion time are reduced. First we need to calculate the extra cost per day for each of the activities for which the special machines could be used:

Activity	C	D	G	H	I	J
Extra cost per day	200	150	200	300	200	250

The method leading to the identification of the optimal, cost-wise, shortest project completion time involves accelerating one or more of these particular activities when they are critical until the saving in daily labour cost is outweighed by the total extra cost of using the machines to achieve the corresponding reduction in completion time. It is advisable to check the length of every network path as the critical activities are accelerated.

		Accelerations		
Path	Normal length	1. D by 2	2. J by 2	3. C and G by 1
ADEIK	12	10	10	10*
ADFL	11	9	9	9
ADGJL	15*	13*	11*	10*
BEIK	7	7	7	7
BFL	6	6	6	6
BGJL	10	10	8	7
CHJL	13	13*	11*	10*

Activity D is chosen first to accelerate since it is critical and is cheapest to accelerate; all paths including D will reduce in length by the 2 days of acceleration. The second acceleration involves activity J because it is on both (now) critical paths ADGJL and CHJL and is the next cheapest activity. Finally, activities C and G are accelerated by one day each so that both critical paths are reduced in length from 11 days; the total cost of such accelerations is £200 for C and £200 for G = £400. Technically, this will not reduce the total cost of executing the project – the 11 day and the 10 day total costs are the same. Attempting to further accelerate the project is impossible because the critical path ADGJL cannot be further reduced.

Acceleration 1. reduces total project costs by 2 × (400 − 150) = £500
Acceleration 2. reduces total project costs by 2 × (400 − 250) = £300
Acceleration 3. reduces total project costs by 1 × (400 − {200+200}) = £0.

Thus, the optimal project completion time is either 11 days or 10 days.

(c) (i) The total project cost for a completion time of 11 days is:

11 × £400 + (2 × £150) + (2 × £250) = £5,200

This compares to a cost of 15 × £400 = £6,000 if the project is completed in 15 days as in (i).

(ii) The critical activities for the optimal project cost are:

A, C, D, G, H, J and L; these activities have zero total float (spare time).

(iii)
Non-critical activity	B	E	F	I	K
Float days	3	1	2	1	1

2 **Top-down budgeting** describes the situation where the budget is imposed 'from above'. Project Managers are allocated a budget for the project based on an estimate made by senior management. The figure may prove realistic, especially if similar projects have been undertaken recently. However, the technique is often used simply because it is quick, or because only a certain level of funding is available.

In **bottom-up budgeting** the project manager consults the project team, and others, to calculate a budget based on the tasks that make up the project. Work breakdown structure (WBS) is a useful tool in this process.

Chapter 5

(a) The operation of the system is studied first to find the procedure for dealing with clients and to obtain the probability distributions of arrivals and services.

The operation is then simulated by following each simulated client through the system, selecting time of arrival and length of service with probability proportional to size. This is achieved by allocating to each probability group a range of two digit numbers, the range being proportional to the probability of the group. Random number tables are then used to select the arrival interval and service time for each client. The times of arrival, length of wait and length of service for each client is recorded on a simulation pro-forma. If the waiting time is longer than 10 minutes this is recorded.

In practice a running average of waiting or service time would be recorded. When this settles down to a steady state, the simulation is finished. This may take many simulations to achieve and is best done on a computer.

(b) Allocation of sampling digits:

Service times			Arrival times		
Service time Minutes	Probability	Digit allocation	Arrival Minutes	Probability	Digit allocation
2	0.05	00 – 04	1	0.2	00 – 19
4	0.10	05 – 14	8	0.4	20 – 59
6	0.15	15 – 29	15	0.3	60 – 89
10	0.30	30 – 59	25	0.1	90 – 99
14	0.25	60 – 84			
20	0.10	85 – 94			
30	0.05	95 – 99			

Simulation table

Client No.	R number arrival	Arrival interval	Arrival time	Start of service	R number service	Length of service	Depart-ure time	Time in queue	See manager
1	03	1	1	1	63	14	15	0	
2	47	8	9	15	71	14	29	6	
3	43	8	17	29	62	14	43	12	✓
4	73	15	32	43	33	10	53	11	✓
5	86	15	47	53	26	6	59	6	
6	36	8	55	59	16	6	65	4	
7	96	25	80	80	80	14	94	0	
8	47	8	88	94	45	10	104	6	
9	36	8	96	104	60	14	118	8	
10	61	15	111	118	11	4	122	7	
11	46	8	119	122	14	4	126	3	
12	98	25	144	144	10	4	148	0	

Tutorial Notes

1 Two equally correct variants are possible.

    (a) The system could be initiated by the first arrival who would therefore arrive at time zero. The random numbers would then be used to determine the arrival times of subsequent clients.

    (b) As the arrival interval probabilities are only given to one significant figure, one digit numbers could have been used for this distribution.

These would give different results for the twelve simulations, although in the long run simulation they would make no difference.

ANSWERS TO END OF CHAPTER QUESTIONS

2 Time of start of service is whichever time is the greater of arrival time and time of departure of the previous client.

3 It has been assumed that those clients who see the manager are still in the system and are therefore allocated their service time. If the manager takes them out of the system and allows the assistant to deal with the next client, the service time of those who see the manager would be zero.

(c) In 148 minutes operation, two clients have seen the manager.

Hence the number seeing the manager in 50 hours $= \dfrac{2}{148} \times 50 \times 60$

$= 40.54$

Cost @ £5 $= 40.54 \times £5$
$= £202.7$

Note. An alternative method is to take $\dfrac{2}{12}$ths of the number of clients who arrive in 50 hours. This is calculated as follows:

Time	Probability	Time × Probability
1	0.2	0.2
8	0.4	3.2
15	0.3	4.5
25	0.1	2.5
Average arrival interval in minutes =		10.4

Number of customers in 50 hours $= \dfrac{50 \times 60}{10.4}$

$\dfrac{2}{12}$ths of these see the manager $= \dfrac{2}{12} \times \dfrac{50 \times 60}{10.4}$

$= 48.08$

Cost @ £5 $= 48.08 \times £5$
$= £240.4$

The difference between the results from the two methods is due to short run random errors. In the long run, the results would agree.

(d) **Advantages** of simulation:

(i) Where the application of analytical techniques would be unsuitable, for instance for strategic planning models, simulation provides a method of at least providing information if not solving problems. It is also more suitable where the user wishes to study a range of possible combinations of variables and the different outcomes that may occur.

(ii) Simplifying assumptions, necessary in both simulation and mathematical models, are not usually so great in the former. This means that more variables can be included providing a more realistic model.

(iii) Some decision-makers place more reliance on simulation methods even where analytical methods are appropriate. This is particularly true where the amount of uncertain variables is large so that EV calculations would give a false view of possible variations in outcomes.

(iv) Simulation can provide an insight into how the system behaves before reaching equilibrium. For example, simulation of a queuing system will show how the system can vary from start-up, whereas queuing formulae will only give the steady state results.

Disadvantages of simulation:

(i) A simulation run uses only a sample of test data. It is necessary therefore, to carry out further runs before the results are sufficiently accurate. Statistical techniques can be applied to the results to estimate their accuracy.

(ii) Since simulation involves the application of test data to a model, it is inevitably a lengthy process, and will usually necessitate the use of a computer.

(iii) Simulation is not an optimisation technique. Whereas other techniques (such as linear programming) determine the optimal solution, simulation only indicates the likely results of taking a particular decision. It is necessary for the decision-maker to evaluate the results according to pre-determined criteria, and to compare the results of different decisions in an attempt to identify the optimal solution. However, by carrying out a large number of simulations with varying values of the inputs, an optimum can sometimes be found. For example, by simulating a stock control system with different re-order levels and quantities, the optimum values can be found, but it is a very lengthy process, only feasible with the use of a computer.

Chapter 6

(a) For each of the years 3 to 7 we can calculate the expected annual profit for each of the alternative uses of the house. The formula

$E(x) = S\ px$

is used, where p represents probability and x the possible annual profit.

For alternative A: $E(x) = (0.2 \times 0.25) + (0.4 \times 0.35) + (0.3 \times 0.45) + (0.1 \times 0.55) = 0.38$ £m

Note that it is conventional to use the midpoint of any interval for x, and to assume that any open-ended class for x is of the same width as the neighbouring classes.

Thus, on average, if the owner chooses to turn the country house into a small conference centre, the venture will return an annual profit of £0.38 million (excluding conversion costs over years 1 to 2).

For alternative B: $E(x) = (0.5 \times 0.35) + (0.3 \times 0.45) + (0.2 \times 0.55) = 0.42$ £m

For alternative C: $E(x) = (0.4 \times 0.2) + (0.5 \times 0.4) + (0.1 \times 0.6) = 0.34$ £m

Thus over the total period of years 1 to 7,

A's expected profit is $-0.8 + (5 \times 0.38) = £1.1$ m
B's expected profit is $-0.7 + (5 \times 0.42) = £1.4$ m
C's expected profit is $-0.5 + (5 \times 0.34) = £1.2$ m

(b) (i) The best option appears to be venture B since it has the highest expected operating profit over the seven-year period. However there is not a great deal to choose between the three alternatives. The owner should be made aware of the limitations of basing a single decision on an expected value analysis.

Firstly, expected values are merely arithmetic averages, in this case of yearly possible returns. As such, the averaging process masks any variations in possible yearly returns, and indeed takes little account of them. Much therefore depends upon the accuracy of the information within the distributions of possible annual profits – both the amounts and the probabilities. Because these are subject to uncertainty they may not reflect accurately the true pictures. It has also been implicitly assumed that the annual profits have identical distributions each year for the five years 3 to 7. No account is taken of risk in the calculation of the expected values. Risk is simply a way of describing the uncertainty/variation in the data. After all, for venture B for example, the actual annual profit could be as low as £0.2 million, or as high as £0.6 million. Either of these extremes would give a different picture for the worth of venture B. Some recognition of risk should therefore be applied and provided to the owner before he makes a choice between the alternatives.

(ii) A measure of risk that can be applied in situations involving probability distributions is standard deviation for which the formula is

$$SD(x) = \sqrt{\{\Sigma px^2 - [E(x)]^2\}}$$

Standard deviation is primarily a measure of the variation or dispersion between figures. It does this by comparing the difference between each actual figure and the average of the figures. The differences are squared to remove the influence of negative differences and then averaged. The act of taking the square root in the formula brings the result back into linear units, in this case £m. The possible profits for each venture are expressed on an annual basis. A more correct standard deviation analysis would require the creation of 5-year profit distributions prior to calculating SD; hence we will be able only to calculate standard deviation for a year's profits in this analysis.

(c) For alternative A, the standard deviation calculation is:

x	p	px	px^2
.25	.2	.05	.0125
.35	.4	.14	.049
.45	.3	.135	.06075
.55	.1	.055	.03025

$E(x) = 0.38$ and $\Sigma px^2 = 0.1525$. $SD(x) = \sqrt{\{0.1525 - (0.38)^2\}} = 0.09$ £m

Thus, the standard deviation of annual profit is £0.09 million.

For alternatives B and C the calculations are:

		B				C	
x	p	px	px^2	x	p	px	px^2
.35	.5	.175	.06125	.2	.4	.08	.016
.45	.3	.135	.06075	.4	.5	.2	.08
.55	.2	.11	.0605	.6	.1	.06	.036
			S = .1825				S = .132

Thus for B, $SD = \sqrt{\{0.1825 - (0.42)^2\}} = 0.078$ £m

And for C, $SD = \sqrt{\{0.132 - (0.34)^2\}} = 0.128$ £m

The smallest annual profit standard deviation is for alternative B at £0.078 million. Alternative B therefore is associated with the highest expected overall profit and the lowest project risk. The owner of the country house should on balance choose to renovate the country house into a quality restaurant if all the data can be reasonably relied upon.

Chapter 7

(a) (i) With three shops it is likely that staff in any one outlet will need to communicate with the other shops, and even contact suppliers electronically. Necessary basic hardware will include at least three microcomputers and printers, a print server, a file server, and a communications server – the latter to support inter-shop and shop-external environment communications. In addition, specifically to create a LAN, the shop owner will also require a high-speed cable to connect the several devices, a network card for each device which is to be connected to the network (and network software to manage data transmission around the network cabling).

(ii) The LAN would be owned and operated by the owner and staff of Jean-Genie, and its operation would be restricted to the confines of this operation, except for possible internet access. The latter is, however, one facility that could be utilised (via a gateway with the public telephone network). Other facilities offered within the network are:

- Use of a centralised shared data and program store held on a file server, perhaps in the form of a database.
- Sharing of several resources by several users connected on the network.
- Use of electronic mail.
- Use of electronic calendar and diary facilities to schedule meetings and events.

(b) Compared with the existing manual administration of the one shop/outlet business, there are obvious advantages of taking the opportunity at business enlargement to automate the administration of Jean-Genie Linking the three shops via a LAN will make communication and co-ordination less labour intensive and simplify a more complex managerial entity. Online stock records may be devised enabling the owner to immediately know the position of stocks at any time; these stock records for all three shops may be accessed from any one shop. The system could be programmed to automatically produce purchase orders when stock falls below a predetermined level. The use of payroll software would simplify the management of staff payment. Accounting software would include allowing Jean-Genie's owner to closely monitor shop performances, produce summary reports of a wide range of accounting measures and balance sheet items, including for example VAT recording. Comparisons of sales by medium of payment would also be possible, thereby providing Jean-Genie with key information on the operation of the business.

(c) Initially, the owner of Jean-Genie may need technical support and advice in operating with a completely new computer-based business system. Perhaps even, the owner should consider employing a specialist to support her over the initial few months. Unless she has reasonably advanced and working knowledge of computing, networks and software capabilities, she is likely to be swamped by the opportunity. Given this, it would be advisable for her to begin simply by acquiring standard accounting and payroll software. Even so, much preparation and lead-in work would be required – manual to automation of business administration is not learned nor applied overnight. Apart from payroll and purchase ledger software, simple nominal ledger software could be utilised, and gradually a range of microcomputer-based business support software. A spreadsheet package would be a distinct advantage in monitoring the performances of the three shops, and in allowing turnover forecasting and budgeting. Database software is another possibility, the use of which over time could be extended from providing an integrated stock record system to other business-wide applications.

The key in this situation would be to start simply and then gradually refine and expand the use of the computerised system.

Chapter 8

(a) A Level 0 data flow diagram is the most general diagram showing only key aspects of the data process. It is important to represent the features of the system correctly – in this case the one process can be called 'process application', the data source is exhibitor (customer) applications, the two data sinks are the Accounting department and the sending out of 'a joining instruction pack', and the data stores are the price list and the previous customers' file. Each of these basic components of the DFD must be shown using the standard symbology, with appropriate connectivity, to indicate the flow of data through the application process.

ANSWERS TO END OF CHAPTER QUESTIONS

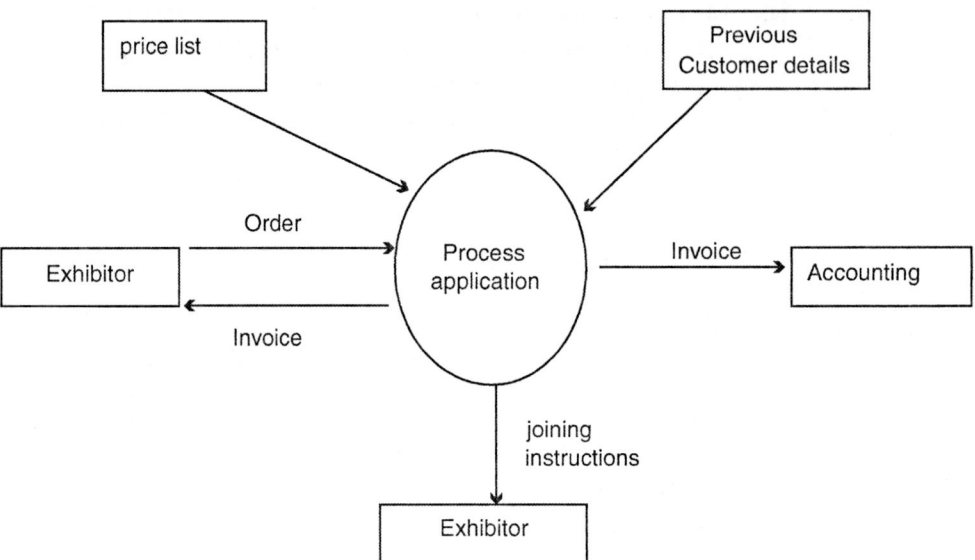

(b) A Level 1 DFD shows the data processing of the exhibitor application process in more detail – the elements for inclusion are listed under the normal headings in the question. Note that there are now three data processes, three data sources or sinks, and four data stores to be included. Again, the correct data flows must be shown – this is the object of the exercise.

Level 1 Data Flow Diagram

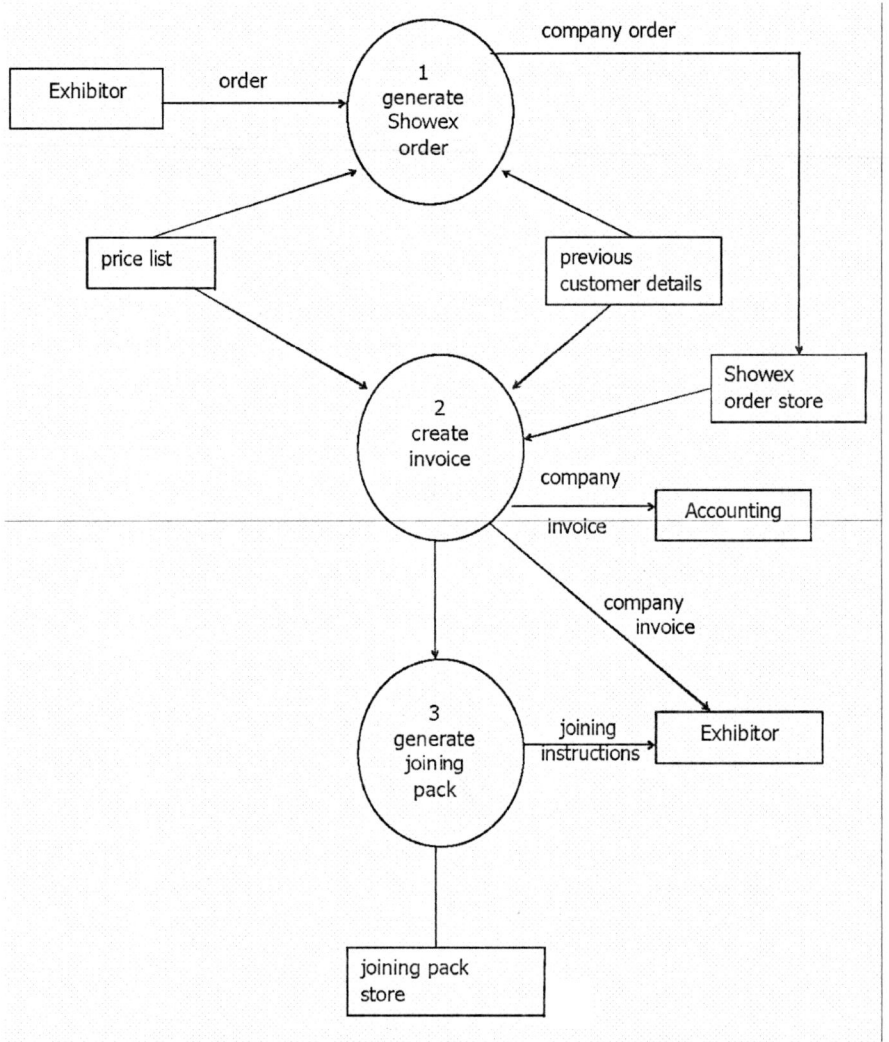

(c) The role of the data dictionary appended to a DFD is to provide definitions of the types and uses of data flowing through the processes within the DFD. The dictionary must be comprised of precise data specifications; it must not include duplications of data descriptions so that consistency is ensured. The data dictionary is used throughout the process of systems analysis and into the detailed design stage, and it is normally stored on a computer to facilitate cross-referencing between data elements.

Typical data dictionary entry

Name: **Type**:

   Exhibitor invoice   Data flow

Structure:

Aggregate: (invoice#, invoice date, exhibitor#, exhibitor name, order#, stand/space [duration, size, location, price], total payable)

Usage characteristics:

Output process 2 – make up invoice

Input to sink – Accounting department

Input to sink – Exhibitor

Chapter 9

(a) Computer software is the general term for a set of instructions that control the operation of a computer. There are two types: applications and system software. All software has to be written in a specialised language or code, ranging from code that the computer can immediately accept and execute to code written in English that a human-being can understand.

Machine code, as the name suggests, is a prime computer language. It allows the computer's CPU to accept data and instructions and 'compute' them. Machine code instructions are written in patterns of binary digits – 0s and 1s – such as 010011011011101 – virtually unintelligible to a human. Machine code is first generation language.

Assembly languages (AL) were developed to make the writing of programmes easier and more intelligible to humans (programmers). However, programmes in AL remain machine (computer)-orientated, and are specific to the manufacturer of the machine. Assembly code uses symbols or mnemonics like 'ADD' and 'STO' (store) instead of the binary digits. An example of an assembly language instruction is ADD R1, R3:R5 – add the contents of registers 1 and 3 and place the result in register 5. All programmes have to be translated into machine code before the computer can execute the instructions – for this an assembler programme is used. AL tends to be used to develop operating systems software; it is efficient and code runs quickly on the computer. ALs are second generation languages.

High level languages (HLL) were developed to increase the productivity of programmers – they are akin to the English language and programmers can write in HLL more quickly. Such languages are task-orientated rather than the machine orientation of machine code and AL. HLL are therefore more portable between different manufacturer's machines. Examples include COBOL: a general-purpose business data processing language, BASIC, C and Java: used in developing internet web-site pages. HLL programmes require translation into machine code before they can be run on a computer. This is achieved through either interpreting (line-by-line each time the programme is run, but each line is executed immediately following interpretation), or by compiling (the whole HLL programme is translated into machine code before being executed by the computer). Compiling creates a machine-based version of the programme that can be stored for execution on future occasions.

Generally, programmes written in HLL run on the computer much slower than those directly in machine code or AL, but allow programmers to be much more productive in developing software applications. HLLs are third generation.

(b) (i) The array of HLLs has done much to support the development of all types of computing, including computing in business. But, modern computing, with decreasing hardware costs yet ever more sophisticated technology, requires increases also in the sophistication of business programmes. While HLLs have greatly increased programmer productivity, the cost of software development has increased as a proportion of the total cost of an organisation's expenditure on its information system. Often the organisation has had to turn to commissioning purpose-designed software.

There is also a need to produce new or replacement information systems quickly – not something that HLLs can achieve readily. And applying more programmers to any one task does not necessarily speed development. A further identified need is to produce systems that meet user requirements rather than being merely technically efficient. More recently, much effort has gone into the correct identification of computing user needs. One approach is to develop quick, cheap versions of prototype systems that users can test before revision and improvement. Thus, thought has also been given to develop languages that are straightforward yet powerful, so that users themselves can develop their own systems. These languages, designed for use directly by end-users are called collectively, fourth generation languages.

(ii) 4GLs are designed for fast applications development, are often end-user orientated and structured for interactive applications development around a database. A prime example is SQL. A feature of a 4GL is the emphasis on instructions to specify what applications are to do rather than how to do them, and the instructions are often written in near-English phrases.

4GLs contain a powerful interface with the user of the language enabling interactive dialogue in applications development. Further, users may specify both input and output screens, and reports; record contents can be specified and graphics incorporated.

Other 4GL features include: interfaces to conventional programming languages for writing special procedures not covered within the 4GL, and special features for model development. 4GLs also use very high-level instructions to reduce the total number of instructions needed in the development of the system – this feature makes them especially different to 3GLs.

(iii) While 4GLs are powerful tools for end-users cancelling the need for commissioning lengthy and expensive new applications software development, this does not mean that 3GLs are replaced. Large investment by companies in current 3GL programmes and programming skills demand continued maintenance and updating (in 3GL). Compared, say, to COBOL (a 3GL), an application written in a 4GL requires more processing power; this can more than offset the savings in development time offered by a 4GL since extra expenditure on hardware may be required to run 4GL programmes to reduce the run time.

A second drawback in the use of programmes written in 4GLs is the potential lack of standardisation of systems development in the organisation – applications developed by different end-users may ignore centralised standard-setting and control.

Chapter 10

1 (a) Information is the key to running a successful organisation almost regardless of size or complexity. Obviously, all information should be timely, accurate and pertinent, and results from data processed for a purpose – generally to support a planning or a control decision. Such decisions are taken by the managers in the organisation who will operate at different levels. There are three broad levels defined – strategic, tactical and operational.

ANSWERS TO END OF CHAPTER QUESTIONS

Operational level planning and control are concerned with the normal day-to-day operations within the organisation, and cover decisions designed to ensure effective and efficient usage of existing resources to achieve budget objectives. Such decisions as hiring or dismissing employees, on inventory and production levels, on (limited) pricing decisions, and on accounting cash and credit controls, are each part of an operational manager's remit.

Tactical level planning and control is usually associated with the middle levels of managers in an organisation. Typical examples include: the allocation of resources within departmental budgets, medium-term forecasting and work scheduling, and the planning of medium-term cashflows. Middle managers also monitor actual production, expenditure against budgets, and analyse variances and decide upon subsequent actions.

Strategic planning is executed by the most senior levels of organisational management and covers broad issues relating to the organisation's development over the longer term. Typical activities and decisions are the allocation of resources to major functions and departments in the organisation, structuring the company's finances; decisions on whether to undertake major investments and bid for large long-term contracts are part of a strategic manager's remit. Further, a strategic manager also contributes to the setting of the organisation's objectives.

(b) All information has characteristics like the period of time to which it relates, how much detail is included, from where it originates, with what degree of certainty it comes, and how often such information is needed. The characteristics will vary with the purpose of the information and with the level of the manager, and indeed the activity to which it is directed.

The time horizon characteristic refers to the length of time to which the information relates – whether it is longer term (several years) as in the case of strategic planning, or (very) short term as in the case of operational planning.

Operational managers generally require highly detailed information to support the often immediate decisions they take, while tactical managers generally need information that is less detailed/in more aggregate form, such as totals (production, expenditure per month or year).

Information to support operational decisions tends to be generated exclusively within the organisation; this is also true to a large extent for tactical information, whereas strategic managers rely on information mainly sourced from outside the company (and not in the control of it), though not entirely.

Information to support strategic managers' activities tends to suffer higher degrees of uncertainty because it often relates to the economy as a whole or general market forces; it is externally sourced and is in aggregate (general) form. At the other extreme, operational managers can rely with certainty on much of the information provided and relevant to their needs; this is due to the short-term, detailed and internal natures of the required information. Fairly obviously, information for tactical managers varies in level of certainty dependent, in part, on whether it is sourced internally and on the time period to which it relates.

Information to support strategic managers tends to be required infrequently (as and when the need surfaces) except appraisal of an organisation's plans and objectives may require regular treatment. Tactical planning and control tend to operate over the medium-term (a few months to one year) so information is more frequently required; operational decisions will, by their nature, require immediate information to support their taking.

(c) (i) Computerised systems offering a management information capability have gradually evolved, at a varying pace, ever since computers were first developed. Initially, computer programmes were written specifically to extract and process the relevant information. As systems' sophistication was developed, so information with greater depth and breadth was able to be produced, including the facilities for querying and reporting.

ANSWERS TO END OF CHAPTER QUESTIONS

Desk-top computers and distributed computing contributed to the greater use of management information systems in all organisations. The latter empowered the decentralised use of systems by users. Further, advances in internet technology have allowed connection between an organisation's location, between organisations and between customers and organisations.

A key factor has been the emphasis on designing a system for transaction processing – the base element in providing relevant management information – with the way the system can be used to generate information as an important objective.

Advances in computing technology have increased computing power with decreasing cost allowing computers to be more used by all organisations for routine processing. Equally, there has been a management culture shift recognising the importance of quick, effective and targeted information for management planning and control.

In summary, the factors contributing to the growth in the use of management information systems are reduced costs, greater speed of provision, interactive querying facilities, and flexibility in allowing managers to decide upon the types of information needed.

(ii) An executive information system (EIS) would be used by senior management to assist in strategic decision-making. Such a system would utilise modelling and simulation in medium- to long-term forecasting and budgeting.

A decision support system (DSS) includes the facilities for short- to medium-term forecasting and budgeting, and inventory control. Middle level managers use these facilities, including also those of creating special reports and ad-hoc querying, for tactical planning.

Lowest down the scale, a transaction processing system (TPS) is used by operational managers to monitor payroll, order tracking and employee records.

2 **Critical success factors** are a small number of key operational goals vital to the success of an organisation.

In general terms Rockart identifies four **sources** of CSFs.

(a) The **industry** that the business is in.

(b) The **company** itself and its situation within the industry.

(c) The **environment**, for example consumer trends, the economy, and political factors of the country in which the company operates.

(d) Temporal organisational factors, which are areas of corporate activity that may cause **concern** from time to time, for example, high inventory levels.

Chapter 11

(a) The risks in operating a computerised information system are multifarious: data entry may be inaccurate, hardware may fail, disks may become corrupted or lost, fire, software may malfunction, fraud and embezzlement may occur. The purposes of controls are to reduce these risks through:

(1) Deterrence and prevention – directed at potential erroneous data processing, and at potential fraud.

(2) Detection – obviously it is advisable to be able to discover when errors or fraud have occurred; the possibility of detection acts itself as a control.

ANSWERS TO END OF CHAPTER QUESTIONS

(3) Minimise loss – if a loss occurs, control needs to reduce the size of the loss such as utilising a back-up file regularly.

(4) Recovery – controlling by creating the ability to re-establish the state of the system before the breach of control or disaster occurred.

(5) Investigation – specifically aimed at general investigation such as internal audit; again, awareness that investigation may be applied acts as a form of control.

(b) (i) Data input controls are designed to ensure that inputted data is true and accurate. The controls can be installed as computer software routines.

Format checks are checks applied upon data entry to ensure that the 'shape' of the data entered is correct. For example, a customer code may always have to be in the form of two numerical digits followed by two alphabetic characters (74BW).

Check-digit verification can be applied to the input of numerical codes (product, account reference). Such checks utilise an extra numerical digit added to the end of the code; this digit has a mathematical relationship with the actual code. Such a check will identify single digit errors, transposition errors, and other like errors. A typical example is the modulus-11 method.

Other accuracy control-types are limit and reasonableness checks, master file checks, and form design.

Two possible completeness controls are batch control totals and field-filling checks. These controls are designed to combat omission errors.

Batch control totals are applied to lots of, say, 100 transactions. The total of all the numerical data values in a particular field is calculated pre-data entry. This control total is then compared to the computer-generated total post-data entry.

Field-filling checks involve the computer checking that in a transaction record the necessary fields have been completed with a value (numerical, alphabetic or alphanumeric). Other completeness controls are batch hash totals, batch record totals, and sequence checks.

(ii) Data storage controls are particularly aimed at erroneous erasure of files and at the provision of back-up and recovery facilities.

One such control is the physical protection against erasure: floppy disks have a plastic tab which may be switched to allow read only, magnetic tape files are provided with rings for insertion if the file is to be written to or erased.

A second storage control is magnetic labelling: such labels are encoded on the medium and identify its contents. A file-header label is placed at the start of the file to identify the file by name and give the date of the last update. Trailer labels at the ends of files contain control totals that are checked against those calculated during file processing.

A third storage control is a file back-up routine: copying important files for security. The grandparent-parent-child method provides security against the mishap of losing both the master and (single) back-up files at the same time. Other storage controls are external labelling (applied to tape reels and disk packs), database back-up routines using tapes to back-up disks, database concurrency controls, and cryptographic storage (scrambling contents).

(c) Data transmission in a computer system happens between the CPU and local peripherals (storage, output devices), and along telecommunications lines between computers or peripherals in WANs. Within the latter, communication can be subject to electronic noise interfering with the reliable transmission of the binary 1s and 0s.

With parity bit controls, an extra (parity) bit is added to a string of bits encoding characters (data). For example, odd parity uses the principle of an odd number of 1s for each coded character.

ANSWERS TO END OF CHAPTER QUESTIONS

The set of bits is tested by computer hardware to ensure that the odd number of 1s exists for each character – failure in this test requires re-transmission of the data.

An echo check is typically applied between the CPU and a printer. It involves the transmitted message from sender to receiver being re-transmitted back to the sender from the receiver. This 'echoed' message is compared with the original – any discrepancy signifies a transmission error.

Chapter 12

1   Data entry devices:

- Optical character reader – to scan documents or price tags in shops and convert to machine readable form.
- Bar code reader or wand reader – a laser scanning device to input information in shops, supermarkets, warehouses etc.
- Magnetic ink reader – used in banks to input the magnetic characters on cheques.
- Optical mark reader – to detect data on questionnaires, answer sheets, meter reading forms etc by the presence or absence of marks on documents.
- Optical scanner – to convert text in reports and articles into digital form.
- Mouse – small, easy-to-use handheld device for highlighting or selecting data on a screen.
- Touch screen – used with a finger on a screen to select items or commands.
- Light pen – pointing device used to select items or highlight items on a screen.
- Joy stick – mainly used with games or simulations.
- Voice recognition device – used to recognise speech to input data in applications such as warehouse and laboratory data entry and security systems.

2   A significant advantage of keyboard input is that the user is able to read and interpret what is being input – the user can exercise some judgement to ensure only valid data is entered.

Other advantages of keyboard input include:

(a) The person keying in the data can be in a remote location, away from the computer itself. Data can be transmitted via a communications link.

(b) The person keying in the data can check for keying errors on-screen.

(c) Keyboard input is convenient for small volumes of data when the time taken up by data input is relatively short.

3   Direct keyboard input has a number of disadvantages.

(a) It is unsuitable for large volumes of transaction data. Keying data manually takes time, so is not appropriate in some situations.

(b) Keyboard input is likely to be error-prone.

(c) There might be security problems. For example, keyboard input may be watched and there is the risk that unauthorised people could access a terminal or PC.

Chapter 13

(a) (i) Electronic commerce may be defined as any business transaction or exchange of information that is facilitated by using information and communications technologies. All sizes of organisations, private and public, and individuals, buy goods and services over the world wide web. Using the above definition of ecommerce allows three categories of systems to be identified:

ANSWERS TO END OF CHAPTER QUESTIONS

Electronic data interchange – establishing electronic communications between organisations to process transactions between them. For example, suppliers and retail outlets. Such electronic communications may be permanent via leased telephone connections, or temporary using the internet to establish connection.

Internet commerce – home computer users (the public) making purchases over the internet (business-to-customer transactions). This category must also include business-to-business transactions involving the purchase of goods and services.

Electronic markets – basically these are information sources that can be searched for particular products or services. They allow customers to examine and compare alternative services and prices before deciding to purchase.

(ii) To an extent, the availability of the internet has revolutionised business activity – the marketplace has become more global, transaction settlement may be automated and 'normal' business hours become wider. Using the internet for/in business is not so much an alternative to more conventional approaches; rather, it should be complementary to existing means of conducting the business of brokering insurance.

Four advantages to the company are:

(1) Ease of updating list of services, product range and prices compared to paper based information.

(2) Cheaper and easier provision of information, including reports, ratings and comparisons of products and prices.

(3) Reaching a wider market not constrained by geographical boundaries; the brokerage will not consist of high street offices available only to passers-by but be able to reach customers throughout the national area.

(4) Reduction in advertising costs: media such as hoardings, newspapers, radio and mailshots are expensive to use and have limited time spans. Running a website, after start-up costs, is comparatively cheap and is available 24 hours a day.

(b) (i) Potential barriers to the insurance brokerage adding a web-based dimension to its business are:

(1) Security: violations of confidentiality, virus attack.

(2) Increased volumes of activity: bottlenecks (delays) slow down access and response times, possibly causing frustration to potential customers.

(3) High telecommunications costs.

Further, there are potential difficulties with the effects on existing modes of business.

(ii) Factors that could encourage the insurance brokerage to enter into web-based business are:

(1) Improved customer service: the business may co-operate more frequently and closely with its customers.

(2) Low level of risk: there is much experience in creating websites and operating them for business purposes. The technology is proven and there is governmental support.

(3) Flexibility: the brokerage may decide for itself the level of involvement it deems appropriate, or, expand from an entry-level approach with experience to transaction-handling systems.

(4) Cost: entry costs are relatively low and running costs not punitive; there is potentially a massive return on a limited investment in hardware and website design.

ANSWERS TO END OF CHAPTER QUESTIONS

Exam question bank

1 Firth Travels (5/12)

The table below shows results of a survey conducted in 2011 by Firth Travels, a small travel agency, on the holiday destination selected by their customers.

Destination	Customers (%)
Europe	65
Asia	21
Africa	11
Middle-East	3

Required

(a) A random survey of 1000 customers in 2012 showed that 820 preferred Europe, 110 preferred Asia, 55 preferred Africa and 10 preferred the Middle-East. Use the chi-squared test at 2.5% significance level to determine whether the pattern in 2012 is different from the previous year.

(12 marks)

(b) The travel agency has been promoting ten of its holidays. The table below shows the amount spent on promotion of holidays by the travel agency (X) and average spent on each holiday by customers (Y).

Holiday	X	y
A	150	160
B	250	145
C	275	180
D	300	200
E	310	200
F	325	250
G	375	220
H	405	275
I	410	300
J	420	330

The owner of the travel agency wants to determine if the promotions have had any impact on the average amount spent on each holiday. Explain and use the coefficient of correlation and coefficient of determination to determine the relationship between the amount spent on promotion and the average spent on each holiday.

(10 marks)

(c) Using the formula for the regression line, calculate how much would be needed to be spent on promotional activities to achieve average sales of £500.

(3 marks)

(Total = 25 marks)

2 Mason and Price (5/14)

Mason and Price have been selling small electronic goods from their stall since 2007. Customers are offered a chance to purchase batteries for their items at a discounted price. The table below shows the number of electronic items and batteries sold in the last seven months.

Month	Sales of electronic goods £m	Number of batteries £m
1	500	100
2	1,000	120
3	2,000	110
4	2,000	160
5	3,000	170
6	5,000	210
7	6,000	220

Additional information based on the above table:

x is number of electronic items sold

y is the number of batteries sold

$\sum xy = 545,250$

$\sum x = 6,400$

$\sum y = 565$

$\sum x^2 = 6,235,000$

$(\sum x)^2 = 40,960,000$

$\sum y^2 = 47,825$

$(\sum y)^2 = 319,225$

Required

(a) Differentiate (without doing any calculations) between the following terms:

    (i) Coefficient of correlation r and Coefficient of determination r^2
    (ii) Linear and curvilinear correlation. **(5 marks)**

(b) Calculate the coefficient of correlation and the coefficient of determination and interpret these two figures. **(5 marks)**

(c) The total sales of electronic items in the twelfth month are estimated at 2600 units. Apply the least squares regression equation to obtain a sales forecast for batteries. **(5 marks)**

(d) Spreadsheets can be used to build business models to assist the forecasting and planning process. Discuss three advantages and two disadvantages of using spreadsheets. **(5 marks)**

(e) A recent random survey of 175 customers revealed that 70% of the customers preferred brand A batteries compared with brand B standard batteries.

    (i) Calculate the 95% confidence limits of all customers in favour of brand A batteries.
    (ii) Discuss the sampling error in relation to the confidence limits. **(5 marks)**

(Total = 25 marks)

3 Huang (11/12)

HuangTronics specialises in the production of mobile phones. The company has recently introduced cost-cutting measures across all operations. Jennifer Huang has reduced the number of staff working on the ten production lines. She wants to check if there is a relationship between cost savings and the number of defective phones produced.

Given

x = average cost savings per phone

y = average number of defective phones produced

n = 10 $\sum x = 430$ $\sum y = 363$ $\sum X^2 = 22,424$ $\sum Y^2 = 15,123$ $\sum xy = 13,052$

Required

(a) Calculate the correlation coefficient. **(5 marks)**

(b) Calculate the coefficient of determination and comment on your answer. **(5 marks)**

(c) Using the method of least squared calculate the formula for the regression line. **(5 marks)**

(d) Next year HuangTronics will introduce two new phones, XL and XXL. The production of these phones is restricted by the following constraints:

– XL requires £10 of components and XXL requires £20.

– A total of £3,000 of components are available for both phones per week.

– Sales staff will not be able to sell more than a combined total of 200 phones per week.

– Each XL phone will make a profit of £15 and XXL £25.

Construct the formula for the objective function and the constraints. **(5 marks)**

(e) Last year's customer survey showed that only 50% of the customers were satisfied with HuangTronics products. This year a survey of 300 customers was undertaken. Calculate the standard error and the z value for a satisfaction rate of 75%. **(5 marks)**

(Total = 25 marks)

4 Kullar Electronics (11/14)

Kullar Electronics have been selling mobile phones since 2011. Customers are offered a chance to purchase insurance cover for accidental damage to their mobile phone.

Assume x is the number of mobile phones sold and that y is the number of customers purchasing the insurance cover in the last 12 months.

$\sum xy = 7350$

$\sum x = 920$

$\sum y = 95$

$\sum x^2 = 71700$

$\sum y^2 = 761$

Required

(a) Differentiate between the coefficient of correlation and the coefficient of determination. Calculate each of these two coefficients. **(5 marks)**

(b) Apply the least squares regression equation to obtain a sales forecast for the number of customers likely to purchase the insurance cover for sale of 120 mobile phones. **(5 marks)**

(c) A random survey of 250 customers revealed that 65% of them preferred pay-as-you-go mobile phones compared with fixed contract phones. Calculate the 95% and 99% confidence limits for a proportion of all customers in favour of pay-as-you-go mobile phones. **(5 marks)**

(d) Kullar Electronics have decided to set up training for all their staff. The following table shows the tasks to carry out the training.

Activity	Duration (days)	Preceding activity
A: Appoint training manager	3	None
B: Carry out training audit	5	None
C: Analyse training needs	2	B
D: Produce training plans	1	A
E: Schedule training events	6	A
F: Carry out training	3	D
G: Carry our review of training	3	C,E

Required

(i) Construct an activity-on-arrow network diagram for the above project.
(ii) Identify the critical path. **(5 marks)**

(e) Kullar Electronics recently carried out a simulation of 6 customers arriving at the shop and results of them getting service from the staff.

Customer	Inter-arrival time (minutes)	Arrival time (clock)	Service time (minutes)	Time service begins (clock)	Time service ends (clock)	Customer waiting time in queue (minutes)	Time customer in system (minutes)	Idle time of server (minutes)
1	0	0	3	0	3	0	3	0
2	6	6	2	6	8	0	2	3
3	1	7	5	8	13	1	6	0
4	6	13	4	13	17	0	4	0
5	8	21	3	21	24	0	3	4
6	8	29	6	29	35	0	6	5

Required

(i) Calculate the average service time.
(ii) Calculate the average time customer in the system.
(iii) Calculate the average server idle time.
(iv) Briefly discuss two advantages of simulation. **(5 marks)**

(Total = 25 marks)

5 JKM Gifts (5/15)

(a) JKM Gifts specialises in providing men's gifts directly to the retailers. Recently they introduced premium and standard quality men's wallets to their current range of products. There are two phases, manufacturing and packaging, for producing both types of wallet.

Manufacturing time: 8 minutes for a premium and 6 minutes for a standard wallet.

Packaging time: 4 minutes for a premium and 2 minutes for the standard wallet.

The total capacity is 48 minutes per hour for manufacturing and 20 minutes per hour for packaging. The company makes a profit of £3 for each premium and £2 for each standard wallet.

Required

Develop the above scenario as a mathematical linear programme and sketch a graph showing the feasible area. **(5 marks)**

(b) During the first six months in the current year the following data for the total number of wallets produced and cost of production was provided.

Month	Number of wallets produced (000s)	Total costs (£)
	X	Y
1	40	60
2	32	48
3	48	72
4	44	66
5	36	54
6	50	75

Required

Calculate the expected costs for a production volume of 65,000 wallets.

Given

$\sum xy = 15{,}990$

$\sum x^2 = 10{,}660$

$\sum y^2 = 23{,}985$ **(5 marks)**

(c) JKM Gifts recently advertised their products in a popular trade newspaper, Gifts for Men. The newspaper claimed that the advert had been seen by 40% of the potential trade customers.

Required

Briefly discuss the purpose of 'sampling for attributes'.

Calculate the sample size necessary to be at least 95% confident that the estimate will be within 5% of the true value. **(5 marks)**

(d) There are eight activities required to manufacture the wallets as shown in the table below.

Activity	Preceded by Activity	Duration (minutes)	Workers required to complete activity
A	–	3	4
B	–	5	2
C	B	2	4
D	A	1	2
E	A	6	3
F	D	3	1
G	C, E	3	2
H	G, F	1	1

Required

Develop a network analysis diagram and show the number of workers required across the manufacturing process. Assume each worker is multi-skilled and capable of working on any of the activities.

(5 marks)

(e) JKM Gifts provides its wallets to UK and overseas customers. These customers may pay the full amount once the order is placed, part payment with the order or pay once they have received the items. Analysis of a random sample of 4,300 of its customers gave the following results.

		UK customers	Overseas customer
Payment method	Full payment with order	250	75
	Part payment with order	300	125
	Payment on receiving the order	200	150

Required

Using chi-squared contingency table calculate if there is a difference in the proportions of the customers paying by different methods.

You have been provided with the following information.

```
        O       E      (O-E)²/E
       250     222      3.64
       300     290      0.36
       200     239      6.26
        75     103      7.80
       125     135      0.77
       150     111     13.40
```

'O' refers to the observed frequencies and 'E' refers to the expected frequencies.   **(5 marks)**

(Total = 25 marks)

6 Tomato sauce (5/13)

A tomato sauce maker produces small sachets of two types of tomato sauce, supreme and premium. The production of supreme sauce uses 40g of tomato powder and 10 minutes of machine time whereas premium sauce requires 20g of tomato powder and 15 minutes of machine time. Altogether 800g of tomato powder is available each day. The sauce making machine is available for a maximum of 450 minutes per day.

To produce the supreme sauce the machine operator is required for 20 minutes and for premium sauce the machine operator is required for 30 minutes. The machine operator works for 600 minutes per day.

The manufacturer makes 5 pence profit for each sachet of supreme sauce and 10 pence profit for each sachet of premium sauce.

Required

(a) Discuss the difference between linear programming and the Simplex method. **(5 marks)**

(b) Derive equations for the objective function and constraints for the above problem. **(5 marks)**

(c) Susan Cox, the company's Marketing Director, believes there are differences between male and female customers in the proportions of customers purchasing the different types of sauces. A recent analysis of sales was undertaken from a random sample of customers.

Susan Cox has been provided with the following information:

Test H_0: there is no association between female and male customers and the type of sauce they purchase

Test H_1: There is some significant association between female and male customers and the type of sauce they purchase

O represents the observed sales and E represents the expected sales.

$$\frac{(O-E)^2}{E} = 12.55$$

At 5% level of significance chi-squared = 5.991 with 2 degrees of freedom

Discuss how the chi-squared contingency table and the test can be used to investigate the assertion that there is no association between female and male customers and type of sauce they purchase. Discuss the conclusions that can be drawn from the information provided. **(5 marks)**

(d) The company is considering using linear regression to forecast future sales. Discuss the conditions suited to the use of linear regression analysis. **(5 marks)**

(e) The table below shows the sales figures for premium sauce.

Year	Quarter	Sales
1	1	2,100
	2	2,940
	3	1,470
	4	2,520
2	1	2,240
	2	3,010
	3	1,470
	4	2,590

Calculate a moving average trend line and the seasonal variations using the additive model for the above sales figures. **(5 marks)**

(Total = 25 marks)

7 Tranter Home Styles (11/13)

(a) Tranter Home Styles manufactures two types of wooden chairs – standard and classic. Production of both chairs requires assembly time, machine time and finishing time. Table 1 below shows the time in hours required to manufacture these chair.

Table 1

	Assembly time	Machine time	Finishing time
Standard	3	4	2
Classic	2	6	4

The factory has allocated at most 60 hours for assembly time, 100 hours of machine time and 100 hours for finishing time per week. The profit per standard chair is £7 and the profit per classic chair is £10. However, the company wants to ensure at least 50% classic chairs are manufactured. The maximum predicted demand for classic chairs is 500 per week.

Tranter Home Styles want to determine how many standard chairs and how many classic chairs should be produced each week to maximise the profit.

Required

(i) Develop the equations for maximisation of profit.
(ii) Produce a graph showing the above problem.
(iii) Discuss why the graphical method is not suitable to solve this problem. **(5 marks)**

(b) Discuss how the simplex technique can be used to solve this problem and interpret the results produced in applying this technique (Table 2).

Table 2:

The following output was produced by computer software using the simplex technique.

Variables in the solution	x	y	a	b	c	d	Solution column
X	1	0	−3	0	0	0	300
Y	0	1	−0.2	2	0	0	400
C	0	0	−1.5	1	0	1	200
D	0	0	1	4	0	1	250
Solution row	0	0	1	4	0	0	3,250

Assuming

X is the number of standard chairs.

Y is the number of classic chairs.

a is the number of unused assembly time

b is the unused machine time

c is the unused finishing time

d is the amount by which demand for classic chair falls short of 500 **(5 marks)**

(c) The data showing the total revenue from sales and the amount spent on marketing per month for the first six months of this year is being analysed by Tranter Home Styles.

Assume the following

x is the total revenue from sales per month

y is the amount spent on marketing per month

$\sum x = 20{,}230$

$\sum y = 2{,}900$

$n\sum xy = 58\ 770\ 000$

$\sum x \ \sum y = 58\ 667\ 000$

$n\sum x^2 = 409762200$

$n\sum y^2 = 8\ 460\ 000$

$(\sum x)^2 = 409252900$

$(\sum y)^2 = 8\ 410\ 000$

Calculate the coefficient of correlation and coefficient of determination between total revenue from sales and the marketing spent. **(5 marks)**

(d) Use the least squares regression equation to calculate how much marketing budget would be required to attain sales revenue of £4,000. **(5 marks)**

(e) The mean and standard deviation of the height of a random sample of 144 standard chairs are 351.25 mm and 5.5 mm.

    (i) Explain the use of Central Limit theorem as the basis of sampling theory and significance testing.

    (ii) Calculate the 95% and 99% confidence intervals for the mean height of all standard chairs.

    (iii) Comment on your answer. **(5 marks)**

(Total = 25 marks)

8 R Kit (5/13)

Rebecca Kit is a specialist Financial Services Management Consultancy offering investment advice and financial loans. The business is divided into two departments; loans and sales.

There has been a significant increase in the number of customers requiring loans. The processing of the loans requires Loans Advisors to spend significant time in assessing each loan application – an expensive process. However, the company is keen to keep these costs down. Whilst the loans department offers a variety of loans, the advisors are expected to follow strict rules. Some of the new members of staff have not been applying these rules consistently.

A recent audit of the sales department noticed discrepancies in the sales and invoice figures and wrong invoices being sent to customers. This has made it difficult for the sales director to manage and plan for the predicted growth in sales. Each department is required to produce quarterly financial statements.

Rebecca Kit offers discounted rates for existing and new customers based on the following rules. For existing corporate customers a discount of 10% is awarded and new non-corporate customers receive a discount of 2%. Existing non-corporate customers receive a 5% discount and new corporate customers receive a 2% discount.

Rebecca Kit uses the following process to deal with customer enquiries. Initially all enquires are received by the Customer Relations Manager. Enquiries are from new or existing customers. Enquires from existing customers are forwarded to the Client Manager who responds to the customer using the email. New customers fall into two possible categories; home or international. For home customers a face-to-face meeting is arranged by the Client Manager. For international customers, a teleconference meeting is set up by the Client Manager.

EXAM QUESTION BANK

Required

(a) Discuss the advantages and disadvantages of an expert system for the loan applications process. **(5 marks)**

(b) Explain how the attributes of an Accounting Information System would be useful to the management of the Sales Department. **(5 marks)**

(c) Develop a decision table showing how the discounts are determined for new and existing customers. **(5 marks)**

(d) Rebecca Kit has commissioned an IT company to the Accounting Information System. Two approaches to analyse and develop this system have been proposed; Object Oriented and CASE tools approach. Compare these two approaches. **(5 marks)**

(e) Produce a flowchart for dealing with customer enquiries. **(5 marks)**

(Total = 25 marks)

9 Excel Enterprises (11/12)

Excel Enterprises is a large business park with over 120 seminar rooms, 5 lecture theatres, 50 meeting rooms, and a number of offices available to hire by local firms. The current information system is used to keep details of all the facilities available at the business including; including room sizes, availability, resources in each room (chairs, tables, audio and visual equipment etc). Additionally the system keeps a record of revenue, cost and profit generated for each room. The administration team are responsible for:

- Allocating the most appropriate rooms to their clients. The customer fills in an electronic resource requirement form and the administrative team allocate the most appropriate room based on the information provided by the client. This is a time-consuming activity as the allocation of a room is dependent on a large number of pre-defined rules.

- Production of reports for Event Manager showing use of resources, expenses and revenue on weekly basis. However, the administration team are expected to provide on-demand reports.

- Forecasting future demand on Excel Enterprises' facilities, carrying out 'what if' analysis to determine the most use of the company's resources.

Required

(a) Identify the essential differences between a Management Information System (MIS) and a Decision Support System (DSS). **(5 marks)**

(b) Discuss how the following reports produced by the MIS would be useful for the Events Manager. Use examples to illustrate your answers.

- Scheduled/Summary report
- Exception report
- On-demand report
- Key indicator report
- Drill down report

(15 marks)

(c) Discuss features of an accounting software that may be useful for Excel Enterprises. **(5 marks)**

(Total = 25 marks)

10 Davenport (11/14)

Chris Davenport has been appointed as an accountant to her local chess club. The chess club has about one hundred and forty members who pay their membership monthly in cash. All records, such as membership records, utility bills and other sundry costs, are maintained manually by the Treasurer of the club. The Treasurer of the club has stated that they have funds to purchase a personal computer (PC) for their accounting and general administrative functions. Chris Davenport who has very little knowledge of modern computers has carried out her own research by talking to IT specialists.

Required

(a) Chris Davenport has been advised to consider Executive Support Systems (ESS), Expert Systems, Decision Support Systems and Management Information Systems (MIS). Discuss whether these systems are likely to be useful for the chess club. **(12 marks)**

(b) Chris Davenport has decided to purchase an off-the-shelf accounting software package. Discuss the benefits and disadvantages of an off-the-shelf package for the chess club. **(6 marks)**

(c) The club offers a 12-month membership. If a new member pays the whole amount immediately a discount of 5% is awarded and if payment is made in 7 days a 2% discount is awarded. If a member introduces a friend to the chess club an additional 1% discount is awarded. Produce a decision table for calculating the total percentage discount for a 12-month membership of the club.

(7 marks)

(Total = 25 marks)

11 Chouhans (5/14)

(a) Chouhans specialises in selling automobiles. During the summer sale, Chouhans offers customers 'Summer Special Offers'. If a customer pays by cash and spends more than £4,000, they receive a free insurance on the vehicle for one year. If a customer pays by cash but spends £4,000 or less then they receive free insurance for 6 months. If the vehicle is over £10,000 then they automatically receive free insurance for 12 months and if they pay by cash then the customer is also entitled to free recovery service for twelve months. If the automobile is over £15,000 then the customer receives 12 months free insurance and free recovery service for one year whether they pay by cash or not.

Required

(i) Discuss the purpose of a decision table and describe its basic components. **(6 marks)**
(ii) Produce a decision table for Chouhans' Summer Special Offers. **(8 marks)**

(b) In the future Chouhans will be offering loans to their customers. The following process will be followed:

- The customer completes a Loan Application Form (LAF).
- The sales administrator receives and checks the form.
- The customer is informed that the loan has been refused if it is over 50% value of the automobile.
- If the loan is for an existing customer then the sales administrator forwards the LAF to the Credit Advisor who checks the credit history of the customer.
- The Credit Advisor checks customer history and determines if the customer is considered to be 'credit worthy'.
- If the customer is credit worthy then the Credit Advisor informs the customer the terms of the loan.

EXAM QUESTION BANK

- If the customer is not credit-worthy the Credit Advisor informs the customer that their loan has been refused.
- If the loan is for a new customer, the Sales Administrator forwards the customer details to a credit agency.
- The credit agency informs the sales administrator if the customer is 'credit worthy'. If the customer is considered to be not credit worthy then the Sales Administrator informs the customer the loan has been refused.
- If the customer is considered to be credit worthy then the details are forwarded to the Credit Advisor who informs the customer of the terms of the loan.

Required

Produce a flowchart for the Loan Application Process. **(11 marks)**

(Total = 25 marks)

12 Huber and Cox (11/13)

(a) Management consultants, working for Huber and Cox, forward their timesheets to the payroll department at the end of each month. The payroll administrator checks the hours worked against the Personnel file that contains the hourly rates for each employee. The Works Manager approves any bonuses earned and informs the payroll administrator who calculates the gross pay. The deductions file is used to calculate the net pay. Payslips are produced by the payroll administrator and these payslips are used to update the wages file. The administrator at the payroll dept. uses the wages file to prepare money to be transferred to the employee's bank account.

Required

(i) Differentiate between Level 0, 1, and 2 data flow diagrams. **(5 marks)**

(ii) Produce a Level 0 and a Level 1 Data Flow Diagram for the payroll system for casual workers at Huber and Cox. **(9 marks)**

(b) At the end of each project details are passed to the accounting and finance department by the team leader. The finance department calculates the gross profit/loss for the project. If gross profit from the project is greater than £250,000 then the project team receive a £10,000 bonus. If customer satisfaction is over 90% and gross profit from the project is greater than £250,000 then an additional bonus of £5,000 is awarded to the team. The team are assigned to a new project whether they receive the £5,000 bonus or not. If gross profit is less than £250,000 and the satisfaction rate is above 90% then £1,000 is awarded to the team and the team are assigned to a new project. If the gross profit from the project is less than £250,000 but project does not make a net loss, team are awarded a bonus of £1,000. If the project makes a loss then the project team have to undergo an additional training course before they are assigned to a new project and no bonus is awarded.

Required

(i) Produce a flow chart showing the above process. **(6 marks)**

(ii) Produce a decision table to show the above actions and decisions and comment on your table. **(5 marks)**

(Total = 25 marks)

EXAM QUESTION BANK

13 Dhillons Office Supplies (5/15)

Dhillons Office Supplies operates through a number of shops which sell their products direct to local business customers. Every 3 months the Marketing Executive, located at the Head Office, sends out new catalogues to each of the shops. The Sales Manager based at the shop, checks if there are any new products in the brochure and, if required, updates the Product File. The brochures are sent to existing and potential new customers. Customers contact the Sales Manager by telephone to place their order and provide credit card details. The Sales Manager checks the customer file for existing customers and forwards the details to the Finance Assistant for checking credit card details and recording the sales details on the Order File. At the end of the week Finance Assistants from each shop forward a summary report to the Marketing Executive showing all the customer orders for the week. The Marketing Executive compiles and forwards a statement to each Marketing Manager showing total sales for each product and bonuses accrued.

Required

(a) In relation to Data Flow Diagrams (DFD), describe the following terms:

    (i) External entity
    (ii) Data store
    (iii) Data flow
    (iv) Data process
    (v) Level-0 DFD
    (vi) Level-1 DFD **(6 marks)**

(b) Draw a dataflow diagram (DFD) showing the procedure described above. **(9 marks)**

(c) There are four Marketing Executives based at the Head Office who support a number of shops. Each shop is assigned a Marketing Executive to support any promotional activities. A Marketing Executive is responsible for a number of Marketing Managers, however, each Marketing Manager only reports to one Marketing Executive. Each shop has a Marketing Manager who looks after a number of sales assistants. A team of sales assistants deal with all queries from a number of customers. Produce an ERM for the scenario described here. **(5 marks)**

(d) Customers are given discounts based on the following rules:

Existing customers with orders above £1,000 will receive a 10% discount and customers (existing or new) within a 20 mile radius of the store warehouse will receive 1%. The higher of the two discounts is always applied.

Draw a decision table for the above. **(5 marks)**

(Total = 25 marks)

14 JKM (5/13)

The JKM is a specialist training company offering advanced IT courses to business. The company organises over 50 courses across 10 different countries in Europe. Most of the courses are delivered in English, however JKM try to accommodate requests by clients to deliver in their native languages; French and German being the most popular of these languages. Most of the courses are approved by professional IT bodies and follow a standard format, however, JKM also provides bespoke training for specialised IT companies. The courses are residential and are held in luxury hotels with conference facilities. These study days vary between five and twelve days. Wendy Price, Director of JKM, has employed four full-time trainers and a number of part-time trainers on a freelance basis. The administrative team is based in Paris and is responsible for course bookings, distributing course material, booking hotels, invoicing and allocating relevant trainers to the courses. Due to the large number of courses the company offers and disparate needs of its clients, the administrative team has to customise its services according to the needs of its customers. Recently JKM invested a significant amount of money in new IT hardware for the administrative functions. The administrative staff have gained experience in dealing with JKM clients and are likely to be resistant to any changes to their work practices.

A recent survey conducted by JKM suggests there is a demand for their online courses in China, India and Hong Kong. This has led Wendy Price to consider marketing their courses in Asia, even though this is not perceived to be a strategic aim of the company.

Required

(a) Explain why information strategy is relevant to strategic planning. **(5 marks)**

(b) In the last 18 months JKM have noticed a significant increase in bookings and the administrative team is having difficulties in managing this growth in business. This has led Wendy Price to consider 'off-the shelf' and 'bespoke software' to manage the administrative functions of the business.

Discuss potential disadvantages of adopting a number of 'off-the-shelf' software packages for JKM's administrative functions (accounting and finance, booking system, allocating tutors etc.).

(8 marks)

(c) JKM has decided to contract the development of a bespoke package to an IT software house. Discuss the four key areas of feasibility (technical, operational, social and economic) in relation to JKM. **(12 marks)**

(Total = 25 marks)

15 Manning and Huber (5/14)

Manning and Huber provides management courses to a number of its corporate clients. Whilst the company manages all the administration and financial aspects, all of the training is outsourced to local colleges and universities. A recent decline in business has been attributed to the rapid growth of online training courses offered by Manning and Huber competitors. The IT Director has proposed that the company installs a new information system. This, she claims, will enable Manning and Huber to offer online training and provide much better management information from the current systems. This would be a strategic change for the company as the new system is likely to require significant financial resources and the company would need to change their infrastructure.

Required

(a) Discuss the differences between strategic, tactical and operations information. **(9 marks)**

(b) Discuss the role of information systems in strategic planning. **(7 marks)**

(c) Using Earl's three leg analysis, discuss how Manning and Huber could adopt business led (top down) and Infrastructure led (bottom up) approaches. **(9 marks)**

(Total = 25 marks)

16 JK Associates (11/13)

The JK Associates is a financial management firm providing services; including financial planning, taxation and auditing and consultancy services, to more than 1,200 medium-sized businesses. There are 9 Accounts Managers, 8 administrative staff and 20 auditing and consultancy staff working in the office. The firm has plans to expand its business through acquisition of a number of medium-sized local financial services in the near future. Many of auditing and consultancy staff work at client sites, thus, require mobile devices (such, as laptops, phones and notebooks) and access to JK databases systems when working off-site. A recent IT/IS audit revealed that JK Associates were experiencing a number of security breaches including loss of financial data, staff members changing data on corporate databases without authorisation and some of the firm's data had been corrupted due to computer viruses.

Required

(a) The IT consultants have recommended that JK Associates develop an information policy. Discuss the key issues that need to be addressed within this policy. **(6 marks)**

(b) The firm operates from a four-storey building and many of the departments are located in open-plan offices. A recent audit of the stock showed that a number of hardware devices; such as PCs and memory sticks had gone missing. Discuss possible physical access controls JK Associates could introduce to avoid the loss of any hardware in the future. **(6 marks)**

(c) JK Associates have secured a contract to provide financial services to the local council. However, the contract stipulates JK Associates must have a disaster recovery plan in place. Discuss the key features that need to be important for this plan. **(8 marks)**

(d) The IT consultants have also recommended that JK Associates install audit trail software. Discuss the purpose and contents of the audit trail software. **(5 marks)**

(Total = 25 marks)

17 Dr Huber (5/15)

Dr Angela Huber has decided to leave her job at the local hospital to set-up an online medical consultancy service for minor illnesses. She has converted her garage into an office space that will house her PCs, printers and internet hardware. Additionally she has bought office furniture including storage units. Dr Huber intends to employ two part-time administrators to help run the business.

Required

(a) Discuss the possible physical security measures Dr Huber will need to put in place. **(8 marks)**

(b) It is now two years since Dr Huber set up her medical consultancy business and it has been a resounding success. A number of her colleagues now want to join her business and help expand the business. Dr Huber realises she needs to consider long term strategic direction for the business and information systems/technology will play an important part in any future planning. Discuss the role of information systems in strategic planning. **(7 marks)**

(c) Discuss how an expert system may be useful for Dr Huber's business. **(5 marks)**

(d) Dr Huber is keen to reduce her staff and IT/IS resources for non-core activities. Thus she has decided to outsource the invoicing and collection of payments to an external IT vendor. Discuss the three levels of service provision; time-share, service bureaux and facilities management. **(5 marks)**

(Total = 25 marks)

18 Dr Appleby (5/13)

Dr Steven Appleby decided to leave his job at the local hospital to set up a new medical centre in his neighbourhood. He purchased a large empty business unit to run his business. All the operations and management of the medical centre will be supported by a standard computer system available from the national medical agency. However, Dr. Appleby will need to consider the security of the computer system himself.

Required

(a) Discuss the possible physical security aspects of setting up his business in the business unit. **(7 marks)**

(b) Dr Appleby expects the practice will require regular access to the internet. Discuss possible internet security issues and how these can be minimised. **(7 marks)**

(c) The medical practice will keep personal data of all its patients. In terms of principles of data protection, discuss the key issues for the practice. **(4 marks)**

(d) Discuss what procedures the medical centre should adopt to ensure system and data integrity.

(7 marks)

(Total = 25 marks)

19 Snowball (5/12)

Mr and Mrs Snowball own and manage a medium-sized grocery shop in a rural village. The business has been in the family for the last two generations and Mr and Mrs Snowball have resisted the use of technology in any of its operations. The business employs six full-time and up to three casual staff who help with stocking the shelves during the peak season. The under- and over-ordering has been a problem, in many cases too much stock or too little stock being ordered. The stock ordering is done twice a week over the phone by Mrs Snowball. Furthermore, on several occasions the stock delivered has not matched with what Mrs Snowball claims she ordered. At the end of each day, Mrs Snowball totals up the sales from the two tills and records these in her sales book. There have been occasions when the total cash from the sales has not matched with the sales receipts. Every month Mrs Snowball's brother collects the sales book and all the receipts and produces a balance sheet which he passes back to his sister three months later. Although there has been a steady increase in sales over the last few years profits continue to fall.

Required

(a) Recently, local property developers have submitted plans to the local council to build 400 new residential properties in the near vicinity of the shop. Mr and Mrs Snowball now have to decide whether to expand the shop to cater for the possible increase in demand. Discuss the characteristics of strategic information Mr and Mrs Snowball would require in making their decision. **(5 marks)**

(b) Mr and Mrs Snowball are considering buying standard off-the-shelf EPOS software. Discuss the advantages and disadvantages of purchasing off-the-shelf software in this case. **(5 marks)**

(c) Discuss how an EPOS could help with stock management in the grocery shop. **(5 marks)**

(d) An IT consultant has advised the Snowballs that they should use SSADM methodologies to develop a system for the grocery shop. Briefly explain the five stages of this methodology. **(5 marks)**

(e) Mr and Mrs Snowball want all their staff members to participate in the proposed accounting information system. Discuss the limitations of Joint Application Development (JAD). **(5 marks)**

(Total = 25 marks)

20 Manning and Bates (11/14)

Manning and Bates is a private data management company that, on behalf of a national bank, holds personal data of customers. The bank sends the customer details to Manning and Bates on an ad hoc basis using a secure internet link. This data is then entered into the data management system at Manning and Bates by the information administrators at the end of each week. The manual task of entering data into the system is a long and complex process prone to errors.

Required

(a) Differentiate between data integrity and systems integrity. **(4 marks)**

(b) Discuss the input controls Manning and Bates could adopt to ensure the data they receive from the bank is entered correctly by the information administrator. **(5 marks)**

(c) Discuss the contents of a disaster recovery plan for Manning and Bates. **(10 marks)**

(d) Differentiate between back-up controls and archiving. **(6 marks)**

(Total = 25 marks)

EXAM QUESTION BANK

21 Payne Associates (11/14)

Payne Associates is a specialist accountancy company providing be-spoke financial services to small and medium sized businesses. The company operates from a number of offices across the major cities in the country providing a unique service to its local clients. Each office provides all administrative functions, such as marketing, pricing, and general enquires from potential new customers. Each office has their own off-the-shelf software to support their functions. The head office, based in the capital city, manages the invoicing and payments. Jane Williams, Managing Director, has decided to centralise the main functions of the business and manage these through the head office. She proposes an integrated system that will deal with marketing, pricing of projects and allocating contracts to each regional office. Jane Williams has noted that recently the financial services sector has become very competitive and to gain any competitive advantage there is a need to develop information systems quickly. The IT department at the head office has been tasked to develop this new system. The IT Director has stated that his team will use systems development methodologies to develop the new system. He is aware that there may be resistance to the new system as regional offices have been using their own systems for a long time and may be reluctant to adopt any new centralised system.

Required

(a) Discuss the characteristics of systems development methodologies. **(8 marks)**

(b) Demonstrate how SSADM could be used to develop the information system at Payne Associates. **(12 marks)**

(c) Discuss the possible advantages of using Rapid Application Development (RAD) for Payne Associates. **(5 marks)**

(Total = 25 marks)

22 Trentham Royal (11/12)

Trentham Royal Hospital is a small hospital providing short-term care for minor illnesses. The hospital has 120 beds with most of the patients staying at the hospital for no longer than three days on average. There are twelve consultants and physicians, twenty-five specialist nurses and twenty administrative staff who work at the hospital. The consultants and physicians are well qualified and have been renowned for their work internationally. However, the administrators are less well experienced due to the large turnover of staff – most complain of poor wages. This has meant the service provided by the Admin staff is quite poor and the Hospital regularly receives a number of complaints. As in most businesses in this sector, there is a continuing pressure to reduce costs, or at the very least, do more with the same resources. The government has recently made it easier for individuals and companies to apply for medical care by offering tax breaks. However, this has resulted in a number of new competitors seeking to break into this market.

The Trentham board are considering providing 'Tele-home Healthcare'. The objective is to reduce the number of days each patient returns to the hospital for follow-up care after their treatment, by using remote consultation technology and encouraging patients to receive care from their homes. If this technology is implemented successfully, it could help to improve the quality of healthcare and reduce costs. The patient will be able to log on to the hospital website and using a videophone speak to the nursing unit, or alternatively, they can enter their query on a specially designed electronic form. Services offered could include:

- Medical consultations;
- Physical therapy instructions;
- Nutritional advice;
- Help with accessing social services; or
- Emotional support.

This strategy option will require a new information system (IS).

Required

(a) Explain the importance of IS in strategic planning. **(6 marks)**

(b) Describe the following types of outsourcing.

    (i) Multiple sourcing
    (ii) Incremental approach
    (iii) Joint venture outsourcing
    (iv) Application Service Providers **(4 marks)**

(c) A number of suppliers are to be invited to tender to supply the specific software. Discuss the possible contents of the invitation to tender document. **(9 marks)**

(d) Discuss how these suppliers would be evaluated. **(6 marks)**

(Total = 25 marks)

23 Nadine Enterprises (5/12)

Nadine Enterprises provides airline travel service to business customers. Over 80% of the customers use the company's e-commerce-based service to search and book their business trips. The company has ambitious plans to expand its operations in Asia in the next two years. The company uses an integrated software package that links the front-end booking services with back-end functions, such as accounting, marketing, and human resources. The IT department is responsible for all IT and IS functions within the organisation. However, the Managing Director of Nadine Enterprises is considering outsourcing the IT functions to an external provider.

Required

(a) Briefly discuss the following four types of outsourcing approach:

    (i) Ad-hoc
    (ii) Project management
    (iii) Partial
    (iv) Total **(4 marks)**

(b) Discuss four areas that Nadine Enterprises should consider before reaching an outsourcing agreement for its IT functions. **(8 marks)**

(c) Discuss the key elements of service level agreement that could operate between Nadine Enterprises and the external supplier. **(7 marks)**

(d) Discuss four possible advantages of outsourcing the IT functions for Nadine Enterprises. **(4 marks)**

(e) Briefly discuss the difference between the services offered by software houses and consultancy firms. **(2 marks)**

(Total = 25 marks)

24 Morris Enterprises (5/14)

Morris Enterprises is a medium sized accounting company that is experiencing a rapid growth. Due to an increase in demand for its services, the company has been able to develop a range of financial advisory services to its growing customer base. The company has a large pool of accountants, financial advisors and consultants who liaise directly with the customers. Currently, the company uses stand-alone desktop computers connected. Davina Morris, the Managing Director, has commissioned an IT firm to evaluate the company's future Information Systems (IS) requirements. The IT consultants have recommended top of the range hardware and software to allow for expansion of the systems to meet the future needs of Morris Enterprises. The new system has been justified by the consultants because it could reduce costs, increase sales revenue and save staff time, although precise details have not been given. Once the system has been installed it is expected that management reporting structures will need to be reviewed.

Required

(a) Discuss why Morris Enterprises should conduct a feasibility study of the IS. **(8 marks)**

(b) The IT developers have indicated that they will be using structured walkthroughs as part of their SSADM approach to developing the new system. Discuss how structured walkthroughs would work at Morris Enterprises. **(8 marks)**

(c) Morris Enterprises have received a number of viable tenders for the development of the IS. These tenders will be compared using benchmark tests and weighted ranking scores. Compare these two approaches. **(9 marks)**

(Total = 25 marks)

25 Grady and Price (5/15)

Grady and Price is a specialist marketing consultancy producing be-spoke web pages for its clients. The company operates from the main office in London but has satellite offices across Europe. Each office has the autonomy to manage their own business portfolio and develop and customised web pages to suit their client needs. Each office are responsible for contracting work to local web-designers. Due to the varied nature of the customer requirements, projects vary significantly in terms of design and requirements. All administrative functions, such as client details, financial terms, start/end dates of project and details of web designers are kept by each office on their own software packages. Additionally some of the offices have reported that, due to poor bandwidth in some European countries, the transferring of data files across public networks can be very slow. Grady and Price have recently decided to centralise these functions using an integrated software system.

Required

(a) Discuss the issues that Grady and Price need to consider in purchasing an off-the-shelf software package. **(8 marks)**

(b) Discuss the five characteristics of system development methodologies. **(5 marks)**

(c) Grady and Price have decided to employ IT consultants to develop a be spoke software package. The project designers intend to employ Joint Applications Development, structured walkthroughs and CASE tools. Compare these three approaches. **(12 marks)**

(Total = 25 marks)

Exam answer bank

1 Firth Travels

Learning Outcome: Apply appropriate techniques and interpret the results to support a range of business decisions. 9.6 Decision theory.

(a) Use the chi-squared test at 2.5% significance level to determine whether the pattern in 2012 is different from the previous year.

The null and alternative hypotheses are.

H_0: The percentage distribution of preferred holiday destination in 2012 is the same as that for the previous year.

H_1: The percentage distribution of preferred holiday destination in 2012 is the same as that for the previous year.

Degrees of freedom df = 4 − 1 = 3

The significance level = 0.025

From the chi-squared distribution table the critical value of X^2 for df = 3 is 9.348.

Category	Observed frequency (O)	Probability (p)	Expected frequency (E = np)	O–E	$(O-E)^2$	$(O-E)^2/E$
Europe	820	0.65	1,000 × 0.65 = 650	170	28900	44.46
Asia	110	0.21	1,000 × 0.21 = 210	−100	10000	47.62
Africa	55	0.11	1,000 × 0.11 = 110	−55	3025	27.50
Middle-East	10	0.03	1,000 × 0.03 = 30	−20	400	13.33
						132.91

The value of the test statistic X^2 = 132.91 is greater than the critical value of X^2 = 9.348 and it falls in the nonrejection region. Hence we reject the null hypothesis and state that the current percentage distribution of the preferred holidays is different from that for 2011. The difference between the observed frequencies and the expected frequencies seems to have occurred only because of sampling error.

(b) The degree of correlation between two variables can be measured by the coefficient of correlation r.

	x	y	x^2	y^2	xy
	150	160	22,500	25,600	24,000
	250	145	62,500	21,025	36,250
	275	180	75,625	32,400	49,500
	300	200	90,000	40,000	60,000
	310	200	96,100	40,000	62,000
	325	250	105,625	62,500	81,250
	375	220	140,625	48,400	82,500
	405	275	164,025	75,625	111,375
	410	300	168,100	90,000	123,000
	420	330	176,400	108,900	138,600
Sum	3,220	2,260	1,101,500	544,450	768,475

Coefficient of correlation (r)

$$r = \frac{n\Sigma xy - \Sigma x \Sigma y}{\sqrt{n\Sigma x^2 - (\Sigma x)^2} - \sqrt{n\Sigma y^2 - (\Sigma y)^2}}$$

$$= \frac{10 \times 76,845 - 3,220 \times 2,260}{\sqrt{10\Sigma 1,101,500 - (3,220)^2} - \sqrt{10\Sigma 544,450 - (2,260)}}$$

r = 0.8732

Firth Travels can conclude that there is a correlation of 0.87, this suggests a strong positive relationship between promotional activities and amount spent on each holiday by the customers.

Coefficient of determination.

The coefficient of determination is a measure of the proportion of change in the value of one variable that can be explained by variations in the value of the other variable.

r2 = (0.8732)2 = 0.7624

Firth Travels can conclude that 76.24% of the variation in the average sales of the holiday can be explained by the amount spent on promotional activities. Factors other than change in the value of x account for 23.76% of the variation in y.

c)   a = 23   b = 0.63

Y = a + bx

Y = 23 + 0.63x

500 = 23 + 0.63x

X = 757.14

Thus Firth Travels needs to invest approx. £757.14 in order to achieve average sales of £500.

2 Mason and Price

Techniques to support business decision: Correlation and regression (9.1). Sampling Theory and Significance Testing (9.2)

(a) (i)   Coefficient of correlation is used to measure the degree of correlation between two variables. This measure gives the strength and direction of a linear relationship between two variables being tested.

        The coefficient of determination is used to measure the proportion of change in the value of one variable that can be explained by the variations in the value of the other variable. The r^2 value provides show how well future outcomes are likely to be predicted by the model.

   (ii) Linear relationship has direct proportionality that causes the dependent variable to change when the independent variable changes thus all the points on the scatter diagram lie near a straight line. Nonlinear relationship does not have proportionality between the dependent and independent variables thus the points on a scatter diagram are depicted graphically by anything other than a straight line.

(b) $r = \dfrac{7 \times 545,250 - 6,400 \times 565}{\sqrt{((7 \times 6,235,000) - 4,096,000) \times (7 \times 47,825 - 319,225)}}$

$= \dfrac{200,750}{\sqrt{2,685,000 \times 155,550}}$

r = 0.982

r^2 = 0.964

The coefficient of correlation value shows there is a strong positive correlation between the sale of electronic items and the sale of batteries.

Coefficient of determination value shows that 96.4% of the variation in sales of the batteries can be explained by variation in the sales of the electronic items.

(c) $b = \dfrac{n\sum xy - \sum x \sum y}{n\sum x^2 - (\sum x)^2}$

$= \dfrac{7 \times 545{,}250 - 6{,}400 \times 565}{7 \times 6{,}235{,}000 - 40{,}960{,}000}$

$= \dfrac{3{,}816{,}750 - 3{,}616{,}000}{43{,}645{,}000 - 40{,}960{,}000}$

$= \dfrac{200{,}750}{2{,}685{,}000}$

$= 0.074767 = 0.075$

$a = \dfrac{\sum y}{n} - \dfrac{b\sum x}{n}$

$= 80.72 - 68.57 = 12.15$

y = 12.15 + 0.075x
= 12.15 + 0.075x 2600
= 207.15 = 207

(d) **Advantages**

Can be used for a wide range of tasks; such as, balance sheets, inventory records, profit projections, tax estimations, job cost estimates market share and planning.

The great value of spreadsheets derives from their simple format of rows and columns and the ability to manipulate data using mathematical formulae. Spreadsheets bring powerful computer modelling within everyday reach of data users.

Disadvantages

A minor error in the design of the model at any point can affect the validity of the data throughout the spreadsheet.

It is possible to become over-dependent on them, so that simple one-off tasks that can be done in seconds with a pen and paper are done on a spreadsheet instead.

The possibility for experimentation with data is so great that it is possible to lose sight of the original intention of the spreadsheet.

Spreadsheets struggle to take account of qualitative factors since they are invariably difficult to quantify.

(e) (i) As the population proportion is not known the sample proportion must be used to calculate the standard error.

p = 0.70 q = 1 – 0.70 = 0.30 and n = 175

standard error = $\sqrt{pq/n}$

$= \sqrt{0.70 \times 0.30/175}$
= 0.03464

95% confidence limits = 0.70 + 1.96 × 0.03464

= 0.76789 or 0.6321

This means that there is a 95% probability that the proportion of all customers of Brand A batteries is between 63% and 77%.

(ii) It is impossible to infer an exact value of the population from a sample. We can only state that there is a specified probability that the population mean is within the specified limits. This uncertainty is known as the sampling error. The only way to eliminate sampling error and obtain an exact value for the population mean is to measure every item in the population.

3 Huang

Syllabus reference 9.1. Chapter 1 (4.4).

(a) Correlation Coefficient

$n = 10 \quad \sum x = 430 \quad \sum y = 363 \quad \sum X^2 = 22{,}424 \quad \sum Y^2 = 15{,}123 \quad \sum xy = 13{,}052$

$$r = \frac{n\sum xy - \sum x \sum y}{\sqrt{\left[n\sum x^2 - (\sum x)^2\right] \times \left[n\sum y^2 - (\sum y)^2\right]}}$$

$$= \frac{10 \times 13{,}052 - 430 \times 363}{\sqrt{\left[10 \times 22{,}424 - (430)^2\right] \times \left[10 \times 15{,}123 - (363)^2\right]}}$$

$$= \frac{130{,}520 - 156{,}090}{\sqrt{39{,}340 \times 19{,}461}}$$

$$= -25{,}570 / 27{,}669$$

$r = -0.924$

(b) **Syllabus reference 9.1. Chapter 1 (4.4).**

Coefficient of determination

$r^2 = (-0.924)^2 = 0.854$

HuangTronics can conclude that 85.4% of the variation in the faulty parts delivered may be predicted by change in the staff cost savings. Factors other than change in the value of x account for 14.6% of the variation in the number of defective phones produced.

(c) **Syllabus reference 9.1. Chapter 1 (6.1).**

$$b = \frac{n\sum xy}{n\sum x^2} - \frac{\sum x \sum y}{(\sum x)^2}$$

$$= \frac{10 \times 13{,}052}{10 \times 22{,}424} - \frac{430 \times 363}{(430)^2}$$

$$= \frac{130520 - 156090}{224240 - 184900} = -0.649 = -0.65$$

$$a = \frac{\sum y}{n} - \frac{b \sum x}{n}$$

$$= \frac{363}{10} - \frac{(-0.65) \times 430}{10}$$

$$= 64.25$$

$Y = 64.25 - 0.65x$

(d) **Syllabus reference 9.3. Chapter 3 (2.0).**

Objective formula

Let   x = the number of XL phones manufactured

y = the number of XXL phones manufactured
Profit = 15x + 25y

Constraints

$10x + 20y \leq 3{,}000$

$x \geq 0$ and $y \geq 0$

$x + y \leq 200$

(e) **Syllabus reference 9.2. Chapter 2 (3.0).**

Syllabus reference 9.2.

p = 0.5 q = 1−0.5 = 0.5 and n = 300

Standard error = $\sqrt{pq/n}$

$= \sqrt{0.5 \times 0.5 / 300}$

= 0.02887 = 0.029

Given sample proportion = 0.75

Standardising the value 0.75

z = √(0.75 − 0.5/standard error)

= √(0.25/0.029)

= 2.94

4 Kullar Electronics

(a) The degree of correlation between two variables can be measured using the coefficient of correlation. The coefficient of determination is a measure of the proportion of the change in value of one variable that can be explained by the variations in the value of the other variable.

$$r = \frac{n\Sigma xy - \Sigma x \Sigma y}{\sqrt{[n\Sigma x^2 - (\Sigma x)^2][n\Sigma y^2 - (\Sigma y)^2]}}$$

$$= \frac{12 \times 7{,}350 - 920 \times 95}{\sqrt{[12 \times 71{,}700 - 920 \times 920][12 \times 761 - 95 \times 95]}}$$

$$= \frac{800}{1{,}223.93}$$

Coefficient of correlation r = 0.6536

Coefficient of determination $r^2 = (0.6536)^2 = 0.4272$

(b) **9.1 Techniques to support business decisions: Correlation and Regression, Regression and forecasting**

Analytical Skills for Business, LO 1.3

EXAM ANSWER BANK

$$b = \frac{n\Sigma xy - \Sigma x \Sigma y}{n\Sigma x^2 - (\Sigma x)^2}$$

$$b = \frac{12 \times 7,350 - 920 \times 95}{12 \times 71,700 - (920)^2}$$

$$b = \frac{800}{14,000} = 0.0571$$

$$a = \frac{\Sigma y}{n} - \frac{b\Sigma x}{n}$$

$$a = \frac{95}{12} - \frac{0.0571 \times 920}{12}$$

a = 7.917 − 4.378 = 3.539

Number of mobiles phones sold x = 120

Estimated sale of insurance cover y = 3.539 + 0.0571 × 120

= 10.391 = 10

(c) **9.2 Techniques to support business decisions: Sampling theory and significance testing, Confidence interval**

Analytical Skills for Business, LO 2.2

n = 0.65

p = 0.65

q = 1 − 0.65 = 0.35

Standard error = √0.65 × 0.35/250

= 0.0301

At 95% confidence level = 0.65 ± 1.96x0.030

Therefore the 95% confidence limit is = 0.59 to 0.71 (2 d.p.)

The 99% confidence limits = 0.65 ± 2.58 × 0.030 = 0.57 to 0.73 (2 d.p.)

(d) **9.4 Network Analysis**

Analytical Skills for Business,

(i) Activity-on-arrow network diagram for the above project.

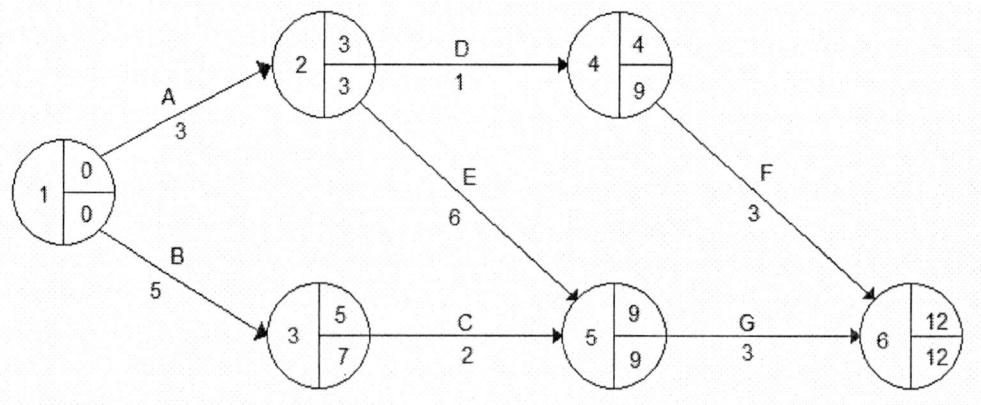

(ii) Critical path: AEG

(e) **9.5 Simulation**

Analytical Skills for Business,

(i) Average Service time = 23/6 = 3.8 minutes.

(ii) Average time customer in the system = 24/6 = 4 minutes.

(iii) Average idle time = 12/6 = 2 minutes.

(iv) Advantages of simulation:

- It provides a means of solving problems in situations where the use of other quantitative methods may not be suitable.
- Fewer simplifying assumptions are used in simulation models compared with other quantitative methods and models.
- Carrying out a properly designed simulation is much the same as observing the real system.
- A computer simulation model can assess the performance of the real world over a lengthy time span.

5 JKM Gifts

Linear Programming 9.3

(a) Maximise profit $3x + 2y$

Constraints

$8x + 6y <= 48$

$4x + 2y <= 20$

$X => 0 \quad y => 0$

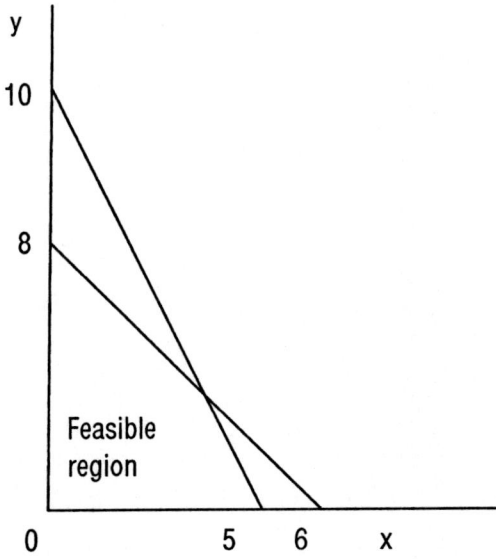

(b) **Correlation and regression 9.1**

$b = (n\sum xy - \sum x \sum y)/(n\sum x^2 - (\sum x)^2)$

$= (6 \times 15{,}990 - 210 \times 375)/(6 \times 10{,}660 - (210)^2)$

$= 17{,}190/29{,}860$

$= 0.8656$

$a = y - bx$

$= (375/6) - (0.8656 \times 210/6)$

$= 62.5 - 30.30 = 32.2$

$y = 32. + 0.87x$

$= 32 + 0.87 \times 65{,}000$

$= 56{,}582$

If JKM Gifts produce 65,000 wallets, they can expect costs to be £56,582.

(c) **Sampling Theory 9.2**

The purpose of sampling for attributes to estimate the proportion of the population who possess the attributes under investigation.

Estimate available of the population proportion is 40% (0.4). This can be used to calculate the standard error.

$p = 0.4$

$q = 1 - 0.4 = 0.6$

Standard error $= \dfrac{\sqrt{pq}}{n}$

$= \dfrac{\sqrt{0.4 \times 0.6}}{n}$

The value of n needs to be such that 1.96 standard errors = 0.05

$0.05 = 1.96 \times \sqrt{\dfrac{0.4 \times 0.6}{n}}$

$n = 368.79$

A sample size of 369 should be taken.

(d) **Network analysis 9.4**

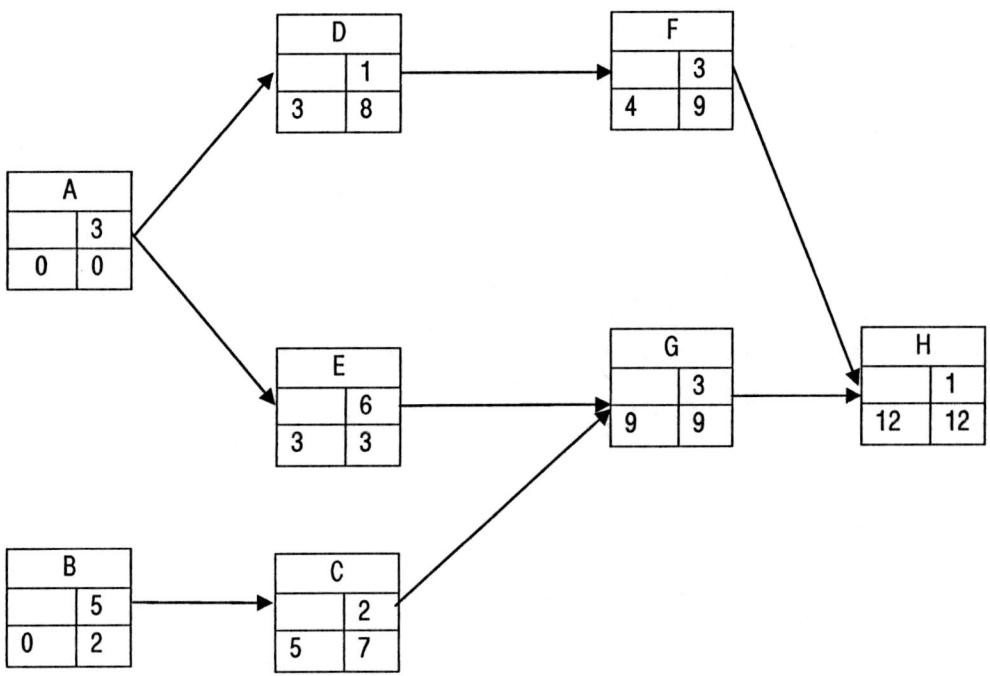

Minutes	0	1	2	3	4	5	6	7	8	9	10	11	12
Activities	AB			EBD	EBF	ECF		3		G			H
Workers required	6			7	6	8		3		2			1

(e) **Significance testing 9.2**

Test H_0: there is no association between UK and overseas customers and the payment methods used.

H_1: There is some significant association between these attributes.

Level of significance: a = 0.05 (5%)

Critical region: reject H_0 if chi-squared >5.991 with 2 degrees of freedom.

Chi-squared = 32.24

Conclusion: since chi-squared = 32.24 is greater than the theoretical value of 5.991, we must reject H_0 at the 5% significance level. It would appear that there is some association between the two attributes of UK/overseas customers and payment method.

6 Tomato sauce

9.3 Techniques to support business decisions: Linear programming, Significance testing, Regression.

(a) Linear programming is a technique for solving problems of profit maximisation or cost minimisation and resource allocation. Since profits generated by different products may vary, it may be better not to produce any of a less profitable line but to concentrate all resources on producing the more profitable ones.

Simplex method is an algorithm that solves linear programming problems with three or more variables.

(b) 5x + 10y objective function

10x + 15y ≤ 450 machine time constraint

40x + 20y ≤ 800 Tomato powder constraints

20x + 30y ≤ 600 operator time constraints

x ≥ 0

y ≥ 0

(c) Significance testing: A relationship is considered statistically significant if it is unlikely to have occurred by chance. A 'statistically significant' difference or relationship means there is statistical evidence of a difference or relationship. Significance test measures the likelihood that the association between variables is caused by chance.

Since chi-squared = 12.55 is greater than the theoretical value of 5.991, Susan Cox can reject the H_0 at the 5% significance level. It would appear that there is some association between the types of customers and the types of sauce they purchase.

(d) A linear cost function is assumed. This assumption can be tested by measure of reliability, such as correlation coefficient and the coefficient of determination.

It is assumed that the value of one variable can be predicted or estimated from the value of one other variable.

It is assumed that conditions which have existed in the past will continue in the future.

The amount of data available is very important. Low pairs of data can result in unreliable forecasts.

Historical data should be accurately recorded so that variables are matched against the correct items.

(e)

Year	Sales	Moving total of 4 quarters	Moving average of 4 quarters	Mid-point of 2 moving averages (Trend line)	Seasonal variations
1	2,100				
	2,940				
	1,470	9,030	2,257.5	2,275	–805
	2,520	9,170	2,292.5	2,301.25	218.75
2	2,240	9,240	2,310	2,310	–70
	3,010	9,240	2,310	2,318.75	691.25
	1,470	9,310	2,327.5		
	2,590				

7 Tranter Home Styles

Techniques to support business decisions (a and b) 9.3 Linear programming, (c and d) 9.1 Correlation and regression; (e) 9.2 sampling and significance testing.

(a) x is the number of Standard chairs produced
y is the number of Classic chairs produced

Maximise profit P = 7x + 10y

Constraints.
3x + 2y ≤ 60 (Assembly time – line a)
4x + 6y ≤ 100 (Machine time – line b)
2x + 4y ≤ 100 (Finishing time – line c)

x ≤ 500 (Maximum demand for classic chairs)
2y ≥ x + y (Manufacture at least 50% classic chairs)
x ≥ 0, y ≥ 0

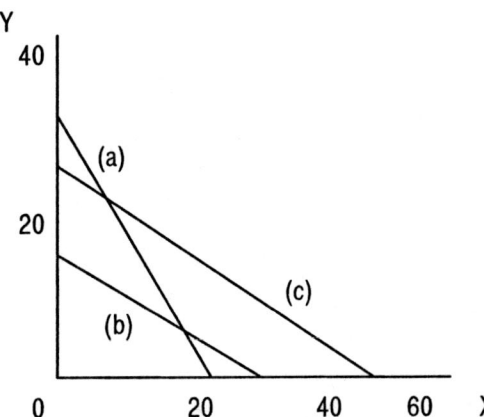

The graphical method cannot be used where there are more than two decision valuables.

(b) A method called the simplex method is available in these circumstances. The simplex technique uses the decision valuables and the slack variable to test a number of feasible solutions to the problem until the optimal solution is found. The technique is a repetitive step-by-step process that test a number of feasible solutions in turn.

The value of the objective function is the total contribution, is in both the solution row and the solution column. Here it is £3,250.

The solution row gives the shadow prices for each variable. The shadow or dual price is the opportunity cost of the scarce resources, which is the amount of benefit foregone by not having the availability of the extra resources.

£1 per hour of assembly time.
This means that if more assembly time could be made available at their normal variable cost per hour total contribution could be increased by £1 for each extra hour of assembly time.

£5 per hour of machine time.
This means if more machine time could be made available, at its normal variable costs, total contribution could be increased by £5 per extra machine hour.

(c) **Coefficient of correlation**

$$r = \frac{n\sum xy - \sum x \sum y}{\sqrt{\left[n\sum x^2 - (\sum x)^2\right]\left[n\sum y^2 - (\sum y)^2\right]}}$$

$$r = \frac{58,770,000 - 58,667,000}{\sqrt{[409,762,200 - 409,252,900] \times [8,460,000 - 8,410,000]}}$$

r = 0.6454 = 0.65

Coefficient of determination

$r^2 = 0.4166 = 0.42$

The coefficient of correlation value shows there is a positive correlation of 65% between revenue from the sales and the amount spent on marketing. Coefficient of determination value shows that 42% of the variation spent on marketing can be explained by variation in the revenue from the sales of the chairs.

(d) $$b = \frac{n\sum xy - \sum x \sum y}{n\sum x^2 - (\sum x)^2}$$

$$= \frac{58,770,000 - 58,667,000}{409,762,200 - 409,252,900}$$

$$= \frac{103,000}{509,300}$$

$$= 0.2022 = 0.20$$

$$a = \frac{\sum y}{n} - \frac{b\sum x}{n}$$

$$= \frac{2,900}{6} - \frac{0.20 \times 20,230}{6}$$

$$= 483.33 - 674.33 = -191$$

$$y = -191 + 0.2 \ast x \, 4,000$$

$$y = 609$$

To generate sales of £4,000 would require a marketing budget of £609. This prediction is based on the assumption that there is a linear relationship between the sales revenue from chairs and the amount spent on marketing activities. It is also worth noting that the correlation between these two variables is not very strong. Other factors may influence the sales of the chairs such as social changes (alterations in fashion and social acceptability of the products).

(e) A statistical theory states that given a sufficiently large sample size from a population with a finite level of variance, the mean of all samples from the same population will be approximately equal to the mean of the population. Furthermore, all of the samples will follow an approximate normal distribution pattern, with all variances being approximately equal to the variance of the population divided by each sample's size. The sampling distribution of sample means will more closely approximate the Normal Distribution as N increases.

As the standard deviation of the population is not known, and n>30, the standard deviation of the sample can be used to calculate the standard error.

$$\text{Standard error} = \frac{5.5}{\sqrt{144}}$$

$$= 0.46 \text{ mm}$$

The 95% confidence limits are $351.25 \pm 1.96 \times 0.46$

This means that there is a 95% probability that the mean height of all standard chairs is between 350.35 and 352.15 mm.

The 99% confidence limits are $351.25 \pm 2.58 \times 0.46$

This means that there is a 99% probability that the mean height of all standard chairs is between 350.06 and 352.43mm.

It is important to note it is impossible to infer an exact value of the population mean from the sample. We can only state that there is a specified probability that the population mean is within specified limits.

8 R Kit

9.7 Information Systems: Types and applications.

(a) An expert system will help provide a consistent loan decision, useful where repetitive decisions are to be made and can help clarify the loans decision. The system can help reduce costs as the system can be used by multiple and non-specialist loan advisors for 'standard' applications.

An expert system lacks common sense needed in complex or unusual loan applications. The system cannot adapt to changing environments, unless the knowledge base is changed. Introduction of the system will require high upfront development costs, training for staff and changes in work processes.

(b) The Accounting Information System would make it easier for the Loans Department to establish internal controls and help detect fraud, theft and other mismanagement.

The Accounting Information System can hold and process information and produce reports that aid managers and owners in the decision making process. This feature would be useful as the loans department is expanding and the management would find it useful to allocate appropriate resources to new business.

An Accounting Information System can provide statistical information that indicates performance of current products or services offered by Rebecca Kit. The management can use this information to make decisions regarding sales, cost of goods sold and efficiency.

The Accounting Information System can help generate year-ending financial statements, such as, balance sheet and income statements.

(c)
Conditions

1. Corporate customers	Y		Y	
2. Non-corporate customers		Y		Y
3. New customer		Y	Y	
4. Existing customer	Y			Y
Actions				
2% discount			X	X
5% discount				X
10% discount	X			

Note. All new customers are offered 2% discount. Thus conditions 2 and 3 can be combined.

(d) Object-oriented programming focuses on 'objects' rather than 'actions' and data rather than logic. This approach identifies all the objects and then determines how they are to be processed and how they relate to each other, this is referred to as data modelling.

CASE (Computer Aided Software Engineering) is software that provides a development forum for computer programming teams. The software offers tools to automate, manage and simplify the programming process, including, capturing initial requirements, producing flow diagrams, scheduling tasks, producing documentation and developing the computer programs.

(e)

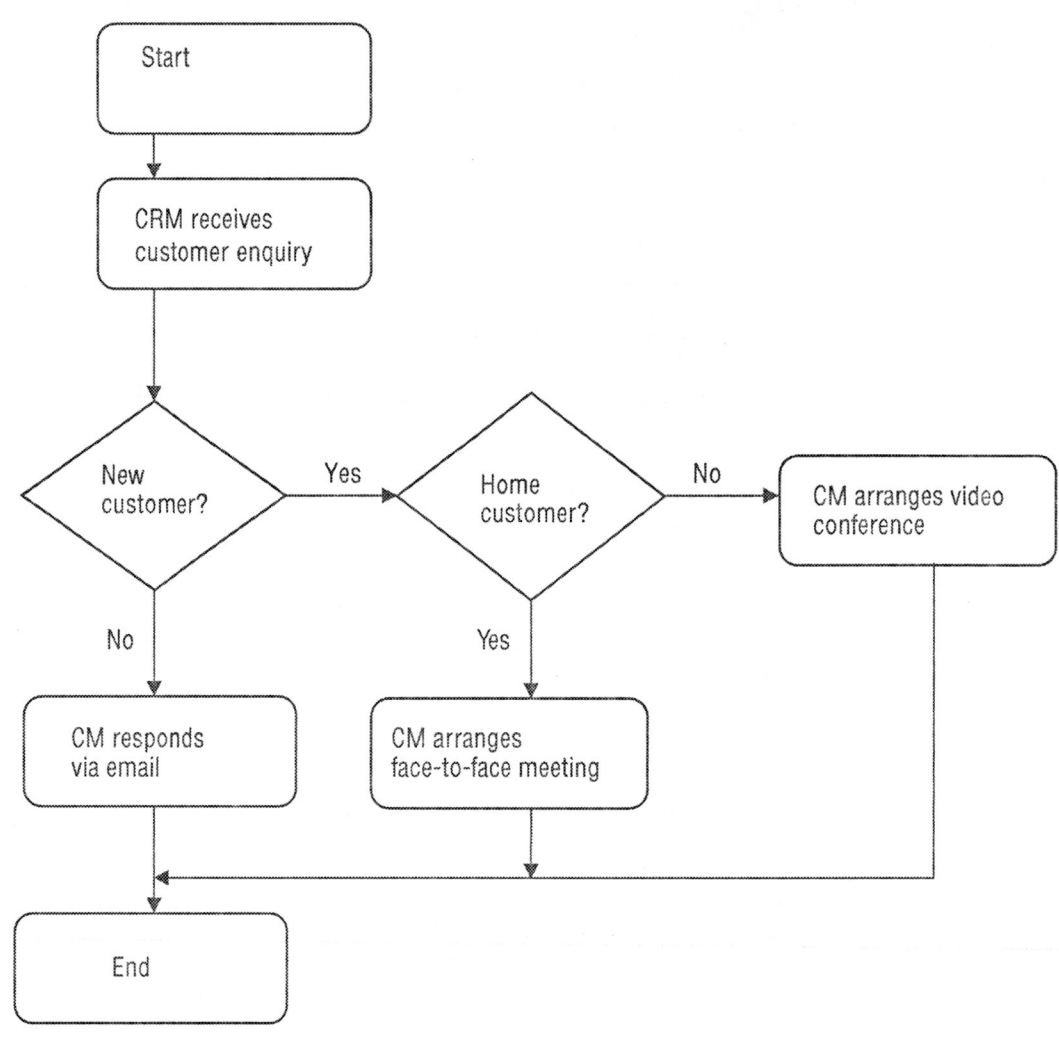

9 Excel Enterprises

(a) **Syllabus reference 9.7. Chapter 7 (9.11, 9.12).**

Identify the essential differences between a Management Information System and a Decision Support System.

MIS	DSS
Support structured decisions	Useful for unstructured situations
Mainly used by managers	Useful for employees at all levels of the organisation
Have little analytical ability	Uses complex models and simulations
Draw on internal operational data	Uses data from variety of sources
Provides pre-defined reports	Provides alternative and flexible decision options

(b) **Syllabus reference 9.7. Chapter 7 (9.11).**

Discuss how the following reports produced by the MIS would be useful for the Events Manager. Use examples to illustrate your answers.

Scheduled/Summary report:

- Exception report
- On-demand report
- Key indicator report
- Drill down report

Scheduled reports are produced periodically, or on a schedule (daily, weekly, and monthly). The MIS can be used to produce the monthly summary reports showing room utilisation. This can help the events manager to plan marketing and pricing strategy for the future.

Example

Monthly Revenue by Room Summary Report
Prepared 10/09/XX

Room	Amount
A123	£2,600
D343	£1,250
E001	£4,150
F341	£3,500

Exception Report

MIS can produce exception reports. An exception report can show rooms that do not generate the expected revenue. For example, the Events Manager may forecast revenue of £1000 per month for each room with a variation of 10%. The MIS will report on rooms that have generated revenue above or below this expected amount. Automatically produced when a situation is unusual or requires management action.

Example

Daily Sales Exception Report – revenue under £100 and over £500

Room	Revenue
D450	£75
G132	£650

On-Demand report

Provides information when requested by the manager. For example Events Manager may request current usage of each room.

Example

Daily Usage Report

Room	Number of Delegates	Capacity
D450	50	50
G132	120	150

Key-indicator report provides a summary of previous day's critical activities.

Example

Monthly Revenue Key Indicator Report

	This Month	Last Month	Last year
Total Revenue per month to date	£5,500	£4,500	£6,000
Forecast Revenue per month	£5,250	£5,500	£7,500

Drill down report

Drill down offer strong reporting and drill down capabilities. Drill-down capabilities provide you with the flexibility to trace problem areas directly to the source. For example, Excel Enterprises may have seen a decrease in revenue in the month. Provide detailed data about a situation.

Example

Revenue per month

	Revenue	Variance	Variance by Room
January	£1,200	+10%	
February	£2,000	-15%	D123 (-20%)
			A122 (-10)
March	£1,500	+5%	
April	£2,000	+10	

The Drill Down report shows rooms D123 and A122 in February were the cause of decrease in revenue.

(c) **Syllabus reference 9.7. Chapter 7 (9.16).**

Discuss features of an accounting software that may be useful for Excel Enterprises.

- Maintain records of all financial transactions, for example, customer orders, invoices, and payments.
- Generally accounting software can help produce and submit government taxes (eg VAT).
- Personalised invoices and statements created for its customers and suppliers.
- Produce scheduled financial reports, for example, monthly revenue and costs for each room.
- Help manage your cash flow. Incoming and outgoing money can be monitored including overview of credit position with creditors and debtors.
- Maintain financial records for Excel Enterprises facilities. For example the software can maintain record of profitability of each room.
- Advanced software can keep record of customer activity, such as, money owed by the customer and their credit history with Excel Enterprises.

10 Davenport

(a) **9.7 IS Types and Applications, Types of IS**

Designing a Management Information System: LO 1.1.

Expert System

An expert system is a computer program that captures human expertise in a limited domain of knowledge. Expert system software uses a knowledge base that consists of facts, concepts and the relationships between them on a particular domain of knowledge and uses pattern-matching techniques to solve problems. This type of software may be useful if the chess club wanted to allow its members to play chess with a computer system. However, it is highly unlikely to be useful for accounting and general administrative functions.

MIS

Management Information Systems (MIS) convert data from mainly internal sources into information that can be used by managers to make timely and effective decisions. Such systems are used for planning and controlling activities within the organisation. MIS may be useful for the chess club as it can provide operational and financial management information. The system can help with the management of membership fees, utilising resources, aiding cash flow, and financial decision making. MIS systems can use the data to run simulations – hypothetical scenarios, such as, the likely impact of increasing or decreasing membership fees. Though the chess club is relatively small in terms of members and the MIS may not be useful in terms of costs and the reports generated from the system.

ESS

An ESS pools data from internal and external sources and makes information available to senior managers in an easy-to-use form. ESS helps senior managers make strategic unstructured decisions. Such systems include flexible but sophisticated data analysis and modelling tools. Such systems are unlikely to be useful for the chess club. The chess club is only considering storage of internal records for management of accounts, the system is not required to make strategic decisions. ESS systems are generally useful for large organisations and where senior managers need to process significant amounts of data before making strategic decisions.

Decision Support systems

DSS combine data and analytical models to support semi-structured decision making on issues which are subject to high levels of uncertainty about the problem. DSS are intended to provide a wide range of alternative information gathering and analytical tools with a major emphasis on flexibility and user-friendliness. DSS have more analytical power than other systems enabling them to analyse and condense large volumes of data into a form that aids managers make decisions.

(b) **9.12 Technology, selection and acquisition, Off-the-shelf software**

Designing a Management Information System: LO 2.4.

The chess club will be carrying out general accounting functions that are likely to be readily available on most off-the-shelf software and would be compatible with most standard PCs. The software is likely to come with a user manual. As funds are limited at the chess club the off-the-shelf software is likely to be relatively cheaper than having a bespoke application. The user interface is likely to be easy to navigate as most applications use Microsoft Windows operating system.

The off-the-shelf software may not fully meet the requirements of the chess club. Furthermore, the software maybe highly complex and some sections may not be relevant to the chess club. The chess club would be dependent on the supplier for maintenance of the package – ie updating the package or providing assistance in the event of problems. The package supplier may go out of business or be taken over which could affect the support the organisation receives.

(c) **9.8 System Modelling, Decision tables**

Designing a Management Information System: LO 1.2.

Condition	1	2	3	4	5	6	7	8
Immediate payment	Y	Y	Y	Y	N	N	N	N
Payment in 7 days	Y	Y	N	N	Y	Y	N	N
Introduction of a friend	Y	N	Y	N	Y	N	Y	N
Discount								
1%	X		X				X	
2%	X	X			X	X		
5%	X	X	X	X	X			

Note. Conditions 1, 2, 7 and 8 are not possible. Therefore the decision can be reduced as shown below.

Condition	3	4	5	6
Immediate payment	Y	Y	N	N
Payment in 7 days	N	N	Y	Y
Introduction of a friend	Y	N	Y	N
Discount				
1%	X		X	
2%			X	X
5%	X	X		
Total discount	6	5	3	2

11 Chouhans

9.8 Systems Modelling

(a) (i) Decision Tables are used as a method of demonstrating the effect of a process or action in a concise manner. Decision tables are useful in deciding what action to take if an error is identified when following a test script.

A decision table consists of four quadrants.

Condition stub	Condition entry
Action stub	Action entry

The condition stub specifies what is being tested.

The condition entry shows the outcome for the condition stub, in the form of Ys and Ns.

The action stub shows the range of possible actions.

The action entry shows the action or actions that will be performed, in the form of Xs.

(ii)
Cash payment	Y	Y	N	Y	N	Y
Automobile price > £4,000	Y					
Automobile price £4,000 or less	N	Y				
Automobile price > £10,000	N		Y	Y		
Automobile price > £15,000	N				Y	Y
Free Insurance (12 months)	X		X	X	X	X
Free insurance (six months)		X				
Free recovery service (12 months)				X	X	X

Note. There are redundancies in the decision table. If customer purchases automobile for over £15,000 it is irrelevant whether they pay by cash or not therefore final two columns can be combined.

(b)

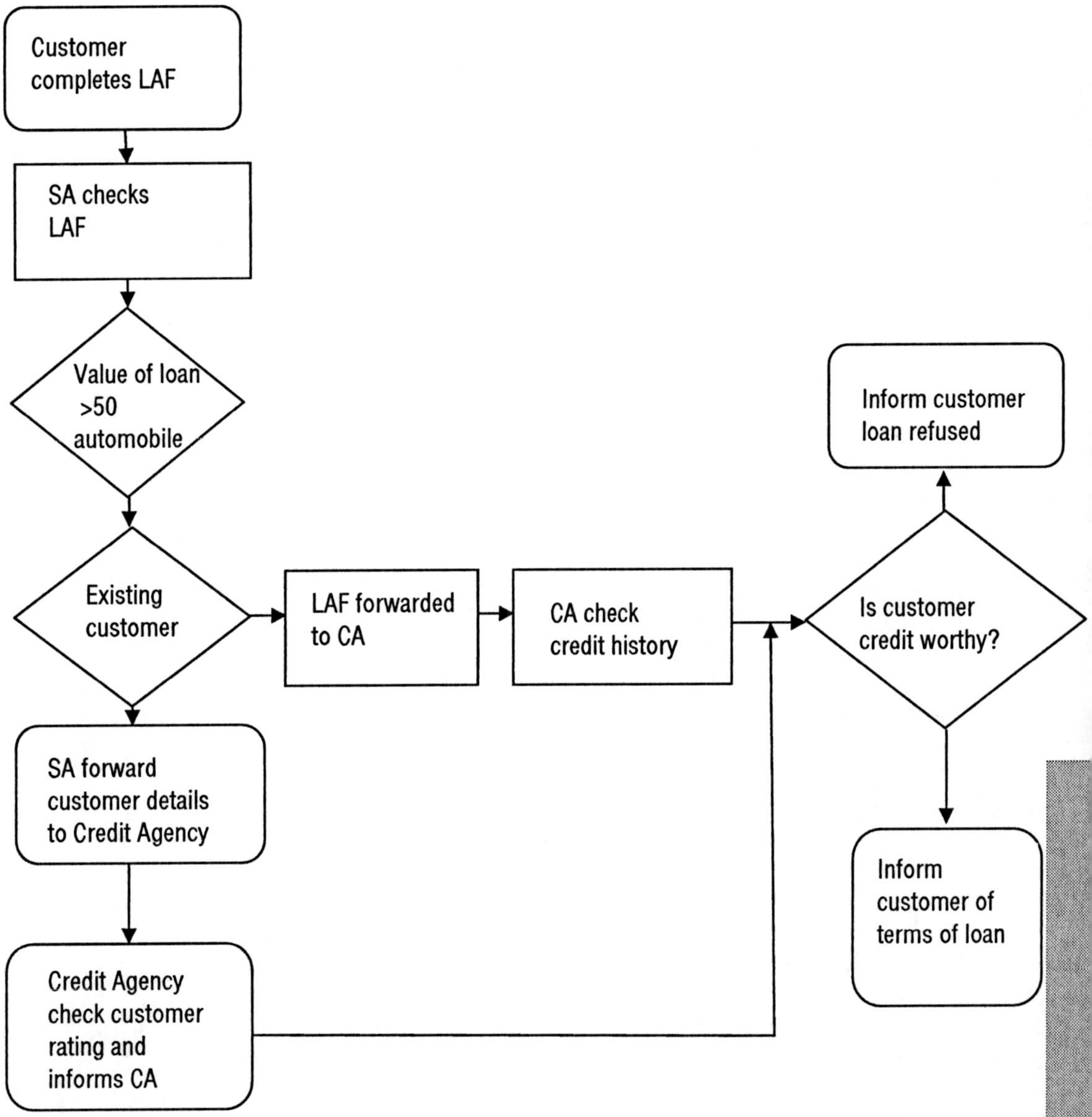

LAF: Loan Application Form
SA: Sales Administrator
CA: Credit Advisor

12 Huber and Cox

Information systems: 9.9 Systems development and organisation.

(a) (i) Level 0: Context diagram shows the total process in a summary form. This diagram is useful in setting the objectives for the system. Additionally, it provides an overview of how information flows through the system. This type of diagram can be useful in discussing the system with the strategic level of management.

Level 1: Low level DFD show each subsystem to be examined in isolation from the rest of the system. This diagram helps in project management and communication between users, analysts and software developers. It is also useful in discussing the system with the tactical or supervisory level of management.

Level 2: DFD is a breakdown of level 1 process. A separate DFD is prepared for each of the numbered processes in Level 1 DFD. This is known as decomposing a process.

(ii)

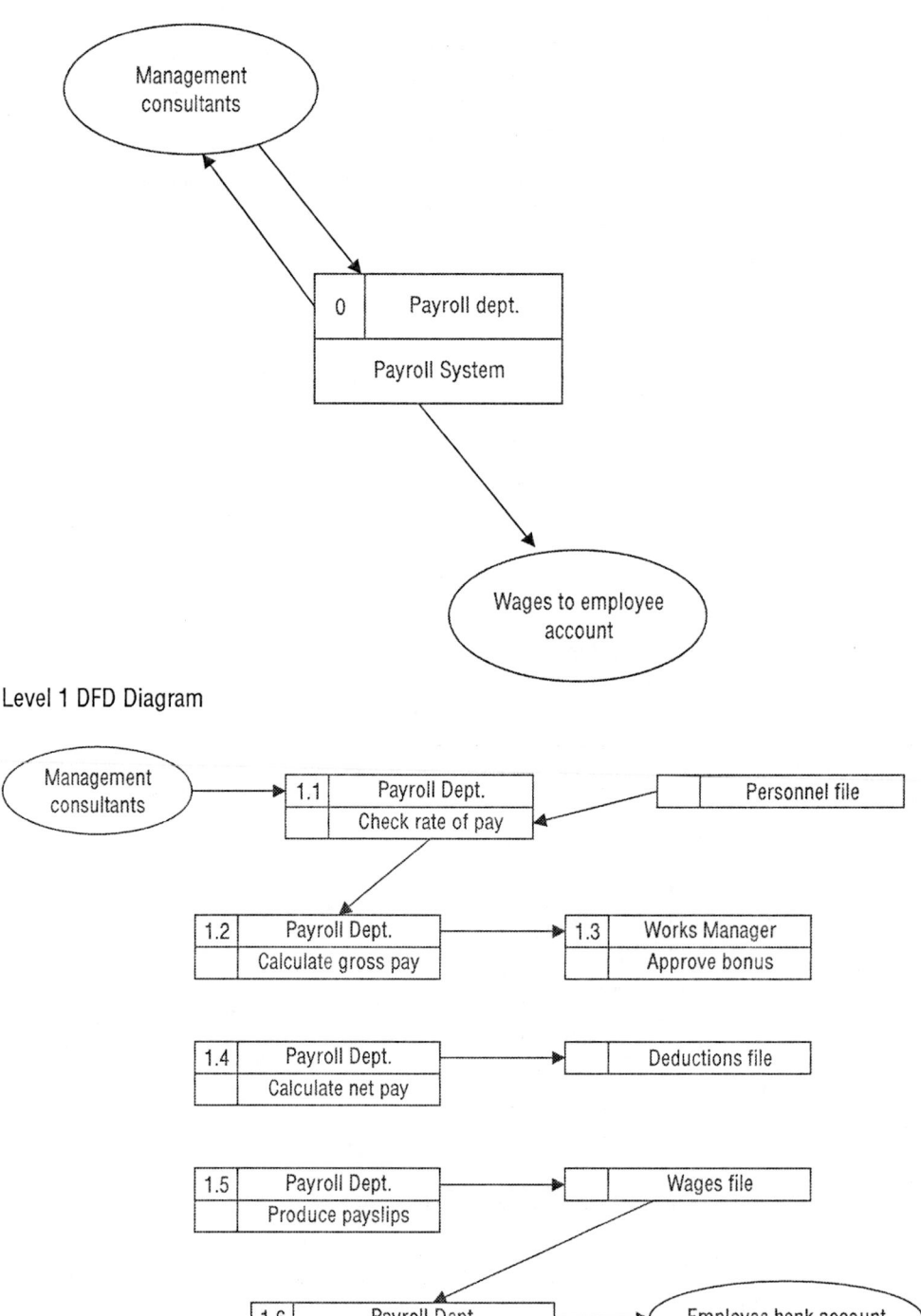

Level 1 DFD Diagram

EXAM ANSWER BANK

(b) (i)

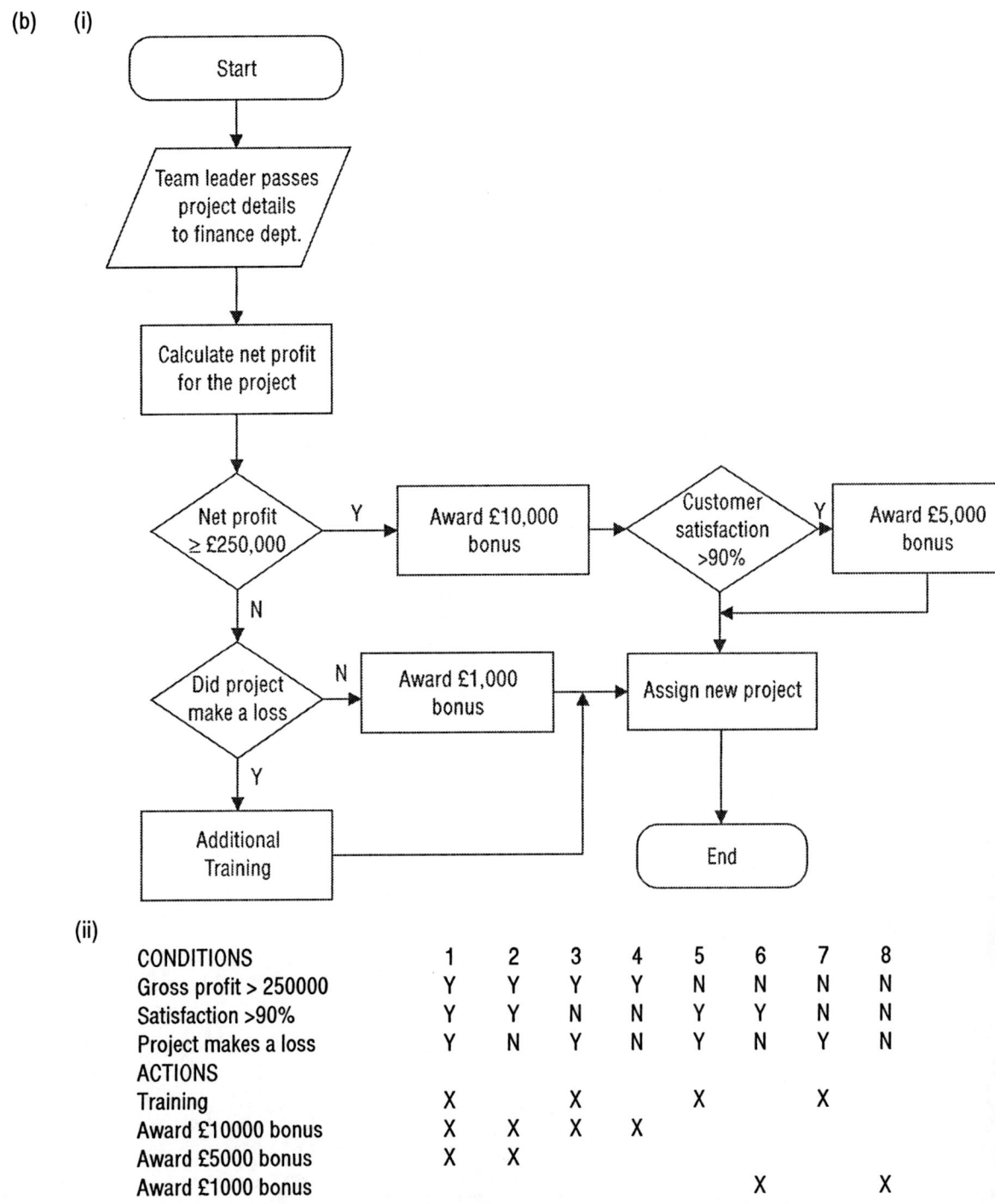

(ii)

CONDITIONS	1	2	3	4	5	6	7	8
Gross profit > 250000	Y	Y	Y	Y	N	N	N	N
Satisfaction >90%	Y	Y	N	N	Y	Y	N	N
Project makes a loss	Y	N	Y	N	Y	N	Y	N
ACTIONS								
Training	X		X		X		X	
Award £10000 bonus	X	X	X	X				
Award £5000 bonus	X	X						
Award £1000 bonus						X		X

Note. Conditions 6 and 8 result in the same action and these two columns can be combined. It is not possible to make a net profit and a loss, therefore columns 1 and 3 can be deleted as they are not logical.

13 Dhillons Office Supplies

9.8 Systems modelling

(a) (i) An external entity is a source or destination of data which is considered external to the system (not necessarily external to the organisation). It may be people or groups who provide data or input information or who receive data or output information.

(ii) A data store is a point which receives a data flow and holds data. Most data stores would be either digital or paper.

(iii) A data flow represents the movement or transfer of data from one point in the system to another.

(iv) Data processes involve data being used or altered. The processes could be manual or computerised.

(v) Level-0 DFD: The top level (least detailed) diagram would show one process only. The sources of the data for this process, and its destination(s) are also shown.

(vi) Level-1 DFD: The Level-0 DFD may be 'exploded' into a more detailed data flow diagram. This will show more individual entities, stores, flows and processes than Level-0 DFD.

(b)

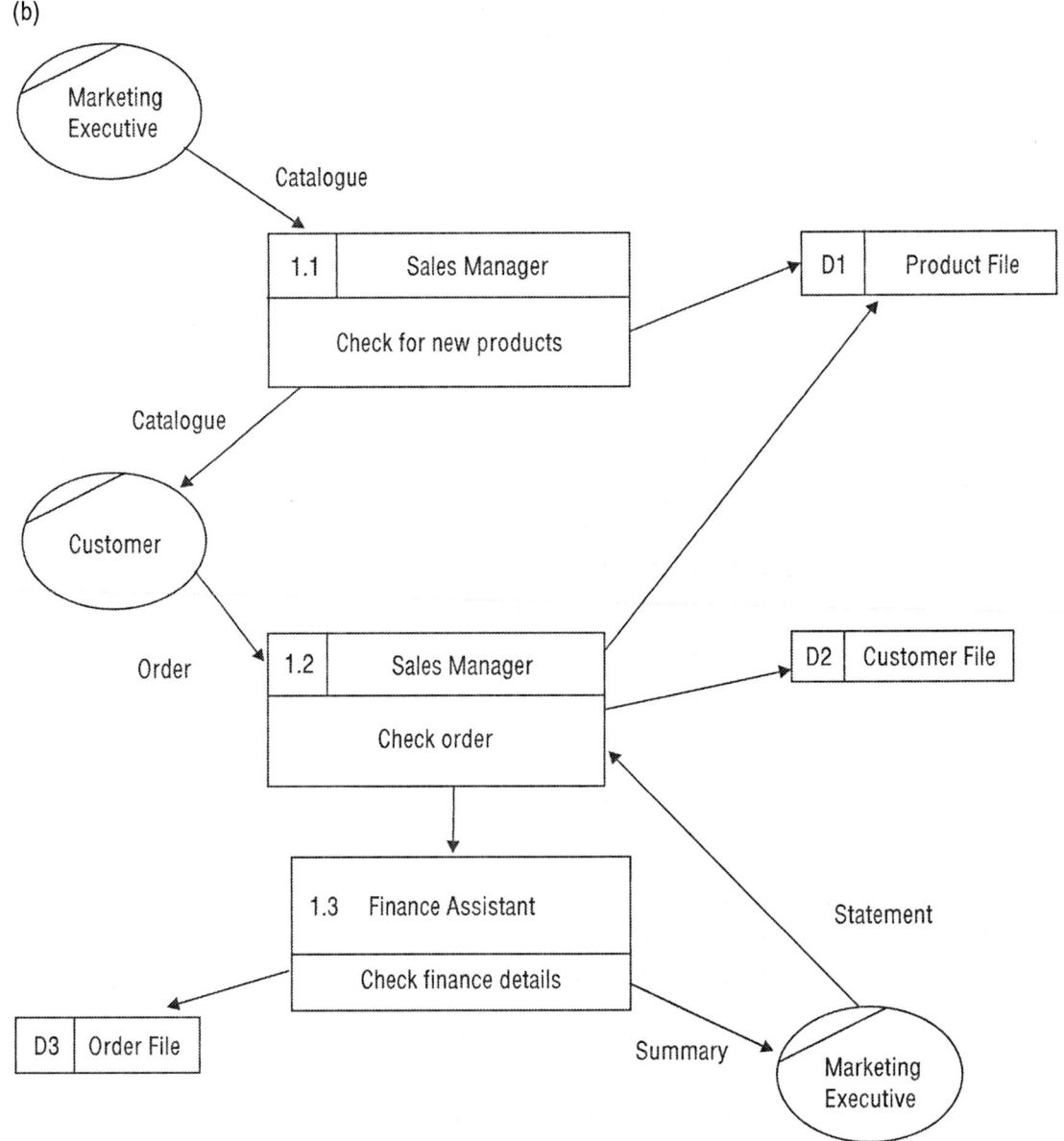

(c)

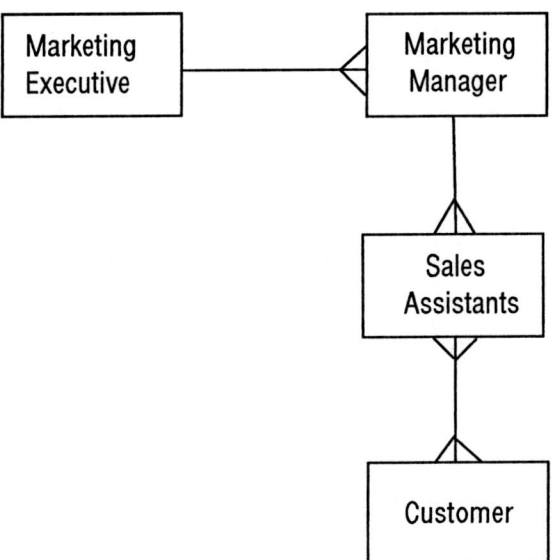

(d)

	1	2	3	4	5	6	7	8
Existing customers	Y	Y	Y	Y	N	N	N	N
Customer order above £1,000	Y	Y	N	N	Y	Y	N	N
Customer within 20 miles	Y	N	Y	N	Y	N	Y	N
10%	X	X						
1%	X		X		X		X	

Conditions 4, 6 and 8 can be deleted.

Conditions 1 and 2 can be combined and 10% discount applied.

Conditions 3, 5 and 7 can be combined.

14 JKM

9.9 **Information Systems: Development and Organisation.**

(a) Reasons why Information Systems strategy is relevant to strategic planning:

- Information Systems strategy may have a major influence on determining corporate and business strategy.
- Information Systems strategy can impact corporate decision making.
- Business strategic planning is becoming more customer focused and Information Systems strategy can help in providing good customer service.
- Many organisations could not fulfil their corporate objections without IT/IS.
- IT/IS can help gain competitive advantage and thus are important in developing business strategy.
- IT/IS can aid business strategy in developing innovation products or services and in reducing costs.

(b) In general, off-the-shelf software is available for business functions that are performed similarly across a range of organisations. However, the requirements of JKM are quite varied and it is unlikely that any off-the-shelf software will meet its requirements.

Purchasing a number of different software packages can result in incompatibility issues. JKM will need to consider whether different packages might produce incompatible data and whether this data can be transferred from one software to another. Furthermore, having data held in each software package can result in duplication making file maintenance difficult.

An off-the-shelf package relies on the supplier for maintenance, support and upgrades. However, if the supplier goes out of business or changes strategic direction this can leave the package without any support.

The decision to purchase a package can be made without adequate recognition of the organisation's requirements. JKM is going through a period of change and it might be difficult to identify the organisation's requirement clearly.

(c) Technical feasibility: JKM recently invested large amounts of money on IT and will need to consider if the proposed system is able to run on this IT hardware. The volume of future transactions to be processed at any given time will need to be considered, including response times and number of users in other locations.

Operational feasibility: If the proposed system conflicts with the way in which the organisation does business, the solution is not operationally feasible. The administrative staff are likely to be resistant to any new proposed system. JKM will need to ascertain the impact of the system on changes to staff responsibilities, regional reporting structures, retraining and reorganisation before accepting the new system.

Social feasibility: JKM will need to consider a number of human resource issues, including; redrawing of job specifications, threats to industrial relations, expected skills requirements and motivation.

Economic feasibility: JKM will need to conduct a cost-benefit analysis and the benefits will need to justify the costs. The proposed system will need to be the 'best' option from those under consideration. The project must compete with other areas of the business for funds, for example, expansion of training courses in Asia.

15 Manning and Huber

9.10 Systems strategies and management issues.

(a) Strategic information is used to plan the objectives of the organisation, and to assess whether the objectives are being met in practice. Such information includes overall profitability, the profitability of significant segments of the business, future prospects, the availability and cost of raising new funds, total cash needs, total manning levels and capital equipment needs. This information is used at the very top level of management within an organisation. These are chief executives or directors who have to make decisions for the long term.

Tactical information is used to decide how the resource of the business should be deployed, and to monitor how they are being and have been employed. Such information includes productivity measurements (output per hour) budgetary control or variance analysis reports, and cash flow forecasts, staffing levels and profit results within a particular department of the organisation, labour turnover statistics within department and short-term purchasing requirements. Tactical information is used by middle management (employees) when managing or planning projects.

Operational information is used to ensure that operational tasks are planned and carried out as intended. The timescale is usually very short, anything from immediately, daily or at most a week. The operational information is usually passed upwards to let the tactical planners evaluate their plans.

(b) Manning and Huber have a vision for the future of the company and information technology/systems can be used to turn this vision into reality and use new technologies for strategic advantage. The role of IT/IS is highly significant as these areas will involve high cost and are critical to the success of the organisation. The role of IT/IS will have an impact on external and internal stakeholders and sufficiently important and widespread to require proper planning.

Developing strategy involves taking a number of steps, from setting strategic objectives right through to evaluating actual performance. Three basic issues are the organisation's overall business objectives and in consequences its IS/IT needs, the organisation's current IT usage and the potential opportunities that IT can bring.

Manning and Huber would need to develop organisational plans and objectives. These may be formed by internal and external analysis. The analysis would include IS/IT trends in online courses, business environment Manning and Huber operate within, political, social and economic factors in each of their locations. Internally Manning and Huber would need to evaluate their resources and capabilities to underpin their organisational strategy.

(c) Business Led Approach: Manning and Huber would need to identify the overall objectives of the business and then IT/IS systems can be implemented to enable these objectives to be met. This approach will require the company to break down the organisation and its objectives into a series of business objectives and processes and to be able to identify the information needs of these. This will involve senior management and specialist teams.

Infrastructure Led approach: Manning and Huber would focus on the systems that facilitate transactions and other basic operations. The people involved are system users and specialists. The coverage and value of existing systems and experience is evaluated through surveys.

Mixed (inside out): The organisation encourages ideas that will exploit existing IT and IS resources. Innovations may come from entrepreneurial managers or individuals outside formal planning process. This is an innovative/creative approach. The people involved are entrepreneurs and/or visionaries.

16 JK Associates

Information systems: 9.11 Control and Security.

(a) JK Associates need to develop a coherent corporate policy that takes into account the nature of current and, as the company has plans to expand, future risks to their information assets. The policy needs to cover procedures and technologies required to address potential risks. However, it will be impossible to alleviate all the risks, therefore, the management need to identify acceptable security goals and the cost to achieve this level of acceptable risk. As some of the equipment is used off-site by the auditors and consultants, the information policy needs to address the acceptable uses of the firm's information resources and computing equipment, including laptop and desktop computers, and mobile phones. The information policy needs also to establish the levels of access to information systems for different levels of employees based on a set of access rules.

(b) The IT department needs to maintain a record of all equipment; including the make, model and serial number of each item, code identifying the department which owns the item, the staff member responsible for the item and its location. Auditors and consultants taking any equipment off-site should book it out and book it back in.

Laptops, tablets, memory sticks and other small items need to be locked securely away. Ensure larger items, such as desktop computers, printers cannot be moved easily by securing them to desks. JK Associates may consider employing site security guards and installing closed circuit camera systems.

Each member of staff can be provided with an individual personal identification number (PIN) which identifies him or her to the system. Based on the security privileges allocated, the person would only be allowed access to certain parts of the building.

(c) JK Associates will need to assign a senior member of the management team to take control in a crisis. This individual can delegate specific tasks or responsibilities to other designated personnel.

The firm will need to determine how best to use its IT resources in an emergency. Some tasks may be more important than others and may need to be tackled first. These need to be agreed in advance.

Back-up and standby arrangements need to be in place; such as, possibility of using other departments to help with the processing, using an external company that provides such services or reverting to manual procedures. Standby procedures need to be in place so that some operations can be performed while normal services are disrupted.

Communication with staff: The problems of a disaster can be compounded by poor communication between members of staff. Therefore, there needs to be communication channels to inform the staff of their role in the recovery plan.

As JK Associates will be working with public information, they need to ensure they have processes to inform the media of the recovery plans.

(d) The aim of the audit trail system is to identify errors and detect fraud. An audit trail enables the manager or the auditor to follow transactions stage-by-stage through a system and ensure that they have been processed correctly. An audit trail is a record and should be provided so that every transaction on a file contains a unique reference. The software package includes the following items; system generated transaction number, transaction types, user ID, transaction details, PC or terminal, date and time of the entry.

17 Dr Huber

9.11 Control and Security

9.10 Systems Strategies and Management Issues

9.7 Information Systems – Types and Applications

(a) Physical aspects: this relates to the security risks associated with the computer hardware.

- Ensure that there are adequate fire systems and procedures in place (fire alarms, fire extinguishing equipment.
- Train staff on relevant policies and procedures, for example, evacuation drills and fire control.
- Ensure steps can be taken to prevent access of unauthorised persons to computer faculties, this may include, using badge readers or coded locks on doors, automatic door closing and electronic tagging of hardware.
- Computer equipment will need to be stored and used in an environment protected from extremes and changes of temperature and humidity.
- Smoothed and uninterruptable power supplies (UPS) will be required. This would ensure the risk of losing power due to failure or disaster can be eliminated. The UPS storage battery automatically takes over when the mains power fails, giving users sufficient time to save their work.

(b) The role of IT/IS is highly significant as these areas will involve high cost and are critical to the success of the organisation. The role of IT/IS will have an impact on external and internal stakeholders and is sufficiently important and widespread to require proper planning. Developing strategy involves taking a number of steps, from setting strategic objectives right through to evaluating actual performance. Three basic issues are the organisation's overall business objectives and in consequences its IS/IT needs, the organisation's current IT usage and the potential opportunities that IT can bring.

Dr Huber would need to develop organisational plans and objectives. These may be formed by internal and external analysis. The analysis would include IS/IT trends in online medical care, business environment the business operates within, political, social and economic factors in each of their locations. Internally Dr Huber would need to evaluate the resources and capabilities to underpin their organisational strategy.

(c) An expert system is a software that captures human expertise in a limited domain of knowledge. An expert system uses a knowledge base that consists of facts, concepts and relationships between them on a particular domain of knowledge and uses patter-matching techniques to solve problems. Medical expert systems can be used to diagnose medical conditions and suggest the appropriate course of action. Such systems can search for facts that match the condition part of the productions that match the action part of the question. The staff at Dr Huber's consultancy can input patient's symptoms the system's search engine searches the knowledge base and provides possible diagnoses.

(d) Dr Huber is keen to reduce her staff and IT/IS resources on for non-core activities. Thus she has decided to outsource the invoicing and collection of payments to an external IT vendor. Discuss the three levels of service provision; time-share, service bureaux and facilities management.

Time Share: The vendor charges for access to an external processing system on time-used basis. As Dr Huber wants to reduce the workload on her staff this service may not be very useful.

Service bureaux: This usually focuses on a specific function. Traditionally, bureaux would provide the same type of service to many organisations. As Huber uses a standard invoicing and payment system this service bureaux may be the most appropriate choice.

Facilities management: The outside agency would manage Huber's IS/IT facilities. All equipment would remain with Huber's, but the responsibility for providing and managing the specified services would rest with the facilities management company. This would not be appropriate for Huber's as they do not want to maintain their own equipment.

18 Dr Appleby

9.11 Information Systems: Control and Security.

(a) Physical aspects: This relates to the security risks associated with the computer hardware. These risks mainly come from outside the system and include theft, fire, dust, humidity, and flood. Computer systems consist of a mixture of electronic and mechanical devices that can be severely impaired when they are subject to fire, flooding and improper environmental conditions.
Dr Appleby will need to ensure that there are adequate fire systems and procedures in place (fire alarms, fire extinguishing equipment). Staff will need to be trained on relevant policies and procedures, for example, evacuation drills and fire control. Additionally, physical access controls will need to be considered to ensure steps can be taken to prevent access of unauthorised persons to computer faculties, this may include: using badge readers or coded locks on doors, automatic door closing and electronic tagging of hardware.

Environmental controls: Computer equipment will need to be stored and used in an environment protected from extremes and changes of temperature and humidity. Smoothed and uninterruptable power supplies (UPS) will be required. This will ensure the risk of losing power due to failure or disaster can be eliminated. The UPS storage battery automatically takes over when the mains power fails, giving users sufficient time to save their work.

(b) Corruptions such as viruses can spread through the network to all computers at the practice. Viruses can spread through the use of free software, pirated software, games software and email attachments. The main protection against viruses is anti-virus software. These programs include an auto-update feature that enables the program to download profiles of new viruses. Additional precautions include disabling CD drives to prevent viruses entering an organisation. However, this can disrupt work processes therefore it is critical to ensure all files are virus checked. External email links can be protected by the way of a firewall that can be configured to virus check all messages and may also prevent files of certain types being sent via email.

Hacking involves attempting to gain unauthorised access to a computer system. Encryption aims to ensure the security of data transmission. It involves the transition of data into secret code.

(c) All personal data must be processed fairly and lawfully and processing of sensitive data is forbidden unless express consent has been obtained. Sensitive data includes data relating to racial origin, political opinions, religious beliefs, physical or mental health or sexual orientation.

Personal data shall be obtained only for one or more specified and lawful purpose and shall not be further processed.

Personal data shall be accurate and kept up to date and not kept for any longer than necessary.

Appropriate technical and organisational measures shall be taken against unauthorised or unlawful processing of personal data and against accidental loss or destruction to personal data.

(d) Data integrity is preserved when data is the same as in source documents and has not been accidently or intentionally altered, disclosed or destroyed. Systems integrity refers to system operation conforming to the design specification despite attempts (deliberate or accidental) to make it behave incorrectly.

Backup systems could be set up to ensure data is not lost in anticipation of future failure or corruption. A back-up copy of a file can be kept separately from the main system. This will ensure that the most recent usable copy of data can be recovered in the event of loss or corruption on the primary storage media.

Dr Appleby would need to have a contingency plan in case of a major disaster that could lead to potential loss of equipment or data. The plan will need to have standby procedures to allow some operations to continue while normal services are disrupted. A recovery procedure to identify and correct the breakdown may be required. A personnel management policy to ensure that the standby procedures and recovery procedure are implemented properly is also required.

19 Snowball

(a) Characteristics of strategic information.

- Derived from internal and external sources.
- Summarised at high levels.
- Relevant to long term planning.
- Concerned with all aspects of the business.
- Both qualitative and quantitative data.
- Uncertain, requiring assumptions to be made regarding the future.

External information could include; profile of potential customers in the future, such as, income and shopping habits of potential customers; products/prices offered by competitors, road/transportation infrastructure, possible increase in local taxes due to expansion of business, competitor wages, products and services.

Internal information could include; cost of expansion, cost of extra stock/staff, potential profits, impact on existing customers, possible pricing structures and profits.

(b) Mr and Mrs Snowball do not have technical staff to develop the software in-house, they could ask a software company to develop bespoke software for their needs. This option could be more expensive than purchasing off-the-shelf software. Off-the-shelf software can be very sophisticated and of high quality as it will be developed by software specialists. The software would be available immediately and come with supporting documentation.

However, the off-the-shelf software may not be well-suited to Mr And Mrs Snowball's business needs. The software is likely to be highly complex and will usually include large sections that may never be required by the business. The owners of the business will always be dependent on the supplier for maintenance, upgrades and support.

(c) Electronic sales tills will handle the calculations involved in sales, issue receipts and maintain historical records.

Stock can be ordered automatically and identify stock levels of top selling products and products that are not selling well.

Help in ensuring accurate pricing, speedier transactions, and reduce human error.

Prices can be changed quickly and easily. The impact of any price changes can be simulated by the system.

EPOS can provide data that can be useful for accounting, marketing and sales purposes.

(d) **Feasibility study:** This would focus on investigating the current systems and conducting cost-benefits of the proposed system.

Requirements Analysis: An analysis of current operations followed by the development and presentation of options for the new system.

Requirements specification: Defining the data and processes that will be used in the system. Documentation would be produced.

Logical system specification: Identification of technical options for hardware and communications technology.

Physical design: The logical data structure is converted to actual physical data specifications.

(e) JAD describes a close relationship between users and developers. The relative inexperience of Mr and Mrs Snowball's understanding of the technology may lead to misunderstandings and possibly unreasonable expectations on the system performance. This could lead to valuable time of IT professional being wasted and could lead to fragmented esoteric information system. Mr Snowball's decision to invite all staff members to participate in the development of the system could lead to the wrong problem being addressed. Having input from all staff members can result in conflicts that compromise the final system.

20 Manning and Bates

(a) **9.11 Control and Security, Integrity controls**

Designing a Management Information System: LO 2.3.

Data integrity in the context of security is preserved when data is the same as in source documents and has not been accidentally or internationally altered, destroyed or disclosed.

Systems integrity refers to the system operation conforming to the design specification despite attempts (deliberate or accidental) to make it behave incorrectly.

(b) **9.11 Control and Security, Input controls**

Designing a Management Information System: LO 2.3.

Data validation involves ensuring that data entered is not incomplete or unreasonable.

Check digits: A check digit can be calculated by the data management software and added to the information being checked to validate it, eg modulus 11 method.

Control totals: A batch total totalling the entries in the batch. Any discrepancies in the expected and entered records can be identified.

Hash totals: The data management software can generate a total that can be used to check processing has been performed as intended.

Range and limit checks can be used to check the value entered against a sensible range, eg account numbers.

Allowed character checks: The system can check that only expected characters are present in a field. For example an account number may only allow the digits 0-9, the customer surname is text only and email address has the @ sign.

Cardinality check can be used to ensure that each customer has a valid number of related records. For example customer must have at least one account with the bank.

Uniqueness check: Checks that each customer record is unique.

(c) **9.11 Control and Security, disaster recovery plan**

Designing a Management Information System: LO 2.3.

Definition of responsibilities: Manning and Bates would need to designate a member of the management to take control of crisis. Additionally there will be a need to delegate specific task or responsibilities to other designated personnel.

Priorities: As limited resources may be available for processing, Manning and Bates would need to develop priorities of tasks in advance. The recovery program would need to indicate the areas which must be tackled first and identify resources to complete these tasks.

Back-up and standby arrangements: Manning and Bates may draw up contingency plans with other data management companies who may be able to carry out non-sensitive work on their behalf.

Communication with staff: The disaster would have an impact on the bank, thus, Manning and Bates would need to identify a member of its staff who will be responsible for communication with the bank. A protocol would need to be established to ensure there is effective communication of the problem and the recovery plan. Additionally, as Manning and Bates hold customer information there will be a need to inform the media.

Risk Assessment: Some way must be found of assessing how big an impact on the organisation a 'contained' disaster would have. For example, would all the systems be fully operation if running on temporary replacement hardware.

(d) **9.11 Control and Security, back-up and archiving**

Designing a Management Information System: LO 2.3.

Back-up controls aim to maintain system and data integrity. Manning and Bates would make a back-up copy in anticipation of future failure or corruption. This back-up copy would be duplicate copy kept separately from the main system and only used if the original fails. Archiving data is the process of moving data from the primary storage, such as hard disk, to tape or other portable means for long-term storage. Archiving provides a legally acceptable business history, while freeing up hard disk space. Once the file from the bank has been used to update the records kept by Manning and Bates the file from the bank can be archived and if data is needed it can be restored from the archived media to a hard disk. Archived data can be used to recover from site-wide disasters, such as floods or fires, where data on the primary storage devices is destroyed. Archiving can also help Manning and Bates to avoid the slowdown in processing which may occur when large volumes of data build up in the main operational storage.

21 Payne Associates

(a) **9.9 Systems development and organisation, Systems methodologies**

Designing a Management Information System: LO 1.3.

A systems development methodology is a collection of procedures, techniques, tools and documentation aids which help systems developers in their efforts to implement new information systems.

Separation of logical and physical: The initial focus is on the business benefits – on what the system will achieve (the logical design). Physical design and implementation issues are looked at later.

User involvement: Users' information requirements determine the type of data collected or captured by the system. Users are involved throughout the development process.

Diagrammatic documentation: Diagram rather than text-based documentation are used as much as possible to ensure the focus is on what the system is trying to achieve – and to aid the user understanding of the processes.

Data driven: Most structured methods focus on the data items regardless of the processes they are related to. The type of data within an organisation is less likely to change than either the processes which operate on it or the output information required of it.

Define structure: Most methodologies prescribe a consistent structure to ensure a consistent and complete approach to the work.

(b) **9.9 Systems development and organisation, SSADM**

Designing a Management Information System: LO 1.1.3.

IT department would need to conduct a feasibility study focusing on the systems requirement and conducting cost-benefit analysis. The feasibility study evaluates the various technical, organisational, financial and business options available to Payne Associates. The proposed project would need to be economically, technically and operationally feasible before moving to the next stage of the SSDAM. Technical feasibility may consider of the system whether the solution can be implemented using existing technology by upgrading or adding to. Additionally, compatibility with existing systems at each regional office, system expansion in the future and security would also be considered. The operational feasibility would consider the possible reaction of employees at regional and head office to possible organisational changes and the level of management support to the proposed system.

Requirement analysis: The IT development team would analysis the current operations followed by the development and presentation of options for the new system. The analysts would investigate the current IT systems at each regional office and identify problems or areas that need improvement. A range of possible options would be developed and the preferred option that meets the requirements of the selection criteria would be identified. During the requirements specification, the IT team would define the data and processes that will be used in the new system. The systems specification document will be produced. The focus of this stage is on identifying the system data, functions and events. Techniques such as Data flow diagrams, entity-event modelling and prototyping would be used by the developers.

Logical system specification stage would focus on the technical options for hardware technology. The IT developers would design the user interface and develop logical rules for processing. In this stage different options for implementing the specification are described in relation to the costs, benefits and internal and external constraints. Each of these options are examined and presented to the management board of Payne Associates.

Once the logical system specification have been agreed, the physical design can commence. The logical data structure is converted to actual physical data specification. The physical environment of the system is considered in this stage in converting from the logical design. The user screens and outputs are designed.

(c) **9.9 Systems development and organisation, Rapid Application development**

Designing a Management Information System: LO 1.3.

Rapid Applications Development (RAD) combines a less structured approach to systems to system development with the use of other tools such as prototyping. As there is likely to be resistance to the centralised information system, RAD involves the end-user heavily in the development process and this may help overcome some of the opposition from the regional offices. RAD can be advantageous to Payne Associates as it recognises the pace of change in business and helps develop systems quickly that provides competitive advantage.

22 Trentham Royal

(a) **Syllabus reference 9.10. Chapter 10 (3.0).**

For Trentham hospital information systems can provide the foundation for new services and ways of conducting business that provides them with strategic advantage over their competitors. The new information system will underpin the planned organisational change involving much more than introduction of a new technology and systems. The change to provide Tele-home health care is likely to include changes in jobs, skills, management, and organisation. Thus the new system needs to be viewed as an important part of the organisational process by the Trentham management board. Arguably, at Trentham hospital, IS may have a significant influence determining the organisational strategy and may provide a possible source of competitive advantage. This could involve technology not available to others or simply using existing technology in a different way. Thus Trentham management team needs to ensure that the development of the information systems plan supports the overall business plan. IS strategy is important to the hospital as the new Tele-home care initiative is likely to be expensive and is critical to the success of the organisation. The IS strategy needs to be developed with the aims of ensuring IS is utilised as efficiently and effectively as possible.

(b) **Syllabus reference 9.12. Chapter 12 (9.4).**

  (i) Multiple sourcing

  This involves outsourcing different functions or areas of IS/IT function to a range of suppliers. Some suppliers may form alliance to present a stronger case for selection.

  (ii) Incremental approach

  Organisations progressively outsource selected areas of their IT function. Possible problems with outsourced services are resolved before progressing to the next stage.

  (iii) Joint venture outsourcing

  Organisation enters into a joint venture with the supplier. The costs and rewards are split on an agreed basis.

  (iv) Application Service Providers

  ASP are third parties that manage and distribute software services and solutions to customers across a Wide Area Network.

(c) **Syllabus reference 9.12. Chapter 12 (5.0).**

The covering letter would include inviting suppliers to tender to develop the software. Basic information, such as contact details for queries and closing date for submitting tenders, need to be included.

Instructions need to be provided informing suppliers of information required in their tender. Suppliers may be required to specify areas of their tender that do not comply with the requirements provided by Trentham hospital, period of validity for the tender, basis for calculating process (estimates or actual), dates when work starts and when the software would be completed.

Detailed software requirements by Trentham hospital need to be specified clearly. This may include the purpose of the system and possible upgrades and future requirements. Additionally, the likely usage of the system in terms of volume of data to be processed, number of potential users, and processing requirements (inputs, outputs, interfaces with other systems etc.) will need to be specified.

Trentham hospital board may also request description of the methodology or systems development model to be used by the supplier. This can be used to evaluate the supplier in terms of quality of the system.

Details of the contract may also be requested (eg delivery date, ownership of the source code, right to make copies, maintenance agreements).

(d) **Syllabus reference 9.12. Chapter 12 (6.0).**

Once the tenders have been received, they should be evaluated against what was requested within the IT. Some of the main factors to consider when evaluating supplier proposal are described below.

Organisation needs: How well does the software meet the requirements of the organisation? If some requirements are not met, how important are they?

Documentation: Is there a full documentation for the user and a technical manual that would allow further development?

Controls: Access and security controls should be included, as should be processing controls that enable the accuracy of processing operations to be confirmed.

User friendly: software should be easy to use and tolerant to user errors. Menu structures should be logical and the software should follow standard user-interface conventions.

Training: Training is essential for the organisation to utilise the software effectively.

Support, maintenance and updates: The availability and cost of software should be considered as should the arrangements for updates and upgrades. This is particularly important if software is likely to be affected by changes in legislation.

Cost: An organisation should aim to purchase a package that will meet their requirements. However a package should not be purchased if the cost outweighs the value of the benefits it should bring.

23 Nadine Enterprises

Learning Outcome: discuss the features of information systems and technology to a given set of requirements. 9:12 Technology selection and acquisition.

(a) (i) Ad hoc outsourcing is generally used on an irregular basis and is a useful option when a company does not use a specific function frequently.

(ii) Project management refers to contracting out a specific project to external vendors. For example, this may be development and installation of a specific IT project.

(iii) Partial outsourcing refers to outsourcing of specific services to a third party. The coordination of the function is managed by the client (the buyer). The major problem is of demarcation of the responsibilities between the buyer and the vendor.

(iv) Total outsourcing refers to external vendor providing a large part of an organisation's services. Total outsourcing transactions are often viewed as strategic partnerships. The responsibility for the execution of the entire function (or activities) lies with the external provider.

(b) Nadine Enterprises need to consider the strategic importance of the activity/function to be outsourced. IT/IS appears to be pivotal to Nadine Enterprises and thus may not be suited to outsourcing. By outsourcing the IT/IS Nadine Enterprises risk leakage of confidential and competitive information.

Ease of isolating the function/activity to be outsourced. The IT function at Nadine's cannot be easily isolated from other functions making it difficult to be outsourced. Functions that have only limited interfaces are most easily outsourced.

Likely changes in the future. As Nadine Enterprises' requirements are likely to change in the future they should avoid tying themselves into any long-term outsourcing agreement.

Loss of management control. Outsourcing of IT/IS will mean Nadine's are turning the management and control of their IT function over to another company. The outsourcing company may not have the same standards and mission as Nadine's, thus, quality of service to customers may be compromised.

(c) **Timescale:** As Nadine's requirements are likely to change in the future it will be important to specify the timescale for the contract.

Service level: As IT plays a significant role at Nadine's, the quality of service provided by the external supplier will need to be monitored. Service level agreements can be set up between the two parties in terms of quality, eg system 'uptime' percentage, response times and deadlines for performing relevant tasks.

Exit route: Nadine's can ensure arrangements are in place if they wish to transfer to another supplier or move the IT back in-house.

Software ownership: Nadine's need to ensure that SLA includes details of software licensing, security and copyright.

Employment issues: If any of Nadine's IT staff are likely to move to the third party, employer responsibilities will need to be specified clearly.

(d) Outsourcing IT companies are likely to have update hardware and software and expertise in managing such projects. Nadine Enterprises can gain access to new technology that may not be available internally.

There is likely to be a reduction in staff costs at Nadine's. The company would save on employment taxes and other overheads. A specialist organisation is able to retain skills and knowledge, whereas, Nadine Enterprises is unlikely to be able to offer IT opportunities for career development.

Freeing up of financial resources can allow Nadine's to concentrate on expanding their business.

Focusing on mission. Rather than expending management's time and effort to build internal information technology/systems, Nadine Enterprises can focus on core and primary processes.

Reduced financial risk. Outsourcing through an external vendor can reduce uncertainties of costs as there is often a long-term contract where services are specified in advance for a fixed price.

(e) Software houses generally concentrate on the provision of 'software services'. These can include feasibility studies, systems analysis and design, development of operating and application software. Software houses can be contracted to deliver some particular software.

Consultancy firms generally provide high level advice to management on the general approach to solving problems and on the types of systems to use. The primary purpose of a consulting firm is to provide organisations with access to specialists and subject matter experts.

24 Morris Enterprises

Systems Development and organisation (9.9). Technology, selection and acquisition (9.12).

(a) The Managing Director needs to be informed whether a project is viable, the feasibility study can help with this. The system is likely to be costly therefore Morris Enterprises need to ensure they are fully aware of the cost implications of the new system. The benefits of the system are not clear and not quantified. A feasibility study will help identify the costs and benefits of the system. The system is likely to require changes to current management structures and roles and responsibility of staff. This may have major impact on the staff; the feasibility study will help address the human costs of the new system.

(b) Structured walkthroughs are a technique used by analysis and programmers to present their design to directors, accountants, financial advisors and consultants. The IT developers would hold formal meetings in which the documentation produced during the development is reviewed and checked for errors or omissions. These presentations would be used both to introduce and explain the new systems and also to offer the users the opportunity of making constructive criticism of the proposed systems, and suggestions for further amendments/improvements, before final system specification is agreed. The staff from Morris Enterprises will be involved in structured walkthroughs because their knowledge of the desired system is more extensive than that of the systems development personnel. At the end of each stage of development, the resulting output would be presented to Morris Enterprises for their approval. There must be a formal sign-off of each completed stage before work on the next stage begins.

(c) Benchmark tests test how long it takes a machine and program to run through a particular routine or set of routines. Benchmark tests are carried out to compare the performance of a piece of hardware and software against pre-set criteria. Typical criteria which may be used as benchmarks include speed of response of a particular operation, acceptable volumes before degradation in response times is apparent. This would help Morris Enterprises asses the speed of responses of any calculations to be performed or transfer of files between themselves and their clients.

Once the performance of the information systems under consideration has been evaluated, the acquiring organisation should consider other features of the proposal, possibly using a weighted ranking system.

A weighted ranking system may be used to evaluate software proposals from a number of different vendors. The factors chosen to be used in the weighted ranking and the relative importance will vary according to the purpose of the system under consideration. Judgements need to be made in the selection of criteria, the weightings applied to the criteria and the scores allocated. These judgements must be made by the employees of Morris Enterprises who have a good understanding of the system requirements.

25 Grady and Price

9.9 System and Development and Organisation

9.12 Technology, Selection and Acquisition

(a) As each office operates differently, it may be difficult to identify suitable packages for all requirements. Given that one package will not satisfy all the Grady and Price requirements, the issue of compatibility arises. The company will have to consider whether different packages might produce incompatible data.

System performance: As the quality of IT infrastructures varies between countries, the functionality of the system must be supported by acceptable performance. Grady and Price need to be sure that the system can cope with the volumes of data that will be processed and stored. Some software packages have tables of performance statistics showing response time of their software under different loadings and configuration.

Compatibility with existing systems: Each office use their own software packages and problems may arise due to compatibility and data conversion from existing packages to the new off-the-shelf software. Grady and Price would need to investigate the willingness of the supplier to provide such facilities and their costs.

(b) **Separation of logical and physical:** The initial focus is on business benefits – on what the system will achieve (the logical design). Physical design and implementation issues are looked at later.

User Involvement: Users' information requirements determine the type of data collected or captured on the system. Users are involved throughout the process.

Diagrammatic documentation: Diagrams rather than text-based documentation re-used as much as possible to ensure the focus is not what the system is trying to achieve.

Data driven: Most structured methods focus on data items regardless of the processes they are related to. The type of data within an organisation is less likely to change than either the processes which operate on it or the output information required of it.

Define Structure: Most methodologies prescribe consistent structure to ensure a consistent and complete approach to work.

(c) Joint Applications Development (JAD) describes the partnership between users and system developers.

Methodology promotes a more participative approach to systems development. It creates a pool of expertise comprised of interested parties for all relevant functions thus there is a reduced risk of systems being imposed on Grady and Price personnel.

The approach increases the user ownership and responsibility for system solutions. The methodology emphasises the information needs of users and their relationship to business needs and decision making.

The relative experience of many users may lead to misunderstandings and possibly unreasonable expectations/demands on the system performance. The danger of lack of co-ordination leading to fragmented, individual, possibly esoteric information systems.

Structured walkthroughs

A structured walkthrough would involve meetings with the Grady and Price users at the head office and the designers would present the output from a phase or stage of development. Structured walkthroughs are formal meetings in which the documentation produced during the development is reviewed and checked for errors and omissions. These presentations are used both to introduce and explain the new systems to users and also to offer the users the opportunity of making constructive criticisms of the proposed systems, and suggestions for further amendments before the final specification is agreed. Grady and Price users would be involved in structured walkthroughs as their knowledge of the desired system is more extensive than that of the system development personnel.

CASE Tools

CASE tools are software tools used to automate some tasks in the development of information systems generating documentation and diagrams. Possible uses of CASE tools include: generating project schedules, production of diagrams (eg DFDs, ERMS), automating screen and report designs and tracking implementation of the information systems.

CASE tools can be quicker and efficient production of documentation, accuracy and consistency in diagrams and documentation enables prototyping and enables re-use of blocks of code.

CASE tools do not necessarily prevent developers from producing poor information systems. Additionally the use of CASE tools requires training and can be difficult to master. There may be other software that can also produce diagrams at lower costs than purchasing CASE tools software.

Mock exam 1 questions and answers

MODULE C

PROFESSIONAL EXAMINATION 1

PAPER 9 - MANAGEMENT INFORMATION

WEDNESDAY 29th NOVEMBER 2017

TIME ALLOWED - 3 HOURS

SECTION A (Management Science)
This question is Compulsory

SECTION B (Management Information Systems)
Answer ALL questions

All questions carry equal marks

In marking, the Examiner takes into account clarity of exposition and logic of argument, effective arrangement, and all presentation

Statistical Tables and a Formulae Sheet are printed at the end of the question paper

You are allowed an additional 15 minutes reading time before the exam begins, during which you should read the question paper and, if you wish, make notes on the question paper. You are **not** allowed to open the exam script booklet and start writing or use your calculator during the reading time.

Section A – Management Science

This question is Compulsory

Question 1

(a) The management of AngloEuro Corporation is interested in using simulation to estimate the profit per unit for a new product. Probability distributions for the purchase cost, the labour cost and the transportation cost are as follows:

Purchase cost (£)	Probability	Labour cost (£)	Probability	Transportation cost (£)	Probability
10	0.25	20	0.10	3	0.75
11	0.45	22	0.25	5	0.25
12	0.30	24	0.35		
		25	0.30		

Assume that these costs are the only costs and that the selling price for the product is £45 per unit. Use the ten random numbers 0.37, 0.58, 0.83, 0.19, 0.74, 0.62, 0.05, 0.11, 0.95, 0.44 to calculate the ten respective net profit values per unit. **(15 marks)**

(b) AngloEuro commissioned a survey to estimate the demand for the new product. In a random sample of 225 people 65% claimed that they would consider buying the product.

Produce a 99% confidence interval for the proportion of the total population likely to buy the product. **(5 marks)**

(c) AngloEuro is considering three options for managing its demand data processing operation: continuing with its own staff, outsourcing to an outside vendor, or using a combination of its own staff and an outside vendor. The cost of the operation depends on the future demand which can be high, medium or low. The annual cost (in £'000s) of each option and the demand probabilities are as follows:

Staffing options	High demand (p = 0.2)	Medium demand (p = 0.5)	Low demand (p = 0.3)
Own staff	650	650	600
Outsourcing	900	600	300
Combination	800	650	500

Which decision should AngloEuro adopt to minimise the expected cost of the data processing operation? **(5 marks)**

(Total = 25 marks)

Section B – Management Information Systems

Answer ALL questions

Question 2

(a) During the analysis phase of systems development the focus is on meeting certain key objectives. In order to realise these objectives some important sequential activities need to be carried out.

Required

(i) Provide a concise list of three key objectives. **(3 marks)**
(ii) Briefly list the activities making up the analysis phase of systems development. **(5 marks)**

(8 marks)

(b) Give a detailed list of the tasks involved in the traditional sequential design process of systems development. **(7 marks)**

c) List a series of possible questions for management to ask during the design of systems development. **(10 marks)**

(Total = 25 marks)

Question 3

(a) Describe in steps a cost-effective hardware/software acquisition and installation process. **(10 marks)**

(b) For each of the following give at least five control measures to protect their security:

(i) User data
(ii) Hardware
(iii) Network **(15 marks)**

(Total = 25 marks)

Question 4

(a) Give a clear definition of a Distributed Data Processing (DDP) system and three basic capabilities such a system provides to its users. **(6 marks)**

(b) Describe four advantages and four disadvantages associated with the use of DDP. **(16 marks)**

(c) Provide a reason as to why DDP might be inappropriate for geographically dispersed warehouse inventory control. **(3 marks)**

(Total = 25 marks)

MODEL ANSWERS

MODULE C

PROFESSIONAL EXAMINATION 1

PAPER 9 - MANAGEMENT INFORMATION

WEDNESDAY 29th NOVEMBER 2017

Question 1

(a) 5 Simulation (Designing a simulation model 9.5), pages 121-128. LO 1.3

(b) 2 Sampling theory and significance testing (The theory of sampling (proportions) 9.2), pages 48-51. LO 2.2

(c) 6 Decision theory (Decision analysis (single decision), 9.6), pages 132-136. LO 3.2

(a)

Random number	Purchase cost (£)	Labour cost (£)	Transportation cost (£)	Net profit (£)
0.37	11	24	3	7
0.58	11	24	3	7
0.83	12	25	5	3
0.19	10	22	3	10
0.74	12	25	3	5
0.62	11	24	3	7
0.05	10	20	3	12
0.11	10	22	3	10
0.95	12	25	5	3
0.44	11	23	3	8

(b) 99% confidence interval $= 0.65 \pm 2.58 * \sqrt{\dfrac{0.65 * 0.35}{225}} = 0.65 \pm 0.08$, 57% <p <73%

(c)

Staffing options	High demand (p = 0.2)	Medium demand (p = 0.5)	Low demand (p = 0.3)	Expected cost
Own staff	650	650	600	635
Outsourcing	900	600	300	570
Combination	800	650	500	635

The least expected cost is £570,000 for the outsourcing option.

> **Additional areas where credit might be given, note this is not an exhaustive list:**
> - Answers to all three parts of Q1 are numerical and marks deducted must be in accordance to the detailed marking scheme in the Outline Marking Scheme. No marks to be given if the process and/or formulae used are wrong.

Question 2

(a) (i) 9 Systems development and organisation (Systems development lifecycles 9.9), pages 213-216. LO 4.3.

    (ii) 9 Systems development and organisation (The waterfall model 9.9), pages 213-216. LO 4.3

(b) 9 Systems development and organisation (Systems development methodologies 9.9), pages 218-242. LO 4.3

(c) 9 Systems development and organisation (User involvement, The feasibility study 9.9), pages 232-242. LO 4.3, LO 5.3, LO 5.4

(a) (i) The three key objectives under focus are:

1. Identify the system owners and users.
2. Define the system's purpose (functional specifications).
3. Determine the technical, economical and operational feasibility of the new system.

    (ii) In the analysis phase the key activities are:

1. Investigate business area of concern.
2. Study current system.
3. Develop initial recommendations.
4. Design a logical model of the new system.
5. Evaluate alternatives.
6. Develop final recommendations.

(b) A traditional system design process:

1. Perform functional decomposition.
2. Define system outputs.
3. Define system inputs.
4. Specify systems processing.
5. Define system databases and files.
6. Define manual procedures to support system operations.
7. Define systems controls to safeguard system and its data.
8. Define emergency alternate procedures.
9. Conduct structured walkthrough.
10. Develop system implementation schedule.
11. Update estimates of systems benefits and costs.

c) Some questions management could ask are:

1. Has the system been designed using structural design and module decomposition with some coupling?
2. Have system users and analysts participated in structured walkthroughs of key system components?
3. Have emergency alternate procedures been developed?
4. Is control of the operation robust?
5. Is the data input process simple?
6. Is there comprehensive and clear documentation in place?
7. Is the design of the logical and physical data base sound?
8. Have system costs and benefits been reviewed?
9. Has a detailed system implementation schedule been developed?

MOCK EXAM 1 ANSWERS

> **Additional areas where credit might be given, note this is not an exhaustive list:**
> - (a) (i) Full 3 marks must only be given if each objective is listed. No additional marks are possible here as the objectives are unambiguous and generic.
> - (a) (ii) Full 5 marks if the key activities are mentioned in the logical order. If other key activities are stated, instead of the ones given above. 1 mark may be allocated per activity if valid. No additional marks are possible for answers that do not address the key points.
> - (b) Full 7 marks if the design process given differs somewhat from the one above but still captures all important stages. Some discretionary marks may be awarded if less important stages are mentioned.
> - (c) All 10 marks if pertinent questions are asked albeit different to the ones here.

Question 3

(a) 12 Technology, selection and acquisition (IIT, Evaluating supplier proposals, 9.12), pages 283-296. LO 5.4

(b) (i), (ii), (iii) 11 Control and Security (Security, Physical threats, physical access control, 9.11), pages 261-281. LO 5.3

(a) Steps in acquiring and installing cost-effective hardware/software.

1. Acquire hardware/software to meet well-defined needs.

    (a) Develop an Invitation To Tender.
    (b) Identify appropriate vendors.
    (c) Submit a request for proposal to the selected vendors.
    (d) Evaluate proposals.
    (e) Select vendor.
    (f) Negotiate contract.

2. Install hardware/software

    (a) Handle personnel issues.
    (b) Prepare the installation site.
    (c) Prepare operating procedures.
    (d) Select and train staff.
    (e) Convert files and system if necessary.

3. Evaluate system, procedures and personnel.

(b) (i) Data: Passwords, input controls, back-up and recovery, archiving (cloud), anti-virus software.

(ii) Hardware: power protection, fire, theft, door locks, alarms, CCTV, card entry systems.

(iii) Network: firewalls, authentication and authorisation methods, system protocols, virus guards, use of intranet and/or Virtual Private Network.

> **Additional areas where credit might be given, note this is not an exhaustive list:**
> - (a) Full marks for capturing the essential steps and contingency measures in the acquisition and installation of a system. Some discretion in marking may be necessary so additional marks may be given if other legitimate steps are mentioned.
> - (b) (i) (ii) (iii) Full marks if at least five key control measures are mentioned, albeit different or additional to the ones here.

Question 4

(a) 7 Information systems (Types of information system 9.7), pages 177-178. LO 4.1
(b) 7 Information systems (Types of information system 9.7), pages 177-178. LO 4.1
(c) 7 Information systems (Types of information system 9.7), pages 177-178. LO 4.1

(a) Distributed Data Processing (DDP) is a method of providing cost-effective computer capability wherever it is appropriate within an organisation via multiple processors that can process independently and can interact by exchanging data. These processors communicate data to a central facility for reviewing, planning and control. The link is provided by either a Local Area Network (LAN) or a Wide Area Network (WAN).

A DDP system provides the following three basic capabilities to meet the needs of its users:

1. Information processing
2. Network processing
3. Database storage

(b) Four possible advantages:

1. Managers in remote locations have more control over the data processing resources.
2. Data transmission costs are reduced as much processing can be done locally.
3. The central computer's processing load is reduced.
4. The risk of a system failure is mitigated since no component of the DDP system can bring the entire network to a halt.

Four possible disadvantages:

1. Local managers may work an expedient solution locally but it may not be cost effective for the whole organisation.
2. Costs may rise if more processors are added to the system.
3. The need for highly qualified staff to manage, control and maintain the devices DDP may increase.
4. Lack of coordination or sufficient communication among various divisions may result in the development of similar but incompatible systems.

(c) A centrally administered inventory control may arrive at a replenishment number which may be different to the individual warehouse needs. As the remote warehouse manager's decision will be overridden by centrally located managers, the remote locations will not have the authority to implement their own decisions and DDP may be inappropriate.

Additional areas where credit might be given, note this is not an exhaustive list:

- (a) Full 3 marks for an adequate DDP definition and 3 marks for its three basic capabilities. No additional marks possible as the three capabilities are well defined.
- (b) Full marks if meaningful advantages and disadvantages, other than the ones in this scheme, are outlined so additional marks may be awarded in this instance.
- (c) Full marks if a satisfactory reason, other than the one given in this scheme, for the unsuitability of a DDP system for warehouse inventory control is given.

MOCK EXAM 1 ANSWERS

Mock exam 2 questions and answers

MODULE C

PROFESSIONAL EXAMINATION 1

PAPER 9 - MANAGEMENT INFORMATION

WEDNESDAY 23rd MAY 2018

TIME ALLOWED - 3 HOURS

SECTION A (Management Science)
This question is Compulsory

SECTION B (Management Information Systems)
Answer ALL questions

All questions carry equal marks

In marking, the Examiner takes into account clarity of exposition and logic of argument, effective arrangement, and all presentation

Statistical Tables and a Formulae Sheet are printed at the end of the question paper

You are allowed an additional 15 minutes reading time before the exam begins, during which you should read the question paper and, if you wish, make notes on the question paper. You are **not** allowed to open the exam script booklet and start writing or use your calculator during the reading time.

Section A – Management Science

This question is compulsory

Question 1

(a) InvestRight, a UK financial investment firm, has been providing funding to a number of countries over the last 15 years. The data below shows the number of countries, X, and the average profitability Y (in £m) per country.

X	Y (£m)
4	47
5	111
6	124
12	240
13	211
13	205
16	276
16	305
17	309
17	302
18	259
19	334
20	302
22	371
24	241

Required

(i) Find the 'line of best fit' relating the average profitability, Y, to the number of countries, X.

(6 marks)

(ii) What is the average change in profitability for every extra country receiving funding each year? **(1 mark)**

(iii) Discuss briefly how well the regression line in (i) fits the actual data. **(3 marks)**

(10 marks)

(b) Over a year InvestRight experiences 100 computer breakdowns. These are classified into the four time slots indicated below.

Time of breakdown	Number of breakdowns
9.00am – 11.00am	22
11.00am – 1.00pm	18
1.00pm – 3.00pm	26
3.00pm – 5.00pm	34

Test the hypothesis that computer breakdowns are spread evenly throughout the working day, using a 5% level of significance. **(8 marks)**

(c) InvestRight's business is expanding and the firm wants to move to new larger premises in order to accommodate new staff to be recruited in the near future. The building contractor in charge of construction has provided a list of activities that need to be completed before InvestRight move in. These activities and durations along with their dependencies are listed below.

Activity	Description	Preceding activities	Duration (weeks)
A	Purchase construction materials	-	8
B	Choose and purchase electronic trading equipment	-	12
C	Recruit technical manager	-	12
D	Prepare site	-	2
E	Construction	A,D	6
F	Install utilities	E	2
G	Internal finishing/decoration	F	1
H	Install electronic trading equipment	B,G	2
I	Recruit staff	C	4
J	Train staff	I,H	1

Required

(i) Draw the project network for the new premises. (5 marks)
(ii) Identify the critical activities path and its duration. (2 marks)

(7 marks)

(Total = 25 marks)

Section B – Management Information Systems

Answer ALL questions

Question 2

(a) Interpret the three categories of management planning and control, called the Anthony hierarchy and draw a diagram to illustrate the hierarchy of an organisation. **(4 marks)**

(b) Discuss in sufficient detail the type of decision structure and responsibilities within each level in the Anthony hierarchy in the context of a manufacturing company's entry into a new market by launching a new product line. **(21 marks)**

(Total = 25 marks)

Question 3

(a) Discuss the characteristics of a Database and a Database Management System (DBMS). **(3 marks)**

(b) Discuss at least three objectives of the database approach that provide a guide to the database requirements processes and data modelling. **(15 marks)**

(c) Produce an Entity-Relationship diagram for the following entities and attributes:

Professional accounting body: Association of International Accountants (AIA)
AIA Student: Name, Student ID
Examiner: Name, National Insurance number
Exam paper: Management Information Systems **(7 marks)**

(Total = 25 marks)

Question 4

A local GP surgery wishes to develop an Expert System for use by its patients. The system would advise the patient on whether his/her poor condition is due to the common cold or something more serious like a flu or viral infection. The GPs would be responsible for entering the knowledge data and for answering any queries beyond the scope of the new knowledge-based system.

(a) Interpret the basic operations of an Expert System and explain the function of each component in detail. **(12 marks)**

(b) Discuss the main disadvantages of Expert Systems in general and the potential issues with the one proposed here in particular. **(13 marks)**

(Total = 25 marks)

MODEL ANSWERS

MODULE C

PROFESSIONAL EXAMINATION 1

PAPER 9 - MANAGEMENT INFORMATION

WEDNESDAY 23rd MAY 2018

Question 1

(a) 1 Correlation and Regression (9.1 Forecasting problems), pages 25-26. LO 1.1
(b) 2 Sampling theory and significance testing (9.2 The Chi-Squared Test) pages 53-56. LO 2.3
(c) 4 Network Analysis, (9.4, 9.5) pages 91-119. LO 3.3

X	Y	XY	X^2	Y^2
4	47	188	16	2,209
5	111	555	25	12,321
6	124	744	36	15,376
12	240	2,880	144	57,600
13	211	2,743	169	44,521
13	205	2,665	169	42,025
16	276	4,416	256	76,176
16	305	4,880	256	93,025
17	309	5,253	289	95,481
17	302	5,134	289	91,204
18	259	4,662	324	67,081
19	334	6,346	361	111,556
20	302	6,040	400	91,204
22	371	8,162	484	137,641
24	241	5,784	576	58,081
$\Sigma X = 222$	$\Sigma Y = 3,667$	$\Sigma XY = 60,452$	$\Sigma X^2 = 3,794$	$\Sigma Y^2 = 995,501$

$$\text{Slope} = \frac{15 \times 60452 - 222 \times 3637}{15 \times 3794 - 222^2} = 13.03$$

$$\text{Intercept} = \frac{3637 - 13.03 \times 222}{15} = 49.62$$

$$R = \frac{15 \times 60452 - 222 \times 3637}{\sqrt{(3794 - 222^2) \times (995501 - 3637^2)}} = 0.872, R^2 = 0.76$$

(a) (i) The linear regression model is Y = 49.62 + 13.03 × X.

(ii) For every extra country the profitability increases on average by £13.03 million.

(iii) The coefficient of determination, R^2, is approximately 76%. The number of countries funded accounts for 76% InvestRight's profitability.

(b)

H_0: breakdowns evenly spread
H_1: breakdowns not evenly spread

O	E	(O – E)	(O – E)²	$\frac{(O-E)^2}{E}$
22	25	-3	9	0.36
18	25	-7	49	1.96
26	25	1	1	0.04
34	25	9	81	3.24
Total				5.60

The test statistic, $X^2 = \sum_{i=1}^{4} \frac{(O-E)^2}{E} = 5.60$. From tables $X^2_{0.05,3} = 7.81 > 5.60$. Accept H_0 that computer breakdowns are evenly spread.

(c) (i)

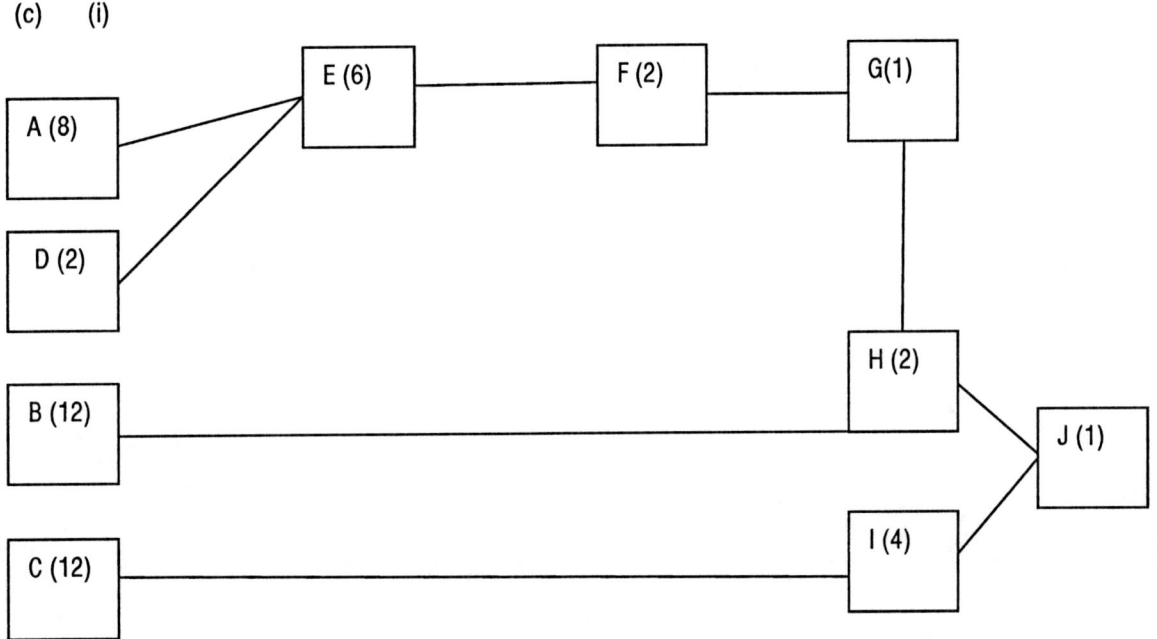

(ii) Critical path $A \to E \to F \to G \to H \to J$ with duration $8 + 6 + 2 + 1 + 2 + 1 = 20$ weeks.

Additional areas where credit might be given, note this is not an exhaustive list:
- Answers to all parts of Q1 are numerical and any marks deducted must be in accordance to the detailed marking scheme in the Outline Marking Scheme. Some marks may be given to answers that indicate correct procedures but with arithmetic errors.

Question 2

(a) 10 Systems strategies and management issues (Organisational information requirements 9.10), pages 244-247. LO 5.1.

(b) 10 Systems strategies and management issues (Organisational information requirements 9.10), pages 244-247. LO 5.2.

(a) The three categories of management planning and control as defined by Anthony are:

1. Strategic planning – long term definition of goals.
2. Management control and tactical planning – planning of activities to achieve goals targeted by strategic planning.
3. Operational planning and control – execution of planned activities.

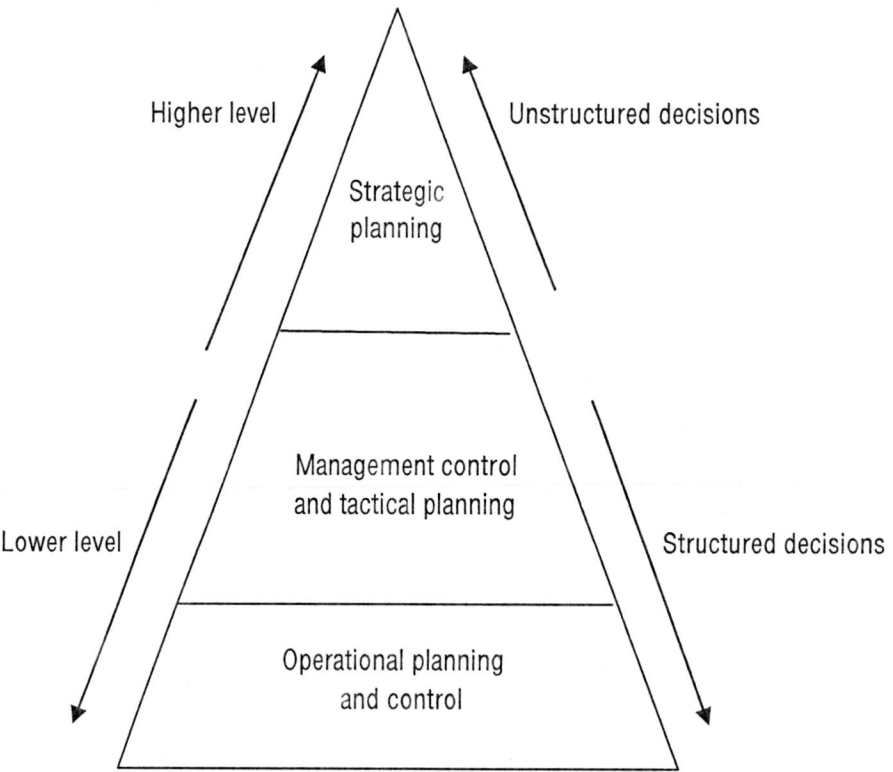

Pyramidal structure of MIS

(b) The three levels of management activity can be differentiated on the basis of the planning horizon for each level. Strategic planning deals with long-range considerations. The decision to manufacture a new and novel product as a means of entering a new market and the associated market strategy is a strategic decision made at the highest level of the organisation. Decisions at this stage are relatively unstructured. A CEO will devote most of the time to strategic planning.

Management control and tactical planning has a medium-term planning horizon. It includes acquisition and organisation of resources, capital expenditure budget, training and acquisition of personnel and allocation of advertising budget in anticipation of the launch of the new product. Particular managers will be responsible for this type of planning.

Operational planning and control is related to short-term decisions for current operations. Pricing, production levels and inventory levels are a result of such planning. Decisions at this stage are highly structured. A shop floor supervisor will be solely responsible for this kind of planning.

> **Additional areas where credit might be given, note this is not an exhaustive list:**
> - Full 3 marks may be given if the essence of each category is captured albeit in different words. 1 full mark may also be given if a pyramid is drawn with only an outline of the operations.

Question 3

(a) 7 Information System: types and applications (Databases 9.7), pages 172-173. LO 4.4.
(b) 7 Information System: types and applications (Databases 9.7), pages 172-173. LO 4.4.
(c) 8 Systems modelling (Logical data modelling 9.8), pages 205-207. LO 4.2.

(a) A database is a formally defined, central collection of data in an organisation. The data base approach is made operational by a database management system (DBMS), a software platform designed to perform the functions of defining, creating, revising and controlling the database.

(b) The database objectives can be captured by the following five characteristics:

1. Availability – Data should be made available for use by applications and by queries.

2. Sharing – Date items prepared by one application are available to all applications. Minimisation of redundancies reduces the need for multiple data stores.

3. Evolution – Database can evolve as applications and queries evolve.

4. Data independence – separating data from the programs that use it, providing facilities for different user views of the data, and the separation of logical from physical design.

5. Data integrity – data are controlled through the database administration function and data creation, access, and updating controlled by the database management software.

(c)

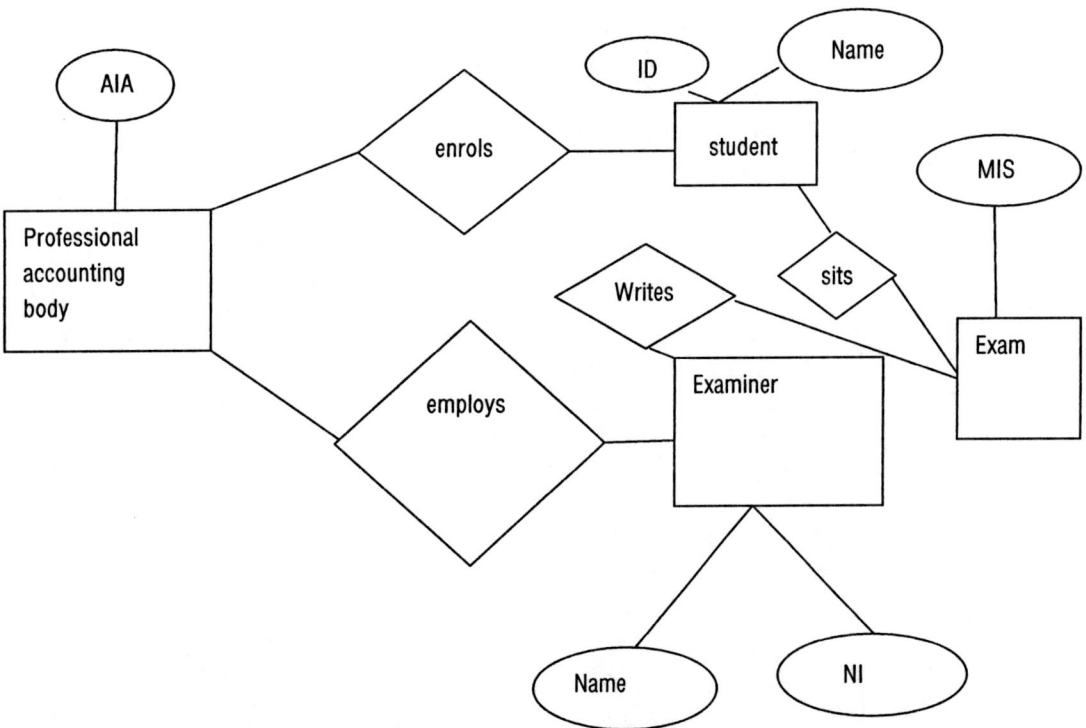

> **Additional areas where credit might be given, note this is not an exhaustive list:**
> - (a) Full marks for a meaningful definition.
> - (b) A maximum of 5 characteristics are given here. Full marks for any 3 out of 5 characteristics even if expressed in different terms as long as they capture the basics.
> - (c) Full marks for a complete diagram with arcs, some marks for correctly identifying entities, attributes and relationships.

Question 4

(a) 7 Information systems (Types of information system 9.7), pages 159-160. LO 4.4
(b) 7 Information systems (Types of information system 9.7), pages 159-160. LO 4.4

(a) An Expert System consists of three basic components:

1. A knowledge base developed by capturing the expert's knowledge. This is the most common form of expert system, which is a rule-based system consisting of a series of IF/THEN rules, with the IF part being the solution and the THEN part is the response. The IF/THEN rules constitute the system's heuristics and is designed to allow deletion of old rules and addition of new ones.

2. An inference engine to simulate the problem-solving process of the human expert. This deals with the way the IF/THEN rules are processed and the order in which inferences are made. The two most common inference methods are backward chaining and forward chaining. Backward chaining starts with the THEN part and searches for the appropriate IF. Forward chaining works in the reverse order.

3. A user interface to provide facts about the problem to be solved. This provides the connection between the user and the expert system.

(b) There are a number of significant problems with expert systems. The logical processes (rules) in the knowledge base are often difficult to identify and communicate to another individual. A long period of thorough and exhaustive testing is required to ensure that the decisions made by the expert system correlate quickly with the human expert's conclusions. As a result expert systems are costly to develop.

An expert system is developed to address only a specific area of knowledge. Rapid changes in the knowledge of rules may render the system invalid. Flexibility needs to be built into the system

Another problem is the need for a simple but flexible interface with a non-expert user.

The common cold and flu are both viral infections of the respiratory system and share some common symptoms but are different in some other ways known to the medical expert. The user of the medical diagnosis expert system in question must provide the system with all these symptoms. The program must have all the symptoms stored in its knowledge base and interact with the user to suggest a course of action, either a diagnosis of common cold or a referral to a GP for proper treatment. There is a distinct possibility of misdiagnosis however due mainly to the commonality of symptoms which might falsely indicate that a normally fit and healthy individual is suffering from a common cold instead of flu. A live simulation test with two patients suffering from each type of infection would attest to the reliability of the expert system.

> **Additional areas where credit might be given, note this is not an exhaustive list:**
> - a) Full marks for listing all three basic components of an Expert System as long as they are stated by their generic labels.
> - b) Answers above are not prescriptive and are only indicative. A thorough understanding of the issues is sought. Answers different to the ones suggested here are acceptable as long as they make sense. Some discretionary marking is allowed.

Mathematical tables

Formulae Sheet

Correlation:

Pearson's product-moment coefficient of correlation

$$r = \frac{n\sum xy - (\sum x)(\sum y)}{\sqrt{\left[n\sum x^2 - (\sum x)^2\right] \times \left[n\sum y^2 - (\sum y)^2\right]}}$$

Regression: Linear form $y = a + bx$

$$b = \frac{n\sum xy - (\sum x)(\sum y)}{n\sum x^2 - (\sum x)^2}$$

$$a = \frac{\sum y}{n} - b\frac{\sum x}{n}$$

Inventory Control: $EOQ = \sqrt{\dfrac{2cd}{n}}$

Significance testing:

Single-sample test on a mean: $z = \dfrac{\bar{x} - \mu}{\sigma/\sqrt{n}}$

Two-sample test on means: $z = \dfrac{\left(\dfrac{\bar{x}_A}{n_A} - \dfrac{\bar{x}_B}{n_B}\right) - (\mu_A - \mu_B)}{\sqrt{\dfrac{\sigma_A^2}{n_A} + \dfrac{\sigma_B^2}{n_B}}}$

Single-sample test on a proportion: $z = \dfrac{\dfrac{x}{n} - p}{\sqrt{\dfrac{p(1-p)}{n}}}$

Chi-square contingency test:

$$x^2 = \sum \frac{(O - E)^2}{E}$$

Risk:

x or $E(x) = \sum px$

$SD(x) = \sqrt{\sum px^2 - E(x)^2}$

Coefficient of variation, $CV(x) = 100 \times \dfrac{SD(x)}{E(x)}\%$

Project Evaluation Review Technique (P.E.R.T.):

Mean duration $= \dfrac{1}{6}(a + 4m + b)$

SD duration $= \dfrac{1}{6}(b - a)$

Normal distribution (areas)

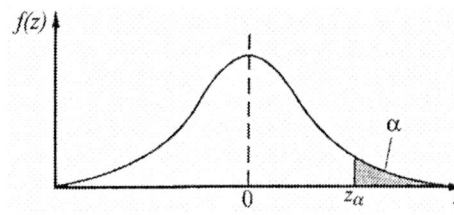

Area (α) in the tail of the standardised Normal curve, N(0.1), for different values of z. Example: Area beyond z = 1.96 (or below z = -1.96) is α = 0.02500. For Normal curve with μ = 10 and σ = 2, area beyond x = 12, say, is the same as area beyond

$$z = \frac{x - \mu}{\sigma} = \frac{12 - 10}{2} = 1 \text{ ie } a = 0.15866$$

z→ ↓	0.00	0.01	0.02	0.03	0.04	0.05	0.06	0.07	0.08	0.09
0.0	.50000	.49601	.49202	.48803	.48405	.48006	.47608	.47210	.46812	.46414
0.1	.46017	.45620	.45224	.44828	.44433	.44038	.43644	.43251	.42858	.42465
0.2	.42074	.41683	.41294	.40905	.40517	.40129	.39743	.39358	.38974	.38591
0.3	.38209	.37828	.37448	.37070	.36693	.36317	.35942	.35569	.35197	.34827
0.4	.34458	.34090	.33724	.33360	.32997	.32636	.32276	.31918	.31561	.31207
0.5	.30854	.30503	.30153	.29806	.29460	.29116	.28774	.28434	.28096	.27760
0.6	.27425	.27093	.26763	.26435	.26109	.25785	.25463	.25143	.24825	.24510
0.7	.24196	.23885	.23576	.23270	.22965	.22663	.22363	.22065	.21770	.21476
0.8	.21186	.20897	.20611	.20327	.20045	.19766	.19489	.19215	.18943	.18673
0.9	.18406	.18141	.17879	.17619	.17361	.17106	.16853	.16602	.16354	.16109
1.0	.15866	.15625	.15386	.15150	.14917	.14686	.14457	.14231	.14007	.13786
1.1	.13567	.13350	.13136	.12924	.12714	.12507	.12302	.12100	.11900	.11702
1.2	.11507	.11314	.11123	.10935	.10749	.10565	.10383	.10204	.10027	.09853
1.3	.09680	.09510	.09342	.09176	.09012	.08851	.08692	.08534	.08379	.08226
1.4	.08076	.07927	.07780	.07636	.07493	.07353	.07214	.07078	.06944	.06811
1.5	.06681	.06552	.06426	.06301	.06178	.06057	.05938	.05821	.05705	.05592
1.6	.05480	.05370	.05262	.05155	.05050	.04947	.04846	.04746	.04648	.04551
1.7	.04457	.04363	.04272	.04182	.04093	.04006	.03920	.03836	.03754	.03673
1.8	.03593	.03515	.03438	.03362	.03288	.03216	.03144	.03074	.03005	.02938
1.9	.02872	.02807	.02743	.02680	.02619	.02559	.02500	.02442	.02385	.02330
2.0	.02275	.02222	.02169	.02118	.02068	.02018	.01970	.01923	.01876	.01831
2.1	.01786	.01743	.01700	.01659	.01618	.01578	.01539	.01500	.01463	.01426
2.2	.01390	.01355	.01321	.01287	.01254	.01222	.01191	.01160	.01130	.01101
2.3	.01072	.01044	.01017	.00990	.00964	.00939	.00914	.00889	.00866	.00842
2.4	.00820	.00798	.00776	.00755	.00734	.00714	.00695	.00676	.00657	.00639
2.5	.00621	.00604	.00587	.00570	.00554	.00539	.00523	.00509	.00494	.00480
2.6	.00466	.00453	.00440	.00427	.00415	.00403	.00391	.00379	.00368	.00357
2.7	.00347	.00336	.00326	.00317	.00307	.00298	.00289	.00280	.00272	.00263
2.8	.00256	.00248	.00240	.00233	.00226	.00219	.00212	.00205	.00199	.00193
2.9	.00187	.00181	.00175	.00169	.00164	.00159	.00154	.00149	.00144	.00139
3.0	.00135	.00131	.00126	.00122	.00118	.00114	.00111	.00107	.00104	.00100
3.1	.00097	.00094	.00090	.00087	.00085	.00082	.00079	.00076	.00074	.00071
3.2	.00069	.00066	.00064	.00062	.00060	.00058	.00056	.00054	.00052	.00050
3.3	.00048	.00047	.00045	.00043	.00042	.00040	.00039	.00038	.00036	.00035
3.4	.00034	.00032	.00031	.00030	.00029	.00028	.00027	.00026	.00025	.00024
3.5	.00023	.00022	.00022	.00021	.00020	.00019	.00019	.00018	.00017	.00017
3.6	.00016	.00015	.00015	.00014	.00014	.00013	.00013	.00012	.00012	.00011
3.7	.00011	.00010	.00010	.00010	.00009	.00009	.00009	.00008	.00008	.00008
3.8	.00007	.00007	.00007	.00006	.00006	.00006	.00006	.00005	.00005	.00005
3.9	.00005	.00005	.00004	.00004	.00004	.00004	.00004	.00004	.00004	.00003
4.0	.00003	.00003	.00003	.00003	.00003	.00002	.00002	.00002	.00002	.00002
α	0.4	0.25	0.2	0.15	0.1	0.05	0.025	0.01	0.005	0.001
zα	.2533	.6745	.8416	1.0364	1.2816	1.6449	1.9600	2.3263	2.5758	3.0902

MATHEMATICAL TABLES

Random digits

Random digits 0 to 9, which are 'blocked' for convenience, may be used in any systematic way; e.g. if a random sample of 5 is required from population consisting of 83 members, the first two columns may be used to identify the members of the population, i.e. numbers 01 to 83, and the selected numbers are: 29, 12, 02, 69 and 11. Numbers greater than 83 may be ignored. When the first two columns are exhausted, columns 3 and 4 may be used etc.

29	32	95	99	57		98	08	36	97	08		65	30	47	22	00		38	60	10	01	10
12	11	80	16	17		01	03	97	59	73		74	98	73	65	85		59	74	66	37	58
87	58	22	25	55		35	72	79	28	15		69	17	42	98	72		05	47	12	40	99
02	92	42	87	57		53	53	34	55	75		83	64	09	10	19		33	29	57	62	98
69	28	63	73	98		45	61	10	43	20		08	10	43	16	81		17	62	99	09	16
11	95	68	77	86		91	76	11	63	34		15	08	35	39	37		12	74	15	00	10
06	43	41	02	13		65	23	94	48	88		88	87	03	90	77		68	98	09	17	22
68	55	98	08	39		59	85	46	66	13		42	90	86	13	29		12	38	48	27	54
41	01	06	65	10		29	29	91	86	24		45	59	04	88	17		68	31	01	91	13
46	75	71	76	88		04	42	94	41	42		39	79	14	46	13		49	37	18	28	08
80	14	13	43	24		47	61	47	42	24		24	82	12	23	54		81	33	18	96	89
30	56	60	77	80		33	67	68	31	67		73	23	45	30	55		81	51	87	68	58
53	50	41	02	98		49	97	32	43	55		75	33	51	20	99		64	76	20	80	98
84	14	75	87	37		58	51	94	06	73		27	94	23	76	77		81	72	90	45	41
08	27	89	33	87		52	24	57	50	22		22	76	60	05	79		86	58	83	88	41
97	08	50	16	41		67	40	56	13	12		68	67	36	22	08		55	76	86	45	67
97	08	37	42	48		95	90	48	34	88		19	66	38	94	64		95	07	78	23	86
70	15	04	10	34		95	57	63	75	82		88	74	28	24	66		99	52	65	36	98
06	38	31	17	38		24	98	52	67	04		95	54	89	79	45		28	05	18	60	17
63	87	79	25	86		56	74	17	45	32		53	62	09	04	86		65	87	48	82	02
17	00	56	31	14		18	56	97	91	78		85	82	06	24	88		49	17	68	51	50
17	76	35	38	19		24	47	21	09	43		09	72	02	64	66		06	78	21	70	41
57	77	32	13	60		37	68	66	11	23		30	62	97	71	02		20	13	22	00	40
35	86	97	84	91		77	73	03	37	77		50	24	54	51	40		20	66	16	34	84
72	68	64	77	89		72	77	67	45	72		25	56	78	69	72		63	86	52	07	43
91	01	78	50	50		91	99	15	36	02		74	42	55	33	19		88	35	17	58	37
70	37	55	94	53		05	78	53	23	29		15	57	70	30	88		63	20	12	64	38
11	06	17	48	24		57	50	76	81	77		30	12	92	27	19		32	63	70	97	80
60	37	89	98	61		05	51	89	47	28		34	83	98	44	66		96	84	64	64	92
37	41	11	09	04		84	38	51	91	49		23	78	53	95	40		17	73	23	04	70
28	97	38	27	97		54	95	94	54	79		93	88	00	82	39		61	93	78	07	88
14	29	17	18	84		03	10	62	15	70		01	15	06	30	97		79	55	98	79	39
81	70	53	83	20		25	26	56	55	56		33	58	74	21	76		94	24	80	12	50
08	20	90	25	43		22	81	74	51	76		53	39	59	35	34		46	55	54	73	50
61	95	25	85	66		34	76	39	98	88		45	57	64	11	17		06	43	35	27	09
64	58	31	05	45		77	25	20	02	09		36	87	63	01	10		08	01	19	19	06
75	49	97	87	79		31	66	57	89	56		56	97	71	43	65		62	36	77	50	87
66	95	10	78	42		24	91	82	74	29		00	53	44	70	18		23	48	09	90	99
85	37	61	48	07		99	13	01	16	94		37	31	28	96	59		77	62	24	95	84
06	87	15	09	48		31	18	66	87	11		19	71	67	20	93		92	02	96	15	65
11	15	95	59	69		81	75	75	88	69		95	12	75	69	18		10	60	35	31	47
03	64	44	33	46		16	02	28	14	33		61	57	28	33	96		47	49	86	85	83
68	89	57	51	94		84	09	80	37	90		52	99	85	52	49		66	63	69	11	31
43	13	09	12	00		65	69	54	11	00		20	94	22	93	90		16	82	64	27	46
42	68	71	56	74		17	71	63	80	81		02	41	49	27	92		44	44	13	45	21
12	55	09	80	30		50	34	96	31	71		19	21	79	42	17		57	04	04	19	00
88	84	87	74	01		39	99	02	75	76		61	88	97	89	06		97	15	70	26	27
49	27	92	08	87		65	12	32	27	96		11	26	30	88	48		89	29	73	50	47
46	51	54	92	06		44	85	83	14	78		68	83	33	17	03		10	99	10	17	34
34	96	78	90	18		41	44	69	10	30		48	98	32	76	12		81	29	83	02	87

χ^2 (Chi-squared)-distribution

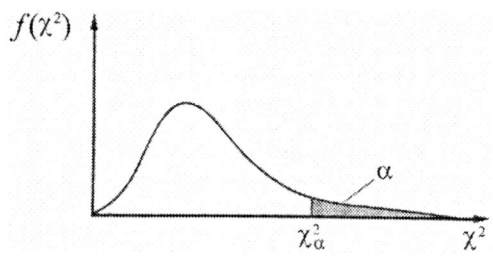

Values of χ^2_α giving area (α) in the right-hand tail for different number of degrees of freedom (v).
Example: For $v = 15$ area beyond $\chi^2_{0.95} = 7.261$ is 0.95 and beyond $\chi^2_{0.10} = 22.307$ is 0.10.

α \ v	0.995	0.990	0.975	0.950	0.900	0.750	0.500
1	0.0⁴3927*	0.0³1571*	0.0³9821*	0.0²3932*	0.01579	0.1015	0.4549
2	0.01003	0.02010	0.05064	0.1026	0.2107	0.5754	1.386
3	0.07172	0.1148	0.2158	0.3518	0.5844.	1.213	2.366
4	0.2070	0.2971	0.4844	0.7107	1.064	1.923	3.357
5	0.4117	0.5543	0.8312	1.145	1.610	2.675	4.351
6	0.6757	0.8721	1.237	1.635	2.204	3.455	5.348
7	0.9893	1.239	1.690	2.167	2.833	4.255	6.346
8	1.344	1.646	2.180	2.733	3.490	5.071	7.344
9	1.735	2.088	2.700	3.325	4.168	5.899	8.343
10	2.156	2.558	3.247	3.940	4.865	6.737	9.342
11	2.603	3.053	3.816	4.575	5.578	7.584	10.341
12	3.074	3.571	4.404	5.226	6.304	8.438	11.340
13	3.565	4.107	5.009	5.892	7.041	9.299	12.340
14	4.075	4.660	5.629	6.571	7.790	10.165	13.339
15	4.601	5.229	6.262	7.261	8.547	11.036	14.339
16	5.142	5.812	6.908	7.962	9.312	11.912	15.338
17	5.697	6.408	7.564	8.672	10.085	12.792	16.338
18	6.265	7.015	8.231	9.390	10.865	13.675	17.338
19	6.844	7.633	8.907	10.117	11.651	14.562	18.338
20	7.434	8.260	9.591	10.851	12.443	15.452	19.337
21	8.034	8.897	10.283	11.591	13.240	16.344	20.337
22	8.643	9.542	10.982	12.338	14.041	17.240	21.337
23	9.260	10.196	11.688	13.090	14.848	18.137	22.337
24	9.886	10.856	12.401	13.848	15.659	19.037	23.337
25	10.520	11.524	13.120	14.611	16.473	19.939	24.337
26	11.160	12.198	13.844	15.379	17.292	20.843	25.336
27	11.808	12.879	14.573	16.151	18.114	21.749	26.336
28	12.461	13.565	15.308	16.928	18.939	22.657	27.336
29	13.121	14.256	16.047	17.708	19.768	23.567	28.336
30	13.787	14.954	16.791	18.493	20.599	24.478	29.336
40	20.707	22.164	24.433	26.509	29.050	33.660	39.335
50	27.991	29.707	32.357	34.764	37.689	42.942	49.335
60	35.535	37.485	40.482	43.188	46.459	52.294	59.335
70	43.275	45.442	48.758	51.739	55.329	61.698	69.334
80	51.172	53.540	57.153	60.391	64.278	71.144	79.334
90	59.196	61.754	65.647	69.126	73.291	80.625	89.334
100	67.328	70.065	74.222	77.929	82.358	90.133	99.334
z_α	-2.5758	-2.3263	-1.9600	-1.6449	-1.2816	-0.6745	0.0000

*e.g. $0.0^4 3927 = 0.00003927$

MATHEMATICAL TABLES

α \ ν	0.250	0.100	0.050	0.025	0.010	0.005	0.001
1	1.323	2.706	3.841	5.024	6.635	7.879	10.828
2	2.773	4.605	5.991	7.378	9.210	10.597	13.816
3	4.108	6.251	7.815	9.348	11.345	12.838	16.266
4	5.385	7.779	9.488	11.143	13.277	14.860	18.467
5	6.626	9.236	11.070	12.833	15.086	16.750	20.515
6	7.841	10.645	12.592	14.449	16.812	18.548	22.458
7	9.037	12.017	14.067	16.013	18.475	20.278	24.322
8	10.219	13.362	15.507	17.535	20.090	21.955	26.125
9	11.389	14.684	16.919	19.023	21.666	23.589	27.877
10	12.549	15.987	18.307	20.483	23.209	25.188	29.588
11	13.701	17.275	19.675	21.920	24.725	26.757	31.264
12	14.845	18.549	21.026	23.337	26.217	28.300	32.909
13	15.984	19.812	22.362	24.736	27.688	29.819	34.528
14	17.117	21.064	23.685	26.119	29.141	31.319	36.123
15	18.245	22.307	24.996	27.488	30.578	32.801	37.697
16	19.369	23.542	26.296	28.845	32.000	34.267	39.252
17	20.489	24.769	27.587	30.191	33.409	35.718	40.790
18	21.605	25.989	28.869	31.526	34.805	37.156	42.312
19	22.718	27.204	30.143	32.852	36.191	38.582	43.820
20	23.828	28.412	31.410	34.170	37.566	39.997	45.315
21	24.935	29.615	32.670	35.479	38.932	41.401	46.797
22	26.039	30.813	33.924	36.781	40.289	42.796	48.268
23	27.141	32.007	35.172	38.076	41.638	44.181	49.728
24	28.241	33.196	36.415	39.364	42.080	45.558	51.179
25	29.339	34.382	37.652	40.646	44.314	46.928	52.620
26	30.434	35.563	38.885	41.923	45.642	48.290	54.052
27	31.528	36.741	40.113	43.194	46.963	49.645	55.476
28	32.620	37.916	41.337	44.461	48.278	50.993	56.892
29	33.711	39.087	42.557	45.722	49.588	52.336	58.302
30	34.800	40.256	43.773	46.979	50.892	53.672	59.703
40	45.616	51.805	55.758	59.342	63.691	66.766	73.402
50	56.334	63.167	67.505	71.420	76.154	79.490	86.661
60	66.981	74.397	79.082	83.298	88.379	91.952	99.607
70	77.577	85.527	90.531	95.023	100.425	104.215	112.317
80	88.130	96.578	101.879	106.629	112.329	116.321	124.839
90	98.650	107.565	113.145	118.136	124.116	128.299	137.208
100	109.144	118.498	124.342	129.561	135.807	140.169	149.449
z_α	0.6745	1.2816	1.6449	1.9600	2.3263	2.5758	3.0902

*e.g. $0.0^4 3927 = 0.00003927$

Index

INDEX

Note. **Key Terms** and their page references are given in **bold**.

Access control, 262
Accidental damage, 261
Activity-on-node diagrams, 95, 96
Additive model, 19
ADSL, 311
Advantages of database systems, 175
Amazon.com, 317
Analysis tools, 222
Analysts' workbenches, 222
Anti-virus software, 275, 313
Application package, 286
Application Service Providers (ASP), 299
Architectures, 163
Archiving, 266
ASCII, 152
Asymmetric Digital Subscriber Line (ADSL), 311
Audio output, 285
Audit trail, 267, 268
Authentication, 275, 312

B model, 214
Back-up, 266
Barcodes, 283
Batch processing, 162
Benchmark tests, 291
Bespoke application, 154, 287
Bespoke development risks, 293
Bespoke software, 286, 292
Bessel's correction, 39
Beta version, 273
Beta versions, 312
BIOS, 152
Birrel and Ould's 'b' model, 214
Bit, 152
Boehm's Spiral model, 215
Bottom up, 253
'Brick or click', 310
Broadband, 178, 311
Browsers, 308
Bulletin boards, 170, 311
Business led, 253
Business to Business (B2B) sector, 309
Business to Business 'infomediaries', 309
Byte, 152

C++, 224
Cache, 152
Call-back buttons, 170, 311
Card entry systems, 263
CASE repository, 222

CASE tool, 191, 222
CD-R, 153
CD-ROM, 153
CD-RW, 153
Central processing unit (CPU), 151
Central server, 164
Character, 152
Check digits, 265
Child segment, 173
Chip, 151
Chi-squared test, 53
Class, 225
Clickstreams, 316
Client applications, 165
Client workstation, 164
Client, 164
Client/server, 151
Client-server architecture, 164
Cluster sampling, 36
Code generators, 222
Coefficient of determination, r^2, 14
Communications, 178
Competitive advantage, 247
Computer Aided Software Engineering (CASE), 221
Computer manufacturers, 298
Computer Misuse Act, 276
Computer theft, 263
Confidence intervals, 44, 49
Confidence level, 44
Confidence limits, 44
Constraint, 79
Constraints, 60, 72
Consultancy firms, 298
Consulting activity, 298
Context diagram, 194
Contingency, 269
Control totals, 265
Controlling, 242
Cookies, 315
Copyright, Designs and Patents Act 1998, 295
Corporate applications, 165
Corporate Over-Use, 295
Corporate server, 164
Corporate strategy, 249
Correlation, 11, 12
 Curvilinear, 13
 Negative, 13
 Non-linear, 13
 Partial, 12
 Perfect, 12
Correlation and causation, 14

Cost control, 105
Cost-benefit analysis, 218, 234, 235
Critical activity, **94**
Critical Path Analysis, 94
Critical success factors, **254**
Cryptography, 319
CSF approach, 256
Customer Relationship Management (CRM), 325
Customer relationship Management Systems (CRM), 177
Customer service, 319
Cyclical variations, 18

Data dictionary, 222
Data flow, **193**
Data Flow Diagram, 193, 195
Data independence, **172**
Data integrity, **265**
Data processes, **193**
Data processing, 150
Data Protection Act 2018, 270, 271
Data protection principles, 271
Data redundancy, **172**
Data store, **193**
Data subject, **271**, 272
Data transmission, 178
Data users, **271**
Database, **172**
Database Management System (DBMS), **172**
Database structures, 173
Database system, 172
Decision analysis, 132
Decision making, 242
Decision point, 141
Decision points, 136
Decision Support System (DSS), **157**
Decision trees, 136
Decision variables, 77
Decisions made under uncertainty, 132
Degree of freedom, 53
Denial of service attack, 276
Departmental server, 164
DFDs, 195
Diagramming tools, 222
Dial-back security, 275, 313
Digital cameras, 283
Digital television, 308
Disaster recovery plan, 269, 270
Distributed Data Processing (DDP), 177
Distribution, 315
Document generators, 222
Document reading methods, 282
Document review, 192
Door locks, 263

Downsizing, 151
Dropper, 274
DSS, 157
DVD, 153, 154
Dynamic pricing, 317

Earl, 252, 253
Earliest event time, 118
Earl's three leg analysis, 252, 253
E-commerce, 170, 314, 317
E-commerce disadvantages, 318
Economic context, 250
Economic feasibility, 234
EDI, 179
Electronic commerce, 170, **314**
Electronic Data Interchange (EDI), 179, **314**
Electronic marketing, 315
Electronic Point of Sale (EPOS), 283
Email, 324
Email tracking systems, 311
Encryption, **275**, **312**
Enterprise servers, 150
Enterprise-wide systems, 177
Entity Life History (ELH), **205**
Entity Relationship Model (ERM), **203**, 204
Entity, **202**, 205
EPOS, 283
Equipment cost, 234
Escrow agreements, 296
ESS, 158
Estimates, 92
Event model, 205, 206
Executive Support System (ESS), **158**
Expected value, **132**
Expert system, **159**
External entity, **193**
Extranet, 169
Extrapolation, **10**

Facebook, 179
Facilitated user workshops, 191
Facilitator, 191
Facilities Management (FM), 297
Fact finding, 188
FAQs, 323
Feasibility study, 212, 218, **230**
Feasibility study report, 236
Feasible area, 63
Feasible polygon, 63
File viruses, 274
Financial services, 318
Fingerprint readers, 267
Fingerprint recognition, 262

Fire, 260
Firewall, 275, 312, 313
Float, 114
Flooding, 261
Floppy disks, 263
Forecasting, 4, 15, 25
Fourth Generation Language (4GL), 224
Free float, 115
Frequently Asked Questions (FAQs), 170, 310

Gantt chart, 93, 102, 104
Gigabytes, 152
GigaHertz, 152
Graphical solution to linear programming problems, 62

Hackers, 273, 312
Hacking, 273, 312
Hard disks, 152
Hash totals, 265
Hierarchical model, 173
Historigram, 17
Hoaxes, 275, 313
Homeworking, 181
HTML (HyperText Markup Language), 308

Identifying IS projects, 230
Incentives, 309
Incremental approach, 299
Independent float, 96
Independent variable, 4
Inequalities, 60
Information centre (IC), 229
Information management, 248
Information ownership, 260
Information superhighway, 169
Information System controls, 264
Information Systems (IS) strategy, 246, 248, 249, 257
Information Systems (IS), 248
Information Technology (IT), 248
Information technology strategy, 249
Infrastructure led, 253
Initial tableau, 79
Input devices, 282
Inside out, 253
Installation costs, 234
Integrated circuit, 151
Integrated Services Digital Network (ISDN), 311
Integration, 172
Integrators, 316
Integrity, 172
Intel, 151

Internet, 169, 247, 273, **308**, 310, 311
Internet distribution, 315
Internet growth, 308
Internet kiosks, 308
Internet marketing, 315
Internet problems, 311
Internet security issues, 311
Internet Service Provider (ISP), 308
Internet uses, 308
Interpolation, 10, 314
Interviews, 189
Intranet, 169
Invitation To Tender, 288
IS/IT strategy, 249
ISDN, 311
Iso-profit lines, 67
Iteration, 206

Java, 224
Join, 175
Joint Applications Development (JAD), 229
Joint venture sourcing, 299

Key encapsulation, 319
Key performance indicators, 254
Key recovery agent (KRA), 319
Keyboard, 282
Keyboard input, 306
Keys, 319
Keyword search, 170, 310
Kilobytes, 152
Knowledge management systems, 176
Knowledge Work Systems (KWS), 158
Knowledge Workers, 158

Laptop, 263
Laser printers, 284
Latest event time, 118
Least squares technique, 7
Levelled DFDs, 194, 195
Licences, 295
Limit checks, 265
Line of best fit, 7, 11
Linear programming and maximisation problems, 67
Linear programming and minimisation problems, 74
Linear programming, 60
Linear regression analysis, 7
Linear relationships, 4
LinkedIn, 179
Local applications, 165
Local Area Network (LAN), 167, 177

Local server, 164
Locks, 263
Logic bomb, 274
Logical design, 216, 217
Logical structure, 172
Logical system specification, 219
Lower CASE tools, 222

Macro viruses, 274
Magnetic Ink Character Recognition (MICR), 283
Magnetic tape, 152
Mainframe, 151
Management, 250
Management information, 250
Management Information Systems (MIS), 156
Many-to-many relationship, 203
Many-to-many relationships, 174
Many-to-one relationship, 203
Mean of the population, 39
Megabytes, 152
Megahertz (MHz), 152
Memory, 152
Memory stick, 153
Methodologies advantages and disadvantages, 217
Methodology, 216
Mixed approach, 253
Mobile communications, 178
Models, 27
Modem, 178
Monitor, 282, 284
Monte Carlo simulation, 126
Mouse, 282
Moving averages, 19
Multiple sourcing, 299
Multi-stage sampling, 35
Mutual adjustment, 215, 216

National Computing Centre, 212
Negative correlation, 13
Network analysis, 94, 102
Network, 163
Network diagram, 94, 104
Network model, 173, 174
Non-negativity constraints, 61, 72
Notebook, 263

Objective function, 61, 71, 78
Object-oriented Programming, 225
Observation, 37, 191
OCR, 283
Office Automation System (OAS), 155

Off-the-shelf applications, 154
Off-the-shelf package, 286, 293
One-to-many relationship, 174, 203
One-to-one relationship, 203
Online processing, 162
Operating systems, 154
Operational feasibility, 233
Operational information, 244
Opportunity cost, 83
Optical Character Recognition (OCR), 283
Optical mark reading (OMR), 283
Optical mouse, 282
Option evaluation, 232
Organisational information requirements, 252
Output, 284
Output devices, 284
Outsourcing, 297

PA Consulting Group, 300
Packaged software, 286
Passwords, 267
Pearsonian coefficient of correlation, 13
Peer-to-peer architecture, 166
Pen drive, 153
Performance indicators, 254
Performance measurement, 242
Personal computers, 151
Personal data, 271
Personal Digital Assistant (PDA), 308
Personal interview, 37
Personnel costs, 234
Physical access control, 262
Physical design, 216, 217, 219
Physical structure, 172
Physical threats, 260
Pixel, 282
Planning, 242
Pointers, 174
Population, 34
Population standard deviation, 38
Portable, 263
Portables, 151
Positive correlation, 13
Postal questionnaire, 36
Power supplies, 261
Primary cache, 152
Printers, 284
Privacy, 270
Problem definition, 232
Problem identification, 212
Problems/requirements list, 232
Process models, 193, 197
Processor, 151
Producers, 316

Product moment correlation coefficient, 13
Programmers' workbenches, 222
Programming tools, 154, 294
Project budget, 92
Project identification, 230
Project Life Cycle, 212
Project management software, 104
Project selection, 230
Proportional (multiplicative) model, 22
Prototype, 226
Prototyping, 191, 226

Questionnaires, 190
Quota sampling, 36

RAM, 152
Random Access Memory (RAM), 152
Random outcome point, 141
Random outcome points, 136
Random sampling, 34
Random variations, 17
Range checks, 265
Rapid applications development (RAD), 229
Ratios, 254
Read-Only Memory, 152
Real time, 162
Reality, 248
Regression, 15
Relational data structure, 174
Relational model, 173, 174
Relationships, 203
Remote working, 180, 181
Report generator, 222
Requirements analysis, 219
Requirements creep, 192
Requirements specification, 219
Resource histogram, 103
Revenue costs, 234
Review and maintenance, 212
Roll back method, 138
Rollback technique, 138
Root segment, 173
Royce's Waterfall model, 212

Sales forecasting, 15
Sample, 34
Sample size for a given error, 46, 50
Sample standard deviation, 38
Sampling (means), 38
Sampling (proportions), 48
Sampling distribution of the mean, 42
Sampling for attributes, 48
Sampling frame, 34

Savings, 235
Scanners, 283
Scatter diagrams, 11
Screen layout generator, 222
Scribe, 191
Search engine, 308
Seasonal variations, 18
Security, 260, 264
Security and the internet, 311
Select, 175
Selection, 206
Server, 164
Service bureaux, 297
Service Level Agreement (SLA), 300
Service Level Contract (SLC), 300
Shadow prices, 83, 85
Signatures, 319
Significance testing, 52
Simplex tableaux, 79
Simulation, 122, 128
Simultaneous equations, 75
Slack variable, 79
Social feasibility, 233
Social networking, 179
Software contracts, 294
Software houses, 298
Software licences, 294, 295
Software package, 286
Software sources, 285
Software supplier proposals, 289
Spiral model, 215
Spreadsheet packages, 27
Stakeholders, 251
Stand-alone, 163
Standard error of a proportion, 48
Static structure model, 202
Statistical enquiries, 36
Statistical significance, 53
Status checking, 170, 310
Stealth viruses, 274
Steering committee, 231, 249
Storage, 285
Storage devices, 285
Strategic analysis approach, 254
Strategic information, 243
Strategic planning, 243
Strategy, 243
Stratified sampling, 35
Structured Systems Analysis and Design Method (SSADM), 217, 218
Structured walkthroughs, 228
Supply chain, 316
Support, 170
Surplus variables, 77
Switching costs, 309

SWOT analysis, 248
System architectures, 163
System benefits, 235
System boundary, 196
System development lifecycle, 212
System justification, 233
Systematic sampling, 35
Systems analysis, 193, 212
Systems design, 212
Systems development lifecycle, 212
Systems implementation, 212
Systems integration, 297, 300
Systems integrity, 265
Systems investigation, 188, 212
Systems specification document, 219

Tableau, 83
Tactical information, 243
Tape streamers, 152
Technical feasibility, 233
Telephone interview, 37
Terms of reference, 231
The high-low method, 5
Three leg analysis, 253
Time bomb, 274
Time series, 16
Time series analysis, 16
Time share, 297
Time/Cost/Quality Triangle, 105
Top down, 253
Total float, 114
Touch-sensitive pads, 282
Touch-sensitive screens, 282
Trackball, 282
Transaction costs, 309
Transaction Processing System (TPS), 156
Transactions, 242
Transparent pricing, 317
Travel agents, 318
Trend, 17

Trojan, 274
Twitter, 179
Two-plus variable models, 77
Types of information system, 155

Uninterruptible (protected) power supplies, 261
Universal Resource Locator, 308
Upper CASE tools, 222
URL, 308
User groups, 229
User involvement, 228
User requirements, 188
User validation, 228
Utilities, 154

Validation, 213
Variables, 71
VDU, 282, 284
Verification, 213
Videoconferencing, 180
Virtual company, 316
Virtual Supply Chain (VSC), 316
Virus, 274, 313
Viruses, 273, 274, 312
Vision, 248
Visual display unit, 282

Walkthrough, 228
WAP phones, 308
Waterfall model, 212, 213
Website, 169, 308
Weighted ranking, 291
What if analysis, 28
Wide Area Networks (WANs), 167, 168, 169, 177
Wizards (interview style interface), 310
Work breakdown structure, 92
World Wide Web, 169, 308
Worms, 274